Creativity and Method:

Essays in Honor of Bernard Lonergan, S.J.

Creativity and Method:
Essays in Honor of Bernard Lonergan, S.J.

Edited By
MATTHEW L. LAMB

Associate Professor of Systematic Theology
Marquette University

MARQUETTE UNIVERSITY PRESS
MILWAUKEE, WISCONSIN
1981

Library of Congress Catalogue Card Number: 81-80327
© Copyright, 1981, The Marquette University Press
Milwaukee, Wisconsin
Printed in the United States of America
ISBN 0-87462-533-5

Foreword

Marquette University celebrated Reverend Bernard Lonergan's seventy-fifth birthday with a symposium during the final week of April, 1980. It was opened with an invocation by Most Reverend Rembert G. Weakland, Archbishop of Milwaukee, and a presentation to Lonergan by the Dean of the College of Liberal Arts, Reverend Frederick Dillemuth, of a pre-publication copy of this volume of essays. Reverend Frederick Crowe then delivered the Pere Marquette Lecture on the significance of Lonergan's *Method in Theology* as a profound challenge to restructure the ways in which theology is done.[1] Eight other lectures—included in this volume—were offered during the symposium by Patrick Byrne, Robert Doran, Tad Dunne, Vernon Gregson, Joseph Komonchak, Frederick Lawrence, William Loewe, and Philip McShane.

In so honoring Bernard Lonergan, Marquette University wished to acknowledge publicly the creative contributions he has made to human culture and religious thought. From his earliest research efforts onwards, Lonergan has been engaged in exploring the sources of human creativity. These he recognized in the restless questioning of human intelligence and in the ceaseless questing of the human heart. Inspired by the great Christian traditions associated with Augustine and Thomas Aquinas, Lonergan has sought to charter for our times, as they had for theirs, how human minds and hearts are not isolated faculties lost in a vast cosmic loneliness but are ultimately orientations towards Infinite Intelligence and Infinite Love. His recovery of Aquinas' central insights into the relationship of

---

[1] This lecture could not be included in this volume since it is published in the Pere Marquette Lecture Series, cf. Frederick E. Crowe, *Method in Theology: An Organon for Our Time* (Milwaukee: Marquette University Press, 1980).

human intelligence and freedom to Infinite Intelligence-Love decisively broke the modern myths which set up oppositions between human freedom and Divine grace. Hence, while his deepening life of prayer led him to experience human consciousness as an image of God, that growing conviction only strengthened his resolve to uncover the inherent orientation of intelligence towards responsibility and freedom.

Lonergan's quest has ranged over many diverse fields of contemporary human inquiry: logic, mathematics, physics, biology, psychology, sociology, economics, education, hermeneutics, history, philosophy, and theology. His guiding interest was not simply focused upon the ever changing contents in these diverse fields, but also upon the underlying dynamic patterns of questioning whereby new discoveries are generated and previous contents are transcended. To appropriate such dynamic patterns holds the hope of overcoming the massive fragmentation of modern consciousness and life, without imposing extrinsic limitations upon creativity which would stifle openness to the new and unexpected. To appropriate such dynamic patterns serves as a basis for effectively criticizing the many empiricist and idealist deformations of reason, without sacrificing the real gains in science and scholarship attainable today. To appropriate such dynamic patterns clears the way for contemporary discoveries of the continuity between mind and heart, as well as of the continuity between reason and faith, without minimizing the public and social dimensions of such discoveries.

Crowe distinguishes between the achievements of Lonergan and the larger, long-term enterprise those achievements have initiated.[2] The achievements are recorded in over fifteen books, and in over one hundred and fifty scholarly articles, published in many languages — not to mention the many as yet unpublished manuscripts. Central to these writings is an invitation to appropriate questioning human consciousness with its dynamic patterns of related and recurrent activities yielding cumulative and progressive results. This is Lonergan's challenging understanding of method, transforming method from a mere following of external rules or axioms into a process of creative collaboration. Why would such a challenging invitation have provoked an enterprise devoted to promoting personal and social self-appropriation? The essays in this volume will address that question in many different ways. The alienating conflicts between creativity and method are experienced in a series of dichotomies which underlie so many of the crises in modern times: subjec-

---

[2] Cf. Frederick E. Crowe, *The Lonergan Enterprise* (Cambridge: Cowley Publications, 1981).

tivity versus objectivity, art versus science, nature versus technology, desire versus control, social change versus institutional order, innovation versus tradition, freedom versus authority. By inviting us to appropriate the common sources of creativity and method, Lonergan's achievements have initiated a profound reorientation of the most basic notions and categories of contemporary self-understanding and social living.

The challenge has not gone unheeded. Today eight research centers located in Australia, Canada, Ireland, Italy, the Philippines, and the United States are dedicated to implementing and extending this creative approach to method. Over one hundred and thirty masters and doctoral dissertations have explored Lonergan's thought. Many others are still in process. The books, articles, and essays dealing with his achievements, or critically probing their implications, number in the thousands. While these centers and texts record something of what Crowe calls the ongoing enterprise, they are— like Lonergan's own work—no more than a small and unpretentious beginning in comparison with the immense task of encouraging human flourishing and creativity in a world marked by terrifying inhumanity and bias.

The following essays celebrate Lonergan's work, not by a complacent repetition of answers, but by a commitment to engage in questions with at least some of the care for attentive understanding, scholarly judgment, and personal responsibility which have marked his own spirit of inquiry. Limitations of space and time prohibited the inclusion of a greater number of essays by many other scholars and seekers influenced by Lonergan's invitation to self-appropriation; nor could I include essays by the large number of distinguished thinkers who have critically and creatively dialogued with Lonergan over the years. The essays express orientations which blend the authors' own areas of expertise and insight into a shared search for the sources of creativity and method in the related and recurrent activities of self-transcendence. The fruitfulness of such orientations is hopefully intimated by the rich diversity of theological and philosophical issues treated: foundational theology, biblical themes, soteriology, ecclesiology, ethics, language and literary criticism, phenomenology, socio-political themes, natural science and mathematics, macroeconomics.

I wish to thank Marquette University, especially its Theology Department, and the Lonergan Trust Fund for the financial assistance which made both the symposium and this *Festschrift* possible. The sudden death of Reverend Eric O'Connor has tempered the celebration of Lonergan's seventy-fifth year with a sorrow deeply felt by those who came to know and love him as a founder and director of the Thomas More Institute in Montreal. It was Eric O'Connor who invited Lonergan to give a series of lectures on "Thought and Reality" to an adult education class at the Institute thirty-five years ago. Those lectures were the first draft of *Insight: A Study of Human Understanding*. Finally, I wish to thank Mr. Mark Lowery and Ms. Elizabeth Dreyer for their help in the initial stages of this project, as well as Dr. Robert Engbring and Mr. Paul McInerny of Marquette University Press who, together with Mr. Norbert Peck and the staff of Central Press, were very encouraging in this publication venture. A very special debt of gratitude is owed Mr. Roberto S. Goizueta for his invaluable and indefatigable editorial collaboration.

Matthew L. Lamb
Associate Professor
Theology Department
Marquette University
Milwaukee, Wisconsin
April 1981

CONTENTS

FOUNDATIONAL THEOLOGY

    Insight and Waiting on God 3
        John Dunne, CSC

    Passages and Conversion 11
        Bernard Tyrrell, SJ

    Theologies of Praxis 35
        David Tracy

    Generalized Empirical Method and Praxis 53
        Matthew Lamb

    Method and Theology as Hermeneutical 79
        Frederick Lawrence

    Theological Grounds for a World-Cultural Humanity 105
        Robert Doran, SJ

    Rahner and Lonergan on Foundational Theology 123
        Michael O'Callaghan

    The Historian of Religions and the Theologian 141
        Vernon Gregson, SJ

    Religious Language and Theological Method 153
        William Shea

BIBLICAL ORIENTATIONS

    Beliefs and Authenticity 173
        Quentin Quesnell

    The Rise of David Story and the Search for a Story to Live By ... 185
        Sean McEvenue

    The "Inside" of the Jesus Event 197
        Ben Meyer

SOTERIOLOGY

    Towards a Responsible Contemporary Soteriology 213
        William Loewe

    For a Soteriology of the Existential Subject 229
        Sebastian Moore, OSB

    Alienation and Reconciliation 249
        Nancy Ring

ECCLESIOLOGY

    Lonergan and the Tasks of Ecclesiology 265
        Joseph Komonchak

    Sacrament: Symbol of Conversion 275
        Stephen Happel

    Consciousness in Christian Community 291
        Tad Dunne, SJ

Ethics

Moral Development: Is Conversion Necessary? 307
    Walter Conn

Bioethics as Anamnesis 325
    David Roy

The Theory and Praxis of Social Ethics 339
    John Raymaker

Aristotle's Notion of Epieikeia 353
    Garrett Barden

Language and Literary Criticism

Lonergan, Wittgenstein, and Where Language
Hooks onto the World 369
    Hugo Meynell

The Question of Belief in Literary Criticism 383
    Mary Gerhart

Phenomenology

The Transcendental Reduction according to Husserl
and Intellectual Conversion according to Lonergan 401
    William Ryan, SJ

Maréchal, Lonergan and the Phenomenology of Knowing 411
    Michael Vertin

Socio-Political Orientations

Method and the Social Appropriation of Reality 425
    William Mathews, SJ

Politics and Self-Acceptance 443
    Geoffrey Price

Horizonal Diplomacy 459
    Mark Morelli

Natural Science and Mathematics

Lonergan and the Foundations of the Theories of Relativity 477
    Patrick Byrne

From Body to Thing 495
    Joseph Flanagan, SJ

A Dialogue on Learning Mathematics 509
    Eric O'Connor, SJ

Macroeconomics

Insight and Emergence 529
    Michael Gibbons

Generalized Empirical Method and the Actual
Context of Economics 543
    Philip McShane

List of Contributors 573
Index of Names 575

Foundational Theology

Insight and Waiting on God

by John S. Dunne

Insight, I would say, is what happens when reasons of the heart become known to the mind.[1] It belongs both to the realm of mind and to that of heart. Lonergan's *Insight* is the log of a voyage of discovery in the realm of mind. It is the work of a "Ulysses of the realms of thought." There is the prospect of an almost unending series of further discoveries in those realms. "Brighter stars will rise on some voyager of the future — some great Ulysses of the realms of thought — than shine on us," Frazer says at the end of *The Golden Bough*. "The dreams of magic may one day be the waking realities of science."[2] Some of those discoveries may arise, though, not so much from exploring the realm of mind itself as from voyaging into the darker realm of heart where dreams have not yet become waking realities. What I would like to try here is an excursion into that darker region. I will use the term "insight," but where Lonergan uses it more in an intellectual context, that of method in science and common sense and philosophy and theology, I will use it more in an existential context, that of making choices and finding one's way in life.

I would like to reflect on the experience of waiting on God. It is, I believe, the heart of prayer. It is a waiting on a God who is hidden in the darkness, not only the darkness that comes before and after life but also the darkness that is found again and again during life whenever one is searching for one's way in life. The waiting is the praying, and the coming of God is the answer to the prayer, and His coming takes the form of a kindling of light in the darkness. This kindling of light I shall call "insight."

---

[1] Cf. my book, *The Reasons of the Heart* (New York: Macmillan Company, 1978), p. xii.

[2] Sir James Frazer, *The Golden Bough,* Part VII (London: Macmillan Company, 1913), vol. 2, p. 306.

Imagine a man who has come to a time of darkness in his life when he doesn't know which way to go. Say it is a question of his lifework, what to undertake, or if he is already well into his work, which way to go from here. Or say it is a question of his relations with others, whether to become part of a movement or a community or instead to try to find his own individual way. Or say it is a question of love, whether to give or to withhold his heart. Ordinarily a person would go through two stages in reaching a decision. First he would explore the possibilities in his mind, imagining himself into them: "If I were to do this, then this and this and this would happen; if I were to do that, then that and that and that would happen." Then at length he would make his choice: "I will do this rather than that." The first stage by itself does not ordinarily lead to a resolution. It only reveals the possibilities and their consequences. The choice still has to be made, and when it is made, there is a feel of something arbitrary about it. A person chooses one path, but it seems he could have chosen another, and he knows this, and the other remains with him as a "road not taken."

Let us imagine then a man who halts between the exploration of possibilities and the choice, and waits for insight. What he is doing when he is waiting is a kind of thinking, different though from the kind he was engaged in when he was exploring the possibilities. I shall call it "meditative thinking." The exploration of possibilities, on the other hand, I shall call "calculative thinking,"[3] for it calculates the consequences of each possible choice.

When he was exploring the possibilities, he was calculating advantages and disadvantages. One way of going with his work may have involved a high risk of failure, a new way of doing things, one he had not mastered. Another way may have had the advantage of being familiar, but the disadvantage of being unlikely to yield any fruit it had not already yielded. Or, if it was a matter of his relations to others, one way, that of becoming part of a movement, may have held the danger of submerging him in a collectivity while the other, that of trying to find his own way, may have held the counter-danger of rendering him isolated and ineffectual. Or, if it was a matter of love, one way, that of giving his heart, may have appeared to risk losing everything by trusting everything to a person who could well undergo a complete change of mind toward him. The other way, that of withholding his heart, may have appeared to risk forfeiting the fullness of life by not daring to trust.

---

[3] These terms are from Martin Heidegger, *Discourse on Thinking,* trans. John M. Anderson and E. Hans Freund (New York: Harper & Row Publishers, Inc., 1969), pp. 46ff., though Heidegger is thinking primarily of the contrast between philosophy and science while I am thinking of the contrast between planning and waiting on insight in a decision.

Now, as he waits for insight, he is not looking for an error in his calculations or for a new balance of advantages and disadvantages. He is looking rather for a new vision of the way. When he was calculating he was working out of the question "What shall I do with my life?" Now, as he waits for insight, he is asking a different question, "Is there something my life wants to do with me?", or if he is confident that his life does have a goal of its own, independent of any purpose he tries to impose upon it, then, "What does my life want of me?" It may be that it is not for him simply to choose this or that lifework but to do the work his life calls for, to accomplish the task his life poses for him. It may be too that it is not for him to decide to be part of some movement or community or to strike out on his own but to take the path his life demands, to find the way that is meant for him. And it may be that it is not for him simply to give or withhold his heart but to give his heart when his life demands that he give it and to withhold it when his life forbids him to give it.

The first question come first, though, "Is there something my life wants to do with me?" Or better perhaps, "Is there something my life demands of me or calls upon me to do?" He fears, let us say, that anything he may find in his life will turn out to be something he has put there himself, that any call he may think he hears will actually be the echo of this wish to be called. A good sign that it is a true call, he reasons, would be if it went against his wishes, if he were like the prophets who did not want to be prophets, like Jonah or Jeremiah. The sign of a true prophet, he is almost ready to conclude, is that he does not want to be a prophet, that the call to prophecy is against his wishes. On further thought it occurs to him that there could be part of him that does not want the call and another part of him that does. Maybe that was true of prophets too; maybe there was something in them that did not want to be prophets and something that did. Anyway, a call that goes against one wish could be in accord with another, could even be an echo of that other. So the fact that a call is against certain of his wishes, he is forced to conclude, is no sign that it is a true call. Indeed maybe a call is always in accord with one's deepest wishes, he reflects, always an echo of one's heart's desire. Maybe the call is the heart's desire and one is led by one's heart.

If that is true, then in waiting for insight, he sees, he is waiting for his heart to speak. What he should be doing while he is waiting is listening to the different voices within himself. Say he begins therefore to listen to his inner voices. He is entering now into the second question, "What does my life want of me?" Or better, "What does my life demand of me?" The first question, nevertheless, is still in the back of his mind and comes to the fore whenever the inner voices seem to conflict and there seems to be no one thing that is called for. Kierkegaard's saying comes to mind. "Purity of heart is to will one thing."[4] The man we are imagining is searching his heart for that one thing, trying to come to purity of heart. He searches and searches, let us say, but does not find it. He hears one voice within himself urging him to break new ground in his work, but another urging him to continue what he has been doing to reach its full fruit. He hears one voice urging him toward participation in a movement or a community but another urging him to set out on his own individual path. He hears one voice urging him to give his heart but another urging him to withhold it.

For a moment he thinks he has fallen back into calculative thinking, for these inner voices are urging the very same things he was considering when he was calculating his possible courses of action. Yet he himself, he realizes now, is no longer calculating but listening. He is listening indeed to inner voices that are calculating, but his interest now is not in the calculations themselves but in the sources of all these calculations. He is trying to find out what part of himself is speaking when he hears a given voice and its promptings. As he listens to the inner voices he realizes that they are taking into consideration the outer circumstances of his life. So he cannot decide between them by introducing something from the outside that they are not taking into account. The only thing that is over and above them is his own listening. That, he reflects, may be the unifying factor, his listening, his waiting for insight. In fact that waiting, he begins to see, is the willing of one thing. He is willing one thing insofar as he is waiting for one thing: the one thing is like the x in an algebraic equation. It is an unknown quantity, the unknown path he must walk, and his willing it is really a willingness to walk it.

Purity of heart for him, he sees, consists in waiting for insight, in waiting for his unknown path to be revealed. Yet he is still in the darkness; the path is still unknown. As he continues to wait now he does not know what to do with his time, whether to continue listening to inner voices in the hope that one of them may prove to be the voice of heart's desire or whether to expect something entirely new to appear on the scene. He continues nevertheless to wait. He begins to worry about the amount of time he is spending in waiting. He begins to fear that he is simply being indecisive, trying to escape the hard necessity of making a decision and of taking responsibility for his path and his life. Still he continues to wait, seeing that the waiting itself is unifying everything in him and giving him a purity of heart.

---

[4] Søren Kierkegaard, *Purity of Heart Is to Will One Thing*, trans. Douglas V. Steere (New York: Harper & Row Publishers, Inc., 1956).

As he continues on in the darkness hoping for some light to appear, he notices that the aspect of his choices is changing. He wonders whether this is a beginning of light or whether his eyes are simply becoming accustomed to the dark. The waiting, he can see, is itself working a change in him. His choices begin to appear in a new perspective, that of the waiting itself. Some of them seem more in accord with the spirit of waiting for insight than others. Some of them seem to have no significance beyond the calculative, but some seem to embody the meditative spirit of the waiting. The saying of Jesus comes to mind, "Blessed are the pure in heart, for they shall see God." [5] He begins to hope that the waiting in darkness is a willing on one thing, a purity of heart, that will enable him to see his way, to see the way God wants him to follow. That seeing of the way, he expects, will be the seeing of God, a seeing of the will of God. The willing of one thing and the will of God, he thinks, must somehow go together. His own waiting for insight is a gathering of all his forces, a coming together of everything within him. If God leads by the heart, then God's leading should come to light, as it seems to be doing, when the heart becomes pure, when the heart begins to will one thing.

He is able now to pose the question of choice in terms of the heart. He has waited long enough for risks and calculations to recede into the background and for the question of the heart to come into the foreground. "Would my heart be in this work?" he asks now of each possible lifework. That question is quite a different one from the original one of success and failure he was asking when he was engaged in calculative thinking. "Would my heart be in this movement," he asks now of each collective trend, "or would my heart be rather in finding my own individual way?" That question is different too from the original one of being submerged in the collectivity or being isolated as an individual. "Would my heart be in giving my heart," he asks now of love, "or would giving my heart only divide my heart?" And that question is different from his former one of losing everything by a mistaken trust or losing everything instead by a failure to trust. He has come, it seems, from trying to find his way between opposing fears to trying to find the way of heart.

These questions he is asking now are so simple that it seems he could have asked them at any time. Still the waiting on insight has been a purification of his heart that has enabled him to pass from his initial fears and calculation of risks to the matter of his heart's desire. The questions of the heart could have been asked at any time but only now have they become upper-most in his mind. They cast a

---

[5] Matthew 5:8.

light upon his alternatives, or the heart itself casts a light upon them, that makes it seem possible now to make a choice that is not arbitrary. Where before it seemed that he could go various ways with his lifework, it seems fairly clear now that there is only one way in which his heart would be fully in his work. Where before it seemed that he could either join in a movement or go his own way, it seems now that one of these would be for him a heartless path while the other would be the path of his heart. Where before it seemed that he could either give or withhold his heart, it seems now there is only one way to follow his heart's desire.

He makes his choice. As he makes it, though, he is aware that he is not entirely sure of himself. There are three things of which he is uncertain. One is whether in willing this thing his heart is whole or whether there is rather some part of his heart that is not included and that does not will this thing at all. He is uncertain, that is, whether his heart is pure in this matter. The second is whether the path he has chosen is indeed the path of his heart's desire. It is conceivable that even if his heart were not pure he may have hit upon the path of heart's desire and has simply the task of purifying his heart and putting his whole heart into the path. On the other hand, he may have made a mistaken choice in spite of all good will and may find after he has begun to travel it that the path is a heartless one. The third is whether the path he has chosen is indeed the will of God and whether the light he thinks he has found in the darkness is really an illumination of mind and heart by God.

He makes his decision with the awareness, therefore, that he may be entirely wrong. In coming to his decision, however, he has not been seeking certainty so much as understanding. He has been waiting for insight, not for certainty. If his heart is not pure, if the path he has chosen is not that of heart's desire, if it is not the will of God for him, then he has hope that this will come to light as he travels the path. His waiting for insight continues on into the carrying out of his decision. He meets his uncertainty not by seeking for certainty, a quest that tends to defeat itself—the more intensely one seeks to be certain the more uncertain one becomes.[6] But by continuing to wait for insight, his whole life becomes a waiting for insight and his hope is that he will be led from one insight to another, that his life will become a voyage of discovery.

---

[6] On the quest of certainty defeating itself and on going over from the quest of certainty to the quest of understanding cf. my books, *A Search for God in Time and Memory* (New York: Macmillan Company, 1969), pp. 217ff., and *The Way of All the Earth* (New York: Macmillan Company, 1972), pp. 42ff.

There is a passage in the *Four Quartets* where T. S. Eliot seems to describe exactly the experience I have been talking about, waiting on God and coming to insight:

> I said to my soul, be still, and wait without hope
> For hope would be hope for the wrong thing; wait without love
> For love would be love of the wrong thing; there is yet faith
> But the faith and the love and the hope are all in the waiting.
> Wait without thought, for you are not ready for thought:
> So the darkness shall be the light, and the stillness the dancing.[7]

To "wait without hope" and "without love" is to wait without setting my heart on this road or that, for that would prevent the true road from appearing. But there is faith and hope and love in the waiting itself. To "wait without thought" is to wait without calculative thought, but the waiting itself is meditative thought. So the mind shall be illumined and the heart kindled, "the darkness shall be the light, and the stillness the dancing."

---

[7] T. S. Eliot, *Four Quartets* (New York: Harcourt, Brace & World, 1971). p. 28 ("East Coker," III).

Passages and Conversions

by Bernard Tyrrell

It is a joy to contribute to this *Festschrift* in honor of Professor Bernard Lonergan, S.J. on the occasion of his seventy-fifth birthday. Bernard Lonergan has enriched my life, in ways which cannot be measured, through the gift of his friendship and the gifts to me and to the whole world of his great philosophical and theological writings. My own contribution to this *Festschrift* is taken from my present "work in progress" tentatively entitled *Foundations and Process of Christotherapy*. Without the aid of Lonergan's powerful cognitional theory and his unique articulations of the processes of religious and moral conversion, I would be incapable of doing the type of foundational thinking and writing which presently engages me. Lonergan's whole approach invites "ongoing collaboration." I offer my present contribution as an instance of one man's effort to respond to Lonergan's call for collaboration and as a "birthday present" to a great thinker and friend.

When I wrote *Christotherapy*[1] my general aim was to offer an initial sketch of a theology of Christ as healer of the whole person—in a beginning fashion in this life and totally in the life of the final resurrection. One of my specific goals was to work out in a relatively popular fashion the rudiments of a Christian approach to counseling and psychotherapy.[2] A key method was to utilize key insights of such psychotherapists as Drs. Thomas Hora, Viktor Frankl, William Glasser, Kazimierz Dabrowski and others as a kind of lens through which I could meditatively consider Scripture and the teachings of Christianity and hopefully highlight and at times make explicit

---

[1] Bernard Tyrrell, *Christotherapy: Healing through Enlightenment* (New York: Seabury Press, 1975).

[2] In my use of the terms counseling and psychotherapy I generally follow the usage of Gerald Correy in his *Theory and Practice of Counseling and Psychotherapy* (Montery, California: Brooks/Cole, 1977).

psychotherapeutic elements present in the revelational event of Jesus Christ.

Regis Duffy, however, in a review of my book,[3] suggested that what I seemed fundamentally to be attempting in *Christotherapy* was to reevaluate in a contemporary context the basics of the Christian spiritual life itself. In reflecting on Duffy's comment and on others of a similar nature I came to agree. In *Christotherapy* I do try to deal with the undergirding principles of Christian existence. I do try to show how true Christian spirituality impacts the human person in all the dimensions of his or her existence, the psychic and bodily, as well as the spiritual. I now see more clearly than before that it is just as valid to look upon *Christotherapy* as a proposed form of spiritual direction which explicitly and methodically makes use of certain tools and insights of psychology and psychotherapy as it is to view it as a type of psychotherapy which makes prayer, God, and the Christ-event central to its authentic unfoldment.

As a result of what I have learned in the past few years, I hope to show in my book in process how the principles of Christotherapy, now in a more mature and nuanced state of development, can be profitably utilized both by spiritual directors and by Christian counselors and psychotherapists, as well as by laypersons who with God's help seek healing and growth for themselves and for others. I presently see Christotherapy as *one* of a number of contemporary attempts to formulate a new science or "new wisdom." This new science seeks to integrate the principles of healing and growth both of Christian revelation and of psychology and psychotherapy in such a fashion that it can become a holistic, generative source both of effective spiritual direction and of Christian counseling. My entire effort, of course, rests on my firm conviction (1) that such a project as a Christian psychotherapy is possible and desirable both in theory and in practice,[4] and (2) that the professional practice of spiritual direction in our highly complex cultural milieu requires as deep a knowledge as possible of the natural laws and processes of the human psyche as well as of the subtle workings of grace in the human spirit.[5]

---

[3] Regis Duffy, "Book Review of Christotherapy," *The American Ecclesiastical Review*, October, 1975, pp. 568-569.

[4] Cf. Bernard Tyrrell, "On the Possibility and Desirability of a Christian Psychotherapy," *Lonergan Workshop,* Vol. I (Missoula Montana: Scholars Press, 1978), pp. 143-185.

[5] Cf. James Gill, "Psychiatry, Psychology and Spirituality Today," *Chicago Studies,* Vol. 15, Spring 1976, No. 1, pp. 27-37.

I. "New Wisdom"

A principal breakthrough insight which has helped me to develop my own example of the new wisdom is the understanding that there exists a powerful analogy and relationship between four key conversion processes to which human beings can be subject. The four conversion processes are: religious conversion, moral conversion, psychological conversion, and the conversion from addiction. All of these processes are truly forms of conversion — *analogously understood.* All of these processes involve two basic stages: radical conversion and ongoing conversion. Further, both radical conversion and ongoing converson consist in twofold movements. In radical conversion there is a "turning from" a fundamentally destructive form of existing or operating and a "turning toward" a basically constructive, life-creating, and fulfilling way of existing and acting. In ongoing conversion there is a confirmation of the "turning from" of radical conversion by a continuously deepening rejection of remaining destructive tendencies and a tranformation of the "turning toward" of radical conversion by an ever intensified embracing of what is life-enriching. Also, God's Holy Spirit and the graces of the Spirit are active in each of these conversion processes in a manner congruent with the type of conversion involved. Likewise, human freedom and decision play a vital role in the unfoldment of each of these processes of conversion. A principal aim, then, in the development of the new wisdom is to show how these four key conversions share in common, though in an analogous manner, certain basic stages of unfoldment and how the grace of God and free decisions play a pivotal, crucial role in each of these processes.

II. Passages

It was in the beginning the sharpness of personal pain that drove me into the series of passages which resulted in my ever deepening insight into the rich relationship and affinities which exist between the diverse conversion processes to which I have referred.

Acute neurotic pain first goaded me into my passing over into the psychotherapeutic world of Dr. Thomas Hora. The latter's emphasis on the centrality of God and prayer in the psychotherapeutic process at first stunned and perplexed me. I looked around somewhat desperately for some living, flesh and blood example, of a neurotic who had found healing in an appeal to God and His Christ. Providentially, I found what I was looking for in Maurice Nesbitt's powerful, autobiographical account of his own healing in his book *Where No Fear Was.*[6] I at once felt a strong personal bond with

---

[6] Maurice Nesbitt, *Where No Fear Was* (London: Epworth Press, 1966).

Nesbitt because fear was the demon with which I too had to struggle in a special way. Nesbitt related how he had a nervous breakdown as a young man of twenty and another as a middle aged man of fifty. The latter experience made him reflect that apparently he had learned nothing in thirty years and that there was nothing ahead of him except misery and despair. At this point he turned to the Scriptures in his search for psychological emancipation and by the grace of God he discovered that Jesus in his words and parables had a psychological and spiritual teaching which can liberate the tormented neurotic from his or her chains. Nesbitt's discovery led to his own liberation. Nesbitt in turn gave me hope, although he taught me at the same time that the healing of neurosis is truly a matter of conversion, that it can be a "bloody" and often lengthy process and that enlightened personal decision or decisions, inspired, sustained, and strengthened by God's grace play an important role in the process.

If neurotic pain provided the initial impetus for my passing over into the worlds of Hora and Nesbitt, the agony of active addiction, in my case alcoholism, drove me to pass over into the world of Guest House, a treatment center for alcoholic priests and religious brothers.[7] At Guest House I also came across the "Big Book" which is the basic text for *Alcoholics Anonymous* and, in fact, bears that latter name as its official title.[8] I should make it clear at once that in my comments on the "Big Book" and various aspects of *Alcoholics Anonymous* I do not write as a member of *Alcoholics Anonymous* but as an individual who has passed over profoundly and with ever growing sympathetic understanding into the basic horizon and worldview which *Alcoholics Anonymous* embraces and embodies.

It was in my meditative reading of the "Big Book" that I first learned that the movement of *Alcoholics Anonymous* had its roots in a powerful conversion experience of its founder, Bill Wilson. My reading of the "Big Book" also gave me the opportunity to pass over into the lives of a whole series of anonymous individuals, pioneers of the *Alcoholics Anonymous* movement, who found healing and high level psychic and spiritual growth by assimilating and living the spiritual principles of *Alcoholics Anonymous*. These readings all served to heighten my awareness that the healing of the addict is a conversion, that it is a dynamic process with stages and that God-given enlightened personal decision is a vital factor in it.

---

[7] The address of the Guest House I attended is as follows: Guest House, RFD 4, Box 954, Rochester, Minnesota, 55901.

[8] Anonymous Authors, *Alcoholics Anonymous* (New York: Alcoholics Anonymous World Services, Inc., 1939).

What struck me most forcefully in my various quests for healing was that I inevitably found myself propelled into a headlong encounter with God. The truth contained in Francis Thompson's daring description of God as the *Hound of Heaven* verified itself for me again and again.

III. Four Conversion Processes

For the present essay to become a reality I needed more than my psychological and spiritual adventures of passing over into the psychotherapeutic worlds of Hora and Guest House, I also needed the type of insight which grasps an analogy and a deep relationship between the diverse forms of conversion I had experienced and continued to experience. As an enthusiastic appropriator of Bernard Lonergan's highly rewarding method of doing philosophy and theology I had a good start in my quest for a unified understanding of my diverse conversion experiences. Lonergan taught me much about the nature of religious and moral conversion. But I needed the further encounters with the famous *Twelve Steps* of *Alcoholics Anonymous,* the writings of Gaston Fessard[9], Andras Angyal[10], and others to provide me with the pivotal insight by which I understood that there exists a powerful analogy and relationship between the four basic conversion processes I mentioned earlier. What I would like to do now is to look at each of thm four conversion processes in some detail, beginning with religious conversion.

IV. Religious Conversion

Webster's New Collegiate Dictionary's (1973) definitions of both the verb "to convert" and the noun "conversion" give these terms primarily a religious denotation. For Webster "to convert" is "to bring over from one belief . . . to another" and the noun "conversion" basically signifies "an experience associated with a definite and decisive adoption of religion." Clearly in the common understanding it is the process of religious conversion which provides the paradigm in the light of which all other so-called conversions are to be analogously understood.

My main concern at present is with the process of religious conversion in the Judeo-Christian tradition. There are, of course, many modes of Christian conversion. There is, for example, the case of the infant who is baptized and then dies. Again, there is the instance of

---

[9] Gaston Fessard, *La dialectique des Exercises spirituels de saint Ignace de Loyola.* 2 vols. (Paris: Aubier, 1956 and 1966).

[10] Andras Angyal, *Neurosis and Treatment: A Holistic Theory* (New York: Viking Press, 1965).

the person who is baptized as an infant and who, upon reaching an appropriate level of psychological and moral development ratifies the gift received in baptism and never deviates thereafter from the path of righteousness. Further, there is the complex situation where an adult baptized Christian shifts allegiance from one Christian denomination to another. In each of these instances the reality of Christian conversion is involved in some manner. I choose, however, to use as my basic example of the phenomenon of Christian religious conversion the case of an adult who is *converted from* a stance of radical denial of God in mind, heart, and actions *to* a state of basic commitment to Jesus Christ in mind, heart, and ethical behavior.

Saint Augustine in his *Confessions* provides us with an eloquent and moving witness to the basic "turning from" and "turning toward" of radical religious conversion and to the initiating, transforming, and consummating role of God in the process. Augustine relates how, in a period of great crisis and inner struggle, "I cast myself down I know not how, under a certain fig tree, giving full vent to my tears."[11] The saint then recounts how he prayed:

> "And Thou, O Lord, how long?" "How long, Lord, wilt Thou be angry, for ever? Remember not our former iniquities," for I felt that I was held by them. I sent up these sorrowful words: "How long? How long? Tomorrow and tomorrow? Why not now? why not is there an end to my uncleanness?"[12]

Augustine immediately added:

> So I was speaking and weeping in the most bitter contrition of my heart, when, lo! I heard from a neighbouring house a voice as of boy or girl, I know not, chanting and oft repeating, "Take up and read; take up and read."[13]

At this point Augustine's glance fell on a volume of the writings of Paul the Apostle. He opened it and read the section on which his eyes fell:

> "Not in rioting and drunkenness, not in chambering and wantonness, not in strife and envying; but put ye on the Lord Jesus Christ, and, make not provision for the flesh," in concupiscense. No further would I read; not needed I: for instantly at the end of the sentence, by a light as it were of serenity infused into my heart all darkness vanished.[14]

---

[11] Augustine, *Great Books of the Western World,* Vol. 18 (Chicago: Encyclopedia Britannica, 1952), p. 60.
[12] Ibid.
[13] Ibid., p. 61.
[14] Ibid.

Augustine's dramatic description of his conversion experience in the garden reflects central elements of the radical conversion process as the Old and New Testaments speak of it. The apostle Peter in an early address to the people of Israel reminded them that it is God who takes the initiative in turning them from the path of evil: "God, having raised up his servant, sent him to you first, to bless you in turning every one of you from your wickedness" (Acts 3:26). Augustine experienced God's initiative through the mediation of the voices of the children who chanted: "Take and read." Again, the Lord Jesus told Paul on the way to Damascus that He was sending him to the Gentiles "to open their eyes, that they may turn from darkness to light, and from the power of Satan to God" (Acts 26:18). Over three hundred years later God used the words of Paul to let Augustine know that he had to renounce the works of the flesh and turn from them once and for all. At the same moment Augustine was told to "put ye on the Lord Jesus Christ." Ezechiel, one of the greatest prophets who spoke of the need for conversion in the Hebrew Testament, described the core moment of radical conversion in the graphic words: "And I will give them one heart, and put a new spirit within them; I will take the stony heart out of their flesh and give them a heart of flesh" (11:19). Paul was depicting this same radical moment when he wrote to the Romans that "God's love has been poured into our hearts through the Holy Spirit which has been given to us" (Rom 5:5). Augustine appears to be describing this core reality Ezechiel and Paul speak of when he writes that darkness vanished from his heart as a light of serenity was infused into it.

Before I shift attention to the twofold "turning from" and "turning toward" of ongoing Christian religious conversion, I would like to indicate why I chose in describing the process of radical conversion to speak first of a "turning from" and subsequently of a "turning toward." A direct citation of Thomas Aquinas' analysis of the "moments" involved in the process of justification will make it immediately clear why I raise this issue here. Aquinas, then, names four elements which are constituents in the justification process: "The infusion of grace, the movement of free choice toward God by faith, the movement of free choice against sin, and the remission of guilt."[15] Aquinas insists that these elements are listed according to the natural and proper order of their occurrence. Aquinas' order of elements appears to contradict my own since he indicates that in the person's response to God's justifying action there is first a turning of

---

[15] Thomas Aquinas, *Basic Writings of Saint Thomas Aquinas*, Vol. II, Edited by Anton C. Pegis (New York: Random House, 1945), *Summa Theologica* I-II, q.113, a.6, response.

free will to God in faith and then a turning from sin. An adequate response to this apparently serious objection to my basic procedure requires that I distinguish between the central moment of radical conversion or justification and the stages which lead up to it and culminate in it.

Basically I am in complete agreement with Aquinas' analysis of the stages involved in the central moment of radical conversion itself. There is no question but that the "turning toward" enjoys a natural priority over the "turning from." As Aquinas succinctly argues: "He who is being justified detests sin because it is against God, and thus the movement of free choice towards God naturally precedes the movement of free choice against sin, since it is its cause and reason."[16] But Aquinas is equally insistent that there is no temporal succession in the core moments of the justification process. They occur simultaneously. Moreover, Aquinas also acknowledges that in the adult who undergoes radical conversion or justification preparatory phases generally lead up to it. For example, Aquinas writes that "before justification, a man must detest each sin he remembers to have committed."[17] Aquinas' doctrine is in accord with the general Roman Catholic belief solemnly professed at the Council of Trent that a person can dispose and prepare himself for the grace of justification by assenting to God's initial calls and awakening graces.

In the case of radical adult Christian conversion God most often begins to move a person toward the core moment of radical conversion or justification by such graces as arousing in the person a sense of disgust with the self-destructive effects of immoral living, a fear of punishments that await a person who perdures in his or her rejection of God, a growing feeling of guilt and shame, an experience of moral impotence and powerlessness.

Apart from God's healing grace, of course, these experiences could lead to despair and even suicide. But when these experiences are enlightened by God's healing grace they become occasions for the beginning of a turning away from a destructive, idolatrous, self-centered type of existence and a turning toward the true source of life. In the Hebrew Testament, for example, we read how again and again God sought to bring his wayward chosen people back to himself by letting them experience the harshness of life apart from Him. In the book of Hosea, for example, Gomer, the prophet's unfaithful wife, is a symbol of Israel in her infidelity to the Lord.

---

[16] Ibid., a.8., response.

[17] Ibid., a.5, reply to objection 3.

And how does the Lord act to draw His disloyal spouse back to Himself?

> I will hedge up her way with thorns; and I will build a wall against her, so that she cannot find her paths. She shall pursue her lovers, but not overtake them; and she shall seek them, but shall not find them. Then she shall say, "I will go and return to my first husband, for it was better with me then than now (Hos 2:6-7)."

Notice the parallel in Gomer's experience with that of the prodigal son in the celebrated Lucan parable. Luke writes that after the son squandered his inheritance in loose living and found himself in the midst of a famine

> he went and joined himself to one of the citizens of that country who sent him into his fields to feed the swine. And he would gladly have fed on the pods that the swine ate, but no one gave him anything. But when he came to himself he said, "How many of my father's hired servants have bread enough and to spare, but I perish here with hunger. I will arise and go to my father. . . . (Lk 15: 15-18)"

The examples from Hosea and the parable of the prodigal son both graphically portray the beginnings of the process leading to radical conversion as a painful turning away from what is destructive. It is true, of course, as Charles Curran and Hans Kung both emphasize, that conversion in the New Testament is basically a joyous affair. Curran writes that "New Testament theology teaches that conversion is the joyful change of heart that comes from hearing the good news of salvation"[18] and Kung states that "aversion from the sinful past and the return of the whole man to God is a joyful event for God and men."[19] Yet, Curran, in bringing the parable of the prodigal son up to date remarks that the son at the end of his tether "experiences only sorrow, slavery and misery."[20] There is, I believe, no contradiction in stressing that there is joy at the core of radical conversion while the initial stage of turning away from what is evil can be quite painful. In both the Old and New Testaments God is often portrayed as utilizing the painfulness of a disintegration process as a means of effecting a turning away from evil and a turning toward the good on the part of the suffering person. And Ignatius of Loyola confirms this initial action of God in the conversion process when he writes in his "Rules for the Discernment of Spirits" that in the case of

---

[18] Charles Curran, "Conversion: The Central Message of Jesus,"*Conversion,* ed. Walter Conn (New York: Alba House, 1978), p. 226.

[19] Hans Kung, "Christian Conversion," *Conversion,* ed. Walter Conn, p. 275.

[20] Curran, "Conversion," p. 227.

persons "who go from one mortal sin to another" the good spirit "rouses the sting of conscience and fills them with remorse."[21]

In my discussion of radical religious conversion in its preparatory and core moments I have focused attention on the classical issue of justification. I would like to point out that Dr. Lawrence Crabb, a Presbyterian clinical psychologist, in his most recent book, *Effective Biblical Counseling*,[22] makes the matter of justification and sanctification the cental concern of his first chapter. Crabb, like myself, is seeking to flesh out a working model of the new wisdom within the context of his own Christian denomination. Crabb clearly recognizes that the issue of Christian conversion, both in its justification and sanctification stages, is central to any attempt to develop a specifically Christian model of counseling.[23]

The mention of the word "sanctification" leads naturally into a consideration of ongoing religious conversion with its continuously deepening confirmation of the "turning from" and its ever richer transformation of the "turning toward" of radical conversion. The process of Christian religious conversion is not finished at the moment of justification when God replaces the heart of stone with the heart of flesh and pours forth his love through the gift of the Holy Spirit. There is also need for an ongoing waging of the daily battle against the world, the flesh, and the devil. Above all, there is an exigency for an ever deepening growth in the love of God and of one's neighbor.

The author of the epistle to the Hebrews exhorts his fellow Christians in words which capture very well the ever intensifying "turning from" and "turning toward" of ongoing religious conversion:

> Therefore, since we are surrounded by so great a cloud of witnesses, let us also lay aside every weight and sin which clings

---

[21] Louis J. Puhl, S.J. *The Spiritual Exercises of St. Ignatius* (Chicago: Loyola University Press, 1951), p. 141.

[22] Lawrence Crabb, *Effective Biblical Counseling* (Grand Rapids: Zondervan, 1977), pp. 22-30.

[23] Dr. Crabb's understanding of justification differs in certain important respects from my own. I agree with the following comment of Cardinal William Baum which he made in his keynote address to the National Workshop on Christian Unity held on April 23, 1979 in Birmingham, Alabama: "Historically, many of the differences that arose at the time of the division of the 16th century concerned the mystery of justification. This seems a good moment to note that the Lutheran-Roman Catholic theological discussions are now dealing with this mystery. With the Lord's help, we will be able to dispel some of the misunderstandings that contributed to our division on this central truth of the faith. It seems to me that the mystery of justification still contains the key to many of our differences in other areas and therefore a greater agreement concerning this mystery will lead to greater unity in our perception of other aspects of divine revelation." This citation is found in *Origins,* National Catholic Documentary Service, Vol. 8, No. 47, May 10, 1979, p. 751.

so closely, and let us run with perseverance the race that is set before us, looking to Jesus the pioneer and perfecter of our faith, who for the joy that was set before him endured the cross, despising the shame, and is seated at the right hand of the throne of God (Heb 2:1-2).

The writer of Hebrews is here reminding his readers of the need to turn away more completely from whatever weight and sin still encumber them and above all to turn with fixed gaze toward Jesus who is now enthroned at God's right hand. The simile of the race is used and Hebrews echoes the words of Paul in his epistle to the Philippians: "Not that . . . I am already perfect but I press on . . . ; one thing I do, forgetting what lies behind, and straining forward to what lies ahead, I press on toward the goal for the prize of the upward call of God in Christ Jesus (Phil 3:12-14)."

It is necessary for the radically converted Christian to take up the cross daily in ongoing imitation of Christ and of his disciple Paul (Phil 3:17) and to seek to share ever more richly even now in the resurrection of Christ by seeking "the things that are above, where Christ is, seated at the right hand of God" (Col 3:1). This process of ongoing conversion, with its continuous "turning from" and "turning toward", its daily dying and rising with Christ, is repeated at ever higher levels in the spiral of transcendence. The reality of the ongoing nature of religious conversion is clearly witnessed to and manifested in the lives and writings of such an early Christian saint as Ignatius of Antioch and of such towering Christian mystics as Theresa of Avila and John of the Cross, with their respective talk of ever richer interior mansions and of a succession of dark nights and ever more luminous dawns.

V. Moral Conversion

Religious conversion and moral conversion are clearly interrelated. Yet, there are grounds both in ordinary experience and in philosophy and theology as well for considering moral conversion in its own right instead of just in its relationship to religious conversion. Thus, there are countless instances of non-believers and of self-acknowledged atheists who live highly upright, moral lives. An essay by Wang Tao-ming, a Marxist instructor in China, shows just how great a moral concern and selfless service of others can manifest itself in professed atheists.[24] Further, it is a fact of life that the human community finds it possible both in everyday affairs and on the

---

[24] Wang Tao-Ming tn *Religion for a New Generation,* ed. Jacob Needleman, A.K. Pierman and James A. Gould (New York: Macmillan Company, 1973), pp. 104-115.

international level of professional discourse, e.g. at the United Nations, to dialogue on moral issues without reference to theology. I believe that this human ability for discussing moral issues independently of an explicit theological context is rooted in the fact that it belongs to the nature of the human being to be able to perform natural moral acts and to discuss moral matters from an experiential and rational perspective. This is why Lonergan is able to offer a definition of moral conversion which is intelligible to theists and atheists alike. In Lonergan's definition moral conversion is a matter of deciding to act responsibly and to be governed fundamentally in one's ethical activities by the criterion of what is truly good and worthwhile instead of by what merely satisfies a person's immediate demands for self-gratification.[25]

But there is the further question regarding the dynamic movement which takes place in radical and ongoing moral conversion. Here I find especially helpful a distinction philosopher Joseph de Finance draws between a "vertical" exercise of human freedom and a "horizontal" exercise of this same freedom.[26] In my application of this distinction, the vertical exercise of human freedom in the case of the adult who undergoes radical moral conversion involves a fundamental about-face in which the person turns from a basically destructive, immoral way of existing and acting in the world to a way of being and operating which is authentically worthwhile and truly good. It is most appropriate to describe this radical shift as a "vertical" exercise of human freedom and decision because by it the individual is catapulted into a new plane or sphere of moral existence, into a fresh world of authentic value, into an entirely novel horizon. The horizontal exercise of liberty, however, as the literal meaning of the term horizontal suggests, is a movement forward or backward along the same plane within which a person is already functioning. There is no basic shift in plane or sphere of existence, no radical passage into a new world or horizon. The horizontal exercise of liberty, accordingly, applies more appropriately in the area of ongoing moral conversion in which the person turns ever more firmly away from any temptations arising from remnants of old destructive allegiances and turns ever more totally to the new world of moral values embraced in radical moral conversion.

It is Christian belief, however, that the effects of original and personal sin so interfere with a person's natural moral functioning that apart from the gift of God's transforming love and His healing and

---

[25] Bernard Lonergan, *Method in Theology* (New York: Seabury Press, 1970), p. 240.

[26] Joseph de Finance, *Essai sur l'agir humain* (Rome: Presses de l'Université Grégorienne, 1962), pp. 287 ff.

enlightening graces no radical or sustained ongoing moral conversion is possible. For this reason Lonergan cogently argues that it is the occurrence of radical and ongoing religious conversion which makes effective moral conversion possible. Religious conversion is, in Lonergan's words, "the efficacious ground of all self-transcendence, whether in the pursuit of truth, or in the realization of human values."[27]

Lonergan and most other Catholic theologians hold, especially in the light of the teachings of Vatican II, that the Holy Spirit is powerfully and transformatively at work in all human minds and hearts, at least in an invisible, hidden, interior fashion. This teaching means that wherever radical and sustained ongoing moral conversion takes place it is due to the presence of an inner religious conversion, effected by the Holy Spirit. This is the case even if the religiously and morally converted person in question is not an explicit Christian believer or reflectively aware of the true inner source of his or her conversions. As Rahner put it:

> Where a man is detached from self . . . loves his neighbor unselfishly, trustingly accepts his existence in its incomprehensibility . . . ; where he succeeds in renouncing the idols of his moral fear and hunger for life, there the kingdom of God, God Himself . . . is accepted and known, even if this occurs quite unreflectingly. In this way the conversion remains implicit and "anonymous" and in certain circumstances Christ is not expressly known (though attained in his "Spirit").[28]

There is, of course, a negative side to the theological view which holds that the Father of Jesus Christ is at work through the power of His Holy Spirit at least in an invisible, anonymous manner in the minds and hearts of all human beings. This is the dark element of sin. I have dodged the issue of sin in the present context because it is a theological notion and I wanted to focus centrally on moral conversion in a non-theological context. Yet, the position of Rahner, Lonergan, and many others on the anonymous working of the Holy Spirit in the hearts of all human beings equally implies that when a person says a radical, "vertical" *No* rather than *Yes* to authentic demands of life and of existence this person is also saying a radical *No* to God and to Christ, even though perhaps not in a reflectively conscious manner.

Ladislas Orsy describes the person who says *No* to the authentic demands of existence through the exercise of a radical, fundamental

---

[27] Bernard Lonergan, "Theology in its New Context," *Conversion,* ed. Walter Conn, p. 19.

[28] Karl Rahner, "Conversion," *Conversion,* ed. Walter Conn, p. 205.

moral option as *"given to evil."*[29] Orsy and others sharply distinguish between the type of radical *No* whereby a person disposes of himself or herself as a whole in a destructive way and thus "sins unto death"[30] and the type of *No* which does not effect a radical deformation in the moral being of the person but merely weakens the person in his or her fundamental commitment to the truly good and worthwhile. Classical Roman Catholic theology expressed this distinction through the terms "mortal" and "venial" sin. Today, however, many moral theologians prefer to speak in more existential, personalist terms of the distinction between a fundamental moral option of a radical nature and more limited exercises of human freedom. These theologians also put more emphasis on basic inner orientations and moral stances rather than on isolated moral acts. Despite this current trend however, Orsy does not hesitate to give examples of individual moral acts which he says tend to betray in a person the presence of a basic radical option against God and hence of "internal death."[31] Among such acts Orsy mentions the following:

> Cooly calculated homicide, the denial of faith for temporal advantages, the contempt of marriage covenant through adultery, the ruining of someone through purjury, the misuse of funds given for the support of orphans and widows.[32]

In these cases there is often enough a need for radical religious and moral conversion.

A final point I would like to make in this discussion of moral conversion is that individuals who undergo radical moral conversion know through bitter experience the particular idol or group of idols which they are prone to worship. This sadly won self-knowledge serves to tip-off these persons about the particular form of turning from and turning toward which their ongoing moral conversion should take. Divine providence thus turns the weapons of the Evil One against himself by utilizing the very character weaknesses and foibles of individuals as a means of drawing them to ever higher levels in the spiral of ongoing moral and religious conversion.

VI. Psychological Conversion

The expression "psychological conversion" is my own. The notion of a conversion of a psychological nature is recent, but not unique to

---

[29]. Ladislas Orsy, *Blessed are those who have Questions* (Denville, New Jersey: Dimensions Books, Inc.), p. 46.
[30] Ibid.
[31] Ibid.
[32] Ibid.

myself. Robert Doran has worked out a theory of "psychic conversion"[33] which is inspired largely by Jung and Lonergan. Donald Gelpi has proposed a theory of "affective conversion"[34] which roots itself in the psychologies of Carl Rogers, Jung, and others. There are certain commonalities between these three theories of conversion, but key differences in emphasis, inspiration, development, and goal preclude any facile identification of the three. Nor do I intend here to discuss the interrelationship of the three theories. But, since the very notion of a psychological conversion is novel and hence almost inevitably controversial, I thought it wise to begin my own discussion by indicating that other theologian-philosophers are doing seminal, creative and, to an extent, convergent work in this same largely uncharted area.

What, then, is psychological conversion?[35] In my definition psychological conversion is a shift from a basically neurotic way of existing and functioning to a dominantly healthy psychic state of being and acting. Further, psychological conversion, like religious and moral conversion, is a process which involves two basic stages: radical and ongoing conversion. Likewise, each of these basic stages involves respectively and with its own individual nuances a twofold "turning from" what is destructive and disintegrative and a "turning toward" what is constructive and integrative. I must reemphasize, however, that it is only by analogy that I speak of the healing of neurosis as a conversion process with diverse stages, etc. Religious and moral conversion remain the paradigmatic instances of conversion and it is in the light of these conversions that I wish the other conversions to be analogously understood.

My theory of psychological conversion involves a precise understanding of the nature of neurosis and the best methods for effecting its healing. In subsequent chapters of my forthcoming book I will present in turn and in detail (1) my ideas about the nature of neurosis; (2) the most useful methods for dealing with neurosis; (3) concrete examples of the healing of particular neurotic difficulties. At present, however, my aim is simply to offer brief sketches of certain models of the process involved in the healing of neurosis which underlie or lend support to my own theory of the healing of neurosis

---

[33] Robert Doran, *Subject and Psyche: Ricoeur, Jung and the Search for Foundations* (Washington D.C.: University Press of America, 1977), esp. pp. 240ff.

[34] Donald Gelpi, *Experiencing God* (New York: Paulist Press, 1978), esp. pp. 179ff.

[35] I choose basically to limit my discussion of psychological conversion to the area of what is classically termed neurosis. I do believe, however, that if proper distinctions are drawn, it can also be applied analogously to the area of what is classically described as psychosis.

as a process of psychological conversion involving two basic stages and twofold movements internal to each of the stages.

Before I initiate my sketch of certain models relevant to my theory of the process involved in psychological conversion I want to make a few basic comments about the application of the term "conversion" to the area of the healing of neurosis. I do this to stave off in advance certain possible, potentially disastrous misunderstandings. First, then, it only makes sense to speak of the healing of neurosis as a conversion process if the healing of neurosis implies a transformation in the suffering individual on the level of meaning, value, and behavior and if it requires, at least at a certain point, the exercise of free choice and decision on the part of the sufferer. I do not believe, for example, that it would be accurate or appropriate to describe the healing of neurosis as a conversion process if all that it involved was the correction of a chemical imbalance through the intussuception of suitable chemicals. Second, although I hold that it is legitimate to describe the healing of neurosis as a conversion process I in no way mean to imply that the initial neurotic state of the individual is necessarily due to personal sins or moral faults on the part of the suffering person. Third, while I maintain that personal, free decisions on the part of the sufferer must occur if radical and ongoing healing is to take place, I do not hold that if psychological conversion does not occur this is necessarily attributable to bad will or sin on the part of the sufferer. The grounds for the assertion I have just made will emerge as my book unfolds. But I thought it best to make my basic position on these vital, fundamental issues very clear from the outset.

In my explanation of the processes of religious and moral conversion I happily had the whole rich Christian tradition to rely on. In the case of psychological conversion, however, I am dealing with a fundamentally new idea. Consequently, I will require an entire book to flesh out my own model of psychological conversion. And even then it will only be a beginning. In this introduction, however, my aim is simply to offer brief sketches of three models relevant to the healing of neurosis which underlie and/or support in some fashion my own model of psychological conversion with its radical and ongoing stages, etc. The three models I have chosen are those of Andras Angyal, Kazimierz Dabrowski, and *Neurotics Anonymous*. I will first focus attention on the Angyal and Dabrowski models. It will be more profitable, however, to delay consideration of the *Neurotics Anonymous* model until I raise the issue of the conversion from addiction.

VII. Andras Angyal

Dr. Andras Angyal, a Hungarian psychiatrist, in his book *Neurosis and its Treatment: A Holistic Theory*,[36] offers a model of the stages in-

---

[36] Andras Angyal, *Neurosis and its Treatment: A Holistic Theory*, esp. pp. 220-260.

volved in the healing of neurosis which strikingly parallels, though in analogous fashion, my own model of the stages involved in the processes of religious and moral conversion.

Angyal first speaks in global terms of the initial and final phases of the healing and growth processes of the neurotic. There is the beginning stage in which the neurotic pattern of living is dominant in the sufferer; and, there is the culminating stage in which the health pattern is clearly in the ascendancy. Between these two stages there occurs what Angyal refers to as "the struggle for decision." As the personal drama of the struggle for decision unfolds there takes place what Angyal characterizes as the "demolition process" in which the neurotic sufferer starts to recognize in a deeply felt manner the destructiveness of his or her neurotic way of existing in the world and begins to turn away from it. Likewise, there is what Angyal depicts as the "reconstruction process" in which the drive for mental and emotional health and wholeness inspires and activates in the individual a dynamic movement toward an integral, truly healthy way of living in the world. The struggle for decision manifests itself in one or most often in a series of enlightened decisions and turning points which lead to the dominance of the health pattern. Yet, even when the health pattern is firmly tn the ascendancy, the process is not completed. Relapses are a real possibility. Consequently, there is need for vigilance and for an ongoing resistance against negative factors and temptations. There can be a sharp recrudescense of symptoms even late in therapy. The potentiality for malfunctioning remains. Moreover, it is immediately activated "when the patient succumbs to conceit, pride, or self-centeredness and retreats into his angry, anxious isolation."[37] Still, though there remains the need to turn away ever more firmly from destructive tendencies in the period of ongoing conversion, there is hopefully an ever greater ascendancy of the integrative and life-enriching elements. There is accordingly, an increasing dynamic inner exigency to turn ever more fully toward the cultivation of healthy patterns of living and genuinely life-enhancing, truly worthwhile values.

It is easy to discern the parallel between the stages of Angyal's model for the healing of neurosis and the stages of religious and moral conversion as I have articulated them. In all three instances there is the occurrence of a radical conversion which consists in a fundamental turning away from a basically destructive way of existing and acting in the world and a turning toward a new, integrative way of being and operating. Similarly, once the radical shift occurs, there is in all three cases an ongoing turning away from

---

[37] Ibid., p. 260.

negative inclinations and seductive tendencies and an ever fuller embracing of life-producing values and patterns of living.

VIII. Kazimierz Dabrowski

It is with caution and a certain reservation that I select Dabrowski's model[38] to provide support for the validity of my own model of psychological conversion with its particular sequence of stages and "turnings." This is so because, as I read Dabrowski, his primary focus is on personality development and the process whereby a person moves from a primitive level of personality integration to a high level of personality development. It is Dabrowski's view that many so-called "neurotic" and even some so-called "psychotic" symptoms are not, in fact, signs of real pathology in the individual. Rather, they are evidence of a process whereby a primitive level of personality integration is undergoing a disintegration so that, with the aid of emerging psychic forces or dynamisms, the creation of a higher level of personality integration can be realized. I myself would tend at time, to see a true healing, a real pathology where Dabrowski would see a form of personality development, effected through a positive type of disintegration of primitive personality structures. Yet, despite certain possible disagreements about what is truly pathological and what is not, I find Dabrowski's model highly useful.

Dabrowski's model is helpful to me for a number of reasons. First, it does in part concern itself with symptoms classically viewed as neurotic; second, it does effectively demonstrate how by means of certain psychic, mental, emotional dynamisms a person can utilize so-called "psycho-neurotic" and at times even "psychotic" symptoms in a highly creative fashion and move beyond them to a rich level of psychic and spiritual existence; third, Dabrowski's model does involve a set of stages and dynamic movements which parallel remarkably, though analogously, my own model of the stages and dynamisms involved in religious, moral, and psychological conversion. Finally, Dabrowski's model is more relevant to my overall enterprise because it does concern itself with high level intellectual, moral, psychic, and spiritual growth and these forms of maturation are of vital concern for Christotherapy as a form of spiritual direction.

The key to Dabrowski's model, as I just indicated, is the view that a certain disintegration of the lower level personality structure is

---

[38] Kazimierz Dabrowski, *Psychoneurosis is not an Illness* (London: Gryf Publications, Ltd., 1972).

required if a higher level of integration is to take place. Thus, for example, in the case of the primitive instinct of self-preservation, a form of disintegration of the primitive form of the instinct is necessary so that at a higher level a willingness to engage in self-sacrifice for others can emerge. Dabrowski argues that the developmental process involves an initial stage in which an individual begins to feel that his or her present level of personality development and functioning is inadequate and restricting the possibility of growth. This initial disintegration expresses itself in an outbreak of so-called neurotic and at times even psychotic symptoms. Also, such psychic dynamisms as shame, guilt, fear, anxiety, disquietude, dissatisfaction, astonishment at oneself begin to manifest themselves. These experiences trigger an endeavor to break away from the present uniform, stereotyped, repetitious, primitive form of personality organization. At the same time the individual begins to be attracted by new values and goals. These dawning positive attractions also dynamically motivate the individual to reach out beyond the confines of the present personality structure. The individual who is dealing positively rather than negatively with the disintegration process grows in insight into himself or herself and makes choices in which certain radically inadequate or negative values are rejected and authentically worthwhile, positively fulfilling values are affirmed and embraced. In this process there is most often a gradual shift from the dominance of the lower level structure to an ever increasing prevalence of qualities characteristic of the higher personality structure. The ideal goal of the whole process is the creation of a new and harmonious organization of all one's psychic, aesthetic, intellectual, emotional, spiritual functions. But, generally, the process that moves one toward the ideal consists in a series of partial higher level integrations which are the result of a series of insight-directed decisions.

It is not difficult to observe certain parallels between the stages of Dabrowski's process of positive disintegration and the stages I have argued to be present in the processes of religious, moral, and psychological conversion. There is the initial stage of radical dissatisfaction and turning away from the inadequate or destructive. There is the increasing attraction of new values and the ideal of a novel personality integration. This radical turning away from the negative and turning toward the positive is effectively consolidated and actualized in a decision or generally in a series of enlightened decisions. There is further the ongoing process in which the movement toward the ideal of high level personality integration is gradually intensified and successfully realized through further rejection of immature or actually destructive elements and the adoption of higher values more in harmony with total personality integration. Dabrowski's overall concern with personality development is a comprehensive one and envisages a holistic high level integration of the human person which is at once psychological, cognitive, affective, social, aesthetic, moral, and spiritual. This means that Dabrowski's greatest contribution to the development of Christotherapy lies in his insights into the forms of healing and growth involved in the successive upward spiralings of ongoing conversion in all of its forms.

IX. Conversion from Addiction

The notion of the healing of addiction as a conversion[39] is comparatively recent, as is the concept of the healing of neurosis as a form of psychological conversion. This means that the exact meaning of the healing of addiction as a conversion is something which I can only gradually explicate and seek to validate in my forthcoming book. There, I will present my own theory regarding the nature of addiction, key healing methods for dealing with addiction, and concrete examples of elements involved in the radical and ongoing healing and growth of the addicted person. In this introduction, however, I deliberately refrain from offering an explanation of the nature of addiction. I simply presuppose for the moment, as I did in the case of neurosis, the common sense understanding of the term. I do, however, wish to make it clear from the outset that it only makes sense to speak of the healing of addiction as a conversion process if the process of healing does indeed involve a transformation of the levels of meaning and value and if it does engage the suffering person in the concrete exercise of acts of enlightened decision and freedom.

My immediate concern here is to offer a model for the healing of addiction which lends support to my own theory of the healing of addiction as a conversion process which consists of radical and ongoing stages, each of which respectively involves a twofold turning from what is destructive and disintegrative and a turning toward what is authentically worthwhile and life-giving. I find a model of this type in the famous *Twelve Steps* of *Alcoholics Anonymous.*[40]

---

[39] In the book *Alcoholics Anonymous,* the founder of A.A. describes the healing of his addiction in terms of a conversion experience. Cf. *Alcoholics Annymous,* p. 14. Dr. Harry M. Tiebout in 1951 wrote an article entitled "Conversion as a Psychological Phenomena in the Treatment of the Alcoholic," *Pastoral Psychology,* Vol. 2, April 1951, pp. 28-34. More recently, C. Roy Woodruff in his book *Alcoholism and Christian Experience* has discussed at length categories of conversion in the area of the healing of alcoholism. (Philadelphia: Westminster Press, 1968).

[40] Anonymous Authors, *Twelve Steps and Twelve Traditions* (New York: Alcoholics Anonymous World Services, Inc., 1952). My citations of the twelve steps are all taken from pp. 5-9 of this book.

The first of the *Twelve Steps* reads: "We admitted we were powerless over alcohol—that our lives had become unmanageable." This admission of personal powerlessness is the first dynamic step which enables the actively addicted person to begin to turn away from the addictive way of being and living in the world. The second step reads: "[We] came to believe that a Power greater than ourselves could restore us to sanity." This is followed by the third step: "[We] made a decision to turn our will and our lives over to the care of God as we understood Him." In the second and third steps there takes place a radical turning toward the value of sobriety and to the Power that can effectively bring about this commitment. The third step is followed by nine more. These steps read as follows: Step four: "Made a searching and fearless moral inventory of ourselves"; step five: "Admitted to God, to ourselves, and to another human being, the exact nature of our wrongs"; step six: "Were entirely ready to have God remove all these defects of character"; step seven: "Humbly asked Him to remove our shortcomings"; step eight: "Made a list of all persons we had harmed, and became willing to make amends to them all"; step nine: "Made direct amends to such people wherever possible, except when to do so would injure them or others"; step ten: "Continued to take personal inventory and when we were wrong promptly admitted it"; step eleven: "Sought through prayer and meditation to improve our conscious contact with God as we understood Him, praying only for knowledge of His will for us and the power to carry that out"; step twelve: "Having had a spiritual awakening as the result of these steps, we tried to carry this message to alcoholics, and to practice these principles in all our affairs." In steps four through ten there is evidence of an ongoing attempt to confirm the radical "turning from" involved in the admission of powerlessness over alcohol and the decision to renounce it; and, especially in steps eleven and twelve, there is an ever more deeply transformed turning toward authentic freedom through the cultivation of authentic, life-enhancing values, the seeking of ever richer contact with God, and a growing commitment to the service of fellow human beings, especially those suffering from active alcoholism.

Certainly the *Twelve Steps* of *Alcoholics Anonymous* are the expression of a profound conversion process touching the human being at the very core of his or her psychological, moral, and spiritual essence. Moreover, there is no need to belabor what is obvious, namely, the striking parallel which exists between the stages of the twelve step model of *Alcoholics Anonymous* for the healing of addiction and the stages I have shown to be at work in the religious, moral, and psychological conversion processes.

Now *Neurotics Anonymous*[41] grounds itself precisely on the same *Twelve Steps* which are the cornerstone of *Alcoholics Anonymous*. The only difference is that members of *Neurotics Anonymous* acknowledge that they are powerless over their emotions instead of over alcohol. But the dynamics stages involved in the healing process of *Neurotics Anonymous* are exactly the same as those involved in *Alcoholics Anonymous*. This means that the basic stages of radical and ongoing conversion, with their respective twofold turnings, are at the core of the healing process of *Neurotics Anonymous* just as they are at the center of the healing process of *Alcoholics Anonymous*. The use of the *Twelve Steps* by neurotics justifies my reliance on the *Twelve Steps* as providing a third model in support of my own model of psychological conversion with its diverse stages and turnings. Finally, the fact that the *Twelve Steps* are utilized by addicts of such disparate character as gamblers and overeaters justifies my use of the *Twelve Steps* to exemplify the stages involved in the healing of addiction generally, and not just in the case of addiction to alcohol.

The salient analogy which exists between the dynamic movement and stages of the four conversion processes I have just scrutinized naturally suggests the question: Why is there such a striking similarity (not to deny, of course, certain dissimilarities) in inner dynamics and structural elements between the four conversion processes? This is a question, of course, to which the entire book seeks to respond. But an initial answer is that all four conversions touch the human person holistically and at the core of his or her freedom. Also, all four involve massive shifts from evil or at least grossly inadequate ways of existing and acting in the world to authentic, excellent, optimally worthwhile forms of being and functioning. There is a further fact that all four conversions involve reformations and transformations on the level of meaning. And I speak here not of the type of meaning that simply informs but of the meaning Jesus spoke of when He said that knowledge of the truth sets people free (Jn 8:32). There is also the fact that religious and moral conversion inevitably play a role in psychological conversion and in the conversion from addiction, to freedom. Finally, there is the fact that some or all of the conversions can be dynamically present and operative in one and the same person. I myself, for example, can tentatively and gropingly and, of course, with the possibility of error — for we are all opaque and mysteries to ourselves — identify elements of all four conversions presently at work in my own concrete adventure in liv-

---

[41] Literature on *Neurotics Anonymous* is available from Neurotics Anonymous Liaison Inc., Room 304 Colorado Bldg., 1341 G. Street N.W., Wash. D.C. 20005.

ing. I am a recovered and recovering alcoholic[42] and neurotic and I experience ongoing struggle and hopefully some growth in these conversion areas; likewise, I experience in myself an ongoing process of positive disintegration in which I seek to let go of fragments of lower level personality integrations and to move toward my own personality ideal. Above all, though none of us really knows how he or she stands before God with an absolute certitude, I experience God's grace in my life deepening in me a yearning for ongoing religious and moral transformation and I see how elements of these two latter conversion processes are deeply intertwined with and at work in the other conversion processes. Such are my initial reflections on conversions and passages.

---

[42] I use the expression "recovered and recovering" to avoid misunderstanding. I speak of myself as recovered in the sense that for a good number of years I have not been actively addicted to alcohol. I speak of myself as recovering because I view the process of realizing an ever more richer sobriety a life-long affair.

Theologies of Praxis

by David Tracy

Many contemporary theologians insist that any theory or argument in theology must now yield to the demands of praxis.¹ This insistence has occasioned both an enrichment and some confusion on the contemporary theologies of praxis. The positive proposals on the meaning of both praxis and theory and their interrelationships, however, are really diverse if not conflicting. The clear negative proposal is this: since any understanding of praxis regards human action as what we actually do or probably or possibly can do, any merely technical understanding of praxis as mere practice (more exactly as mechanically and routinely applied theory) must be negated.² Hence the employment of the ancient Greek word praxis rather than the more familiar practice.

One clear positive proposal also unites theologians of praxis before the major differences occur: any proper understanding of praxis demands some form of authentic personal involvement and/or commitment. Any individual becomes who he/she is as an authentic or inauthentic subject by one's actions in an intersubjective and a social-historical world with other subjects and in relationship to con-

---

¹ Background work on the concept: Nicholas Lobkowicz, *Theory and Practice: History of a Concept from Aristotle to Marx* (Notre Dame: University of Notre Dame Press, 1967); Richard Bernstein, *Praxis and Action* (Philadelphia: University of Pennsylvania Press, 1971); idem., *The Restructuring of Social and Political Theory*, (New York: Harcourt, 1976). In theology, see the several essays on this theme of Matthew Lamb, esp. "The Theory-Praxis Relationship in Contemporary Christian Theology" in *CTSA Proceedings* (1976): 147-178; Johann Baptist Metz, *Faith in Society and History*, (New York: Seabury, 1979), pp. 48-88; Hermut Peukert, *Wissenschaftstheories — Handlungstheorie — Fundamentale Theologie* (Frankfurt: Suterkamp, 1978). On the latter work, see Rudolf Siebert, "Peukert's New Critical Theology," in *The Ecumenist* 16/4, pp. 52-58; 16/5, pp. 78-80. A more expanded version of this present essay will appear in my forthcoming book, *The Analogical Imagination* (New York: Crossroads, 1981).

² Cf. Lamb, op. cit., pp. 150-52.

crete social and historical structures and movements. Praxis, therefore, must be related to theory not as theory's application or even goal, as in all conscious and unconscious mechanical notions of practice or technique. Rather praxis is theory's own originating and self-correcting foundation since all theory is dependent, minimally, on the authentic praxis of the theorist's personally appropriated value of intellectual integrity and self-transcending commitment to the imperatives of critical rationality. In that sense, praxis sublates theory, not vice-versa.

If we desire to determine criteria of adequacy for meaning and truth, therefore, we must understand the foundational role of praxis in relationship to theory.[3] We must, by theory's own internal imperatives, pay constant attention to the authenticity or inauthenticity (at the limit, the radical alienation) of the truth-teller's subjectivity. For some theologians of praxis the clearest, sometimes the sole test for the authenticity or inauthenticity of the subject's truth-telling is whether one speaks the truth by doing the truth.[4] We can discern the reality of the latter by our actual involvement in some particular social, cultural, economic, political, or religious movement where true or authentic praxis lives. The more particular forms of theologies of praxis range from emphases upon involvement in particular cultural-historical activity (as in many "theologies of culture") to liberal socio-political reform (as in Social Gospel theologies) to radical Marxist revolutionary praxis (as in some liberation theologies).[5]

---

[3] For most of the practical theologians (clearly for Baum, Metz, Lamb, and Francis Schüssler Fiorenza), this also implies some form of primacy to practical reason.

[4] Notice, for example, the relative and earned ease with which Gregory Baum can move from his praxis-oriented Blondelian "method of immanence" in *Man Becoming* (New York: Herder and Herder, 1971) and its concerns for individual, personal self-transcendence to his praxis-oriented social-critical work in *Religion and Alienation,* (New York: Paulist Press, 1975).

[5] Note, moreover, how, in each of these instances, the praxis involved is *faith*-praxis transforming personal, social, and historical praxis. This reality in the American tradition need not prove merely an import from German and Latin American sources. Indeed one of the dominant characteristics of much of the American philosophical tradition is the emphasis on praxis — whether largely individual (as in William James) or social-historical (as in John Dewey). On the latter, note Bernstein, *Praxis and Action,* op. cit., pp. 165-230 and William Shea, "Matthew Lamb's Five Models of Theory-Praxis and the Interpretation of John Dewey's Pragmatism" in *CTSA Proceedings* (1977): 125-42. Moreover, not to note the "political" theological character of many of the classic American theologians is also to miss a native resource worth further exploration: note, in American Protestantism, Martin Marty's essays on Reinhold Niebuhr, in *Journal of Religion* (1979): 154-69. In the American Catholic tradition, note especially the positions of J. A. Ryan and John Courtney Murray. For interpretations of the latter, see John Coleman, "Vision and Praxis in American Theology," *Theological Studies* (1976): 3-40.

The most familiar form of praxis-oriented theologies in contemporary theology are the various political theologies and the theologies of liberation.⁶ In the latter case, for example, one often finds the insistence that *only* personal involvement in and commitment to the struggle for liberating transformation of some particular societal evil (economic exploitation and dependency, sexism, racism, anti-semitism, elitism, exploitation of the environment) will free the theologian to see and speak the truth by doing the truth in solidarity with all those in the cause. For many theologians of liberation, for example, it follows that the major problematic of most forms of fundamental theology, the problem of the truth-status of the cognitive claims of both Christianity and modernity, cannot in principle be resolved by better theories. For the norms of all theories are, in fact, grounded in the value of theorizing. Those norms include a non-objectified reality which is not theoretical (viz., the theoretician's own emancipated or alienated subjectivity). Norms are ultimately grounded not in the self-evident axioms of further theories but in the concrete intellectual, moral, and religious praxis of concrete human beings in distinct societal and historical situations.

In fundamentally classical, usually Aristotelian, formulations of this emphasis upon praxis, like those of Bernard Lonergan or Eric Voegelin, the position will emphasize the constant need for personal

---

Moreover, the American tradition, in figures like Abraham Lincoln and Martin Luther King, is strongly praxis-oriented (in contrast to the largely theory-oriented political theories of many European political theorists). On Lincoln, see William Wolf, *Lincoln's Religion: This Almost Chosen People* (Philadelphia: United Church of Christ Press, 1963) and Reinhold Niebuhr's tribute to Lincoln as America's classic theologian (of praxis) in *The Irony of American History,* pp. 170-74, and the creative use of Lincoln's vision for a theology of liberation in Peter Hodgson, *New Birth of Freedom: A Theology of Bondage and Liberation* (Philadelphia: Fortress, 1976). The work on King's relationship to the praxis-tradition (as distinct from other aspects of King's thought) is, to my knowledge, yet to be written. I do not mention these American resources in a chauvinist spirit to suggest that American theologians do not need to continue to learn from European and, more recently, Latin American theologies in these matters, nor to suggest that these praxis-traditions are identical, as they are not—as any reader of both Dewey and Habermas or Niebuhr and Metz soon discovers. I do mention them, however, to observe a curious American irony: what was once considered a major "failure" of American theology by European commentators and their American followers—viz. its "practical character"—is now largely ignored rather than reclaimed by many recent American "political" and "liberation" theologians in favor of denouncing the "academic" and "theoretical" character of American theology. *Plus ça change . . .*

⁶ For an excellent analysis of the similarities and differences of these theologies, see Francis Fiorenza, "Political Theology and Liberation Theology: An Inquiry into Their Fundamental Meaning," in *Liberation, Revolution and Freedom: Theological Perspectives,* ed. Thomas McFadden (New York: Seabury, 1975): 3-29.

transformation or "conversion" in all theoreticians.[7] Indeed, the theologian, in Lonergan's judgment, grounds the truth-status of all properly theological discourse ultimately on the "foundations" of the concrete, radically personal but neither private nor individualistic basis of the theologian's own self-transcending subjectivity as one who is intellectually, morally, and religiously "converted."[8] The cognitive "therapy"[9] provided by a book like *Insight* must be matched by a moral therapy from satisfactions to values and a religious therapy grounded in the radical and transformative gift of God's grace experienced as a state of "being-in-love-without-restriction."

Philosophical meaning and truth is irreducibly grounded in the intellectual conversion of an attentive, intelligent, rational, and responsible self-appropriating thinker.[10] Moral meaning and truth is grounded in the moral conversion of an agent possessing a character that recognizes true values along with a reflective *phronesis* grounding all moral judgments.[11] Religious meaning and truth is grounded in the gift of God's grace transforming our "hearts of stone into hearts of flesh" and enabling us thereby to cooperate with that graced state through religious actions and a reflective discernment of spirits. In that sense, Lonergan joins such quite different theologians of praxis as Edward Schillebeeckx and Johann Baptist Metz to insist that orthopraxis must ground orthodoxy. Like them, however, he is careful to insist that "doing the truth" also involves "saying the truth."[12]

---

[7] For Bernard Lonergan, see his *Insight,* and *Method in Theology,* and his explication of his own praxis-position in "Theology and Praxis" in *CTSA Proceedings* (1977): 1-17. For the article on which Lonergan reflects, see Eric Voegelin, "The Gospel and Culture" in *Jesus and Man's Hope,* ed. D. G. Miller and D. Y. Hadidian (Pittsburgh: Pittsburgh Theological Seminary, 1971).

[8] *Method in Theology,* pp. 267-71. Lonergan's "conversion" language, I assume, can be changed into "transformation" language (i.e., the radical transformation of the subject's "horizon," not perspective, occasioned by intellectual, moral, and religious transformation, not mere development of the same).

[9] The expression is David Burrell's as applied to Lonergan's work.

[10] Note how Lonergan can appeal here as well to his own earlier interpretation of Thomas Aquinas in *Verbum: Word and Idea in Aquinas* (Notre Dame: University of Notre Dame Press, 1967). Metz could also appeal to his own earlier interpretation of Aquinas' "anthropocentric" (in contrast to "cosmocentric") horizon to show how his later political theology is in some continuity with his earlier more "individualist" and "metaphysical" work—see *Christliche Anthropozentrik: Über die Denkform des Thomas von Aquin* (München: Kasel-Verlag, 1962).

[11] In Lonergan, *Method In Theology,* pp. 47-55. For a creative study retrieving "character" for Christian ethics, see Stanley Hauerwas, *Character and the Christian Life: A Study in Theological Ethics* (San Antonio: Trinity University Press, 1975).

[12] Bernard Lonergan, "Theology and Praxis," op. cit.

In terms of claims to truth, theologies of praxis employ what I believe can be labelled a transformation model for truth. More exactly they argue that theological truth is ultimately grounded in the authentic and transformative praxis of an intellectually, morally, and religiously transformed human subject. Although Lonergan rigorously criticizes Aristotle's formulation of science in the *Posterior Analytic,* he joins the Aristotle of the *Ethics* and the *Politics* to insist upon a tranformative ethic of agency, character, and *phronesis* and joins the mainline Christian tradition in understanding the transformative reality of faith as first a matter of orientation, trust, and loyalty *(fides qua)* that grounds all right beliefs *(fides quae).* The imperatives of "speaking the truth" (alternatively, the problem of "cognitive claims") are real. Yet they will only be treated as the reality they in fact are by a transformed subject involved in doing the truth.[13]

The role of the practical theologian on this view, moreover, must not be misunderstood as the application of theological theories worked out elsewhere.[14] For every form of "mediated theology" is, in fact, grounded in the transformative *praxis* of the authentic intellectual, moral, and religious conversion of the individual theologian and community.[15] For Lonergan, only an interdisciplinary collaboration among properly transformed theologians can assure that any individual or communal theological study of concrete issues will pay sufficient attention to the personal and communal self-correcting process of both self-transcending learning and self-transformative action.

Any attempt to formulate criteria for theological truth which ignores the foundational reality of *praxis* as transformed authentic subjectivity is likely to fail. For inattention to the necessary transformations of the theologian's subjectivity will eventually mean that the foundational and highly personal but not individualistic praxis element ultimately grounding the meaning and truth of theory itself will be neglected. The theoretician will then be left with theories which may or may not emerge from these authentic praxis criteria.

---

[13] A good overview of Lonergan's position on the subject may be found in *The Subject* (Milwaukee: Marquette, 1969).

[14] It is worth recalling here the praxis-character of tnterpretation itself—insofar as application is intrinsic to interpretation: see Hans Georg Gadamer, *Truth and Method* (New York: Seabury, 1975): 274-305.

[15] Note the implicitly social reality operative from the ecclesial character of faith to the collegial or collaborative character of theology. The first Lonergan develops through his notion of "mediating theology" whereby, in dialectics, "religious conversion" is not solitary but communal. The second Lonergan develops through his notion of theology as a collaborative enterprise encompassing eight functional specialties.

All theoretical claims to meaning and truth in theology, therefore, must be subject to a dialectical analysis forged to discern the presence or absence of intellectual, moral, and religious "conversions."[16] Only radical and enduring personal transformation can assure the presence of truth.[17] This may seem peculiar, Lonergan admits, to those concerned with an objectivity so pure that it does not recognize its own character as a "self-transcending" subjectivity. Yet the destructive innocence of any notion of objectivity ungrounded in the transformative reality of authentic subjectivity is exactly what theologians most need to exercise in their pursuit of truth. Indeed, "interest in praxis in the academy," Lonergan affirms, "is only likely to occur after the age of innocence has passed."[18]

The more familiar use of a praxis insistence for determining the truth-status of theological statements, however, may be found not in such classical understandings of praxis as those of Lonergan, Voegelin, and others but in the theological use of some form of Hegelian-Marxist analysis on the dialectical relationships of theory and praxis. Whether concentrating upon infrastructural elements in society as in more traditional forms of Marxism or upon both infra and suprastructural or cultural-political elements,[19] many "political theologians" in Europe and North America as well as liberation theologians in both the Third World and among oppressed groups in the First World, employ some variant of Marxian analysis for understanding the praxis. Sometimes that form is straightforwardly Marxist, as in attempts to unmask the latent economic and class contradictions present in contemporary society through the critical analysis of present oppressive and alienating structures and their attendant ideologies. Sometimes one finds appeals to the earlier, more "humanist" writings

---

[16] *Method in Theology,* pp. 237-45.

[17] For a development of this theme from resources in Lonergan, Voegelin, Gadamer, and Strauss, see Frederick Lawrence, "The Horizon of Political Theology," in *Trinification of the World* (Frederick Crowe Festschrift), eds. Thomas Dunne and Jean-Marc Laporte (Toronto: Regis College Press, 1978), pp. 46-70.

[18] Quoted in Matthew Lamb, "The Theory-Praxis Relationship in Contemporary Christian Theologies," CTSA Proceedings (1976): 172.

[19] The key remains here the revisionary Marxism of the Frankfurt School: see Matthew Lamb, "The Challenge of Critical Theory," in Gregory Baum (ed.), *Sociology and Human Destiny* (New York: Seabury, 1980); for background works, see Martin Jay, *The Dialectical Imagination* (Boston: Little, Brown, 1973); Susan Buck-Morss, *The Origins of Negative Dialectics* (New York: Free Press, 1977); on Habermas, Thomas McCarthy, *The Critical Theory of Jürgen Habermas* (Cambridge: MIT Press, 1978). On Marxism, cf. Leszek Kolakowski, *Main Currents of Marxism,* 3 Volumes (Oxford: Clarendon, 1978), esp. Vol. 3, *The Breakdown,* pp. 341-420; Shlomo Avineri, ed., *Varieties of Marxism* (The Hague: Nyhoff, 1977); Alvin Gouldner, *The Two Marxisms* (New York: Seabury, 1980).

of Marx along with various revisions of Marx's own analysis of the "alienating role" of religion.[20]

Most of these Christian theologians of praxis, whatever their other differences, will employ some form of Christian and Marxist ideology-critique upon present church, academic, and societal structures.[21] Often they will demand that theologians be committed to a particular praxis situation (e.g., some "base community") to assure the "truth" of their claims to speaking the Christian truth to the powers of the prevailing oppressive ideologies. By either assuming or arguing that Christianity is not ultimately an ideology in the Marxist sense,[22] they will insist that Christian faith, hope, and that love concretized as justice should situate the theologian in an objective conflict with society, church, and academy. Thereby will we actualize the truth of the conflict already present, the contradictions really inherent in the situation we in fact face.[23]

The spectrum of praxis-positions is wide indeed. Indeed the full range is as wide as the spectrum of specific reformulations of the Hegelian and Marxist notions of praxis; the spectrum of specific symbols or themes chosen from the Christian tradition for critical-hermeneutical use (Exodus, liberation, redemption, social sin); the

---

[20] For some examples here, see the study by Peter Hebblethwaite, *The Christian-Marxist Dialogue* (New York: Paulist, 1977).

[21] See Johann Baptist Metz, *Faith in Society and History*, pp. 119-35, for an excellent analysis of the dialectical relationships of redemption and emancipation. It bears repeating to note that almost all the political and liberation theologians are clearly not reductionist: faith-praxis transforms Marxian and other forms of ideology-critique. In the language of the present work, Metz establishes mutual critical correlations between the praxis informing ideology-critique and Christian faith-praxis.

[22] Juan Luis Segundo, for example, uses the phrase "ideology" in an explicitly non-Marxist sense to speak of faith and ideology, in *The Liberation of Theology,* (Maryknoll: Orbis, 1976): 97-125. For a recent study of the generic characteristics of ideology (as both positive and negative), see Alvin Gouldner, *The Dialectic of Ideology and Technology: The Origins, Grammar, and Future of Ideology* (New York: Seabury, 1976). For an informative history of the complexities of the concept "ideology" (in both its pejorative [distorted consciousness] and more positive senses) in Marxist thought from Marx and Engels to the present, see Martin Seliger, *The Marxist Conception of Ideology: A Critical Essay* (New York: Cambridge University Press, 1977). For a positive, cultural, anthropological view of "ideology" as a "symbolic template" for periods when the "received tradition" is called into question, see Clifford Geertz, "Ideology as a Cultural System" in *Interpretation of Cultures,* (New York: Basic Books, 1973) pp. 193-234. For a creative and clarifying use of the work of Gouldner and Geertz here to determine the "genre" of "liberation theology," see Charles Strain, "Ideology and Alienation: Theses on the Interpretation and Evaluation of Theologies of Liberation," *Journal of the American Academy of Religion* (1977): 473-91.

[23] For expressions of this conflict orientation, see Charles Davis, "Theology and Praxis", in *Cross Currents* (1973): 154-68; and Gustavo Gutierrez in *CTSA Proceedings* (1978): 30-35.

spectrum of particular issues chosen for the major focus of the situation (sexism, racism, classism, elitism, economic exploitation and dependency, energy or environmental crises, etc.); the spectrum of particular prophetic stances or systemic analyses[24] of the relationships between the alienating and/or oppressive "situation" in its infrastructural roots and suprastructural fruits and the transformative possibilities provided by Christianity.

Despite these significant differences, all theologians of praxis will implicitly or explicitly insist that personal transformation ("doing the truth") is the key to theological truth as speaking the truth. Far more than alternative Aristotelian formulations of the same basic position, the liberation and political theologians will, of course, ordinarily demand explicit analysis of the infrastructural and suprastructural realities affecting any possibility of personal authenticity. Implicit in this insistence will be some propositions like the following: insofar as praxis sublates theory; insofar as the speaking of the truth demands doing the truth; insofar, therefore, as truth is always best understood as basically transformative in character rather than either metaphysical or disclosive, praxis-theology sublates the claims to truth of all alternative formulations articulated in non-praxis oriented fundamental and systematic theologies. It may still prove helpful for purely methodological reasons to continue to distinguish fundamental, systematic, and practical theologies. Substantively, however, all claims to truth in all forms of theology are determined by alienated or emancipated praxis and should be judged on those transformative praxis criteria.

Such seems to be the implicit and sometimes explicit understanding of truth present in most theologies of praxis. Although a fuller treatment of this issue is not possible here, the analyses of later chapters on the relationships between disclosure and transformation models of truth may aid an initial study of the conflicting claims on the nature of theological truth present across the spectrum of contemporary theologies. For the present, a brief analysis of the same kind of dispute present in one clearer but analogous contemporary philosophical discussion may clarify the more fluid and more confusing theological situation.

Indeed, the recent German discussion between the hermeneutical approach of Hans Georg Gadamer and the praxis-orientation of Jürgen Habermas may be taken as a singularly clear example of a distpute over arguments of relative adequacy for contemporary

---

[24] For an example of the latter, see Rosemary Radford Ruether, *Liberation Theology* (New York: Paulist, 1972).

praxis.²⁵ For Gadamer's familiar insistence upon the disclosive power of the classical Greek tradition has led him to reaffirm his trust in conversation and in the persuasive power of classical rhetoric as sufficient in the public forum. If Gadamer were correct on this matter, it follows that hermeneutical reflection would suffice not only for questions of aesthetic meaning but also for the more difficult question of a relatively adequate strategy for societal praxis. Yet Habermas' counter-argument must also be noted: a purely hermeneutical approach can too often serve simply to affirm a tradition, to disallow the emancipatory function of critical reason, and eventually to capitulate to, not transform, the status-quo. He argues, for example, that our present social, political, and cultural situation is not sufficiently analogous to that more harmonious situation of the Greek polis wherein public discourse, personal *phronesis,* and the power of rhetorical persuasion could still be assumed. Rather we find ourselves in a technologically dominated political and social situation wherein systematically distorted communication on a mass scale seems to hold sway. The persuasive power of classical rhetoric seems well-nigh powerless in that all-too-easily manipulated situation. We need, therefore, some form of a critique of ideologies that can perform a critically emancipatory function on a societal level by unmasking those ideological distortions in the same way psychoanalysis unmasks the distortions and illusions of any individual.

Just as we no longer assume that a neurotic or psychotic individual can be radically transformed by intelligent, rational, and rhetorically persuasive discourse, so we cannot now assume that a societal situation of systematically distorted communication can be transformed merely by hermeneutical reflection and rhetorical persuasiveness. The criteria for relative adequacy, for truly public discourse and practice in that situation is one that demands, for Habermas, the development of both a critique of ideologies and a theory of communicative competence correlating language, work, and power into a public whole.²⁶

---

²⁵ Cf. *Hermeneutik und Ideologiekritik* (Frankfurt: Suhrkamp, 1971). Part of the exchange is published in *Continuum* (1970). For two commentaries, see Paul Ricoeur, "Ethics and Culture," in *Political and Social Change,* eds. David Stewart and Joseph Bien (Athens: Ohio University Press, 1974) and Dieter Misgeld's analysis in *On Critical Theory,* ed. John O'Neil (New York: Seabury, 1976) pp. 164-84.

²⁶ The "negative" moment of ideology-critique is represented in Habermas' early work, *Knowledge and Human Interests.* The more recent, complex, and still developing positive proposal on criteria for communicative competence is carefully analyzed in Thomas McCarthy, *op. cit.,* pp. 272-387. A use of Habermas' positive proposal for communicative competence to develop a public theology may be found in Dennis McCann's work; Metz and Lamb tend to make more use of the earlier, more "theological" thinkers of the Frankfurt School, especially Adorno, Horkheimer, and Benjamin. Note also Peukert's (op. cit.) appeal to both "early" and "late" schools.

I have presented this extra-theological dispute over criteria of relative adequacy for contemporary praxis largely in the hope that it may serve to illuminate the analogous, if ordinarily less sharply formulated, dispute between hermeneutical and political theologians. Briefly stated, in terms of criteria and modes of argument, several contemporary theological discussions seem to take the following form: some theologians basically appeal to the disclosive power of the languages of story, myth, symbol, metaphor, parable, analogy, etc. Their position implies the need for the kind of disclosive model of truth. Their position also implies a trust in the sufficiently persuasive power of good hermeneutical work and rearticulated Christian rhetoric to transform contemporary praxis. Indeed, the same kind of rhetorical persuasiveness which Gadamer wishes to accomplish by means of his retrieval of classical Greek texts is what these systematic theologians effectively argue for by means of their hermeneutical and literary-critical retrieval of classical Christian texts. This position does not lack argumentative force. When analyzed in terms of criteria, in fact, the position constitutes an argument for the relative adequacy, that is, the disclosive and persuasive power, of those retrieved Christian texts and symbols.[27] Yet unlike their philosophical analogue, Gadamer, the hermeneutical theologians seem too content with a relatively unexamined trust that the rhetorical persuasiveness of those retrieved meanings will prove sufficient to transform individual and societal practice.

---

[27] This position is basically an appeal to poetics and rhetoric as distinct from dialectics (in fundamental theology) and ethical and political praxis (in practical theology). The praxis of the value of theory and argument is also operative in fundamental theology and the praxis involved in all interpretation in systematics. The real difference between the third position and the first two, therefore, is not that only the third appeals to praxis but that the third accords a *primacy* to praxis and indeed to a specific form of praxis—faith-praxis with an ethical-political emphasis (or, as Metz and Lamb name it, mystico-political praxis). One way of formulating arguments among these three distinct but related forms of praxis would be in terms of abstract-concrete distinctions. In those terms, practical theology is the most concrete yet should, by its own criteria, be open to the necessary correctives provided by the authentic praxis informing the arguments and theories of fundamental theology and the authentic praxis informing the disclosures of systematic theology. Gadamer, for example, is singularly clear on the reality of praxis—and thereby of ethical and political philosophy—in his insistence on the inner relationship of *intelligere, explicare,* and *applicare:* note, for example, his appeal to Aristotelian *phronesis* as praxis in his essay "Hermeneutics and Social Science" in *Cultural Hermeneutics* (1975), pp. 308-319, and "Hermeneutik als praktische Philsophie," in *Zur Rehabilitierung der praktischen Philosophie,* ed. M. Riedel (Freiburg: Rombach, 1972), pp. 325-44. Practical theology can, I believe, sublate the other two disciplines as long as the sublation also includes the truth-claims operative in fundamental and systematic theologies. In more strictly theological terms, "faith working through love and justice" (the mystico-political praxis of practical theology) does sublate "faith" only by really including that faith. I hope to return to these issues in a future volume on practical theology—a volume intended to complete this "trilogy", initiated by *Blessed Rage for Order,* by its move to the more fully concrete concerns of practical theology.

The political theologians, on the contrary, seem to assume, like Habermas, that a fair analysis of the contemporary societal situation forces any observer to admit to the relative powerlessness of all rhetorical persuasion in a situation of systematically distorted communication.[28] What will prove more relatively adequate to that situation, they effectively argue, is some form of a Christian critique of ideologies, often named liberation or political theologies. It is of no little interest to note that both the philosophers Gadamer and Habermas and their theological analogues, the hermeneutical and political theologians, can unite on certain questions of criteria and argument. For example, these theologians do unite with one another and with the metaphysical theologians to attack various forms of positivism only to go their separate ways again when further questions emerge about an adequate model for truth, the proper strategy, the relatively adequate arguments and practices needed to transform the present political and societal situation.

As the analysis indicates, there are, in fact, several distinct kinds of claims present in this theological dispute. The basic dispute, I have suggested, is a fundamental one: what constitutes truth for a theological statement? Would the criteria be correspondence, empirical verification or falsification, coherence, adequacy to proper language use or to common human experience, consensus, disclosure, disclosure-concealment, transformation; or, perhaps, a quiet announcement of a plague upon all these models from a skeptical observer masked as "jesting Pilate?"

A second but often overlooked discussion amidst the theological skirmishings should be more empirical and sociological than theoretical.[29] For example, the empirical evidence for our present situation as systematically distorted (however illuminating the

---

[28] Most of them, in fact, struggle implicitly or explicitly against the privatization of religion. Few of them seem to relate that privatization to the marginalization of art: Metz's use of Benjamin here and his use of "narrative theology" being one exception to the more general rule.

[29] I take this correct demand for empirical social scientific evidence to be the chief objection of Andrew Greeley against many theological uses of social science. This objection seems to me entirely sound, assuming (with Greeley) (1) that the empirical social scientist also employs theory (including, *in principle,* therefore, theories like the praxis of ideology-critique or a theory of communicative competence, etc.) to assure that empirical social science does not end merely affirming the *status quo* and (2) that in the conversation between sociology and theology, the philosophical (fundamental) and faith-praxis concerns of theology proper also play their necessary roles. For examples of American empirical and theoretical social science in conversation with theology, see the essays by William McCready, Pastora San Juan Cafferty, Bruno Manno, and Teresa Sullivan in *Towards Vatican III: The Work that Needs to be Done,* ed. David Tracy with Hans Küng and Johann Baptist Metz, (New York: Seabury, 1979).

analogy with psychoanalysis for many aspects of our felt experience of contemporary life) should not be allowed to assume a descriptive and implicitly prescriptive force in theology without rigorously empirical social scientific support. I may find Jacques Ellul's analysis of technology illuminating about the contradictions and conflicts I sense or experience in this society. That does not absolve me or anyone else from seeking out empirical social scientific evidence which supports, qualifies, or refutes this "prophetic" insight.

I may, in fact, I do, agree with the need to employ some form of ideology-critique in social science, philosophy, *and* theology.[30] On the presumption that this agreement is based not on personal preference grounds but on arguments on common methodological grounds, any use of ideology-critique should possess a healthy hermeneutic of suspicion upon its own stance. On any standard, after all, the surest sign of strictly ideological thought is the refusal of that thought — ironically sometimes under the banner of ideology-critique — to face and account for the complexity of conflicting empirical evidence. All claims for the primacy of praxis over theory, if they are to prove consistent, must allow for empirical social-scientific analysis to check all theories on our societal situation.

A second area of dispute among all three kinds of theology is more properly theological. Indeed, it has already been investigated in the analyses of fundamental and systematic theologies. There we noted the distinct appeals to different aspects of the Christian tradition: the universalist strain for fundamental theologians; the confessionalist strain for systematic church theologians. It is clear that practical theologians may also appeal to the tradition to warrant their position. Is it not the clear and consistent teaching of the scriptural and later Christian tradition, for example, that "conversion" is central to the Christian life, including the life of thought? Is it not the case that Christian faith, hope, and love are first praxis-realities for a transformed agent and community before they are expressed in cognitive claims or right beliefs? In that sense, is it not the case that orthopraxis does in fact ground orthodoxy? The scriptural and traditional warrants for a transformation model of religious and theological truth, therefore, seems to back the kind of praxis-emphasis desired by both the distinct Aristotelian and Hegelian-Marxist modern formulations.

Moreover, the case for the social-political dimensions of Christian faith has equally clear scriptural warrants, especially, of course, in

---

[30] Christian ideology-critique is intrinsic to any recognition of the de-familiarizing, de-legitimating, de-mythologizing, and de-ideologizing character of the prophetic and the mystical strands in both Judaism and Christianity.

the prophetic and apocalyptic strands of the tradition and their assumptions of God's activity in history for the oppressed.[31] These are public claims, let us note, focused on God as acting in church and world in publicly intelligible ways. Indeed the notion of God's activity in history in and through prophetic action in past, present, and future seems to be the chief strictly theological assumption for publicness in these theologies.

Finally, the political and liberation theologians have warranted their positions through uncovering sometimes hidden and masked, sometimes forgotten or half-remembered, aspects of the Christian tradition.[32] Their understanding of the crisis in the public of contemporary society (or "world") impels them to search in the church tradition for resources, almost always prophetic and eschatological, often apocalyptic, to help transform, liberate, emancipate, save the present "demonic" situation. Romans 13, it seems, has been allowed to play its theme long enough. It is time to consider Revelation 13. The Constantinian and medieval sacralism implied in models of "Christendom" has (*pace* Belloc, Dawson, Danielou, T. S. Eliot, and others)[33] long since been unmasked by many theologians, including political and liberation theologians, as an inadequate model for the church. That same kind of church model, even when recast into more liberal forms, has also been unmasked as really a "cultural Christianity" in unholy alliance with a modern, truncated

---

[31] One obvious issue that fundamental theology should pose for practical theologies (especially liberation theologies) employing the "God acting in history" paradigm is the question of the correct way to speak that language. Otherwise, liberation theologies may be repeating the same difficulties exposed by Langdon Gilkey in the earlier biblical theology of G. Ernst Wright, et al.: cf. Langdon Gilkey, in "Cosmology, Ontology, and the Travail of Biblical Language," *Journal of Religion 41* (1961): 194-205. For some distinct, constructive responses to that question, see Langdon Gilkey, *Reaping the Whirlwind*, pp. 239-318; Schubert Ogden, "What Sense Does It Make to Say 'God Acts in History'?" in *The Reality of God*, (New York: Harper and Row, 1966) pp. 164-88; David Mason, "Can We Speculate on How God Acts?" in *Journal of Religion* (1977): 16-33. For two biblical studies on the "privileged" character of the oppressed, see Norman Gottwald, *The Tribes of Yahweh* (Maryknoll: Orbis, 1979) and Richard Cassidy, *Jesus, Politics and Society: A Study of Luke's Gospel* (Maryknoll: Orbis, 1978).

[32] This is especially true of the political theologians' retrieval of apocalyptic (Metz) and the left-wing of the Reformation (Moltmann) as well as the liberation theologians' retrieval of the Exodus motif and the "privileged" status of the oppressed in the prophetic traditions. For an example of the latter, see James Cone, *A Black Theology of Liberation* (Philadelphia: Lippincott, 1970). Philosophically, it might be added, the left-wing Hegelians are the philosophical tradition most often employed by Metz and Moltmann in their political theologies and, either explicitly or by implication, in the liberation theologies.

[33] It seems fair to observe that, in all four of these figures, Europeanism was the crucial component of Christendom: as stated with the fewest qualifications, for example, in Belloc's famous statement: "Europe is the faith and the faith is Europe."

secularism.³⁴ Any "mystical communion" model of the church which involves "flight from the world" has been treated to the scorn of the Marxist charges of rank "idealism" and "alienation." The "sect" model, once so marginal to mainline Christian consciousness, may now be reexamined, retrieved, and, to be sure, reformulated into an effective praxis model of "church" as a mission fighting for liberation and emancipation.³⁵ Thus will Jürgen Moltmann reinterpret the Christian doctrine of eschatological hope and the centrality of the cross to formulate a new and vital form of Christian praxis theology and a new ecclesiology. Thus will Johann Baptist Metz provide rigorous and persuasive criticisms of the "individualism" of much contemporary theology while formulating a praxis political theology and ecclesiology honoring the "subversive memory" of freedom and suffering embedded in the central texts, events, and witnesses of the Christian tradition. The black theologians, the feminist theologians, the liberation theologians of the Third World, as we shall see below, all warrant their positions by appeals to often overlooked aspects of the Christian tradition. They aid us all by speaking from and to the concrete conditions of oppression, alienation, and suffering in their particular societies. In sum, all theologies of praxis will ordinarily be concerned with society as their primary referent group, yet not without substantial warrants from the church tradition itself.

Some realities, to me at least, seem clear in the complicated disputes raised by theologies of praxis. First, as mentioned above, strictly social scientific claims are to be judged by social scientific, not theological criteria. On those criteria, both strictly empirical *and* theoretical positions (including theories of praxis like ideology-critique or theories of communicative competence) are necessary. Without that empirical base, the theories are literally groundless as social scientific evidence and should be treated, and respected, as proposals and hypotheses awaiting empirical testing. Without critical theory and transformative praxis, empirical social scientific studies are always in proximate danger of simply affirming the pre-

---

³⁴ For two careful defenses of "liberal Christianity" against these now familiar charges, see George Rupp, *"Culture Protestantism",* (Missoula: Scholars Press, 1977) and William R. Hutchison, *The Modernist Impulse in American Protestantism* (Cambridge: Harvard University Press, 1976). The fact is that the political and liberation theologians also exist as heirs of that admittedly ambiguous liberal and modernist tradition as much as their more "individualist" predecessors, the existentialist neo-orthodox theologians did. The historical relationship is nicely stated in Wilhelm Pauck's comment: "Neo-orthodoxy is not orthodoxy but the self-criticism of the liberal tradition." Methodologically, as I have suggested here, practical theologies continue to need the correctives of fundamental theology as much as the latter needs sublation into the praxis concreteness of practical theology.

³⁵ See Roger Haight, "Mission," *Theological Studies* (1976):620-49.

sent, possibly alienating and oppressive, status-quo and in remote but real danger of disallowing any real critique of society (including, therefore, genuinely prophetic theological critiques) in favor of what can become a "fetishism of facts."

Second, the tendency to separate, even dichotomize disclosure and transformation criteria for truth is mistaken. Any real distinction (like that between disclosure and transformation, like that between theory and praxis, like that between faith and faith working through love, like that between liberation-emancipation and redemption) is never a separation. Distinctions remain distinctions, serving the cause of clarity and a need for emphasis through a process empowered by the necessary and enriching power of abstraction grounding all proper intellectual distinctions. As the too easily despised Scholastics correctly insisted, sometimes *"debemus distinguere."*

In present terms: of course, all good theory is grounded in the authentic praxis of intellectual integrity and cognitive self-transcendence. Of course, all real knowledge is in some sense participatory. Yet those realities—denied only by the strictly positivist theories of theory and strictly instrumentalist misunderstanding of praxis as mechanically applied theory—can be distinguished without being separated. "Saying the truth" is distinct from, although never separate from, "doing the truth." *Fides quae* is distinct from, though never separate from *fides qua.* Cognitive claims are distinct from, though never separate from, their grounding in particular historical concrete situations and social structures. More concretely, there is never an authentic disclosure of truth in authentic praxis without also discerning some disclosure of what is now recognized as the case (i.e., true). To attempt to separate truth as disclosure from truth as transformation is damaging to the fuller understanding of truth itself. If adhered to, it could eventually prove fatal to the more comprehensive, the non-positivist and non-instrumentalist, notions of rationality operative in both models of disclosure and models of transformation.

To distinguish these models of truth is entirely appropriate. Sometimes the distinction is put forward to indicate a shift of emphasis in major concerns. Unfortunately, sometimes this is also misunderstood as an entirely novel, revolutionary notion of truth itself. For example, a plausible case can be made that, since the Enlightenment, theology has been concerned too exclusively with the "crisis of cognitive claims." Theology's single-minded concern, perhaps even obsession, with this Enlightenment crisis may have involved theologians unconsciously in those structures of alienation reaching their apotheosis in instrumentalist notions of reason as purely technical and notions of practice as mere technique and application: notions which the initially liberating Enlightenment concept of "autonomous" reason helped to unleash. In that situation, a shift of emphasis from theory (since theory can seem trapped in positivist and instrumentalist categories) to praxis can be and is emancipating, *even for theory*. This same shift of emphasis can clarify that the major question in our situation is not the crisis of cognitive claims, but the social-ethical crisis of massive suffering and widespread oppression and alienation in an emerging global culture. Again, an emphasis upon praxis helps to refocus theological attention on that situation rather than upon the crisis of the modern Christian intellectual analyzing the cognitive claims of the Christian tradition.

However, if praxis effectively becomes identified with some particular cause, movement, program, then neither praxis nor theory, nor the cause itself, are well served. For praxis soon becomes uncritically mediated practice of whatever form. And any theories daring to be critical of the cause—even, indeed especially, critical theories generated from within the cause—are too quickly dismissed as pre-revolutionary, "bourgeois," or "academic." The cause itself may become yet another hardened ideology more than open to conflict, yet closed to the actuality of critique and even the ideal of conversation. The "eschatological proviso" of most political theologies, to be sure, provides a good theological check upon these temptations (not inevitabilities) of any praxis-oriented theology. The internal developments of most forms of liberation theology seem to be providing the same kind of theological check on the same temptations.[36]

And yet almost any exclusive emphasis upon praxis for truth needs other checks than the strictly theological ones as much as alternative theological models of truth need, as they do, the checks provided by models of truth as transformative praxis. In the case of a transformation model of truth, the following realities need to be reemphasized: the very notion of praxis is grounded in a distinction, not a separation; truth as transformation always also involves truth as disclosure; speaking the truth is never separable but is distinguishable from doing the truth; cognitive claims are not simply validated through authentic praxis any more than causes are validated through the presence of martyrs; the crisis of cognitive claims does not simply dissipate when the shift of emphasis to the social-ethical crisis of a global humanity comes more clearly into central focus; the need for argument, criteria, warrants, evidence, the

---

[36] The major theological proviso demanding publicness remains the doctrine of God present in all three theological disciplines. Indeed, the "theistic proviso" (to thus name it) impels the eschatological proviso and the "God acting for the oppressed" provisos of political and liberation theologies.

need for certain necessary abstractions from the concrete, the need for the ideal of conversation embodied in most forms of contemporary fundamental and systematic theologies remain in force as necessities and ideals even in a situation that is possibly systematically distorted.

In sum, the emergence of theologies of praxis in our time has aided the search for criteria of truth for all theologians by their emphasis upon truth as transformation. In principle, that emphasis may prove complementary to the emphasis upon disclosure in systematic theologies or the emphasis upon metaphysical and existential adequacy to experience in fundamental theologies.[37] In fact, all these theologies are more often in conflict than in conversation or genuine argument. However, it is also true that the distinction among three major disciplines in theology may yet yield a clarification of both the major differences and the major similarities among all existing theologies. Then the possibilities of collaboration (including, of course, argument over the more relatively adequate theological criteria for meaning and truth) might become real again. Then, as well, there might prove a communal recognition of the real need for all three disciplines in theology: really distinct, never separated; each grounded in and ultimately judged by the drive of *all* to the publicness impelling every theology.

---

[37] This would especially be the case if, as suggested above, one reflected upon this matter in terms of the following complementary emphases in each discipline. 1) Fundamental theology: the transcendental — metaphysics; the major mode of conversation — argument or dialectic. 2) Systematic theology: the transcendental — the beautiful (and *as* true) related to the religious or holy; the disciplines poetics and rhetoric; the major mode of conversation — interpretation as conversation with the religious classics. 3) Practical theology: the transcendental — the good (and *as* true) related to the religious or holy; the disciplines — ethics and politics related to a transforming faith-praxis; the major mode of conversation — Christian ideology-critique or conflict (the negative moment) and some positive proposal of a future ideal situation articulated in ethical-political-theological ways. This proposal for the possibility in principle of complementariness, if successful, would validate a general analogical pluralism on the spectrum abstract-concrete as distinct from an eclecticism or a univocal monism. It would not solve the inevitable conflicts and disputes emerging in the results on particular issues from each discipline (e.g., consider how all three disciplines would provide distinct interpretations for the theological concept "The Reign of God").

Praxis and Generalized Empirical Method

by Matthew L. Lamb

"He would have been the perfect incarnation of the last scholastic. A tireless worker and a great *savant,* he knew the world more in theory than in practice." Many would take these words as a description of Bernard Lonergan, while finding his more recent interest in praxis and his extensive work in macroeconomics somewhat disconcerting. The quotation, however, is the description of Karl Marx by one of his erstwhile close friends.[1] The difficulty in understanding Lonergan's contributions to themes associated with praxis can be traced to his concern with consciousness and rational self-appropriation. This concern is often suspected of retreating from the suspicions of consciousness generated by the work associated with Freud and Marx. Freudian insights have called into question a whole range of suppositions regarding conscious motivations, uncovering as they do the unknown psychic infrastructure of instinctual desires and fears operative in conscious living and action. Analogously, Marxian insights have called into question the supposed independence of consciousness and ideas, uncovering the social and economic interests which condition and constitute consciousness.

The resolution of these critical questions to the work of Lonergan depends upon the extent to which his concern with consciousness and self-appropriation does or does not fall behind the insights into the psychic and social conditioning of conscious intentionality. The work of such scholars as Robert Doran, Vernon Gregson, Sebastian Moore, and Bernard Tyrrell argues persuasively that Lonergan's concern with conscious intentionality is capable of creatively and critically integrating the insights into the psychic infrastructure associated with contemporary forms of psychology. The orientation

---

[1] Cf. David McLellan, *Karl Marx: His Life and Thought* (New York: Harper and Row, 1973), pp. 102 f.

of these scholars' writings indicates how a concern for uncovering the unknown determinations of conscious human activity by attending to psyche can indeed be integrated within the project of self-appropriation, once the latter is understood as inclusive of psychic as well as of intellectual, moral, and religious conversions. The integration is transformative, not only for our knowledge of conscious intentionality, but also for our understanding of psychic processes. For the manifold efforts to understand and to analyze the human psyche within the psychological and psychiatric movements are themselves efforts constituted by the related and recurrent operations involved in the transition from consciousness to knowledge.[2]

In what follows I should like to spell out some of the major implications in relating Lonergan's work to the context and consequences of Marx's call to praxis. The first section will deal with primarily philosophical issues, while the second section will indicate how Lonergan's work provides categories for a critical retrieval of theological teachings from the perspective of praxis.

I. Praxis and Generalized Empirical Method

Some might argue that assessing the contributions of Lonergan to the themes of praxis and method is to slant the dialogue too much toward Kantian or Hegelian perspectives. After all, was not Marx's resounding call to praxis precisely a critique of the transcendental and theoretical critiques of Kant and Hegel? Is not Lonergan a transcendental Thomist and so rather removed from concerns with praxis? I believe that such objections fail to appreciate both Lonergan's work and the project envisaged in Marx's call to praxis.

To begin with the latter, Marx's lifelong efforts to sublate philosophy into social praxis was by no means a complete negation of the transcendental projects associated with German idealism. If there are few issues on which the many divergent schools of Marxist scholarship agree, this would be one of them. Indeed, I would agree with Alvin Gouldner's assessment in his Marxist analysis of Marxism, and with others, that a basic element in the contradictions and anomalies imbedded in the development of Marxist theory and praxis can be traced to German idealist traditions.[3] As the young Marx stated with regard to Kant, and the mature Marx with regard to Hegel, the aim of his control of theory through social praxis was

---

[2] Cf. the articles by Robert Doran, Vernon Gregson, Sebastian Moore, and Bernard Tyrrell in this volume, with the references to their other works provided there.

[3] A. Gouldner, *The two Marxisms: Contradictions and Anomalies in the Development of Theory* (New York: The Seabury Press, 1980), pp. 177-98; see also pp. 8-37. L. Kolakowski, *Main Currents of Marxism*, vol. I, *The Founders* (Oxford: Clarendon Press, 1978). D. McLellan, *Marx before Marxism* (New York: Harper & Row, 1970).

not to replace theories or ideas with some kind of mindless activism, but to understand idealists like Kant and Hegel as unknowingly and uncritically reflecting in their theories concrete social values and disvalues.⁴ As I argue at much greater length in a book I am now writing on the foundations of religious theory and praxis, the modern "turn to the subject" initiated by Kant and German idealism is singularly important for an adequate understanding of contemporary efforts at elaborating a methodologically grounded praxis enlightenment.⁵ All too briefly stated, the "turn to the subject" has two major phases: the transcendental-idealist phase (Kant, Hegel, right-wing Hegelians) and the dialectical-materialist phase (left-wing Hegelians, Marx, Marxists). Common to both these phases was a concern to promote the responsible freedom of humankind in the face of the increasing cognitive, social, and cultural domination of the natural sciences with their empirico-mathematical techniques of observation, verification and industrial application.⁶ Kant's critiques, especially the *Critique of Practical Reason,* sought to protect the realm of moral praxis and freedom as a noumenal realm over against the phenomenal realm of necessity. Hegel recognized the inconsistency of this phenomenon-noumenon dichotomy and sought to develop a conceptualistic intellectual praxis aimed at sublating all meanings and values into the constitutive meaning of *Geist* as a coherent and complete system.⁷ The decisive discovery by Hegel of history as constituted by meaning—Lonergan once remarked to me that the earliest expressions of this can be found in Hegel's early theological writings—was a heady experience indeed.

---

⁴ Cf. J. O'Malley's "Introduction" to his trans. of Marx's *Critique of Hegel's 'Philosophy of Right'* (Cambridge: The University Press, 1970), pp. ix-lxiii. Compare, for example, Marx's early poem on Hegel in K. Marx and F. Engels, *Collected Works,* vol. *1* (New York: International Publishers, 1975), pp. 576 f:
  "Kant and Fichte soar to heavens blue
  Seeking for some distant land,
  I but seek to grasp profound and true
  That which - in the street I find."
with his analysis in *The German Ideology* of how Kant's critique of practical reason fully reflects the contradictions of political liberalism, *Collected Works,* vol. 5 (New York: International Publishers, 1976), pp.193-96; and his remarks on Hegel's dialectics in the "Afterword to the Second German Edition" of his *Capital* (New York: International Publishers, 1967), pp. 19 f.

⁵ The book is on the foundations of religious theory and praxis. On the praxis enlightenment, cf. M. Lamb, "Theology and Praxis: A Response (II) to Bernard Lonergan," *CTSA Proceedings* 32 (1977), pp. 22-30; and "Dogma, Experience and Political Theology" in E. Schillebeeckx and B. van Iersel (eds.), *Revelation and Experience* (New York: The Seabury Press, 1979), pp. 79-90.

⁶ Cf. G. Baum, *Religion and Alienation* (New York: Paulist Press, 1975), pp. 21-61; M. Lamb, "The Challenge of Critical Theory" in G. Baum (ed.), *Sociology and Human Destiny* (New York: The Seabury Press, 1980), pp. 183-213.

⁷ Cf. W. Oelmüller, *Die Unbefriedigte Aufklärung: Beiträge zu einer Theorie der Moderne von Lessing, Kant und Hegel* (Frankfurt: Suhrkamp, 1969); O. Schwemmer, *Philosophie*

While the right-wing Hegelians attempted to maintain that the factual institutions of society in Church and State incarnated constitutive reason, the left-wing Hegelians had, perhaps, drunk more deeply of the discovery and tended to follow Feuerbach's call for an absolute negation of existing historical and social institutions in order to re-create society and history in the anthropocentric image of a radically secularized constitutive rationality.[8] The "turn to the subject" passed from the transcendental-idealist phase, with its emphasis on moral praxis (freedom) and intellectual praxis (concept), to the dialectical-materialist phase. The young Hegelians promoted a historical praxis aimed at realizing concretely in history (or materially) constitutive rationality. The empirical methods of the natural sciences, as Feuerbach stated, once united to the new philosophy will collaborate in creating a new truth and new freedom: autonomous *secularized* humankind.[9]

If Marx could write that "there is no other road for you to *truth* and *freedom* except that leading *through* the brook of fire (the Feuerbach),"[10] he soon recognized that the heady optimism of the young Hegelian emphasis on historical praxis aimed at meaning was neither dialectical nor concretely material enough. The "turn to the subject" would, for Marx, only be real and concrete insofar as a social, revolutionary praxis would aim at realizing the *value* of human life by transforming society from its capitalist alienated stage of production and social relations of domination to a socialist stage of freely associated producers.

As Prof. O'Malley and others have indicated, Marx's *materialist conception* of society and history (Marx never wrote of "dialectical materialism") aimed at fusing natural science and dialectical criticism by materially inverting Hegel's discussion of the ethical life

---

der Praxis: Versuch zur Grundlegung einer Lehre vom Moralischen Argumentieren in Verbindung mit einer Interpretation der praktischen Philosophie Kants (Frankfurt: Suhrkamp, 1971); M. Riedel, *Theorie und Praxis im Denken Hegels* (Stuttgart: Kohlhammer, 1965); M. Theunissen, *Hegels Lehre vom absoluten Geist als theologisch-politischer Traktat* (Berlin: de Gruyter, 1970); C. Taylor, *Hegel* (New York: Cambridge Univ. Press, 1975), pp. 510-33; W. Becker, *Hegels Begriff der Dialektik und das Prinzip des Idealismus* (Stuttgart: Kohlhammer, 1969).

[8] K. Löwith, *From Hegel to Nietzsche: The Revolution in Nineteenth-Century Thought*, trans. by D. Green (New York: Doubleday Anchor Books, 1967), pp. 50-134; M. Xhaufflaire, *Feuerbach et la théologie de la sécularisation* (Paris: Les éditions du Cerf, 1970).

[9] L. Feuerbach, *Anthropologischer Materialismus: Ausgewählte Schriften*, Vols. I and II, ed. and introduced by A. Schmidt, (Frankfurt: Europäische Verlaganstalt, 1967); esp. vol. I, pp. 5-64, 75-162.

[10] D. Easton and K. Guddat (eds.), *Writings of the Young Marx on Philosophy and Society* (New York: Doubleday Anchor Books, 1967), p. 95. S. Avineri, *The Social and Political Thought of Karl Marx* (New York: Cambridge Univ. Press, 1968), pp. 8-40, 124-49.

in *The Philosophy of Right*.[11] If social praxis aims at a unity of theory and praxis in terms of concrete human values, then Marx was convinced that simple-minded moralisms against greedy capitalists was just so much nonsense. Ignorance of infrastructural value-conflicts rather than greed was at fault. Marx envisaged a massive empirical-dialectical study of economic values as the concrete embodiment of Hegel's abstract ideas. The conceptions of Hegel's discussion of civil society would be materialized in Marx's analysis of capital, landed property, wage labor. Hegel's conceptions of state constitution would be materialized in a treatment of the economic activity of the state. Hegel's ideas on international law would materialize in Marx's analysis of international trade. And, finally, world history would be concretized in terms of an analysis of the world market.[12] Marx never lived to complete even the first part of the first part (capital) of this ambitious project. He was constantly revising his dialectical analyses in the light of ever new empirical studies which, as the correspondence over the last thirty years of his life attest, were simply too many for any one person to keep up with.[13]

The purpose of this all too quick overview of the "turn to the subject" in its transcendental-idealist and dialectical-materialist phases is twofold:

First, it intimates an abiding, deep-rooted, dichotomy between the determinism increasingly operative in 18th and 19th century empirical natural sciences and the concerns of these philosophers of praxis for human freedom. As Alvin Gouldner amply demonstrates in *The Two Marxisms,* the anomalies in Marx's development itself (e.g., *materialist conception* of history; the infrastructure as juxtaposing both the *forces* and *relations* of production; the necessary empirically analyzable laws of capitalism would inevitably lead to its own breakdown and replacement by socialism *versus* the need to organize the revolutionary cadres to overthrow capitalism) have not been resolved in the subsequent history of Marxism. We are still confronted in theory and praxis with the two poles of Scientific Marxism (determinism, object-oriented) and Critical Marxism (voluntaristic, subject-oriented); for example, Lenin-Stalin versus Trotsky-Gramsci, Structuralist Marxism versus the Frankfurt School.[14]

Nor is this rift only troublesome for Marxists. In philosophy there are trends either to erect the logical techniques of the natural sciences into the canon for all valid knowledge (e.g., positivism,

---

[11] J. O'Malley, "Marx, Marxism and Method" in S. Avineri (ed.), *The Varieties of Marxism* (The Hague: Martinus Nijhof, 1977), pp. 7-41.

[12] Ibid., pp. 18-25.

[13] Ibid., pp. 25 f., 40-41.

[14] A. Gouldner, op. cit., pp. 32-63, 289-389.

naturalism, logicism, linguistic analysis of the Vienna circle, historicism, structuralism) or to preserve some domain for freedom which could not be invaded by the sciences (e.g., idealism, some forms of phenomenology, existentialism, personalism).[15] Human sciences such as psychology and sociology are marked by similar dichotomies, e.g., behaviorism vs. humanism, functionalism vs. symbolic interactionism, and most recently sociobiologism vs. anthropologism.[16] Nor are *we* immune from this, as is all too evident in the tensions between religious studies and theology, between historical-critical exegesis and doctrinal systematics.[17]

Second, I believe the *philosophical* contributions of Lonergan can be differentiated from those, e.g., of a Karl Rahner, according to how each of them directed their own retrievals of Aquinas toward overcoming the dichotomy from differing perspectives. Rahner's cognitional metaphysics in *Geist in Welt* essayed a quasi-Heideggerian transcendental retrieval of Aquinas which would attempt an ontological mediation of primordially originating experience and conceptualization through an *existential* thematization of the prior unthematic *existentiell* of transcending experience. Against Kant, Rahner would hold that the "ought" of moral and metaphysical principles were not beyond the range of human experience; against Hegel, he would affirm the unity-in-difference of reality and ideality to be in prethematic experience open to the transcendent rather than in conceptualization *per se*.[18] If from Aquinas Rahner saw the inexhaustible ground and goal of all questioning in God as Mystery, and from Heidegger how the question is the piety of thought, then it is little wonder that his achievements were to roam over the manifold questions confronting Christianity and Catholicism seeking to shift the *status quaestionis* from the ontic categories of a cosmological metaphysics to the ontological categories

---

[15] M. Lamb, "The Exigencies of Meaning and Metascience," in T. Dunne and J.-M. Laporte (eds.), *Trinification of the World: A Festschrift in Honor of Frederick Crowe* (Toronto: Regis College Press, 1978), pp. 15-45; H. Peukert, *Wissenschaftstheorie, Handlungstheorie, Fundamentale Theologie* (Frankfurt: Suhrkamp, 1978), pp. 229-300.

[16] M. Gross, *The Psychological Society* (New York: Simon & Schuster, 1978); T. Bottomore and R. Nisbet (eds.), *A History of Sociological Analysis* (New York: Basic Books, 1978), pp. 237-86, 321-61,457-98, 557-98; E. Wilson and M. Harris, "The Envelope and the Twig," *The Sciences*, vol. 18 (1978), pp. 10-15, 27.

[17] C. Davis, "The Reconvergence of Theology and Religious Studies," *Studies in Religion* 4/3 (1974-5), pp. 205-21; and the five responses to this study, *ibid.*, pp. 222-36. G. Sauter, *Vor einem neuen Methodenstreit in der Theologie?* (Munich: Kaiser, 1970); D. Kelsey, *The Uses of Scripture in Recent Theology* (Philadelphia: Fortress Press, 1975). V. Harvey, *The Historian & the Believer* (New York: Macmillan, 1966).

[18] P. Eicher, *Die Anthropologische Wende* (Freiburg: Universitätsverlag, 1970), pp. 13-33; F. Fiorenza, "Introduction: Karl Rahner and the Kantian Problematic," in K. Rahner, *Spirit in the World*, trans. by W. Dych (New York: Herder & Herder, 1968), pp. xix-xlv; A. Carr, *The Theological Method of Karl Rahner* (Missoula: Scholars Press, 1977).

of a cognitive metaphysics.[19] Where Rahner's transcendental turn to the subject essayed a creative Catholic response to, and critical appropriation of, the transcendental-idealist phase, Johann B. Metz's political theology has attempted to articulate a foundational theology appropriate for those questions and challenges posed by the dialectical-materialist phase of the turn to the subject.[20] While the originating primordial experience as openness to Mystery through the *Woraufhin* of human questing is indeed a foundational orientation of human experience, still for Metz Rahner has paid too little attention both to the *problematic* character of human experience, especially in its intrinsically social and historical-dialectical dimensions, and has conceded too much to the conceptional-ideational aspects of transcendental-idealist traditions in dealing with the many disputed questions in theology.[21] For Metz Rahner's achievements were too conceptually immune from the natural and human sciences, not to mention from the concrete histories of suffering associated with the struggles for liberation and redemption.[22]

Lonergan's retrieval of Aquinas, on the other hand, was not in terms of a cognitional metaphysics but rather a theoretical articulation of the cognitive praxis or performance underlying both the transitions from consciousness to knowledge and from knowledge to action.[23] Instead of moving away from the empirical sciences toward an ontological refuge of human freedom and self-determination, Lonergan proceeded to uncover the dynamic and heuristic performance of questioning as grounding all advances in empirically scientific knowing.[24] From this he dialectically challenged the notions of deterministic necessity and axiomatic deductivism, which not only misled so many articulations of empirical science, but also alienated social and cultural living. It did this by attempting to impose concep-

---

[19] P. Eicher, op cit., pp. 115-199; A. Carr, op. cit., pp. 59-123.

[20] V. Spülbeck, *Neomarxismus und Theologie: Gesellschaftskritik in Kritischer Theorie und Politischer Theologie* (Freiburg: Herder, 1977); R. Johns, *Man in the World: The Theology of Johannes B. Metz* (Missoula: Scholars Press, 1976); M. Xhauflaire (ed.), *La pratique de la théologie politique* (Tournai: Casterman, 1974).

[21] J. Metz, *Faith in History and Society,* trans. by D. Smith (New York: The Seabury Press, 1980), pp. 154-68; also Metz's "An Identity Crisis in Christianity? Transcendental and Political Responses" in W. Kelly (ed.), *Theology & Discovery: Essays in Honor of Karl Rahner* (Milwaukee: Marquette Univ. Press, 1980), pp. 169-78; also the responses to Metz's study by D. Tracy and M. Lamb, ibid., pp. 179-87.

[22] R. Johns, op. cit., pp. 132-49; M. Lamb, *History, Method and Theology* (Missoula: Scholars Press, 1978), pp. 1-54.

[23] B. Lonergan, *Verbum: Word and Idea in Aquinas,* ed. by D. Burrell (Notre Dame: Univ. Press, 1967), pp. vii-xv, 1-95; D. Tracy, *The Achievement of Bernard Lonergan* (New York: Herder & Herder, 1970), pp. 45-103.

[24] B. Lonergan, *Insight: A Study of Human Understanding* (New York: Harper & Row, 1978 edition), pp 3-172. Also M. Vertin's contribution to this volume.

tual necessities through the use of technocratic and bureaucratic techniques.[25] If Lonergan learned from Aquinas that proportionate being as the *concrete universal* is shot through with contingency, he creatively transposed those insights in terms of a complementarity of classical and statistical procedures in empirical science. These yielded, not a universe whose laws could be theoretically deduced according to some iron necessity, but a universe of emergent probability open to the rhythms of limitation and transcendence, and constitutive of the dialectical tensions between essential and effective human freedom.[26] Lonergan's work through *Insight* is a massive transposition of the basic presuppositions underlying the transcendental-idealist phase of the turn to the subject. The Kantian dichotomy between phenomenal necessity (known by the empirical sciences) and noumenal freedom (oriented to moral praxis) is overcome by adverting to the actually related and recurrent performance of what we do when we know.[27] Such attention to cognitive praxis discloses the alienations operative in believing that we know the real through sensitive intuition *(sinnliche Anschauung)*. If knowing is not taking a good look but verifying insights into sensible and imaginative data, then moral praxis is not voluntaristically following the categorical imperatives encapsulated in noumenal subjectivity. Rather, moral praxis positively sublates the underlying sensitive flow of desires and fears, through practical insight and evaluative reflection, to reach decisions on contingent courses of action whereby we can extend the range of effective human freedom.[28].

The Hegelian shift from sensitive to intellectual intuition *(intellektuelle Anschauung)* with its orientation toward a conceptualistic intellectual praxis dominated by knowledge and theory is replaced in Lonergan by an attunement to the related and recurrent operations of conscious intentionality which shifts attention from logic to method, and acknowledges the coherent but *radically incomplete* (and so ongoing) character of the human spirits' *(Geist)* quest for meaning and value.[29] The problematic ambiguity of concrete human experiences in history cannot, Lonergan reminds us, be overcome by the equally problematic ambiguity of abstract human knowledge in his-

---

[25] *Ibid.*, pp. 207-44; M. Lamb, *History, Method and Theology*, pp. 254-81. Lonergan developed a strong critique of bureaucracy as illustrative of sin in the social process in his unpublished *Lectures on the Philosophy of Education* (Cincinnati: Xavier University, 1959), lecture three, pp. 10-13.

[26] *Insight*, pp. 103-39, 607-33; M. Lamb, *History, Method and Theology*, pp. 480-85.

[27] Lamb, ibid., pp. 56-93.

[28] G. Sala, *Das Apriori in der menschlichen Erkenntnis* (Meisenheim: Verlag Anton Hain, 1972), pp. 41-68, 297-389.

[29] J. Nilson, *Hegel's Phenomenology and Lonergan's Insight* (Meisenheim: Verlag Anton Hain, 1979).

tory.³⁰ The metaphysical logic of an Hegelian type, presupposing as it does an eventual completeness of system and theory, cannot be *die Gesamt- und Grundwissenschaft*. Lonergan's transcendental method strives for coherence but frankly admits its radical incompleteness. The operations of conscious intentionality are indeed both factual ("is") and normative ("ought"). Yet this fusion of the factual and the normative is not the indicative ("always already") possession of *Geist* within the world of theory but is the imperative ("not yet") beckoning of concrete human strivings toward attentiveness, intelligence, reasonableness, and responsible love.³¹ The fusion is a *project*, not a possession. The foundations of intellectual praxis in transcendental method are not some set of theories, however brilliant, but questioning human beings living within the multiple and changing patterns of natural and historical processes.³² Idealism, as Lonergan mentions, is only a halfway house between empiricism and such a critical realism.³³

If Lonergan's early work can be seen as transposing the basic presuppositions of the transcendental-idealist phase, then I believe his later work (from *Method in Theology* to his present work in macroeconomics) can be viewed as a creative and critical response to the challenge of the dialectical-materialist phase of the "turn toward the subject."

In *Method in Theology* Lonergan indicates the pressing need for dialectical criticism to inform historical and social praxis:

> There are deviations occasioned by neurotic need. There are the refusals to keep on taking the plunge from settled routines to an as yet unexperienced but richer mode of living. There are the mistaken endeavors to quieten an uneasy conscience by ignoring, belittling, denying, rejecting higher values. Preference scales become distorted. Feelings soured. Bias creeps into one's outlook, rationalization into one's morals, ideology into one's thoughts. So one may come to hate the truly good, and love the really evil. Nor is that calamity limited to individuals. It can happen to groups, to nations, to blocks of nations, to mankind. It can take different, opposed, belligerent forms to divide mankind and to menace civilization with destruction. Such is the monster that has stood forth in our day.³⁴

The monster of contemporary alienation intimates how the age of innocent criticism, i.e., criticism innocent of its own presupposi-

---

³⁰ W. Loewe, "Dialectics of Sin: Lonergan's Insight and the Critical Theory of Max Horkheimer," in *Anglican Theological Review* vol. 41, n. 2 (1979), pp. 224-45.
³¹ B. Lonergan, *Collection*, ed. by F. Crowe (New York: Herder & Herder, 1967), pp. 198-220.
³² Lamb, *History, Method and Theology*, pp. 254-72, 424-48.
³³ *Insight*, p. xxviii.
³⁴ B. Lonergan, *Method in Theology* (New York: Herder & Herder, 1972), pp. 39 f.

tions, has begun to end. As Lonergan later wrote "the more human studies turn away from abstract universals and attend to concrete human beings, the more evident it becomes that the scientific age of innocence has come to an end: human authenticity can no longer be taken for granted . . . It is only after the age of innocence that praxis becomes an academic subject . . ."[35] Empirical human sciences are not sufficiently objective to the degree that they ignore the complex dialectics of decline in which (1) "the data may be a mixed product of authenticity and unauthenticity," and (2) "that the very investigation of the data may be affected by the personal or inherited unauthenticity of the investigators."[36]

With increasing frequency over the last six years, Lonergan has referred to his work not as "transcendental method" but as "generalized empirical method." His empirical method is *"generalized"* in two radical ways: (1) it attends to both the data of sense and the data of consciousness; and (2) the data of consciousness involve not only a genetically related series of sublations from data through understanding and judgment to decision and action, but also the need for an ongoing series of dialectically operative methods which are grounded in decisions and actions aimed at promoting good and overcoming alienation.[37] The dialectically operative methods are what Lonergan terms "method as praxis". Where empirical methods move from experiential data, through ranges of understanding relative to the data, and through judgments discerning whether such understandings are correct or not, to decisions and actions, method-as-praxis has a reverse orientation. It seeks to explicate the value commitments, or value-conflicts, operative in decisions and actions. People respond to value in actions embodying love or hate even though they cannot explain fully what they are responding to. The knowledge flows from the loving or hating actions; and it flows in terms of judgments of value or disvalue wherein they judge concrete situations in the light of the values they love, and the disvalues they hate. From such judgments they engage in what Ricoeur calls a hermeneutics of recovery (regarding values) and a hermeneutics of suspicion (regarding disvalues) on the level of understanding. Finally, from such decisions, judgments, and hermeneutics, they engage

---

[35] B. Lonergan, "The Ongoing Genesis of Methods," *Studies in Religion*, 6/4 (1977), pp. 341-55; here, 341 and 351.

[36] *Ibid.*, p. 349.

[37] *Insight*, pp. 469-82, 530 ff.; *Method in Theology*, pp. 27-55, 235-66. On the significance of this shift to a generalized empirical method which emphasizes the dialectics of the human good, cf. R. Doran, *Subject and Psyche: Ricoeur, Jung and the Search for Foundations* (Washington, D.C.: University Press of America, 1977), pp. 17-113; also his essay in this volume.

in an empirically transformative action which changes both human hearts and human social and cultural institutions.[38]

Although one could claim that all of Lonergan's work in method is praxis insofar as it is concerned with the question of what we *do* when we know, still Lonergan himself also acknowledges a more transformative sense of *praxis* in which decision and action precede and ground a knowledge of values, lead to understandings which engage in a hermeneutics of suspicion as well as of recovery, and thereby engages in a transformation not only of the data of sense but also the data of consciousness itself.[39]

Now such a generalized empirical method, with its attention to dialectics and praxis, critically responds to the concerns of the dialectical-materialist phase of the "turn towards the subject." With the young Hegelians it acknowledges the centrality of constitutive meaning in historical praxis. History is constituted by human meanings and values which not only grow and flourish but also disintegrate and decay. While the self-appropriation that is foundational to generalized empirical method is intensely personal, it is not private or monadic. Quite the contrary. Such self-appropriation is intrinsically related (as all persons are) to the ongoing history of humankind itself.[40] Thus Lonergan can write that generalized empirical method is indeed experimental. "But the experiment is conducted not by any individual, not by any generation, but by the historical process itself."[41] Unlike the young Hegelians, however, our 20th century has profoundly shaken secularist faith in humankind's ability to carry off the experiment on its own. In an unpublished essay of 1974 on "Sacralization and Secularization" Lonergan indicates how the undifferentiated sacralism of the Middle Ages led

---

[38] B. Lonergan, "The Ongoing Genesis of Methods," pp. 348-52.

[39] Doran, *Subject and Psyche,* pp. 253-309; Lamb, *History, Method and Theology,* pp. 422-53.

[40] B. Lonergan, "The Ongoing Genesis of Methods," pp. 345 and 348: "...privacy in the world mediated by meaning has to be contrived and defended and even then it is limited. In that world one is taught by others and, for the most part, what they know they have learnt from others, in an ongoing process that stretches back over millennia....None of us is an Adam living at the origin of human affairs, becoming all that he is by his own decisions, and learning all that he knows by personal experience, personal insight, personal discernment. We are products of a process that in its several aspects is named socialization, acculturation, education." All human persons are intrinsically related to other human persons. Both the personhood question (Who are we?) and the nature question (What are we?) can only be answered in relation to the ongoing processes of human history. But where the nature question admits of explanatory understanding in terms of the universe of emergent probability, the personhood question admits of narrative-symbolic understanding heuristically oriented into Mystery.

[41] Lonergan, ibid., p. 345.

from the 17th century onwards to a defensive clerical sacralism in Roman Catholicism which tended to extend "the mantle of religion over the opinions of ignorant men."[42] Such an undifferentiated and defensive sacralism provoked, especially from the 19th century onwards, an equally undifferentiated and offensive secularism. We have witnessed as Max Weber intimates, the alienating transition from a hierarchic *sacralist* authoritarianism to a bureaucratic *secularist* authoritarianism.[43]

Like all authoritarianisms, the two tend to reinforce one another over the heads of people and communities. The illusion of a god identical with ecclesial-social institutions is not radically different from the illusion of a humankind identical with political-economic institutions.[44] The need of our times is for a differentiation of sacred and secular attune to the genuine and the pathological in both. Lonergan's reflections on the structure of the human good and the dialectic of religious experience will be helpful in such a task of differentiation.[45]

The creative and critical responses to the ongoing challenges of Marxist social theory and praxis by generalized empirical method are extensive and deeply transformative. I have already referred to Alvin Gouldner's *The Two Marxisms* which traces the origins and development of the contradictions and anomalies between Scientific Marxism and Critical Marxism. The former is characterized by an empirical determinism convinced that necessary laws of social development would, irrespective of human freedom, lead to the demise of capitalism. The objective creates the subjective. Critical Marxism, on the other hand, is characterized by a dialectical voluntarism convinced of the need to instill a revolutionary messianism in peoples in order to change existing social structures. The subjective creates the objective.[46] Gouldner sees these two Marxisms as two extremes, both present in Marx, and defining (as idealtypes) the ends of a continuum towards one or the other of which all subsequent Marxist theory and praxis has vacillated.[47] Nor is he alone in

---

[42] Lonergan, "Sacralization and Secularization," (unpublished lecture in 1974), p. 24.

[43] M. Weber, *Economy and Society: An Outline of Interpretative Sociology*, ed. by G. Roth and C. Wittich (Berkeley: Univ. of California Press, 1978), vol. 2, pp. 956-1003; M. Weber, *The Protestant Ethic and the Spirit of Capitalism*, trans. by T. Parsons (New York: C. Scribner's Sons, 1958), pp. 155-84; G. Baum, *Religion and Alienation*, pp. 162-92; D. Martin, *A General Theory of Secularization* (New York: Harper & Row, 1978).

[44] M. Lamb, "The Challenge of Critical Theory," pp. 205-08.

[45] *Method in Theology*, pp. 27-55, 108-12.

[46] Gouldner, *The Two Marxisms*, pp. 3-31.

[47] Ibid., pp. 32-79.

such a formulation; he points to similar studies by Karl Korsch, Lucio Colletti, Merleau-Ponty, Mihailo Marković, Dick Howard, Karl Klare, Eric Hobsbawm, and Perry Anderson.[48]

Generalized empirical method exposes the cognitive and epistemological misunderstanding regarding so-called necessary deterministic laws in nature and history by its articulation of concrete cognitive performance and its attendant emergent probability. It also maps out the interlocking mediations of empirical and dialectical methods capable of radically displacing the dichotomies of scientistic determinism and voluntaristic decisionism.[49] In place of these alienated and alienating dichotomies, generalized empirical method elaborates an ongoing complementarity of empirical methods (classical, statistical, genetic) and dialectical methods in which the results of empirical investigations provide the data for a dialectical discernment of the values and disvalues they exhibit.[50] The dialectically foundational articulation of genuinely humanizing praxis promotes a value critique, and systematic understandings of the ramifications of values and disvalues, in order to transform the social situations from which empirical human sciences in turn draw their data.[51] This, in very abbreviated fashion, is the metascientific Theory-Praxis Mediation based on Lonergan's functional specialties I have developed in *History, Method and Theology*.[52]

Moreover, this is not only relevant to the dichotomy within Marxist social praxis and theory, but also to analogous dichotomies that bedevil both philosophy in general and scientific methodologies.[53]

In a letter to Walter Benjamin, Theodor Adorno wrote in 1935: "A restoration of theology, or better, a radicalization of the dialectic into the very glowing core of theology, would at the same time have to mean an utmost intensification of the social-dialectical, indeed economic, motifs."[54]

During the past few years Lonergan has taken up again the work in macroeconomics he began during the 1930's. To those skeptical of self-educated economists, I would recall how neither Adam Smith nor Karl Marx nor for that matter, many of the key figures in

---

[48] Ibid., pp. 155-63 and references given there.

[49] *Insight*, pp. 86-102, 115-139, 259-62, 458-83, 607-18.

[50] *Method in Theology*, pp. 36-47; Lamb, *History, Method and Theology*, pp. 388-441.

[51] Lonergan, "The Ongoing Genesis of Method," pp. 348-52.

[52] Op. Cit., pp. 195-209; also J. Raymaker, "The Theory and Praxis of Social Ethics," in this volume.

[53] Lamb, *History, Method and Theology*, pp. 156-209, and the references given there.

[54] Adorno, *Über Walter Benjamin* (Frankfurt: Suhrkamp, 1970), p. 117.

Schumpeter's massive *A History of Economic Analysis,* had Ph.D.'s in economics. If Marx's concern with social praxis was guided by a concrete understanding of value as at bottom economic value, then Lonergan has understood how a genuinely dialectical critique of Marxist materialism should meet head on the problems of massive economic oppression and exploitation that materialist dialectic sought to remedy.[55] Marx tried to discern criteria for economic progress or decline immanent in the economic infrastructure constituted by the industrializing forces and relations (the human relations to nature and to other human beings) of production. In a critically similar manner, Lonergan's macroeconomics connects his dialectic of the observance or non-observance of the transformative transcendental imperatives (be attentive, be intelligent, be reasonable, be responsible, be loving) immediately with his macroeconomic analysis. His *Circulation Analysis* tries to discern the *criteria* immanent in production processes with their alternating stages of surplus expansions and basic expensions. "But the dialectic arises from the contradiction that arises when the criteria are adverted to or not, understood or not, affirmed or denied, observed responsibly or disregarded, by a community of love or a community of egoists."[56]

Contemporary Catholic social teaching has continually criticized the alienating shortcomings of both late capitalism and state socialism. But, as liberation theologians are quick to point out, if these criticisms however justified in themselves, are not to degenerate into a value-neutral legitimization of the status quo, then we must elaborate an accurate and critical economic theory and praxis capable of concretely and dialectically overcoming the alienations so massively present in both.[57] Moralistic appeals to the common good, subsidiarity, and the just wage are hardly sufficient. As I have argued elsewhere, Lonergan's macroeconomics is as insightfully challenging in its potential contributions to really humanizing economic processes, as his earlier work in method is in regard to basic cognitive issues. Just as the latter offers us a way to unmask the myriad forms of empiricism and idealism not as opposites but as different aspects

---

[55] Lonergan, *An Essay in Circulation Analysis* (Boston College: unpublished manuscript, 1978-80), p. 2: "In other words, the productive process itself contains implicit criteria, and if these criteria are unknown or ignored, things may go from bad to worse. And as we all know, such an eventuality has already occurred." J. Schumpeter, *History of Economic Analysis,* 8th printing (New York: Oxford Univ. Press, 1974) pp. v-xiii, 1-1260.

[56] Lonergan, *An Essay in Circulation Analysis,* p. 2.

[57] Cf. J. Segundo, "Capitalism versus Socialism: Crux Theologica," in R. Gibellini (ed.), *Frontiers of Theology in Latin America* (Maryknoll: Orbis Books, 1979), pp. 240-59; G. Baum, *The Social Imperative* (New York: Paulist Press, 1979), pp. 3-38, 70-98.

of a radical neglect of transformative cognitive praxis, so his macroeconomics will help us to understand how the many forms of late capitalism and state socialism are the alienated and alienating results of a deep-seated ignorance of the criteria constitutive of the alternating basic and surplus stages of the production process. As I have argued elsewhere, late capitalism is a bad materialization of idealism, whereas state socialism is a bad idealization of materialism.[58] What humankind doesn't know has hurt it, for this ignorance continues to spawn the economic misadventures (as Lonergan terms them) of colonialism, welfarism, and multi-nationalism.[59] Such are the economic monstrosities which have stood forth in our day generating widespread poverty, unemployment, inflations, recessions, militarisms, depressions. The terribly dehumanizing effects can be read all too easily in the massive sufferings of millions of human beings.[60]

II. Orthopraxis and Theological Method

Within the above context I have sketched some of the main critical contributions Lonergan's generalized empirical method has made to the theme of praxis in the "turn to the subject" with its transcendental-idealist and dialectical-materialist phases. As a result, Lonergan's articulation of generalized empirical method seems to be especially helpful in sorting out the many methodological misunderstandings that haunt not only philosophy in general, and the philosophies of praxis in particular, but also the human sciences and scholarships.

In the light of these contributions one can, perhaps, appreciate why Lonergan can bluntly write that "orthopraxy has a value beyond orthodoxy" and that the profound change in the structures and procedures of theology articulated in method "places orthopraxis

---

[58] M. Lamb, "The Production Process and Exponential Growth: A Study in Socio-Economics and Theology," in F. Lawrence (ed.), *Lonergan Workshop*, vol. 1 (Missoula: Scholars Press, 1978), pp. 257-307; also Lamb, "The Challenge of Critical Theory," pp. 198-208.

[59] Lonergan, *An Essay in Circulation Analysis,* pp. 70-107. For illustrations of the misadventures of the multinational corporations, Lonergan draws upon primarily R. Barnet and R. Müller, *Global Reach: The Power of the Multinational Corporations* (New York: Simon and Schuster, 1974). Lonergan's *Circulation Analysis* decisively advances the Post-Keynesian positions represented in A. Eichner (ed.), *A Guide to Post-Keynesian Economics* (N.Y.: M. E. Sharpe, 1979).

[60] For a descriptive account of some of these sufferings, cf. P. Lernoux, *Cry of the People: United States Involvement in the Rise of Fascism, Torture, and Murder and the Persecution of the Catholic Church in Latin America* (New York: Doubleday, 1980); also S. George, *How the other Half Dies: The Real Reasons for World Hunger* (Montclair: Allanheld, Osmun & Co., 1977); F. Lappé and J. Collins, *Food First: Beyond the Myth of Scarcity,* revised & updated (New York: Ballatine Books, 1979), and Lonergan's review of the first edition of this book, *Theological Studies*, vol. 39, n. 1 (1978), pp. 198 f.

above orthodoxy."⁶¹ Orthopraxis in this sense has, I believe, two meanings. Its primary meaning refers to the genuine practice of religion whereby humans appropriate the genuine religious meanings and values transmitted by their religious tradition. In this primary sense, then, orthodoxies can be expressions of the orthopraxis of religious communities at particular places and times. This primary orthopraxis is the concrete realization in history of religious conversion as an ongoing withdrawal from sinful hate and indifference.⁶² As genuine (or "ortho-") praxis, it can never be simply taken for granted or automatically guaranteed in any religious tradition. It is the fruit of God's grace and free, human, and communal response. Such orthopraxis is foundational to the ongoing religious traditions in history.⁶³

A second meaning of orthopraxis might be termed reflective, dialectical orthopraxis. This second meaning moves orthopraxis from its conscious primary meaning to a known and explicit thematization in order to aid theology in a move toward the "third stage of meaning" marked by the modern emergence of historical consciousness and the contemporary emergence of dialectical consciousness.⁶⁴ Lonergan sketches the relationship between these two meanings of orthopraxis when he writes:

> For religious communities are historical realities. Their authenticity is the resultant not only of the authenticity of their contemporary members but also of the heritage transmitted down the centuries. Whatever the defects of any such heritage, it comes to be accepted in good faith. Good faith is good not evil. It needs to be purified, but the purification will be the slow product of historical research into the screening memories and defense mechanisms and legitimations that betray an original waywardness and a sinister turn.⁶⁵

Lonergan sees both religious studies and theology challenged by a contemporary need to develop dialectical and critically practical methods for discerning genuine from alienated aspects in the histori-

---

⁶¹ Lonergan, "A New Pastoral Theology," (unpublished lecture, 1973), p. 22; "Theology and Praxis," *CTSA Proceedings* 32 (1979), pp. 1-16; also the responses by E. Braxton and M. Lamb, *ibid.*, pp. 17-30. On how Lonergan's theological method acknowledges how "orthopraxy has a value beyond orthodoxy," cf. Lonergan, "Mission and Spirit," *Concilium* 9/10, n. 10 (London: Burns & Oats, 1974), pp. 69-78, here p. 75.

⁶² *Method in Theology*, pp. 105-07, 237-44, 267-71.

⁶³ Lonergan, "Mission and Spirit," pp. 69-78; also his "Healing and Creating in History," in *Bernard Lonergan: Three Lectures* (Montreal: Thomas More Institute, 1975), pp. 55-68.

⁶⁴ *Method in Theology*, pp. 85-99.

⁶⁵ Lonergan, "The Ongoing Genesis of Methods," p. 353.

cal realizations of religious traditions. Based upon his own work on the relationships between intellectual and religious conversions, Lonergan views the orientations of religious studies and theology as heading toward an overlapping and interchangeability. A reflectively dialectical orthopraxis calls for a creative openness to a "whole battery of methods" which, to the extent that they are operative in both religious studies and theology, will lead both sets of disciplines towards overlapping and interchangeability.[66]

This reflective, dialectical orthopraxis is "method as praxis". Lonergan writes of it:

> . . . it discerns a radically distorted situation; it retreats from spontaneous to critical intelligence; it begins from above on the level of evaluations and decisions; and it moves from concord and cooperation towards the development of mutual understanding and more effective communication.[67]

The radical oppositions distorting the global situations of humankind means that both religious studies and theology must "undertake dialectic, a dialectic that will assemble all the dialectics that relate religions to organized secularism, religions to one another, and the differing theologies that interpret the same religious communion."[68]

An illustration of such a dialectics now emerging in Christian theologies is the conflicts in interpretation between historical-critical and social-critical orientations towards past traditions. The conflicts between conservative "orthodoxy" (which might more accurately be termed "palaeodoxy") and liberal or modernist theologies in the early part of this century could be traced to a common (mis)understanding of revelation. Orthodoxy was viewed principally as affirmations of certain revealed *factual* truths demanding intellectual assent. These were times when, in Lonergan's phrase, "contemplative intellect, or speculative reason, or rigorous science were supreme, and practical issues were secondary."[69] Conservatives appealed to a contemplative or speculative "pure" reason which would assent to revealed, a-historical facts as dogmas. Liberals would reject the latter in favor of reading scripture as essentially reducible to secular moral values.[70] Liberal historians developed historical-critical techniques which pre-

---

[66] Ibid., pp. 354-55.
[67] Ibid., p. 354.
[68] Ibid.
[69] Ibid., pp. 351-52.
[70] M. Lamb, "The Theory-Praxis Relationship in Contemporary Christian Theologies," *CTSA Proceedings* 31 (1976), pp. 149-78, esp. pp. 154-62 and references given there.

scinded from the faith (or lack thereof) of the exegete and/or historian. These techniques appealed to rigorous science or scholarship which sought to disclose how religious texts and orthodoxies were primarily expressions of the plausibility structures of the cultures or societies in which the texts emerged. Hence we had the themes of liberal historical criticism on the "hellenization of Christianity" during the patristic and conciliar periods.[71]

As Quentin Quesnell has observed, this factual orientation toward revelation, with its consequent reduction of values to secular moral values (a là Neokantians like Ritschl), tended to overlook the rather massive evidence in the Scriptures of a revelation of values transformative of the conduct of the believing communities.[72] In line with this shift, exegetes and historians are now developing social-critical methods which interpret religious texts and doctrines, not as merely reflecting the plausibility structures of the cultures in which they emerged, but more importantly as criticizing those very plausibility structures. For example, there is Norman Gottwald's *The Tribes of Yahweh* or Gerd Theissen's *Urchristliche Wundergeschichten*, Phyllis Trible's *God and the Rhetoric of Sexuality* or Richard Cassidy's *Jesus, Politics, and Society* or Ben Meyer's *The Aims of Jesus*.[73] These are all very different exegetical and historical works; they raise many methodological issues which will be disputed and discussed for some time. In common, however, are their various critiques of, and corrections to, the presuppositions of liberal historical criticism. They refuse, in various manners, to interpret texts as doing no more than mirroring the plausibility structures and values of the surrounding cultures; instead they indicate the value-conflicts expressed in the text.[74]

---

[71] Lonergan, "The Dehellinization of Dogma," in his *A Second Collection,* ed. by W. Ryan and B. Tyrrell (Philadelphia: Westminster Press, 1974), pp. 11-32; W. Kümmel, *The New Testament: The History of the Investigation of its Problems,* trans. by S. Gilmour and H. Kee (Nashville: Abingdon Press, 1972), pp. 120-308; A. von Harnack, *Lehrbuch der Dogmengeschichte,* vols. I and II, reprint of 4th edition (Darmstadt: Wissenschaftliche Buchgesellschaft, 1964), vol. I, pp. 496-796.

[72] Q. Quesnell, "Beliefs and Authenticity," in this volume. On Kantian secular moral religiosity, cf. I. Kant, *Religion within the limits of Reason Alone,* trans. by T. Greene and H. Hudson (New York: Harper Torchbooks, 1960); A. Wood, *Kant's Moral Religion* (Ithaca: Cornell Univ. Press, 1970); on the Neo-Kantian Ritschlians, cf. D. Mueller, *An Introduction to the Theology of A. Ritschl* (Philadelphia: Westminster Press, 1969).

[73] N. Gottwald, *The Tribes of Yahweh* (Maryknoll: Orbis Books, 1979); note how Lonergan's critical realism is capable of sublating both the idealism and cultural materialism alternatives Gottwald operates within. G. Theissen, *Urchristliche Wundergeschichten* (Göttingen: Gütersloher Verlaghaus G. Mohn, 1974); P. Trible, *God and the Rhetoric of Sexuality* (Philadelphia: Fortress Press, 1978); R. Cassidy, *Jesus, Politics, and Society: A Study of Luke's Gospel* (Maryknoll: Orbis Books, 1978); B. Meyer, *The Aims of Jesus* (London: SCM Press, 1979).

Dialectics move beyond the aims of historical reconstruction. A reflectively dialectical orthopraxis takes seriously the need to thematize value conflicts within the heuristic of discerning values and disvalues capable of distinguishing genuine historical progress toward freedom and humanization from dehumanizing decline. Dialectics, therefore, have to thematize horizons and breakdowns in terms of ongoing heuristics of histories and societies. William Loewe has shown how Lonergan's soteriology based upon the law of the cross is integrated within his philosophy of history with its practical intent.[75] Just as generalized empirical method is an experiment carried on by the historical process itself, so is this method far from being "value-neutral" with regard to psychic, moral, social, intellectual, and religious values and disvalues.

Take, for instance, Lonergan's outlines of dialectical analysis in his "The Origins of Christian Realism" and *The Way to Nicea*.[76] These studies are concerned with a dialectical analysis of intellectual value conflicts. Lonergan is interested neither in historical reconstructions of what the fathers wrote nor in providing fresh data on past historical events. Rather his dialectics is based upon the intellectual appropriation of the cognitive dimensions of orthopraxis, aiming to discern how the values and disvalues such an appropriation uncovers are present in the pre-Nicean movements. He is quite explicit that the fathers "did not intend or desire" the intellectual value conflict he is analyzing.[77] He traces the conflict of values from Tertullian's naive empiricism, through Origen's Middle Platonist idealism, to Athanasius' hesitant affirmations of the critical realism of the Christian Kerygma. While none of the fathers in question explicity knew or intended this conflict, it is one which underlies the ongoing differentiations of consciousness in human history.[78]

---

[74] On the debates the social-critical approaches are occasioning, cf. J. Gager's review essay of recent books by R. Grant, A. Malherbe, and G. Theissen in *Religious Studies Review*, vol. 5, n. 3 (1979), p. 174-180. Also, L. Cormie, "The Hermeneutical Privilege of the Oppressed," *CTSA Proceedings* 33 (1978), pp. 155-81; D. Harrington, "Sociological Concepts & the Early Church," *Theological Studies* 41 (1980), pp. 181-90.

[75] W. Loewe, "Lonergan and the Law of the Cross," *Anglican Theological Review* 59 (1977), pp. 162-74; also Loewe's as yet unpublished dissertation, *Toward the Critical Mediation of Theology: A Development of the Soteriological Theme in the Work of B. Lonergan* (Milwaukee: Marquette Univ., 1974). Also the reference in note 30 above.

[76] Lonergan, *The Way to Nicea: The Dialectical Development of Trinitarian Theology*, trans. by C. O'Donovan (Philadelphia: Westminster Press, 1976); "The Origins of Christian Realism," Lonergan, *A Second Collection*, pp. 239-61.

[77] *The Way to Nicea*, p. viii. Remember that the experiment of generalized empirical method "is conducted not by any individual, not by any generation, but by the historical process itself." Lonergan, "The Ongoing Genesis of Methods," p. 345.

[78] *The Way to Nicea*, pp. 105-37. *Method in Theology*, pp. 305-18.

Lonergan's dialectical analysis takes a critically grounded stand on the transformative values of Be Attentive, Be Intelligent, Be Reasonable, Be Responsible, Be Loving. From that stand within intellectual or noetic orthopraxis, it moves on to judgments of value and of disvalue, and to a hermeneutics of suspicion regarding the disvalues of neglecting or truncating those transformative values, and to a hermeneutics of recovery regarding the instances where those values found concrete expression.

What Lonergan's brief analysis offers is, in his words, "a dialectic that, like an X-ray, sets certain key issues in high relief to concentrate on their oppositions and interplay."[79] Now, an X-ray is certainly no substitute for a full color picture. Patristic scholars who have labored long on research, interpretation, and historical reconstructions of the period in question, delicately assembling all the hues and tones of an author or event, could be shocked and disappointed at Lonergan's X-ray—especially if they had hardly a clue as to the values in conflict the X-ray highlights.[80] But X-rays are extremely useful in knowingly discerning pathological aberrations from genuine developments provided the practitioners know what to attend to. In Rosemary Haughton's phrase, "the present researches the past for the sake of the future."[81] Where historical-critical methods tend to move from empirical research through exegetical interpretations to historical reconstructions, those social-critical methods which are dialectical tend to move from decisions appropriating certain basic values, through judgments of value and disvalue based upon those decisions, to a hermeneutics of recovery and a hermeneutics of suspicion regarding values and disvalues in traditions in order to promote the communication of historical actions fostering the basic values decided upon. Such social-critical methods are, thereby, emergent realizations of what Lonergan terms "method as praxis" or what I have called a reflectively dialectical orthopraxis.

It would extend far beyond the scope of this study to analyze the many instances of social-critical methods now emerging in theology.

---

[79] *The Way to Nicea*, p. vii-viii.

[80] There is, of course, a critical complementarity between historical and dialectical analyses as Lonergan brings out in his functional specialties of how research, interpretation, and history provide results for dialectics, cf. *Method in Theology*, pp. 125-45, 235 ff.

[81] R. Haughton, *The Catholic Thing* (Springfield: Templegate, 1979), p. 17. Note how Haughton's narrative reconstructions here are dialectically oriented to orthopraxis in the present for the sake of the future. On how such an orientation is constitutive of political theology, cf. Lamb, *History, Method and Theology*, pp. 30-53. For another recent study of this aspect of Catholicism, cf. E. Braxton, *The Wisdom Community* (New York: Paulist Press, 1980). Braxton acknowledges: "Indeed, much of the dynamic of this book can be understood as an attempt to translate and apply many of the methodological insights of Lonergan and Tracy into a pastoral context." Ibid., p. viii.

There is an increasing debate among exegetes and theologians concerning the social-critical analyses of scripture and doctrine on the part of political and liberation theologians.[82] In political theology there are the differences between Metz's social-critical dialectics (aimed at moving from both conservative, paternalistic and liberal, middle-class forms of church to the liberating, basic community form of church) and Hans Küng's historical-critical reconstructions aimed at liberal, democratic reforms of the church.[83] There are also the debates among patristic scholars and theologians relative to Erik Peterson's studies on monotheism as a political problem and the Trinitarian and Christological doctrines as expressions of a spirituality and revelatory transformation of values at odds with Roman political religion.[84] Critics of Latin American liberation theologies claim that they fail to observe the distinctions between witness and rigorous reflections, thereby slipping into types of ideological advocacy.[85] Those who argue theologically for the full incorporation of women into Church ministries are sometimes criticized for slighting the symbolism of sacramental traditions.[86]

While not entering into these and other debates, I would ask to what extent various forms of political and liberation theologies are committed to values neglected in other theologies, to what extent they are calling attention by their hermeneutics of suspicion and of recovery to "the screening memories and defense mechanisms and legitimations that betray an original waywardness and a sinister turn." The criticisms of their projects which appeal to historical-critical methods might themselves be unaware of the dialectical presuppositions of their own supposed scholarship and the need for a

---

[82] Cf. references in note 72 above. Also the articles in a forthcoming issue of *Concilium* on Neo-Conservativism edited by G. Baum, esp. M. Fleet, "Neo-Conservativism in Latin America." Also A. Hennelly, *Theologies in Conflict: The Challenge of Juan L. Segundo* (Maryknoll: Orbis Books, 1979); R. McAfree Brown, *Theology in a New Key: Responding to Liberation Themes* (Philadelphia: Westminster Press, 1978).

[83] Cf. Hans Küng and Johann B. Metz, "Perspektiven für eine Kirche der Zukunft," *Publik-Forum,* vol. 9, n. 13 (Juni 1980), pp. 15-21.

[84] A. Schindler (ed.), *Monotheismus als politisches Problem? Erik Peterson und die Kritik der politischen Theologie* (Gütersloh: G. Mohn, 1978).

[85] Besides the references in note 82 above, cf. S. Ogden, *Faith and Freedom: Toward a Theology of Liberation* (Nashville: Abdington Press, 1979), pp. 33-37, 44-65, 115-24. For an enlightening discussion of Marxism and liberation theologies, cf. A. McGovern, *Marxism: An American Christian Perspective* (Maryknoll: Orbis Books, 1980).

[86] For example, D. Keefe, "Sacramental Sexuality and the Ordination of Women," *Communio* 5 (1978), pp. 228-51; also his "The Ordination of Women," *New Oxford Review* 47, n. 1 (1980), pp. 12-14.

social-critical dialectics of historical criticism itself.[87] The contributions of Lonergan to orthopraxis and theological methods, in my judgment, indicate the importance of complementing and correcting the historical-critical methods by engaging in the development of dialectical, foundational, and critically practical methods attune to the transformation of values revealed in biblical narratives and the praxis of religious conversion. To the degree that the scriptures and church doctrines expressed genuine (ortho-) religious praxis of communities in the process of conversion or *metanoia* as an ongoing withdrawal from dehumanizing and depersonalizing sin, to that degree we need today a reflectively dialectical orthopraxis methodologically capable of articulating the dialectic of values and disvalues unknown but consciously operative in scriptural and doctrinal orthodoxies. Lonergan once remarked that faith is indeed a leap, but not a leap into irrationality; faith is a leap away from the biased irrationalities of dehumanizing and depersonalizing social and historical scotosis *into reason*. The emergence of practical reason as reason yet to be realized in history—an emergence which can be read in the critiques of economic exploitation, racism, sexism, militarism—should be retrieved theologically by showing how religious faith, hope, and love are constitutive elements of this reason not yet realized in human social living.[88]

An important aspect of this retrieval involves the positive sublation of church doctrines or orthodoxy in a reflectively dialectical orthopraxis. It is within the functional specialty of doctrines that Lonergan analyzes the ongoing discovery of mind or reason in history. Doctrines are judgments of truth and falsity, of value and disvalue, heuristically anticipating the reign of God redemptively transforming human history. For "the intelligibility proper to developing doctrines is the intelligibility immanent in historical process. One knows it, not by *a priori* theorizing, but by *a posteriori* research, interpretation, history, dialectic, and the decision of foundations."[89] For

---

[87] Cf. B. Meyer, *The Aims of Jesus*, pp. 13-110 on the hermeneutical issues involved in the historical-critical quest for the historical Jesus. Also, Lamb, *History, Method and Theology*, pp. 41-93, 518-30. An adequate social-critical reconstruction of historical criticism yet to be written. Note, however, G. Bauer, *Geschichtlichkeit: Wege und Irrwege eines Begriffs* (Berlin: de Gruyter, 1963); and L. von Renthe-Fink, *Geschichtlichkeit* (Göttingen: Vandenhoeck & Ruprecht, 1968); H. Baumgartner, *Kontinuität und Geschichte* (Frankfurt: Suhrkamp, 1972).

[88] Besides the references in notes 5 and 6 above, cf. K.-O. Apel, *Towards A Transformation of Philosophy*, trans. by G. Adey and D. Frisby (Boston: Routledge & Kegan Paul, 1980), pp. 136-79, 225-300; and the theological critique and retrieval of Apel by H. Peukert, *Wissenschaftstheorie, Handlungstheorie, Fundamentale Theologie*, pp. 300-55. Also M. Lamb, "Contemporary Education and Sinful Social Structures," to appear in a forthcoming issue of *Lonergan Workshop*.

[89] *Method in Theology*, p. 319.

Lonergan discerning doctrinal development is discerning the transformatively religious judgments constitutive of practical reason as reason yet to be realized in history. By way of an all too brief illustration, I would aver that the intellectual values and disvalues Lonergan has dialectically analyzed in the pre-Nicean movement can be correlated with the socio-political values and disvalues Erik Peterson has analyzed in his "Monotheismus als politisches Problem", and the socio-sexual values and disvalues Elizabeth S. Fiorenza has initially discerned in "Early Christian History in a Feminist Perspective." [90] Naive empiricism or materialism and idealism are not just vague abstractions. As disvalues influencing cultural attitudes and social living, they alienate human beings and destroy effective personal and social freedom.

From the perspective of orthopraxis the *real* problems within Christianity today are not the result of real distinctions between natures and persons expressed in traditional orthodoxy. The real problems result from a failure of Christians to pay the cost of discipleship (Bonhoeffer) or the price of orthodoxy (Metz). That is, the real problems result from failures to sublate orthodoxy in an orthopraxis commensurate with the dialectics of values unknown but consciously operative in orthodoxy. How different, for instance, would the history of Christianity have been if Christians more genuinely lived the religious values expressed in the Trinitarian and Christological creeds. At a time when political and cultural forces were bent upon deforming Christianity into just another form of Roman imperial religion with a monistic monarchical one god, one emperor, one world, one religion, Nicea affirmed how God is a trinitarian community of Persons. Instead of hellenizing Christianity such credal confessions expressed a spirituality and a call for *metanoia* at odds with the plausibility structures and disvalues of the *Imperium Romanum*.[91] But how genuinely was this orthodoxy lived?

Analogously, today, I would argue that the real problems liberation theologies uncover in the disvalues of class oppression, racism, and sexism do not stem from the traditional distinctions between natures and person in Christ, nor are those disvalues reinforced by such distinctions. The massive exploitations of class, race, and sex within Christianity have resulted rather from failures to live up to

---

[90] Besides the references in notes 76 and 84 above, cf. E. Schüssler Fiorenza, "Feminist Theology as a Critical Theology of Liberation," *Theological Studies* 36 (1975), pp. 605-26; and "You are not to be called Father: Early Christian History in a Feminist Perspective," *Cross Currents* 29 (1979), pp. 301-23.

[91] E. Peterson, "Monotheismus als politisches Problem" and "Christus als Imperator" in *Theologische Traktate* (Munich: Kösel, 1951), pp. 45-147, 150-64; F. Fiorenza, "Critical Social Theory and Christology," *CTSA Proceedings* 30 (1975), pp. 63-110.

the orthopraxis expressed in Christological orthodoxy. For the critical realist distinctions between nature and personhood are capable of exposing the alienations resulting from the illusory opposites of naively empiricist forms of dualism and idealist forms of monism. The revelatory transformation of values narratively communicated in, e.g., chapter twenty-five of the gospel of Matthew is indicative of the critical realism of the Christian Kerygmata.[92] Similarly, as I have attempted to show elsewhere, the ecological plundering of nature now going on in industrialized societies is hardly a consequence of Judaeo-Christian values (*pace* Lynn White), rather it results from forms of naive empiricism and idealism rampant in secularist social and economic policies and practices from the nineteenth century down to our own day.[93] I have mentioned these issues in order to indicate how, in the framework of Lonergan's generalized empirical method, the dialectical methods needed for a reflective orthopraxis aim at knowingly realizing the transformative value orientations which are unknown but consciously operative in orthodoxy.

III. Conclusions

Lonergan is preeminently a methodological theologian. His lifelong work has transformed method from its empiricist and idealist reifications as sets of axioms, principles, or systems into its concrete embodiments in the related and recurrent activities of ongoing communities of knowers and doers in history. Because of this, Lonergan cannot be accused of trying to immunize theology from critical human sciences and studies. He has initiated a framework for a reflectively dialectical orthopraxis critically open to the ongoing procedures and results of empirical and dialectical human sciences and scholarly disciplines. The intrinsic relationships between religious conversion processes and intellectual conversion processes, which he has articulated, challenge us to work out the constitutive interchangeability and overlapping of praxis, as practical reason yet to be realized in history, and the transcendental imperatives of human questing and questioning for the divine.

---

[92] Q. Quesnell, "Beliefs and Authenticity," as in note 72 above. Theologians who try to legitimate the exclusion of women from ministry (cf. note 86 above) by claiming that males sacramentally symbolize transcendence and females sacramentally symbolize immanence fail, because of their naive empiricism, to live up to the critical realist values expressed in classical orthodoxy—as though the personalizing orientations of transcendence and immanence could be known by taking a good look at the already-out-there-now-real.

[93] "The Production Process and Exponential Growth," pp. 284-97.

Lonergan's contextualization of orthopraxis and theological method within his work on generalized empirical method and macroeconomics is especially relevant in overcoming the long range problems and basic alienations which are at the root of the massive sufferings and victimizations which various political and liberation theologies seek to respond to. Karl Jaspers once observed: "For more than a hundred years it has been gradually realized that the history of scores of centuries is drawing to a close."[94] That aptly describes the epochal implications of the "turn to the subject" which, while it holds the promise of an ever fuller humanization and personalization of life on this planet, is also fraught—as any epochal transition is—with the risks and dangers of refusing to meet the challenges to intelligence, to love, and to freedom which such a turn demands. Neither reflection on theology nor reflection on method are ends in themselves. They are meant to promote a creative and critical collaboration with all humans in the tasks of transforming ourselves and our world into more attentive, intelligent, reasonable, and responsibly loving life. And, as Christians, we are called to incarnate our struggles for humanization and personalization in the transformative values of doing the truth in love revealed in the life, death, and resurrection of Jesus Christ.

---

[94] K. Jaspers, *Philosophy and the World: Selected Essays and Lectures* (Chicago: Henry Regnery Co., 1963), p. 22.

Method and Theology as Hermeneutical

by Frederick Lawrence

I. Theology as Hermeneutical

Claude Geffré's little book, *A New Age in Theology,* summarizes his point that even Roman Catholic theology has become non-authoritarian and non-metaphysical by speaking of theology as *hermeneutical.*[1] Thus, the word, hermeneutics, has become a more or less accurate shorthand for depicting the differences between theology before and after Vatican II.

Geffré's use of the term non-authoritarian smacks of the Enlightenment "prejudice against prejudice"; and his use of the word non-metaphysical, I believe, is no less under the sway of enlightened periodizations of the development of human intelligence *á la* Comte. If his own biases leave something to be desired, it remains that the point of his message is not so far off the mark. That point has been sketched out in far less tendentious terms for us by Frederick E. Crowe in his lucid exercise in what Lonergan has described as the functional specialty of history—namely, his book, *Theology of the Christian Word: A Study in History.*[2] What Geffré means by the advent of theology as hermeneutical, then, is the transition both from the thematization of the Word of God as truth as instantiated by the Councils of the pre-medieval period (Crowe's Chapter 3); and from the notion of that truth as being grounded in the authoritative sources or *loci* as represented by both Reformation and Counter-

---

[1] C. Geffré, *A New Age in Theology* (New York: Paulist,1974). See too: C. Geffré, "Declin ou renouveau de la théologie dogmatique?" *Recherches Actuelles - 1,* (Paris: Beauchesne, 1971), pp. 21-49; and Ibid., "Du savoir a l'interpretation," *Recherches Actuelles - III* (Paris, 1977), pp. 50-79.

[2] F.E. Crowe, *Theology of the Christian Word: A Study in History* (New York: Paulist, 1978).

reformation modes of argumentation (Chapter 4); to a growing realization concerning (a) the sources as "Word across space and time" (Chapter 5); (b) the emergence of a theology of history as Word (Chapter 6); and (c) the inner Word of the Spirit as at work in religious experience (Chapter 7).

Crowe's account implies a recontextualizing of the question of authority rather than a simple debunking of authority *tout court*. If from the contemporary viewpoint the link between teaching authority, juridical power, and the radical demands of personal and institutional authenticity can admit of no extrinsic solution,[3] this can never mean the utter dissolution of differences between those who know more and those who know less, between center and periphery, between those inclined to take thought and those who are not, between those who are open to learn and those who are closed, between those living lives of self-sacrificial love and those who serve only themselves, between the salt of the earth and that which it seasons. As Balthasar once put it so well, only love is truly credible, and in that deep sense, legitimate.

Once again, if Crowe's analysis implies a willingness to subject the authoritative sources to the honest investigation of scholars deploying historical-critical methods and to accept without reserve Pere Chenu's *dictum* that "[l]e plus petit *fait,* du moment qu'il est authentique, est regulateur,"[4] it in no way entails either the historicist implication that theology is intellectually honest precisely to the degree that it is confined to tracing the history of the Christian community's beliefs and behavior; or the closely allied notion of theological application as a short circuit between textual exegesis and sermon or deed.

Similarly, Crowe's account implies a recontextualizing of the question about the "end of metaphysics." For if our thematization of the Word of God is at the threshold of taking seriously the emergent probabilities of cosmic and historical process as Word of God, Crowe explicitly admits that the implications of this for theology are not *contra* the views of Thomas Aquinas, but *praeter* those views.[5] That is, if Crowe himself envisages the possibility of a transposition of the metaphysics of Aquinas, it remains that the statute of reason on the basis of which the Angelic Doctor's metaphysics rested has been radically called into question; that, as one consequence of this, metaphysics as a matter of fact no longer provides the *Grund- und*

---

[3] See Bernard Lonergan, "The Dialectic of Authority," *Authority. Boston College Studies in Philosophy III,* Frederick J. Adelmann, ed., (The Hague: Nijhoff, 1974), pp. 24-30.

[4] M.-D. Chenu, *La foi dans l'intelligence,* (Paris: Cerf, 1964), p. 246.

[5] See Crowe, op. cit., pp. 104-143 at 112.

Gesamt- horizont for theology, and we may not reasonably expect that it ever will again; and that, as another consequence, Christian theology has come to be considered by all but a few in academe to be hardly anything more than the critical explication of just one among many worldviews.

Thus, if I may restate Geffré's thesis, theology as hermeneutical indicates (1) the radical questioning about the *de facto* (in contradistinction to *de jure*) legitimacy of both authoritative teaching offices and authoritative texts within the Christian community of worship and witness; (2) the heightened awareness of the rootedness of theology within each individual's or community's conscious solution to the problem of living in a universe mediated and to a crucial extent constituted by meaning and value.

With respect to the second and more basic issue, theology as hermeneutical implies not just the mediation between Christianity and its cultural matrix, but, further, the increasingly felt need to come to grips with the fact that the contemporary quest for an *intelligentia fidei* is being increasingly peopled by those who have elected to get into the business of making sense of the way people make sense of their lives, but do not understand themselves as believers in any usual sense. Rather, they may be simply wondering with Nietzsche whether nihilism may be overcome at all; or they may be in the process of overcoming the oblivion of being mystically by way of something akin to the secularized eschatology of Heidegger; or they may have devoted themselves to life in the tension of the Metaxy with Voegelin; or to the unconventional piety of questioning all conventions and beliefs aside from the conviction that a life devoted to questioning alone is most choiceworthy as is exemplified by some of the followers of Strauss; or they may be inspired by the radical sort of fidelity that simply defies all pigeonholing in terms of faith-traditions like Simone Weil and Walter Benjamin; or again, by the project of enlightenment and emancipation that fails to understand itself in religious terms such as that of Habermas; or perhaps by the example of taking seriously by way of philosophy the truth of existence that addresses us in the works of art, history, and religion afforded by Gadamer.

In terms of their own self-understanding, then, none of these people fit into the mold of (religious) faith seeking understanding as that has been traditionally understood, i.e., more in terms of belief, in Lonergan's sense, rather than of faith.[6] In varying ways, the cri-

---

[6] For this fundamental distinction, see Lonergan, *Method in Theology* (New York: Herder and Herder, 1972), pp. 115-119 and 41-47.

tique of beliefs[7] carried on by figures like those named in the preceding paragraph has carried them beyond the boundaries of, say, Jewish or Christian communities of worship and witness. What binds them, however, is the undertaking of the awesome task of making sense of the way people make sense of their lives for the sake of confronting for themselves and for their fellow human beings the question of life's meaning and value within a climate of opinion that Voegelin has described as one of deculturation, but which since Nietzsche has been more commonly called nihilism.[8] The hermeneutic question, then, is not adequately met on the level of mere text interpretation or history; of doctrines or ideologies; or even of systems or communications techniques. It is a question that is only addressed with any adequacy on the level of what Lonergan has called dialectics and foundations.[9] And the reason why the question regarding the radical oblivion of meaning and value, of being and God, is called hermeneutical rather than dialectical at all is that it is more properly a foundational than a dialectical question; a question touching the most radical and mysterious intersection of human speaking and listening with divine transcendence. Such a question, then, is as trans-institutional or -traditional (in the sense of faith-traditions as accessible to students of comparative religion) as it is trans-cultural. It is not surprising, then, that the most radically *hermeneutical* of contemporary theologians in the older sense of faith seeking understanding, say, a Protestant like Paul Ricoeur, or Roman Catholics like Johann B. Metz and Bernard Lonergan, have learned constantly and deeply from figures like those mentioned above who are not confessionally aligned. Their consequent radicality in carrying out the hermeneutic task of mediating between their religious faith and the modern cultural matrix leaves them with nothing to apologize for in relation to the specific hermeneutic response to nihilism.

In what follows I would like to suggest some ways the work of Lonergan in method has so met the hermeneutical issue as to have earned a hearing from anyone trying to make sense of the way we humans make sense of our lives. I wish to do this by contrasting his methodical approach with the paradigm of correlation almost universally adopted by theologians who are not just historians today. I am aware that I have given exceedingly short schrift to the theologians whom I have chosen to use as examples of the correlation paradigm. I have not meant to caricature their positions; my

---

[7] See Bernard Lonergan, *Insight: A Study in Human Understanding* (New York: Longmans, Green and Co., 1957), pp. 713-718.

[8] See Eric Voegelin, "On Classical Studies," *Modern Age* 17 (1973): 3-8.

[9] See Lonergan, *Method,* pp. 235-293, 128-132.

interest is rather to clarify weaknesses inherent in the paradigm of correlation and its concomitant model of experience and symbolization.

II. Correlation as the Dominant Paradigm for Theology as Hermeneutical

As I implied in my introductory remarks, the most obvious meaning of the contemporary crisis of theology as hermeneutical is the transition from the *authoritarian* theologies of either old Protestant scholasticism or Tridentine or manualist theologies in the style of Melchior Cano to theologies mediated by historical-critical scholarship. As a bishop, Cano failed to distinguish faith from theology; and as a theologian, he was basically out to *prove* the doctrines in the light of Holy Scripture, the traditions of Christ and the apostles, the authority of the Catholic Church, of the Fathers, of the theologians and canonists; and then by reason, the thought of the philosophers and jurists, and history.[10] The theologian was to demonstrate the presence of doctrinal propositions within authoritative documents (those of Scripture and Tradition being absolute in authority; and those of the Fathers and theologians and canonists being only probable in weight), and to buttress these demonstrations by arguments drawn from reason and history which were held to be only extrinsic sources for theology and of only probable authority. Hence, the *probatur ex Scriptura, probatur ex Traditione,* and the *probatur ex ratione* of the manualist tradition. On the Protestant side, the tradition radiating from Melanchthon's *Loci communes rerum theologicarum, seu Hypotyposes theologicae* operated in fundamentally the same authoritarian style. Eventually, under the pressure of the Enlightenment and the radicalization of the Reformers' intuition that the way to renewal lay in getting behind decadent accretions under the auspices of Rousseau into a doctrinaire suspicion that anything that is not original or primitive must thereby be inauthentic, the transition was made from old Protestantism to new Protestantism. The appearance of Richard Simon's critical histories of Old and New Testaments; of the works of Voltaire, the philosophes, Lessing; of Spinoza's rules for the interpretation of Scripture, gave rise to a line of predecessors to Schleiermacher, the epitome of liberal Protestantism: Arnold, Franck, von Mosheim, Spener, and Semler. The upshot of this

---

[10]. See Crowe, op. cit. pp. 75-79, esp. p. 78; M.-D. Chenu, "Les lieux theologiques chex Melchior Cano," *Recherches Actuelles - III: Le deplacement de la théologie* (Paris: Beauchesne, 1977), pp. 45-50; Quentin Quesnell, "The Foundations of Heresy," *Lonergan Workshop II*, 1980; and B. Lonergan, "Review: *Le lieu théologique, 'Histoire,'* " by Jean-Marie Levasseur. *Gregorianum* 44 (1963):370-371.

transition has been the virtual absorption of the hermeneutical cry of the original Reformers—*Sola Scriptura!*—by the historicist presupposition that what is original is (a) most authentic; and (b) to be mediated chiefly by historical scholarship.[11] Consequently, the noble role of theology has been for the most part, in Van A. Harvey's words, "subcontracted out to the specialized disciplines of biblical study, church history, ethics, the philosophy of religion, etc."[12] Meanwhile, within Roman Catholicism, the gradual incursion of the methods of critical history into patristic, liturgical, and scriptural studies was only very recently met by the cautious approval of *Divino Afflante Spiritu* (1943) together with the flood of articles on doctrinal development and on the relationship between exegesis and dogma more or less under the sign of *Humani Generis* (1950); whereas a decade after Vatican II it takes some doing to distinguish Protestant from Catholic faculties of theology.

In the wake of the dissolution of the authoritative sources of Christian theology into a flux of ever changing hypotheses on the part of historical scholars, some theologians have tended, as Harvey once put it, to become "free-floating intellectuals who were primarily devoted to the culture of the secular universities."[13] But there are others who, looking up to their great forebears like Barth, Bultmann, Niebuhr, Tillich, and Rahner, have attempted to "work out the problems in the faith of a community."[14] I am thinking of the work of people like Langdon Gilkey, Schubert Ogden, John Macquarrie, John Cobb, Peter Berger, Richard McBrien, Avery Dulles, and David Tracy in the United States; or in Europe, of people like Helmut Gollwitzer, Jürgen Moltmann, Wolfhart Pannenberg, Dorothee Sölle, Eberhard Jüngel, and Heinrich Ott.

I would like to suggest that each of these theologians (as well as many, many others not mentioned) in their differing ways has opted to face the question of theology as hermeneutical in terms of the paradigm more or less adequately expounded by Tillich in terms of "correlation." Whereas a former generation of more confessionally based theologians may indeed have blended "edifying discourse, biblical exegesis, preaching, and technical theological scholarship" as "member[s] of a theological faculty [with an] . . . ethos . . . still determined by students and peers who primarily defined themselves

---

[11] See E. Hirsch, *Geschichte der neueren evangelischen Theologie*, 5 Volumes. (Guetersloh: C. Bertelsmann, 1949-1954).

[12] See his "What is the Task of Christian Theology?" *Christianity and Crisis* 36 (1976):119-121.

[13] See Van A. Harvey, "Review: Anders Nygren, *Meaning and Method*," *Religious Studies Review* 1 (1975):13-18, at 14.

[14] Ibid.

in reference to a religious community";[15] these theologians as operating within the correlation paradigm, were ever so much more sensitive to the problems of correlating the results culled from historical-critical scholarship on the one hand with the questions of contemporary men and women precisely as people in all likelihood affected no more than indirectly by answers constitutive of the Christian community. They tend to work outside the old assumption of "from faith to faith."

Perhaps the key characteristic of such correlating theologians is not any prior agreement about their subject matter (as for example liberalism's religious [or human] experience as more or less epitomized in the consciousness of Jesus of Nazareth, or Neo-orthodoxy's revelation as it occurred in Jesus Christ as witnessed to by Scripture), for they usually hold for a pluralism of options. Rather, beyond the commitment to both critical-historical retrieval and the questions of contemporary people—or rather their procedural basis for correlating the two—is the ontological structure or model of experience and symbolization.

Just as people seek direction within the movement of life by actuating this structure, so, too, the business of making sense of the way people do this is an enactment of this model. For it articulates the transcultural framework for the actuation of human being. Consequently, as far as the correlating theologians are concerned, whether they are retrieving past meanings and values or creatively restating or applying these meanings and values in the present, they are entering into and actuating more or less adequately the complex interplay of performative intention and symbolic expression in both the past and the present for the sake of offering elucidations of possibilities of living as a contribution to a heightening of individual or communal self-awareness.

A. The Core of Correlation: Model of Experience and Symbolization

On account of the terrific pluralism among the theologians mentioned and unmentioned whom I would claim to be meeting the issue of theology as hermeneutical in terms of the correlation paradigm and the implicit or explicit model of experience and symbolization, I am perhaps treading on thin ice in trying to sort them out in such brief compass. The vast diversities in intention, theme, tone, and orientation make it necessary to think about an extremely broad spectrum of enactments of the common model of experience

---

[15] Ibid.

and symbolization. I can only hope that the model is not a "straw man". I merely have to risk the opinion that in my own reading of and discussions with contemporary theologians, this model seems to form the latent or explicit limit towards which the theologians who are unwilling to be fundamentalist—by which term I do not refer to Evangelical, "born-again," or charismatic Christians, but to any persons of whatever persuasion who would for whatever reason obscure the implications of the fact that the proximate sources of interpretation are in the mind and heart of the interpreter—tend to converge.

A paper like this does not permit an adequate treatment of the differences among those within the spectrum of users of the model of experience and symbolization. But because of the post-critical awareness on the part of these theologians, it is probably fair to say that they cluster about three poles or versions. The more moderate and most broadly gauged version I would characterize as Kantian; and it would embrace perhaps the dominant group of correlating theologians. Its exponents would pretty much agree with Kant's strictures on metaphysics and buy into his project of grasping the limits of reason in order to make room for faith. The more extreme pole or version—which is understandably marginal in theology—I would call the Nietzschean, because its exponents would tend to reduce the intentions of reason or of rational faith (in the Kantian mode) or of religious faith to their pre-conscious conditions of possibility. Finally, falling within the spectrum of those who rely upon the model of symbol and experience but outside the range that extends as it were between the Kantian and Nietzschean poles are those who willy-nilly have been drawn beyond metaphorical and non-technical symbolization of beliefs towards conceptual explication. This I would name the systematic pole or version. The more consequent of these theologians, like Ogden or Tracy, have moved into a process metaphysics; or like Walter Kasper have adopted the speculative idealism of Schelling. The less consequent, like Gollwitzer, Jüngel, and Moltmann, have nevertheless also tried to move from, to use the classical terminology, the *priora quoad nos* in speaking about God to the *priora quoad se* of statements with an explicitly metaphysical or ontological function. Of chief interest to our present purpose of contrasting Lonergan's methodical approach to theology as hermeneutical with the correlation paradigm, therefore, are the Kantian and systematic versions of the model of experience and symbolization.

1. The Kantian Version of the Model of Experience and Symbolization

In general, the Kantian version of the model of experience and symbolization usually involves a not necessarily reflected upon syncretism of Kant's doctrine of the antinomies along with his handling of the concept of infinity there with the symbolic constructs drawn from the Christian religious tradition—whether from Paul, Augustine, Luther, or Kierkegaard makes no real difference. Again, one might recall Karl Jasper's hitting upon Kant's discussion of "die schoene Chifferschrift der Natur" in section #42 of the *Kritik der Urteilskraft*—a motif taken up by Schelling and the Romantics and indeed generalized by Jaspers in his doctrine of ciphers. But perhaps the most influential theological use of the Kantian version of the model was that of the two great Neo-Kantians also very much influenced by Heidegger, Hans Jonas and Rudolf Bultmann.[16] A later and quite influential exponent of this position has been Paul Ricoeur.[17]

The three key components of this model are (1) engendering experience; (2) expressive symbol; (3) reifying hypostatization of symbolic expression. According to this version of the model, the heart of theological interpretation is to bring to speech the subject matter of a text by recovering within one's own experience the originating experience out of which the symbols have emerged in their specificity. Thus, we can reconstruct as did Augustine the meaning of Romans 7 if we move through all the usual philological techniques (of understanding the words, the author's context, and the author) to be ourselves, with all our different preoccupations and predilections, called into question and even perhaps challenged to a new life-orientation by the text, so that "the world in front of the text" becomes our world *inquantum possibile*. This version of the model, then, avoids the extrinsicism of supposing that the truths by which Christians live get along without the minds and hearts of those who "have eyes to see and ears to hear."

Moreover, this version of the model has the added virtue of being open to the range of human experience as exceeding the limits of Descartes' *res extensa* or Kant's phenomenon. The answers of the Christian religion to the questions, Why is there being and not nothing? and Why are things the way they are? are not susceptible of verification the way hypotheses in physics, chemistry, botany, and

---

[16] See Hans Jonas, "Über die hermeneutische Struktur des Dogmas, Anhang 1," *Augustin und das paulinische Freiheitsproblem,* (Goettingen: Vandenhoeck and Ruprecht, 1965²; 1930¹), pp. 80-89. The reasons for pairing Jonas and Bultmann are laid out in James M. Robinson's Einleitung to the second edition, pp. 11-22. The Neo-Kantianism of Jonas's position is rather obvious; but Bultmann's has been pinned down in scholarly fashion by Roger A. Johnson, *The Origins of Demythologizing* (Leiden: Brill, 1974). See also my own more expanded version of this model: "Experience and Symbol: Between Kant and Nietzsche," to appear in proceedings of the Symposium entitled, Merging Horizons: Hermeneutics and Structuralism, held at York University, Toronto, Fall 1978.

[17] See for example, *Biblical Hermeneutics: Semeia 4* (1975):27-148.

zoology are. But this renders neither the questions nor the trail of symbolisms responding to those questions either meaningless or sheerly arbitrary. The appropriation of the symbols involves a radical and existential truth or falsehood.

A third strength of the Kantian version of the model is an aspect of its diagnostic of the degeneration or decay of symbols in relation to their truth intention as proceeding from an engendering experience that is more or less authentic. One can verify empirically within both individuals and traditions cases in which the dissociation of symbols from their experiential matrix is further aggravated by their displacement to a less authentic mode of experience and a subsequent reduction of their intention to the naive realist's image of an "object" as an "already-out-there-now/or in-here-now" entity or to a framework of such entities.

This version is on more authentically Kantian and less solid footing to the extent that it would condemn any and every systematic or metaphysical re-thematization of the experience to the dustbin of reifying hypostatization. Thus, Augustine's doctrines of grace and free will, or providence, etc. are judged by Hans Jonas to be beside the point; and so, in general, would any instance of the movement from the world of common sense to the world of theory within theology.

For all its strengths, the Kantian version of the model also tends toward the faulty implication that the root of meaning and value is experience in the sense of unmediated immediacy: in other words, experience as pure perception.[18] Not that there isn't a dimension of immediacy to experience, but for human beings—and this, incidentally, is perhaps the chief contention of the hermeneutic style of phenomenology represented by Heidegger and Gadamer—experience as sheer immediacy is rather more of a limit case; because once one has learned one's mother-tongue, one's experience is always also mediated by language, symbol, and image. In Lonergan's expression, the world of immediacy is but a small segment of one's world as mediated by meaning. Experience as referring to the primary process of human life includes insight, reflective understanding, and judgment, existential freedom, and probably grace as well. Nor may the immediacy of human questioning and questing be adequately conceived along the lines of sense perception.

As a result of this implication that experience = immediacy as pure perception, the truth-intention of any mythic or symbolic or

---

[18] See Bernard Lonergan, "Christ as Subject: A Reply," *Collection. Papers by B. Lonergan,* F. E. Crowe, ed. (New York: Herder and Herder, 1967), pp. 164-197.

metaphorical answers to the most practical, basic, and comprehensive questions of humankind gets subordinated by this model to the Kantian dichotomies of noumenon and phenomenon/*Denken-Vorstellen-Glauben* and *Erkennen*. The consequent immanentist reading of religious and philosophical symbols makes the referent of the symbols experience in a subjectivist sense. Conversely and equally suspect from the perspective of a more adequate phenomenology of human knowledge and action like Lonergan's cognitional theory, the model of the reifying or objectifying conception and affirmation of an "already-out-there-now or in-here-now" entity is not an adequate account of the way we reach answers to questions about sub-human reality, but just a fiction conventionally accepted by many theologians for the sake of rhetorically legitimating the status of knowledge in the moral, aesthetic, and religious spheres.

2. *The Systematic Version of the Model of Experience and Symbolization*

The systematic version of the model of experience and symbolization shares with the Kantian version the quite positive features: its dissatisfaction with extrinsicism in interpretation; its antipositivist openness to the range of human experience; and even the complaint against reifying objectification or hypostatization. These emphases are evident in the works of people like Gollwitzer, Jüngel, Moltmann, Ogden, Tracy, and Ott. The principle difference between this version and the Kantian is that instead of permitting the anti-reifying/objectifying/hypostatizing concern to eliminate metaphysics or ontology altogether in favor of a re-symbolizing, revitalizing unpacking of the stories, symbols, and metaphors of the Christian tradition, its exponents tend to distinguish between good and bad ontology and proceed to make the move from the descriptive world of common sense and religious interiority to the explanatory world of theory and system.

The two rather different Barthians, Helmut Gollwitzer and Eberhard Jüngel, each acknowledge non-metaphorical, non-symbolic but rather systematic aspects to the being of God. So Gollwitzer can state that the goal of the question about the meaningfulness of reality ". . . could only reach an end, if it were to issue in a ground-giving Being that is itself no longer a premise of meaningfulness by one outside itself, that itself has no need of another and higher being, that lacks no bestowal of meaning whatsoever, because it is meaningful in itself, i.e., it is not a functional means for something else, but rather everything else is a functional means for it, precisely because it is meaningful 'for itself,' not relatively, but absolutely meaningful: absolute Meaning."[19] In the same vein, Jüngel:

"Every statement about the knowledge of God and hence about the objective Being of God *(Gottes Gegenstaendlich-Sein)* has a thoroughly ontological character. This holds no less true for Barth's doctrine of the Trinity. And so the application of the concept of being for dogmatics is unavoidable." [20] If Jüngel rather dogmatically measures the concept of being against the concept of God as gleaned "from the interpretation of revelation as the self-interpretation of God," he nonetheless is unequivocal that "onto-logical statements in theology are not only legitimate, but indispensable."

Similarly, when Jürgen Moltmann shifts from his earlier stance in the *Theologie der Hoffnung* of regarding salvation history almost exclusively in terms of a dialectic of past promise and future fulfillment to his explicitly Trinitarian theology of the cross, not only does he acknowledge the need for a movement from the economic Trinity to the immanent Trinity that is replete with statements like this: "The Being of God is in suffering, and suffering is in the Being of God itself, because God is love;" but he can boldly assert that it makes "no sense to enlist the 'end of metaphysics' proclaimed by Nietzsche for the sake of driving metaphysics out of Christian theology, if, in the experience of world and self of humankind, one cannot put anything in its place." And again: "Christian theology is not the 'end of metaphysics.' Precisely because metaphysical theism is not applicable to it, theology for its part is free to take over metaphysics as the task of theology and to make faith with its consequences thoughtfully responsive in the realm of the experiences and hopes of the world." [21]

Schubert Ogden, despite his willingness to opt for Whitehead's complicated perceptualism rather than a coherent intellectualism,[22] is nevertheless well known for his effort to ground the human experience of basic trust in an objective reality, the adequate explanatory framework for which he borrows from Whitehead and Hartshorne — the so-called neo-classical metaphysics. His replacement of the systematic concepts of "substance" and "being" (as he considers

---

[19] See Helmut Gollwitzer, *Krummes Holz — aufrechter Gang. Zur Frage nach dem Sinn des Lebens* (Munich: C. Kaiser, 1970) at p. 52; similar affirmations throughout *Die Existenz Gottes im Bekenntnis des Glaubens* (Munich: C. Kaiser, 1963).

[20] See Eberhard Jüngel, *Gottes Sein it im Werden* (Tübingen: J. C. B. Mohr, 1966) at pp. 39, 76, 77, 80, 110. Also see his *Gott als Geheimnis der Welt: Zur Begruendung der Theologie des Gekreuzigten im Streit zwischen Theismus und Atheismus*. (Tübingen: J. C. B. Mohr 1977).

[21] See Jürgen Moltmann, *Der gekreuzigte Gott* (Munich: C. Kaiser, 1972²) at pp.203, 214.

[22] See Schubert Ogden, "Lonergan and the Subjectivist Principle," *Journal of Religion* 51 (1971):155-173; and his key systematic work, *The Reality of God* (New York: Harper & Row, 1964).

them to have been traditionally understood) by those of "development" and "creative becoming" is no less ontological or metaphysical. Ogden's maneuver is enormously enriched by the differentiated linguistic considerations of David Tracy. But for Tracy, too, the appropriate formulation of the truth and meaning of God is reached by what he calls an explicitly transcendental or metaphysical mode of reflection.[23] Indeed, Tracy, Ogden, and all the other authors mentioned in this section (as well as many who are not) would have a fundamental sympathy for the following affirmation of Heinrich Ott: "The label, 'metaphysics,' need not disturb us! Many problems are of course unresolved, and we can't be satisfied with word games or ambitious speculative constructions of history ('secularization,' etc.); but we simply have to ask: What is the status of the reality in question? Either someone will have to give me an excuse for getting rid of such questions or he or she will have to show me how one can put such questions if not in a 'naively metaphysical' fashion!"[24]

The systematic versions of the model of experience and symbolization possess an overwhelming strength that is missing from the Kantian versions: They intend to advance beyond the question of the *intention* of religious discourse to that of its *reference*. Unlike the Kantian versions, they do not want to collapse the reference of religious speech back into its intention. Not content with a metaphorical or symbolic thematization of the truth intention of the trail of symbols, they recognize a further task of giving an account of the referent that is systematic or theoretical or conceptual and terminological. All well and good. Let us consider more carefully now the purpose of the account being given by the systematic versions of the model.

It might be justly claimed that the purpose of the correlations worked out on the basis of the Kantian version of the model is *rhetorical:* to unpack and deliver the intention of the original metaphors and symbols through reenacting their engendering experiences in order to re-symbolize or create fictionalized redescriptions which might elicit or evoke appropriate feelings and imaginative reorientations in the present.

Now on account of the concern for the referential reality meant by the symbols and metaphors of the texts, the systematic versions of the model demand a more than rhetorical correlation. Two motivations or issues seem to loom large for these attempts: the Nietzschean or nihilist *reductio ad absurdum* of the intrinsic metaphoricity

---

[23] See David Tracy, *Blessed Rage for Order: The New Pluralism in Theology* (New York: Seabury, 1975), esp. pp. 52-56.

[24] See Heinrich Ott, *Wirklichkeit und Glaube II* (Göttingen and Zürich, 1969), p.6f.

(or symbolic nature) of language; and the question of theodicy (less in the mood of a Leibniz, to be sure, than of Dostoevsky's Ivan Karamazoff). Consequently, the tenor of the systematic versions' correlation is more *apologetic or argumentative.* By reflecting upon the experiences of limits and/or data from the Christian tradition, they attempt to lay bare their conditions of possibility. The tone is redolent of the Anselmian *demonstratio,* even if the procedure turns out to be less a matter of proof for the existence of God than of disengaging the presence or givenness of an infinite horizon in the experience of human finitude; it turns out to be less a matter of "explaining away" the evil and suffering in the world than of constructing an idea or image of the ground of being that is disclosive of the human experience and/or Christian message of salvation. The point, however, is that the task of attaining a further understanding of the mystery tends in the systematic versions of correlation to be conflated with or at least inadequately distinguished from arguing the truth of the mystery of God. It would seem, therefore, that this sort of correlation is an historically conscious approximation of the old scholastic *probatur ex ratione.* For Scripture and Tradition have been transformed from authoritative sources into a tissue of shifting consensus among exegetes and scholars; and "reason" has been replaced by the structures displayed by a phenomenology of experience and language; and the old-style "proof" has been carried out by way of the working out of a system of categories that would account for common human experience and/or Scriptural teachings. And if we understand ontology or metaphysics to mean not so much an integral heuristic structure in Lonergan's sense as a comprehensive framework for answering the general question, Why is there being and not nothing?, then this conceptual network may be said to be ontological or metaphysical.

I find it emblematic that the metaphysical framework elaborated by each of the theologians I have mentioned (not to mention others, like Rahner and Schillebeeckx, whom I have not discussed), is a species of process theology. Each has arrived at a set of basic categories that expresses the relationships among consciousness, proportionate being, and the transcendent ground of being that uses the language of world-immanent process or what used to be spoken of as panentheism. If one were to wonder why their basic categories in the last analysis seem to be rooted firmly within an imaginative context of "imaginable entities moving through imaginable processes in an imaginable space-time,"[25] one cannot help suspecting that this in turn is a consequence of the fact that the meaning of "experience"

---

[25] See Lonergan, *Insight,* pp. xx-xxi.

on this model systematically excludes any aspect or feature of reality that—even if such experience be strenuously not reduced to sense perception—is not intrinsically conditioned by space and time. It would seem, then, that although their categories would be antinomies for Kant, they use the experienced meaningfulness of limit experiences or Christian transformation to spring to a basic conceptuality that still remains in the grips of what Lonergan has called "the umbilical cord that tied [these thinkers] to the maternal imagination of man."[26] Otherwise they would not have been bound to conceive and affirm processes within the ground of being as intrinsically conditioned by space and time.

In the theology of Aquinas, the fundamental issue of divine transcendence had been a matter of what might be called a limit theorem or axiom whose intelligibility and reasonableness depended upon a technical grasp of the analogy of matter.[27] But if one's foundations do not allow for a phenomenologically accessible instance of creaturely being that is not intrinsically conditioned by space and time, then there can be no critically grounded break from matter at all (the famous "judgment of separation"[28]); and so no theoretically rigorous and coherent analogy of matter.[29] Certainly the feeling of finitude that evokes and in a sense presupposes a sense of the infinite does not allow for a sufficiently precise and verifiable apprehension of the difference between beings which are merely intelligible and those which are intelligent as well,[30] or of the priority of the act of understanding to concepts, etc. Without the control of meaning that arises only from a more exhaustive account of interiority as experienced, the intention at least implicit in each of the systematic versions to differentiate the model of symbol and experience into one of—to quote the title of the book by John E. Smith that rather typifies the efforts of the systematic version—experience and analogy will inevitably run aground. The systematic versions' background of understandings, conceptions, reflective insights, and judgments is not differentiated enough to muster the control of meaning nuanced

---

[26] Ibid., p. xxi.

[27] See B. Lonergan, *Verbum: Word and Idea in Aquinas*. D. Burrell, ed. (Notre Dame, Ind: University of Notre Dame Press, 1967), pp. 142-147.

[28] See Jean-Marc Laporte, "The Evidence for the Negative Judgment of Separation," *The Modern Schoolman* 41 (1963):17-43.

[29] See D. Burrell, "Articulating Transcendence," *Exercises in Religious Understanding* (Notre Dame, Ind.: University of Notre Dame Press, 1974), pp. 80-140; and *Analogy and Philosophical Language* (New Haven: Yale University Press, 1973); Bernard Tyrrell, *Bernard Lonergan's Philosophy of God* (Notre Dame, Ind: University of Notre Dame Press, 1974); Philip McShane, *The Shaping of the Foundations* (Washington, D.C.: University Press of America, 1976).

[30] See Lonergan, *Insight,* pp. 236, 267, 269.

enough to generate the explanatory framework in terms of which the reference of religious and Christian discourse is laid out. As far as I know, the sets of terms and relations that have emerged in these formulations do not differ in any fundamental way from the symbol systems that have been characteristic of process theologies within that venerable trajectory that stretches back at least to Pythagoras and comes through the early Christians, gnostics, and Fathers, right down to the speculations of the kabbalah, Boehme, and Schelling.

Such explicitations tend to have three characteristic shortcomings. First, as I have just suggested, in spite of a certain internal coherence, that coherence still does not meet the requirements of the systematic exigence in the ways only pointed to in the preceding paragraphs. But secondly, neither do they in my opinion function as well as the rhetorical correlations of the Kantian versions in evoking the transformation of people's dominant life-orientation spoken of by Ray Hart under the rubric of the intention of the imagination; or more recently and more adequately by Robert Doran in terms of an imaginal and affective and hence psychic conversion.[31] Correlatively, and thirdly, such explicitations tend not to be directly relevant for or accessible to the problematic of praxis. This does not mean that thinkers like Moltmann, Ott, Gollwitzer, Jüngel, Tracy, Rahner, et. al., are not concerned with changing reality rather than merely interpreting it; for they all do have profoundly practical and political and pastoral concerns. But because their respective correlations of theology and anthropology end in a certain half-way house between rigorous theoretization and whole-hearted re-symbolization, they are in the last analysis more like what Metz has termed "transcendental-idealistic" theologies rather than instances of the "narrative-practical" sort of theology he has been advocating.[32]

B. THE HERMENEUTICAL WEAKNESS OF THE CORRELATION PARADIGM

We have considered rather sketchily leading aspects of two styles of correlation as responses to the issue of theology as hermeneutical: on the one hand, correlation in accord with the Kantian version of the model of experience and symbolization; and on the other, correlation in accord with the systematic version of that model. I have chosen not to discuss correlation in accordance with a third major version of the model of experience and symbolization—the Nietzschean—both because of space limitations and because in general

---

[31] See Ray Hart, *Unfinished Man and the Imagination* (New York: Herder and Herder, 1968); Robert Doran, *Subject and Psyche: Ricoeur, Jung, and the Search for Foundations* (Washington, D.C.: University Press of America, 1977).

[32] See Johann Baptist Metz, *Glaube in Geschichte und Gesellschaft: Studien zu einer praktischen Fundamentaltheologie* (Mainz: M. Grunewald, 1977), pp. 136-148.

the collapse of theology into Christian atheism and the radical displacement/deconstruction of the question of meaning and value it espouses has been rather widely resisted within mainline theology. I have also not emphasized the important development by which mainline Roman Catholic and Protestant theologians have been coming to terms with what C. Wright Mills called "the sociological imagination."[33] This is not merely on account of space, but because in its (to my mind) most serious figures like Gollwitzer, Moltmann, and especially Metz, that very pressure of the question about the social and political relevance of theology has forced them to come to terms with the issues of cross, meaningfulness, suffering, and nothingness with respect to the very meaning of humankind, world, and God in a manner that fits fairly much within the paradigm of correlation. (In Metz's case, the option for the "narrative-practical" style has pushed his theological articulations towards the Kantian end of our spectrum; but his moorings in Rahnerian transcendental theology with its out and out ontological claims — a side not yet foundationally integrated with the more recent "narrative-practical" style — would suggest that he would be located somewhere on the spectrum between systematic and Kantian versions.)

The bias of the Kantian version against concepts, systems, and theory in general as derivative, secondary, and inauthentic because of their having been won at the price of dissociation from their originating experiential matrix, manages to highlight — in a way the systematic versions do not seem to have done — the aspect of the most crucial experiences of our lives as bearing upon our total life-orientation. The dialectical thrust of this bias is to stress that such experiences cannot be discussed in terms of a merely horizontal exercise of liberty; and that the reference of the language used to speak about these experiences (e.g., God, free will, free action, commitment, radical self-alienation on account of sin, etc.) is irreducible to the limits of perceptual experience. But since for this version the limits of referential speech = the limits of objectification = the limits of sense perception (E.g.: The desk is in this room. The particle is in the chamber. The stars stood in such and such a constellation at a certain time.), the dimension of reference tends to be reduced back into the dimension of intention. On this view, then, one is left to fictionally redescribe what is of utmost concern to one and so correlate rhetorically for today in a re-symbolization that would stand in a relationship of intentional identity/difference with the authentic self-interpretations of the past.

---

[33] See reference at note 12.

In the systematic versions the bias against concepts, systems, theories of being, etc. is overcome more or less coherently. The existential question of the meaning of God (i.e., the question of God correlative to vertical exercises of liberty) is acknowledged to be intimately related to the question of God's *being* — and that means not only God's being *for me* (intentional dimension). In moving beyond intention to reference, however, theologians who apply systematic versions of the model intend in no way to diminish or reduce the truth-intention of the symbolic-metaphorical discourse about religious experience to the limits of what can be perceived by the senses. But they still try to account for the reference of such speech in systematic, theoretic, or explanatory terms or concepts. Moreover, the fundamental categories of such systems are meant by these theologians to be safeguarded from reifying, reductionist objectification because of being experientially grounded — in the Christian experience of listening to the Word of revelation; or in the (neutrally) religious experience of limit; or in some more or less clearly acknowledged combination of the two.

The bottom-line issue with respect to this approach is simply: Do these various attempts at a theoretic or systematic correlation offer an adequate account of divine transcendence? If they don't, then their intention of doing justice to the "folly of the cross" has to shatter. If they don't, then despite non-reductionist asseverations and a readiness to speak of God as the "infinitely qualitative Other," or as the "transcendent ground of being, of basic trust, or of the meaningfulness and worthwhileness of life," it is difficult to see how the real rather than just notional transcendence of God is salvaged. If they don't, then the symbolic power for resisting evil or for absorbing the effects of evil in the world would be illusory; and so the basis in reality for anything like Metz's mystical and political discipleship would be lost. For theological virtue presupposes a transcendent objective: a hope beyond hope, a faith that is "the assurance of things hoped for, the conviction of things unseen," (Heb. 11.1) and a being in love with an otherworldly as well as a terrestrial term.

C. Correlation and Model of Experience and Symbol vs. Method as Hermeneutical

My thesis on correlation as a paradigm for meeting the issue of theology as hermeneutical is this: Correlation as a paradigm for the hermeneutical task of theology is defective to the extent that its underlying models of experience and symbolization fail to resolve adequately the radical issue of method as hermeneutical.

Method's importance, as Heidegger once expressed it in his critical remarks on K. Jaspers's *Psychologie der Weltanschauungen,*[34] is not merely "in so far as a more radically methodical heightening of awareness is *needed* if a given tendency is to be able to reach a genuine issue, but and especially because the objective toward which one's intentional anticipation *(Vorgriff)* is headed is so constituted that only in virtue of a primordially appropriate 'method' not imposed extrinsically from without but actually co-constitutive of its reality *is* it what it is."[35]

Heidegger went on to describe this issue of method in a way that is suggestive and prescient for my present argument here:

> If this 'rigorous' consciousness of such an *Explikationsproblematik* is missing, then the objective in question can still be somehow genuinely intended in such a way, at any rate, that an intuitive and conceptual surrogate is put ahead of the objective, which (motivated by well-meaning but unsuccessful intentions) nonetheless then makes for its cognitive efficacy the claim that it will be handled from a variety of perspectives. In the end, though, the surrogate is so pressed to the fore that it presents itself as the genuine phenomenon, which itself then virtually disappears, except verbally....
>
> The proper objective in question may be formally staked out as *Existenz*. In such a formally indicated meaning, the concept ought to point towards the phenomenon of the 'I am,' the meaningful being that lies within the 'I am' as the point of departure both of the phenomenon that affords the archetectonic framework and of its own cognate problematic. With the formal indication (whereby a methodical...*Grundsinn* of all philosophic concepts and conceptual frameworks is to be envisaged), one ought to be placed on guard against an uncritical falling back on some determinate conception of *Existenz*, say, of Kierkegaard or Nietzsche, precisely for the sake of gaining the possibility of pursuing a genuine meaning of the phenomenon of *Existenz* and of explicitating that pursuit.[36]

As the reader will have guessed by now, I believe the model of experience and symbolization so dominant in the area of foundational reflection in theology today plays the role of surrogate for the authentic outcome of a hermeneutics of facticity or a transcendental method. The latter would probe the primordial "meaning of the factual 'I am' " by reflecting upon "the factual, performative history of

---

[34] See Martin Heidegger, "Anmerkungen zu Karl Jaspers' 'Psychologie der Weltanschauungen', (1919/21)," *Karl Jaspers in der Diskussion,* Hans Saner, ed. (Munich: Piper, 1973), pp. 70-100.

[35] Ibid., p. 76.

[36] Ibid.

(one's) life within the factual how which resides in the problematic of the how of the concerned self-appropriation of the self."[37] This would be radical and basic in the sense of Heidegger's statement from the same critical essay: "This meaning of *Existenz* is, if pursued to its origin and its genuine *Grunderfahrung*, precisely the meaning of being."[38] It is a *Daseinsanalytik* in the form of "an arduous exploratory journey,"[39] a voyage of "discovering, identifying, becoming familiar with the activities of one's own intelligence."[40] The model of experience and symbolization is deficient to the extent that it is not the fruit of this prior hermeneutics of interiority.

But the hermeneutics of interiority I have in mind has to be more than a global and compact elucidation of conditions of possibility such as Heidegger himself managed. What is at stake is the phenomenological thematization not merely of what is immanent and operative in the subject as subject *(Existenz)*, but of what is normative there as well: the sharp and effective distinction "between the knowing men share with animals, the knowing that men alone possess, and the manifold blends and mixtures of the two that are the disorientation and ground the bewilderment of people as they are."[41]

An adequate hermeneutics of interiority would regard two major dimensions of human being, the first of which would be cognitive.

The hermeneutics of interiority as cognitive would start with one's concerned involvements, with "the actual texture and complexion" of one's mind; it would address the question not of "whether knowledge exists but what precisely are its two diverse forms and what are the relations between them."[42] In a painstaking and time-consuming meditative procedure that builds up within one the capacity "to discriminate with ease and from conviction between one's purely intellectual activities and the manifold of other, 'existential' concerns that invade and mix and blend with the operations of intellect to render it ambivalent and its pronouncements ambiguous;"[43] it would bring about such a reorientation and reorganization of mind and living as to be tantamount to a *conversion*. Method as a hermeneutics of interiority as cognitive is self-knowledge as self-appropriation: a preeminently practical affair that intersects existentially with the practical and political question concerning the right way to live—let alone the right way to do theology!

---

[37] Ibid., p. 93.
[38] Ibid., p. 90.
[39] See Lonergan, *Insight*, p. xvii.
[40] Ibid., p. xix.
[41] Ibid., p. 397.
[42] Ibid., p. xvii.
[43] Ibid., p. xix.

The models of experience and symbolization currently in vogue do not explain how metaphysics arises; they do not aid us in discriminating true from false metaphysical statements on the basis of accurate self-knowledge. The Kantian version restricts theology's scope to things as correlative to practical concerns of common sense and interiority; the systematic versions would permit theology to deal with things as correlated to one another in explanatory hypotheses and as tested according to public criteria of a specialized community of discourse. But their path from common sense and interiority to ontology/metaphysics is a short circuit inasmuch as it is not mediated by the set of basic terms and relations and the basic orientation that emerges not from any epistemology but only from a cognitional theory that is expressive of a hermeneutics of interiority as cognitive.

But since the basic method as I have been describing it not only disengages basic terms and relations but also realizes a basic orientation; and since radical change in one's orientation is a matter of personal decision, of radical commitment—indeed of a vertical exercise of liberty— a hermeneutics of interiority as cognitive is not enough. Besides that there is needed a hermeneutics of interiority precisely *as existential* as well. Credit must be given the Kantian version for taking seriously Kant's own avowal of the primacy of practical reason; similarly, it is clear that most systematic versions have been motivated to articulate a metaphysics and theology of process in order to do justice to the dispositional immediacy at stake in human relationships of love. Then, too, a central insight of hermeneutic philosophy gained by Heidegger and even more consistently stressed by Gadamer is the way a radical thematization of *Existenz* goes hand in hand with an ever more sensitive attunement to all the dimensions of human becoming cognate with what Lonergan in recent years has been calling "development from above downwards."[44]

The attainment of cognitive objectivity is an achievement of authentic subjectivity; and authentic subjectivity is an achievement of real self-transcendence; and the key to most concrete instances of real self-transcendence is not as much the "development from below upwards" that moves through perceiving, understanding, judging, and deciding in accord with whatever one has already affirmed to be true; even more, it is due to the influence upon one's life-orientation of the experience of reconciliation and love. With a rather high statistical regularity, such love is experienced as not exactly sym-

---

[44] See Bernard Lonergan, "Christology Today," *Le Christ, hier aujourd'hui et demain,* R. Laflamme and M. Gervais, eds., Quebec: Presses de l'université Laval, 1976), pp. 45-65; and "Healing and Creating in History," *Bernard Lonergan: 3 Lectures* Thomas More Institute Papers/75, Montreal, pp.55-68.

metrical with the love of intimacy or the love congruent with one's social and cultural ethos (the laws, institutions, customs, etc. of one's home). It is felt rather to be the effect within one of something like a mysterious pull from an unknown source. And so the hermeneutics of interiority as existential thematizes the experience of real self-transcendence in its subjective and trans-subjective conditions.

III. Method as Hermeneutical and Theology as Hermeneutical

A. Basic Method and Philosophical Hermeneutics

I have been trying to convey the thrust of Lonergan's method in terms of a hermeneutics of interiority as cognitive and as existential. But method has not conventionally been conceived of as hermeneutical. It might help to reduce the novelty of this idea if we recall that neither had philosophy commonly been thought to be hermeneutical; nor had hermeneutics been traditionally thought of as anything more than the art of interpretation. The genesis of philosophical hermeneutics is rather similar to the rise of method in Lonergan's perhaps unusual sense. For philosophy has come to be thought of as explicitly hermeneutical in response to (1) the separation of philosophy from science in the 17th century; (2) the devolution of philosophy into (a) the epistemology of positive sciences, and (b) a meta-worldview concerning the multiplicity of worldviews as a result of the ascendancy of historicism in the 19th century. These same factors have caused hermeneutics in the sense of the time-honored art of interpretation to become ever more involved with philosophic issues. As we have become ever more profoundly aware of meaning and value in history as problematic, the double transformation of philosophy and hermeneutics has arisen as a way of resisting the progressive deculturation of contemporary climates of opinion.

Philosophical hermeneutics (in the sense of Heidegger and Gadamer) has been an attempt to get behind the philosophic alternatives of transcendental reflection in the German idealist mold (as realized by the various schools of Neo-Kantianism and by Husserl) and empiricism/pragmatism. Either of these approaches offered no direct and adequate response to the practical and political question of the right way to live, and so philosophical hermeneutics has addressed itself to experiences of recognition, solidarity, and love with respect to history, art, and religion for the sake of illuminating the way that practical application of past meanings and values in the present is not governed by objectifiable rules or methods in the more quotidian sense. As attentive, intelligent, reasonable, and responsible, any historical concretization of truth and value of the tradition is an instance of (the notoriously forgotten) knowledge by identity: the coming to light of the tradition is one with the coming to light of the concrete self. And so philosophy as hermeneutical is not simply the serious reading of classical texts of philosophy; but it is also and integrally the lifting up into fullest possible luminosity of just what is going on when one does this "reading" authentically: What I *do* as a matter of fact when I read, understand, interpret, translate, etc. is intimately bound up with what I *am*. Heidegger was gesturing toward the core hermeneutic problematic when he wrote:

> Because today we do not properly see the phenomena of *Existenz*, we no longer experience the meaning of conscience and responsibility that lies in historical reality itself *[das Historische]*. It is not merely something one has knowledge of or about which books have been written; it is what we are and that within which we bear ourselves along.[45]

Meeting this issue squarely means crossing over the threshold into the hermeneutics of interiority as cognitive and existential. And that is basic method in Lonergan's sense.

But we must not delude ourselves. The issue may not be squarely met by socially dominant individuals in our day. The Kantian and the Nietzschean versions of the model of experience and symbolization as well as the adoption/elaboration of process metaphysics on the part of the proponents of the systematic versions of the model have been the styles of meeting the hermeneutic crisis accepted by the vast majority of contemporary theologians/ As far as mainline theology is concerned, both philosophical hermeneutics and basic method are marginal influences both in the doing and the teaching of theology.

B. Method in Theology as Hermeneutical

Besides the hermeneutical nature of basic method, Lonergan's work has also been hermeneutical in the sense of his unique realization of the Leonine program of *vetera novis augere et perficere*. I cannot here go into the many phases and dimensions of Lonergan's hermeneutic transactions with Aquinas.[46] I will restrict myself to a brief discussion of the significance of Lonergan's existential appropriation of Thomas's performance of mediating between the Christian religion and its matrix in Western European culture in the Middle Ages.

---

[45] See Heidegger, "Anmerkungen..." op. cit., p. 92.

[46]. See David Tracy, *The Achievement of Bernard Lonergan* (New York: Herder and Herder, 1970).

In meeting the issues of the medieval context, Aquinas helped to work out (1) the threefold distinction of functions between *lectio, disputatio,* and *praedicatio* (today often rendered as: exegesis, theology, and pastoral application); and (2) the distinction within the form of *disputatio* or speculative theology proper of the *ordo inventionis* from the *ordo doctrinae*.[47] These functional distinctions were grounded upon the performative basis of (a) differentiations of consciousness (world of common sense/world of theory); and (b) the emergence within Christianity of a *dogmatic theological context,* inasmuch as the reference of Christian religious discourse became of central and focal importance in the movement by which conflicts called forth a thematization of the Word of God as *true*.[48]

I have already mentioned above how Aquinas's clear and precise specification of theology as in search of understanding as distinct from certitude and proof has been clouded over by the desire for proofs within late medieval and modern scholasticism, as well as by the fact that many people doing theology today are less in a stance of faith seeking understanding than of reason seeking faith within a more or less rationalist or historicist perspective. Lonergan, however, has carried out two great campaigns towards understanding Aquinas. These have resulted in two masterful thematizations of what might be called the hermeneutics of developing understanding *(Grace and Freedom* and *Verbum: Word and Idea in Aquinas).* Anyone who seriously reads these works may well become sensitive, as did Lonergan himself, to the ambiguous attitude towards understanding as such on the part of most practitioners of theology today.

But the ambiguous attitude towards understanding has been matched in our time by the obnubilation of the dogmatic aspect of theology. The latter is probably due to the dialectical reaction to the ossification and manipulation of the truth element of Christian belief within the authoritarian tradition of Roman Catholic theology from Cano and Baroque scholasticism through the anti-modernist reaction right down to our own day. The anti-dogmatic impulse, however, has been itself bedeviled by an underlying incapacity to deal with the relationship between true propositions of belief and their ongoing matrix in the *sensus ecclesiae*. The makeshift development within Church theology of the division between (a) a *positive* discipline that would carry out a step-by-step inventory of the authoritative documents containing the truths of faith, and (b) a

---

[47] See Bernard Lonergan, "Theology and Understanding," *Collection* (New York: Herder and Herder, 1967), pp. 127-141; *The Way to Nicea: The Dialectical Development of Trinitarian Theology* (Philadelphia: Westminster, 1976).

[48] See also William Johnston, *The Inner Eye of Love* (New York: Harper and Row, 1978).

speculative side which deduces conclusions in a manner intended to merit for theology the name "science" in the strictest Aristotelian sense has at length been discredited by the rise of historical-mindedness and the demise of the Aristotelian ideal of science. In brief, theology has been caught between the "overkill" of ahistorical orthodoxy and the "overkill" of subjectivist and relativist reaction.

The usually accepted way out of this impasse we have been discussing, i.e., correlating the results of the historical-critical investigation of texts with the concerns of modern human beings, does not really make good this truth-element of doctrine. The Kantian versions reduce reference to intention and propositional truth to the authenticity of existence; the systematic versions do not fully or accurately answer questions like the following: How can Christian theologians take seriously the truth dimensions of doctrines without also being abstract deductivists; and so that understanding is adequately distinguished from proof, and difficulties of theology are not equated with doubts in religion? How can they come fully to terms with non-Aristotelian science and even displace metaphysics from its former position of centrality without giving up on knowledge in every serious sense of the word? How can they be genuinely historically minded without being historicist? Lonergan's answers to these questions have a unique value on account of his thoroughgoing encounter with the hermeneutic achievement of Aquinas.

Lonergan alone, as far as I know, has envisaged answers to the hermeneutical questions facing theology at the present time in terms of a transposition of the ideas of order of Aquinas (as opposed to decadent scholasticism's or Neo-scholasticism's) — I mean the *via analytica/via synthetica* — in accord with a framework that has arisen from the most comprehensive and thorough execution of the hermeneutics of interiority as both cognitive and existential (for which he is on both counts always also indebted to the prior breakthroughs of Thomas Aquinas as well) yet available to us.

Aquinas had of course explicitly worked out a solution to the question of the nature of theology within a classicist culture: his idea of *intelligentia fidei* as a *scientia subalternans*. Just because he was operating within a classicist framework, Aquinas's own well-documented ventures into the hermeneutics of interiority as cognitive and existential were done only for the sake of ulterior, theoretic motives, as for example, to elaborate theologies of the Trinity and grace. For the same reason, his quest for understanding was satisfied to start from *articula fidei* — or beliefs, in Lonergan's technical sense of the word. But when culture is conceived empirically, not only does the question of theology shift from its nature to its method; but also the mystical basis of theology in religious *faith* (as distinct from beliefs) has to become explicit. This is what occurs in Lonergan's chapters on "Religion" and "Foundations" in *Method in Theology.*

Similarly, when theology's authoritative texts are transformed from objects of belief into documents to be investigated by historical method, then the presence or absence of Christian/religious, moral, and intellectual conversion may no longer be taken for granted among theologians. Indeed, *these conversions become the hermeneutical and methodical crux of theology across the board.* For as I have more than intimated already, the issue of method is a question regarding the praxis of theologians.[49]

From the vantage of Aquinas's speculative theology with its scheme of *lectio* and *quaestio,* the matter of pastoral application was an external addendum. Not so from the standpoint of *Method.* Just as theology conceived in accord with the method as hermeneutical is expressly rooted in the mystical experience of faith, so too do moral, practical, and political issues become integral to the theological task. And this not only in the functional specialty of communications, but in dialectic, foundations, doctrines, and systematics as well.

In closing, theology as a component in the ongoing realization or actuation of the meanings and values of the Christian message may be conceived as a functionally specialized, intrinsically inter-disciplinary process which involves research, interpretation, history, dialectic, foundations, doctrines, systematics, and communications. For Lonergan, I take it, this is the differentiated model for the hermeneutics of history as lived and remembered that is a coherent expansion of an empirically verifiable (and verified) hermeneutics of interiority as cognitive and existential when brought into explicit relationship with the many dimensions of the inner and outer Word of Love.[50]

---

[49] See Lonergan, *Method,* "Index," under *Conversion,* q.v.

[50] Ibid., pp. 112, 119; and Bernard Lonergan, "Mission and the Spirit," *Experience of the Spirit. Concilium 9* (1974/6):69-78.

Theological Grounds for a World-Cultural Humanity

by Robert M. Doran

My efforts over the past eight years have been devoted to trying to establish that the intentionality analysis of Bernard Lonergan renders possible a reorientation of the science of depth psychology. I have argued in addition and as a consequence of this first conviction that the change in the human subject that results from bringing the differentiated operations of conscious intentionality to bear upon human psychic sensitivity constitutes a dimension of conversion. I have called this psychic conversion.[1] I have tried to integrate psychic conversion with the intellectual, moral, and religious conversions whose objectification constitutes the theological functional specialty, foundations.[2] My work has thus been devoted to the two functional specialties of communications and foundations: communications, in so far as the objectification of the conversions can ground a reorientation and integration of the human sciences;[3] and foundations, in

---

[1] See Robert Doran, *Subject and Psyche: Ricoeur, Jung, and the Search for Foundations* (Washington, D.C.: University Press of American, 1977): *Psychic Conversion and Theological Foundations,* to be published by Scholars Press; "Psychic Conversion" *The Thomist,* (1977): 200-236: "Subject, Psyche, and Theology's Foundations," *Journal of Religion,* (1977): 267-287: "The Theologian's Psyche: Notes toward a Reconstruction of Depth Psychology," *Lonergan Workshop I,* (1978): 93-141: "Aesthetic Subjectivity and Generalized Empirical Method," *The Thomist,* (1979): 257-278: "Jungian Psychology and Lonergan's Foundations: A Methodological Proposal, *Supplement to the Journal of the American Academy of Religion,* (March, 1979): G23-G45; "Dramatic Artistry in the Third Stage of Meaning," to be published in *Lonergan Workshop II.*

[2] Bernard Lonergan, *Method in Theology* (New York: Herder and Herder, 1972), Chapter 11.

[3] Ibid., pp. 364-367.

so far as the particular human science to which I have addressed myself studies a dimension of that same human interiority whose differentiations and conversions constitute the foundational reality of theology. If the application of the differentiated operations of intentionality to the states of the human psyche represents the psychic conversion that I have tried to articulate, then this articulation constitutes a dimension of theological foundations. Such has been my argument.

In the present paper I wish to speak briefly to these same two concerns. But I have an ulterior purpose. For I am convinced that the implementation of the theological method that is provided us in Fr. Lonergan's extraordinary and indeed improbable set of achievements[4] must take the form not only of a new statement of Christian doctrines and of a new systematic understanding of the divinely originated solution to the problem of evil, but also of a reorientation of the human sciences through the interdisciplinary collaboration of human subjects whose self-understanding is mediated by the same intellectual, psychic, moral, and religious self-appropriation that would inform, originate, and ground the new doctrinal and systematic theologies. This interdisciplinary collaboration will be essential even for work in the functional specialties of doctrines and systematics as these are conceived by Fr. Lonergan.

Philip McShane, in his book *The Shaping of the Foundations,* says: "Without the personal labor involved in arriving at one's own adequate general theological categories,...sets of special categories relative to religious interiority, authenticity, and redemptive history may well emerge, but they run the danger of being a new nominalism."[5] General theological categories are categories that theology shares with other disciplines.[6] The theological nominalism indicted by Professor McShane would presume that Christian experience and development occur independently of the secular experience of persons and communities, and so can be spoken of without reference to the objects of other intellectual and scientific activity, to psychological and social reality, and to political and economic transactions. It is especially to psychological reality that I have addressed myself. But even here I have been developing not so much general theological categories as transcendental categories that would guide the

---

[4] Improbable in the sense that the dimension that Michael Polanyi said would remain always tacit has been objectified. See John V. Apczynski, "Integrative Theology: A Polanyian Proposal for Theological Foundations," *Theological Studies,* (1979): 23-43.

[5] Philip McShane, *The Shaping of the Foundations: Being at Home in the Transcendental Method* (Washington, D.C: Univerity Press of America, 1976), p. 19.

[6] Bernard Lonergan, *Method in Theology,* pp. 281-288.

generation of the general categories. These latter must be derived in an interdisciplinary collaborative effort of psychologists, psychiatrists, neurophysiologists, biochemists, biophysicists, and so on. Again, I am indebted to Professor McShane for his constant reminder that I not so address myself to the concerns of psychology as to imply that this hard scientific labor can be dispensed with now that we are equipped with adequate heuristic grounds. Far from dispensing with this labor, I wish to insist that it represents an indispensable element for implementing Fr. Lonergan's method, even as that method is pertinent to constructing a new theology *in oratione recta* that addresses itself to the present and to the future. An interdisciplinary reorientation of the human sciences on the basis of Fr. Lonergan's theological foundations represents one dimension of the functional speciality, communications.

It is my purpose in this paper, then, to situate this interdisciplinary collaboration within the dialectic of history that sets the concrete conditions of our responsibility for the future of humanity. Such collaboration will be a dimension of the suprastructure of a global effort to create a humane crosscultural alternative to the various social, political, and economic monstrosities that are the systemic structural objectifications and agents of inauthenticity with which we must come to terms in these latter stages of the longer cycle of decline. I wish to speak of this global effort and of the pertinence of Fr. Lonergan's work to its concerns. In doing so, I will try, finally, to suggest how the collaborative scientific and scholarly praxis that is grounded in theological foundations can have far-reaching ramifications and implications even for the everyday transactions that constitute the infrastructure of our global social, cultural, and economic life.[7]

I. The Reorientation of Depth Psychology

The contributions of Fr. Lonergan to the reorientation of depth psychology are both clear and momentous. The higher viewpoint on the human subject that emerges in his own disengagement of the distinct quality and privileged position of existential responsibility as both grounding and sublating cognitive authenticity, opens us heuristically upon the possibility of what Eric Voegelin has called a psychology of orientations.[8] We can now envision the possibility of

---

[7] On cultural infrastructure and suprastructure, see Bernard Lonergan, "Belief: Today's Issue," in *A Second Collection,* ed. Bernard Tyrrell and William Ryan (Philadelphia: Westminster, 1974), esp. pp. 91-97.

[8] Eric Voegelin, *The New Science of Politics* (Chicago: University of Chicago Press, 1952), p. 186.

elaborating a psychology that would order the entire stream of our sensations, memories, images, emotions, conations, bodily movements, associations, and spontaneous responses to persons and situations, and so the whole of our sensitive psychic undertow, in accord with the participation of the human sensitive psyche in the normative order of the search for direction in the movement of life. This order is disengaged in Fr. Lonergan's thematization of the creative vector of human consciousness and in his more recent anticipation of a discernment of the healing vector within that same consciousness.[9] Such a psychology would be sharply contrasted with the various psychologies of passional motivation that have dominated the modern academic psychological milieu, and that, says Voegelin, could understand without remainder only a certain pneumopathological type of person. These psychologies of motivation acknowledge no higher order of values than the social value of the good of order. Even their contribution to the pursuit of social order calls for a cynical manipulation of more elementary passions. What is missing from the grounding of such psychologies is an understanding of the self-transcendent objectives of human intentionality, objectives whose pursuit is the condition of the possibility of human psychic flourishing. Consequently these psychologies consider what are in fact autonomous religious, personal, and cultural values to be at best purely particular values, and in some instances particular values of the sort that threaten the social control that motivates the pragmatic engineers of our political and social Leviathans.

The elements in Fr. Lonergan's work that I have drawn upon to ground a reorientation of depth psychology are sufficiently well-known that I can simply list them here. They include: the differentiation of intentional from nonintentional feelings;[10] the differentiation within intentional feelings of responses to value from responses to mere satisfactions;[11] the further differentiation within responses to values of various degrees of affective self-transcendence isomorphic with an objective hierarchy of values in which religious, personal, and cultural values condition the possibility of a sustained pursuit of justice in the social order and so of an equitable distribution of particular goods;[12] the establishment of the normative order of intentionality as a grid for the existential discernment of

---

[9] On the two vectors, see Bernard Lonergan, "Healing and Creating in History," in *Bernard Lonergan: Three Lectures* (Montreal: Thomas More Institute, 1975), pp. 55-68. Most of Lonergan's work, of course, is concerned with objectifying the creative vector.

[10] Bernard Lonergan, *Method in Theology*, pp. 30-31.

[11] Ibid., p. 31.

[12] Ibid., pp. 31-32.

affective self-transcendence;[13] conversely, the use of affective self-transcendence as a criterion for discerning whether one is indeed being attentive, intelligent, reasonable, responsible, and loving; the reciprocal relationship between feelings and symbols and between affective development and symbolic transformation;[14] and the at least implicit acknowledgment of an aesthetic base in the normative order of intentionality for the character of a person's religious, moral, and indeed even cognitive authenticity.[15] On the basis of these elements I have attempted to generate the further transcendental categories of second immediacy,[16] the imaginal,[17] and psychic conversion,[18] to establish the distinction of three orders of elemental symbolism: the personal, the archetypal, and the anagogic,[19] and on the basis of this distinction to engage in an ongoing dialectic with Jungian archetypal psychology.[20]

Recently I have discovered that Fr. Lonergan's paper on healing and creating in history[21] suggests a model for understanding the transformation of the aesthetic quality of our religious, moral, and cognitive being,[22] and that the far-reaching explanatory potentials of his talk of limitation and transcendence in the discussion of genuineness that appears in *Insight*[23] can become the basis of a psychology of religious discernment. The various operations that constitute the creative vector in human consciousness are permeated by feelings. To the extent that these feelings are not congruent with the self-transcendent objectives of their corresponding operations, to the extent that one does not *desire* meaning, truth, the real, the good, and attunement with a world-transcendent God whose Word and

---

[13] Ibid., pp. 33-34.

[14] Ibid., pp. 64-69.

[15] Ibid., pp. 31-32.

[16] Robert Doran, *Subject and Psyche*, Chapter Two.

[17] Ibid., Chapter Four.

[18] Ibid., Chapter Five.

[19] Robert Doran, "Aesthetic Subjectivity and Generalized Empirical Method."

[20] In addition to the articles mentioned in footnote 1, see Robert Doran, "Psyche, Evil, and Grace" *Communio*, (Summer, 1979):192-211; "Jungian Psychology and Christian Spirituality," *Review for Religious*, (1979): pp.497-510; 742-752; 857-866; "Primary Process and the 'Spiritual Unconscious,'" to be published in *Lonergan Workshop IV*; and "Christ and the Psyche," in *Trinification of the World*, ed. Thomas A. Dunne and Jean-Marc Laporte (Toronto: Regis College, 1977), pp. 112-143.

[21] See above, footnote 9.

[22] See Robert Doran, "Jungian Psychology and Christian Spirituality: I," *Review for Religious*, (1979): 497-510.

[23] Bernard Lonergan, *Insight: A Study of Human Understanding* (New York: Philosophical Library, 1957; paperback New York: Harper and Row, 1978), pp. 472-479.

Love are incarnate in Christ Jesus, to that extent these *operations* of conscious intentionality are inhibited from reaching their objectives. The automatisms and complexes of our psychic sensitivity interfere with the spontaneous unfolding of the normative order of the search for direction in the movement of life. The universal willingness that can initiate and sustain schemes of recurrence that would meet the problems set by decline must originate elsewhere than in the development from below upwards of our intentional capacities.[24] The absolutely supernatural conjugate form of charity, of the gift of God's love, however it is mediated through the universal instrumentality of all proportionate being,[25] is radically a healing of the convulsive aesthetic undertow whose spontaneous energic compositions and distributions propel us to displace in one direction or another the tension of limitation and transcendence whose cognitive and existential acknowledgment would constitute our genuineness. A displacement in the direction of limitation heads in the limit to a state of psychotic depression, while a displacement in the direction of transcendence heads to schizophrenic inflation. But we can be anywhere on the continuum toward one or the other of these pathological disintegrations, and we can even oscillate from one displacement to the other in manic-depressive inconsistencies. The internal time-consciousness that constitutes the sensitive psyche and its imaginal productions must be converted to a taut participation in the intentions of being and the good that are not bounded by the horizon of time. Only a transparent grounding in God, only being in love in an unrestricted fashion, can unify the otherwise Protean commingling of opposites that results from the fact that our interiority is both spiritual and psychic. A third-stage-of-meaning[26] conversion of affectivity to such participation in the normativity of the intentional quest is precisely what I mean by psychic conversion. In psychic conversion the story structured by memory and anticipation, the story of the creative tension of limitation and transcendence, of its various displacements and its continual re-establishment in the gift of God's forgiving love, is not only healed but also appropriated with something approaching explanatory precision. Elaborations of the model of limitation and transcendence thus permit a reinterpretation and reformulation of both the axial and the Christian traditions of

---

[24] On universal willingness, ibid., pp. 623-624.

[25] On the absolutely supernatural conjugate form of charity, ibid., pp. 698-700, p. 726, p. 741. On universal instrumentality, Bernard Lonergan, *Grace and Freedom: Operative Grace in the Thought of St. Thomas Aquinas,* ed. J. Patout Burns (New York: Herder and Herder, 1971), pp. 80-84.

[26] On the third stage of meaning, Bernard Lonergan, *Method in Theology,* pp. 93-96.

discernment. Much of my current research is devoted to developing such a psychology of discernment.

II. Psychic Conversion

The explanatory self-appropriation of the story structured by the creative tension of limitation and transcendence, particularly as that story is told in the trustworthy elemental symbolizations of one's dreams, constitutes a defensive scheme of recurrence around the advances of the human spirit attained in Fr. Lonergan's objectification of the normative order of the search for direction in the movement of life. We know from *Insight* that a scheme or a series of ranges of schemes of recurrence that have already emerged within the concrete universe whose immanent intelligibility is an emergent probability can place around itself a defensive scheme that increases the probability of its survival.[27] The psychic conversion that I have labored to effect in myself, to understand, and to articulate, brings the pulsing flow of psychic sensitivity forward to a share in the self-transparency of the subject achieved in Fr. Lonergan's transcendental method. In this way it offers one both affective and symbolic indications of the likelihood of the genuineness or inauthenticity of one's present cognitive, moral, and religious stance: affective indications, in that the tension of limitation and transcendence is *felt* by a sensitive psyche that mediates between the relatively fixed schemes of recurrence of the material organism and the spiritual intentionality whose objective is unrestricted by the space and time that are the field or matter or potency in which emergent probability is the immanent form or intelligibility;[28] symbolic indications, in that the energic complexes that constitute these mediating psychic affects are both expressed and transformed in the spontaneous elemental symbolizations of our dreams.[29] Through the appropriation of these affective and symbolic indications, a defensive scheme is placed around the advances in self-transcendence that accrue from the self-appropriation of one's cognitive, moral, and religious exigencies. In this sense psychic conversion is foundational. Since it unifies the normative order of inquiry with our psychic sensitivity, it provides a dimension, not so much of the materials to be integrated in the rest

---

[27] "Schemes might be complemented by defensive circles, so that if some event, F, tended to upset the scheme, there would be some such sequence of conditions as, if F occurs, then G occurs; if G occurs, then H occurs; if H occurs, then F is eliminated." Bernard Lonergan, *Insight*, p. 118. On the probability of emergence, the probability of survival, and the role of defensive circles in survival, ibid., p. 121.

[28] Ibid., pp. 170-172.

[29] Robert Doran, "Dramatic Artistry in the Third Stage of Meaning."

of human knowledge, including theological knowledge, as of the integrating structure of the subjects who will articulate an explicit semantics of the real.

In a recently completed book entitled *Psychic Conversion and Theological Foundations,* I propose that a methodical psychology grounded in self-appropriation would be a transcendental aesthetics, that is, an explicit integration through self-appropriation of our intention of the beautiful with our notions of the intelligible, the true, the real, and the good. The integration of psychic and neural energy into the normative unfolding of the pure question of the human spirit completes, I believe, the therapeutic intention of Fr. Lonergan's transcendental method to effect a mediated return to immediacy on the part of the self-appropriating cognitive and existential agent.[30] A further retrieval of the medieval heritage in the mode of interiority would substantiate this claim. For the medievals did not limit the transcendental field to the intelligible, the true, the real, and the good. They included also the beautiful, the objective of the aesthetic intentionality of the sensitive psyche. Sensitive consciousness is itself intentional, and its intentionality is not obliterated or displaced, but rather sublated, by any genuine intention of meaning, of truth, and of the human good. As there is a transcendental notion of the intelligible, of the true, of the real, of the good, so there is a transcendental notion of the beautiful. It resides in our sensitive consciousness. As the other transcendental notions are revealed in the unfolding of the normative order of inquiry, so the notion of the beautiful resides in the intentional feelings that give to the intention of meaning, the reflective grasp of truth, and the existential discernment of values their momentum, their drive, their satisfaction, and their specifically human drama. One's story is a matter of the satisfaction or frustration of one's desire for meaning, truth, reality, and genuinely ordered values. That the story is human is a function of the specifically differentiating normative order of inquiry, the source of transcendence. But that it is a story at all is perhaps a function of the transcendental notion of the beautiful that resides in a sensitive consciousness that cannot be left behind or displaced in any genuine human exercise of intelligence, rationality, and deliberation, but that is the very condition of the genuineness that lies in a creative tension of limitation and transcendence.

---

[30] Robert Doran, *Subject and Psyche,* Chapter Two.

III. Toward a World-Cultural Humanity

As with everything else in the transcendental method that establishes the third stage of meaning, so too the retrieval through self-appropriation of the intention of the beautiful is not an end in itself. Fr. Lonergan speaks in *Insight* not simply of conceiving and affirming the integral heuristic structure of proportionate being, but also of implementing it, and of doing so in such a way as to effect "a transformation and an integration of the sciences and of the myriad instances of common sense."[31] Moreover, there can be found in the development of Fr. Lonergan's thought a movement from speaking of the cognitional-theoretic foundations of this implementation, as in *Insight,* to proposing a set of theological foundations for an interdisciplinary reorientation of the human sciences, as in *Method in Theology:* theological foundations that include the cognitional-theoretic positions of *Insight* within a higher viewpoint that is explicit in its articulation of positions on the moral and religious as well as on the cognitive subject.[32] In *Insight,* the disclosive and transformative praxis of constructing an explicit semantics of the real is a function of implementing the three basic philosophic positions inherent in cognitional theory: the positions on knowing, being, and objectivity.[33] The development that appears in *Method in Theology* expands the list of basic positions, so that the foundations of the transforming and integrating activity that Fr. Lonergan has in mind when he speaks now of integrated studies are not simply philosophic but properly theological foundations. The intellectual conversion that articulates itself into the three basic positions of *Insight* is itself grounded in a moral conversion, and this moral conversion follows upon a religious conversion.[34] The modality of psychic conversion that is to be included as a dimension of these theological foundations follows upon intellectual conversion and enables the self-appropriation of moral and religious conversion.[35]

Now to speak of the theological foundations of a transformation and an integration of the sciences and of the myriad instances of common sense is to imply a new synthesis of faith and culture. It is also to indicate both the suprastructural component of this new his-

---

[31] Bernard Lonergan, *Insight,* p. 396.

[32] Chapter Two of my book, *Psychic Conversion and Theological Foundations,* is devoted to establishing this interpretation of Fr. Lonergan's development.

[33] Bernard Lonergan, *Insight,* pp. 387-388.

[34] "Bernard Lonergan Responds," in *Foundations of Theology,* edited by Philip McShane (South Bend, Ind.: University of Notre Dame Press, 1972), pp. 233-234.

[35] As with all aspects of genuineness, psychic conversion is analogously realized. I am speaking of psychic self-appropriation.

torical synthesis — the transformation and integration of the sciences — and its infrastructural component — the transformation and integration of the myriad instances of common sense. And to speak of a movement from philosophic foundations to theological foundations that include but sublate the philosophic is to suggest a distinction between the integral heuristic structure of proportionate being and the transcendental notion of value: a distinction that is not afforded us in *Insight* but that is present both in *Method in Theology*'s disengagement of the fourth level of consciousness and in the affirmation that appears in the same book that, while the structure of judgments of value is identical with that of judgments of fact, the respective contents or meaning of such judgments differ from one case to the other.[36] Thus it is that one can approve of what does not exist and disapprove of what does. This recognition of the distinctness of the existential dimensions of foundations from the cognitive dimensions established in *Insight* grounds a further distinction between the real human world as it is and the good human world as it is to be brought into being. This good human world is in the limit a new historical synthesis of faith and culture. I call it a world-cultural humanity. I locate its suprastructural component in the interdisciplinary collaboration that, grounded in theological foundations, would intend a transformation and an integration especially of the human sciences, and its infrastructural component in the transformation and integration of the myriad instances of common sense through a further implementation of the same theological foundations.

The term, world-cultural humanity, is borrowed from Lewis Mumford's book, *The Transformations of Man*.[37] After tracing in descriptive fashion some of the major cultural forms that have constituted what Eric Voegelin would call the substance of history,[38] Mumford raises the question of where we go from here. What may we anticipate? What ideal-types may we use to help us describe our contemporary options? He proposes two dialectically alternative courses that confront us today on a cosmopolitan scale. The first he calls post-historic humanity, and the second world-cultural humanity. His argument is to the effect that, short of a global transformation of human consciousness and of cultural values similar in its impact to the various localized axial differentiations of the order of reason and of the world-transcendent measure of human integrity that occurred in the millenium 500 B.C.-500 A.D., humanity is condemning itself — and here I use other terminology than that

---

[36] Bernard Lonergan, *Method in Theology*, p. 37.

[37] Lewis Mumford, *The Transformations of Man* (New York: Harper Torchbooks, 1956).

[38] Eric Voegelin, *The New Science of Politics*, p. 78.

employed by Mumford — to a cumulative and irreversible determination of its neurophysiology, memory, imagination, intelligence, and existential praxis in inflexible schemes of recurrence fixed by neural, psychic, social, economic, political, conceptual, and linguistic determinisms. The alternative to this post-historic humanity is suggested in the contrary ideal-type of a world-cultural humanity that is grounded in a self-understanding of human subjects that can so mediate the differentiations of consciousness achieved in the past as to bring them forward to a new and cross-cultural unity rooted in an explicit appropriation of the common and so transcendental constituents of human genuineness.

Mumford's ideal-types are precise enough to evoke in us the same persuasion that some, including myself, have arrived at by studying and pondering and being changed by the work of Bernard Lonergan: namely, that we are challenged by the unfolding course of intelligent emergent probability to an agency that would mediate a new axial development in human consciousness, that new control of meaning grounded in interiorly differentiated consciousness that Fr. Lonergan has called the third stage of meaning.[39] For the appropriation of the transcultural roots of human genuineness that would ground a world-cultural humanity is precisely what is rendered possible by the transcendental or generalized empirical method that gives us what Fr. Lonergan calls theological foundations. What Mumford's ideal-type of a world-cultural humanity enables us to envision in an imaginative form that can stir the affective momentum and drive of our intentional operations is a global community grounded in analogously realized attainments of the human genuineness that Fr. Lonergan enables at least us suprastructural practitioners to appropriate through interiorly differentiated consciousness. This global community would be an emerging alternative, especially to the principal agents in today's world of a post-historic humanity: namely, to the two escalating and competing totalitarianisms that lie in an overly centralized and bureaucratic form of socialism such as is paradigmatically manifested in the Soviet bloc, on the one hand, and in the correspondingly monolithic network of transnational corporations that has assumed effective control of the capitalistic world and of many of the developing nations of the Third World, on the other hand. The anticipation of a world-cultural community that is not a homogenization of cultural differences but a grounding of crosscultural enrichment in interiorly differentiated consciousness envisions the formation of a humane

---

[39] I have presented my interpretation of Lonergan to this effect in *Subject and Psyche,* pp. 17-48.

alternative to our present and seemingly exhaustive options between a state-controlled monopoly and a monopoly-controlled state,[40] both of which violate on the level of systemic social-structural objectifications the law of the tension of limitation and transcendence that constitutes the intrinsic intelligibility of all genuine development in this concrete universe of proportionate being.

The interdisciplinary effort at a transformation and reorientation of the human sciences that would constitute the suprastructural component of a world-cultural community would go forward simultaneously on several fronts. Its intention would be, I believe, to redirect the scientific understanding of humanity in accord with the constituents of genuineness that are mediated by the differentiation of intentional and psychic interiority, and especially with the law of limitation and transcendence that is intrinsic to all genuine personal and social development. I have argued that the reorientation of depth psychology is part of the very foundations of this implementation of Fr. Lonergan's method in the human sciences. But the implementation must extend to a reorientation of the social, anthropological, and political sciences, under the guiding orientation of an intention to ground crosscultural understanding and cooperation in the transcendental constituents of human genuineness in all cultures; and to a reorientation of the science of economics in accord with the same vision of crosscultural communication and enrichment. We can only be grateful that Fr. Lonergan is presently turning his attention to a transformation of economic knowledge that, in so far as I understand it, would have economic transactions embody the law of limitation and transcendence whose progressive articulation is simultaneously a promotion of genuine human development.

As we come into possession of this law through interiorly differentiated consciousness, we will find its transformative impact also upon the myriad instances of common sense.

The original experience of the search for direction in the movement of life is variously differentiated or compacted in the different cultural communities whose sets of meanings and values constitute the substance of our history. Eric Voegelin has distinguished three modes of symbolization through which cultures have expressed their self-understanding: the cosmological, the anthropological, and the soteriological.[41] I will try to understand these modes of symbolization in accord with the law of limitation and transcendence, will imply the relevance of psychic conversion to an integration of the

---

[40] Matthew Lamb, *History, Method, and Theology* (Missoula: Scholars Press, 1978), p. 49.

[41] Eric Voegelin, *Order in History, volume I: Israel and Revelation* (Baton Rouge: Louisiana State University Press, 1954).

truth of these various modes, and will indicate the pertinence of Fr. Lonergan's work not only for the transformation and integration of the sciences but also for the development of the common sense of a world-cultural community.

In terms of Fr. Lonergan's differentiations of the constituents of human genuineness, we might say that cultures that exist under the forms of cosmological symbolization, where the prime analogate for the cultural order lies in the rhythms and processes of nonhuman nature, have not differentiated the theoretic and world-transcendent realms of meaning, to say nothing of the interior, scholarly, and soteriological realms, from the compactness of the aesthetic and ecological sensitivities that inform their common sense. Due to their non-differentiation, especially of theory and of world-transcendent reality, these cultures effectively displace the tension of limitation and transcendence in the direction of limitation, and so they are effectively prevented from assuming responsible control over their future course of history by reason of a too compact identification with the schemes of recurrence operative in nonhuman nature. But there is an abiding truth in the cosmological symbolizations of pre-axial cultures. While it is true that for these cultures today to remain under the dominance of cosmological symbolization is for them to become the easy prey of the competing and escalating totalitarianisms that, left unchecked, would institute a post-historic humanity, it is no less true that the abiding truth of cosmological symbolization must be mediated through interiorly differentiated consciousness to a crosscultural community that would counteract the contrary displacement in the direction of transcendence that characterizes the exploits of the competing and escalating totalitarianisms. The characteristic features of cosmological symbolization, as these are disengaged by such scholars as Voegelin and Mircea Eliade, bear striking resemblances to what the psychologist Carl Gustav Jung has called the archetypal symbols of the collective unconscious. While I have emphasized in my own work that Jung fails to distinguish these archetypal symbols from the anagogic symbolizations that both give rise to and express a transcendent and then a soteriological differentiation of consciousness, it can in no wise be denied that Jung has provided us with the principal instrument for mediating through interiorly differentiated consciousness the ecological exigencies for creative tension with the schemes of recurrence of nonhuman nature that, however compactly, form the truth of the cosmological mentality. The recovery through what I have called psychic conversion of these archetypal expressions of the exigency for a balanced relation between nature and culture will mediate to an emerging crosscultural community, among other things, an ecological differentiation of consciousness that will preserve and yet transform by sublation the abiding truth of the cosmological societies.

Fr. Lonergan's mediation of intellectual conversion, on the other hand, is, I believe, at least in part a disengagement through interiorly differentiated consciousness of the axial insights into the order of the soul as the measure of the integrity of a society, and of the world-transcendent measure of the order of the soul itself, that came to expression in anthropological symbolization. And a further mediation of the substance of history through interiorly differentiated consciouness is present in Fr. Lonergan's paper on healing and creating in history. For this paper enables us to distinguish between the eros of an interiority that is well-ordered because of its attunement in ultimate concern with the world-transcendent measure of integrity and the charity of a person who has been healed by the gracious initiative of this world-transcendent measure in one's own regard. A soteriological differentiation is thus implicitly distinguished from the differentiation of world-transcendent Being. This further differentiation, however, does not displace but only radicalizes the tension of limitation and transcendence that is established to the extent that one is grounded in God. The soteriological truth adds to the anthropological insights, disengaged in a new fashion through intellectual conversion, several differentiating characteristics.

First, the world-transcendent ground and ultimate referent of the original experience of the search for direction in the movement of life is now known, not simply as the source of a movement in our hearts and minds through which we are inclined to attunement with God, but as the agent of startlingly new developments in history through which God establishes a saving partnership with His people.

Secondly, the anthropological differentiations represented noetic advances that, however much they may originally have been grounded in revelatory experience, were easily attributed to the immanently generated advances of human knowledge that constitute the ordinary development of this knowledge; and the power of truth regarding the normative order of inquiry led the culture that was built on an analogy with the well-ordered soul to regard its own order as normative and permanent for other cultures as well; but if the measure of the order of the community finds its root in the astonishing interventions of a God who not only raises up prophets and brings down kings, but humbles Himself unto death on a cross to redeem His people from bondage, then no established human order can be regarded either as permanent or as invested with the normativity that would license it to deal with other orders on its own terms alone.

Thirdly, the anthropological truth placed such a premium on

human integrity in the search for direction in the movement of life that it established an aristocratic notion of human worth and of human community. But the soteriological surprise that in fact does meet the anthropological eros, but in such manner as to be a scandal and a stumbling-block to the soul that comforts itself on its disengagement of the normative order of attunement to the measure of integrity, acknowledges that the poor and the enslaved are those whom God favors as most His own, in fact whom He intervenes not only to save but to make into the very instruments of His salvation for others and even for their aristocratic oppressors. Until one has acknowledged in one's own person the same victimization and helplessness that is objectified in the historical bondage of the oppressed, one cannot inherit the Kingdom of God.

Fourthly, a shift is thus introduced in the tradition of discernment, which indeed has its origins in the pre-Christian disengagement of the order of attunement with God. Under anthropological self-understanding, discernment is a matter of discriminating those inclinations that draw us to attunement with the world-transcendent measure of integrity from those inclinations that draw us away from such attunement. Under soteriological self-understanding, the detachment that is the precondition of anthropological discernment is sublated into a participation in the law of the cross that the Word of God has assumed and revealed as the most complete embodiment of attunement with the measure of integrity under the concrete conditions of a history distorted by the social and personal surd that we know as sin.

Exclusively soteriological symbolization, however, contains an inherent danger that was perhaps first manifested in the Christian variants of Gnosticism, but that can also work its way into the community that would assume the vocation of building a humane cross-cultural alternative to the escalating totalitarianisms. Fr. Lonergan alludes to this danger when he speaks of the healing vector without the creative vector as a soul without a body.[42] Eric Voegelin points to it in his talk of the modern Gnosticisms,[43] with their metastatic understanding of human history. An exclusive reliance on soteriological self-understanding would repudiate the truth of anthropological symbolization, a truth that is mediated in explanatory fashion in Fr. Lonergan's articulation of transcendental method. Such a repudiation would neglect the exigencies for integrity that characterize what Fr. Lonergan has called the creative vector in human consciousness. Despite the fact that these exigencies cannot

---

[42] Bernard Lonergan, "Healing and Creating in History," p. 65.
[43] See, for example, his book, *The New Science of Politics*.

be fulfilled in an unbiased and undistorted fashion except to the extent that we are healed by the saving love that moves from above downwards in human consciousness, a neglect of these exigencies shortchanges the demand for radical integrity that is inherent in the covenant that is God's partnership with His people.

Here too we find, I believe, the acute pertinence of Fr. Lonergan's work for the concerns that have come to expression in the various theologies of liberation and in political theology, concerns that also obviously lie behind my own vision of a crosscultural community committed to schemes of recurrence that provide a genuine alternative to the deculturation that would head in the limit to a post-historic form of human existence. The history of ancient Israel is ample witness to the fact that a culture need not have reached the noetic disengagement of individual integrity in order to be visited by soteriological truth. And it surely has been a mistake in missionary endeavors to insist on the anthropological disengagements as somehow essential for Christian evangelization. But a theology of liberation that would revert to a denigration of the integrity of the individual as the measure of cultural values and of cultural values as the condition of a just social order — and by no means do I want to imply that this is the case with all such theologies[44] — would be guilty of a regression within the history of soteriological self-understanding itself. It is true that such self-understanding originally emerged, not out of anthropological differentiations, but as a leap beyond the compactness of cosmological symbolization. Thus soteriological self-understanding only gradually differentiated the radical significance of individual integrity, whereas anthropological truth was constituted by this differentiation. In soteriological history individuation moved into the light only against the backdrop of social apostasy. The community informed by soteriological self-understanding learned only gradually the truth that the integrity of a community is measured by the integrity of the individuals who compose it. But this constitutes no warrant for us to repeat the failures that gave rise to this insight. The denigration of the significance of cognitive and existential integrity that would display itself in a too easy marriage with Marxist analysis and praxis would not only relegate to oblivion the Christian tradition of contemplation through a disparagement of the spirituality of the individual; this loss of attunement with the God who is not only the objective of our longings but the saving partner under whose protection we walk humbly but upright through life

---

[44] But see Alfredo Fierro, *The Militant Gospel: A Critical Introduction to Political Theologies* (Maryknoll, N.Y.: Orbis, 1977).

would become an agent by default of that final collapse of all intellectual and existential synthesis that is our distinct contemporary option.

IV. Conclusion

Fr. Lonergan's mediation of the transcultural constituents of integrity has provided me with the conviction that a humane global alternative to the escalating totalitarianisms is a distinct possibility that has already emerged in the course of the unfolding of intelligent emergent probability. But, lest we ourselves violate the law of limitation and transcendence, let us keep in mind that axial transformations of consciousness and of culture take centuries to establish schemes of recurrence with a high probability of survival. The foundations of a world-cultural humanity have already been laid in Fr. Lonergan's disengagement of the crosscultural exigencies of human intentionality and, I believe, in the work of Carl Gustav Jung and others to identify the cross-cultural symbolic indicators of the participation of psychic sensitivity in, or of its derailment from, the normative order of the search for direction in the movement of life. But we still must be concerned with the probability of survival for the already emergent schemes of recurrence grounded in self-appropriation. I take great comfort in this regard from Jung's suggestion that the formation of a stable crosscultural community grounded in the elements of transcendental subjectivity that are in part differentiated in his work would take 600 years.[45] We stand today at the very beginning of a quite new venture in the history of the human community: a venture whose urgency is established by the dreadfulness of the alternatives that are inevitable if we do not assume our responsibility for transforming and integrating both the sciences and the myriad instances of common sense. But we will not witness in our own lifetimes the results of our efforts to consolidate the already emergent foundations and to begin to build upon them. I would hope only that my own disengagement of a psychic conversion as a defensive circle around Fr. Lonergan's differentiation of the exigencies of human authenticity helps to increase the probability of the survival of the third stage of meaning that comes to expression in his work. But for all of us the universal willingness of agapic consciousness that must inform our labors if they are to be truly detached and disinterested and so in harmony with the normative order of inquiry is the work of the healing vector that moves, not from below

---

[45] See Max Zeller, "The Task of the Analyst," *Psychological Perspectives*, (Spring, 1975): 74-78. See also my article, "Aesthetics and the Opposite," *Thought*, (1977): 117-133.

upwards in human consciousness, but from above downwards. This specification applies as well to the suprastructural labor of transformative interdisciplinary praxis as it does to the infrastructural reorientation of our everyday dramatic intersubjectivity. In either set of instances, the law of the healing vector, moreover, is the law of the cross, and the criterion of discernment is a taut affective balance of limitation and transcendence that is only radicalized when we discover that attunement with the world-transcendent measure of our own noetic and existential integrity is embodied in the cross and resurrection of Jesus as the pattern that this world-transcendent measure assumed in becoming human flesh.

I experience a real inadequacy in expressing my admiration and gratitude for Fr. Lonergan's work and for the encouragement that he has provided me over the past seven years. But I hope that the foregoing remarks are some small indication of the tasks that he has enabled me to assume and to anticipate.

Rahner and Lonergan on Foundational Theology[1]

by Michael O'Callaghan

It is highly useful to compare the thought of Karl Rahner and Bernard Lonergan on the topic of foundational theology. Rahner is a theologian concerned with working out the general and special categories of a foundational theology. Lonergan is a methodologist concerned with how these categories are to be worked out. A comparison of their work not only provides us with a rather complete framework for the new foundational theology, but also tends to eliminate the difficulties that Rahner has expressed about Lonergan's methodology.

I. Rahner's Theological Foundation

Karl Rahner is determined to acknowledge the fact of the Enlightenment. He would accept its turn to the human subject, and he would overcome its rejection of revealed religion and theology precisely by proposing a notion of theology rooted in the anthropological turn of modern thought. Theology simply cannot operate as if the Enlightenment never occurred, or as if it could be dealt with by a global condemnation.[2]

---

[1] This article is based largely on the author's doctoral dissertation, *Theology in a New Key: The Unity of Theology in its New Context, in the Thought of Bernard Lonergan*, completed at Tübingen in 1978 under the directorship of Dr. Walter Kasper. The dissertation has been offered for publication.

[2] For example, see Rahner's "Reflections on Methodology in Theology" in Karl Rahner, *Theological Investigations 11* (London: Darton, Longman and Todd, and New York: Seabury, 1974), pp. 68-114, esp. pp. 84ff.

For Rahner, accepting the challenge posed by the Enlightenment means first and foremost coming to terms with modern philosophy. Negatively, this means that theologians have to admit the inadequacy of scholastic and neo-scholastic philosophy as a tool for constructing their theological systems. Positively, it means that theologians have to turn to transcendental method if they wish to provide theology with a foundation adequate to the modern context, especially to the context provided by modern philosophy. It is clear to Rahner that modern philosophy, as exemplified in the work of Descartes, Kant, the German idealists, and in existentialism, represents a complex of quite contradictory systems; accordingly, when Rahner says that modern philosophy may be studied as a series of efforts to develop a transcendental philosophy, he is quite aware of using the word "transcendental" in an inexact, descriptive manner. Having noted this, Rahner describes the mode of enquiry of modern philosophy (and hence of a modern theology) as follows:

> Quite simply, therefore, and in a sense that is almost prephilosophical, we shall make the following statement: A transcendental line of enquiry, regardless of the particular area of subject-matter in which it is applied, is present when and to the extent that it raises the question of the conditions in which knowledge of a specific subject is possible in the knowing subject himself. The fact that an enquiry of this kind is in principle possible, legitimate, and under certain circumstances even necessary hardly needs to be discussed in general terms or at any length. In any act of cognition it is not only the object known but also the subject knowing that is involved. It is dependent not only upon the distinctive characteristics of the object, but also upon the essential structure of the knowing subject. The mutual interconnection and the mutual interconditioning process between the subject knowing and the object known precisely as known and as knowable are in themselves the object of a transcendental enquiry.[3]

The question about "the conditions in which knowledge of a specific subject is possible in the knowing subject himself" is of course very complex and it may be answered in a variety of ways. The question may be raised in the context of idealism, and the result is a series of philosophies that take their stand on the priority of speculative reason. The question may be raised in the context of existentialism, and the result is a series of philosophies that take their stand on the priority of practical reason. Amidst such philosophical pluralism it is extremely difficult for the theologian to appeal to transcendental method and to pinpoint the conditions of the possibil-

---

[3] Ibid., p. 87.

ity of theological knowing: the disagreements are so pronounced that trying to build theology on this or that modern philosophy seems doomed to failure even before the project is undertaken. Nevertheless, the lack of agreement among modern philosophers in no way detracts from the fact of their unanimity in insisting that the central question concerns human knowing— what knowledge is and what we are to do with the knowledge that we have.

Karl Rahner is very much aware of the pluralism of modern philosophies. Moreover, he is extremely conscious of the complexity within modern theology itself, caused especially by the introduction of critical-historical methods in studying the Christian message and tradition. At the same time, however, he is convinced that there is a way of reflecting on the Christian fact that at once does justice to the spirit of modern philosophy, and also provides the various theological specializations with the categories they need to perform their highly technical and scientific work. It is my conviction that Rahner himself practiced this foundational theologizing in almost all of his work as a theologian over the past forty years. But it is also my conviction that Rahner first began to thematize adequately his foundational theology in 1976, when he published his *Grundkurs des Glaubens*.[4] There, he speaks of foundational theology as a first level of reflection, distinct from second levels of reflection that characterize the various technical and scientific specializations within theology.

What, for Rahner, is the foundational reality that is to be thematized and objectified by this first level of reflection? There seems no doubt that it is the human subject as experiencing divine mystery— this is the reality to be thematized in foundational theology.[5] It is

---

[4] Karl Rahner, *Grundkurs des Glaubens: Einführung in den Begriff des Christentums* (Freiburg: Herder, 1976). (ET: *Foundations of Christian Faith: An Introduction to the Idea of Christianity,* New York: Seabury, 1978).

[5] There would seem to be several different ways of answering the question regarding what is fundamental in Rahner's theology. A theoretical answer would identify the basis in the central *category* of Rahner's theology, and I agree with B. van der Heijden (*Karl Rahner: Darstellung und Kritik seiner Grundposition* [Einsiedeln: Johannes, 1973]) that Rahner's main category is God's self-communication *(Selbstmitteilung Gottes).* A variation on this would further specify the category as Christological, for in Christ the self-communication of God to the human subject achieves its fullness; thus Peter Eicher, *Die anthropologische Wende* (Freiburg: Herder, 1970), and *Offenbarung: Prinzip neuzeitlicher Theologie* (Munich: Kösel, 1977), pp. 347ff. As well one can shift from categories to the way (method) in which Rahner arrived at the categories, or the way that each of us could reach categorical expression; with this shift one speaks of the process from religious experience by drawing on the categories of the Christian tradition. What now is central is the reality of the human subject as experiencing divine mystery, and the process of self-appropriation. This approach to Rahner is found in the work of Klaus Fischer, *Der Mensch als Geheimnis: Die Anthropologie Karl Rahners* (Freiburg: Herder, 1974), 2nd ed.

crucial to note here that it is not the human subject alone, nor divine mystery alone, but the human subject as related to divine mystery that is the foundational reality. This relatedness is at the heart of transcendental reflection. Moreover, it is important to remember that the human subject's experience of divine mystery, in its radical simplicity, is just given: it is conscious without being known, meaning that it is not the human subject knowing she or he is experiencing divine mystery or knowing that it is divine mystery that is experienced. Rahner explains this in connection with his commentary on Ignatius of Loyola's "consolation or trust that has no previous cause":

> From this it is now possible to grasp what is meant by the consolation "without previous cause". What is decisive is not any particular suddenness of the experience but, to put it quite plainly, its absence of object. What this means will have to be explained. There is no *algun obiecto* present, not even in the experience of consolation itself. Now if someone were to intervene at once here with the objection that this involves asserting an objectless, therefore unconscious experience, and this is a *contradictio in adjecto,* the whole teaching of St. Ignatius would have been quite misunderstood. The absence of object in question is utter receptivity to God, the inexpressible, non-conceptual experience of the love of the God who is raised transcendent above all that is individual, all that can be mentioned and distinguished, of God as God. There is no longer "any object" but the drawing of the whole person, with the very ground of his being, into love, beyond any defined circumscribable object, into the infinity of God as God himself....[6]

This radical experience of divine mystery is, for Rahner, the horizon or the very condition of the possibility of cognitional operations which intend any particular object or category. It is the preapprehension *(Vorgriff)* as distinguished from the concept or idea *(Begriff)*. It is the human subject in *existentiell* encounter with divine mystery, as the prior and illuminated reality of the subject—prior to this subject's objectification, prior to the subject as *existential*.[7]

---

[6] Karl Rahner, *The Dynamic Element in the Church* (Montreal: Palm, 1964), pp. 134-35.

[7] For example, see Karl Rahner, *Foundations,* pp. 14ff, and esp. pp. 19-20; also pp. 51ff., for Rahner's distinction between transcendental and *a posteriori* knowledge of God; the former is the knowledge of immediate experience and is pre-reflexive, prior to questioning what is experienced. See also Rahner's eleventh volume of *Theological Investigations,* where his essay "On the Theology of the Ecumenical Discussion" includes a listing of references on this distinction, p. 38, footnote 13.

While a great deal could be said at this point regarding Rahner's notion of religious experience, [8] I wish only to draw attention to the relation of this experience to theologizing. What characterizes Rahner's notion of theology is his insistence that foundational theology is the work of human subjects objectifying their encounter with divine mystery. Foundational theology is the indirect or transcendental reflection by the theologian on his or her religious tradition in light of the theologian's own experience of divine mystery.[9] It is this insistence on the theologian's own experience as being the "specifically theological principle" that I now wish to clarify.

First, Rahner notes that the context of theology is the believing church in the world. Theology is tied to the one abiding creed of the church, so that theology is to reflect upon this creed in the light of the new situations that confront believing and thinking people.[10] Such is the ecclesial or confessional dimension of theology, but it would be a serious oversight to restrict Rahner's meaning to some sort of external link between theology and the living church. What is meant by Rahner is something deeper, and this brings us to a second factor:[11] the relation between orthopraxis and orthodoxy, as set forth by Rahner on several occasions.[12]

There is, then, such a thing as a practical "knowledge" *(Wissen)* that Rahner identifies with experience of divine mystery. Such praxis is pre-reflective and, indeed, can never be captured fully by our reflective thinking:

---

[8] The substance of Rahner's thought on religious experience is found in his *Foundations,* Chapter Two. Among his richest presentations on the topic is his *The Dynamic Element in the Church,* already mentioned. See also his essay, "Reflections on the Experience of Grace", in Karl Rahner, *Theological Investigation — Volume Three,* (London: Darton, Longman & Todd, and New York: Helicon, 1967), pp. 86-90.

[9] I cannot here venture into the complex issue of the meaning of "transcendental" for Rahner, nor even give an account of his "first level of reflection". What I wish to emphasize is Rahner's insistence that foundational theology is reflection involving a human subject (religious consciousness) as related to a religious tradition.

[10] See Karl Rahner, "The Future of Theology", in *Theological Investigations 11,* pp. 137ff; and, in the same volume "Reflections on Methodology...", pp. 79-84.

[11] To date there has been no extensive study of Rahner's "transcendental experience". For some preliminary reflections see Leo J. Donovan, ed., "A Changing Ecclesiology in a Changing Church: A Symposium on Development in the Ecclesiology of Karl Rahner", in *Theological Studies* 38 (1977):736-62. My own opinion is that Rahner's understanding of "church" is co-extensive with the community of those who are responding to God's gift of his love in experience of mystery, whether this experience is given a Christian focus or a focus in some other religious tradition.

[12] See Rahner's own bibliography in his "On the Theology of the Ecumenical Discussion", p. 38, footnote 13.

> All of us "know" in the Spirit of God something more simple, more true, and more real than that which we are capable of knowing and expressing in the dimension of our theological concepts.[13]

This is true, not only for the individual in her or his own religious experience, but as well for the religious community living in history. For there is a lived praxis of the community of those responding to experienced mystery and confessing this response, but it is a praxis that itself is not reflected upon, made thematic, conceptualized. Rahner insists that theology is to be embedded in such praxis, for praxis is the context of theology: each theologian is to weigh his or her own views against the societal convictions of the believing community, realizing that orthopraxis has a certain primacy. For truth can be measured by its effectiveness as a social force, meaning that practical reasoning and decision-making are not simply derivatives from speculative reason.[14] So the theologian is to be rooted, not just in the confessional statements of a believing community, but also in the confessional praxis of a community living out in history and society its relatedness to divine mystery. Foundationally, then, theology is no privatized hobby of an individual but rather a reflection on the lived and confessed faith of a church—of a church living and acting *(handeln)* by virtue of its very faith. Rahner clarifies this in the following important statement:

> This does not mean that we are canonizing a collective (as opposed to an individual) subjectivism or pragmatism, but simply that we are applying to the nature of theology the insight that that which is subjective in a radical sense (which is necessarily the intercommunicative subjective) is also that which is most objective, and that the highest truth remains in practice only attainable in that love which is most all-embracing and free. From this point of view it is obviously part of any sound theological method to take as its starting-point the average and representative awareness of faith to be found in the Church as it exists in the concrete.[15]

Here, Rahner is hinting that theology at its starting-point (foundational theology) is a matter of the theologian entering into the loving praxis and confessional beliefs of a religious community. Orthodoxy is important, yet its importance is dependent on the prior entry of the theologian into the lived mission and praxis of the church—on the theologian's participation in the community's experience of

---

[13] Ibid. Also, see Rahner's *Foundations,* p. 2.
[14] See Rahner's "Reflections on Methodology...", pp. 80ff.
[15] Ibid., p. 81.

mystery in history. This brings us to a third and final dimension of Rahner's ecclesial foundational theology, as he explicitly reflects on the interplay between the theologian as subject and the lived praxis of the community.

Rahner's thinking on this matter permeates his *Grundkurs,* but a brief summary of this "transcendental" interplay appears in a letter written by Rahner to Klaus Fischer.[16] Here, Rahner emphasizes the depth and breadth and rich complexity of life and praxis, that no person can ever fully explicitate, objectify, thematize, justify. Hence, all orthopraxis and thus all lived faith can never be simply the carrying out of a reflexive and objectified orthodoxy. Accordingly, reflexive and reflecting theology can never articulate or objectify fully and completely the meaning and worth of lived faith. And this is precisely where Rahner locates foundational theology. The various technical and highly specialized disciplines in theology are indeed needed to perform the ongoing tasks involved in thematizing lived and confessed faith. But there is an additional need—for a somewhat pre-scientific though methodical grasp of the central categories that emerge in the interaction of my religious experience and the praxis/confession of a religious community. Hence, foundational theology is a first level of reflection, in the sense that the believing person, reflectively aware of her or his rootedness in the experience of divine mystery, comes to an ever-developing understanding of this mystery by drawing upon the resources of the believing community.

Such first-level reflection is critical. It is a matter of the human subject objectifying the meaning of his or her own praxis (encounter

---

[16] The letter from Rahner is found in K. Fischer, *Der Mensch. . .,* pp. 400-10. See esp. pp. 404-05: "...kein Mensch kann das Ganze seines Lebens, seiner Grundentscheidung voll zu einer expliziten, ausdrücklichen Aussage bringen. Er lebt immer aus mehr, als er sich selbst und anderen reflex sagen kann. Er kann sein Tun trotz aller notwendigen Reflexion und reflexen Rechenschaft, die er sich und anderen über sein Handeln gibt und geben muss, nie adäquat reflektieren. Darum ist alle Orthopraxis (aber so auch alles konkrete, gelebte Glauben) nie die blose Execution der (reflex ausgesagten, satzhaft vergegenständlichten) Orthodoxie. Das gilt für das christliche Leben und Glauben. Die refllektierte und reflektierende Theologie holt nie den im Leben vollzogenen Glauben ein. Theologie als argumentierende Reflexion muss sein, darf sein, darf entwickelt und auch mit eigentlich wissenschaftlicher Methodik durchdacht und dargestellt werden. Aber das Christsein und sein Glaube ist immer mehr, als was bei solcher Theologie zum Vorschein kommt. Doch auf eben diese Tatsache der Differenz zwischen Theorie und Praxis, zwischen Glaube (als Tat der Freiheit des Lebens) und Theologie kann und muss nochmals reflektiert werden. Die nie adäquate Reflektierbarkeit des Lebens und des Christseins ist selbst noch einmal ein Gegstand der Reflexion und so der Theologie. Nicht als ob sie dadurch diese Diastase aufheben würde. Aber die Theologie kann aus dieser reflektierten Diastase Konsequenzen ziehen. Und eine davon ist eben die Möglichkeit und das Recht einer Theologie der ersten Reflexionsstufe."

with divine mystery, lived faith), and employing this objectification as the criterion for critically evaluating the community's awareness of faith *(Glaubensbewusstsein)*. But at the same time, it is a matter of allowing the community's awareness of faith—its intersubjectively lived and confessed faith—to evaluate critically the human subject's self-appropriation of experienced mystery.

Rahner stresses this fact again at a later point in his letter to Fischer. Rahner does not at all deny that the objectification of religious experience is legitimately expressed in the Christian history of salvation and revelation. Such is the context of the interpretation integral to foundational theologizing, for it is the horizon in which the individual lives and finds the categories needed to express religious experience in history and society. But the contrary is also true—and this is crucial to foundational theology: because the individual in fact is conscious of religious experience, it can happen that the objectification by the individual of this experience can be a principle for critically evaluating the religious tradition in its praxis and beliefs. In other words, Rahner maintains that foundational theologizing is a matter of reflecting on one's religious tradition by attending, not only to the historically given tradition, but as well to one's own objectified experience of divine mystery as a critical principle by which that tradition is evaluated and further inserted into history and society.[17]

It is in this sense that Rahner conceives of foundational theology (and theology itself) as *"reductio in mysterium"* : not in the sense of some neutral and impersonal contemplation of a far-away divine mystery, but rather as a manner of reflection that *begins from* religious experience. It is the self-appropriation of a subject-experiencing-mystery, a preliminary, first-level reflection by this subject in categories drawn from the lived and confessed praxis of a believing community. For Rahner, theology is properly theology only to the extent it remains rooted in divine mystery. Theology as foundational is that human activity in which a person relates the multiplicity of the realities, experiences, and ideas in her or his life to that experienced yet ineffable mystery that we call God. In a word, "...every theological statement is only truly and authentically such at that point at which man willingly suffers it to extend beyond his comprehension into the silent mystery of God."[18]

Rahner, then, would understand both the Christian church and Christian theology as realities intelligible only in reference to their

---

[17] See ibid., p. 409.

[18] Karl Rahner, "Reflections on Methodology...", p. 103; see ibid., pp. 101ff., for the relation of theology to mystery.

source in the experienced mystery of God. Most especially, he has drawn attention to the vital relationship between the religious subjectivity of the foundational theologian and this theologian's task of objectifying this subjectivity in reference to the lived and confessed truth of the Christian tradition. In doing this, Rahner has prepared the way for a foundational theology that is profoundly religious, truly confessional, and solidly academic.

II. Lonergan's Foundational Theology

According to Karl Rahner foundational reality is the human subject as experiencing divine mystery; and foundational theology is this subject's first-level reflection objectifying this experience of mystery in categories available in a particular religious tradition.

According to Bernard Lonergan foundational reality is religious, moral, and intellectual conversion.[19] Because Lonergan insists that this threefold conversion is not a set of propositions uttered by a theologian, but a fundamental and momentous change in the human reality that a theologian is,[20] I would conclude that both Lonergan and Rahner agree on the identity of foundational reality: the human subject as experiencing divine mystery, i.e., as religiously converted. Although the notion of moral and intellectual conversion is not mentioned by Rahner, the reality of these further conversions in the human subject's adherence to value and truth would seem integral to Rahner's thought.[21]

The further question however, is whether Lonergan and Rahner agree on the notion of foundational theology. An answer to this question demands a brief consideration of Lonergan's thought on this topic. In this regard I would like to situate Lonergan's functional specialty "foundations" in the context, not merely of the other functional specialities, but also of Lonergan's generalized empirical method. "Foundations", as a functional specialty within theology, is not directly concerned with uncovering the conditions of the possibility of religious or theological knowledge and language. This has led some authors to the conclusion that Lonergan's foundational

---

[19] See Bernard Lonergan, *Method in Theology* (London: Darton, Longman and Todd, 1972), p. 267.

[20] See ibid., p. 270.

[21] For example, see Chapter One of Rahner's *Foundations,* that discusses the human subject as intending truth and as responsible and free.

theology is dogmatic, not critical.[22] But I disagree, for Lonergan's "foundations" itself rests on the prior foundation of generalized empirical method, as do all the functional specialties operative in Lonergan's notion of theology. To be sure, one could call such foundational methodology "philosophic", but only while realizing that it is integral to theological reflection. In other words, the functional specialty "foundations" does not represent the entire foundation of all theological reflection; rather, it thematizes only the "added foundation" needed to ground the further specialties of doctrines, systematics, and communications. "Foundations", as functional specialty, presupposes, and is a further determination of, the foundation of generalized empirical method. "Foundations", as functional specialty, also presupposes ongoing work in the historical and dialectical foundation provided by research, interpretation, history, and dialectic.

Lonergan's "foundations", then, is critical and normative to the extent that it rests on the prior foundations of generalized empirical method and the specialized methods of history and dialectic. Lonergan's generalized empirical method is an identification of the conditions of the possibility of religious and theological meaning, for it embraces the realities of the human good, human development, and religious experience. To borrow and adapt a phrase of Rahner, Lonergan's generalized empirical method could be called a first-level reflection by human subjects objectifying their experience of mystery in categories available from cognitional theory (including ethical and religious categories): what Lonergan calls general theological categories.[23]

Such foundational methodology is further determined in the specialized methods employed in theology. In general terms there are three specialized methods: historical, dialectical, and praxis-oriented. Historical methods are foundational to the task assigned dialectic. Both historical and dialectical methods are foundational to praxis. And, for Lonergan, praxis has four dimensions: "foundations" would make known the horizon of such praxis, "doctrines" states the truth of praxis, "systematics" would reach some understanding of that truth, and "communications" would relate praxis to

---

[22] Both David Tracy and Wolfhart Pannenberg are examples of authors who think that Lonergan's foundational theology is "dogmatic" rather than "critical". See David Tracy, "Lonergan's Foundational Theology: an Interpretation and a Critique", in P. McShane, ed., *Foundations of Theology* (Dublin: Gill and Macmillan, 1971), pp. 197-222; and *Blessed Rage for Order* (New York: Seabury, 1975), passim. And Wolfhart Pannenberg, "History and Meaning in Bernard Lonergan's Approach to Theological Method", in Patrick Corcoran, ed., *Looking at Lonergan's Method* (Dublin: The Talbot Press, 1975), pp. 88-100, esp. 97-99.

[23] See Bernard Lonergan, *Method in Theology*, pp. 281-88.

the cultural contexts. So, after an account of method in mediating theology (research, interpretation, history, and dialectic), Lonergan makes the transition to mediated theology (foundations, doctrines, systematics, and communications). Mediating theology evaluatively reconstructs the Christian past; mediated theology evaluatively constructs the Christian present and future. That construction or praxis is a matter of pronouncing which elements of the Christian tradition are true, how they can be reconciled with one another and with the conclusions of science, philosophy, history, and how the truths of tradition can be communicated effectively to the members of each class in every culture.[24]

The difficulty currently facing theology is of course the movement from past to present, from evaluative reconstruction to evaluative construction. On what basis, on what foundation, is theology to take a stand in order to state what is true in the tradition? It is one thing to reconstruct and evaluate the Christian tradition; it is something else for theology to translate that tradition and to influence the cultural context by projecting that tradition into new mentalities and new situations. The need, then, is for a theology that is not only historical and dialectical, but also critically practical. Lonergan realizes that this critical function of theology must include a foundation ultimately in cognitional theory and proximately in history and dialectic. Theology will be all the more critical, the more that it rests solidly on an evaluative reconstruction of the Christian tradition.[25] But he would add that foundational methodology and mediating theology cannot provide the *whole* foundation for a theology that would be critically practical. Theology needs an added foundation in order to move from the evaluative reconstruction of the convictions and opinions expressed in the Christian tradition to the constructive or direct discourse that states what is so.[26]

This added foundation is needed, then, inasmuch as the dialectical evaluation of the Christian tradition does no more than reveal the deep and irreconcilable oppositions present within the tradition. This challenges theologians to take a stand regarding the tradition —to be critical about the tradition, deliberately choosing what is authentic Christian tradition and proceeding to transpose that tradi-

---

[24] See ibid., p. 267. Note that my mention of "Christian" in connection with mediating and mediated theology intends simply to relate my discussion of Lonergan's foundational theology to the Christian heritage; his methodology is relevant as well to other religious traditions—as I'll note later in this article.

[25] See "Bernard Lonergan Responds", in McShane, ed., *Foundations of Theology*, pp. 230-31; and Lonergan, *Method in Theology*, p. 333.

[26] See Lonergan, *Method in Theology*, p. 267. Here, Lonergan highlights the centrality of responsible judgment by theologians who are to be concerned with the evaluative construction of the Christian heritage in the present and future.

tion to the world today. Such is theological praxis, described by Lonergan as follows:

> Dialectic confronts us with the problem of the irrational in human life and, as well, provides a technique for distinguishing between authentic and unauthentic evaluations, decisions, actions. Praxis, finally, raises the final issue: What are you to do about it? What use are you to make of your knowledge of nature, of your knowledge of man, of your awareness of the radical conflict between man's aspiration to self-transcendence and, on the other hand, the waywardness that may distort his traditional heritage and even his own personal life?[27]

Here, the crucial question concerns the critical principle. To what does the theologian appeal in order to ground his or her particular stand vis-á-vis the Christian tradition? For Lonergan, that appeal cannot be to divine revelation, to the inspiration of Scripture, to the authority of the Church, to the consensus of patristic and theological writers, to the *sensus fidelium*, etc. All of these are doctrines, and what is required is the critical principle whereby these or other doctrines are selected as true by theologians.[28] And so Lonergan urges that the foundation of critical theology objectively is found in the evaluative reconstruction revealed by dialectic, but subjectively is found in the religious, moral, and intellectual authenticity of the theologian. The critical principle or foundational reality is conversion. It is in light of one's own authenticity in appropriating the Christian heritage that one is to pronounce which doctrines are true, how they are to be reconciled with one another and with the conclusions of science, philosophy, history, and how they are to be communicated effectively to the members of each class in every culture.

Accordingly, foundations as a functional specialty (foundational theology) is a matter of the theologian objectifying conversion (experience of mystery) in categories made available in the functional specialty, dialectic. It is the task of foundations to objectify religious subjectivity, in special theological categories.[29] So Lonergan notes that foundations derives its first set of categories from religious experience, a second set from community witness in history, a third from the God who is the source of our love, a fourth from dialectical

---

[27] Bernard Lonergan, "The Ongoing Genesis of Methods", in *Studies in Religion/Sciences Religieuses* 6 (1976-1977):351; also *Method in Theology,* p. 268.

[28] See "Bernard Lonergan Responds", in McShane, ed., *Foundations of Theology,* p. 229; also *Method in Theology,* pp. 269-70.

[29] See Bernard Lonergan, *Method in Theology,* pp. 288-91. Of course, the foundational theologian is also to objectify religious subjectivity in *general* theological categories inasmuch as these are foundational and relevant to theology: so the work of the foundational theologian and methodologist would here be especially intertwined.

conflict, and a fifth from redemptive praxis in history. And Lonergan writes:

> The derivation of the categories is a matter of the human and the Christian subject effecting self-appropriation and employing this heightened consciousness both as a basis for methodical control in doing theology and, as well, as an *a priori* whence he can understand other men, their social relations, their history, their religion, their rituals, their destiny.[30]

III. Rahner Revisited

As methodologist, Lonergan is concerned principally with the task of indicating the qualities desirable in theological categories, and the manner in which such categories are to be obtained. He readily acknowledges that the task of actually working out the general and special categories pertains, not to a methodologist, but to the theologian working in the functional specialty of foundations.[31] Here, Karl Rahner may be considered just such a theologian. If my assessment of Rahner's theological foundation is accurate, then he has been principally concerned with the derivation of the categories relevant to a specifically Christian theology. Rahner, of course, has gone beyond such derivation to the other specialties that Lonergan calls "doctrines", "systematics", and "communications"; but Rahner's uniqueness is his attention to working out the categories foundational to Christian theology. Two aspects of this achievement merit attention: the manner of self-appropriation, whereby Rahner derives theological categories; and the eminent usefulness of the categories suggested by Rahner.

Firstly, then, Rahner operates in the manner of a self-appropriation of his Christian religious experience. His first level of reflection *(erste Reflexionsstufe)* is a matter of heightening consciousness, of bringing to light an experience that is simply experienced (conscious) but not adverted to, not questioned, not interpreted, and not known. Accordingly, Rahner's *erste Reflexionsstufe* is remarkably similar to the sort of reflection that Lonergan names generalized empirical method. Probably the main difference between the two types of reflective thinking lies in the fact that Lonergan's method is in fact generalized, while Rahner's *erste Reflexionsstufe* is formulated in specifically religious and theological categories. To put this in another way, Lonergan's generalized empirical method is the work of a methodologist, uncovering the core of conscious and intentional operations common to all human enquiry including theological

---

[30] Ibid., p. 292.
[31] See ibid., p 282.

reflection; Rahner's first level of reflection is the work of a theologian, objectifying conscious intentionality in specifically religious and theological categories. For this reason Rahner may be considered an example of what it means to be engaged in the functional specialty, "foundations"; he is concerned with theological method as praxis and, indeed, as praxis in its foundational function.

Secondly, the categories derived by Rahner for Christian theology seem to be eminently useful and comprehensive. One has only to study the massive extent of Rahner's writings over the years to confirm this fact and to find the categorical structures of a Christian theology that is truly a theological anthropology. Moreover, Rahner himself has given this structure a coordinated integration in his *Foundations of Christian Faith,* that moves from human religious experience to the other-worldly source of that experience, to the revealed Word of Jesus Christ interpreting that experience, and to the togetherness in community of those bearing witness to Christ in the world. All this provides Christian theology with a solid core of foundational categories that will help theologians to take a stand on what is authentic in the Christian tradition and to mediate this tradition to the whole of human affairs.

I am suggesting, then, that Rahner's first level of reflection is coextensive with Lonergan's notion of the functional specialty "foundations". I should perhaps add that foundations, as a functional specialty, stands within the context of method as history and method as dialectic. It seems to follow, then, that Rahner's work might eventually be understood as complementary to that of theologians concerned with factual and evaluative history. This would allow Rahner's first level of reflection to be situated *methodically* within the context of the Christian tradition — a need that has been indicated by many commentators of Rahner's thought.[32]

In light of these admittedly brief and incomplete remarks, it is possible to resolve some of the problems that Rahner has with Lonergan's notion of method in theology.[33] Rahner's criticism was occasioned by the publication in *Gregorianum* of Lonergan's chapter from *Method in Theology* on functional specialties.[34] This occurred

---

[32] For example, see P. Eicher, *Offenbarung: Prinzip...,* pp. 419-421; ibid., "Du sollst Dir kein Bildnis machen. Möglichkeiten und Grenzen theologischer Anthropologie heute", in G. Bitter and G. Miller, eds. *Konturen heutiger Theologie* (Munich: Kösel, 1976), pp. 34-36. Also, B. Wenisch, "Zur Theologie Karl Rahners", in *Münchener theologische Zeitschrift* 28 (1977):383-97; A. Schilson and Walter Kasper, *Christologie im Präsens* (Freiburg: Herder, 1974), pp. 80-89.

[33] See Karl Rahner, "Some Critical Thoughts on 'Functional Specialties in Theology' ", in McShane, ed., *Foundations of Theology,* pp. 194-96.

[34] See Bernard Lonergan, "Functional Specialties in Theology", in *Gregorianum* 50 (1969):485-504.

prior to the appearance of *Method in Theology,* and the article was accompanied by a note to the effect that "functional specialties" was to be the second chapter of Lonergan's book, following an initial chapter on "method" as generalized. This led Rahner to wonder about the specifically religious, Christian, and theological dimensions of Lonergan's theological method: for Lonergan to "leap" directly from generalized empirical method to the structural organization of theology into functional specialties left unanswered the crucial question about the *proprium* of theology and, secondly, about the *proprium* of Christian theology.

After the appearance of his article in *Gregorianum,* and prior to the publication of *Method in Theology,* Lonergan seems to have acknowledged the legitimacy of such criticism. To highlight the *proprium* of theology, Lonergan made the chapter on "functional specialties" the *fifth* chapter of *Method in Theology,* preceded now by chapters on generalized empirical method, the human good, meaning, and religion. Thus, the relevance of generalized method to theology is clarified by formulating a notion of method in theology in terms of reflection on *religion,* thereby highlighting the *proprium* of theology amidst the various academic disciplines. Lonergan himself clarified this further in an interview in which he directly referred to the criticism of Rahner. I wish to quote this clarification at some length for it treats, not only the *proprium* of theology, but also the crucial distinction between methodology and theology:

> To the question whether *Method in Theology* was restricted to theology or to a particular theology Fr. Lonergan replied:
>
> "Karl Rahner, in his paper, remarked he thought it could be applied to any human science that was fully conscious of itself as depending on the past and looking towards the future. I think that's true. But I'm not working it out in those terms. I'm working it out in terms of a theology. That chapter on functional specializations is not going to be chapter two (as was said a year and a half ago when I sent this paper to *Gregorianum*) it's chapter five now. The four background chapters are: 'Method', 'The Human Good', 'Meaning', and 'Religion'. So it's a theology because it's a reflection on religion, as said in *Functional Specialties.*
>
> Now it is doing *method* in theology; it is *not* doing theology. It aims at avoiding settling any theological question. Is it the Koran? Or the Old Testament? Or the Old and the New? Or the Old and the New and the Fathers? Or does it include the whole Christian tradition? Those are questions that theologians have to settle. I'm not going to settle them. So it's a structure, and you can have an analogy to it in Piaget's *Le Structuralisme* — a very thin little book in which he conceives this structuralism as a matter of interdependent, self-regulating, ongoing process.

> The eight functional specialties are a set of self-regulative, ongoing, interdependent processes. They're not stages such that you do one and then you do the next. Rather you have different people at all eight and interacting. And the interaction is not logical. It's attentive, intelligent, reasonable, responsible, and religious. The responsibility includes the element not only of morality but also of religion. I conceive religion as total commitment."[35]

Lonergan, then, says that his notion of functional specialization, as set forth in *Method in Theology,* is theological inasmuch as the various specialties are integral components in the process of reflecting on religion. Properly understood, Lonergan's notion of religion can be related to Rahner's demand for a *theological* method — a method that takes account of the "formal object" that distinguishes theology as properly "discourse about God as such". According to Lonergan, the specifically theological principle is religious conversion — the gift of God's love resulting in the free and total commitment of a person. It is what Rahner names "mystery", and it is what both Lonergan and Rahner understand to be the source and goal of reflection on religion.

It would seem, then, that there is a fundamental agreement between Lonergan and Rahner concerning the meaning of a method that is specifically theological. Both agree that when one conceives theology in terms of material and formal objects, a discipline is "theological" when it treats of God and of all things in relation to God. But Lonergan would add that when one shifts to a new key, to method — attending both to objects and to reflecting subjects — then the religious dimension of a theologian's horizon has to be taken into account. Hence, a discipline will be theological, not just because it reflects on God, but also because the theologian is operating on the basis of religious conversion — something that makes reflection on God profoundly meaningful. Nor is it likely that Rahner himself would disagree with this attention to the theologian as religious subject, for his first level of reflection is simply the effort of a religious subject to articulate her or his own existential reality, in light of a given religious tradition.

This mention of religious tradition, however, raises the second criticism by Rahner of Lonergan's theological method. For Rahner, theology has a specifically Christian dimension, centered on a unique relationship to the concrete person of Jesus Christ as a proper "material object" in theology.

---

[35]. Bernard Lonergan, "An Interview with Fr. Bernard Lonergan, S.J.", in W. F. J. Ryan and B. J. Tyrrell, *A Second Collection: Papers by Bernard J. F. Lonergan, S. J.* (London: Darton, Longman and Todd, 1974), pp. 210-11.

In this regard, Rahner is quite correct in designating the chapter on "functional specialties" as not specifically concerned with the *proprium* of Christian theology. Lonergan's self-understanding is that of a methodologist, and not that of a theologian. Thus, the various functional specialties could be applied to reflection on any of mankind's religious traditions, to the extent that these traditions sought an understanding of their past in order to guide their future.[36] Again, even the published *Method in Theology,* that was not available when Rahner wrote his criticism, cannot be said to be centered on the *proprium* of Christian theology; rather, Lonergan is very much concerned to present a notion of theology that stresses, and builds on, what is common to the great religions of mankind, thereby paving the way for dialogue among these religions and among their theologians.

The question, then, as to the *proprium* of specifically Christian theology is a question that is not answered by Lonergan in any explicit fashion in his *Method in Theology.* It would, however, be wrong to conclude that Lonergan denies a *proprium* to Christian theology. He readily acknowledges that there is a distinctive dimension to Christianity not found in other world religions; that distinctive component is not some original philosophy of life, not some original ethical code, but rather the fact that God's grace is given in Christ Jesus — something that Karl Rahner has himself emphasized.[37] This means, for Lonergan, that the religious experience of the Christian is specifically distinct from religious experience generally, inasmuch as Christian religious experience is intersubjective with Christ Jesus confessed as God.[38] For Lonergan, accordingly, Christian theology is distinct from non-Christian theologies to the extent that the former is a reflection on specifically Christian religious experience from within the specifically Christian religious tradition. But Lonergan himself has not given a great deal of attention, in his formal publications, to the derivation of the categories appropriate to specifically Christian theology. Hence, in discussing specifically theological categories, he refers to a first set of categories being derived from religious experience, and does not refer explicitly to that specific religious experience intersubjective with Christ Jesus. He mentions a second set of categories that is concerned with the togetherness of the religious community, but does not explicitly advert to the Christian

---

[36] See Bernard Lonergan, "Bernard Lonergan Responds", in McShane, ed., *Foundations of Theology,* p. 233.

[37] See Bernard Lonergan, "The Future of Christianity", in Ryan and Tyrrell, eds., *A Second Collection,* p. 156.

[38] See Bernard Lonergan, *Philosophy of God, and Theology* (London: Darton, Longman and Todd), 1973, p. 67.

church. In noting a third set of categories, concerned with the source of religious experience, Lonergan explicitly mentions that he is drawing upon the Christian tradition by identifying this source in trinitarian terms.[39] Other examples could be given, but Lonergan's intention is obvious. Without at all denying the *proprium* of Christian theology, and urging the need for specifically Christian theological categories, he quite simply has written about a notion of theology that would first establish a basis of dialogue and cooperation, before moving into the properly theological issues of what is unique in each religious tradition.

I have been discussing two aspects of the criticism voiced by Rahner about Lonergan's notion of method in theology. On the one hand, such criticism was perhaps unavoidable and to some degree legitimate in light of the ambiguity surrounding the placement of Lonergan's chapter on "functional specialties" within his theological method. On the other hand, Lonergan in fact understands his method to be specifically theological, inasmuch as it is a reflection on religion. Further, there is the possibility, not worked out by Lonergan, of developing the categories appropriate to a specifically methodical and *Christian* theology — drawing upon the Christian tradition and upon specifically Christian religious experience. Finally, it was noted that this latter task is assigned by Lonergan to Christian theologians working in foundational theology, and I have suggested that Karl Rahner might be considered paradigmatic among those theologians concerned with working out the categories central to a specifically Christian theology.

In Rahner, then, there seems to be an example of what Lonergan means by a theologian who takes a methodical stance on religious, moral, and cognitional authenticity, and who objectifies this horizon, employing it as the normative and critical foundation for mediating the Christian tradition to the world of today. It is clear, however, that Rahner is chiefly concerned with the *foundations* of theology as praxis. This is a key element in contemporary theology, yet the foundational is but one of many theological tasks. Indeed, one of the main benefits of Lonergan's work is precisely to highlight the uniqueness of each specialty in theology, yet also its need for further completion by other specialties. In a word, not only does foundational theology presuppose history and dialectic; as well, it is followed by further specialties that relate theological praxis to its concrete historical and cultural contexts. Such further specialties will function all the more effectively, the more they build on a foundational theology seeking to further the insights of both Karl Rahner and Bernard Lonergan.

---

[39] See Bernard Lonergan, *Method in Theology,* pp. 290-91.

The Historian of Religions and the Theologian: Dialectics and Dialogue

by Vernon Gregson

The relationship between history of religions and theology is a sensitive one.[1] For the theologian, coming to terms with the history of religions is not only an instance of the difficult task of situating empirical studies in relation to faith, but it is especially the difficulty of integrating a discipline which appears to challenge, even if only implicitly, any exclusivist claims of one's own and of any one particular faith. The problem for the theologian is further exacerbated by the reductionist tendencies of some of the schools of the sciences used in the history of religions, e.g., psychology, history, and sociology. Theologians, then, are wary of the entrance of an apparently alien and threatening body of knowledge. The historians of religion, on the other hand, are frequently not interested in correlating their scientific and "objective" discipline with the obvious "subjectivity" of theology.[2] The theological question is also not immediately or clearly relevant to their work.

I have located the problematic status of the relationship between the history of religions and theology in the practitioners of the two disciplines, for disciplines cannot cooperate, only people can. What impedes working correlation between the two disciplines is that too few persons have been interested in the sets of questions asked by each, and thus have been unable to formulate the questions which

---

[1] Cf. Joachim Wach, "The Place of the History of Religions in the Study of Theology," *Types of Religious Experience* (Chicago: The University of Chicago Press, 1951); Wilfred Cantwell Smith, "Comparative Religion: Whither—and Why?" in *The History of Religions: Essays in Methodology,* ed. by Mircea Eliade and Joseph M. Kitagawa (Chicago: The University of Chicago Press, 1959); Bernard Lonergan, *Religious Studies and/or Theology,* The Donald Mathers Memorial Lectures presented at Queens University, Kingston, Ontario, 1976, unpublished.

[2] Smith, "Comparative Religion," pp. 44-45.

would lead an individual from one to the other and back again. The history of religions has been for some an alternative to theology and theology has frequently not experienced the need for, or has been fearful of, history of religions.

There are surely sets of questions proper to each.[3] And those questions of fact and of value are not on the face of it incompatible. When we have a stand-offishness of these two disciplines it is frequently because the horizon of faith is unable to cope with the horizon of modern scientific and historical consciousness, and the horizon of modern consciousness is indifferent to or lacking in comprehension of the horizon of faith. A general merging of horizons is still only dawning. Bernard Lonergan's work offers much to one who would attempt such a merger. So does the work of Joachim Wach and Wilfred Cantwell Smith. In the following reflections I will rely on each of them. In the first case, we have a theologian open to the history of religions. In the second, we have historians of religion open to theology.

To write of a merging or fusing of horizons on the part of the theologian and the historian of religion is not to advocate a drawing back from the hard-won separation and distinction of disciplines. That would be all loss and yet the same person can (and should?) ask both sets of questions and hence can discover how they do indeed correlate with one another. Only chaos would result from confusing the sets of questions proper to each discipline.

I. The Horizon of History of Religions

The dispute—mostly resolved now—about what to call the scientific study of religions,[4] highlights a significant facet of the perspective operating in the discipline. The scientific discipline which has developed is by strict intent descriptive and not evaluative. Typologies are indeed employed to relate the various constellations of characteristics of one religion to another—organizational, cultic, doctrinal patterns, etc.—and in that sense comparison is used. But comparison here is a method which serves for greater clarity of description and is not intended to be value laden. Value questions are not denied; they are simply not asked in the discipline.

The questions which are operative in the scientific study of religion are "What is...?" questions,[5] rather than "How do I evaluate

---

[3] Wach, "The History of Religions," pp. 27-29.

[4] Joseph Kitagawa, "The History of Religions in America," *The History of Religions,* p. 15.

[5] These questions particularly relate to the goals of the disciplines which Lonergan calls respectively, research, interpretation and history; cf. Bernard Lonergan, *Method in Theology* (New York: Herder and Herder, 1972), pp. 149-234.

what is?" questions.⁶ "What is?" questions do not demand on the part of the inquirer adherence to a religion. And in fact if the inquirer did adhere to a religion he would have to prescind from — not deny — the value judgments of his religion in his descriptive work.⁷

"What is?" questions do not imply the invalidity of further questions, nor do the further religious questions imply the invalidity or uselessness of "What is?" questions. In fact the further religious questions presuppose answers to the "What is?" questions for the integrity of their own answers.

Historians of religion are "modern" persons. The sets of questions which they ask have only become precise through the development of the various sciences. Their techniques are shared with or borrowed from other scientific disciplines.⁸ What is unique to them is the data they deal with and the perspective from which they deal with it. As to their attitude toward the data, an openness toward the validity of religion would seem a prerequisite for understanding the uniqueness of the data involved. But in itself, the horizon necessary to engage in the history of religions does not logically demand that the historians have come to grips with questions of the type mentioned earlier: "Where do I stand personally with regard to what I have uncovered?" The impetus to the faith question, the theological question, does not derive from the demands of the discipline of history of religions but comes to the historians as persons facing the necessity of taking a stand with their lives.

In summary, the history of religions is an integral discipline in its own right. There is a horizon of questions proper to it. That horizon is available to modern historical and scientific consciousness. That horizon does not logically demand or presuppose a religious or faith horizon on the part of the historians of religion. A failure to have an empathy for the religious horizon, however, can block insight into the unique data being dealt with.

II. The Horizon of Theology

If the horizon of the historians of religion methodologically

---

⁶ Decisional questions relate to the disciplines Lonergan calls dialectics and foundations. Dialectics evaluates the past, foundations expresses the value positions now chosen; cf. Lonergan, *Method,* pp. 235-93.

⁷ "While these commitments are bound to color his understanding to some extent, he can make an effort to distinguish in his own mind between his commitments and his attempts to understand the conscious response of others. On the other hand, the illusion of complete non-involvement, with all the deceptions it nourishes, is more detrimental to objectivity than a lively sense of involvement controlled by the desire to understand." Benjamin Swartz as cited in Kitagawa, "The History of Religions in America," p. 28.

⁸ Lonergan, *Religious Studies,* pp. 54-58.

prescinds from a faith commitment, the horizon of the theologians is founded upon it. The theologian's faith stance establishes both the primary reality that he or she reflects on and the context—the community—within which he or she reflects. Historians of religion depend on modern scientific and historical consciousness for their horizon; theologians did not have to wait for this intellectual breakthrough to ply their trade, though today they ignore it at the peril of irrelevance and escapism. Theologians can and most frequently have operated from other intellectual horizons than historical consciousness. It is the faith stance which is the recurrent feature. The theologians' horizon is established intrinsically by their religious commitment itself and by the shared symbols and values of the community of which they are a part and upon which they reflect.[9]

Even such a preliminary contrast of horizons points out a built-in tension between the historian of religion and the theologian. For historians of religion do not need a faith commitment for their work and theologians do not depend, in principle, on modern scientific consciousness for theirs. And yet theologians as persons in the twentieth century must come to terms with historical consciousness both for the integrity of their personal development as well as to communicate to those who have developed historical consciousness; and the historians of religion need to adopt a stance toward faith not for the sake of their discipline but for their own sake. The questions raised by the history of religion call for answers which the historians of religion can dodge only at the price of their own authenticity. The tension between historians of religion and theologians does not come, then, from their having adopted *incompatible* horizons, but only from their limiting themselves to their own horizons.

Another source of tension is the particularity of theologians. It is true that simply by their religious horizon theologians share an analogous perspective with all believers in any religion, for they and all believers are functioning as such not at the level of intellectual or moral or aesthetic consciousness but at the plane of radical openness to the Ultimate which characterizes religious consciousness. But religious consciousness is always embodied, always concrete. Theologians are opened to it through the images, symbols, teachings of those to whom they are exposed. They also do their own reflection and express their own faith in concrete symbols. Theologians do not create the symbols of their faith nor can they alter them alone or at will. Theologians both receive their faith from and express it in a

---

[9] Lonergan, *Religious Studies,* p. 65.

community.[10] Theologians' symbols are always the particular ones of their community — even when they are expanding the horizon and enriching the symbols of the community. The historian of religion's field of vision, on the other hand, includes in principle all the particular religious symbols of every community. Theologians must integrate and adopt affectively and personally the symbols that they employ. Historians of religion do not integrate and adopt all of the symbols they analyze and examine. They cannot and their work does not call for it. They need not resolve multiplicity, they must only accurately describe it. With this understanding the apparent confinement of the theologian, in contrast to the openness of the historian, can be appreciated. For the theologian's task is to integrate and not only to analyze.

Perhaps an example will clarify this difficult matter further. It is one thing to know a particular language and quite another to know the structure of language. The historians of religion must know the general structure of religion (language) and of a number of particular religions (languages); they need not as historians engage in any one religion (language) or still less create a new religion (language) which combines all the religions (languages) that they know. Theologians as such need not know the general structure of religion (language) or of more than one particular religion (language), but they must practice a religion (language).

It might help to pursue our language analogy a bit further to avoid the possible implication that there are absolute and *a priori* boundaries between languages (religions). History bears out that there is no such thing. New languages do emerge from the commerce of people. Indeed, new religions arise and religions in proximity to one another experience the influence of one another. There are no *a priori* limits on how languages or religions might change. There are, however, the present actual states and the past actual states of different religions which historians of religions do describe and analyze. And there are the present actual horizons of the religions theologians belong to, however much they may be intending or succeeding in broadening those horizons. One must not lose sight of either element, the actual or the potential in a religion.

It is beyond the human capacity of theologians to achieve in themselves the lived integration of all religions. Even if one world religion were a possible or even ideal goal, it would also be the work of centuries and of generations of believers. This clearly does not mean that theologians should not take the lead in opening the horizons of their religion to the religious values of other faiths. In-

---

[10] Ibid.

deed, they should and must. But they cannot do the impossible. They must enrich their own communities and not isolate themselves by moving completely out of the religious horizon of their communities.

The historian of religion is under no such burden of personal synthesis, simply as historian. Faced, however, with taking up a life-stance toward religion, historians would encounter in this dimension of their lives the same particularizing and enrichment as the theologian. And it would indeed be enrichment. For there is an arbitrary and unnatural confinement in limiting oneself to "What is?" questions and not asking the further "Where do I stand?" questions. Asking both sets of questions does not mean confusing them. Each set pertains to a different horizon. But there is every reason for a person to exist on both planes since both correspond to genuine human capacities and aspirations.

If the historian of religion is enriched by asking value questions, so is the theologian enriched by asking descriptive religious questions. That they have not in fact often let themselves be so enriched is a lamentable aspect of much of even current theology.

In summary, the theological horizon is quite as valid as the horizon of the historian of religion. The one is essentially grounded in a faith-stance, the other must prescind from such a stance. The historians of religion have done their work when they have arrived at accurate description and understanding. The theologians, on the other hand, must take a position on what they have understood about religion, and they must reflect on the nature and consequences of their stand and of the stand of the communities in which they participate. The history of religions is not an intrinsic constituent of the horizon of the theologian. Its methods and results, however, can enrich the theological horizon by providing the broadest possible base for the theologian's own decisions and by illuminating structural elements of religion. Historically the theologian often has been reluctant to accept that broader base and the historian of religion has often shied away from the particularity consequent upon taking a faith stance. The breadth afforded by the history of religions has yet to be adequately received by theology.

III. The Horizon of Dialectics

We have pinpointed the basic experience which grounds theology as "taking a faith-stance," being converted. If the historian of religion has not taken a faith-stance, he or she cannot operate in the horizon of theology. We have also described what would principally accrue to both the theologians and the historians of religion if they were also able to function on the other horizon. Something more needs to be said, however, about the evaluative horizon which can mediate between theology and the history of religions. Lonergan refers to this level as "dialectics."[11] It partakes of some of the qualities of each but can rightly be called a separate horizon. It is more than descriptive but it is still preparatory to adopting a faith stance or operating in one. It does involve a comparing and contrasting of religions, not for descriptive purposes but as evaluation. Its questions are, "What are the weaknesses and strengths of individual religions?", "What is at the core of religions?", "What elements are simply cultural particularizations and what incompatible features of different religions?" These questions are more than merely descriptive. They provide the intelligent mediating step between descriptive history of religions and normative theology.

The horizon of dialectics is a little developed one and yet an obviously crucial one if the horizons of the theologian and of the historian of religion are to be merged and the riches of one pass to the other. Historians need to evaluate before they can commit themselves. But how are they to do that evaluation without asking some such questions? Theologians must likewise evaluate and compare the different religions if they are to let them enrich rather than confuse their own theological horizon.

The frequent dichotomy between the faith horizon and historical consciousness has prevented the adequate development of this horizon of dialectics, yet it is precisely this horizon which can mediate between the other two. The historians are reluctant to evaluate lest they appear to compromise the objectivity of their descriptive work. The theologians are reluctant to compare their religion with other religions lest they seem to relativize their own faith position.

The development of this dialectical discipline does not become the less necessary, however, because it becomes the more difficult. Its necessity comes not primarily because of the existence of a lacuna between two disciplines but from the more basic human drive to ask all relevant questions. Its necessity comes from the logic of the progression of the mind's own inquiry: "What is it?" "What is significant about it?" "Where will I stand toward it?" The development of this discipline will help to fulfill this human and scientific gap. It will likewise save the theologian and the historian from the compromise they rightly seek to avoid. Bernard Lonergan has done significant work to flesh out this new discipline, to open up the new horizon.

A specific point of exegesis of Lonergan might serve to further

---

[11] Lonergan, *Method*, pp. 235-66.

clarify the discipline of dialectics. Lonergan indicates that religious conversion is not necessary to engage in dialectics or in the three prior specialties of research, interpretation, and history.[12] But he means that in a very precise sense. He does not mean that it is indifferent whether one is converted or not. What he says is that conversion "does not constitute an explicit, established, universally recognized criterion of proper procedure in these specialties."[13] Lonergan chooses his words carefully. Conversion is not part of the "procedure" in doing research or writing history, even the history of religions. It is certainly not "explicitly" and "universally" acknowledged as a "criterion" in those disciplines. The religiously indifferent write history as well as the religiously committed. And of course commitment to a religion does not by itself imply the full meaning of self-transcendence which is Lonergan's understanding of conversion. And non-commitment to specific beliefs does not mean the absence of such religious self-transcendence. One cannot deny the name history to what an historian whom one considers to be unconverted has written. However, for Lonergan, conversion means the long process of overcoming of one's biases: intellectual, moral, psychic, and religious; and to be unconverted means to be operating out of one's biases, and most probably out of unacknowledged biases.[14] To be unconverted does not mean that *one's procedures* are unsophisticated but that *one's ability* to acknowledge the data, to interpret it with understanding, and to evaluate it accurately can be sorely askew. These are not irrelevant dimensions to the value of a work. Lonergan is simply then acknowledging facts when he says, "anyone can do research, write history, line up opposed positions."[15] His own words acknowledge some place for conversion, but he seems to downplay it: "when conversion is present and operative, its operation is implicit: it can have its occasion in interpretation, in doing history, in the confrontation of dialectic."[16] I would interpret his remark about conversion having "its occasion" as having two purposes. One is simply to recognize that history is indeed written from all imaginable perspectives. Conversion has its occasion but non-conversion also has its occasion. The second purpose is that in the later disciplines of dialectics and foundations biased perspectives from the writing of history can in principle be exposed and rooted out. In other words, there is a discipline which is capable of

---

[12] Lonergan, *Method*, p. 268.
[13] Ibid.
[14] Cf. Lonergan, *Method*, p. 53-55; for a thorough development, cf. Bernard Lonergan, *Insight: A Study of Human Understanding*, (New York: Philosophical Library, 1958), pp. 218-44.
[15] Lonergan, *Method*, p. 268.
[16] Ibid.

evaluating history and which attempts to overcome the effects of biases or distorted viewpoints. The evaluative perspective in dialectics is precisely based on the criteria of the conversions: religious, psychic, moral, intellectual authenticity.[17]

Anyone who can write the following about conversion and about horizons, which the conversions or the lack of them open or close us to, cannot be indifferent to the presence or absence of conversion in those who do history of religions or the history of Christianity.

> Conversion, as lived, affects all of a man's conscious and intentional operations. It directs his gaze, pervades his imagination, releases the symbols that penetrate to the depths of his psyche. It enriches his understanding, guides his judgments, reinforces his decisions.[18]
>
> ...horizons may be opposed dialectically. What for one is found intelligible, in another is unintelligible. What for one is true, for another is false. What for one is good, for another is evil.[19]
>
> Horizons then are the sweep of our interests and of our knowledge; they are the fertile source of further knowledge and care; but they also are the boundaries that limit our capacities for assimilating more than we have already attained.... What does not fit will not be noticed, or if forced to our attention, it will seem irrelevant or unimportant.[20]

Historians whose eyes and hearts are not open to what is can hardly accurately present or interpret reality in their writings.

But if I understand why Lonergan in the interest at least of common usage indicates that historians in their work need not be converted, I would take exception to his statement that conversion is also not necessary, though doubtless helpful, in dialectics. "Anyone can...line up opposed positions." Yes, anyone can, but if the procedure is not to be a method which can be performed by rote, and particularly if the procedure of dialectics is to line up positions on the basis of the intellectual, moral, religious, and psychic conversions involved, those same conversions to some degree would seem to be prerequisite for performing the task at all adequately. Admittedly

---

[17] "Not only do the transcendental notions (the intelligible, the true, the good) promote the subject to full consciousness and direct him to his goals. They also provide the criteria that reveal whether the goals are being reached. The drive to understand is satisfied when understanding is reached but is dissatisfied with every incomplete attainment and so is the source of ever further questions. The drive to truth compels rationality to assent when evidence is sufficient, but refuses assent whenever evidence is insufficient. The drive to value rewards success in self-transcendence with a happy conscience." Lonergan, *Method*, p. 35.

[18] Ibid., p. 131.
[19] Ibid., p. 236.
[20] Ibid., p. 237.

dialectics as dialectics does not actually make choices among the horizons but simply exposes them. Still, without the conversions as a personal horizon, I fail to see how the dialectician can even accurately expose the positions. This point of the necessity of conversion in dialectics is important since unlike history which is an established discipline, dialectics is not established and it would be well in encouraging its development to indicate the irreplaceable necessity of the conversions and the role of subjectivity for performing it properly. One's horizon is important, and the more explicitly this can be acknowledged and the broader the values one is sensitive to, the more significant will be the work and the more liberating it will be for others.

IV. Dialectics and Dialogue

Beyond dialectics there is dialogue. Dialectics is the analysis and evaluation of the past, of others' actions and postures, in the light of one's own values. One must evaluate if one is to clarify one's own values in relation to the wisdom and foolishness which is one's own inheritance. But the emphasis in dialectics is best placed, I would suggest, not on critique of the past but on valuing the past. Dialectics is *e*-valuating, it is *co*-valuating, letting the values of the past reveal themselves and in the process letting one's own values come to light. Dialectics is best understood then as dialogue. One's own development is never complete. If the past stands in need of critique, which it does, so do you and I stand in need of critique. The humility which the fact of our own incompleteness, if not also our own willfulness, should engender is a dialogic rather than a dialectic stance toward the past. In dialogue, one can expect to be challenged by the values one had not yet discovered or perhaps had even uncrtically rejected. This is to be as much an expected part of the process of evaluating the past as the discovery that in the past certain values had been dismissed or not yet uncovered. "...the very people that investigate the dialectic of history also are part of that dialectic and even in their investigating represent its contradictions. To their work too the dialectic is to be applied." [21] And the dialectic which is healing is called dialogue. "While the dialectic of history coldly relates our conflicts, dialogue adds the principle that prompts us to cure them." [22] The disposition to dialogue is a precondition for an accurate and empathetic appreciation of the other's values and affirmations. But the disposition to dialogue is not only a precondition

---

[21] Bernard Lonergan, "Natural Right and Historical Mindedness" (unpublished, n.p., 1976), p. 20.
[22] Ibid.

for the understanding of the other, it is also the same disposition which allows one to grow in appreciation of one's own tradition and in the personal appropriating of that tradition. The disposition to dialogue is a value stance — as is also, obviously, the disposition not to dialogue — but the receptivity involved in a dialogical being-in-the-world indicates a growth posture. It acknowledges one's own historicity as well as that of one's partner and affirms not only that the past can be understood but that the future can be created out of the interchange.

Dialectics, then, is an evaluative discipline necessary both for the historian of religion and the theologian in order to mediate between their horizons. It needs a development comparable to the development in each of these disciplines since it too asks a significant set of human questions. It need not compromise either discipline since a merging of horizons does not mean a confusion about what question is being asked in what context but is simply the development of the latent ability to ask questions which are consequent upon one another. The authenticity of the person who attempts dialectics is even more important than the authenticity of those engaged in research, hermeneutics, and history. Dialectics come to full term will be dialogue not only with the past but with present exponents of different traditions. And the disposition to such dialogue will itself be the type of personal and communal achievement that will have already moved one beyond the past. Wilfred Cantwell Smith has strikingly expressed the direction of this cooperative movement: "The culmination of this progress (of dialogue) is when 'we all' are talking *with* each other about 'us.' "[23]

---

[23] Smith, "Comparative Religion," p. 34.

Religious Language and Theological Method: The Contribution of Horace Bushnell

by William Shea

Horace Bushnell (1802-1876) was, through his adult life, the pastor of a Congregationalist church in Hartford. By all accounts he was an active and attentive pastor. He was certainly an unusually talented man, one who stood quite self-consciously between his Puritan and Calvinist tradition and the new world of thought and action coming to birth in America. He made a unique contribution to the reshaping of the American Protestant doctrinal and theological tradition then under way. He has received insufficient scholarly attention from Protestant thinkers and almost none from Catholics. This essay attempts to call attention to his work on one key issue that is of concern to contemporary theologians, language theory and the foundations of theology. The essay proceeds under four headings: the context of his work; his position on language, religion, and theology; my own reservations and questions on his resolution of the problems; and the perduring implications and value of his work on the subject.

I. The Context

New England theology faced, in mid-nineteenth century, a doctrinal deadlock and a methodological deadend. Princetonian orthodox Calvinism, the Edwardsian theology of Yale, and Harvard Unitarianism, in their various hardened dogmatisms, their traditional attacks on one another, and their common and unwavering devotion to an unworkable theological method, presented a man of Horace Bushnell's intelligence and sensibilities no mean problem. New England and Bushnell needed a new theology and a new theological method.[1]

Secondly, Bushnell was a participant in the nineteenth century transcendental movement. He received his dose of Kant, Schelling, and Fichte through Schleiermacher and Coleridge. For Bushnell, as for the others, subjectivity became the key to the status of the object. However, Emerson's transcendentalism was not Bushnell's.[2] There was little of the nature-romantic in him, and none of the pagan. He was a much harder-headed person than the great blatherer from Concord, and a better philosopher and theologian. Bushnell's romanticism was more of the Coleridgean variety. He aimed at a theoretic recovery of the aesthetic values of the Christian tradition and an end to the Enlightenment ideal of detached and abstract Reason, a recovery and an end still devoutly wished by many of us today.

Thirdly, there were several theorists of language who agreed with Bushnell that the prevalent conception of language needed a critical overhaul, among them Roland Hazard, A. B. Johnson, Henry Goodwin, and Edwards Amasa Park of Andover Seminary.[3] The issue under debate can be put in two ways: is logic or poetry the basic form of human speech, or, is eloquence an adornment and a device or is it intrinsic to authentic human speech? The inherited Lockean and Scots Common Sense theories of language had given primacy to clear and simple ideas and to logic as hermeneutic, and relegated eloquence to entertainment.[4] Unless the hold of the

---

[1] Sydney Ahlstrom, *A Religious History of the American People* (New Haven: Yale University Press, 1972), 583-614. For the classic study, see: F. H. Foster, *A Genetic History of New England Theology* (New York: Russell and Russell, 1907).

[2] On Emerson see Joel Porte, *Representative Man: Ralph Waldo Emerson in His Time* (New York: Oxford University Press, 1979). The influence of Coleridge on both Emerson and Bushnell was large; see Ahlstrom, 599-613. Coleridge's theological position and contribution are matters of renewed interest to theologians; see the recent and, I suspect, definitive analysis by Stephen P. Happel, *The Function of Imagination in Religious Discourse: A Historical-Critical Study of the Theological Development of Samuel Taylor Coleridge* (doctoral dissertation, Faculty of Theology of the Catholic University of Louvain, 1977), 4 vols. For a study of the Coleridge-Bushnell relationship see Mildred Kitto Billings, *The Theology of Horace Bushnell Considered in Relation to that of Samuel Taylor Coleridge* (Doctoral dissertation, Chicago Divinity School, 1959).

[3] Rowland Hazard, *Essays on Language and Other Papers* (Boston: Phillips, Samson, & Co., 1857); A. B. Johnson, *A Treatise on Language,* ed. D. Rynin (Berkeley: University of California Press, 1959); Henry Goodwin, "Thoughts, Word, and Things," *Bibliotheca Sacra* VI (1849), pp. 271-300; and Edwards Amasa Park, "The Theology of Intellect and that of the Feelings," *Bibliotheca Sacra* VII (1850), pp. 533-39.

[4] On the background, see Donald A. Crosby, *Horace Bushnell's Theory of Language: A Historical and Philosophical Study* (doctoral dissertation, Columbia University, 1963), ch. V.

inherited view could be broken, New England theology would go to its grave along with the clarity and simplicity of New England logic.

Fourthly, the debate over the roots of religious faith between Enlightenment Reason and over-heated evangelical affections had preoccupied New England since Chauncy and Edwards had had their go a century before.[5] Bushnell, in his time, saw that the views of rationalist and conversionist theologies alike abandoned any adequate understanding of human experience. Against the Enlightenment he would insist that experience is the context for and referent of religious language, that the heart has reasons which may escape the notice of heartless Reason; and (with Edwards) that the proper and healthy life of reason in religion rests upon graced affections. Against the revivalists he retrieved a Catholic sense of the organic character of religious life, of nature and grace, of growth and continuity in spiritual life.

Finally, Bushnell's attack on the problem of language opened wide and definitively for American theology the issues of interpretation theory and theological method. Inserting himself between the schools of New England theology, he raised several basic questions: what kind of speech is religious language? How shall it be interpreted? What is the subject-matter for theological reflection? Of what use is theology? What are its conditions and limits? In his attempt to answer such questions he forced upon American theology Herder's insight that the Bible is poetry. He made it unmistakeably clear that aesthetics is crucial to theology. And he began the long, uneven, and as yet incomplete transcendental turn in the American conception of theology.

Several things about Bushnell's life are worth keeping in mind. He was himself an evangelical. There was his conversion in a Yale revival in 1831 and his subsequent application for ministerial studies at the Divinity School. In 1849 he underwent a second spiritual experience in which, according to his wife, he "saw the gospel," and received a "clearer knowledge of God and his inspirations, which I have never wholly lost. The change was into faith—a sense of the freeness of God and the ease of approach to Him."[6] Within the year

---

[5] The two works which cast the debate on the Great Awakening into its definitive form for a century of New England theology are: Jonathan Edwards, *Some Thoughts Concerning the Present Revival of Religion in New England* (Boston: 1742); and Charles Chauncy, *Seasonable Thoughts on the State of Religion in New England* (Boston: 1743). The question at stake is whether religion is grounded in affectivity or moral reason.

[6] For the description and an affectionate portrayal of her father's life, see Mary Bushnell Cheney, *Life and Letters of Horace Bushnell* (New York: Scribners', 1905). For a biography see Barbara M. Cross, *Horace Bushnell: Minister to a Changing America* (Chicago: Chicago University Press, 1958).

he published *God in Christ* and became the center of yet another New England theological debate.[7]

At Yale Bushnell was instructed by Nathaniel Taylor in a liberal understanding of grace and sin.[8] He was deeply moved by his second reading of Coleridge's *Aids to Reflection* (he was mystified by the first—a not uncommon experience) and by Schleiermacher. These are among the major theological influences on his language theory and theology. It is also probable that he read and possible that he was influenced by Emerson's essay on language, although he does not mention Emerson in connection with language theory.[9]

His pastoral concern for his strife-torn Hartford congregation and for the other congregations of New England gave impetus to his search for a theology which would transcend the impasse of literalist use of Scripture.

Finally, together with several other reformers of the Calvinist tradition such as Charles Grandison Finney and the Arminian evangelicals, Ralph Waldo Emerson and the other transcendentalists, and William Ellery Channing and the Unitarians, Bushnell attempted to overthrow the nature-supernature dualism that had been so powerfully and effectively symbolized for the Puritan ancestors in the doctrines of limited election and predestination.[10] Like Finney, Bushnell taught that grace is given to all. Like Emerson, he reconstituted nature as the locus and means of salvation, and was driven to a doctrine of the symbolic character of scriptural language. Like the Unitarians, he understood that moral practice flowed from faith and built it up. Yet like the great Calvinist Jonathan Edwards, he turned to experience, individual and communal, for a source of cor-

---

[7] Ahlstrom, ibid. For discussions of Bushnell's doctrinal theology, see Crosby and James Edison Young, *The Expressionistic Theology of Horace Bushnell: A Study of the Approach, Grounding, and Form of his Theology* (Doctoral dissertation, University of South Carolina, 1968).

[8] On Bushnell and Taylor, see Ahlstrom, pp. 610-11. The visage of both men now adorn the walls of the Yale Divinity School refectory. If thinking shapes a face and portraits capture life, I regret that I cannot hear them both.

[9] Ralph Waldo Emerson, "Language" in *Nature: Addresses and Lectures* (Cambridge, Mass.: Riverside Press, 1883), 31-41. Edwards' work on language was not in print when Bushnell was writing the dissertation. See Edwards' *Images and Shadows of Divine Things,* ed. Perry Miller (New Haven: Yale University Press, 1948).

[10] Charles Grandison Finney, *Systematic Theology,* ed. J. H. Fairchild (Minneapolis: Bethany Fellowship, 1976). Finney was the major revivalist of the Second Great Awakening, the originator of the methods of revivals which still obtain, and a solid if not original theologian. See J. M. Cafone, *The Role of the Holy Spirit in the Theology of Charles Grandison Finney* (doctoral dissertation, Catholic University, 1978). William Ellery Channing founded the Unitarian Association; see his "Essence of the Christian Religion," in Sydney Ahlstrom, ed., *Theology in America: The Major Protestant Voices from Puritanism to Neo-Orthodoxy* (Indianapolis: Bobbs-Merrill, 1967), and Ahlstrom, *Religious History,* pp. 397-402.

rection of a tradition which had lost touch with American, and indeed, human experience. In effect, Bushnell wrote a concluding chapter to New England Calvinism and a long first chapter to the liberal tradition in American Protestant theology.[11]

II. Language, Religion, and Theology

The essays in Bushnell's *God in Christ* (1849) on the divinity of Jesus, the atonement, and the nature and function of dogma were delivered first as lectures at Yale, Harvard, and Andover. The three stand on their own as signal contributions to the development of American theology. But we are concerned with the introduction to *God in Christ*, "The Preliminary Dissertation on Language," and with Bushnell's views of language, religion, and theology.[12]

But first let us recall briefly Emerson's essay, "Language." For Emerson, words mean things. "Natural facts" meant by words can become "symbols of spiritual facts." Emerson maintained that images are derived from nature, and that spirit speaks to and of itself in terms of nature and "natural facts." Thus, though language in the first instance means things, it can mean spirit. When it does the latter it is metaphorical, analogical, poetical, and re-presentative.

Secondly, for Emerson poetry, proverb, the language of ordinary speech is basic; and language in its purest form arises from the experience of nature. While Emerson often echoes the standard Jacksonian anti-urban rhetoric in his praise of nature,[13] his position on the primacy of poetry in human discourse is a solid achievement of the Romantic era. Here both he and Bushnell owe much to Coleridge.[14]

Finally, for Emerson the whole of nature is a metaphor of spirit, human and divine. In this Bushnell would concur. Neither man is or pretends to be a metaphysician, yet this metaphysics of nature and spirit lies close behind their analyses of language.

---

[11] Ahlstrom, *Religious History*, p. 613.

[12] *God in Christ: Three Discourses Delivered at New Haven, Cambridge, and Andover, with a Preliminary Dissertation on Language* (Hartford: Brown and Parson, 1849). The three major positions of Emerson are taken up by Bushnell without attribution. A commentator explains Bushnell's uncharacteristic failure to mention Emerson by the fact that to each side of Bushnell's audience, orthodox and Unitarian, Emerson was a heretic; Crosby, ch. V.

[13] On the rhetoric, see Marvin Meyers, *The Jacksonian Persuasion: Politics and Belief* (Stanford: Stanford University Press, 1957).

[14] To Coleridge they may owe as well their affirmation of the moral condition on authentic understanding and speech. Both men aimed at recovering the moral foundations of primary and reflective language.

With Emerson, Bushnell holds that language is natural, not artificial; social, not individual. Noun is the basic form, denotation the basic operation. Words mean things (nouns) or the qualities of things (adjectives). Verbs are the "nouns of actions," adverbs their qualities. Again, with Emerson, Bushnell affirms that the key human moment in language, differentiating it from the noises of animals, is self-presentation through named things and named acts which offer the possibility of self-reference. Words, then, not only mean things and acts; they can mean the self, or spiritual meanings: "there is a vast analogy in things," writes Bushnell, "which prepares them, as forms, to be signs or figures of thoughts" and there is a "Logos in the outward world, answering to the logos or internal reason."[15] Internal states are mediated by gestures and named things. The word and its associated image mediate self-understanding.

Not only do things (or at least their image) come to be used reflexively through their words, but the grammar of a language answers to the "external grammar of creation." Nature shapes the grammar of any language, for the relations of things in space are mirrored in the structure of the grammar of the language for things — in prepositions and conjunctions. The relations of things in time shape the tenses of verbal speech. There is, according to Bushnell, a logos in the relations of things which structures human language: "The outer world which envelopes our being is itself language, the power of language." Nature is a "dictionary and grammar of thought."[16] Bushnell's Aristotelian metaphysical approach to grammar is complemented by a nod to Platonism: nature is the expression of God. Nature's intelligibility makes God unavoidable — He is immediately available in things and their relations and is mediated by their images.

For Bushnell, spirit, both human and divine, is immaterial or, in his usage, "formless." Both spirits are spoken or imaged in "forms." The term and its image, which directly and literally mean a thing presented to the senses, can by reflexive and metaphorical use mean an aspect of human and divine spirit. So we come to utter such words as in-sight, con-ception, in-spiration, and the term spirit itself. There is a "fitness" in the image, an "analogy" in things, which enables their metaphorical use, a fitness instinctively felt but which cannot be theoretically uncovered and justified.[17]

---

[15] *God in Christ*, pp. 76-77, 89. Note the peculiar usage of "form." It seems to mean body, material thing, and is distinguished from soul; e.g. "For the body is a living logos, added to the soul to be its form..."

[16] Ibid., p. 30. For the discussion of nature, language, and thought see especially pp. 16-38.

[17] Ibid., p. 89.

But images applied to spirit are always to some extent false, for the image is material and finite while spirit is infinite and formless. This constitutes the fatal threat to a literalist interpretation of religious language, and the necessity of dialectic and paradox to any true speech about spirit. Image must be balanced and contra-dicted by image.[18]

The language for spirit, then, is necessarily and invariably figurative, analogical, imaginative, symbolic. This is not to say that *some* words are figurative when so used. Language itself is figurative *whenever* used for spirit.[19] The theologian's mistake is to suppose that *some* linguistic usage in religious language is literal and some figurative. Theologians are thus trapped into logic. The deductive theological method is invalidated by the poetic nature of religious speech. For Bushnell, logic is a purely formal instrument, not actively intelligent and interpretative.[20] The proper language for spirit is poetry.

The Bible, then is truth poetically uttered. Even its historical parts tend to be poetical. It offers symbols, not proofs, a truth which contains its own evidence and "finds us."[21] Dogmatic and "scientific" (i.e., logical) theology is inadequate to the truth of Scripture, for Scripture's poetic truth fits neither logic nor theological "dialectics."[22]

In addition to the poetic character of language, another condition of understanding and interpretation obtains: history. Not only are primary religious language, creed, and doctrine poetry; they are the poetry in time and place. They cannot be mindlessly lifted from their time and place and repeated without awareness of their historical character. They divide communities rather than unite them unless their historical and symbolic status is recognized. Bushnell's solution: insist in doctrines and creeds that the language used stay close to ordinary and poetic usage, and let ten thousand creeds bloom![23]

The salvation for systematic theology, if indeed it can be saved, is abandonment of logic as method, an "aesthetic" turn in theological study, and a return to the practical situation of religious language use.[24] Theologians ought to affirm that the very possibility of theology rests on "the competence of natural man to understand spiritual things..." and in "an immediate, experimental knowledge of

---

[18] Ibid., pp. 93-94.

[19] Ibid., p. 87.

[20] Ibid., p. 95.

[21] Ibid., p. 75. the words are Coleridge's.

[22] "Dialectics" is used pejoratively and is equivalent to "logic"; for his favorable view of paradoxical speech, see ibid., p. 55.

[23] Ibid., p. 82-84.

[24] Ibid., p. 102.

God...."[25] The meaning of Scripture cannot be captured by logic but only by grace-inspired inquiry. Theological knowing rests on Christian loving. Is this a "mystical" teaching, asks Bushnell? Yes, but language itself is mystical: "...there is a mystic element, as there should be in what I have represented as the source of meaning in language...Man is designed, in his very nature, to be a partially mystic being; the world to be looked upon is a mystic world."[26]

There are several points in Bushnell's discussion of language on which I would like to make evaluative comments. First, I confess that I appreciate Bushnell's important, if brief and minor, excursion into metaphysics. On the one hand he must ground all his talk about analogy and about the mysterious correspondence between the language for objects and the language for spirit. He accomplishes this grounding operation by a fairly straightforward metaphysical argument, namely, that the very existence of the languages for spirit and objects demands as its condition of possibility a divinely established logos in things.[27] He establishes, then, that nature is God's self-expression. All grammars hinge for their possibility as well as their concrete structure on an eternal Speaker. On the other hand he argues, or better asserts, that God is immediately present to human experience in the experience of nature. On the surface it seems difficult to reconcile the argument with the claim of immediate presence; if the second, why the first? Yet Bushnell is following the time-honored and still utilized Christian apology to the effect that God is present to all experience but the content of none, and the equally time-honored methodological position that metaphysics thematizes the unthematic and immediate. What is immediate is taken-for-granted and unnoticed and in need of clarification. The metaphysical argument is needed in Bushnell, as I am convinced that it is needed in any theology which would avoid fundamental incoherence, and is carried off with a certain style and grace by a person whose abilities in metaphysics are clearly limited. And it is minor, a backdrop piece, a cast in the direction of consistency — which is exactly the way metaphysical arguments ought to be placed in theological work.

Secondly, on the significance of the language issue for theology, Bushnell was uncannily prescient. His discussion of the symbolic character of religious language and the central role he gives to metaphor in it anticipates by one hundred years the work of contem-

---

[25] Ibid., p. 103.
[26] Ibid., p. 104.
[27] Ibid., p. 30.

porary figures such as Paul Ricoeur.²⁸ And although Ricoeur's is by far the better run, the track is Bushnell's. So also with recent work on imagination in religion. Until fairly recently we do not have theologians such as Bushnell, Schleiermacher, and Coleridge who understand that religious language is initially imaginative, that the imagination's chief function is to give shape to the shapeless and possibility to the ideal. And again, in sharp contrast with many in his own age and in ours, Bushnell understood that the fundamental achievement of language is self-presentation. Let us listen to him on this:

> [Persons set to inventing language]...will be struggling out into speech, in the simplicity of children, guided not by reflection, but more by instinct. A very large share of the signs by which they interpret their thoughts one to another, will consist of bodily gestures and actions—all as natural to the internal activity as a blush, or any flush of passions, to the inner state, represented and depicted by it in the face. For the body is a living logos, added to the soul, to be its form, and play it forth into social understanding....The soul that is struggling to utter itself, flies to whatever signs and instruments it can find in the visible world, calling them in to act as interpreters, naming them at the same time, to stand, ever after, as interpreters in sound, when they are themselves out of sight.²⁹

Nature, then, is the self-expression, the self-presentation of God—and it becomes, in speech, the self-expression and self-presentation of human beings.

Bushnell's basis for a theology of revelation is quite secure. He achieved a balance rare in evangelical theology between nature and history as *loci* of God's revelation. As the cosmos is conceived as God's self-revelation, Christ is conceived as God's metaphor, His final figure of Himself in finite existence.³⁰ The conception is remarkably similar to that at work in Rahner's now classical essay, "The Theology of the Symbol."³¹

Bushnell's work, finally, might be considered apologetic but it is not defensive. Christianity, although in an organizational and intellectual miasma, was hardly at death's door in mid-nineteenth century New England. Nor is Bushnell's audience the cultured despisers that attracted Schleiermacher's attention. Rather, Bushnell is

---

²⁸ For an exposition of Ricoeur, see Camille Zaidan, *Ricoeur's Conception of Language and its Implications for Foundational Theology* (Doctoral dissertation, Catholic University, 1980).

²⁹ *God in Christ*, p. 23.

³⁰ *Building Eras in Religion* (New York: Scribner's, 1881), 249-285.

³¹ K. Rahner, "The Theology of Symbol," *Theological Investigations* 4 (Baltimore: Helicon, 1966), pp. 221-52.

addressing theologians of various shades who were ignorant in various ways of the questions and problems that undercut their every effort, their every remark on the nature and meaning of Christian speech. He was attempting not only to recover Christianity for his fellow Christians but, as well, with Coleridge and a few other Romantics, to recover consciousness for Christianity. For example, his work on the relation between the natural and the supernatural can, from this point of view, be understood as a root-and-branch rejection of the ontological dualism lying heavy on the back of the Christian church and as a redefinition of the supernatural as a moment in and facet of human experience.[32] In this world of nature, he taught, the supernatural is human freedom!

Again, in his attempt to redefine the relationship between feeling and thinking he joined both the Romantics and Jonathan Edwards in a rejection of Enlightenment Reason as an abstraction and situated human intelligence in its experiential and experimental context, that is, in relation to the moral, affective, and political context of human existence. In spite of his attacks on the "logikers" and on systematic theology, he can hardly be construed as anti-rational or even a-rational. He simply knew that the myth of the Enlightenment needed doing in.

And from this point of view one can understand a great deal of his work—on nature, family, ritual, biblical language, doctrines, and education—to be a recovery of symbolic consciousness for his colleagues and his people. However one may wish to argue with him on particulars, and I will, one cannot gainsay this remarkable effort by a New England pastor to flesh out in theory a brilliant insight, that symbol cannot be understood apart from its function in consciousness and that religious language is first "God's Gift to Our Imagination."[33]

III. Problems

But it is from this very point of view, which I believe best interprets Bushnell's work, that he can be most sharply criticized. In the transcendental turn, the turn to human consciousness as the context for interpretation of human speech and even the speech of God, the turn which Bushnell inaugurated in New England (if we except only Edwards' work on affection), there are some mistakes and a major failure.

---

[32] W. A. Johnson, *Nature and the Supernatural in the Theology of Horace Bushnell* (Studia Theologiae Ludensia # 24, 1963).

[33] *Building Eras*, pp. 249-85.

In the first place, and running against the main flow of his work, he is guilty of a verbal atomism parallel to the sense atomism of Locke and Hume. He gives a certain primacy to the "objective" in noun use. What nouns, what language, most basically means is "out there," what can be seen and pointed to, what can be demonstrated. Only the demonstrative use of language is literal; what cannot be designated by gesture must be imaged. And when imaged, meaning is no longer literal. It becomes impossible, then, to use language accurately to mean what cannot be seen. In effect, he gives primacy to the noun over the sentence, to the speech unit over human intentionality. Although he is clear that the poetic and the figurative use of language is the more valuable, he does not ask whether it is primordial. Although he knows that the intersubjective and communal functions of language are the more important, he does not ask whether they are the founding and grounding uses. His "first department" of language, the literal, is an abstraction. For language is intersubjective before it is objective, expressive before it is demonstrative, a sentence before it is a name, a judgment before it is a term. Language is a meaning *with* images before it is a meaning of images.

What lies behind Bushnell's position here? He thought that only a *datum* of sense can be meant literally, while *data* of consciousness, that is, what he called spiritual or intellectual, can only be dealt with metaphorically. Now to argue that the divine is "formless," that it does not and cannot become an "object" in the field of sense is one thing. To so argue leads one quite directly to a distinction in the way one speaks about the divine and the finite. But though one can argue that the acts of human consciousness never become objects in the field of sense, it is quite a different matter to claim that such acts can never become objects of inquiry and terms of an accurate use of language.

In an odd way, then, Bushnell was bound by a sensationalist theory of knowing: you know what you can see and point to but you can only guess at or imagine what you can't see. Yet Bushnell knew perfectly well that we do know the human and the divine spirits. Bushnell's affirmation is correct. But his technical unfolding of the grounds for his affirmation is faulty. Let us look at two small but significant cases of his mistake.

He remarks in reference to the metaphorical use of images for the world of spirit:

> ...there is always some reason in every form or image made use of, why it should be used; some analogical property or quality which we feel instinctively, but which wholly transcends speculative inquiry...it is the instinct of our nature to feel some

correspondence between these images and the states they represent. ...Here we come to our limit. All we can say is, that by a mystery transcending our comprehension, the Divine Logos, who is in the world, weaves into nature types or images that have an inscrutable relation to mind and thought. On the one hand, is form; on the other, is the formless. The former represents, and is somehow fellow to, the other; how, we cannot discover.[34]

This is, I think, a mystification. The possibility of metaphorical speech about the spiritual rests on a metaphysics too quickly done. And then a door to an examination of this mysterious analogy, this mysterious correspondence between objects and spirit, is too easily closed. If the language for spirit, whether human or divine spirit, is uncritically asserted to be unanalyzable, if the unknown remains unqualifiedly unknown or uncritically known by some direct and immediate insight, then have we moved the question of human consciousness and its knowledge of itself and the divine one step beyond the old dichotomy of reason and faith? Are we mired again in mystery and mystification?

Secondly, he asserts, in a discussion of the possibility of exact speech about human consciousness, that in "mental science" no exactness is possible, that words in such a science will only be shadows of the truth, and that only poets can provide us with any complete science of man.[35] What Bushnell himself does is provide a language theory based on philological and etymological studies and some very astute guesses at the role of imagination in human speech. Two questions must be asked: first, how is it that Bushnell is in the main so patently correct if exactness is impossible? The answer is that exactness is not at all impossible and Bushnell proves it by his performance. Second, we must ask whether a language theory can be grounded if there is no mental science. Now Bushnell meant by mental science the common sense introspection of the New England and British theologians and philosophers, the ones who expected to find "in there" what Hume said he could not find. Of course there can be no mental science if it is modeled after the physical sciences. Bushnell knew nothing of the human sciences of meaning; and nothing of the strides of his successors—Husserl on time-consciousness and intentionality, James on feeling and thinking, Dewey on scientific method, Lonergan on realms of meaning and interiority. These advances, now quite secure, indicate to all but the most obtuse positivists that mental science, while still difficult, is not at all

---

[34] *God in Christ,* pp. 42-43.
[35] Ibid., pp. 72-73.

impossible and is, in fact, essential to theory of language and to theological foundations.

In my view both the mystification of analogy and the denial of the possibility of mental science indicate that Bushnell's transcendental turn was incomplete. The heart of the question for one of Bushnell's position seems to be this: can human spirit and its operations be dealt with theoretically and accurately? Can the operations of consciousness, for Bushnell shrouded in mystery, be intended in inquiry and characterized accurately in theory? Or can we only vaguely and inconclusively allude to them? Bushnell would have it that a *datum* of sense can be meant literally, a *datum* of consciousness cannot, and so the latter must be imaged or analogued: the language for spirit is necessarily inexact, composed of images and figures only.[36]

On the level of religious language his solution to the question of how we can mean what we cannot point to is a dialectic of images and paradox which gives form to the Formless. The theory is fine. And, when complemented by a metaphysical argument for a referent of images and paradox, is acceptable. But does not the process of multiplication, complexification, and mutual correction of images require an informed intentionality? Bushnell's assumption, and his sometimes explicitly stated view, is that we do know whereof we imagine.[37] But how? And can the answer to this question be uncovered without a version of the mental science which Bushnell rejected? Even when we wholeheartedly agree with Bushnell that the truth cannot be grasped apart from images, neither is it grasped apart from questioning, understanding, reflecting, and judging. Bushnell hovered on the edge of a theory of the human subject, he crossed over into the realm of interiority and mental science with his work on imagination, but he hesitated. The logos in things requires a full study of the logos in human subjectivity if it is to be understood. The analyses of human intentionality that have filled our philosophic coffers over the past seventy-five years bring us nearer to the goal that Bushnell set for American theology, but by a route he thought closed.

IV. Implications

Bushnell singled out a pair of common viruses to which theologians are susceptible: self-defense which issues in dogmatism; and logical method which mistakes the very nature of religious speech and which, in the service of dogmatism, makes any genuine theological reflection impossible. Together they turn theology from a quest for understanding into a war—a war between confessional groups

---

[36] Ibid., pp. 72, 75-77.
[37] Ibid., pp. 55-56, 71.

and a war against the primacy of feeling and poetry in human life. This theology is a monster. Bushnell was skeptical about the possibility and the advisability of systematic theology, so choked was it by the biases and mistakes of its practitioners. Unsparing in his criticisms of and pleas to his Calvinist, Edwardsian, and Unitarian confreres, he wished to liberate theological inquiry from its self-imposed and self-destructive method. But more, he wished to liberate religious speech from its thraldom to theological logicians and credal dogmatists. From the charges he made and the pleas he uttered we have some few lessons to learn in our own situation.

In the first place, his charge is a moral one. Theological practice was immoral. It not only missed the point of religious language; it falsified it for the sake of self-protection and narrow group concerns. Such an immoral stand destroys the value of theology and throttles authentic religious language. The impoverished imagination and language he discovered among the Unitarians, for example, could be overcome only when the value of a common witness is put above the inner assuredness and religious gentility of Harvard Enlightenment rationality. Such a reshuffling of values implies a moral conversion, one which most of his theological colleagues refused. Bushnell recognized that there is a moral condition on authentic religious language and on theological language. He realized that since speech is first and finally self-presentation, the effectiveness of both religious and theological speech will depend largely on the self of the speaker. How, he would ask, can the unreflective and uncritical participant in an inherited version of the Christian language be expected to speak an authentic and authentically contemporary Christian language, or to speak about that language in an authentic theological discourse? Can anyone who puts the value of the survival of a religious and theological tradition above a common quest for truth or a common witness to the gospel, can such a one understand, speak, or, indeed, hear the gospel? Moral conversion from self-satisfaction, self-defense, and group bias is a condition for authentic religious and theological speech. Bushnell's own stand on the matter is clear:

> ...truth is to be gotten by a right beholding of the forms or images by which it is expressed. Ingenuity will miss it by overdoing; mere industry will do scarcely more than muddle it; only candor, a gracious open, clean candor will find it. We can take the sense of its images, only by offering a perfectly receptive imagination to them, a plate to fall upon that is flavored by no partisanship, corrugated by no bigotry, blotched by no prejudice or passion, warped by no self-will. There is nothing that we cannot make out of them, by a very little abuse, or perversity. They are innocent people who can never vindicate themselves when wronged, further than to simply stand, stand and

> wait for a more ingenuous beholding. And it is to be a very great part of our honor and advantage in the truth, that we have it by the clean docility and noble reverence that makes us capable of it. We shall not be afraid of worshipping its images; for they are not craven images, but faces that express the truth because they are the faces of God. We want, in fact, as a first condition, a mind so open to truth that our love and reverence shall open all our sympathies to it and quite indispose us to any violent practice on its terms.[38]

I do not recall any passage in Christian literature which better or more forcefully states the moral character of the theological enterprise.

Secondly, his charge against his contemporaries is aesthetic as well. The Unitarians and the Edwardsians alike had lost the Calvinist and Puritan sense of the glory and beauty of God, a sense so admirably and effectively put by Edwards himself in his *Treatise on Religious Affections* and the *Nature of True Virtue*.[39] The charge seems to me to be several-fold:

a. that religious language was aesthetically impoverished in the New England congregations;

b. that the theologians, even those flying Edwards' banner, failed to feel the beauty of God and the poetic power of Christian language;

c. that aesthetic, and not logical, criteria need to be brought to bear if the meaning of the Christian language is to be uncovered;

d. and that theology itself as a form of speech has an aesthetic character, any slighting of which turns it into a bore.

Bushnell felt the beauty of the biblical language. This aesthetic sense of his appeared in his theological prose, and broke down the wrong-headed and aesthetically wooden style of his contemporaries. He judged that the theology of his time had not come to grips with its own sensibilities, its feelings. An aesthetic conversion is called for, and no less in our time than in his. Theology and religion studied with little or no sense of the beauty of the divine, the beauty of human speech, and the beauty of its own quest and language would as well lapse into logic as method. Bushnell's advice is this:

> ...showing that the advancement and real amount of true theology depends not on logical deductions and systematic solutions, but principally on the more cultivated and nicer apprehension of symbol, it may turn the industry of our teachers more in this direction, giving a more esthetic character to their studies and theories, and drawing them as much closer to the practical life of religion.[40]

---

[38] *Building Eras,* 266-267.

[39] On aesthetics as the leading idea of American thought on religion from Edwards through James, see William A. Clebsch, *American Religious Thought: A History* (Chicago: University of Chicago Press, 1973).

[40] *God in Christ,* p. 92.

Thirdly, the charge was intellectual and theoretic as well. The intellect of his world was as cramped as the imagination. In fighting his way through the intellectual jungle he made a few simple and important discoveries that served him well in theological criticism, given the paucity of resources for a full formed theory of interiority:

a. he discovered that being is not limited to what can be seen or sensed, nor even to what can be imagined;

b. and that being is, in the final analysis, unimaginable;

c. that, paradoxically, the unimaginable *must* be imagined and the unspeakable *must* be spoken about;

d. and that such speaking, whether it be called figurative, metaphorical, or dialectical, goes on *intelligently* and with remarkable accuracy and aptness in religious discourse. How, he could not explain. But his discovery and affirmation I would call an intellectual conversion of the first order, a philosophical conversion necessary for every theologian and student of religion if they are to avoid the blunders we are prone to, namely, on the one hand to dismiss religious language on the grounds that it means itself to be taken literally; and on the other that, since religious language is necessarily and gloriously imaginative, it cannot mean what it says.

Finally, what is the norm for theology, the source of its claims and their authority? If, as Bushnell would agree, the authority is not "out there" in a creed, a dogma, a tradition, a deduction, then where is it? In the religious conversion of the theologian! Bushnell reminds us that religious truth is not subject to the analyses of organic chemistry (we need no reminder of this today, God knows!), but religious truth has "a concrete, vital nature inherent in all fact and symbol around us — a vast, mysterious, incomprehensible power which best we know when most we love."[41] Love, then, is a condition not only for authentic religious speech but theological speech as well, the disciplined speech of the student of religion. Donald Crosby points out that for Bushnell neither logic nor Lockean common sense is the arbiter of religious meaning; rather, the regenerate heart is.[42] L. C. Foard put it neatly: "The only authority here [in Bushnell's theology] is consciousness; the only possibility here for language about God is consciousness informed by Jesus Christ; the only work of Jesus Christ here is his work upon consciousness."[43] Or, in Bushnell's own words: "It has not been held, as a practical, positive, and earnest Christian truth, that there is a *perceptive power* in spiritual life, an unction of the Holy One, which is itself a kind of

---

[41] Ibid., p. 94.
[42] Crosby, ch. VI.
[43] Foard, p. 92.

inspiration — an immediate, experimental knowledge of God, by virtue of which, and partly in the degree of which, Christian theology is possible."[44]

Now there are many ways in which one might define this love, this regenerate heart made by Bushnell a condition for theological inquiry. Lonergan's suggestion, "love without restriction or reservation," does nicely. Perhaps the terms offered recently by Schubert Ogden and David Tracy might qualify: faith in the worthwhileness of existence. I do not mean to ignore the difficulties involved in an explication of the condition. I certainly do not mean, as I am convinced Bushnell himself did not mean, that the perceptive power, this love, is equivalent to any naive acceptance of the beliefs of the Christian confessions. But it remains nonetheless impossible for me to conceive theological inquiry proceeding fruitfully without the religious conversion of the theologian in heart as well as mind. Religious conversion is a prerequisite for authentic religious speech about the Mystery revealed only to our hearts and minds in images and symbols. It is as well a prerequisite for theological reflection and discourse about the effects of the revelation in our common life.

In summary, my reading of Bushnell leads me to the conviction that he has left us a solid legacy and a challenge as yet unfulfilled:

a. first, that language theory is a central consideration in the foundations of theology;

b. second, his abandonment and critique of logic as method for theology and his nudge in the direction of a theory of subjectivity grounding theological method urge complementing and correcting his theory of religious language with a phenomenology of conscious operations and an intentionality analysis capable of an adequate interpretation of the role of imagination in religious speech;

c. perhaps most importantly, Bushnell urges upon us the need to attend to and work out an adequate statement of the conditions for the possibility of an authentic theology and religion study, i.e., the conditions in the moral, aesthetic, intellectual, and religious conversion of the inquirer.

---

[44] *God in Christ,* p. 93.

Biblical Orientations

Beliefs and Authenticity

by Quentin Quesnell

In a subject-centered theology based on conversion, the classic problem of faith and reason becomes the concrete, personal question: How shall I respond authentically to God's gift of love without betraying authentic reasonableness as a knower and a questioner? For conversion and faith do not come pure and unmixed. They always appear linked with some belief system, some set of teaching about God and God's relations to the world and to you. Conversion itself may be just falling in love with God; and faith itself may be the new, heightened perspective on reality which is inseparable from love: the "eye of love."[1] But these always come linked with some preceding notion of the God you are in love with.

This notion is normally part of a system of beliefs you yourself did not create. It comes to you within an integrated religious picture provided by the religious tradition with which you are most familiar—the one you grew up with or one which has more recently been convincingly presented to you by someone eager to foster your conversion. After a fourteen year lapse, you attended midnight mass in the cathedral; you read the Krishna literature handed you in the airport; you listened to an evangelist preaching on Sunday morning TV. One way or another, your conversion did not happen without some preceding image of God, and your conversion happened in terms of that image. With this God, not with God-in-general, you have found yourself in love.

---

[1] B. Lonergan, *Method in Theology* (New York: Herder & Herder, 1972), p. 115.

Yet the pure desire to know cannot stop its restless questioning. The drive to understand and above all to judge the truth or falsity of whatever you experience cannot be suppressed without major inauthenticity.

The tension is inescapable. By awareness of my conversion

> "Whether at once, as once at a crash Paul
> Or as Austin, a lingering out sweet skill" [2]

a given image of God has come to life for me. I have come, without knowing adequate grounds for it, to perceive the God of the religious tradition as my God, the one who has given me infinite love and stirred in me a desire to return that love without measure. But since I am aware that this image is not the result of my own reflection on experience, nor the result of evidence generally available, widely confirmed or universally accepted, I cannot help questioning it, at least in details. For if it came to me as part of my education, it must have come accompanied by the imperfections of my education. I must sort these out. Yet it came accompanied by demands for belief, and now serious critical thought in regard to that belief has become serious critical thought in regard to my living God.

Worse, according to the belief system itself, serious reflective criticism of the revealed objects of belief is an offense against the God who has so generously revealed. In Tertullian's classic statement: "You seek and go on seeking for such time as you fail to find. But when you have believed, you have succeeded in finding. Those only seek who either never possessed, or else have lost what once they had. If you think there is something else to be found, you either have not believed or else have ceased to believe." [3]

This view is emphasized for modern Catholics by the First Council of the Vatican, which teaches that Catholics, unlike followers of other religions, never have a just reason to change or doubt their faith; never have a just cause to suspend assent to the faith they have once received from the Church's teaching, calling it into doubt while they work out a scientific demonstration of its credibility and truth. [4] This would imply that in whatever belief system you found yourself when you came to faith, in that you would have to remain for the rest of your life. The belief system itself could never be subjected to serious significant criticism and reform by you. But this is

---

[2] G. M. Hopkins, "Wreck of the Deutschland," in *Major Poems of Gerard Manley Hopkins* (N. Y.: Dutton, 1979).

[3] Tertullian, *On the "Prescription" of Heretics*, trans. T. H. Bindley (London: SPCK, 1914), paras. 10-11.

[4] Cf. Vatican I, Dogmatic Constitution *Dei Filius,* Chapter 3, "De fide" in H. Denzinger (ed.), *Enchiridion Symbolorum* (Freiburg: Herder, 1963), 32 edition, pp. 590 ff., # 1790 (= DS [33 edition] #3009).

such a contradiction of the way our inquiring minds work that there results a very real problem.

Someone might try to deny that a reasonable person would ever get into such a precarious intellectual situation; might claim that unless one had successfully laid the reasonable premises for the move into faith, conversion and the accompanying beliefs, one should never have made the move. This is logical but utterly unreal.

The model in an old-fashioned textbook of apologetics might indeed think through all evidence and decide coolly at the proper time that now was the moment to proceed to a justifiable act of faith. But in fact human beings are not logical thinking machines. They do not with the dawn of reason reach out for a first premise or celebrate their seventh birthdays by explicitly formulating the principle of contradiction. In fact, by the time we begin to ask the right questions we are already deeply embroiled in many wrong answers.

We are each of us born into a world which preexists us and which, from the moment we begin to learn anything at all, overwhelms us with a great flood of doctrines—commonsensible, scientific, historical, philosophical, and theological. We are handed a world, or more exactly we are socialized into a world already organized for us by others, and our task as responsible human beings is to try to sort it all out and decide how we stand in its regard, what sense we think it makes, how much of it we judge to be true. We must decide how much of it we will concede is beyond the capacity of our single lifetime to settle for ourselves and how much therefore we will calmly take on faith so that we have some time left to enjoy the world and the one life we have.

Since that is the real project, the real starting place for serious reflection is ourselves where we actually are—within or outside of, for instance, the religious traditions which we personally have received some knowledge of. Therefore the question from which our discussion began is not singular or rare. It must arise for every thinking person who is religious and for every religious person who thinks: If I am loyal to this conversion/love/faith experience I feel to be mine, to what extent must I yield unthinking commitment to the religious tradition in which this faith experience has come to me? And how can I then be loyal to myself as a seeker after truth, a lover of wisdom, an honest human being?

To reflect profitably on this issue in a subject-centered, conversion-based theology, the terms of the problem must be more concretely specified. For instance, distinctions must be drawn among various religious traditions as to how much of the tradition can or cannot be questioned without betraying the conversion itself. In a young cult the answer may be that absolutely nothing may be questioned. All is done as willed by God and revealed here and now through the leader. Most religions tend to be like that in their earliest stages, but all develop some role for reasoning by at least the end of their first generation if they are to continue. In an extremely liberal tradition, where there is minimal emphasis on conversion, it may be correspondingly difficult to discern what limits on questioning a conversion might impose.

As representative of the Catholic tradition, one can safely follow the First Council of the Vatican, as Lonergan does in his treatment of "The Permanence of Dogma" in *Method in Theology*.[5] Then that which I have to believe without questioning are the mysteries; and the mysteries are defined in terms correlative to my lack of knowledge and need of revelation: they are the truths so hidden in God that they could not be known except by revelation. Analyzing this, as Lonergan does, against the background of Aquinas' orthodox teaching in S. T. II-II, q. a. 4-5, one concludes that loyalty to the Catholic tradition requires that I believe what I do not yet know and what no human being can ever know.

There are some not insignificant consequences. Believing, and not reasoning, is the proper response only to truths so hidden in God that they could not be known without revelation. These are truths that do not leave tracks. There is not by definition any evidence for them; but there is not by definition any evidence against them. Whether there is one person in God or three or a baker's dozen there are no compelling evidences one way or the other; nor is anyone able to specify in what exactly such evidences might consist. That God was or was not incarnate in this man, Jesus of Nazareth—how would you prove it? Besides the intrinsic philosophic absurdity of the attempt, so powerfully described in Kierkegaard's *Postscript,* there is the fact that the belief system itself says you could not prove it and must not try: it is a truth hidden in God.[6] There is no natural effect to be checked out, and therefore there is nothing for reason to do.

That each of us is conceived in original sin; that one woman, some two thousand years ago, was conceived without it; that God does or does not sanctify us with his grace, elevate our good actions, will punish our bad ones—not one of these is evidential. If any of them were evidential, they would not be objects of belief. As soon as there is anything for reason to work on, reason ought to get to work. If there is contrary evidence, or seems to be, that is to be reasoned upon. If a religious teaching said the moon is made of green cheese, that would not be a mystery to be believed, but a thesis to be inves-

---

[5] *Method,* pp. 320-324.
[6] Vatican I, op. cit., p. 594, canon 5.

tigated. If it were Catholic teaching that human society functions better under capitalism than communism, with a wider distribution of wealth, security, and happiness, this might be something to be checked out. But if the belief is that a certain woman many centuries ago conceived a child without the intervention of a male, the *a priori's* may be strongly against it, but the fact itself cannot possibly be checked.

If it is said that the same might happen to anyone who believed, that could perhaps be subjected to some checking. When Jesus said: "If anyone eat of this bread, he will live forever," and if that meant would not experience natural death, this was not something to be believed but to be tested. When the test failed, as it did when Christians continued to die in the same percentage as others, then the saying had to be reinterpreted, as it was, along with similar statements like: "Some of those standing here will not die before the son of man comes in his kingdom."

The principle then is clear: you believe only what you do not know and what you cannot know. The mysteries of faith calling for belief and restricting your right of investigation must by definition be teachings on matters for which there is no evidence either pro or con. Those revealed mysteries are not to be verified, modified, or substituted for. No major figure in the history of Catholic theology, not even Abelard, has denied those limits. But on the other hand, as soon as any claim is made which could produce perceptible effects or evidence, that claim is to be met not by belief but by critical reflection, and accepted if found true, rejected if found false.

Within the limits suggested, what room is left for thinking and judgment? First, there is left everything which purports to be a matter of evidence—to have concomitant or subsequent measurable effects or indispensable measurable antecedents. As soon as an effect or a cause in the world of experience is appealed to, all judgments are to be rationally determined. Who ruled Israel in such and such a year, if the biblical texts contradict each other? Did Jesus teach freedom from the law or conformity to it? Written texts are evidence and to be handled as such. So also are all historical, literary, sociological, economic, geological questions; everything except mysteries so hidden in God that they cannot be known unless divinely revealed.

But secondly, the Catholic tradition itself specifies another base from which the converted person can criticize the tradition. For the tradition teaches, with Augustine and Aquinas, that in infused faith "the light of your countenance is signed upon us, Lord" and "in your light we shall see light." This is considered to be a fulfillment of Jeremiah's prophecy that "they shall have no need for any man to teach them; for they shall all be taught of God." It is confirmed by the modern teaching of Vatican II on the role of charisms, and is implied in the same council's teaching on the infallibility of the faithful.[7]

The point here is that your faith/love/conversion constitutes in you a new eye for recognizing truths and values you might otherwise have missed. As such, your conversion becomes, like the light of intelligence itself, an internal source of ultimate judgment whose manner of operation provides an inescapable norm. That norm finds concrete expression only in material from the religious tradition in which the conversion occurred, but the norm itself exceeds any concrete expression, and, as an internal norm in a living person, stands in tension with any existing version of the tradition as presently expressed. So too in natural reasoning, our critical powers come to birth within a given culture, but we are not helpless to reflect critically upon that culture and to contribute by our criticisms to its improvement.

This happens in the theological area in at least three ways: first, insofar as current teachings are always incomplete; second, insofar as current teachings are always imperfect; third, insofar as it is the task of the theologian at any given moment to rank the teachings in order of importance.

First, the current teachings are incomplete. This is manifest from the fact that the act of faith is related to the mysteries; but the current teaching, rather than include all the mysteries, tends to be summed up in the dogmas. Now the dogmas are not the mysteries. The mysteries are the revealed truths. The dogmas are not the revelation. The dogmas come later, much later. Many Christians lived and died before the dogmas existed; many Christians and Catholics live and die without hearing more than a few of the dogmas.

The dogmas are not the revealed mysteries, constitutive of the religion. They are the rules for speaking correctly about the mysteries. The dogmas are the grammar of faith. They tell how to use correctly the words and relate correctly to one another the sentences that abound in the Scriptures and in the tradition about the mysteries themselves. That is why the dogmas are phrased, "If anyone shall *say...* let him be anathema [or let her be anathema]." To define a dogma is not to proclaim a truth, but to specify exactly how to speak and think about a truth which was always believed.

---

[7] Vatican II, Dogmatic Constitution *Lumen Gentium,* chapter 2, "The People of God," n. 12, in W. Abbott, ed., *The Documents of Vatican II* (New York: Guild Press, 1966), pp. 29-30.

The mysteries are behind the dogmas and are more than the dogmas. Theology, as the understanding of faith, demands engagement with the mysteries. But to that engagement the dogmas are, at most, a help and certainly only a partial help. If we allow them to play too prominent a part in our thinking, their effect can be crippling. That is what has always been wrong with doing theology in terms of an outline of dogma or even a history of dogma. It is like learning a language by reading grammars. Theology wants to understand the religion itself, the language as lived and spoken, not some collection of the rules most frequently violated in using that language.

Theological surveys in terms of dogmas are understandable insofar as theology is done within a religious community whose history of bloody wars of mind and spirit is recorded in its dogmas. But the dogmas do not necessarily outline the most essential abiding characteristics, and may miss some important points entirely.

The mysteries are conveyed not only in dogmas and creeds, but also in the preaching and worship of the Church, in the Scriptures, in the lives of the saints, in the prayers, devotions, and Christian lives of the faithful of every age. We might consider here, for example, some instances just from the Scriptures, which appear in no creeds and have never been defined as dogmas, but are just as truly mysteries constitutive of Christianity.

Take, for example, such a statement as "As long as you did it to one of these my least brothers, you did it to me." No evidence is offered or expected. No reasonable, human verification is possible now or was possible when the words were first spoken or written. If accepted and believed, it is believed on the authority of God revealing. It is the revelation of a mystery. Its importance in the history of Christianity is acknowledged by all. Yet it has never been defined. It is not a dogma or the theme of any dogma.

Take another: "He laid down his life for us; we also ought to lay down our lives for one another." Except as the revelation of a mystery, an exposition of God's values for our lives, it does not follow. God may want us to draw that conclusion from Christ's death, and we may believe that is the proper conclusion to draw; but we draw it, not because it follows reasonably, but because we believe God has revealed that it should follow for us.

Teachings like these are mysteries in the fullest sense. Their truth could not be known by any human means or by any rational analysis. For if taken seriously they point in the direction of self-diminution, self-sacrifice, and self-destruction. But if reason shudders at any suggestion of limits being placed on the freely inquiring spirit, how much more must reason repine at the suggestion that it move toward terminating itself, imposing an absolute end to all its inquiring forever. Never to ask another question about anything at all? Never to give the benefits of one's wisdom to another, in the present or in future generations? Lay down one's life? Without even a Plato at one's side to record the event?

A milder example may illustrate the irrationality more clearly. If one were exhorted to submit oneself in certain special circumstances to a brain operation which would render one a vegetable, could this truly be accepted as a reasonable course of action? The horror which the thought provokes in a mind devoted to free inquiry is an indication of how little reasonable would be the more extreme conclusion that one might lay down one's life for a friend. It is the conclusion that never follows logically from principles of reason alone.

A similar analysis can, I believe, be done on many another gospel command or promise. Most of them turn out to be affirmations in one form or another that if you go to the cross you will find salvation, resurrection, and life. As such they are revelations of something which could not be known except by revelation. It might be dreamed of, guessed at, hoped for, even occasionally aspired to or practiced, but it could not be known. That happy are the poor, the lowly, those who weep and mourn, suffer persecution for justice's sake — if anyone believes these they believe them because of faith in the word of God; that is, they believe them as revealed, and from that alone comes their certainty. For they certainly are not logical conclusions of reason.

"Sell what you have and give to the poor, and you will have treasure in heaven." "Resist not evil. Take no thought for tomorrow." "Forgive one who offends you, not seven times a day, but seventy times seven times." "Turn the other cheek." "Go the extra mile." "Give to everyone who asks of you." "If anyone takes away your cloak, give him your tunic as well." "It is more blessed to give than to receive." "It is easier for a camel to pass through the eye of a needle than for a rich man to enter heaven." "Love your enemies, do good to those who hate you." "When you give a banquet, don't invite your friends or relatives or anyone able to repay you by inviting you in return; but invite the poor and the crippled and the lame and the blind, because they cannot repay you, and you will receive your reward in the resurrection of the just." "Happy are you when they curse you and revile you and speak all manner of evil against you for my name's sake. Be glad and rejoice, for your reward is very great in heaven."

There is not a one of these which can be validated by reason. There is no evidence to support the truth of any one of these statements. They are mysteries, as great as the revealed mysteries of the Trinity, Incarnation, redemption. In fact, they may be greater. A theology which gave even equal time to these other mysteries might be revolutionary. In fact, to some extent such a theology is being produced in our time or at least being dreamed of by some liberation theologians, and it is revolutionary.

(It will be noticed that the sort of mysteries just outlined, to which less explicit attention has been paid in classical theology, are revelations of mysteries of value. Previously, attention was paid primarily to mysteries which were revelations of matters of fact. Though both types are mysteries and revealed, it may be well to be able to distinguish them by separate terms: mysteries of fact and mysteries of value. The distinction will be of some importance in the third point, below.)

Second, we said that any existing formulation of belief is always imperfect. In some ways this needs no explanation. It follows from the very goal set for theological reflection by the First Vatican Council, quoting the fifth century Vincent of Lerins: that without betraying the same teaching, the same sense, the same opinion, it was still possible that "each and all, every single person as well as the entire Church, should in the course of generations and of centuries grow and make extraordinary progress in understanding, wisdom and knowledge."[8] If each of us and all together are to grow and make extraordinary progress, the implication is that we are going to leave behind previous states of understanding, wisdom and knowledge for better ones to come.

But more fundamentally still, the mysteries cannot be known apart from divine revelation. But all revelation is in sensible forms or in human words, and so is necessarily imperfect. As the Fourth Lateran Council taught in 1215, no matter how great a similitude of God with a creature is ever expressed, the dissimilitude will be still greater.[9]

Third, the Second Vatican Council encourages theologians to remember that "there exists an order or hierarchy of the truths of Catholic teaching, according to their diverse connection with the foundation of Christian faith."[10] Now what the Council meant by the foundation of Christian faith they tell us often enough. It is the Christian mystery, the salvation event, the Christ event. It is the death and resurrection of Christ, preached by the Christian community from the beginning as a message from God to us. Vatican II sums up that message as the "perfection of revelation"; namely, that God is with us to save us out of the darkness of sin and death and to

---

[8] Vatican I, op. cit., p. 592.
[9] In Denzinger, op. cit., # 432 (= DS # 806).
[10] Vatican II, op. cit., *Unitatis Redintegratio*, n.11 p. 354.

lift us up to eternal life."[11] The work of the theologian then will be to rank the mysteries according to their closeness to that central revelation.

Another way of identifying the foundation of Christian faith is ontologically. In theological ontological terms, the foundation of faith for me, the individual, is that the love of God is poured forth in my heart by the Holy Spirit who is given me. Or again, psychologically, from the side of my consciousness, that foundation is the conversion event. The theologian can and should rank the mysteries in relation to that.

Whichever criterion one uses to rank the mysteries — closeness to the preached mystery of Christ's death and resurrection; closeness to the central revelation that God is with us to save us out of the darkness of sin and death and to raise us up to eternal life; closeness to the ontological fact of God's pouring out his love in our hearts; or closeness to one's own experience of conversion, it seems apparent that the mysteries of value stand closer to the center than most of the mysteries of fact. To the extent that they are closer, they rank higher; and one can take up the Council's suggestion that the lower ranked mysteries may be for the sake of the higher ranked ones.

At any rate, the work of the reasonable and responsible Catholic thinker or theologian becomes that of attending directly to the mysteries of value as well as to the mysteries of fact; identifying them, clarifying them, embracing and even incarnating them in practice. Theology means looking for interconnections of the mysteries of value with the infused and recognized love of God, with one another, and with the mysteries of fact. It involves perceiving how the mysteries of value flow from and towards conversion, and how the mysteries of fact are linked to conversion through them; how the mysteries of fact illustrate and exemplify the mysteries of value and motivate their acceptance and practice. The work of theology becomes finally also searching for natural analogies to all the mysteries, those of value as well as those of fact, so that a fruitful insight and progress in them may be made ever easier for all the faithful.

Insofar as the mysteries of fact, the traditional beliefs, are subordinate to the mysteries of value, the belief system may in fact be revealed only in the sense that it shows itself to be a secure embodiment of the mysteries of value; expresses them well, though only implicitly; and makes it possible or easier to live by them. The history of Christian thought could be analyzed as a preserving and safeguarding of the mysteries of value, passing them on primarily in life within the "incarnate meanings"[12] which are the lives of Christ

---

[11] Vatican II, op. cit., *Dei Verbum*, n.4 p. 113.
[12] *Method*, p. 73.

and of Christians. Explicit recognition, definition, and formulation of mysteries of fact in dogmas would come about only gradually and only insofar as those were found necessary to preserve and safeguard the mysteries of value in various cultural situations.

Traditional beliefs in mysteries of fact can thus be appreciated as products of human culture without betraying one's conversion experience. For the direct effect of an awareness of conversion is an inclination to accept new values. True, these values too have their antecedents in human thought and culture, and to that extent might also be subject to critical reflection. But the accepting of values is not a function of critical judgment (Is it so? True or false?), but of responsible choice (Armed with just the knowledge I have here and now, what am I to do?). The setting of values is not (to use the language of *Insight*) a matter of purely rational consciousness, but of rational *self*-consciousness. Its criterion is not evidence, but moral attractiveness. One learns to be open to moral attractiveness by consistently trying to choose responsibly with readiness to reform as new moral horizons open up, just as one learns to judge well and find truth by consistently trying to be critical, reasonable, attentive to evidence and to possible ways of synthesizing it.

Love itself will incline us immediately to accept a new set of values. Love itself only indirectly and mediately inclines us to accept new beliefs about matters of fact. The values will indeed come within a belief system, carried by a tradition. Loyalty to the God revealed to us will incline us to continue in that tradition that we may continue to cherish the values his love reveals. But anything within that tradition which is a matter of true and false, any supposed facts which imply evidence, will have to be judged by the evidence. Mysteries of fact which are real mysteries, completely independent of evidence, will be accepted to the extent that they are inseparably linked to the conversion experience through the values.

Attending separately to the mysteries of fact and the mysteries of value may add force to Lonergan's demonstration that he is "departing not from the older doctrine but only from the older manner of speaking" when he distinguishes faith and beliefs.[13] If one attends to the mysteries of value, beliefs may be identified with faith and be ideally invariable, as in the "older and more authoritative tradition." If one attends to the mysteries of fact, beliefs obviously differ according to cultural situations and backgrounds, and do so without any harm to faith.

---

[13] *Method*, p. 123.

The Rise of David Story and the Search for a Story to Live By

by Sean McEvenue

If Lonergan is right in claiming that scholarship has sealed off all the familiar avenues between theology and Scripture,[1] then it seems misleading to speak of biblical theology and it appears a deception to teach the Old and New Testaments, as presently understood, in departments of theological studies. However, Lonergan himself has made notable use of Romans 5:5. Moreover many otherwise sensible scholars cannot make head or tail of Lonergan's approach, and in reading the Lonergonians they find little which they can understand, reason about, or deliberate upon! A seventy-fifth anniversary, twenty-two years after the publication of *Insight*, is a fitting occasion for at least one student of the Bible both to acknowledge gratefully that Lonergan's thought has been perking through the grains in his cranium and to rise to the colossal challenge of "migrating from a basis in theory to a basis in interiority".[2]

---

[1] Cf. B. Lonergan, *Method in Theology*, (New York: Herder and Herder, 1972), p. 276, "Scholarship builds an inpenetrable wall between systematic theology and its historical sources, but this development invites philosophy and theology to migrate from a basis in theory to a basis in interiority."

[2] I did not, and could not have, risen to the challenge without the continuous encouragement and guidance of Philip McShane, Visiting Fellow at Lonergan College during 1979-80.

The *Rise of David Story* is a redactional unity stretching roughly from 1 Sam 16 to 2 Samuel 8.[3] The story ends with a triumphant summary, rounding off David's accession to power over an empire. Its opening chapter contains an editorial creation which clearly makes a point: the outcome was determined by Yahweh from the very beginning, when Samuel, after finding the boy Cinderella-fashion and noting that he "was ruddy, and had beautiful eyes, and was handsome," anointed him at the Lord's command. The organizing theme is that David blamelessly replaced Saul as the dynastic head of Israel. The full theme appears most clearly, perhaps, in the twice recounted confrontation between David and Saul, in which Saul is the persecutor and David asks only to be spared.[4] The confrontation ends with Saul asking David's forgiveness, and recognizing David as his son (i.e., legitimate successor), and as destined to be king over Israel.[5]

Now if one allows oneself to interpret this story in a cynical frame of mind, a frame of mind all too easily adopted by critical-historical methodists, one can see here a purely political intention: to support David's kingship first by stilling whisperers who must have argued that David had come to power through bloody assassinations, and second by claiming divine authority for the outcome. But this is a massive anachronism: no author in the ancient world had purely political intentions. We must read for compact mentalities in which religion and politics and history are not adequately differentiated.

---

[3] The literary criticism of the book of Samuel has a complex and inconclusive history. For a summary cf. Brevard Childs, *Introduction to the Old Testament as Scripture.* (Philadelphia: Fortress, 1979), pp. 266-271. That a *Rise of David Story* is a unity which can be recognized is not universally adverted to, but it is generally agreed upon by those who look for redactional units beyond original sources: v.g. M. Noth, *Überlieferungsgeschichtliche Studien,* 1943, 3rd edit. (Tübingen: J. C. B. Mohr 1967), p. 62; Sellin-Fohrer, *Introduction to the Old Testament* (Nashville: Abingdon, 1968), pp. 220-221. The exact limits of this unit are debated. 2 Sam 6-7 are often thought to introduce the Succession Narrative (2 Sam 9-20; 1 Kings 1-2), and not to be a part of the *Rise of David Story:* Cf. v.g., David Gunn, *The Story of King David: Genre and Interpretation,* (Sheffield, 1978), who gives a thorough review of opinions and reasons. I would contend that 1 Sam 15 became part of the *Rise of David Story* at some redactional point, since the links with ch. 16 are marked, and since there is a very similar framing of a Saul story and of a David story by the concluding summaries of 1 Sam 14: 47-52 and 2 Sam 8:15-18. None of these points bear on the discussion we will pursue in this paper.

[4] Cf. 1 Sam 24 and 26. The accounts are introduced by divergent "travelling legends" (24: 1-7 and 26: 1-12), which serve to base dramatic confrontations of very similar content.

[5] There can be no doubt that the author strives to establish these postures throughout the narrative. Cf. David's relationship with Jonathan (1 Sam 18: 1-4; 20:13-17 and 30-31). Cf. also the author's constant concern to point out that David could not have killed Jonathan or Saul, or Abner or Ishbosheth (1 Sam 29; 31; 2 Sam 1; 2: 31-39; 4).

Similarly if one indulges in facile forms of biblical theology, one might point out a purely theological intent, an intent made visible by the last editor who, in writing 1 Sam 16: 1-13, has drawn materials from the heroic legend of David and Goliath (cf. 1 Sam 17: 12-15 and 42) in order to spin a yarn about an anointing of David at the hands of Samuel.[6] This approach relieves any anxiety we may have about the unhistorical tone of this tale. Moreover, by making its author a "late" interpreter of this material, we can easily imagine such a process of theological abstraction and fabulation. This is the line taken for example by Gerhard von Rad.[7] It has two drawbacks: first it is once again untrue to the compact mentality of ancient authors, who express religious experiences not theological doctrines; and second it gets us into a theological trap. If this were a theological doctrine, namely that God acted with prevenient grace in the case of David's kingship in a manner paralleling the vocation narratives (e.g., Jer 1: 5), then we are committed to a certain form of divine causality. It could seem true, indeed, *de fide divina,* that God foreordains the salvific acts of at least certain of his saints, and maybe *proxima fidei* that he foreordains all gracious acts. However, we need not fall into this trap, if we insist that the author was not writing doctrine, but rather compactly expressing the meaning of experience. Interpretation, then, would need to reach into the historical socio-cultural context to imagine creatively and feelingly the experience which was conveyed to the first readers of this story.[8]

What general historical context should be indicated? Scholarship leads to a dating in a period after David and prior to the end of the monarchy. The story was composed after David because some time must be allowed during which the David stories could grow variants (v.g., 1 Sam 16: 14-23 and 17: 55-58; 1 Sam 24 and 26; 1 Sam 21: 10-15 and 27: 1-7), and one could forget just who had killed Goliath (cf., 2 Sam 21: 19). And it was composed before the end of the monarchy because the core text of the Deuteronomistic history is generally viewed as having been completed under the monarchy.

A socio-cultural context involves a specification of the role of the king of Israel, and most particularly the centralizing role of the monarchy of Jerusalem. First of all, kings in the ancient world, and

---

[6] In the rest of the *Rise of David Story* there is no sign that David was aware of such an anointing. In fact in 2 Sam 2, 4 David is king of Judah, and in 2 Sam 5, 3 he is anointed king over all Israel.

[7] Cf. Gerhard von Rad, *Old Testament Theology,* Vol. 1 (Edinburgh and New York: Oliver and Boyd, 1962), p. 309. The same line of thought is implicit in recent commentaries, v.g. Peter Ackroyd, *The First Book of Samuel,* Cambridge Bible Commentary on the New English Bible (Cambridge: Cambridge University Press, 1971), pp. 131-132.

[8] Cf. B. Lonergan, op. cit., pp. 172-173.

right up to the turn of this century, were very powerful symbols. That Psalm 2 could be written, and retained in the canon, shows that Israel appropriated the near idolatry surrounding kings in the ancient world. We North Americans tend to think of kings in comical terms, and we do not easily go beyond words like "superstition" in trying to recapture feelings about the monarchy which we come across in history. The overwhelming feelings and passions which link us with parents, as analyzed by Freud, and which are ruled by archetypes, as described by Jung, were once quite unanalyzed and overpoweringly present in relation to kings. Like all powerful symbols, the kings of Israel were ambiguous figures.

What then would a Judean feel about the king at any point during the monarchy?[9] One could easily imagine a subject tortured with doubts: "If I obey the king's orders, will I be doing the will of God or cooperating with the devil?" Our own religious experience extends very easily to important uncertainty in religious matters. We can sympathize with an ancient Judean's anxiety when Hezekiah stopped all sacrifice in the homes and villages, centralizing religious practice in Jerusalem (2 Kings 18:22). "We can no longer expiate our sins, and commune with God, in the country....Has Hezekiah, like Saul before him, come under an evil spirit, receiving instructions from the witches at Endor? This king in Jerusalem now, is God on his side? Didn't David usurp power from the Benjaminite Saul. Was it not the Benjaminite Joshua who conquered this country for Yahweh? Are there not many Benjaminite families living here now who have never trusted the Ephrathites? Oh for the days when kings went to war, and we could soon know whose side Yahweh had chosen...."

This situation is significantly mirrored in the Deuteronomistic historian (Dtr) for whom the monarchy remained theologically ambiguous. He has absorbed the *Rise of David Story* into his work, a story in which David appears as beautiful to look at, a military darling and super-hero, successful in everything, enhanced by the contrast with Saul, chosen and anointed by Yahweh and by all Israel to be king. But Dtr has then placed beside it the *Succession Narrative* (2 Sam 9-20; 1 Kings 1-2). In this, David is presented as weak in dealing with Bathsheba (2 Sam 11; 1 Kings 1), with Absalom (2 Sam 13:39; 19:1-8), with Adonijah (1 Kings 1:6); David is presented as politically devious in dealing with Ziba and Mephibosheth (2 Sam 9:9-13; 16:1-4; 19:24-29); David is presented as hypocritically vicious in dealing with his enemies (1 Kings 2:5-9); and finally he is presented as

---

[9] Clearly we are raising questions here which, as indicated below, demand extensive new research.

criminal in dealing with Uriah the Hittite (2 Sam 11). Even more important in the *Succession Narrative* is the fact that the choice of Solomon to replace David is not seen as blameless or directly influenced by God, but rather as the result of a corrupt court life in which rivals have been murdered; and the weak, doddering, impotent, old king David has been manipulated by Bathsheba and a secularized Nathan (1 Kings 1). Moreover, Dtr has retained the admiring tradition regarding Solomon (1 Kings 3-11), but he himself has evaluated Solomon negatively: into the law for kings in Dt 17: 14ff he has introduced warnings which clearly aim at Solomon (vv 16-17); and he has written a programmatic speech for Samuel in the same terms (1 Sam 8:4-22). Again, Dtr presented Hezekiah and Josiah in a favorable light precisely because of their centralizing reform, but condemned virtually all the other kings of Israel and Judah for sins to the contrary. Other texts in his work and in the book of Jeremiah, (despite Dtr editing), retain clear evidence that not every contemporary Judean agreed with such views (2 Kings 18:22; Jer 44:15-19). Finally, the Deuteronomistic historian clearly felt that the kingship was over (2 Kings 25: 27-30) and yet he retained the prophecy of Nathan that there would always be a son of David on the throne (2 Sam 7: 11b-16).[10]

All of this is a schematic indication of what was surely a far more complex chaos at times in the minds and hearts of villagers under the king; political uncertainty, religious confusion, personal anxiety, social chaos, all contributing to one another. At some stage there emerged a creative unifying vision: "The power of the king in Jerusalem comes from Yahweh, and has been so willed since he chose David. Our present confusion is due to our failure to believe that Yahweh alone has brought about the present political-religious structure." The vision is expressed and written, not in analytic terms, but through the accumulation of stories about the origin of the Jerusalem monarchy, and their selective integration in a manner which supports this vision. The *Rise of David Story* catches on, unifying the country, comforting souls, releasing creative energies, renewing faith throughout Judah. Even a modern theologian could not quarrel with this: whatever the nitty gritty human facts, and whatever the theory of divine causality, it remains true that in so far as the kings' power was real it came from God. One could only praise God in it, and proceed to deal with it.

It must be pointed out that the author did not write a parable. He has not created a timeless paradigm in order to teach a lesson.

---

[10] For further discussion cf. Georg Fohrer, *History of Israelite Religion,* (New York: Abingdon, 1972), pp. 149-150; M. Noth, *Überlieferungsgeschichtliche Studien,* Tübingen, 1967, p. 56-58.

Rather he has creatively gathered carriers of "incarnate meaning",[11] to form a new meaning relevant to issues which tortured his community. The writer discovered and portrayed a personal vision of contemporary reality within community memories. This is not timeless: it is his world as he felt and meant it. It is not a lesson, but a transformed and transforming interpretation of reality. It was not a doctrine, but primarily a faith-perspective for himself and communicated to others. He has not made a judgment, but retold a story. He has not just had an insight, but rather has undergone an incarnate conversion. He is not thinking about prevenient grace, but feeling toward order in the world he inhabits.

At this point, let us see where we stand with regard to functional specialties. We have made use of the functional specialty of research in establishing a text for interpretation. Research has progressed beyond the work of Wellhausen and Eissfeldt who exhausted the possibilities of identifying continuous strands in the sources of the books of Samuel and Kings. It has established redactional unities which existed prior to the final Deuteronomistic redaction. A unity, which could be described as the *Rise of David Story*, with the theme we have indicated, certainly can be discerned. Research is still active in determining the exact boundaries and text of this unity, but the further determinations which are possible will probably not change much in the discussion.

We have further initiated work on the functional speciality of *interpretation*, focusing on 1 Sam 16: 1-13, and drawing out its meaning on the understanding that it is itself a summary of the meaning of the whole unit.

In interpreting we appealed to *history*, but not as something "going forward" — rather as cross-sectionally delimiting a social context. We also entered into some *dialectic* in so far as we pointed out the cynical bias implicit in any "purely political", etc. interpretation of this story, and we adduced the notion of "compact consciousness"[12] to establish a perspective on interpretation alternative to both the purely political and the purely theological perspectives from which interpretations have been attempted. However, all of this has been done in order to point towards interpretation. Within that pointing there has been no attempt at theology, and one might conclude that the product of this considerable effort is merely interesting or curious, valuable for a scholarly article to be published in a review to be deposed in the many tombs of university libraries.

---

[11] B. Lonergan, op. cit, p. 73.

[12] Cf. Eric Voegelin, *The Ecumenic Age* (Baton Rouge, La.: Louisiana State University Press, 1974), p. 2.

My training as a "scholar", and my bias as an "academic", would indeed lead me to stop there. And I would note that all further inquiry on my part will be incompetent to begin with and unprofessional as well. However as a human being I am dissatisfied, and if I dare call myself "theologian" instead of "scholar" then it will not be unprofessional to go further with due caution about competence. I am dissatisfied on two minor points and one major.

My first dissatisfaction is around the psychological, social, religious role of the king of Israel. Current social science has a great deal to say about this, and it has not been said. Because my foundations include a hermeneutic which requires a scientific perspective on reality, I have to be dissatisfied with the very vague description I gave about the role of the kings in a Judean's consciousness. The social history of Israel has yet to be written. Roland de Vaux began the task with his study of the institutions of Israel, and the first volume of his *Histoire Ancienne d'Israël*.[13] His death has been a monumental loss to this enterprise. The sporadic attempts of psychologists to enter the field have not dealt with the psycho-dynamics of a divinely appointed king, and in biblical areas have been singularly lacking in critical sense for history.[14] Norman Gottwald has applied sociology to the Old Testament,[15] and in conjunction with Frank Frick has formed a study group within the "Society of Biblical Literature" with the title "Social World of Ancient Israel Group."[16] So far their attention has been directed to pre-monarchial Israel. Still a social study of the tribes, and particularly of their relations to each other, will eventually be essential to an understanding of the role David played between Judah and Benjamin, and the other Northern tribes, as he established regal power in Jerusalem. My dissatisfaction will have to wait.

A second dissatisfaction lies in the functional specialty of history: what was going forward at the time of David? First of all did David kill off the Saulides, or was he really as open to God's will as portrayed in some texts? In any event, what can be said of the religious meaning of the execution of political enemies in fundamentalist

---

[13] Roland de Vaux, *Ancient Israel: Its Life and Institutions* (New York: McGraw-Hill, 1961); *Histoire ancienne d'Israël: des origines à l'installation en Canaan.* (Paris: Lecoffre, 1971).

[14] Notably Sigmund Freud's, *Moses and Monotheism* (New York: A. A. Knopf, 1939), and C. J. Jung's, *Answer to Job; Collected Works,* vol. 11 (Princeton, N.J.: Princeton University Press, 1969), pp. 355-470.

[15] Cf. Norman K. Gottwald, *The Tribes of Israel: A Sociology of the Religion of Liberated Israel, 1250-1051, B.C.E.* (Maryknoll, NY: Orbis, 1979).

[16] This group proposes to prepare a complete bibliography in this area for the AAR-SBL meeting next year.

theocracies today or in Israel during David's life time? Secondly, what institutions and social phenomena created a national consciousness of which we have evidence in the biblical document written by "the Yahwist"? These questions arise because my foundations include a heuristics of revelation and tradition: my knowledge of God is dependent on those who knew Him before me, and specifically on the affirmations about God made by David and David's era. Were those people credible only because later ages lived through the culture they created, or were they worthy of belief in themselves?

However, my main dissatisfaction with stopping at interpretation arises in the area of politics and religion. My foundations include heuristically an imperious demand for knowing God now. I do not believe that God appoints political leaders now, and establishes civilizations for me to enjoy spiritually. Did He ever do this, and if so what can I conclude about political theology for the present? This question invites the theologian to participate in a *dialectic* which is visible in our tradition.

Immediately following the *Rise of David Story*, we had a very different religious experience in the area of Israel's king, namely the *Succession Story* which (as indicated above) presents the kingship of David without any trace of direct divine interference, and little trace of human virtue,[17] and in particular presents the selection of Solomon (1 Kings 1) as the result of manipulation of David once he is impotent in every sense. This presentation would tend to deny rather directly any idea that God's will for David as expressed in 1 Sam 16:1-3 was repeated in the anointing of subsequent kings of Israel. The Deuteronomistic editor ends up by relegating the whole experience of the Jerusalem monarchy to an irreversible past,[18] even though he leaves uncommented, and as yet unfulfilled, the Nathan prophecy in 2 Sam 7 that there will always be a son of David pro-

---

[17] For this reason this story has often been called "The Court Narrative" emphasizing the tone rather than the point of the story. David Gunn, op. cit., characterizes this story as "serious entertainment", and, although I cannot accept his conclusion, the term itself suggests the point I am trying to make.

[18] Discussion of the Dtr's intentions has its own history. Cf M. Noth, *Uberlieferungsgeschichtliche Studien* (Tübingen, 1943), and G. von Rad, "Die deuteronomische Geschichtstheologie in den Königsbüchern", *Deuteronomium Studien; Teil B* (Göttingen, 1947) and reprinted in *Gesammelte Studien zum Alten Testament* (Munich: C. Kaiser 1965); H. W. Wolffe, "Das Kerygma des deuteronomistichen Geschichtswerkes", *ZAW* 73 (1961): pp. 171-186; N. Lohfink, "Bilanz nach der Katastrophe: Das deuteronomistische Geschichtswerk", *Wort und Botschaft* (Würzburg: Echter-Verlag, 1967), pp. 196-208; P. R. Ackroyd, "The Deuteronomic History", *Exile and Restoration* (Philadelphia: Westminster, 1968), pp. 62-83; F. M. Cross, "The Themes of the Book of Kings and the Structure of the Deuteronomistic History," *Canaanite Myth and Hebrew Epic* (Cambridge, Mass.: Harvard University Press, 1973), pp. 274-289.

tested by God upon the throne. The Deuteronomist's vision includes a succession of eras with clear transitions: a golden age of Joshua, a charismatic era of judges terminating in 1 Sam 8, and a decisive era of the monarchy. His vision for the despairing Jews in exile embodies both a disastrous past in which God is shown as nevertheless fully in command, and a few glimmers of hope for the future. For purposes of the present dialectic, his experience supports the view that Yahweh's involvement in politics as known in the past is now over.

The Bible presents other experiences subsequent to this. In *Chronicles,* salvation centers around the Temple and its cult, and this salvation has been placed on earth by God working through the political power of David. Another, and probably parallel vision, makes the High Priest take over the robes and role of the king, and in that sense fulfill Nathan's prophecy.[19] In the New Testament, of course, Jesus is the Messiah, and the multiplicity of meaning around this word as used in the NT has been the subject of an infinity of recent scholarly literature. For our purpose it will be sufficient to say that Jesus was indeed king, and his kingdom was not of this world.[20] St. Augustine believed that there was an earthly kingdom, and a *civitas Dei* beside it. In all of this tradition, God sent the priest, the crucified Messiah, the Pope, the Church, etc., and had a direct will in their work, but really He left the rest of life to the Seleucides, or the Romans, or the kings.

There followed another tradition drawn from both biblical and pagan sources, in which the Emperor at Constantinople was divinely appointed, as were Charlemagne and the leaders of the Holy Roman Empire. This tradition survived in the Russian empire right up until the abdication of the last Romanov, Tsar Nicholas II, March 16, 1917. In the West, Boniface VIII believed that he held the "two swords" in his own hand in so far as spiritual power was more excellent than temporal. (DB 469) As the Medieval papacy lost ground, a new basis for divinely directed temporal power was built upon the doctrine of "the divine right of kings", as set forth most cogently in *Basilikon doron* by James VI of Scotland (James I of England), and contested by Suarez and Bellarmine.[21]

---

[19] Cf. the supplements to the Priestly document in Leviticus 8 where the priest wears a crown and is anointed, and the extended praise of Simon son of Onias in Sirach 50.

[20] Cf. John 18: 33-38

[21] For the medieval period, cf. discussion and bibliographical information in J. J. Ryan, *The Nature, Structure, and Function of the Church in William of Occam* (Missoula, Mont.: Scholars Press, 1978), pp. 26 and 49. For the divine right of kings, cf. v.g. *New Catholic Encyclopedia,* vol. IV (New York: McGraw-Hill, 1967), under the entry "Divine Right of Kings", *Catholicisme* (Paris, 1952) entry "Droit divin des rois"; or James Broderick, *Robert Bellarmine: Saint and Scholar,* London, 1961, chapter 10. For a moving portrait of the religious self-awareness of a Tsar, cf. R. K. Massie, *Nicholas and Alexandra,* (New York: Atheneum, 1971).

All of this dialectic would require more reading than a biblical scholar could easily undertake before publishing the present article. And yet even this leaves completely untouched such areas as theories of divine kingship in Egypt and the Ancient Near East, Plato's *Republic* and the continuous outpouring of commentary on it, Macchiavelli and his very real influence on irresponsible forms of bureaucratic governments in the West, all controversy about individual rights versus state rights, not to mention forms of government sacral and otherwise in the Orient. Yet all of this clearly lies within the horizon of inquiry which is relevant to determining a doctrine about God and political authority. It bases solidly the case for functional specialization.

One could conclude from this discussion that it is absurd to devote time to studying the Bible. The Bible is so demanding, and yet so remote that no *doctrine* about God and politics could arise from it. No biblical argument could in any case have more than a straw's weight in such a massive study. However, this is refuted at the personal level. This Bible set in motion a personal *dialectic* which must be pursued with a hermeneutics of suspicion: why do I absolutely not believe that God appoints civil governments, and why have I, over several decades of reading theology, read so little in the area of political theology? And why am I so upset at the biblical writer's insistence that David was beautiful to look at? And why did I use the words "biblical argument" above? There is a lot to examine here: being brought up as a defensive Roman Catholic in Toronto with its Protestant establishment; a Manichean-Jansenist tradition of rejecting the body; a tradition heavy with deductivist rationalism; a scholarly tradition detached from modernity; etc. These are important biases, which disable my reading of the *Rise of David Story,* and which have closed my mind to a huge area of intellectual and religious concern. My foundations[22] are in need of significant correction. The Bible text, and the questions which it elicited in this case, demand conversion of me. And the acknowledging of that demand itself is a conversion which has made me a member of a

---

More recently Christian political thought has moved from divinely appointed authority to divinely motivated insurrection: Marxist insight has enriched the debate, spearheaded by the political theology of J. B. Metz and worked out in Europe through the Christian-Marxist dialectic of the "Paulus Gesellschaft". In South America liberation theologies have been developed by G. Gutierrez and others. For recent discussion and publication cf. v.g. J. M. Bonino, *Christians and Marxists: The Mutual Challenge to Revolution,* (Grand Rapids, Mich.: Eerdmans, 1976); J. G. Davies, *Christians, Politics and Violent Revolution* (Maryknoll, NY: Orbis, 1976).

[22] I have not here explicitly gone beyond indications regarding the first five functional specialties. Clearly, however, the discomforts expressed reach into doctrines, systematics, communications, and life.

modern theological community ready to support the advance into modernity in the areas I now perceive to be neglected. And while such an initial conversion and its follow-up may not enable me to make up for wasted years, it will alter important areas of my present experience, understanding, reasoning, and deliberation, in living, in scholarship, and in teaching.

The question why one should start with the Bible, however, returns in a new form: granted on the one hand that the Bible is both demanding and remote and on the other that one can draw some profit of conversion from reading it, why should one choose to begin one's questioning with the Bible rather than with a more immediately promising source such as Rahner or Weber? Here are some tentative sketches of an answer. First, the Bible is the collection which the Jewish and Christian communities recognized as authentically expressing their beginnings. It is a collection of those texts which contained the collective memory and self-appreciation of the "factions" within Judaism and Christianity which emerged as dominant and normative. These texts have influenced, in more or less valid ways, all significant phases in the development of our communities. We would lose our roots, and suffer collective amnesia, if at least some part of our scholarship were not dedicated to biblical studies. Secondly, the Bible is the only text common to Jews and Christians, and the only text common to all Christians. It is the place where divisions of Western civilization can discuss most radically what they hold in common and what irreducibly separates them. It is also the text for worship in all these communities. Thirdly, the Bible objectifies compact consciousness's experience of God which our differentiations of consciousness have caused us to fracture in some degree, and which we aspire to repossess when consciousness is finally reintegrated after some centuries of this migration through interiority.

The "Inside" of the Jesus Event

by Ben F. Meyer

What can history do for Christology? Or, rather, with reference to Christology, what can history do for us?

A telling answer would take account of past and present, old and new. History done competently and honestly offers the kind of entrée to tradition that accords with the critically differentiated consciousness of the contemporary West. We have become aware that the very act of inheriting demands that one's heritage be translated into one's own cultural language; and this perhaps more than anything else is what has brought about developments in doctrine.

Long before the rise of the historical consciousness this process of translation had proceeded apace. It generated the worlds of Christological meaning that came to expression in early Christianity, e.g., when the Easter faith of the Jerusalem church was translated into a thematization of the pre-existence of Christ on a par with God (cf. the Philippians hymn, Phil 2:6-11). This was a startling translation but (as Gregory Dix recognized)[1] still a merely adequate translation of the original Easter faith into another range of wondering and questioning, a new conceptual idiom and aesthetic pattern.

For centuries this process of translation or transposition was carried on not only without benefit of an accompanying theory of development but without even the hint that something new was taking place and that some account of it was in order. Ancient and medieval Christians overlooked or disavowed the novelty regularly

---

[1] Dom Gregory Dix, *Jew and Greek: A Study in the Primitive Church* (Westminster: Dacre Press, 1952), pp. 77-81.

emergent in the transpositions that allowed each culture and each age to appropriate its religious heritage, safely relocating the most innovative aspects of their own historic experience in God's original act of revelation.

In our own changed situation it is history that allows whoever among us is able to enlarge and enrich the old with the new *(vetera novis augere et perficere)* to discern what the old really was so that the new might enlarge and enrich rather than just displace, diminish, or destroy it. Bernard Lonergan has persuasively commended this principle by realizing it in practice.[2] Though his words on the *vetera* and *nova* had the ring of a consciously and reassuringly traditional formula, they have made room for a problem barely entertained and a solution barely hinted at in classical Catholic tradition.

The problem is summed up in the conditionedness of acts of meaning by historical contexts of meaning. True, St. Thomas "was quite accurate on the matter of eternal truths. They exist, but only in the eternal and unchanging mind of God"[3] (S. T. I, q. 16, a. 7). Still, neither Thomas nor, much less, the Renaissance scholasticism prolonged by manuals down to our own time drew the conclusion that theology, if it was to make our religious heritage truly and thoroughly intelligible to us, would have to undertake the vast historical task of recovering the contexts in which religious formulations were originally embedded, of tracing through subtly shifting semantic centers of gravity the transpositions of religious themes from one context to another, and of thereby helping to meet the conditions for distinguishing between successful and failed transpositions in the past as well as for effecting successful transpositions in the present, with both the new developments they entail and the concomitant sloughing off of untransposable "period trash."[4]

Shorn suddenly of the protection of its conceptualist premises, of the illusion of meaning without context, objectivity without subject, truth without mind and so without time, Catholic theology is newly and finally positioned to capitalize on the discovery that, far from being the enemy of the truths of philosophy and religion, the swelling tide of historical knowledge is a condition of their transposability from context to context and hence of their lasting validity. What

---

[2] *Insight* and *Method in Theology* are the outstanding but not the only examples. For Lonergan's statement of the ideal, see the end of the *verbum* articles and the end of *Insight*; *Verbum: Word and Idea in Aquinas*, p. 220; *Insight: A Study of Human Understanding*, p. 748.

[3] Bernard J. F. Lonergan, "Philosophy and Theology," *A Second Collection*, pp. 193-208, p. 193.

[4] The phrase in inverted commas is borrowed from Austin Farrer, *Finite and Infinite: A Philosophical Essay* (Westminster: Dacre Press, 1943; repr. 1964), p. ix.

history can do for us with reference to Christology is nothing less than to allow us to enter into our rightful Christological heritage in the recognition that this very act of inheriting recurrently requires an enlarging and enriching of the old with the new.

The present essay, I hasten to add, does not itself ambition anything so grand. It remains at the level of determining what the old really was. It is an effort to recover a single but crucial moment in the emergence of Christological meaning. It undertakes to consider Christ as Subject, not at that threshold where one conducts the inquiry into "subject" and "consciousness" (and where Lonergan realized in a particularly striking way the ideal of enlarging and enriching the old with the new)[5] but beyond that threshold in the properly historical sphere, where Christ is the subject of horizons, perspectives, purposes, and purposeful words and acts.

II.

The central act of the Jerusalem church was to interpret the Easter vindication of Jesus as messianic enthronement. But how did this interpretation relate to the historic career of Jesus? Was messiahship tacked onto the figure of Jesus after the fact? Or was it inevitable, in the light of his historic words and acts, that divine vindication should be construed in just this way? In either case the resourceful historian of religions may make the interpretative act of the Jerusalem church historically comprehensible. But this must not be allowed to conceal the chasm between messianic enthronement as one interpretative option out of many, and messianic enthronement as the uniquely coherent, the "inevitable," interpretation of Jesus' vindication.

Clearly relevant to this issue (the resolution of which cannot but determine in large part how one will understand both Jesus and the Jerusalem church) is the question of where to locate the beginnings of thematic Christology. On this there are two positions in contemporary scholarship, one locating these beginnings in the Easter experience of the disciples, the other positing the historicity of the disciples' pre-Easter confession of Jesus as Messiah (cf. esp. Mk 8:27; Mt 16:16; Lk 9:20; Jn 6:68f.; 1:41f.) and, still more fundamentally, the messianic self-understanding of Jesus himself (Mk 8:27c, 29: Mt 16:13c, 15; Lk 9:18c, 20; Mk 14:62; Mt 26:64; cf. Mk 15:2; Mt 27:14; Lk 23:3; Jn 18:37). These two views represent a complete disjunction: thematic Christology either did or did not originate earlier than Easter. Between these contradictory alternatives there can be no middle ground or third position.

---

[5] Bernard J. F. Lonergan, *De constitutione Christi ontologica et psychologica* (Rome: Gregorian University Press, 1964), pp. 83-148. See also "Christ as Subject: A Reply," *Collection,* pp. 164-97.

Nils Alstrup Dahl, to be sure, has presented in his well-known essay "The Crucified Messiah"[6] what at first looks like a third position. But in fact it is a combination in which pre-Easter thematic messiahship is affirmed but in so weak a sense as to be left virtually unaffirmed. At Jesus' trial before the Sanhedrin (if there actually was a trial before the Sanhedrin) and at his trial before Pilate, "Messiah" (or "king") figured in an accusatory question. Out of a willingness to accommodate to the categories of the questioner (for he "could not deny the charge that he was the Messiah without thereby putting in question the final eschatological validity of his whole message and ministry"),[7] Jesus acknowledged, either by a word "extorted" from him or at least by silence, that he was the Messiah.[8]

Dahl, it should be noticed, did not ask precisely why it was that Jesus thought he would put his whole ministry into question unless he were to accept a title that he did not otherwise find appropriate. Moreover, one cannot but wonder whether this supposed dilemma of Jesus is coherent with the view that "Messiah" in the Judaism of Jesus' time was merely one among many parallel figures and by no means "the necessary contemporary expression" for "eschatological bringer of salvation."[9] Dahl's view had the merit of insisting once again on the great significance of the *titulus* on the cross as attesting that there had indubitably been some messianic thematization of Jesus, however grounded and by whomever sponsored, in the pre-Easter period; that it played a key role in Jesus' condemnation; and that this itself was of lasting significance for the post-Easter church. Nevertheless, his view as it stands neither represents a genuine third position between the two we have distinguished nor exhibits the internal coherence of an historically plausible account. Leaving it aside, then, we shall consider only the clearly stated alternatives; thematic Christology either did or did not originate earlier than Easter.

For either of these views the price of probability is to concede meaning and importance to the data on which the opposing view is based. For, even should it be made plausible that prior to the Easter event Jesus himself deliberately elicited from his disciples acknowledgment as "the Messiah" *($m^e\bar{s}ih\bar{a}$' = ho christos)* or that he was referring to his own future destiny and role in evoking "the Man" *(bar ^{e}nāšā' = ho huis tou anthopou)* foreordained to bring the eschatological ordeal to an end (see, e.g., Lk 17:22-30), it nevertheless remains

---

[6] N. A. Dahl, "The Crucified Messiah," *The Crucified Messiah and Other Essays* (Minneapolis: Augsburg, 1974), pp. 10-36.
[7] Ibid., p. 33.
[8] Ibid.
[9] Ibid., p. 26.

implausible that, as it stands, the gospels' presentation of the use of such titles literally transcribes the pre-Easter past. There are some indisputably non-historical uses of the titles (on "Messiah" or "Christ" see Mk 9:41; Mt 23:10; on "Son of man" see, e.g., Mk 2:10; Mt 9:6; Lk 5:24; Mk 2:28; Mt 12:8; Lk 6:5; Mt 8:20; Lk 9:58); there are still more instances in which historicity is doubtful; and, in any case, those who find the beginnings of thematic Christology in the time of Jesus' ministry must still acknowledge that the Easter event triggered a Christological explosion. Conversely, even if it should be plausibly argued that thematic, titular Christology dates only from the Easter experience of the disciples, it is still altogether implausible that the dramatic emergence of such Christology lacked solid roots in the pre-Easter career of Jesus.

This is not to minimize the significance of the debate or the difference between the two stands it has brought to light. In terms of the history of religions the debate is significant both as history and as the history of a religion. It is the function of history to settle matters of fact and the condition of historical achievement is a passion for getting things straight. But the question of who and what stood at the beginnings of thematic Christology not only bears on a matter of fact but on a hinge fact of great significance to Christianity as a religion. For, the history of Christianity is the history of a people bonded not by blood but by meaning, and struggling to achieve its own summoning selfhood by finding its way to the center of that meaning. The relation of Christological confession to the Jesus of history and, indeed, to his self-understanding belongs inalienably to that center. As Franz Mussner once put it, this is a *Schicksalsfrage* for Christianity. If Christology has no roots at all in the consciousness of the historical Jesus, how in the end could it vindicate its claim to be other than and much more than mere ideology?[10]

Behind myth, urges one school of research, stands ritual. But behind the Christ myth—that is, behind the affirmation of Jesus as messianic Lord—stands not just ritual but a disruptive flesh-and-blood figure, a man with a public career and definable mission, a charismatic hero to the depressed elements of the society he addressed, a defendant accused of a political crime and executed by a known official. How one answers the question of whether the Jerusalem church's interpretation of him as Messiah reflects Jesus' own understanding of his mission or is a wholly independent conception of his person and work tends to settle how one will answer such ulterior questions as whether Christianity originated with Jesus or his

---

[10] F. Mussner, "Wege zum Selbstbewusstsein Jesu. Ein Versuch," *Biblische Zeitschrift* 12 (1968):161-72, p. 161.

disciples, whether public events in the history of Israel pertained to its foundations, whether the categories appropriate to understanding Christianity in its origins and root structures are supplied by Torah and prophets (Messiah, covenant, remnant, etc.) or by gnosis or the mysteries or other cults of Hellenistic Egypt, Greece, and Rome. If these are matters of moment, they only underscore the importance of accurately locating the beginnings of thematic Christology. Obviously, this project is far too large to be undertaken here in its full scope. In what follows we shall be obliged to do no more than indicate in summary fashion certain grounds for locating these beginnings in Jesus himself. With particular reference to the temple riddle (Mk 14:58 para.) we shall correlate the aspects of weal *(Heil)* and woe *(Unheil)* in Jesus' conception of his mission. Finally, we shall return to the issue of whether or not there is an intrinsic connection between thematic Christology and Jesus' actual career.

III.

The complexity of the question "did the historical Jesus understand himself to be the Messiah?" derives, ironically, from the disciples' Easter proclamation of his messiahship, for this proclamation grounds the possibility that the Easter church might have merely retrojected messiahship and messianic consciousness to the days of Jesus' public life. The methodical sceptic (that is, the critic who argues that, of words and acts attributed to Jesus, only that is historical which contradicts practices or convictions of both Judaism and the early church) immediately infers from the continuity between the Easter proclamation and the messianic texts of the gospels the impossibility of showing historically that Jesus understood himself to be the Messiah. The restrictive or negative side of the methodical sceptic's principle (*"only* that is historical which...") is arbitrary and invalid[11] and no historical critique consistently observing it could be anything but self-defeating.[12] In its positive moment, however, and in the following formulation, the principle is valid: those words and acts attributed to Jesus that are discontinuous with the practices and convictions of the early church do derive from him. It follows that the critic interested in the issue of Jesus and messiahship should pay particular attention to traditions that relate to messiahship but fail to correlate with the early church's own characteristic messianic themes.

---

[11] See B. F. Meyer, *The Aims of Jesus* (London: SCM Press, 1979), pp. 81-84; p. 277 n. 8.

[12] See M. D. Hooker, "On Using the Wrong Tool," *Theology* 75 (1972), pp. 570-81.

The leading candidate for such status may well be the riddle apparently taken up out of the Jesus tradition with mortal effect by Stephen and the *hellēnistai* (cf. Acts 6:14). Approximating the formulation which it receives in the account of Jesus' own trial, we have:

> I will destroy this sanctuary
> and within three days I will build another.[13]

Limitations of space do not permit here a full-dress review of scholarship on this saying from Dalman to the present day. Let it suffice to make three remarks on this exegetical history and to follow them with a few further observations on the interrelation of the themes of weal and woe.

First, it is an extraordinary fact that scholarly opinion since Dalman is practically unanimous in favor of historicity. Given this or that qualification on the wording, the critics are at one in attributing the saying to Jesus himself.

Second, the effort to locate in the history of religions the field of meaning to which the saying is related has been at least partly successful. But the hope of finding a pre-Jesus model in which the motifs of destroying and building the sanctuary were already conjoined has not been met. Neither the proposal of Reitzenstein,[14] accepted by Bultmann[15] and Goguel,[16] on a background in the eschatological myth of the primaeval man (= "Son of man") nor the proposal of J. G. H. Hoffmann,[17] following Engnell's studies in divine kingship,[18] on a background in Canaanite ritual (and thence in the royal messianism of the Bible) has proved out. In both cases something is lacking either in the data or in the argument or in the

---

[13] For the various textual forms see Mk 14:58; Mt 26:61; Mk 15:29; Mt 27:40; Jn 2:19; cp. Acts 6:14. Aramaic retrotranslation, slightly revised from G. Dalman, *Orte und Wege Jesu* (Gutersloh: Mohn, ^{4}1924; repr. Darmstadt: Wissenschaftliche Buchgesellschaft, 1967), p. 324:

'ănā' sātar hêk^e lā' hādēn
ûlit^e lātā' yômîn nibnê ḥōrānā'

[14] R. Reitzenstein, *Das Mandäische Buch des Herrn der Grosse und die Eveangelienüberlieferung* (Heidelberg: Winter, 1919), pp. 63-70.

[15] R. Bultmann, *The History of the Synoptic Tradition,* trans. J. Marsh (Oxford: Blackwell, 1968), pp. 120f.; p. 401.

[16] M. Goguel, "La parole de Jésus sur la destruction et la reconstruction du Temple," *Congrès d'histoire du christianisme I,* ed. P. L. Couchoud (Paris: Rieder and Amsterdam: Van Holkema & Warendorf, 1928), 117-36, pp. 135f.

[17] J. G. H. Hoffmann, "Jésus messie juif," *Aux sources de la tradition chrétienne* [M. Goguel Festschrift] (Neuchatel/Paris: Delachaux & Niestlé, 1950) pp. 103-11, p. 105.

[18] Ivan Engnell, *Studies in Divine Kingship in the Ancient Near East* (Oxford: Blackwell, 1967^3; original: Uppsala, 1943), p. 150.

two together.[19] That classical messianism, on the other hand, offers a relevant background for the motif of building the sanctuary has several times been noticed, beginning with the observations of Dalman and culminating in those of Otto Betz.

Dalman made the fundamental observation that Jesus "spoke of the building of the temple (cf. Matt. 26:61, Mark 14:58) in the same sense in which the Messiah is the builder of the temple according to Zech. 6:12, 13."[20] The building of the temple was the task of the son of David (i.e., Solomon) according to the oracle of Nathan (2 Sam 7:13f., repeated in 1 Chron 17:12f.) and this motif was actualized by prophets (Hag 1:1f.; 2:20-23; Zech 6:12f.) intent on the post-exilic rebuilding of the temple. But was Jesus' adoption of the temple-building motif meant "in the same sense" as that of Zech 6? Was he to build a physical temple? The latter question Dalman left unanswered; but he did show that the riddle of Jesus may well have had a scripturally grounded messianic significance.[21]

Betz pointed to the fact that the text of Nathan's oracle had been interpreted messianically by the Essenes (4QFlor 1-13, admittedly without a messianic interpretation of the precise words 'he shall build a house for my name" in 2 Sam 7:13).[22] He articulated the correlations in the Christian reading of the oracle between the motifs of Davidic Messiah, Son of God, resurrection, enthronement, and the building of the temple. He rooted the crucial tie between messiahship and the building of the temple in the historical Jesus' own symbolic actualization of biblical tradition. Betz was thus able to recognize the significance of age-old biblical tradition for understanding both the Markan trial-scene before the Sanhedrin (esp. Mk 14:58-62) and the celebrated "Thou art Peter" pericope (esp. Mt 16:16-19).

---

[19] M. Lidzbarski, *Das Johannesbuch der Mandämr* (Giessen: Töpelmann, 1915), p. 242 n. 4, was probably right in the first place that the Mandaean text is dependent on Jesus' saying. The key word *hek^e la'* differs, however, in meaning in the two texts. In Jesus' saying it is the sanctuary of the Jerusalem temple; in Enoš's word it is 'palace' as symbol of the world. Again, Engnell has attempted to reconstruct the Canaanite pattern for the Sukkot festival. But even if the reconstruction were more certain than it is, its relevance to Jesus' word remains doubtful. Thus, Hoffmann can appeal to a vague and uncertain parallel but can offer no textual support for it.

[20] G. Dalman, *The Words of Jesus,* trans D. M. Kay (Edinburgh: Clark, 1902), p. 307.

[21] Dalman also took notice of the scripturally grounded (Ps 2 and 110) identification of "Messiah" and "Son of God," ibid.

[22] O. Betz, "Die Frage nach dem messianischen Bewusstsein Jesu," *Novum Testamentum* 6 (1963), 20-48; also, *What Do We Know About Jesus?,* trans. M. Kohl (Philadelphia: Westminster, 1968), pp. 83-112. On the one hand, the Essene congregation was already the sanctuary of God prior to the coming of the Davidic Messiah (cf., e.g., 1QS 8:5-9; 1QH 6:25-28); on the other, God himself would build a new temple "at the time of blessing" (11Q Temple 29:8-10; cf. 5Q13 2:6).

Third, the effort to say how the motifs of destroying "this sanctuary" and building another fit in with other data on Jesus' view of the future was crowned with success—a success largely overlooked by subsequent scholarship—in the work of C. H. Dodd and Joachim Jeremias. Dodd found that he could easily fit the phrase on destroying the sanctuary into the framework of Jesus' vision of events destined to take place in history (all of which belonged to "the eschatology of woe"); but, finding himself unable to fit into the same historical framework the phrase on building another sanctuary, he posited a complementary framework of post-historical "apocalyptic" events (Jesus' "eschatology of bliss") to which it must have been meant to refer.[23] These events would be opened by the day of the Son of man: at once resurrection, enthronement, and parousia. Dodd's achievement was thus to set the temple saying in the fully coherent context of a two-phase vision of the future: first, woe, rooted in the response to Jesus' ministry and epitomized in the destruction of the temple; then bliss, inaugurated by the day on which the Son of man is revealed (Lk 17:30) and epitomized in the new temple.

Jeremias offered a critical appreciation of this analysis.[24] The critical aspect was evident in his disengaging the reconstruction from Dodd's one-sided system of "realized eschatology." But the positively appreciative aspect was evidenced by the way in which Jeremias added the high gloss of technical precision to Dodd's insightful reconstruction.

The eschatological scheme of early Christianity differentiated perforce between resurrection and parousia, for the consummation of history did not take place with the resurrection. The "three days" sayings, on the other hand, supposed an eschatological scheme in which "the third day," the great turning point, was a global undifferentiated whole. This, together with the motif of Jesus as the destroyer of the temple, made the temple saying problematic to the early Christian community. Since the triumph imaged in the new temple had not come with Jesus' resurrection, the promise to build it in three days looked like unfulfilled prophecy. (The fourth gospel solved the problem by reinterpreting the new temple as the body of the risen Christ; cf. Jn 2:19-21).

Jeremias had never doubted the messianic sense of the temple saying or its transcendent and symbolic perspective.[25] And thirty

---

[23] C. H. Dodd, *The Parables of the Kingdom* (London: Nisbet, 1935), see chapters two and three.

[24] J. Jeremias, "Eine neue Schau der Zukunftaussagen Jesu," *Theologische Blätter* 20 (1941), pp. 216-22.

[25] J. Jeremias, *Jesus als Weltvollender* (Gütersloh: Bertelsmann, 1930), p. 35-40.

years after his article on Dodd's reconstruction of Jesus' vision of the future, he completed the analysis by offering a convincing treatment of the three days motif as designating the interval between the climax of the eschatological ordeal and its resolution with the coming of the reign of God.[26]

The end-result of research and reflection on the temple riddle from Dalman to the present day is to have vindicated its historicity; to have located at least one element of its background in the history of religions, namely, in biblical texts identifying the Messiah as that son of David/Son of God (2 Sam 7:13f.; 1 Chron 17:12f.; Ps 2:7; 89:27; 110:3; cf. 4 Q Flor 11) who is appointed to build God's house (2 Sam 7:13f.; 1 Chron 17:12f.; Hag 1:1f.; 2:20-23; Zech 6:12f.); and, finally, to have set the saying in the context of the historical Jesus' own view of the future as divided between the eschatological ordeal (here epitomized in the destruction of the temple) and its swiftly following ("in three days") resolution (here epitomized in the building of the new temple, i.e., the transfigured community of Jesus' followers).

The saying is a consciously enigmatic disclosure of Jesus' mission as comprehending both weal and woe. The enigma lies in the antithesis "destroy"/"build," which correlates with Israel's divided response to him, seen now as settled. The antithetical structuring recalls two images from the classic tradition of the prophets. The first is that of Jerusalem, the temple city set high on the mountain, under attack by the nations but inviolable under the protection of Yahweh (Is 8:9f.; 17:12-14; 14:26f.; Joel 2:1-20; Zech 12:2-4). The second is that of Yahweh bringing the nations up against Jerusalem (Zech 14:2; Ezek 38:14-17) or himself laying siege to the city (Is 29:2f.; Zeph 3:8b).[27] The basic theme is that Yahweh protects Jerusalem; Yahweh against Jerusalem is a thematic reversal grounded in the prophetic conviction that the inviolability of the city was conditional on its allegiance to God (e.g., Is 7:9b; 14:32; 28:16). This is simply a variation on the basic thematic reversal effected by the prophetic movement as a whole: far from being an unconditional guarantee of security, the day of Yahweh would see his judgment turned against Israel itself.

The riddle of Jesus gave this thematic legacy a new shape. In the ordeal about to break out unbelieving Jerusalem would go under.

---

[26] J. Jeremias, "Die Drei-Tage-Worte der Evangelien," *Tradition und Glaube. Das frühe Christentum in seiner Umwelt* [K. G. Kuhn Festschrift], ed. J. Jeremias, H.-W. Kuhn, H. Stegemann (Göttingen: Vandenhoeck & Ruprecht, 1971), pp. 221-29.

[27] See Hanns-Martin Lutz, *Jahwe, Jerusalem und die Völker. Zur Vorgeschichte von Sach 12,1-8 und 14,1-5* (WMANT 27; Neukirchen/Vluyn: Neukirchener Verlag, 1968), for text-critical, exegetical, and tradition-historical treatment of the texts.

But at the center of Jesus' eschatology stood the messianic remnant, the unique beneficiary of God's saving act. This surely is the key to the remarkable phenomenon of Jesus' consistent *application to the disciples* of the imagery of the city on a mountain (Mt 5:14; [28] cf. Thomas, 32), the cosmic rock (Mt 16:18; cf. Jn 1:42), and the new sanctuary (Mk 14:58; Mt 26:61). *Here* was the inviolable city streaming light onto the world; here was the temple built on rock, secure against the assaults not of the nations but of death; here was the sanctuary to be built by the newly enthroned king.

IV.

R. G. Collingwood distinguished between the "outside" and the "inside" of an event.[29] The outside is what can be described in terms of time, place, and movement. The outside of the Jesus event is easily summarized: a public figure in his mid-thirties, Jesus was itinerant in the regions of Galilee and Judea in the days of the Roman prefect Pontius Pilate (A.D. 26-36) at whose command he was executed by crucifixion on the charge of claiming to be a king.

This summary is not historical knowledge in the proper sense but data for historical knowledge. Knowledge adds to data the effort to understand the data and the effort to secure that understanding as correct. Such efforts entail the quest of ever fuller data, deeper understanding, more detailed and circumstantial cross-checking. The result, inevitably, is to discover something of the "inside" of the event under investigation; that is, to grasp it as motivated in some way, moving in some direction, significant in some context. This internal factor, which gives the event its human and historical density, can only be described in terms of meaning. The meaning of the event—the meaning intrinsic to and constitutive of it—has two sources: the intention of its author(s) and the context of its actualization.

Prescind from their differences and actions are all the same. But consider actions, not abstractly in their physical reality alone, but concretely in their properly human integrity, and they are all unique. This concrete approach to action, typical of history as distinct from science, is equally the key to the historian's scepticism of "laws" purporting to explain a given action and to his interest in recovering the particular perspectives and purposes that account for the coming to be of the action and its unique contour. Thus, the

---

[28] See K. M. Campbell, "The New Jerusalem in Matthew 5.14," *Scottish Journal of Theology* 31 (1978), pp. 335-63.

[29] R. G. Collingwood, *The Idea of History* (Oxford: Oxford University Press, 1946), pp. 213-15.

historian is positively concerned with action not only as taking place in a given context and having a given impact on it but also as a revelation of the agent. For, action is symbolic. Its meaning is irreducible to its pragmatic effect—what Michael Novak, echoing William James, has called its "cash value." Every action, argued Novak, "also means what the agent intends it to mean, i.e., what he is symbolizing by it....Action is like speech: each life utters a unique word."[30] This corresponds to the category of "incarnate meaning" and is obviously central to "the inside of the event."

At this point we might recall, for purposes of illustration, the novelty of Jesus' initiative toward notorious sinners (*hamartōloi;* cf., e.g., Mk 2:14; Mt 9:9; Lk 5:27; cf.19:5). Apart from the cleansing of the temple, no other feature of his public career so startled his contemporaries. To the sinners themselves his free entry into contact and communion (cf. "dining" in Mk 2:15f.; Mt 9:10f.; Lk 5:29f.; cf. 5:2) with them was irresistible (cf. "friend" in Mt 11:19; Lk 7:34; cf. Mk 2:14c; Mt 9:9d; Lk 5:27c; 7:37f.) but to the upright *(dikaioi)* it was indefensible (e.g., Mk 2:16; Mt 9:11; Lk 5:30; Mt 11:19; Lk 7:34; 7:36-50; 15:1f.). Now, Jesus no more intended to write off the upright than he did the sinners; hence a set of memorable words, several of them in the form of "I have come" sayings, addressed to the upright and meant to explain, justify, and commend his initiative toward the sinners. These texts present Jesus' behavior toward the sinners in the images, first, of the physician:

> It is not the healthy but the sick who need the physician
> (Mk 2:17a; Mt 9:12; Lk 5:31),

second, of the messenger (cf. Lk 14:16f.) commissioned by his master to tell the invited guests that the banquet is ready:

> I have not come to summon the righteous but the sinners
> (Mk 2:17b; Mt 9:13; Lk 5:32),

and third, of the shepherd who, having counted his sheep and found one missing, sets out in search of the straggler:

> The Son of man has come to seek and to save the lost
> (Lk 19:10).

Now, the point of the images of physician, messenger, and shepherd is to make the "inside" of Jesus' actions intelligible: to reveal the purposes that fill them and to present them in a swiftly sketched parabolic setting designed to illuminate and commend them. As the physician goes to the sick because they need him, as the messenger

---

[30] M. Novak, "The Christian and the Atheist," *Christianity and Crisis* 31 (1966), pp. 51-55, p. 52.

summons the guests at his master's bidding, as the shepherd for whom every sheep counts sets out for the straggler—so I go to the sinners. The images unravel an enigma; no enigma remains in Jesus' behavior toward sinners if one takes account of the sinners' need (Mk 2:17a; Mt 9:12; Lk 5:31), of the claim on God of every child of Abraham (Lk 19:9f.; cf. 13:16) and, finally, of God's own will, benevolence, good pleasure (Mk 2:17b; Met 9:13; Lk 5:32; cf. Lk 15:11-32; *thelein* in Mt 12:7; 20:14f.; *thelēma* in Mt 18:14; *chara* in Lk 15:7, 10). The images are designed to offer the explanatory perspectives in which Jesus' startling, enigmatic comportment toward sinners suddenly becomes transparent, a luminous epiphany of divine love.

If we allow these explanatory images to function as patterns on which to understand "Messiah," the question arises: what action of Jesus is "Messiah" meant to explain?

The answer lies half-hidden in traditions we have already alluded to: the confession at Caesarea Philippi (Mt 16:13-20; Jn 1:41f.; cf. Jn 6:68f.; Mk 8:27-30; Lk 9:18-21) and the trial before the Sanhedrin (Mk 14:57-62; Mt 26:60-64). For these traditions suggest, as we have noted, that "Messiah" should be defined in accord with the most classical biblical messianism as that Son of David and Son of God who is appointed to build God's house; second, that we should understand the whole mission of Jesus, divided between a present earthly and future heavenly phase, as the building of the new sanctuary or (to translate the metaphor) the bringing into being of the eschatological covenant and people of God.

The point at which all the words and acts of Jesus' public career converged was the eschatological restoration of Israel. "Messiah" in the sense of the above texts adds nothing to this except to specify it, under the image of the new sanctuary, as the appointed task of the messianic son of David/Son of God. "Messiah," in short, is explanatory. As "physician" or "messenger" or "shepherd" explains Jesus' initiative to sinners, "Messiah" explains the totality of his words and acts and affirms their interconnectedness as facets of one purpose. To predicate "Messiah" of Jesus in the sense he himself intended is to grasp the "inside" of the Jesus event as the single task of re-creating Israel—and the nations by assimilation to Israel—in fulfillment of the Scriptures. To this messianic mission belonged, above all, Jesus' death as "ransom" (Mk 10:45; Mt 20:28; cf. Is 43:3f.), expiatory offering (Mk 14:24c; Mt 26:28b; Lk 22:20c; Jn 6:51; cf. Is 53:10), and covenant sacrifice (Mk 14:24b; Mt 26:28a; Lk 22:20b; cf. Ex 24:8; Jer 31:31-34), not only for Israel but for the nations (Mk 10:45; Mt 20:28; Mk 14:24; Mt 26:28b; cf. Jn 6:51; Is 15:13-53:12).

If Jesus himself thus saw to it that his messiahship be defined by his destiny, a like intention imposed itself in the confessions of the post-Easter church. "Messiah" had originally provided the heirs of the biblical tradition with a world of meaning taken over by Israel from "sacral kingship" and thematizing enthronement, restoration of temple and cult, judgment, and the universal reign of justice and peace. Messiahship did not lose its sacral and royal aura everywhere in early Christianity, witness the gospels. But the death and resurrection of Jesus established the new soteriological pattern that early defined the messiahship of Jesus and so dominantly that the predicate "Christ" became rather the *subject* of predication, a cognomen, a name. At the springs of this development, however, stood the historic figure whose real task, despite appearances, was caught parabolically and comprehensively in the royal images of master-builder and temple (Mt 16:18; Mk 14:58; Mt 24:63; Jn 2:19).

Soteriology

Toward A Responsible Contemporary Soteriology

by William P. Loewe

Each evening my wife and I perform the American ritual of dining, putting the baby to bed, and watching the news. At the time of this writing the people of Cambodia are starving to death by the thousands; already, in the past few years, war, political upheaval, famine and disease have conspired to kill more than two million of them. Their plight has at last moved the nations of the world, and relief supplies are piling up on the Cambodian border. Thus far the current rulers have allowed only a small, inadequate portion of the supplies to trickle in.

Meanwhile, for a minute or so each evening, my wife and I watch the Cambodians die. Then as the image of their agony fades from the screen, we receive a word from the sponsors of the newscast—Cadillacs will please those who want more, not less, out of life, and a chubby entertainment celebrity cannot commend a certain dietetic aid too highly. The newscaster returns, smiling, for a final light-hearted anecdote from the day's happenings. I return to the comfort of my study for an evening of work. The Cambodians continue dying. As one newscaster likes to conclude his program, that's the way it is.

Can that be the final word? This spectacle of the unfolding of human affairs includes my own. Images of starvation and of mindless affluence mingle in casual obscenity. Stupidity, indifference, and murderous politics dictate a major part of the script. Is such a spectacle to be simply registered and acknowledged as the way things are? In the context of this question, I think, the seriousness and urgency of Christian talk of salvation become evident. Or, perhaps, the triviality of such discourse is unmasked. Christians claim that the life, death, and destiny of Jesus of

Nazareth have made a radical difference in human affairs. Jesus, they announce, has saved the human race. What sense, if any, does that claim make?

This essay rests on two convictions. I am convinced, first, that despite the virtual disappearance of classical soteriology from the recent theological scene, the soteriological question remains of central importance. If one raises the pragmatic question of what difference Christianity makes to the course of history, then an understanding of what it means to affirm that Christ has wrought the salvation of the world leads quickly to the heart of the matter. Second, I am equally convinced that the work of Bernard Lonergan provides elements of enormous value for the task of constructing a responsible contemporary soteriology.

Classical soteriology, the doctrine of Christ as Savior—of which Fr. Lonergan has offered a specimen in his *De Verbo Incarnato*[1] — was defined by a single question: How did the God-man, Jesus Christ, effect the salvation of mankind? The logical position for soteriology lay at the conclusion of the treatise on Christology which, assuming a prior treatise on the Trinity, focused on the dogma of Chalcedon to determine the ontological constitution of the Second Person in his incarnate state. Next there could be deduced the consequences for Christ's human nature of its assumption into hypostatic union with his divinity; in this phase of the treatise the various noetic and moral qualities with which that humanity must have been endowed were amply demonstrated. Finally one was prepared to inquire how the agent of redemption, thus equipped with the beatific vision, special infused knowledge, sinlessness and the rest, in fact fulfilled his task. Some authors chose to find an answer in the biblical image of sacrifice,[2] while others took a broader approach indicated by the post-Reformation doctrine of Christ's triple office as priest, prophet, and king.[3] In his own treatise Lonergan preferred to follow the mainstream of the Roman Catholic tradition in seizing upon the Anselmian doctrine of satisfaction, and the lack of unanimity in the understanding of the term manifest among his Catholic colleagues left ample room for the exercise of Lonergan's systematic acumen.

Soteriology of the sort just described is not much practiced today, and the reasons for its decline are numerous. Avery Dulles has noted a problem of terminology: because the biblical view of redemption is expressed in images like that of sacrifice, the biblical view has

---

[1] Bernard Lonergan, *De Verbo Incarnato* (Rome: Gregorian University Press, 1964).

[2] See, for example, *A Catholic Catechism: 2. Of God and Our Redemption* (New York: Herder and Herder, 1959), pp. 65-71.

[3] See L. Ott, *Fundamentals of Catholic Dogma* (Cork: Mercier, 1957), pp. 179-90.

become practically unintelligible in a culture to which such cultic ritual is foreign. As for Anselm's satisfaction theory, Dulles hazards that it evokes downright repugnance from contemporary sensibilities.[4] If the language of classical soteriology poses problems, it is also apparent that Christology, which provided its immediate context, has undergone a sea-change in recent years. The dogmatic starting point set by Chalcedon has been relativized, and many theologians have been seeking instead to ground their projects in the concrete historical particularity of Jesus of Nazareth.

This is not to imply that any simple translation of traditional terms, biblical or medieval, or even an inversion of the "high, descending" approach to Christology will of themselves open the way to a responsible contemporary soteriology. And yet the question persists: How is the Christian claim to Jesus' salvific importance to be mediated to the contemporary world and tested against the grim, desperate realities which make up that world?

The question itself can, of course, serve a number of functions. On one level it may signify an identity crisis in religious circles,[5] a quest for the palpable relevance which might reassure those Christians who find themselves disoriented and bewildered by cultural shifts affecting their ecclesial bodies. On this level the question discloses a valid human concern for identity, but the same concern renders it vulnerable to distortion and trivialization. For if the interest which guides the question is restricted to the retrieval of a formerly enjoyed personal and communal stability, if the answer obtained serves merely to reestablish the coherence of world view which it is the general business of religion to deliver, then one might fairly conclude that the question has lost its seriousness, debased by the dynamics of individual or group narcissism. Yet this need not be the case. The quest for Christian identity, to which, I believe, the question of Jesus' redemptive significance provides a key, may arise not merely from cultural malaise but from a sober confrontation with the realities of malice, stupidity, and untold suffering which dominate vast segments of human history. In that case the question transcends narcissistic self-absorption to stake out the arena in which fatalism and despair wrestle with hope. Is the newscaster's "that's the way it is" really the final comment on our days and months and years?

---

[4] Avery Dulles, *The Survival of Dogma* (Garden City, N.Y.: Doubleday, 1971), p. 178.

[5] J. Moltmann, "The Identity and Relevance of Faith," *The Crucified God* (New York: Harper and Row, 1974), pp. 7-31; F. van Beeck, "From Ecclesiological Fatigue to Christian Identity," *Christ Proclaimed* (New York: Paulist, 1979), pp. 13-29.

The soteriological question of Christian theology thus becomes a matter of hope for the course of history. The present moment, together with as many of its predecessors as the memory of the race can recall, abounds with cruelty and suffering. Does the massive facticity of these phenomena endow them with some sort of natural necessity? Can anything else be expected from the course of history? With this shift to an historical perspective emerges the decisive reason for the muting of classical soteriology: concern with history precisely as such rests on cultural developments which were simply unavailable to the era in which that soteriology took shape. Historical consciousness was not a feature of the biblical, patristic, or medieval epochs.

Today, however, a culture informed by historical consciousness, and any theology which would function within that culture, find themselves troubled on two fronts. Continuity with the Christian past has been broken, and the unproblematic reception of tradition and Scripture which Paul Ricoeur identifies as the "first naivete" of an earlier age has given way to the various forms of a hermeneutics of suspicion. Nor is the relation of contemporary culture to the future any easier. That culture has perceived clearly the character of history as a human product and thus glimpsed the possibility of responsibly shaping history to human ends. Yet the dynamics of history continue to elude man's grasp. Invested with a demonic autonomy of their own, they mock the impotence of his efforts. And even while those efforts meet frustration, the same culture which promotes them harbors within itself forces which head not to the humanization of history but toward its extinction, prompting some commentators to speak already of the dawning of a post-historical epoch.[6]

I. Authenticity, Conversion, and the Law of the Cross

The genre of the Roman seminary textbook left little room to address the issues raised by historical consciousness, but even in *De Verbo Incarnato* Lonergan moves beyond the confines of classical soteriology. Of the three theses which he devotes to the topic, the first two correspond to the five headings under which St. Thomas had dealt with it. Not content with the *vetera* of tradition, Lonergan proposes a further thesis. It reads as follows:

> The Son of God thus became man, suffered, died, and was raised because the divine wisdom ordained and the divine goodness willed, not to take away the evils of the human race through an exercise of power, but to convert those evils into a certain highest good through the just and mysterious Law of the Cross.[7]

---

[6] M. Horkheimer and T. Adorno, *Dialectic of Enlightenment* (New York: Herder and Herder, 1972).

[7] Lonergan, *De Verbo Incarnato*, p. 552.

Scholastic theology determines the language and perspective of the thesis. It operates within the framework of a descending Christology, and the major moments in the economy of salvation, namely, the incarnation, passion, death, and resurrection of the Son of God, are affirmed as facts in a recital untroubled by questions of myth and history. The question which the thesis addresses is the Thomist question of *convenientia:* Given this set of "facts," theology in the Thomist mode seeks not their necessity but their congruence with the divine wisdom and goodness from which they issue; it follows that theological understanding consists in grasping the intelligibility of the contingent matter of fact.

What intelligibility does Lonergan discern in the Christian story of Jesus? The answer provided by his thesis transcends the confines of its scholastic context. Put in somewhat different terms, the thesis affirms that the story of Jesus re-presents a basic trust that the evil in the history of the human race is not the final word. There is a condition for this trust; if God exists, evil can somehow be converted into a greater good. And Lonergan specifies the dynamic of that transformation in what he calls the Law of the Cross. He formulates this "law" in quasi-biblical terms. Sin incurs the penalty of death; death, however, can be transformed if accepted in loving obedience, and such loving obedience receives the blessing of new life. The embodiment of this principle of transformation in the Christian story of the death and resurrection of Jesus is obvious, but two further comments which Lonergan makes deserve note. He claims that the Law of the Cross constitutes the "essence," the "intrinsic intelligibility" of biblical affirmations that Jesus has effected salvation;[8] in addition, he assigns the Law of the Cross the logical status of a precept addressed to human freedom.[9]

The heart of Lonergan's direct contribution to soteriology lies in the Law of the Cross. If the meaning of the formula remains somewhat indeterminate in *De Verbo Incarnato,* Lonergan's other works provide ample material from which a full and precise statement of the meaning of the formula might be constructed. Because the performance of that exegetical task would exceed the scope of the present essay,[10] I shall content myself with the following clarificatory suggestions.

To begin with a formal observation, we have noted Lonergan's assertion that the intrinsic intelligibility of Christian discourse about salvation takes the form of a precept. With this assertion he is reject-

---

[8] Ibid., pp. 576-77.
[9] Ibid., p. 574.
[10] See W. Loewe, "Lonergan and the Law of the Cross: A Universalist View of Salvation," *Anglican Theological Review* 59 (1977), pp. 162-74.

ing any purely contemplative approach to the soteriological question which would satisfy itself with speculative understanding of a past salvific deed or event. Such may have been the force of the Anselmian doctrine, but Lonergan's third soteriological thesis moves beyond Anselm toward a further stage of theological development. If Christian soteriology becomes a matter of hope in face of the historical phenomenon of evil, soteriology acquires a practical intention which finds fulfillment not in understanding but in action. By the fact that it culminates in a precept, Lonergan's theory points toward action not as an afterthought, not as an inference to be drawn, but directly and intrinsically.

This shift from a speculative to a praxis-oriented soteriology corresponds to a larger development and refinement in Lonergan's own thought which can be documented in the writings after *Insight* and which is consolidated in *Method in Theology*.[11] In the former work Lonergan quite properly restricted himself to cognitional analysis, and the result was a brilliantly transposed statement of the Thomist position on human knowing. At the same time, however, he easily created an impression that knowing was the privileged human activity *par excellence,* particularly as its operations become specialized within the intellectual pattern of experience. Lonergan's subsequent works thoroughly overcome this impression. By the time of the appearance of *Method in Theology* Lonergan had expanded cognitional analysis into intentionality analysis, differentiated a distinct notion of value and located the operations through which it finds fulfillment, and thus reached a fuller, more adequate statement on the human subject.

In this later stage of Lonergan's thought the cognitive operations through which one transcends oneself through objective truth to arrive at the actual world of being constitute only a step along the way to the achievement of one's humanity, a step which demands to be sublated into the real self-transcendence which occurs with the evaluations, decisions, and actions by which one constitutes both oneself and one's world in the realization of value. The crucial business of human living occurs in the realm of value, decision, and activity, and while recognition of that fact neither alters the rigor of the immanent norms which govern the rationality of human knowing nor disturbs the relative autonomy of the world of theory, it does establish an ultimate finality for the subject of knowledge and theory which lies beyond cognition. Unlike the spokesmen for the classical Greek tradition, Lonergan locates the fulfillment of humanity

---

[11] On this development in Lonergan's thought see Robert Doran, *Subject and Psyche: Ricoeur, Jung and the Search for Foundations* (Washington: University Press of America, 1977), pp. 29-48.

beyond knowing in the activity which strives for the actualization of value.

What significance does the Law of the Cross acquire within the context of this development in Lonergan's thought? As is evident from the pivotal role assigned dialectic and foundations in Lonergan's understanding of theological method, the idea of authenticity governs his full statement on the human subject.[12] Authenticity is an achievement, not a given, and if self-transcendence designates the complex and dynamic process through which authenticity is attained, the Law of the Cross specifies the working out of that process under the concrete conditions of actual historical existence. The real self-transcendence which presses cognition into the service of value cannot consist simply in the progressive actuation of human potential through a series of successively richer integrations. To be born into this world is to be born into an historical process which is, among other things, shot through with dehumanizing dynamics. The familial, social, and cultural situation into which one is born contains elements which concretize a previous history of the refusal of fidelity to the demands of self-transcendence. These elements constitute an objective surd; they embody human oversight, irrationality, unreasonableness, and irresponsibility. And they are sure to combine with the structural disequilibrium resulting from the complexity of the ordered systems which compose human nature to ensure the occurrence of bias and distortion in the individual's development.

Hence the Law of the Cross. The refusal of self-transcendence dehumanizes one and corrupts the world one constructs; in biblical terms, sin leads to death. Is the process reversible? Yes, but only through a deeper entry into death. The cycle of dehumanization can be broken only through the loving obedience of which Lonergan's formula speaks, through a fidelity to the demands of self-transcendence which crucifies what is biased, distorted, and closed within oneself. Death of this sort turns out to be a liberation; it frees one for the qualitatively new life which is the reward of authenticity.

The Law of the Cross formulates a principle of transformation required for the attainment of human authenticity under the concrete conditions of existence in a sinful world. Lonergan's understanding of authenticity distances him from any mere humanism. While he can describe the fulfillment of human self-transcendence phenomenologically as a state of being in love without restrictions, a state of unreserved openness to value, he also interprets this

---

[12] "Indeed, the basic idea of the method we are trying to develop takes its stand on discovering what human authenticity is and showing how to appeal to it." Bernard Lonergan, *Method in Theology* (New York: Herder and Herder, 1974), p. 254.

fulfillment religiously as the result of God's prior self-gift in grace. It follows that strictly speaking the achievement of authenticity lies beyond man's unaided grasp; all his striving for it consists in fact in cooperation with a prior gift. And if Lonergan is ready to demonstrate that at least the question of God lies within the horizon of human inquiry, he also affirms soberly that only if God exists does the fact of evil become a problem in the technical sense, that is, one for which a solution may reasonably be sought.

Lonergan's identification of religious conversion as the event in which the human drive to self-transcendence is gifted with fulfillment not only distinguishes his thought from a humanist position. He describes conversion as a transvaluation of all one's values, and he locates its occurrence on a level of consciousness prior to that of rational inquiry and reasonable judgment. Religious conversion consists first of all in a transformation of the felt meaning which shapes one's experience and directs one's living. With this description it also becomes clear that Lonergan is no rationalist.

Feeling both provides the mass and momentum of human living and serves as the medium through which value is first disclosed. This applies to transcendent value as well, apprehended in a state of being in love in an unrestricted fashion. But if that state is to take root and find consolidation, if it is to become the center and not one more phase in the shifting tides of one's affective life, it requires the stability which appropriate expression renders possible. Lonergan defines symbol as an image evoked by or evoking feeling, and the transformation of felt meaning which constitutes religious conversion requires the work of the symbolic imagination if it is to find completion. A set of symbols which evokes and is evoked by the felt meaning operative in religious conversion can serve to integrate the psychic infrastructure of conscious intentionality with the drive to self-transcendence. The fidelity to transcendent value which constitutes human authenticity finds its strength and power in the symbolic imagination. Hence the primordial expression of religious conversion takes the form of what contemporary scholars refer to as myth and for which Lonergan reserves a more technical term, mystery.[13]

For this reason it should come as no shock even to those who make of orthodoxy a shibboleth to recognize in the Christian story of Jesus a myth, that is, a narrative expansion of symbol through which the properly religious significance of Jesus is apprehended, expressed, and communicated. The story of Jesus is proclaimed as good news

---

[13] B. Lonergan, *Insight: A Study of Human Understanding* (New York: Philosophical Library, 1958), pp. 723-724.

and presented as an invitation. People are called to become followers of Christ, to find in his story the meaning of their own lives. In imaginatively identifying with the figure of Christ they are grasped by a symbol which mediates that state of unrestricted love which is religious conversion. Metanoia, the transformation of felt meaning, is the proper effect of the Christian gospel.

Against this background a first, partial statement of the Christian contribution to history may be offered. The Christian myth operates on the level of the symbolic imagination to integrate human affectivity with the drive toward self-transcendence so as to make possible the fidelity to God's self-gift through which authenticity is achieved. By thus mediating the grace which empowers human beings to live the Law of the Cross Christianity introduces into history transformed subjects who constitute a counter-principle to the dynamically expanding surd which would make of history a reign of sin.

II. Collaboration In Redemptive Praxis

Thus far our comments have focused somewhat artificially on the individual. One misapprehension must immediately be overcome. We have contended that in Lonergan's thought the Law of the Cross expresses the condition for human authenticity imposed by existence in a sinful world. The term, authenticity, derives from existentialism, and that philosophy has evoked widespread criticism of late. The charge has been made, and rightly, that existentialist thought entertains an abstract, ahistorical understanding of the human subject; transposed to the theological context, most notably by R. Bultmann, this would promote an effete, privatized Christianity.[14] It by no means follows, however, that because of the emphasis Lonergan places on human authenticity, his understanding of salvation proves vulnerable to this line of criticism.

First, Lonergan's religiously converted subject is no isolated monad. Religious conversion, the response to God's self-gift in grace, requires mediation by meaning. To the inner word of God's love there corresponds the outer word which thematizes it, and we have argued that the primordial form of the outer word lies appropriately in myth. Now the mediation by meaning of religious conversion makes possible community, and in the tradition carried by a community one finds the vital symbols which restructure one's imagination in consonance with the transformation of felt meaning effected by God's love. Indeed, the members of the community are likely themselves to be among the most important and effective of such symbols. In this respect religious conversion proves no

---

[14] D. Sölle, *Political Theology* (Philadelphia: Fortress, 1974).

exception to the general manner in which culture advances; there is no need for each individual to re-invent the wheel for himself. And if Lonergan assigns the Law of the Cross the logical status of a precept, the conditions for its fulfillment exceed what can be expected from the insight and good will of any isolated individual. By the very makeup of our humanity, with its psychic infrastructure and spontaneous intersubjectivity, the incarnate witness of an authentic community is required.

Next, salvation is from sin, and Lonergan elaborates a notion of sin to which no ahistorical, privatized remedy is possible.[15] The root of sin lies in the individual, but from that root there issues a tangled growth which can penetrate society and choke entire cultures. Where St. Thomas spoke gloomily of the individual and his passions, Lonergan points to the human psyche. We have basic needs to be met, and the psyche proves indispensable when it loads appropriate images with the affective force which ensures action to meet those needs. But human desire is ambiguous, and the infantile criteria by which we identify the good with what immediately satisfies and the real with what our senses contact become entrenched long before we learn better. The lasting effect of these criteria is to severely limit our freedom. In the essential order our destiny may lie in an unrestricted openness to being and value, indeed, in an orientation to the divine mystery, but effectively, to the extent that infantile criteria of reality and value hold sway, that destiny evaporates like a vague illusion. Of themselves those criteria would commit one to a life-long project of egotism, and egotism stands in sharp contrast to the genuine human freedom won by self-transcending authenticity.

If individuals have their desires, groups have vested interests. Practical intelligence calls for a society composed of functionally specialized groups cooperating harmoniously to achieve a good of order through which the needs of all are cared for. But the primacy which each group tends spontaneously to accord its special interests generates distrust and competition. There emerges a stratified society with a political arrangement which seeks to contain, by one means or another, the tension between dominant and oppressed classes. That tension is likely to grow, because the vested interests of the dominant group act as a screen for creative proposals which warps material progress and heads eventually toward the breakdown of the good of order. As this draws near political stability disintegrates, power shifts, and a new dominant group with vested interests of its own appears to begin the cycle anew.

---

[15] Lonergan, *Insight*, pp. 218-42.

The work of individual and group bias is completed by what Lonergan terms general bias. Men—and, increasingly, women—of common sense conduct the daily business of the world. Each day poses its set of practical problems, to which those with the requisite know-how, skills, and experience provide equally practical solutions. Common sense directs these myriad commercial, social, and political transactions, and rightly so. To pause for lengthy and arduous theoretical reflection in their midst would constitute an unwarranted, even ludicrous, distraction. Common sense, not theory, confers the competence to deal with the immediate, practical problems of daily living.

Yet common sense has its limits, and Lonergan ascribes to general bias the tendency to ignore these limits and claim omnicompetence for common sense. General bias is operative when people of common sense canonize a crude realism in which practicality becomes the ultimate norm, when they dismiss theoretical and critical reflection as useless speculation, when they demand that the facts of the situation determine how every problem is to be solved. What they fail to discern is that not all so-called facts are objectively intelligible. Some situations, because they arise from human stupidity and irresponsibility, because they concretize the refusal of self-transcendence, require a dialectical analysis to uncover their irrationality. Common sense, however, has no patience for so abstruse an exercise, and by making facticity normative for action, common sense allows the objective surd constituted by the refusal of self-transcendence to determine the further course of history.

The myth of the way things are thus draws its power from the general bias of common sense, and the result is a perversion of culture. Although the facts of the situation exhibit a merely specious intelligibility, the only sort of theory which enjoys plausibility is that which can appeal to common sense by systematizing those facts. With the emergence of such pseudo-theory, the corrupt praxis which has engendered the situation finds itself dignified as an ideal. Meanwhile the human need for meaning and value persists, but the morality or religion which would supply them must conform to the same standard of realistic practicality. There springs up a flourishing market for the exotic managed by purveyors of private fantasy who offer escape but no remedy for the increasingly opaque, irrational social situation.

Lonergan arrives at the specter of an anti-history. In their compounded effect individual, group, and general biases generate an increasingly irrational social situation which feeds back on the human subject through a mass culture dominated by the myth of the way things are. The power of the myth reduces imagination to harmless fantasy and confines intelligence to registering and manipulating facts. Thus are neutralized the sources of creative and responsible change which might counter and reverse the process. At its limit this anti-history results in moral impotence; in religious terms, it constitutes the reign of sin.

With this analysis of sin as an historically mediated dialectic between human subjects and the world they construct, a dialectic which heads toward the extinction of human freedom, Lonergan indicates the full dimensions of the redemptive task. If that task includes and even pivots on the interior transformation of individual human beings, the process through which such transformation occurs can be neither ahistorical nor private, nor does it reach its term with the individual.

Individual conversion, we have seen, requires the incarnate witness of an authentic community. Now individual conversion is no secure possession. Because the roots of bias lie permanently embedded in the depths of human interiority, because the world in which one lives contains some blend of rationality and irrationality, of value and pseudo-value, fidelity to God's self-gift involves one in a process of transformation which is only gradual and which is subject to both advance and regression.

Much the same holds true for the community as well. Like any society, the Christian community has needs best met by the collaboration of functionally specialized groups. The Catholic Church, for instance, has evolved a priesthood, a hierarchic structure of officers, and a rich variety of religious orders. But this practical division of labor mandated by the common good constitutes also the condition for the emergence of group bias, of the jealousy for rank, privilege, and power which stratifies the community into dominant and deprived groups. The possibility of group bias is no abstract, remote possibility. Surely the full meaning of clericalism exceeds its significance as an interesting datum for sociological analysis of the supposedly value-free sort. Rare is the religious order which would presume to simply identify its past or present history with the greater glory of God. Group bias can be expected within the Christian community, and it proves particularly insidious when it succeeds in transforming religious symbol into an ideology, in the pejorative sense, for self-interest. Authenticity is as little a given for the community as for the individual, and in its corporate life the community, too, will discover that fidelity to the gift that gathers it subjects each of its component groups to the Law of the Cross.

The corporate life of the Christian community can be no closed, intramural affair, for the community exists within and to serve a larger society, so that one measure of the community's authenticity will be the degree to which it experiences its relationship to the host society as one of dialectical tension. The commitment to transcendent value, fidelity to God's self-gift, sets the community in opposition to those elements of the larger society produced by the dynamics of bias. Sin finds embodiment in social, political, economic, and cultural institutions, and hence there devolves upon the community a task of discernment and criticism. If sinful structures and dehumanizing belief systems draw their plausibility from the myth of the way things are, the Christian community possesses in its own myth and ritual the imaginative resources with which to challenge the power of that myth in prophetic denunciation.

Here again a number of ambiguities must be overcome. Because the Christian community itself comprises a set of institutions within society, it is likely to compromise its prophetic task with special pleading for the institutional interests upon which group bias fastens, reducing the Christian voice within society to one more expression of self-interest in a chorus of competing voices. Furthermore the fact of institutionalization implies dependence on the dominant political and economic powers within society; general bias is quick to suggest the impracticality of criticizing those powers. As the adage has it, you don't bite the hand that feeds you. Performance of the community's prophetic mission will be costly, and the major obstacle is likely to arise not from the hostility of those criticized but from within the community itself, from the narrow vision and false prudence which confuse service of the Kingdom of God with institutional self-service.

The demands of authenticity impose on the Christian community a prophetic mission. Sin in all its concrete manifestations must be discerned and denounced. The meaning and value mediated through the Christian symbol system can bring into contrasting focus the irrationality and disvalue embodied in the larger social reality, but the prophetic task requires further resources. If the Christian critique of society is not to be dismissed as mere religious rhetoric, it will have to be worked out in dialogue with the disciplines which possess the competence for social, economic, political, and cultural analysis. Without such collaboration a critique couched in purely religious terms, if it intends to address a concrete situation, is apt to oversimplify issues, miss the mark, and evoke the easy dismissal accorded amateurish intrusions. Lonergan has remarked that "There is a developing and penetrating criticism of sin outside the Church, a criticism that's true in all its aspects,"[16] and the Chris-

---

[16] Bernard Lonergan, "The Philosophy of Education" (Lectures delivered at Xavier College, Cincinnati, Ohio, 1959. Text from tape recording.)

tian community needs to discover and enter into dialogue with that criticism for the sake of its own prophetic mission.

Finally, for all its necessity, the voice of prophetic denunciation makes but a partial contribution. Negative criticism in itself is sterile, and so there comes into play the other pole of the dialectical tension between the Christian community and its host society. Besides denouncing sin, the community must also foster the forces in society which would overcome and reverse the dynamics of bias. Here again religious rhetoric proves insufficient; there must be real collaboration on many levels. If, for example, an economic system proves unjust, the Christian community must offer more than anathemas; it falls within the community's redemptive task to promote the theoretical research which might discover how the system could be corrected or transformed. In far broader terms the Christian community, with its commitment to the objectivity of truth and value, surely has a contribution of crucial importance to make to the scientific world in an age dominated by neopositivism and relativism. That contribution can, of course, only be made through those who possess the necessary scientific expertise.

One wonders whether the Christian community has begun even to imagine the scope of the intellectual responsibility inherent in its redemptive task. So often Christian universities, for example, seem governed by a compromise; they claim their identity from the presence of required programs in theology and philosophy and of a ministry team to foster the devotional life of staff and clients; meanwhile the secular disciplines to which the vast majority of students are attracted remain just that, untroubled mirrors of the prevailing social and cultural world.

III. Conclusion

If I have concluded with the commitment to collaboration in theoretical pursuits to which the redemptive task of the Christian community impels it, I would in no way slight the importance of the political collaboration required to render effective both prophetic criticism and intellectual creativity. A whole body of political and liberation theology makes the point cogently.

But I have been attempting to suggest the singular value of Fr. Lonergan's work toward constructing a responsible, praxis-oriented soteriology. The heart of his contribution lies in the invitation to appropriate a religious vision of human authenticity which highlights the necessity of the Law of the Cross and which illumines the ordinary form of the mediation of grace through the myth, tradition, and incarnate witness of a religious community. The application of dialectical method to the position on authenticity yields an understanding of sin as an objective surd generated by individual, group, and general biases which expands to pervert the social and cultural world of man's making and heads toward the extinction of human freedom. This understanding of sin in turn suggests the dimensions of the redemptive praxis which would counter it.

The fact remains, however, that the real demonstration of the value of Fr. Lonergan's work consists not in its exposition but in the creative, collaborative performance of the manifold tasks to which it so clearly urges.

For a Soteriology of the Existential Subject

by Sebastian Moore

"The turn to the subject" is one description of the massive shift in thought that Lonergan has made, sustained, and enjoins. It also describes my approach to soteriology, an approach that I have been enabled to deepen and refine over a period of twenty years. This work has now reached the point where I feel able to name, to describe, and to appropriate, the climactic experience of those historically privileged "subjects," the disciples of Jesus. The disciples then experienced Jesus as doing for them what only God can do, of being for them what God alone is. Thus:

> One who does for us what only God can do must be God, and Jesus has done and is doing for us what only God can do. Therefore Jesus is God.

It is the minor that was overwhelmingly experienced by the disciples: the experienced minor is the new life that transforms the abstract major, whose intention is to declare an impossibility into a concrete and all-transforming reality.

In this paper I hope to show the steps whereby I arrive at this appropriation of the central belief of Christians.

The first step is, as I have just implied, a form of "turn to the subject." I have had to explore the existential subject.

Foundational to the existential subject, I believe, is the conviction of having a unique and absolute value or worth. It is a conviction, not a wish. A mature relationship, for instance, is one where the persons have got beyond saying to each other "I am worthless. Help me to feel worthy" to saying "I am valuable and I am for you, and you for me." It is precisely because a person fundamentally *knows* that he is worthfull that he experiences, as his central desire, the desire to enrich another with himself. It is also because of this fundamental conviction that he experiences desire for another person *as* the enlargement of his own sense of worth. Essentially we are selves desiring to enrich others with ourselves; essentially, then, we are in our own estimate rich. And "essentially" means that we experience this way of being as that to be deprived of which is what Hilaire Belloc once called "the worst thing in the world." In other words, we experience this essence. We know it.

Becker's view, that our foundational sense is one of unworth and that we are essentially beings who are trying, never quite successfully, to deny this, is in my view mistaken. I shall return to him, however, at a later stage when my picture has been filled out.

But we need to be much more precise about his conviction of personal worth. We know now, for instance, that a small child's rapid beginnings in language, and in the coeval sense of his body as his, is unaccountable for in terms of stimulus-response and the other behaviorist jargon. We know that the child is enormously characterized at this stage by "object interest" which is quite other than response to stimuli. But we have to take the further step of appropriating this stage in an imaginative retrospection, and recognize that yes, I did step out of I know not what into a brave new world, of things *called* things, of limitless wonder, of other selves, of shared dreams. The only difference between us and Wordsworth in this matter of "trailing clouds of glory" is that he knew how to recognize it and talk about it. "The primacy of joy," says Dan Maguire, "is a minority report filed by Christians and children."

It is the unnoticed, unrecognized inheritance of a spacious world of meanings, mysteriously more than the animal's world of prospects and dangers, that grounds the sense of having a unique and absolute value. I take the beautiful images of Heidegger—of language as the house of being, of man as the shepherd of being—and I ask "Who am I, of whom these strange things are true?"

In other words, the *kind* of thing that the sense of personal worth is is understood by recognizing and owning our multiple initiation into "a world mediated by meanings and motivated by values," owning it *as* a theme for awe and wonder which makes its inescapable statement about who and what I am. Every deepening of this initiation, every clearing up of the sludge of confused values, every liberation of affectivity, every reconciliation with enemies, endorses the conviction of personal worth and, cognately, of responsibility to the world.

It has even been suggested that the reason why a scientist chooses, among the limitless number of available images, the few that contain promise is that the human brain, the most sophisticated product of the universe, is somehow the key that unlocks its secrets. J. C. Eccles talks very much that way. Perhaps the idea only appears so wild because for centuries we have been culturally world-alienated. Well, then, who am I, that am somehow the meaning of, or the clue to, the universe? This, again, is the sort of self-scrutiny that I am using when I say that the human person has an inalienable conviction of personal value.

The sense of self-worth becomes distorted when, to the neglect of our whole context of wonder, of mutual recognition, of communication, of shared dreams, it is privatized and becomes what people in the last decade called "feeling good about myself." The phrase by itself is a fair description of psychic and spiritual well-being. But its use in pop psychology narrows and therefore fatally distorts it. There is an apocryphal saying of Jesus to which Hopkins refers in a sermon: "Never rejoice but when you look on your brother with love." I don't think the usual contemporary meaning of "feeling good about myself" has much to do with looking on my brother with love! The only true way to feel good about oneself is to experience oneself as enriching another whom one loves.

That the person's sense of their absolute worth is a matter of conviction and not just of wish is confirmed in a vivid and nearly unbearable way by the following reflection on Auschwitz.

What can I do about Auschwitz? Not much, but this at least: I can take to heart its dire and clear lesson as to the main intention of evil, which is, to persuade persons that they are worthless and die like cattle. I can then ask: What is the conviction of being worth-*full*, that the evil power of Auschwitz was bent on extinguishing? If it is ultimately an illusion, as many respected philosophies of human being aver, then what was done at Auschwitz was only the dissipation of an illusion. And so any philosophy of human being that regards the conviction of human worth as an illusion or a creation of meaning, where in reality there is none, is equivalently the statement that no great evil was done at Auschwitz. At least I owe it to those numberless tortured persons not to mock them with a trivial philosophy of human being.

What has happened for me recently is a big shift towards the conviction of worth as opposed to the mere desire for worth as the basic human condition, and, what really comes to the same thing, towards the notion that the worth of which we are convinced is found in my radical self-experience as a self among selves, a being in relationship and in communication, a dreamer of shared dreams, a co-celebrant of the being of things through language. A book that has been largely responsible for this shift is *The Message in the Bottle* by Walker Percy. Percy's insight into the unnoticed and uncelebrated miracle of language has pointed me to the *type* of self-experience which grounds the conviction of worth, of dignity, of significance, as opposed to the mere wish for these things.

The next step is as follows. A true self-appropriation on the above lines leads to a question: "When the others are withdrawn and I am alone, what of that aloneness? Is it an absolute aloneness? Is it as though the self that I have discovered progressively in relationships, in communication, in the midst of a world revealed as being through language, were succeeded then by a self in total isolation? In my relationships I discover myself to be an absolute, and other selves to be absolutes. When alone, does this absolute exist in isolation, unrelated to any other? If it does, then it resembles the scholastic concept of God, who is absolute and without any "real relation" to creatures. So if I am absolutely alone when I am alone, then I am God. A very strange god, indeed, for this negation in solitude of all the self-properties that I discover in community makes of me an animal. And Becker does describe man as "the god that shits." This paradox is the coming-to-roost of a whole culture that has failed to see the human as a new ontological level of being. Since the whole vast world of culture and meanings has not been allowed to *constitute* the human as a new level of being, take away the surrounding human world and all that is left is the animal, alone with his godlike pretension, and his mocking anus.

My argument then proceeds: If I am alone, then I am God. But clearly I am not God. Therefore I am not alone. A student in my class commented on this argument that God appears in it by name only "on the side," only as "what I would have to be if the thesis of ultimate solitude were to be sustained," and indeed, I would add, as the scholastic God in a very simplistic form; whereas God in the conclusion is hidden in, implied in, the strange statement that "alone, I am not alone." I believe this hint of relationship, as constitutive of selfhood, with another whose name has already appeared "on the side," suggests a fresh discovery of God as the ultimate meaning of self-awareness and self-esteem. This will be of incalculable importance for theology. On the one hand, it leads, as we shall see, to the conclusion that any and every movement against self-esteem is a negating of the person's God-orientation, so that the concept of sin is immeasurably widened and deepened. And it prepares the ground for the central assertion of this paper, that at the climactic moment of the Jesus story God is known to be present and active *by* a return, in superabundance, of the sense of their worth on the part of the disciples of Jesus.

The argument might also go as follows:

My radical self-esteem generates the question "Am I, who know myself in relatedness as an absolute, alone?" and tends towards the answer "No." But to what could such an answer refer? Who could be the other, the companion? To approach an answer, I must ask another question: *Why* do I value myself? *Whence* is this miracle of self-awareness that is I? And to keep my eye on the ball here, I must remember one of the most surprising, valuable, and culture-critiquing things Lonergan ever said: "*Conscientia nihil addit supra ens.*" The conscious I am. I, conscious, am. Voegelin is making the same critique of our banal mentality when he says that "existence is not a fact," a fact that may or may not be meaningful. And so it is of the conscious, self-aware, meaningful I, and of the whole world of being to which it is the opening, that I ask "Why?" and "Whence?" And thus, conjoining the two questions "Am I alone?" and "Why am I, aware?", we get the hint that the "other" of my not-aloneness is indeed "the ground of my being," or, as Dame Julian of Norwich put it with mystical foresight, "the ground of my beseeching." This *is* foresight, for "beseeching" connotes being in its fullness as self-aware and questing, of which God is "the ground" rather than the narrower "cause."

The next step is to say that, as well as my inalienable sense of my worth I have a sense of unworth. The sense of my worth remains foundational: the two senses are not on a par. My sense of unworth is essentially corrosive of my sense of worth, so that to give it parity would be like giving to a cancer parity with the organ it diseases. Indeed, so foundational is my sense of my worth, so indispensable to psychological survival, that it forces into the deeper regions of consciousness my sense of my unworth. This combination of corrosiveness with inaccessibility to normal consciousness is exactly described by Eliot in "The Family Reunion":

> It goes a good deal deeper than what people call their conscience;
> It is just the cancer that eats away the self.

People generally give an inaccurate account of this business of unworth and concealment. They say something like this: "I suspect that at bottom I may be worthless and therefore do not look into myself for fear that this might prove to be the case." In reality the sense of my unworth is something much stronger than the suspicion that I may be worthless. It is an *inclination* to be worthless, a preference for worthlessness or perhaps for animal oblivion, an approving feeling that I am worthless, a consent to unworth: and precisely because this movement of consent to unworth erodes my sense of my worth, I am compelled to conceal it from myself. It is self-denigration, not the self, that I conceal. I think well of myself, but deep down I harbor another feeling. We think meanly of ourselves, and so we do evil. Even our deeds, public though they are, we hide from ourselves. How much more the mean self-estimate whence they proceed!

This was brought home to me reading a student's paper in which he described a conversion experience. What was fascinating about the description was that he blended two things: his own realization that he had always regarded himself "as shit" and treated other people accordingly, and the evangelical language of "not wanting Jesus to come into my life because I think I'm shit." It suddenly flashed upon me that if it is the conviction that I am worthless that keeps Jesus out, then it is the conviction that I am worthless that is sin! This conclusion the evangelical theology does not draw, presumably because it implies a fundamental goodness in the person which Lutheran theology cannot allow.

Once the sense of worth is thought of as the sense of being a self among selves and connected with the whole universe that we recreate, Godlike, through language, and then as producing the "crisis of divinity" which leads to the mysterious conclusion "I am not alone," it becomes much easier, and not at all far-fetched, to identify its opposite as sin. We have an adequate context for defining sin as a fundamental pull towards worthlessness, which, in this full context, is seen as the pull away from God. This seems to me to be what Voegelin means by the counterpull.

The consent to worthlessness, to animality, the desire for animal oblivion, the "wish not to be" that Hopkins wrestles with in one of the great late sonnets, lies very deep. It lies beyond the reach of our self-control, as Paul tragically noted in the famous passage in Romans (7:15-20). Can it, then, be called consent? It has to be, for to deny to it the quality of consent is to deny our freedom. A dark consent to nothingness that lies beyond our moral control—that is an odd, apparently a contradictory notion. Yet it is oddly descriptive of people's lives, the irrationally destructive actions that they occasionally do. A friend of mine, who comes closer to my ideal of the intellectual than almost any of my other acquaintances, said the other day that sin has to be regarded as a dark, tragic, beyond-moral force or fate. Indeed, might it not be that the Christian mind incorporates the pagan idea of fate—too real to be disavowed—under the name of sin? That same friend, who is Jewish and has a wonderful feel for the Scriptures, said of the famous Romans passage: Paul, on the road to Damascus, was blinded by the light of Jesus which penetrated his inmost soul and let him see the life-thrust and the death-thrust all intertwined, and he said "I don't know what is going on."

And with regard to the "consent" part, I find that when I look back on the evil in my life—and I don't mean just the evil deeds and omissions but their root in affectivity—the element of consent now becomes rather clear. Not at all clear at the time, it differentiates itself to some extent for memory.

There is a chorus in Eliot's "Murder in the Cathedral" which describes sin much as I am describing it:

> I have smelt them, the death-bringers; now is too late
> For action, too soon for contrition.
> Nothing is possible but the shamed swoon
> Of those consenting to the last humiliation.
> I have consented, Lord Archbishop, have consented,
> Am torn away, subdued, violated,
> United to the spiritual flesh of nature,
> Mastered by the animal powers of spirit,
> Dominated by the lust of self-demolition,
> By the final ecstasy of waste and shame,
> O Lord Archbishop, O Thomas Archbishop, forgive us,
> forgive us, pray for us that we may pray for you,
> out of our shame.

According to the scholastic tradition, sin itself is irrational and unmotivated; there is a "mystery of iniquity." While this is importantly true, it tends to be understood in too metaphysical a fashion. Phrases like "tending to nothingness" get used. The point about a notion of sin as willed worthlessness is that it earths this airy language in something just perceptible. The "nothingness" in question is the valuelessness, the meaninglessness, which something in us hankers for. The strict scholastic doctrine has no place for hankering, for that implies some motivation, some "good." My notion is on the fine edge where the motivational element in sin (the pursuit of a "good") is just disappearing into the mystery of iniquity. I think that is where Paul is in that extraordinary passage. And of course I think it is important for us to be there.

An important point in favor of this notion of sin as willed worthlessness is that it enables us to point to the real evil in oppression and all forms of the degrading and violating of persons. The real evil in oppression is that it awakes, calls forth into sympathetic resonance with itself, the oppressed person's own sense of worthlessness, for relief from all the pain of dignity gets a strong boost from injury unjustly inflicted. A person may be more sinned against than sinning, but the sin within the person will catch up. I am struck by the moral ineptitude of the comment that one sometimes hears on the fact that the Jews in the death camps connived at their degradation and reinforced it in the degrading of each other—as though this somehow *spread* the evil from the Nazis to the Jews so that it "wasn't all on one side." Evil doesn't work that way. The evil I call forth in the person I injure *adds* to the sum of evil, it does not *subtract* from my own. There is no Law of the Conservation of Evil. Evil's law is one of progression: in the case of Nazi Germany, of geometrical progression.

Sin, to repeat, is a radical self-disesteem that erodes that true self-esteem which is built into self-awareness as an implication of the latter's flourishing as a self among selves. In more common sense language I would say that the human being is basically good and hopelessly vulnerable to evil. A more theoretical language is necessary to clear up the ambiguity in "vulnerable." In it I would say that the self-aware being is, necessarily, convinced of having absolute value and so demanding of recognition. This conviction is indefinitely erosible, but not totally so. This limitless erosibility accounts for our limitless capacity for evil.

With this definition of sin we are in a position to name the sinfulness that lies at the root of consumerism. To extol an experience over whatever is producing it is an effect of sin. The self esteemed seeks to be recognized in the enrichment of others: the self disesteemed seeks alleviation by "good experiences." This critique bears on popular psychology, with its other-ignoring way of understanding the phrase "feeling good about myself." In so far as a "feeling good about myself" is not other-directed, it means filling the hole that is constituted by a fundamental feeling of the self as worthless to others. Popular psychology is the palliative for sin.

And this is the point at which to reintroduce Becker, as I promised to do. Becker's concept of the human being as radically unconvinced of his or her value and driven to *acquire* value, to build a livable lie, is in fact a description not of the human reality but of the cancer of sin that "eats away the self." One glory of Christianity is: that which the world calls reality it calls sin.

With our definition, too, we can appropriate the Old Testament language about man's utter worthlessness before God. This language is hateful to the liberal Catholic mentality for which "God loves me just the way I am" (on which C. S. Lewis once commented "God, I hope not!"). Properly, what it describes as worthless is that whole apparatus of self-esteem which a person builds to coverup a fundamental self-disesteem which is sin. What God "detests" is the cosmetization of sin which perpetuates its tyranny over us. A similar sense of worthlessness is experienced by the person who comes into a great love-relationship, in respect of all the dodges he used to use to feel good about himself. Now that his true value has been invited out by another, he rejects joyfully the counterfeit, like Paul who described as "dung" all his former observances now that he had fallen in love with Jesus Christ. The liberal Catholic mind tends to miss this dimension. Being, as it thinks, specifically committed to "openness" and honesty, it does not easily recognize that, while we think we think well of ourselves, deep down we allow disesteem to erode the self.

With this definition of sin, I am at last able to say where I stand in relation to Jung's important idea of the shadow. For Jung, the shadow, which equates with evil, is the dark side of myself that I fear to acknowledge as mine. Since it is clearly desirable to acknowledge and own the dark side, the fully developed person will, according to Jung, embody a synthesis between good and evil, a synthesis which God himself realizes in the Jungian scheme. For some time now I have thought that, contra Jung, it is not the shadow that is evil but my non-acceptance of the shadow, my failure to own it. I now think that the human evil, or sin, is my tacit *agreement* with the shadow as representing who I truly am. Certainly *non*-acceptance or repression plays an important role here; but what is repressed is not just the shadow, but my tacit self-identification by it.

The tacitness, the repression, of self-disesteem, is my next theme. My self-esteem is so essential to my psychological survival that I cannot afford to recognize the powerful tendency in me to indulge its opposite. It is really scary to think of an interior self-destruct button, a red telephone of the psyche. The human deathwish is the hardest thing to unearth. And so self-disesteem, the love of death, is buried. I bury that in me which wants nothing of life or of others. But from its buried position, self-disesteem makes itself felt *in my relationship with life and with others*. It produces there a complex malaise, which combines a feeling of failing others with resentment at them. This malaise is guilt.

Guilt at once hides sin and extends it. It *hides* sin's intolerable nihilism in the other-related, life-oriented, feeling of failing the other. And its negative quality, its wretchedness, is the *extension* of sin.

In an earlier position, I see "generic guilt" as our radical evil, and sin as its fruit. My present position is much more satisfactory in that it accords with both tradition and common sense, two allies not lightly to be set aside. For tradition and common sense see *guilt* as the feeling that results on *sin*. With an adequate concept of sin, it is possible to restore this order and to agree with a tradition that has always seen in guilt a sign of life as well as of death, to be welcomed as the doctor welcomes pain as a sign that the organism is still alive and resistant. Of course there is the guilt that is neurotically or otherwise induced, and is not the sign of sin. But our readiness to accept such guilt is itself the sign of our deep self-disesteem, our sin.

It is this ambivalence of guilt, its capacity at once to hide sin in an other-directed sadness and to communicate its venom to the other, that accounts for the limitless negative complexities in human relations, especially sexual relations. Perhaps the sexual chaos of today represents the dead-end of a culture that has denied to itself any public recognition of the transcendent, that infinite opposite to the limitless power of sin.

While we're on sex, I cannot resist quoting an authority not too much in favor with theologians at this time, Pope John Paul II—at least as paraphrased by Andrew Greeley. Greeley's weekly boutades have been rather fun recently for obvious reasons. In this one, he recommends "the Roman inquisitors" to turn their attention to a dangerous thinker, who turns out to be John Paul. I quote:

> He argues that when the Genesis author speaks of human nakedness, he is dealing wtth our basic experience of being persons with bodies that are sexual and indeed male and female combined, "the experience on the part of man of the femininity that is revealed in the nakedness of the body and reciprocally the similar experience of masculinity on the part of the woman."
>
> In the experience of shame, he goes on to say, we have a "liminal" experience of the unity of human nature as male and female. The negative implications of shame are the result of sinfulness; we become "ashamed" of our incompleteness vis-a-vis the other because of our fear and insecurity, but we also perceive, however dimly, that beyond this "ashamedness" there is fundamental truth about the mixture of femininity and masculinity not only in the human species but in each individual human.

I would go on to say that sin is the resentment at my incompleteness, my being only half of the human reality. The incompleteness is "rubbed-in," and the resentment reinforced, by the evidence, in my naked body, of femininity as well as masculinity. But the root-sin is not the resentment at my incompleteness, but my *interpretation* of my incompleteness *as meaning* invalidity, second-rateness. The bias in favor of my worthlessness fastens onto my sexual incompleteness and imposes on the latter its own negative meaning. This is the trick that is always missed. We recognize sin so much more easily in the grandiose schemes it dictates for cosmetizing itself than in its inner espousing of emptiness. We are happier with a denunciatory rhetoric than with the reality. Which is, for God's sake, that reality of which "Humankind/Cannot bear very much."

But as sin hides itself and prolongs itself in guilt, so guilt hides and prolongs itself. If sin is unbearable, guilt too is very painful. To the dishonesty that denies "that we have sin" is added the lesser dishonesty of hiding our guilt from ourselves. So what do I do? I persuade myself that the other, whom my guilt is making to appear ugly to me, really *is* ugly, and that *that* is why I dislike him or her. This is exquisitely caught by Dostoevski when he has the old father in *The Brothers Karamazov* say "I did him a bad turn years ago and I've had a grudge against him ever since."

Thus sin, guilt, and projection are the three "places" of evil in human beings. All three are combined, I think, in Scheler's powerful concept of resentment, whose parable is the Aesop fable of the Fox. The fox attempts to reach the grapes and, failing to do so, pronounces them sour. The failure represents sin, that deep withdrawal from life into the isolated self. The failure is buried: but the sight of another succeeding in just that area, the sight of life where for me has been death, revives the buried feeling of failure, causes me to re-feel (re-sent) it *in* the spectacle of another's success rather than the *cause* of it. But palpably it is all the same system.

The final stage of this part of the paper is to work out the above-elaborated meaning of sin, guilt, and projection, in relation to God. We have already explored the notion of sin as a sense of worthlessness, of meaninglessness, of isolation. We have now to recognize that, as the sense of my worth provokes the question "Am I, thus absolute, alone?", so the sinful sense of my unworth generates the answer "Yes, you *are* alone." And as the question calls to its aid the other question "Why, whence, am I, aware?", so the sinful answer undermines this question too and says that there's nothing special in this self-awareness, that we have nothing to learn from children, that reality is banal and sad. Thus sin closes my mind both to the mysterious other and to the mysterious other's "grounding" of an experience that, fundamentally trivial, needs no "ground."

A curious thing is to be noted about this logic of sin. At one and the same time, it leads me to conclude, from "I *am* alone," that I am God, that each of us in this secularist culture is God in respect of all that is, and it leads me to disavow that very sense of my value which *generates* the question "Am I alone?", and this leads to the opposite conclusion that, far from being God, I am just an animal. This ambivalence affords perhaps the crucial insight into a traditional demonology that sees the powers of evil as at once, and without a mediating humanity or humor, sublime and animal. It also accounts for Becker's despairing description of man as "the god that shits." If I am, as my secularist culture tells me I am, ultimately alone, then indeed I am "the god that shits." And I have to confess that so deeply alienated have I become to Christian joy that, not too long ago, I accepted that wretched phrase as a valid description of man. It is a *very* good description of what sin makes man thinks he is.

Now if sin cannot be faced directly and so hides in guilt, making of guilt its ambivalent carrier, how totally shall we see this process at work when that from which sin withdraws us is not just other humans and human life generally but the mysterious other that seems to befriend self-awareness and to ground it! And in fact, in spite of all indignant pretensions to the contrary, our relationship with God is the most ambivalent, contradictory, and stormy of all our relationships.

We can in fact trace the negative relationship to God through the three "places" of evil in the human being: sin, guilt, and projection.

In the first place, then, and most radically, my opposition to God is directed against myself. It is the movement that simultaneously undoes the sense of my greatness as a self-aware being and usurps divinity. Of these two contradictory qualities of the movement, we tend, in our analysis of sin, to emphasize the usurpation of divinity. This releases a flood of homiletic rhetoric which serves to disguise the other quality, the sheer lowness of sin, which is the trick that is always missed. As between sin as self-exaltation and sin as self-destruction, we fasten onto the former. The reason for this is that the moralist and preacher is as fearful of his hidden self-destructive tendency as is the man or woman in the pew. Sin can hide its true nature in a sermon as well as in a bank robbery.

In *The Crucified Jesus is No Stranger,* I placed the main emphasis, in this matter of sin, on the willed destruction of the self in its deepest orientation toward God and life, which I saw acted-out preeminently in the rejection and crucifixion of Jesus. I believe this position was correct. I only moved away from it because it seemed to swallow up the crucifixion, in all its historical banality, in the believer's wrestle with himself as God-oriented being, of which Jesus became the symbol. Thus *The Crucified Jesus is No Stranger* is haunted by the question as to whether its theology would not work equally well had Jesus never existed, a question once made explicit and, according to one perceptive reader, never satisfactorily dealt with. I have subsequently (in a book shortly to be published) succeeded, I hope, in getting history to the center by "recovering" the experience of the disciples of Jesus. But it was harder to see the self-destructive quality of sin in the disciples than to see it *symbolically* in the action of the crucifiers. But this in turn was only because I was still not clear about the self-destructive quality itself. It was still clouded by rhetoric. Once I began to grasp the real self-destructive-movement of sin, it appeared with terrifying clarity as that which was totally unleashed in the followers of Jesus when God had died on them.

In the second place, we have guilt. It hardly needs pointing out how prominently guilt figures in all religion. According to my analysis, it is our *positive,* self-awareness-dynamized attitude to God jarred and complicated by the hidden and never fully avowed hatred of the life into which God is calling us, which is sin. As sin hides in guilt in our interhuman relationships, so it does in our relationship with God, with the important difference that sin here is more opposing to the positive relationship than it is in the case of our other relationships. In religious guilt, the friction and self-contradictoriness which is never absent from guilt is at a maximum.

In the third place, we have projection. As sin hides in guilt, so guilt hides in the apparent ugliness of God. The prototype of this is the story of Abraham and Isaac. The goodness in Abraham meets a God who demands everything. But the sin and guilt in him hears this demand as a command to murder his firstborn. He has to work through this painful conflict. On the hill of sacrifice a light dawns on him that was to be *the* light of Israel which came to full brightness in Jesus: a God not of guilt and blood-payment but of people, of a people, who turns blood-payment inside out since the blood is his own.

The ugliness which the religious find in their God they dare not attribute to him. Instead it is projected onto the heretic and in the case of Christians, the Jews. The history of Christianity is heavily featured with persecutions and religious wars. People who never seriously pray find it easy to see this fact as invalidating Christianity's enormous claims. They resemble someone who, never having felt the violent attraction of the opposite sex, contemplates a fight between a husband and wife and wonders what all the fuss is about. The fact is that to take religion seriously is to become involved in our tortuous negative mechanisms at their worst. Is it worth it? If there is a God, emphatically yes.

My strategy for the rest of this paper is as follows. First, I shall use the concept of sin here developed to work out a soteriology based on Jesus as the person without sin. This soteriology will be found to generate a crucial question, which is *the* question for Christian belief, as to how the followers of Jesus knew his conquest of death, which they experienced, *as* the swallowing-up of sin and the consequent enfleshment of God for us. This will involve a fuller treatment of the sinless person, that is, as liberated not only in the first "place" but also in the second and the third. The whole mechanism of sin, guilt, and projection will have to put in reverse, the effect of this on the disciples studied, and their final exposure to the God who is love defined. There follow, then, two concentric soteriological circles.

1st Soteriological Circle

Jesus is the sinless one. In him there is no dark inclination to worthlessness. Nothing in him betrays the word he hears "You are my beloved." This means that the rejection of him, the degrading of him, the "setting him at naught," found nothing *in* him to agree with it, to move in sympathetic resonance with it. He "opened not his mouth": sin found in him no resonance.

Now sin in a person moves in sympathy not only with others' rejection of him but also with death. "The wages of sin is death" means that death is all that the being that sin declares me to be is worth. "The wages of sin is death" objectifies, exposes the inner voice that says "You are alone and ultimately meaningless. You will crawl into a hole and die like the animal you are." Whereas the inner voice says "Death is appropriate *for you*," the saving word says "Death is appropriate *for sin's version of you,* but that version is a lie, for you are mine."

Now I am sure there is a connection between sin's sympathetic resonance with rejection and sin's sympathetic resonance with death. Death is the great public sign that sin is right, that sin's word is the last word. Death is not *per se* the corroboration of what sin says in us, but sin sees it and uses it as corroborative, and sin is universal. Death swells the voice of sin in us to choric volume. And that is why the Nazi movement was really enamored of death. One of the mysteries I am teased by these days is the death wish which sometimes shows itself in some political movements. It has been observed in Europe's Left at this time. What on earth is all this about? Who wants extinction? Who courts death? Who wants to bring everything down in ruins? Answer: sin does, and sin is in all of us.

After his execution, Jesus appeared to his disciples victorious over death. What does this mean? It means that he who did not swell sin but swallowed it up in an unimaginable wholeness and holiness did something similar with death, sin's chosen symbol; and that the people who *saw* him *knew* was that their sin, their sense of worthlessness, had been swallowed up *as* death had been swallowed up. It was the resurrection that was *experienced* as "wiping the slate clean." It was the resurrection that *showed* that the slate had been wiped clean. Death had not done to Jesus what its prospect does to us: spoken to sin, questioned his ultimate worth to God. And in failing to do this, it had manifested the opposite: the intimacy of the human being to God that nothing, not even death itself, can alter. In the risen one we see death stripped clear of all that sin has put into it. Thus stripped clean, it is the way to God, the Father. But is not this simply allowing death to be itself, free of sin's projection onto it? We might try saying that Jesus did not *open* death, he only showed that it *is* open, *"revealed* the resurrection." But this runs into difficulty. The true nature of man, for which death *is* open to God, is not experienced by us in the pure state. Our experience of nature, our existential essence, is shot through with universal sin. Only a divine act that dissolves sin, therefore, can open death to God. Thus what Jesus is experienced as doing in respect of death *must* be described as "opening" it. It is not adequately described as "showing it to be *open.*" Existentially, culturally, it is *not* open. It is the wages of universal sin. The whole law of the spiritual life is here. Union with God liberates all the deepest potential of the human being: but we experience this liberation consequentially to the spiritual consummation of a love-relationship, not directly as its content or purpose.

Theologians who tend to spirtualize the resurrection, who dismiss the empty tomb as irrelevant, who make the correct observation "not the resuscitation of a corpse" do far more work than it is capable of, really have to ask themselves this question: If the sign, for the disciples, that Jesus had swallowed up sin in a new age of humankind, was that he had swallowed up death, how could this latter fact have become known to his disciples? Death, which sin has universally accepted as ruler and measure, had succumbed to the man who could "accept" sin without reproducing it. The succumbing of death, or conversely the conquest of death, is a most ancient rhetoric for the resurrection. It presents, as is the way of such rhetoric, the problem as to what exactly it means. It seems to me that the question "What does this mean?" is really the question "What did the disciples experience?" How did *they* know, after the death of Jesus, his "conquest" of death, which objectified for them, which jolted them into, his wonderful embracing and dissolving of all their sense of fundamental human unworth? If we think of the depth and universality of this sense of unworth, its pervasion of all human culture, above all its self-symbolization in the universal silent fact of death, how were people convinced, by a man recently dead, that this universal cancer had been dissolved and death thus robbed of its power to endorse it? Surely Jesus had to be known to have *done something with death.* At least this must be said: the conviction that the corpse of Jesus, the evidence that he was dead as all the dead are dead, had disappeared from its last resting-place, which is clearly the conviction of the New Testament and has been the conviction of the Christian Church ever since, *symbolizes* more adequately the total change that the resurrection was believed to mark, than do any of the spiritualizing "Jesus lives on" accounts of the matter. The concept of "living on" leaves death exactly where it was. It leaves intact the whole ambivalent condition of human culture in respect of our ultimate meaning and destiny.

Schillebeeckx has undoubtedly found the new direction for thinking about the resurrection when he sees the disciples' experience of the risen Jesus as a being reconciled to him. But the reconciliation was only possible at the spiritual depth at which it occurred because of something that the reconciler showed them about himself: that he was not bounded or measured by death, as sinful man thinks he is: that death did not have that power over him which sin gives it. It was in that context of freedom from death that he showed them the love that swallows up all injury in its enormous wholeness and intimacy with the source of meaningful existence.

And of course there is—though one feels vaguely improper mentioning it in theological circles—the Shroud of Turin, which goes on quietly getting straight A's in all the tests that the most sophisticated modern science can derive for it.

The treatment of sin so far has issued in a first soteriological runthrough, with the conclusion that the encounter with the risen Jesus must have shown the disciples that the slate was wiped clean, that sin had been swallowed up in the love of the sinless one. This first soteriology, however, does not really say *how* the disciples knew, from the *risen* Jesus, that *sin* had been swallowed up. To answer this question, we need a fuller treatment of sin and its symptom guilt, and a reconstruction, in the light of this, of the *experience* of the disciples of Jesus.

2nd Soteriological Circle

The essentials are as follows. First, the sinless person, being totally free of the self-destructive denial of God, will experience God as his very life. This will be an intimacy with God that is a quantum leap beyond all other religious experience. Secondly, this person will be free of guilt, and of the projections that guilt creates both onto God and onto the neighbor. Thirdly, this person's experience will be, for the person, so overwhelmingly and obviously "right" that the conviction will be generated that this is the way human life is meant to be and that the only significance of this person's unique experience is to be the agent, in God's plan, that is to bring this about. These three characteristics, of unique divine intimacy, of freedom from projection, and of eschatological self-understanding, are in fact the salient features of the figure of Jesus as portrayed in the gospels. God is Abba. There is table fellowship with sinners. There is the imminence of the Kingdom.

The next question, which I have only recently learned to ask, is crucial: What would have been the effect of this Jesus on his disciples? They "caught" from him a sense of who God really is, that none had ever had before. They saw through the traditional words and symbols to the burning reality. More dangerously, they "caught" from him the conviction that this new experience of God was shortly to change the world, that the Kingdom was "at the very doors," and that their movement was its inauguration. Jesus did nothing to inhibit this infection. On the contrary, he fomented it with his Kingdom preaching. His followers were on an ecstatic journey into Apocalypse, in which ecstatic condition the reality blotted out all questions as to *how* the final step was to be taken.

There was an implication in all this that was not and that could not be made explicit. If the movement failed, then the God of Jesus would be no more. And the God of Jesus had supplanted forever all previous ideas of God: there would be no going back to traditional religion. God would be dead. Really.

Which is precisely what happened. The Good Friday experience was, for the disciples of Jesus, the death of God.

Now with God dead, the soul's last hold on life is gone. Everything that is positive in the soul, the whole force of self-esteem that is built into identity, tends, we have seen, toward God. Jesus, uniquely, made this whole tendency explicit: so that with the God in whom it centered dead the soul would know nothing in itself but the voice of sin saying "You are alone, and without meaning. You will crawl into a hole and die like the animal you are."

Now once the soul's *whole* tendency to live has been revealed to it as a tending towards God, then the removal of God would remove from the soul *all* its resources for meaningful life. This, in a lesser figure, is the lesson of bereavement. So much of the bereaved person's life is invested in the other lost to him or her that there is no consolation in anything. Augustine has immortalized this condition in his account of the death of a friend, in the *Confessions*. In the Good Friday condition, all is reduced to sin and meaninglessness.

There is an important implication in all this. What we are considering is an experience of sin in the pure state, *without guilt to give it meaning,* without guilt for it to hide in. We must distinguish between the ordinary sinful condition and the Good Friday sinful condition. In the ordinary condition, God has not revealed him or herself to the soul as the goal of *all* its appetite, and thus the sin that is denying him or her can hide itself in a guilt that makes him remote and, ultimately, unlovable. Thus the God of guilt is a curious hybrid of intimate and alien. We might say that the meaning that guilt gives to sin it takes away from God. In the Good Friday condition, the escape-hatch into guilt is shut down: there is nothing now except the intimate of God with no God.

Now in this condition, if God is to reappear, to be alive again, this can only be *as* the soul's total *life* rallying from the total death to which it has become subject. And conversely, *if* such a rallying is experienced, that can only *be* the presence of God. In this case there would be a psychological displacement of divinity from its habitual position, its guilt position as intimate-and-alien, into the very movement of the heart and into this very humanity of ours that appeared to us alien to him.

The resurrection encounter effects both these vectors of the one displacement: in Jesus alive they saw our humanity as God's home not death's home; in the consolation they knowingly attributed to the Holy Spirit, they knew a joy that is the sufficient evidence of God's presence.

It was in this experienced connection between the risen Jesus and the movement of the heart with the Holy Spirit that the disciples knew Jesus' swallowing-up of death in life *as* the swallowing-up of sin in the mysterious love of which the whole event is nothing but the revelation. They knew that Jesus, in overcoming death, overcame sin, because they experienced the resurrection encounter as doing precisely that for them. This also is the basis of the belief that Jesus is God: he had perceptibly done for them what only God can do. It should follow from this that the more profoundly I am able to recognize and name sin in myself and in the culture, the more free I am to confess the godhead of him who is freeing me of sin. The optimistic liberal mind, so unperceptive of these obscure depths, easily settles for a Jesus who is less than God.

Thus, so far as I can see, the wider soteriological circle resolves the question generated by the narrower one.

A very important point remains to be made, or rather emphasized. It is indispensable to this whole account that the God that dies with Jesus is the real God, the God that Jesus lived by and lived for. It is only in this way that the experience of sin in the pure state as the cutting-off of *all* meaning-resources was possible; and only sin in the pure state could be the threshold for that revelation of God as the soul's intimate life against sin and death, which is the meaning of the incarnation and of the Holy Spirit, and which enables Christianity to crown the whole movement of Israel with its dogged insistence on the heart as the ultimate and sufficient evidence for God in this world. I mention this because for the psychological armchair Christianity of Jung, which beguiles many Christians, the God that died at Calvary was the old guilt-inducing God. The heresy of course is a very old one — in fact the oldest. Its name is Gnosticism.

Coda and Summary

The self-esteem of another claims my respect. It is not just his value, it is his sense of his value, that claims my respect. There is something at the heart of it that I may not ignore.

That "something" is made totally explicit by him who is totally explicit about his own value, saying "I and the Father are one."

Thus all contempt shown to persons is contempt shown to him who spoke up for each person's concealed sense of infinite worth and dignity. It was he who was packed into the cattle-trucks and carried off to the death camps.

And the converse is true. All down-grading of him is a down-grading of all. To muffle the one explicit human voice is to deprive all of their voice already enfeebled by the brutality of life.

Auschwitz is the first blasphemy. "No Christology after Auschwitz" is the second.

A person's self-esteem is the beginning of his or her dialogue with God, which Jesus brings to fruition.

Alienation and Reconciliation: The Theological Methods of Paul Tillich and Bernard Lonergan

by Nancy Ring

A primary concern of Christian theology in the twentieth century has been and remains the place and function of belief in a secularized culture. The appropriate relation between faith and culture has been addressed by Karl Barth, Rudolph Bultmann, Edward Schillebeeckx, Karl Rahner, David Tracy, Johann Metz and countless others.[1] It was the major concern of the late eminent theologian Paul Tillich and remains the concern of Fr. Bernard Lonergan, whose massive and demanding works, in their very density as well as simplicity, sometimes conceal the revolutionary character of his analysis of the human subject, Christian faith, and culture.

Theology, whether done in apostolic, medieval, or modern times, is always a response to the desire of every human person to experience personal and societal unity and reconciliation. Otherwise stated, alienation is the common experience of humankind, a condition which elicits a continuum of responses as different in nature as asceticism, contemplation, stoic acceptance, and hedonistic rebellion. Theology seeks to respond to the condition of human alienation

---

[1] Representative of the works of these theologians which are relevant to the subjects are: Karl Barth, *Church Dogmatics,* (1961); Rudolph Bultmann, *Kerygma and Myth,* (1961); Edward Schillebeeckx, *The Understanding of Faith,* (1974); Karl Rahner, *Hearers of the Word,* (1941); David Tracy, *Blessed Rage for Order* (1975); and Johann Metz, *Theology of The World,* (1968).

by analyzing its causes and explaining how Christian faith operates as a principle of reconciliation.

The purpose of this essay is to explicate the manner in which the theological methods of Paul Tillich and Bernard Lonergan respond to this human dynamic of alienation and reconciliation. This will be accomplished in the following manner. First, the analysis of each regarding the human subject will be explored. Since one's conception of being is foundational to one's understanding of the subject, and since both theologians write extensively on this matter, the way in which being is understood by each will be the starting point of the comparison.

Because being is understood differently by Tillich and Lonergan, each will differ in his understanding of the causes of alienation from oneself, from society, and from God. An explanation of this difference in understanding will comprise the second part of this essay. If the cause of alienation is understood differently, so will be the dynamic of reconciliation. Consequently, this will be the material treated in the third section. Finally, an evaluation of the contribution of each theologian will be offered.

I. The Conception of Being in Paul Tillich and Bernard Lonergan

According to Tillich, the question, What is being? is the most fundamental of all philosophical questions, and its meaning is universal in scope.[2] Since everything participates in being, one can gain understanding of being through a study of the human situation, the structural principles of which yield knowledge of the nature of the being in which it participates.

The question, What is Being?, occurs when one becomes aware that it is not ontologically necessary that any particular finite being exist. The question, Why is there something and not nothing?, establishes a tension between nonbeing and Being that results in Tillich's describing Being as that which resists nonbeing.[3] It further establishes a tension between subject and object in that a human subject asks about something in which one existentially participates, but from which one is distinct.[4] Consequently, an analysis of the subject/object relationship provides an entrance into the study of Being, although Being is itself not a being, nor in any way a generic

---

[2] Paul Tillich, *Systematic Theology*, 3 vols. (Chicago: University of Chicago, 1951-63), 1:163.

[3] Ibid., pp. 163-64.

[4] Ibid., p. 164.

reality. It is that which, because it precedes any being, is beyond all specific being.[5]

This approach places Tillich squarely in the philosophical tradition concerned with the turn to the subject, but it also shows his concern with the question of transcendentals: What is there in the human structure that is both given and precedes and organizes ontic concepts? Such notions Tillich terms ontological concepts and the most basic of such concepts he names the concept of self/world.[6] Obviously, then, if the most fundamental ontological concept, and that in which the others are implicit, is a polarity, it can be said that Tillich's experience and interpretation of reality is one of polarity. So, because polarity characterizes Tillich's ontological concepts, and because as ontological concepts they are constitutive of being and present in everything that exists, it may be stated that polarity is the structural element of the mind which grasps and shapes reality, and reality's foundation: being.

Reflecting on the self/world polarity, Tillich observes that the dynamic of polarity means that neither polar element can exist without its corresponding element. Either both poles exist or neither exists. Each appears simultaneously with the other in one's experience. The important factor, then, is that neither element is considered an independent entity, but rather a factor in a dynamic principle by which one experiences being.[7] To the extent that the polarities do not exist in a complementary balance, one is faced with the possibility of dissolution.

But, according to Tillich, such polar complementarity never exists in the existential situation. What is, known in existence, is a definitive contradiction of what should be, the essential order, an order which is manifested only sporadically in one's existence.[8] Tillich establishes a distinction between essence and existence on the basis of the manifest inconsistencies one experiences in existence. Consequently, any incompleteness or lack of perfection in humankind is interpreted as being an estrangement from one's essential nature which is the norm of humanity, a norm known theoretically rather than existentially, a norm realized in existence only momentarily and under special conditions.[9]

---

[5] Ibid., p. 163.

[6] Ibid., p. 164.

[7] Ibid., p. 165.

[8] Paul Tillich, *The Interpretation of History* (New York: Charles Scribner's Sons, 1936), revised and published as *On The Boundary* (New York: Charles Scribner's Sons, 1966), p. 83.

[9] These special conditions are those of revelation, miracle, ecstatic reason, and Mystery. They are treated in *Systematic Theology* 1:106-18.

Bernard Lonergan, on the other hand, posits that the basis for one's analysis of being resides in the dynamic structure of the human subject which is grounded in the pure and disinterested desire to know.[10] This pure desire to know is oriented to the totality of all that can be known. Until one arrives at a complete set of answers to a complete set of questions, there will always be a further relevant question arising from the true (or false) judgments one has already attained. Thus, the object of the pure desire to know includes all that one knows as well as all that can be known.[11] This object of the pure desire to know is what Lonergan names "being", which reality, consequently, is all-inclusive or universal as well as concrete because it includes the totality of any one thing as well as of all things.[12]

One's encounter with being is mediated by experience and understanding and known in judgment.[13] Experience, understanding, and judgment are termed by Lonergan "transcendental notions" because they govern and direct one's *eros* toward the knowledge of being and because they are indigenous to the structure of each human person. Despite the biases and prejudices of the human psyche, despite the fact that the *eros* directed toward being can be circumvented, truncated, and distorted, the original impulse of any person is to know that which is, in fact, so.

One never experiences the totality of being because all of one's questions concerning reality are never exhausted. The incompleteness of one's experience of being is rooted in one's finitude but not in the fact that there exists a realm of nonbeing that is in potency to being and which is a threat to existential being, nor in the fact that one's existential experience of being is qualitatively different from being as it essentially is.

In regard to the understanding of being, then, Tillich and Lonergan are dialectically opposed. Because Tillich conceives reality from an essentialist point of view, and since Tillich posits, against Hegel, that existence is not a manifestation of essence, but following Schelling, declares that existence is the contradiction of essence, what one experiences in virtue of one's status as a human person is always the contradiction of essential being, of that which should be.[14] One experiences estrangement; one seeks the union of oppo-

---

[10] Bernard J. F. Lonergan, *Insight* (London: Darton, Longman and Todd, 1957), p. 348.

[11] Lonergan, *Insight,* p. 350.

[12] Ibid., p. 356.

[13] Bernard J. F. Lonergan, *Collection,* Ed. F. E. Crowe, S. J. (New York: Herder and Herder, 1967), p. 223.

[14] Paul Tillich, *Dynamics of Faith* (New York: Harper and Row, 1957), p. 63.

sites as this was conceived by the nineteenth century philosophers of romanticism.[15]

Lonergan's understanding of the subject's experience of being is dialectically opposed to that of Tillich because Lonergan proceeds from a perspective of critical realism: being is the virtually unconditioned known in judgment,[16] not an essence or norm inferred from existence. Consequently, one's experience of being is an experience of the union of the subject and object.

Existentially, one may very well experience the threat of the dissolution of the polarities which, according to Tillich, constitute the fundamental polarity of self/world; individuality/participation; dynamics/form; freedom/destiny.[17] In fact, Tillich's acute perception of the sources of existential anxiety and consequent alienation is among the greatest contributions he has made to modern self-understanding. One who, as Lonergan does, however, questions the idealist identification of perception and knowing must challenge the adequacy of Tillich's identification of the experience of polarity with the structure of being.

From Lonergan's point of view, the point at which Tillich is vulnerable is in his failing to distinguish between experiential truth, normative truth, and the constitution of truth in a grasp of the virtually unconditioned.[18] In Lonergan's view, the sublation of experience by understanding while retaining experience adds a new element not present in the elemental experience: intelligence. In like manner, the sublation of understanding by judgment adds the previously absent element of rationality. Consequently elemental experience, as spontaneously known, is not the full experience of being, but only, but very importantly, the inception of the full experience of being.

The basic differences of Tillich and Lonergan in regard to the conception of being which both propose have been outlined. Now, more detailed attention must be directed toward the dynamics of alienation which follow on the position of each.

---

[15] In a lecture on July 5, 1972, at Middlebury College Monsieur Michel Haar stated, "Le point du départ du romantisme, c'est la fusion des contraires." Professor Haar named Rousseau, Schelling, Mme. de Staël, Fichte, and Schlegel, among others, as those who attempted this fusion of the "moi et le non-moi."

[16] Lonergan, *Insight*, p. 280.

[17] Tillich, *Systematic Theology* 1:174-86.

[18] Lonergan, *Insight*, p. 375.

II. Alienation in the Theology of Tillich and Lonergan

In Tillich's view, existential estrangement is a function of the tendency of the ontological elements to separate as well as the fact that in the state of existence there exists a definitive gap between essence and existence. One is consequently faced with the fact that separation from one's essence is the cause of estrangement, but that such separation is what it means to exist. This dilemma is related to two of Tillich's most fundamental concepts: non-being (mē on) and the separation of essence (Being-itself) and existence (being in actuality).

Nonbeing, for Tillich, is a concept of limits. One arises out of non-being, and goes toward nonbeing. In the existential order, the limit toward which one goes may be either the limits imposed by the ontological concepts, or by death itself. Therefore, the concept of nonbeing is intimately connected to one's finitude. "Being, limited by nonbeing, is finitude. Nonbeing appears as the 'not yet' of being and as the 'no more' of being." [19]

The *mē-ontic* concept of being is dialectical in that it represents what is potential but not yet actual due to its lacking existence. This is its "not yet" aspect. In its "no more" aspect it represents that which may result in the dissolution of existent being. Consequently, being and nonbeing are in perpetual dialectical tension. It is thus that Tillich can say that nonbeing is a threat to being and that being is the power that resists nonbeing. Within the human structure as human, there is no answer to the threat of nonbeing. This understanding situates Tillich in the Platonic, Augustinian, Lutheran tradition.

If one accepts the dialectical relationship between being and nonbeing, as Tillich does, then the definitive separation of essence and existence must also be posited. For Tillich, to stand outside of pure potentiality and to exercise one's finite freedom in order to do so has the inevitable consequence of separating oneself from essence. This exercise of freedom, then, is the basis of the subject/object dichotomy which is expressed in the experience of moral freedom and universal destiny, tragic because of its separation from essence.[20]

Tillich employs the myth of The Fall to illustrate his thesis. Tillich interprets The Fall to be a dramatic account of the "first fact": the world exists, one exists within it, this is the situation. It is one's destiny to exist in a world which is given, which is estranged from its essence, but within which one is responsibly free. By the very fact of

---

[19] Tillich, *Systematic Theology* 1:189.
[20] Ibid., p. 255.

one's destiny, then, one is estranged, separated from Being-itself. "To be outside the divine life means to stand in actualized freedom, in an existence which is no longer united with essence. Seen from one side, this is the end of creation. Seen from the other side, it is the beginning of the fall. Freedom and destiny are correlates." [21]

Tillich's point in making this affirmation is to maintain, simultaneously, the non-temporal character of human estrangement (there is no "before") and the existential situation of moral freedom and universal destiny: "...theology must insist that the leap from essence to existence is the original fact—that it has the character of a leap and not of structural necessity. In spite of its tragic universality, existence cannot be derived from essence." [22]

Since estrangement is the separation of essence and existence, the ontological elements and categories are in jeopardy from the outset. Unbelief, *hubris,* and concupiscence are the terms Tillich uses to characterize the human person in the state of existence. All three imply one's tendency to establish oneself as the center of existence, to become one's own ground and depth, and to find ultimate meaning and power in oneself, in one's desires, at the expense of the rest of reality, of the "world". In such a situation, one has turned others into objects, and, consequently, one cannot experience participation. Thereby, one loses one's world (though not one's environment).[23] Since the self-world correlation is basic, the loss of one's world results in self-loss. So, self-loss is experienced through the destruction of the self-world polarity. This disintegration is expressed and further constituted by the separation of the ontological elements and categories: When freedom and destiny are separated, there remains no deciding center. When dynamism is separated from form, there results either chaotic rebellion or suppression. Individualization divorced from participation causes one to become either an isolated object or an amorphous part of a collective.[24]

It can be concluded, therefore, that, if one follows Tillich, one must accept the fact that a structural function of existence is estrangement from oneself, from others, from the ground of Being.

In Lonergan's view, on the other hand, since all activities of the human subject are unified and directed by the *eros* toward being and value, and since this *eros* is manifested in experience, understanding, judgment and decision, there can be no definitive, unbridgeable separation between what one is and that which one should be. To

---

[21] Ibid., p. 255.
[22] Tillich, *Systematic Theology* 2:59-65.
[23] Ibid., pp. 59-65.
[24] Ibid., pp. 62-65.

the extent that one knows being and value [25] — and this is possible in one's existential situation — one is what one should be. Just as one is not threatened by an ontological movement toward separation within oneself, neither is one's freedom necessarily a function of one's separation from the source of one's being, as it is with Tillich.

In Lonergan's view, one is alienated from oneself and from the possibility of union with others and ultimately with God to the extent that one fails to realize one's *eros* toward knowledge and value. Alienation, for Lonergan, is experienced when one separates oneself from one's most fundamental orientation, when one engages, actively or passively, in the flight from understanding.[26] Otherwise stated, the fact of human alienation resides in one's freedom to frustrate oneself, to deprive oneself of the possibility of realizing oneself in self-transcendence rather than, as in Tillich's view, residing in ontological necessity.

Lonergan speaks of the flight from understanding in terms of various biases: dramatic, personal, group, and general.[27] To the degree that one actively reinforces or passively accepts one's relationship to these elements of distortion, one alienates oneself which, in Lonergan's schema, insures alienation from others as well as from one's destiny.

The various forms of bias, all rooted in the flight from understanding, manifest distortions of reality on various levels. Dramatic bias is the least conscious and consequently the most devastating of the biases. In such a case, the subject refuses to admit to consciousness the images necessary for insight into how best to make her life a work of art.[28] Consequently, one's decisions are a reinforcement of one's spontaneous, unexamined fears and desires. Judgment is impaired due to the impaired or inappropriate formulations of intelligence. Left to its natural course, dramatic bias expands to the point where neurosis is the predominant characteristic of the subject.[29]

---

[25] Here, a new term, value, is introduced. Lonergan's early work was concerned with cognitional theory which results in the knowledge of being. This has been explicated. In his later work, principally in *Method In Theology* (New York: Herder and Herder, 1972), he outlines the notion of value which retains and sublates the knowledge of being. The knowledge of value responds to the question, Is it worthwhile?, and implies decision in relation to truth. It is in considering Lonergan's notion of value that Fr. Robert Doran, S.J., has explicated the role of the symbolic and the role of feeling in the imperative to be attentive to one's experience.

[26] Lonergan, *Insight,* pp. xi, xii.

[27] Ibid., pp. 191-203; 218-42.

[28] The term "work of art" is introduced into the understanding of the dramatic subject by Robert Doran, S.J. who has done extensive work in expanding Lonergan's concept of dramatic bias. Included in his publications in this area are: *Subject and Psyche* (Washington, D.C.: University Press of America, 1977), and "Christ and The Psyche" in *Trinification of the World* (Toronto: Regis College Press, 1978).

[29] Lonergan, *Insight,* p. 192.

Personal, group, and general biases are more conscious flights from understanding. In each case, self-interest, fear, and intersubjectivity are dynamically interrelated. Egoism results in self-deception and alienation in that it consistently disregards the realm of intersubjective feelings such as co-operation and compassion in order to promote personal self-interest. Thus, although the egoist can quite intelligently understand how to actualize personal desires, she does so by consciously suppressing any admission of the intersubjective meaning of human life into her understanding of the situation and consequently her decisions regarding appropriate action.[30] Unexamined and spontaneous fear plays a role in the decisions dictated by personal bias since one fears that by allowing one's intersubjectivity to play a part in one's decision-making, that one's desire to succeed, to be on top, will be frustrated.

Group bias, on the other hand, is a function of intersubjectivity. It can be expressed in ideologies which prevent the group to which one belongs from initiating intelligent social change. The fear determinative of group bias is that intelligent change would either limit one's power or, if the group is powerless, that change would demand that one initiate responsible action to change the oppressive situation. Group bias, then, is the collective reinforcement of the tendency to consider as irrelevant any data, the consideration of which may lead to a judgment that one's group should initiate action that would lead to a change in one's present status.[31]

General bias results from accepting as one's fundamental orientation to life the point of view that the realm of common sense[32] is coincident with the realm of the real. Since decisions made in the realm of common sense are exclusively concerned with the concrete and particular, there is in general bias, a disregard for issues that are concerned with more universal and theoretical aspects of life. The systematic disregard which general bias evinces toward those issues that transcend the realm of common sense leads to the decline of society, the promotion of which demands insight into the general dynamics of social evolution. Social change requires that intelligence address itself to that which goes beyond the concrete and particular. Decline is especially apt to occur when there is mutual reinforcement of general and group bias.

It can be stated that Lonergan's understanding of alienation is rooted in praxis rather than in theory. Alienation results from the conscious distortion and limiting of the free play of one's understanding, judgment, and decisions.

---

[30] Ibid., pp. 222-25.
[31] Ibid.
[32] Ibid., pp. 226-28.

Since alienation is structural in Tillich's understanding, it is therefore necessitated. In order to proceed with the dialectic of methods, one must ask if alienation is also structural and necessary in Lonergan's understanding. We have seen above that alienation is not structural. There is nothing in human structure which necessitates alienation. Significantly, though, Lonergan's understanding leads to the observation that, although alienation is not structurally necessitated, it is inevitable. It is inevitable because the basis of evil is irrationality. Since human structures are orientated toward rationality, there is no human structure that can organize residual irrationality and sublate it into a higher viewpoint.[33] Thus, there is no operation within the human structure which can overcome evil and it is within the environment of evil that the various biases flourish.

Consequently, the principle of sublation or of the emergence of a higher viewpoint reaches an impasse when the human person is found to be in a situation in which the evil which results from bias as well as from the inability to sustain uninterrupted development cannot be handled by an appropriate human structure. Because they cannot be solved by the operations of human structures, the problems of human bias and human subjectivity inevitably result in alienation. This alienation results in increasingly less comprehensive viewpoints with the possible result that flight from understanding becomes more characteristic of the person than one's *eros* toward understanding.

III. Reconciliation in Paul Tillich and Bernard Lonergan

Within the context of Paul Tillich's theological method, reconciliation is effected by the recognition of existential estrangement and the courage to accept the tension which results from the tendency of the polar elements through which one is constituted to separate.[34] This courage to be that which one is finds sustenance in faith, allowing oneself to be grasped by Ultimate Concern.[35] The possibility of living courageously in the face of estrangement is further aided by the knowledge that one's experience of being is grounded in Being-itself,[36] and that one's reason has Depth even if this Depth of Reason is not transparent to one's actual reason.[37] Thus, faith is that which

---

[33] Ibid., pp. 666-68.

[34] Paul Tillich, *The Courage to Be* (New Haven: Yale University Press, 1952), p. 155.

[35] Tillich, *Dynamics of Faith,* p. 17.

[36] Tillich, *The Courage To Be,* pp. 178-81.

[37] Tillich, *Systematic Theology* 1:79-81.

makes existence possible. Faith is the experience of Mystery and of wholeness which allows one to live without fear of dissolution. Faith is that by virtue of which one's constitutive polarity is maintained in balance. Given *to* existence, it, nevertheless, is not present *within* existence. Faith, therefore, does not eliminate estrangement and alienation, but it guarantees that the New Being in Christ has overcome estrangement. Faith overcomes; it does not transform being so as to eliminate the sources of alienation and estrangement.[38] Reconciliation, then, is the experience of Mystery through which one accepts one's existential state because one knows that existence is not finally determinative of reality and that existence can be harmonious because of the presence of the New Being in Christ to it.[39]

In Lonergan's understanding, reconciliation is effected by the reversal of the flight from understanding and the elimination of bias. Because, however, there is no human structure that is proportionate to resolving the irrationality of sin and evil, a solution which is supernatural to the structures of natural proportionality must be posited.[40] "It follows that the newer and higher collaboration is not the work of man alone, but principally the work of God."[41]

It is the work of God understood in this manner: One's *eros* toward the knowledge of being, even the highest being, occurs within one's natural horizon, but the structure proportionate to the attaining of the higher viewpoint is beyond one's natural horizon, or, otherwise stated, beyond one's horizontal freedom.[42] In Lonergan's view, this higher viewpoint, given to humankind and which empowers one to deal with and go beyond the irrationality of sin, is the free gift of God's love. Within the context of God's love, one is empowered to reverse the flight from understanding and to eliminate or at least to drastically lessen the influence of dramatic, personal, group, and general bias. Thereby, one can attain the fulfillment of one's *eros* which includes not only personal reconciliation but the reversal of the process of social decline.

Lonergan explains the dynamics of the gift of God's love philosophically in terms of contingent necessity and theologically and religiously in terms of conversion. Contingent necessity is concerned with world order. God, as God, could envision all possible world orders. He freely chose to actualize the world order in which humankind is oriented toward self-transcendence. Consequently, the gift of

---

[38] Tillich, *Dynamics of Faith,* p. 79.
[39] Tillich, *Systematic Theology* 2:161.
[40] Bernard Lonergan, "Mission and Spirit," (Mimeographed), p. 4.
[41] Ibid., p. 11.
[42] Ibid., p. 15.

His love is necessarily, not contingently, bestowed on all of humankind. God's love is the environment of world order.

The effect of one's appropriation of God's love is known in conversion: religious, psychic, moral, and intellectual. Religious conversion is the experience of God's love; it is religious experience. The human experience of God's gift of His love is the state of being-in-love with God.[43] Just as it is beyond the power of the human person to circumvent the fact that God has established a world order which He loves, it is also beyond the power of the person not to experience his love within her being, her psyche. So, in one sense, the person has no choice about her being "being-in-love." However, she has the freedom and the will to decide whether or not she will correspond to the exigency of God's love or even to admit it to self-consciousness. When one does respond to this exigency, one falls in love. So whereas one has no choice as to the finality of one's being, which is love, one does have the choice whether or not to allow oneself to actualize one's inherent potency to love. As Lonergan expresses it: "That capacity (for self-transcendence) becomes an actuality when one falls in love."[44]

Even though this realization of being in love may be inchoate and nonobjectified, when it is nevertheless experienced as love flooding one's heart, then it becomes the first principle of living. Since one's intentionality is directed toward that which is in vertical and supernatural finality to it, and since falling in love with that finality is equivalent to responding to the exigencies of one's being, then simultaneous with experiencing falling in love with God, one experiences the basic fulfillment of one's intentionality. This is the experience of religious conversion. It is the experience of reconciliation.

Lonergan is careful to note that such authenticity or reconciliation is never achieved in this life once and for all. Self-transcendence is always a dialectic between the transcending moment and the reality-to-be-transcended. Since in this life (and possibly after death) the human person is directed toward the apprehension and love of being, and since being is exhaustive of reality, no human person ever becomes consonant and coincident with, never exhausts her *eros* toward being. Nevertheless, one's consciousness of being-in-love, of being oriented to love, can become the controlling impetus of life.[45]

The consciousness of being loved creates an environment in which the other conversions are facilitated. They are facilitated, but they

---

[43] Bernard J. F. Lonergan, *Method In Theology* (New York: Herder and Herder, 1972), p. 105.
[44] Ibid.
[45] Ibid.

rarely take place without struggle. God's love has a healing effect on one's affectivity to the extent that one may become willing to deal with affectivity as it is communicated to one's consciousness through feelings, dreams, and symbols. This attention to one's symbolic consciousness is the prelude to the resolution of dramatic bias: the repression of unwanted images. Allowing such unwanted insights to emerge makes possible the reintegration of who one says one is and of who one actually is. It results in one being able to consciously direct one's own life. Psychic conversion, then, reverses dramatic bias.

In like manner, moral conversion reverses personal bias. Within the exigence of God's love, value rather than ego-satisfaction is established as a directing principle in one's relations with others. Since "love casts out fear," the fear which necessitates maintaining one's position by power and domination loses its force.

Intellectual conversion consists in the realization that knowledge occurs when one has grasped the virtually unconditioned in an act of judgment. Knowledge is experienced as transcending both perception and thinking. It is an activity of self-transcendence and it is consequently concerned with more than the concrete and practical. Since knowing is not merely "taking a good look at something," reality is not confined to the concrete; rational reflection and long-term planning come to be seen as eminently practical.

To summarize Lonergan's position, then, reconciliation is to actualize one's natural impulse toward self-transcendence. This takes place within the world order in which the gift of God's love, not one's alienation, is the first fact.

The reader cannot have failed to notice that more attention was given to Lonergan's understanding of reconciliation than to Tillich's. This is not so much indicative of the author's bias as it is of the difference between Tillich and Lonergan. Since Tillich's methodology is theoretically controlled, once theoretical limits have been established, praxis is determined. No degree of self-sacrificing love can change the posited gap between essence and existence nor, consequently, can conversion be a category of transformation.

Since Lonergan's methodology is controlled by praxis, it sets only one limit on human possibility: whatever is human occurs within the environment of love. Since love transforms one's conscious and unconscious experience, understanding, and judgment are capable of continual transformation. Reconciliation is not only God's presence *to* life, but His presence *in* life. Reconciliation does not overcome alienation; it transforms the very structures of alienation through "a normative pattern of recurrent and related operations yielding cumulative and progressive results."[46]

---

[46] Ibid., p. 4.

Where Tillich posits the primacy of faith as the fundamental relationship between God and the person, Lonergan posits the primacy of love. Where Tillich shows the possibility of the Christian message overcoming existential *angst,* Lonergan shows the possibility of such *angst* being transformed in this life.

IV. A Postscript

It is a tribute to Lonergan's genius that he has given present-day theology and theologians the insight that transformed praxis not only affects one's life, but one's theory, and consequently, that one's theory is open-ended and not absolutely or necessarily determinative of one's life.

If this is so, the possibility is opened to theologians of critically retrieving the meaning of dogma as a function of human interiority and of expressing Christian faith in terms of interiority. If theology is post-theoretic, it can be expressed in a symbolic and poetic form which does not necessitate a return to a pre-critical stage of development. If the theologian is personally reconciled to and appropriating her intentionality and interiority, such post-theoretic expression of faith appears to be the next step in the development of theology. Tillich was sensitive to such a necessity and indeed attempted such a project. Since, however, his exposition of Christian symbol was theoretically determined and dogmatically opposed to the possibility of fundamental transformation, it could not activate the religious imagination of the believer.

No greater tribute could be given to Fr. Lonergan than that those theologians who recognize in his work a key to theological creativity proceed with the same disinterestedness and love which have marked his life and work. In pursuing the consequences of their own religious experience, understanding, judgment, and decision as these have been transformed by Being-in love, they will be doing just that.

Ecclesiology

Lonergan and the Tasks of Ecclesiology

by Joseph A. Komonchak

Bernard Lonergan has never made the Church the object of sustained theological study. Among his writings, one will find scattered references to the Church in early essays, the provocative suggestion in the Epilogue to *Insight* that ecclesiology look to history for the fundamental terms and relations of a theological treatise,[1] and the short chapter on "Communications" which concludes *Method in Theology,* in which Lonergan makes use of categories derived in earlier chapters to propose understanding the Church to be "a process of self-constitution."[2]

If an ecclesiologist cannot turn to Lonergan for an elaborated theology of the Church, he can, if he reads attentively enough, find a good deal that is of great heuristic value, particularly for suggesting how one might go about laying foundations for ecclesiology. It will be the purpose of this essay to indicate how a reading of Lonergan has brought one theologian to conceive the object, the foundations, and the goal of a critical systematic ecclesiology.

---

[1] Bernard Lonergan, *Insight: A Study of Human Understanding* (New York: Longmans, Green and Co., 1958), pp. 742-43.

[2] Bernard Lonergan, *Method in Theology* (New York: Herder and Herder, 1972), p. 363.

I. The Object of Ecclesiology

"The Christian church is the community that results from the outer communication of Christ's message and from the inner gift of God's love."[3] In Lonergan's view "the inner gift of God's love" is experienced as the reorientation of a person's subjectivity, forming a new self looking out upon a new world, establishing a new basis for community when those so blessed discover one another and together try to understand, to celebrate, and to live out the gift now experienced also as transformed intersubjectivity.[4]

That potential for full community is given form, actuality, and realization as the Christian Church when the wordless inner gift is matched by the outer gift of God in Jesus Christ whose word mediates the movement of transformed immediacy and intersubjectivity into the world mediated by meaning and thus founds the community of experience, understanding, judgment, and decision which is called the Church.

If in general the message of Christ interprets the inner gift, then the message about the Church may be said to interpret the experienced transformation of intersubjectivity. Both inner gift and transformed intersubjectivity are experienced, are events within consciousness, but they are not necessarily understood or known. Historical revelation is a further gift which enriches greatly the original gift in both its inner and its intersubjective dimensions. The enrichment is greater with regard to the latter dimension, for while the inner gift can operate as a principle of life even without being understood or known, intersubjectivity expresses itself immediately in gesture and word, address and welcome, invitation and response, love and deed, and all these are in a sense already "words" and call for words of understanding and judgment.

The community we call the Church arises when the gift of the Spirit enables a group of people to say "Jesus is Lord." In that common confession, prior to any other words or deeds, the Church has already come to be. Nils Dahl has argued that "the church-consciousness of the first Christians is the reflection of their faith in the Risen One," and that it developed in three moments: (1) the conviction that Jesus had been exalted, (2) the commissioning of the apostles, (3) the reception by faith of their proclamation.[5] Dahl omits what is not a separate moment, but the condition of all three:

---

[3] Lonergan, *Method in Theology*, p. 361.

[4] Lonergan, *Method in Theology*, pp. 112-19; see *Insight*, pp. 723-24, 741-42.

[5] Nils Dahl, *Das Volk Gottes*, 2d edition (Darmstadt, 1963), p. 176.

the work of the Spirit in the apostles ("Did not our hearts burn within us?" [Lk 24:32]) and in their hearers ("No one can say 'Jesus is Lord' except by the Holy Spirit." [1 Cor 12:3]).

In the community of confession so produced, there are already realized—prior to any self-reflection—the common world of experience, understanding, judgment, and decision and the patterns of interrelationship that constitute and distinguish the Church. It is these that are studied by the historian, sociologist, and ecclesiologist; but they are themselves the first expression of the Church, the first and constitutive *logos* of the *ekklesia*.

All reflection on the Church—"ecclesiology"—is reflection on this constitutive self-expression and self-realization. The initial appropriation of terms like "the saints," the choice of *ekklesia* as a self-designation, the gradual differentiation of the Church as a *tertium genus*—all these refer to and derive from the constitutive self-expression and self-realization. This is even more the case with regard to the fuller "ecclesiologies" of the New Testament, of Paul, Luke-Acts, Matthew, the Pastoral Epistles.

But these initial exercises in reflection are, of course, themselves new moments in the self-realization of the Church. To the inner and intersubjective gift of community under the Lordship of Jesus are now added the words, statements, deeds that articulate that gift in the world mediated by meaning. When the understanding, judgment, and decision of the Church regard not only the inner and outer gifts but their intersubjective and social effect as well, the Church takes a further step in the process of its self-constitution. The process continues when the views of a Paul, a Luke, a Matthew become common currency, when these and other writings are gathered together and received as an apostolic canon, when a catholic and apostolic *regula fidei* is developed and received, when an apostolic form of ministry and an apostolic shape of the liturgy are devised and received, and when all these combine to form a received notion of a normative expression of the Church. What is given to the ecclesiologist to study, then, is not only *what is said* about the Church in the New Testament, in the apostolic Symbol, in the liturgy, in descriptions of the ministry, but also *what was coming to be* as the Church in the formation and reception of all four elements.

Although this broad apostolic self-realization of the Church is regarded by Catholics as of unique authority, the process of self-constitution does not end with it. The Church cannot but realize, constitute itself, and it is the self-constitution of the Church that is going forward when, for example, councils begin to be held and their authority received, when norms of orthodoxy are introduced, when the penitential discipline is relaxed, when the baptism of heretics is received, when sectarianism is repudiated, when the authority of the See of Rome develops and is received, etc. The history of ecclesiology is, then, not only the history of statements and texts, but also the history of successive self-realizations of the Church, expressed in statements and texts, of course, but also through choices, actions, and events, through the development of institutions and the differentiation of roles, through the elaboration of rites and the codification of laws, and in a thousand other ways. The Church so realized in the past and so realizing itself today is the object of ecclesiology.

II. "Common Sense" and "Theory" in Ecclesiology

Some measure of reflection is intrinsic to the initial and especially to the derived self-realizations of the Church, as it is to other social bodies. But the degrees and kinds of reflection would appear to have varied greatly. Central celebrations of their new community would naturally lead the early Christians to put their distinctive experience into words and particularly to try to understand it by reference to their religious heritage and their heritage by reference to it. So, for example, the use of the word *ekklesia* to designate their community served both to relate themselves to Jewish messianic and apocalyptic hopes and to differentiate themselves from the contemporary Jewish *synagoge*.

The need for reflection would change and the process would accelerate when disputes with others or within the community itself or when the simple passage of time would force the Church towards various forms of what sociologists call "legitimation." Some Scripture scholars maintain that all three of Max Weber's types of legitimation can be found in the New Testament—the charismatic in Paul, the traditional in Luke, the rational in the Pastoral Epistles. Paul's use of the Body of Christ theme seems at times to draw on sacramental experience, at times on the Stoic apologia for social order, at times on cosmic speculations. In the First Epistle of Clement, Jewish and Roman commonplaces about order are drawn upon to reprove the disorderly Corinthians. In Tertullian and Cyprian, Roman legal institutions and vocabulary vindicate episcopal authority. Leo I devises the classic vindication of Roman authority by applying Roman hereditary law. Much later, Gregory VII operates much more self-consciously when his reform defends the *libertas Ecclesiae* by collecting laws and constructing a juridically articulated notion of a Church in which all authority derives from the Bishop of Rome. Corporation-theory plays a major role in the disputes between papalists and conciliarists. Late medieval canonists and theologians will use Aristotle and Pseudo-Dionysius to construct the first formal treatises on the Church. Scholastic ecclesiologists after Trent often appear to work with a sort of *sociologia perennis*. In the nineteenth century, while some ecclesiologists turn to Romanticism or Idealism for a framework within which to understand the Church, others employ a theory of sovereignty owing much to Bodin and Hobbes to assist and vindicate the triumph of ultramontanism.

Where, in all these instances of reflection on the Church, "theory" may be said to have been differentiated from "common sense" is a nice question. Some very sophisticated political or social theory was employed in the medieval disputes. But in earlier and later reflection (at least in what is sometimes called "classical" ecclesiology), something similar to what Lonergan calls the "post-systematic" seems to have been operating:[6] the language of theory is often used, but outside a theoretical context, for a practical purpose, and, often enough, without its theoretical content. Theory had become simple commonplace, the taken-for-granted.

Examining the taken-for-granted in ecclesiology can serve not only to differentiate common sense from theory but also to differentiate among theories. The social theory which from the Middle Ages on was employed to understand and to defend contemporary self-realizations of the Church usually reflected what Lonergan calls the classical ideal of science. This ignored history and historical variation among societies, and it understood and defended the Church and particularly Church-order by political and social theories, Aristotelian, Dionysian, and others, which it took to be normative. Normative notions of the generative and regulative principles of society controlled what responses could be given to questions and objections. Often enough the disputes concealed an over-arching agreement about the taken-for-granted presuppositions.

Now as it is already a modification of the self-realization of the Church when theory or what passes for theory replaces common sense in the legitimation of the Church, so further self-realization of the Church is greatly affected (1) when the theory is not simply reflective on previous or present practice but regulative of future practice as well, and (2) when such regulative theory is conceived in classical terms. By virtue of the first movement, theoretical control begins to direct what before had happened through the more spontaneous and unself-conscious operations of common sense. But, while this might be considered a benefit in itself, that benefit is severely compromised when theory does not make the critical turn and classicist assumptions rule the interpretation of history and the assessment of present possibilities.

---

[6] See Lonergan, *Method in Theology*, pp. 276-79, 304-5, 311-12, 314.

Today, of course, classicist assumptions are no longer taken-for-granted in the social sciences. These are resolutely empirical; they do not regard themselves as disciplines subalternate to philosophy; they do not have normative ambitions. Historical consciousness permits them to luxuriate in the enormous variety of the self-realizations of the human in society and history. They have contrived their own techniques of observation and correlation, their own methods and models of theory-construction, their own technical vocabularies and expressions. Their theories are more or less probable attempts to understand what happens to be and not certain judgments about what not only is but must be.[7]

Unfortunately, few churchmen or theologians seem eager to explore the implications for ecclesiology and for the self-realization of the Church of this differentiation within social theory. The reasons for this are complex. To some degree it reflects the not surprising reaction of the Church to a program often assumed or proclaimed to imply the discrediting of the Church's claims. To some degree it reflects the retreat of theology into a defensive and dogmatic classicism. Whatever the reasons, post-Reformation and post-Enlightenment ecclesiology has been much more estranged from developing social theory than had been the case before; and in the last century, just as the new sciences of the social were developing, the argument has been made more frequently than before that the Church, both as Mystery and as social order, has more to fear than to hope for from a use of the methods and standards of social theory in ecclesiology. The displacement of a narrowly juridical understanding of the Church by various more fully theological understandings leads thus to a curiously abstract ecclesiology which neglects the concrete self-realizations of the Church in favor of an interpretation or simple reproduction of biblical or doctrinal statements. So the Church is said to be an "event" or a "community" rather than an "institution;" "law" is contrasted to "Spirit," and "office" to "charism;" and the "essence" of the Church is said to be "Mystery," imperceptible except by faith in the "forms" of its empirical self-realizations—all of these being distinctions which only the estrangement from social theory could permit theologians and churchmen to make so confidently.

---

[7] See Lonergan, *Method in Theology,* pp. 85, 93-96, on "stages of meaning."

III. "Foundations" and Ecclesiology

Some of this retreat into "theological reductionism" (to use James Gustafson's phrase[8]) may be forgiveable, particularly when social theorists attempt their own "reductions" or when empirical observation is assigned normative significance. But it is less forgiveable when the reluctance of churchmen rests simply on the taken-for-granted assumptions of the classical ideal of theory, for then theology easily degenerates into ideology. And it is still less forgiveable when the reluctance of theologians rests on a failure or a refusal to work out for themselves basic positions — on individual and community, community and meaning, meaning and history — that could equip them to engage in critical and dialectical conversation with social theorists.

It may help to locate the suggestion being made here to say that it calls for the expansion of the foundational effort beyond the question of the hermeneutics of texts to the question of the hermeneutics of social existence. Without working on the latter question, the ecclesiologist will not be able to interpret the texts which speak of the social existence of the Church. A theologian inclined to pursue the suggestion being made need not fear that he is entering completely alien territory, for a little acquaintance with some of the first-rate literature on the methods of political and social theory will introduce him to sets of questions already familiar from more commonly pursued discussions — the nature of *Verstehen,* the role of presuppositions, the possibility of explanation, the questions of objectivity, verification, and the mediation of conflicting claims, etc.[9] He will find, in other words, an extraordinary verification of the fact that foundational questions really are *foundational* and therefore basic not only to the interpretation of texts but to the interpretation also of society and history, including the society and history of the Church.

Approaching the foundational enterprise with this expanded interest will enable the ecclesiologist to understand and appreciate the significance of what Lonergan calls the "critical" and "methodical" exigences and the realm of "interiority" which they yield and mediate. For entry into that realm is the only way to work through the issues which now vex the social scientists as they wrestle

---

[8] James Gustafson, *Treasure in Earthen Vessels: The Church as a Human Community* (New York: Harper & Row, 1961), p. 100.

[9] For an introduction, see Anthony Giddens' two works, *New Rules of Sociological Method: A Positive Critique of Interpretative Sociologies* (London: Hutchinson, 1976) and *Studies in Social and Political Theory* (London: Hutchinson, 1977) and Richard Bernstein, *The Restructuring of Social and Political Theory* (Philadelphia: University of Pennsylvania Press, 1978).

with the problem of a method for understanding theoretically what is already understood in and by common sense and for constructing a truly critical social theory. Working through those issues will equip him (1) to understand, evaluate, and criticize the methods and conclusions of the social sciences, (2) to undertake his own understanding of the social and historical expressions and self-realizations of the Church, and (3) to articulate that understanding in the terms of a critical and methodical theology.

Readers of *Method in Theology* may have observed that this project suggests the equivalent for ecclesiology of the transposition which Lonergan effects with regard to the theology of grace. Lonergan regards the medieval, particularly the Thomist, theology of grace to have been an impressive theoretical achievement. The theory, however, was constructed in terms of a metaphysical psychology characteristic of what he calls the "second stage of meaning." When, in the "third stage," metaphysics is no longer considered the initial and grounding science but is itself derived from intentionality-analysis, then interiority and not metaphysics yields the categories of a critical and methodical theology. "Sanctifying grace" is now conceived as the founding religious experience of other-worldly self-transcendence. So conceived, it can even be used to enable people to recognize in themselves the experience to which the biblical, doctrinal, and theological language of grace refers. So recognized and conceived by the theologian, it can become the base from which other special theological categories can be derived.[10]

Applied to ecclesiology, this transposition would suggest the movement from a normatively conceived social theory to a critical and historically conscious theory founded in intentionality-analysis. Such an analysis would involve the theologian's self-appropriation of his social and historical existence both in general and in its religious form. This will mean, first, a recognition of the differentiation of common sense by theory both in his own experience and as reflected in the construction of social realities. It will mean, second, a recognition of the differentiation of common sense by transcendence, both in his own experience and in the construction of social realities. Thus, the basic categories of an ecclesiology will be derived from a self-appropriation of the realm of transcendence, only not of a private interiority, but of an interiority whose religious transformation is inescapably a transformed *intersubjectivity*, interpreted and socially and historically expressed and realized in the Church.

Such a foundational effort might enable the ecclesiologist to bring the more recent theologies of the Church, which have displaced the

---

[10] Lonergan, *Method in Theology*, pp. 281-93.

classical juridical theology, down from the dogmatic and theological heights to the concrete communities in which is realized what is meant by the "Mystical Body," and "People of God," the "Temple of the Holy Spirit," *una persona mystica,* the *Ursakrament,* etc. Working out foundational issues might permit the theologian to differentiate among those and other statements of what the Church is, to discriminate between common sense and theoretical expressions so that one set will not be judged by the standards of the other, to test the critical character of what theory is discovered, to search out and describe the experiences to which both common sense and theoretical expressions refer, and to work out an ecclesiology that neither reduces theology to empirical observation nor forgets that the biblical, traditional, dogmatic, and theological language always refers to a concrete social reality constructed around the transformed intersubjectivity of concrete persons in the world. Ecclesiology badly needs something of the concreteness achieved when medieval theology spoke of "created grace" and when contemporary theologians evoke its equivalent in religious experience. Take, for example, the notion of the "Body of Christ": if this cannot simply be identified with the "institutional" Church" (as in *Mystici Corporis),* to what does it refer? What experience or sets of experiences in redeemed intersubjectivity realize it in the world? Can other experiences of intersubjectivity and social existence illumine it and the process of its self-realization? What words, gestures, rites, affections, etc. mediate it? Etc.

It is perhaps clear from this example that the ecclesiological project outlined here does not intend a "reduction" of the Church to simply another social reality in the world. The Church remains the creation of the mysterious God's self-gift in Word and in Spirit. But the project does not forget that it is not God but Christian men and women who constitute the Church, that the Church is constructed when divine favor transforms and promotes conscious acts of human intentionality and intersubjectivity—feelings, experience, understanding, judging, speaking, deciding, loving, acting, believing, remembering, celebrating, hoping, etc.—that these conscious acts are the referent in the world to which image and symbol, doctrine and theory refer when they speak about the Church, and that, thus, ecclesiology has for its object of investigation and reflection not only such images and symbols, doctrines and theories, but also the concrete "process of self-constitution" by which the Church comes to be in Christian men and women.

Sacrament: Symbol of Conversion

by Stephen Happel

Paul Tillich has remarked that the genius of Hegel was "that he created the categories in terms of which others could attack him."[1] Thus, although it might seem ungracious in this context to cite criticisms of Bernard Lonergan, such disagreements may be registered with full knowledge that the framework of the dialogue has already been achieved. Lonergan himself has said several times that even if particular elements of his explications of cognitional theory, metaphysics, or theology require revision, that revision must nonetheless take place within the already stated imperatives of inquiry.[2] Indeed, adjustments I would wish to make to Lonergan's *Method in Theology* are actually by way of extension to positions already taken; such further elucidation makes clear not only my personal intellectual debt to Lonergan's transforming clarity, but also the generally recognized conclusion that this magisterial philosophy and theology have produced collaborative investigations rather than sycophantic disciples.[3]

---

[1] Paul Tillich, *Perspectives on 19th & 20th Century Protestant Theology*, ed. C. E. Braaten (New York: Harper and Row, 1967), p. 123.

[2] Bernard Lonergan, *Method in Theology* (London: Darton, Longman and Todd, 1972), pp. 18-19 or earlier in *Insight: A Study of Human Understanding* (New York: Longmans, 1967), p. 568; hereafter cited as *Method* and *Insight*.

[3] See for example the "foreword" to *Foundations of Theology*, ed. Philip McShane (Dublin: Gill and Macmillan, 1971), pp. xv-xvi and Fred Lawrence, ed. *Lonergan Workshop I* (Missoula, Montana: Scholars Press, 1978), p. v, hereafter cited as *Foundations* and *Workshop I*.

The questions of image and symbol addressed in this essay have caused not inconsiderable unease among a number of thinkers. Some believe that the absence of an elaborated doctrine of symbol and a positive notion of myth have unqualifiedly flawed Lonergan's enterprise.[4] Some wish to complement a hermeneutic of demystification and its pursuit of utter intelligibility with an interpretation theory recovering metaphor, symbol, and story.[5] Others question the ecclesial context, the socially determining registration of image.[6] And yet others attempt to extend through amplification of particular methods the mediation of symbolic consciousness.[7] In general, Schiller speaks for this group of critics:

> While the philosopher may allow his imagination and the poet his power of abstraction to rest, I am obliged when working in this manner to maintain both of these powers in an equal state of tension, and only by a constant movement within me can I keep the two heterogeneous elements in a kind of solution.[8]

They believe that although theory and common sense, art and thought can be differentiated Lonergan has not distinguished to unite, but that he has divided to conquer symbol by thought.

---

[4] See for example, J. P. Jossua, "Some Questions on the Place of Believing Experience in the Work of Bernard Lonergan," in Patrick Corcoran, ed., *Looking at Lonergan's Method* (Dublin: Talbot, 1975), pp. 171-2, hereafter cited as *Lonergan's Method*. For general criticisms, see Edward Braxton, "Bernard Lonergan's Hermeneutic of the Symbol," *Irish Theological Quarterly* 43 (1976): 186-197, which is a condensation of his doctoral dissertation: "Images of Mystery: A Study of the Place of Myth and Symbol in the Theological Method of Bernard Lonergan" (S.T.D. Dissertation, Katholieke Universiteit te Leuven, 1975).

[5] See David M. Rasmussen, "From Problematics to Hermeneutics: Lonergan and Ricoeur," in Philip McShane, ed., *Language, Truth, and Meaning* (Dublin: Gill and Macmillan, 1972), pp. 236-271, a project which is at least partially being followed and revised by David Tracy, *Blessed Rage for Order* (New York: Seabury, 1975), esp. pp. 91-145, hereafter cited *Language* and *Blessed Rage*.

[6] See Langdon Gilkey, "Empirical Science and Theological Knowing," *Foundations*, pp. 99ff.; David F. Ford, "*Method in Theology* in the Lonergan Corpus," *Lonergan's Method*, pp. 15, 20-23 and B. C. Butler, "Method in Theology," *Clergy Review* 57 (1972) 8:579-596.

[7] See Robert Doran, *Subject and Psyche: Ricoeur, Jung, and the Search for Foundations* (Washington, D.C.: University Press of America, 1977) and his articles subsequent to the dissertation: "Psychic Conversion;" *Thomist* 41(1977):200-36, hereafter cited as "Psychic Conversion;" "Aesthetic Subjectivity and Generalized Empirical Method," *Thomist* 43 (1979) 2:257-278, hereafter cited as "Aesthetic Subjectivity;" "The Theologian's Psyche: Notes Toward a Reconstruction of Depth Psychology," *Workshop I*, pp. 93-141, hereafter cited as "The Theologian's Psyche;" and "Dramatic Artistry in the Third Stage of Meaning," *Workshop II* (forthcoming). I shall return to this reinterpretation of Lonergan later in this essay.

[8] Letter to Goethe (17 Oct. 1795) as quoted in Friedrich Schiller, *On the Aesthetic Education of Man*, trans. Reginald Snell (London: Routledge, Kegan, Paul, 1954), p. 6.

Although I find myself sympathetic to such concerns, I am also convinced that extension and revision rather than revolution are at stake in the discussion. In the following essay, therefore, I will outline what I believe are intrinsic symbolic dimensions of Lonergan's position on religious conversion, describe the symbolic structure of prayer as the foundational objectification of that conversion, and extend that through a description of sacrament as religious rhetoric.

Conversion. Religious conversion is the ultimate experience of intersubjectivity. It is being-in-love with another without restrictions, without conditions, without measuring the experiential cost to oneself. Although it is the most complete expression of self-transcendence, it reflects and sublates other kinds of being-in-love, such as familial intimacy, friendship, and philanthropy.[9] Like all intersubjectivity, it appears first as a spontaneity, a primordial "we" which emerges as the horizon in the pattern of a *Gestalt* and the language which interprets it. All intersubjectivity is first an action, a feeling, and then a meaning.[10] Purely human spontaneous intersubjectivity is the base for the good of society, the sense of belonging which is the dynamic basis for the common human enterprise.[11] Human intersubjectivity is later raised to the level of achieved participation, chosen spontaneity. Thus intersubjectivity is an intentional state, not simply "vital contagion" or "emotional identification" with the other without personal differentiation. In authentic intersubjectivity, one adverts to the other of the action while it is occurring, to the other whose feelings are shared by common cause, or to the subject whose gestures are transparent self-presence.[12]

Being-in-love with God is not different from this basic human intersubjectivity. In fact, just as the culmination of human intersubjectivity is to love others for their own subjectivity rather than their reflection of one's own; so too, other-worldly falling-in-love is a self-surrender to a mysterious uncomprehended Other who cannot be an "object out there," but is rather a non-understood "who", given in a "mystical mode."[13] But just as human intersubjectivity is experienced as a spontaneous meaning yet demands articulation (patterning) so that it may appear, so too being-in-love with God requires

---

[9] *Method,* pp. 105ff; "Theology in its New Context," in B. J. F. Lonergan, *A Second Collection,* ed. William F. J. Ryan and Bernard J. Tyrrell (London: Darton, Longman and Todd, 1974), pp. 65-67, hereafter cited as *Collection II.*

[10] *Method,* pp. 57ff.; B. J. F. Lonergan, *Collection,* ed. F. E. Crowe (New York: Herder, 1967), pp. 238, 250, 264; hereafter cited as *Collection I; Collection II,* p. 190.

[11] *Insight,* pp. 212-216.

[12] *Method,* p. 58.

[13] Ibid., pp. 106, 122, 273, 341; *Insight,* pp. 546-549, 723-4; *Collection II,* pp. 172-3.

expression for visibility.[14] The expressions of religious meaning may be art, symbol, or language but they are preceded by the word spoken by the Transcendent Other who is available in an "unmediated experience of the mystery of love and awe."[15] The spontaneous expression of religious intersubjectivity becomes that "incarnate meaning" by virtue of which one *is* in all one's modes of being. Incarnate meaning covers the whole range of human actions, feelings, expressions, etc.; as a created being, one is a word already spoken.[16] The mystery of personal identity is that which precedes, is the basis of, and witness to, the authenticity or inauthenticity of all other subjective expressions.[17] Religious intersubjectivity is the encompassing envelope for all human expressions; it does not die in articulation — rather the primordial "vector" of religious intersubjectivity, the "fateful call to a dreaded holiness," remains as matrix for all other religious expressions, and speaks in that expression.

So the "interior" word spoken by God prior to our response is not irrespective of history, society, or persons. The role of the "outer" word is constitutive. Unspoken, unmediated love is not yet self-surrender and self-gift.[18] Free revelation of oneself to God and God's prior word of love remove one from a purely cognitive context, and unite one's affective behavior in a single piece.[19] As John Dixon, Jr. says in a similar context: "To love truly is to generate the kind of self that is generated only by love."[20] This distinguishes religious conversion from the austerity of intellectual conversion and the affirmation of God in *Insight* as Unrestricted Act of Understanding. Indeed, even in *Insight,* it is difficult to discern that God's only act of understanding in relation to creation is the affirmation of its existence as true![21] The ultimate abolition of the problem of evil in human experience can be accomplished only by "collaboration" with God, which is principally the work of God.[22] The name for that cooperation is Faith, called in *Method* the "knowledge born of religious love."[23]

---

[14] *Insight,* pp. 723-4; *Method,* pp. 112-3.

[15] *Method,* p. 112; *Collection II,* pp. 173-4

[16] *Method,* p. 73; *Collection II,* pp. 61, 85.

[17] See the entire essay, "The Subject," *Collection II,* pp. 69-86.

[18] *Method,* pp. 112-115.

[19] Ibid., p. 39; *Workshop I,* p. 314.

[20] John W. Dixon, Jr., *The Physiology of Faith* (San Francisco: Harper and Row, 1979), p. 311 and 194.

[21] *Insight,* pp. 634-686; see Lonergan's remarks in *Collection II,* pp. 224, 277; or more at length in B. J. F. Lonergan, *Philosophy of God and Theology* (London: Darton, Longman and Todd, 1973), pp. 11-14, hereafter cited as *God and Theology.*

[22] *Insight,* p. 720.

[23] *Insight,* pp. 703-718; *Method,* pp. 115-118. Lonergan distinguishes between faith and beliefs; *Method,* pp. 123-4.

Although Lonergan describes conversion as the centerpiece and basis for a method in theology which in principle applies to all religions, to all cultures, and to every individual without exception, he tends to describe that conversion in Christian terms.[24] In his functional specialty called foundations, he distinguishes between special and general categories,[25] but most often speaks with Christian theological terms and relations. Although the gift, power, exercise, and acts of love are the product of a dynamic religious state, nonetheless they convey the Christian joy and eschatological peace of Romans 5:8, Mark 12, and Galatians 5.[26] The importance of this articulation is clear from his assurance that "an intersubjective element to love...is present in Christianity [as contrasted with other religions], inasmuch as God is expressing his love in Christ as well as giving you the grace in your heart, and this element is missing when the Incarnate Lord is missing."[27] Thus the proper explication of religious being-in-love is Christian conversion, the conscious turning to a God who speaks to us.

The "content" of that intersubjective love or the proper paradigm of that intersubjectivity is the transforming love of Jesus of Nazareth. Christ died for our sins! In his *De Verbo Incarnato,* the tract on Christology and soteriology, Lonergan outlines the nature of satisfaction, which should be understood not through the eyes of vindictive justice, but through the affection of a divinely initiated friendship which "bears all burdens."[28] The very essence of Christian conversion is an intersubjectivity which transforms the converted. It is the "law of the cross" transfiguring the ordinary biases of ordinary human intersubjectivity (fear, hatred, the flight from understanding, etc.) into the resurrected experience of attraction, union of love, and the inquiry for truth at whatever risk to oneself.[29] In fact, what was before experienced as limit and end becomes threshold and means. Final absence (death of the beloved) becomes an agent of presence.

This intersubjectivity of Christian meaning is founded in the mutual relations of the Triune God.[30] The "dynamic presence of

---

[24] *Method,* pp. 282-3, 332-3.

[25] Ibid., pp. 288-291.

[26] *God and Theology,* p. 9 for example.

[27] Ibid., pp. 20, 67; *Method,* p. 119.

[28] B. Lonergan, *De Verbo Incarnato* (Rome: Pontificia Universitas Gregoriana, 1964), pp. 486-552, esp. pp. 510-513 on vicarious satisfaction; hereafter cited as *De Verbo Incarnato.*

[29] Ibid., pp. 552-586.

[30] See his argument that the contingent predications *ad extra* are a participation in the mutual relations of the Triune God in *De Deo Trino,* 2 vols. (Rome: Pontificia Universitas Gregoriana, 1964), II, esp. pp. 232-235.

God in God" is not mere love toward God, but is God.[31] This presence (the Holy Spirit) is not presence as "reproduction," but as a "goal is in tendency to the goal" *(movere per modum causae efficientis* vs. *movere per modum finis).*[32] Indeed, the love which God bears us, the "Spirit poured forth in our hearts," must surely be, first of all, the immediacy of goal-directedness *(per modum finis),* as well as the creaturely dependency upon efficient causality. To use Lonergan's less scholastic vocabulary, the unrestricted desire to know and love has its "object" not in concept or judgment, but in someone.[33] "To be in love without qualifications or conditions or reservations or limits is to be in love with someone transcendent. When someone transcendent is my beloved, he is in my heart, real to me from within me."[34]

This interpretation coheres, as Lonergan notes, with contemporary readings of classical mysticism.[35] So Maréchal describes a contemplative union with God beyond ritual and simple interior prayer;[36] and James registers within his research a mode of otherworldly "reconciliation."[37] The yearning of one's being is not that of thought, but of love,[38] a desire for union beyond simple physical self-transcendence.[39] This union is ordinarily described as a non-spatial reduction of images in which there is no dualism of Ego and non-Ego.[40] This love for the Other knows no moderation.[41] But where Kierkegaard would invite the reader into an experience of nothingness, and the *Cloud of Unknowing* describes the goal as "nowhere,"

---

[31] Most readily available in B. J. F. Lonergan, *Verbum: Word and Idea in Aquinas,* ed. David B. Burrell (Notre Dame: Notre Dame Press, 1967), p. 203.

[32] Ibid., p. 204, fn. 89.

[33] *Method,* p. 109.

[34] Ibid., pp. 109-110.

[35] Ibid., pp. 242; 342, fn. 7 where William Johnston's *The Mysticism of the Cloud of Unknowing* (New York: Desclee, 1967) is cited as a position coherent with his own; cited hereafter as *Mysticism.*

[36] See Joseph Maréchal, *Studies in the Psychology of the Mystics,* trans. Algar Thorold (Albany, N.Y.: Magi, 1964), pp. 155-195, hereafter cited as *Studies;* cf. *Mysticism,* pp. 31-65; it is helpful to parallel these discussions with A. Vergote, *Dette et Desir: Deux Axes chrétiens et la Dérive pathologique* (Paris: Seuil, 1978).

[37] William James, *The Varieties of Religious Experience* (New York: Collier, 1961), p. 306; hereafter cited as *Varieties.*

[38] For examples, see *The Cloud of Unknowing,* ed. William Johnston (Garden City, N.Y.: Image, 1973), pp. 54, 90, hereafter cited as *Cloud;* Søren Kierkegaard, *Purity of Heart,* trans. Douglas V. Steere, hereafter cited as *Purity;* or Douglas V. Steere, *On Listening to Another* in *The Doubleday Devotional Classics,* ed. E. Glenn Hinson (Garden City, N.Y.: Doubleday, 1978), pp. 108, 222-224; and *Varieties,* pp. 298-336.

[39] *Cloud,* p. 128; *Studies,* pp. 28-31, 102-135.

[40] *Studies,* pp. 165-167; see James on the detachment from outer sensations, *Varieties,* p. 319; *Mysticism,* pp. 162-172.

[41] *Cloud,* p. 100; *Purity,* p. 89.

and "to-be-lost in nothingness,"[42] Lonergan (and Rahner) would prefer to speak of a "known-unknown," a mediated immediacy, whose expression may be "caught" so to speak only in act, which yet remains the condition of all self-transcendence.[43] The proper mediation of this Christian conversion is "adoration."[44]

Prayer: Symbol of Conversion. Symbols, for Lonergan, are images intending objects which invite affect or are its product. They can mediate intersubjective love; they provide the communication for the hearts and minds of lovers.[45] In extending the meaning of "symbol" to the mediation of intersubjectivity, I am aware that in *Method,* Lonergan states that the proper context for determining the meaning of symbol is "internal communication."[46] However, in *Insight,* symbol can take on a broader meaning.[47] It has its role in the context of the "heuristic structure" of the solution to the problem of evil. Human orientation toward the known unknown requires a symbol that both propels and guides the individual and group toward the goal. Without such symbols, human sensitivity would remain locked in its patterns of bias, and hope and self-sacrificing love would be denied. The symbol for one's interior communication with God, for one's religious conversion, for one's being-in-love with God becomes the symbol for another.

Christian conversion is fundamentally intersubjective; as other-worldly falling-in-love, it requires figuration to allow it to appear.[48] So just as conversation with a beloved whether enthusiastic gesture, quotidian speech, or lyrical poetry, symbolizes the intersubjective moments of human love, so prayerful words, whether spontaneous, ritual, or sacramental, embody the fundamentally intersubjective character of religious conversion. By their inherent grammatical structure, an irreducible language of first and second person address, prayers articulate the dimensions of the finite subject and

---

[42] *Cloud,* p. 136; *Purity,* pp. 30-32; on apophatic experience, see *Varieties,* p. 299f.; *Studies,* pp.189-195.

[43] Karl Rahner, "The Concept of Mystery in Catholic Theology," *Theological Investigations,* trans. K. Smyth (Baltimore: Helicon, 1966), vol. IV, pp. 36-73; "The Hiddenness of God," *Theological Investigations,* trans. David Morland (New York: Seabury, 1979), Vol. XVI, pp. 227-243; and his remarks about Lonergan's method in this context, in "Some Critical Thoughts on 'Functional Specialties in Theology,'" *Foundations,* pp. 194-196, and Lonergan's response, *Collection II,* p. 229.

[44] *Method,* p. 344; cf. also *Collection II,* p. 217: "Religious conversion is transferring oneself into the world of worship."

[45] *Method,* p. 64.

[46] Ibid., pp. 66-67.

[47] *Insight,* pp. 723ff.

[48] So see the remarks about the state of being in love which is "inferred" when it becomes "knowing," *God and Theology,* p. 38.

the Transcendent Other. Prayer is the primordial word which links inner and outer expression: the inner word spoken to the lover and the word of response.[49] As spontaneous, they share the mediated immediacy of all intersubjective expressions; as formally repeated in assembly, they register the shifting subjectivities of the individuals speaking and the intended divinity addressed. Prayer as a pure intending is the prime objectification of religious being-in-love.[50] As such, it requires dialectical examination in theological method and inclusion in the theological specialty Lonergan names foundations. This assertion however will demand a "methodological detour."

Foundations, Prayer, and the Negotiation of Conversion. The inclusion of the intersubjective language of prayer in foundations is based upon two important positions which I believe to be coherent with Lonergan's own argument. The first is that theology is not purely a cognitive self-appropriation. It is reflection upon religion in a cultural matrix. As such, it requires the apprehension of values which are beyond those of pure intellect, including discrimination, moral enactment, refined sensibility, and delicate feelings.[51] The gross differences upon the level of value which clash in dialectics and are resolved in conversion are more than simple concepts or judgments of fact. They are an encounter with persons, beyond ordinary empirical science.[52]

What is at issue, therefore, at the level of dialectics and its objectification in foundations is neither abstract concept, nor disincarnate idea; rather research into data, interpretation, and ongoing movements of history has revealed potential and actualized intersubjective positions, incarnate values which encompass the conceptual and sentential moments of religion. To appropriate those non-conceptual, non-sentential elements of dialectics, one must not merely have a grasp of one's knowing, but also of one's loving—and of one's various expressions in non-conceptual form: feelings, images, symbols, gestures, and stories. As Lonergan correctly argues, to understand both the sense and reference of religious actions and texts requires the enactment of the religious person and theologian beyond intellectual self-appropriation. Self-appropriation requires the appropriation of aesthetic subjectivity.[53]

---

[49] See *Method,* pp. 112-115, and the problems which Torrance has with this distinction in "The Function of Inner and Outer Word in Lonergan's Theological Method," *Lonergan's Method,* pp. 101-126.

[50] "Prayer in itself properly is naught else but a devout intent directed unto God, for the getting of God and the removing of evil." *Cloud,* p. 191.

[51] *Method,* p. 245; See Doran, "The Theologian's Psyche," pp. 98-111.

[52] *Method,* pp. 247, 252.

[53] See the difference between Doran's use of "aesthetic subjectivity" and Gadamer's in "Aesthetic Subjectivity," p. 258, fn. 4, where he refers to *Method,* pp. 30-31. I have

Now up to this point, Professor Doran has already marked this field as his own — and with a great deal of success. He has argued, it seems with Lonergan's agreement, that a particular method of psychotherapy recovers the images and symbols of one's dreams, thereby liberating the dramatic pattern of one's affect from its various biases.[54] Symbols, as Lonergan articulates his position in *Method*, have a power for revealing the tensions, conflicts, and struggles which logic wishes to eliminate.[55] Indeed, symbol complements logic and dialectic, thus preceding and following upon their clarifications. But in addition to dreams, pictorial art, sculpture, dance, drama, novels, and various forms of poetry also help negotiate one's self-appropriation. And even though it is possible that such expressions may have a base in some archetypical realm of the psyche,[56] it might also be argued that these expressions are the texts from which the psyche fashions its dreams. Whichever is prior (it is more likely that "inner" and "outer" aesthetic self-possession [or dis-possession] is simultaneous), what is surely the case is that although all people dream, not all can, or will undergo psychotherapy to appropriate their affective life. Rather the demand of "internal communication" is fulfilled by personal crafts, public work (the "job"), and play. All may be alienated, but therapy will not release all forms of the imagi-

---

argued that even the most abstract human experiences are "image-dependent" and "spatial" in "The Structures of our Utopial *Mitsein* (Life-together)," *Heaven*, ed. Bas Van Iersel and Edward Schillebeeckx (New York: Seabury *Concilium*, 1979), pp. 92-101. The issue remains an epistemological and ontological one: Does the "I" reduce to non-spatial temporality? Does temporality always precede the spatial? Just as there is a characteristic temporality of human existence, so there is a characteristic spatiality; the two are named incarnate, language which could be interpreted to mean a-spatial temporality taking on the limits of space. Rather in the classical framework, it must mean the eternal taking on the limits of both space and time simultaneously. See Martin Heidegger, *Being and Time*, trans. J. Macquarrie and E. Robinson (New York: Harper and Row, 1962), pp. 418-421; for the earlier reflections of E. Husserl, see *The Phenomenology of Internal Time-Consciousness*, ed. Martin Heidegger, trans. James S. Churchill (Bloomington: Indiana University Press, 1966), esp. pp. 117-122, 164-169; compare the remarks of J. Derrida on Husserl's *Phenomenology* (p. 100) in *Speech and Phenomena*, trans. David B. Allison (Evanston: Northwestern University Press, 1973), p. 84, fn. 9. See the commentary of Gerd Brand, *Die Lebenswelt: Eine Philosophie Des Konkreten Apriori* (Berlin: de Gruyter, 1971), esp. pp. 49-55, 127-133, 354-372.

[54] Doran argues at length but not uncritically that Jungian psychotherapy, when modified dialectically with Lonergan's theories of self-transcendence, will negotiate the symbols of one's inner communication; see "Psychic Conversion," pp. 213-222.

[55] *Method*, p. 66; the remarks on symbolic consciousness in *De Verbo Incarnato*, pp. 534-5, are identical (1964!).

[56] See Joseph Flanagan's use of Northrop Frye's *Anatomy of Criticism* in "Aesthetic Conversion," *Workshop II*.

nation.[57] Work requires the critique of political praxis;[58] and artistic *poiesis* requires the work of literary critics, art interpreters, *et al.*[59] In both worlds, feelings abound; but even if psychotherapy (Jungian or Freudian) allows one to appropriate one's own "interior" communication,[60] it will not supply the absolute resolution of the realms of

---

[57] *Method*, pp. 55, 357-59.

[58] I envision this critique of Doran's revision of Lonergan on image and symbol as akin to J. B. Metz's critique of the "privatization" of earlier use of Transcendental Method in Rahner in *Theology of the World*, trans. W. Glen-Doepel (New York: Herder, 1969), pp. 125-130; and *Faith in History and Society: Toward a Practical Fundamental Theology* (New York: Seabury, 1980), pp. 32-48; and an excellent, if difficult, reinterpretation of Lonergan's method in Matthew L. Lamb, *History, Method, and Theology: A Dialectical Comparison of Wilhelm Dilthey's Critique of Historical Reason and Bernard Lonergan's Meta-Methodology* (Missoula, Mont.: Scholars Press, 1978), esp. pp. 30-54, 479-536; and its concrete application by the same author, "The Production Process and Exponential Growth: a Study of Socio-Economics and Theology," *Workshop I*, pp. 257-307.

[59] For a brief history of the development of the discipline known as Religion and Literature in the United States from one of its founders, see Nathan A. Scott, Jr., "Introduction: Theology and the Literary Imagination," in *Adversity and Grace: Studies in Recent American Literature*, ed. Nathan A. Scott, Jr. (Chicago: University of Chicago Press, 1968), pp. 1-25. A seminal volume was Rollo May (ed.), *Symbolism in Religion and Literature* (New York: George Braziller, 1960). "Schools" of the discipline have grown under Scott, Giles B. Gunn ("Introduction: Literature and its Relation to Religion" in *Literature and Religion*, ed. Giles B. Gunn [New York: Harper, 1971], pp. 1-33, although the entire volume is helpful); Stanley R. Hopper (see "Introduction", *Interpretation: The Poetry of Meaning*, ed. S. R. Hopper and D. L. Miller [New York: Harcourt, Brace and World, 1967], pp. ix-xxi); and Amos Wilder (see *Theopoetic: Theology and the Religious Imagination* [Philadelphia: Fortress, 1976]). The work of biblical critics (awakened in the United States by Robert W. Funk, *Language, Hermeneutic and the Word of God* [New York: Harper and Row, 1966]) adapted literary critical tools to theological texts (see J. D. Crossan, *The Dark Interval: Towards a Theology of Story* [Niles, Ill.: Argus, 1975]); see the original work of John Dunne *(A Search for God in Time and Memory* [London: Sheldon Press, 1974] or John Navone *(Towards a Theology of Story* [Slough, England: St. Paul Publications, 1977]). The more theoretic work of Ray L. Hart, *Unfinished Man and The Imagination* (New York: Herder and Herder, 1968) and P. Ricoeur, "Biblical Hermeneutics," *Semeia* 4(1975):29-148, and its utilization in *Blessed Rage*, pp. 91-145 are essential; an example among European parties interested in this dialogue may be seen in Dorothee Sölle, "Zum Dialog zwischen Theologie und Literaturwissenschaft," *Internationale Dialogszeitschrift* 2(1969)4:296-318 and Ernst Josef Krzywon's comments in "Theologie als literarische Realisation," *Stimmen der Zeit* 192(1974):60-63, and "Literaturwissenschaft und Theologie," *Stimmen der Zeit* 193(1973):299-304; a caveat is offered by R. G. Gill, "Theology and Literary Criticism," *Theology* (London), 74(1971): 456-460.

[60] *Method*, p. 34; for an interesting specific study bearing general results for cognitional theory, see Itamar Yahalom, "Sense, Affect, and Image in Development of the Symbolic Process," *International Journal of Psychoanalysis* 48(1967):373-383; and the reflections of P. Ricoeur, *Freud and Philosophy: An Essay on Interpretation*, trans. Denis Savage (New Haven: Yale University Press, 1970), pp. 159-177; see the introduction, "Le symbole médiateur nécessaire de toute créativité" by Jean Dierkens (pp. 3-5) and the entire number of *Cahiers internationaux de symbolisme* (Genéve) 22-23 (1973):85-106.

public discourse. Thus, alone it cannot "unblock" the biases against self-appropriation or religious conversion. It could be argued that the post-dramatic recitation of oneiric narrative is already an artform, itself in need of liberation.

The appropriation of aesthetic subjectivity, therefore, emerges as an element of religious conversion. A theory of artistic expression which does not exclude the inter-subjective element should be included as the objectification of the dialectics of value. This will permit, even demand, explicit attention to the structure of "adoration," of prayer in foundations.[61] In fact, prayer is what permits the subject to recognize the self as converted. It is the prime "negotiation" of conversion, as the "sustaining flow of expression." Prayer is the "loving attention" to the other which marks the very identity of the converted subject.[62] Its literary expression will operate for Lonergan between symbol and logic.[63] The links between prayer and other forms of primary religious expression will be stated in a generative poetics of religious discourse.[64]

It is a logic of Christian prayer that Lonergan has already articulated in an unpublished lecture concerning the mediation of Christ in prayer.[65] During introductory remarks on the nature of "mediation," he distinguishes mediation in general, mutual mediation, self-mediation, and mutual self-mediation. It is the latter two which concern our topic. Self-mediation is the "structuring" which labels the organic growth of a human being. It involves differentiation and specialization—all in service of a whole. There is also the self-mediation "inwards" which is the intending subject, the consciousness which is presence to oneself, the condition of all knowing and doing. It is ultimately the development of this mediation Lonergan has described in *Insight* and the early chapters of *Method*. Mutual self-mediation has its prime example in falling-in-love. But there is also mutual self-mediation in the education of children, the relation-

---

[61] *Method*, p. 344; *Collection II*, pp. 150, 155-6.

[62] *Method*, pp. 255, 109; see the remarks of A. Vergote, *Interprétation du langage religieux* (Paris: Seuil, 1974), pp. 209-210, hereafter cited *Interprétation*.

[63] *Method*, p. 72.

[64] See Paul Ricoeur's ordering in a genetic way of the genres of revelation: P. Ricoeur, "Toward a Hermeneutic of the Idea of Revelation," *Harvard Theological Review* 70(1977): 1-37, which I believe mistakes the original moment of religious expression as "prophetic" rather than "prayerful." An excellent introduction to the call for a "generative poetics" may be seen in Erhardt Güttgemanns' remarks in *Semeia* 6(1976):esp. pp. 1-21. Hans Urs von Balthasar's personal project for an aesthetic, dramatic, and poetic of revelation (see *La Gloire et la Croix*, trans. R. Givord [Paris: Aubier, 1964]) should be interpreted in this context.

[65] The mimeographed text is labelled a transcription of TC 369, consisting of 13 pp.

ships of parents to child, in friendship, commerce, professions, and politics.[66] One decides to reveal one's self to an other.

But the capacity of self-donation to the absolute Other in conversion cannot be accomplished by oneself alone. The immediate sense of gift evoked in conversion requires mediation, not by Christ as object, but by Christ as subject, as one who developed, grew in mediation of his own personal appropriation.[67] His self-mediation was always in relation to others.[68] The reference of Christian conversion is not to an abstract principle of loving, but to a person who embraced the Cross. What is essential to this interpretation of conversion, prayer, and foundations is that incarnate and intersubjective meaning which is at stake in Christian conversion. It is not concept, abstract idea, nor a speakerless language (text) which is the object of conversion requiring thematization in foundations, but a person, who is the only adequate public symbol (sacrament) of self-mediation. Address to and through Christ is the adequate public symbol (sacrament) of self-mediation. Address to and through Christ is the adequate expression of Christian conversion.

Sacrament: Symbol of Christian Conversion. I have stated that the intersubjectivity of conversion issues in an argument for symbolic mediation of aesthetic subjectivity, and that symbolic mediation is prayer. In Christian conversion, that mediation becomes prayer to and through Christ. As James states: "The genuineness of religion is thus indissolubly bound up with the question whether the prayerful consciousness be or be not deceitful."[69] I should like to call this language of mutual self-mediation the rhetoric of love.

By the use of the word rhetoric, I do not mean mere decoration, ornament to hide underlying truth or falsity.[70] This latter position may be inherent in some classicist understandings of rhetoric,[71] but it is even explicitly denied by Quintilian. "Let us take the greatest care in expression with the principle that nothing is to be done for the sake of words—words having been introduced for the sake of

---

[66] *Collection II,* pp. 170-73.

[67] See the parallel remarks in *Collection II,* p. 156.

[68] For a highly scholastic discussion of this issue, see "Christ as Subject: A Reply," *Collection I,* pp. 164-197.

[69] *Varieties,* p. 362.

[70] Even in the late classical period, the decline of proper eloquence and the rise of ornamental speech was recognized; see Harry Caplan, "The Decay of Eloquence at Rome in the First Century," in *Of Eloquence: Studies in Ancient and Mediaeval Rhetoric,* ed. Anne King and Helen North (Ithaca: Cornell Univ. Press, 1970), pp. 160-195.

[71] See for example, Augustine, *De Doctrina Christiana,* Bk. I, c. 2.

content."[72] But in the shift of meaning which we describe as historical consciousness, we are fundamentally aware of the authenticity of speech and gesture. The ultimate issue is for us the honest relation of speaker to word; and so, in our contemporary world, the final issues seem to be faith in the political or religious leader and trust in the commercial product. What is often at issue is "what counts" for warrants in this human interchange. Rhetoric is the logic of the world of common sense;[73] it articulates the inter-subjective character of all speech, a public language which incarnates common political, social, and cultural values. Rhetoric is the thematization of the primary avenue of human understanding and interpretation. Affective as well as cognitive, its primary objective is persuasion of the other to the truth of our self-presence in gesture and word. More often in tone, rather than in explicit cognitive appeal, rhetorical language announces the authenticity of the speaker; it attempts to inform about our self-involvement in our own expressions. Truly effective rhetoric means that the hearer cannot identify either the other or self without it; it becomes mutually self-implicating language.

Classically,[74] the logic of rhetoric is described by Aristotle as part of the achievement of practical wisdom *(phronesis)*. Convincing rhetoric is accomplished by a speaker whose language embodies good sense *(phronesis)*, virtue *(arete)*, and goodwill *(eunoia)*.[75] If the principles are clear, then only amplification is necessary. If deliberation *(symboules)* is required, examples are needed so that the past may be discerned and the future judged. If arguments are at stake, then *enthymemes,* i.e. partial syllogisms, are used in which the hearers involve themselves by completing the logical movement personally.[76] To outline a contemporary inventory of rhetorical patterns in speech (or in religion) would require a much longer work.[77] To interrelate

---

[72] *The Institutio Oratoria of Quintilian,* trans. H. E. Butler, 4 vols. (Cambridge, Mass.: Harvard University Press, 1943), III: 195 (Bk. VIII, Praef., 32-33); or as he says elsewhere: *Curam ergo verborum, rerum volo esse sollicitudinem. Nam plerumque optima rebus cohaerent et cernuntur suo lumino; at nos quaerimus illa, tanquam lateant semper seque subducant* (VIII, praef., 21).

[73] I am here using the word "common sense" in Lonergan's usage as an analogue to Ordinary Language or *Lebenswelt.* For the notion of world, see H. L. Dreyfus and S. J. Todes, "Discussion: The Three Worlds of Merleau-Ponty,"*Philosophical and Phenomenological Research* 22(1961-2):559-565.

[74] We shall take Aristotle's *The "Art" of Rhetoric,* trans. John Henry Freese (Cambridge, Mass.: Harvard University Press, 1975), esp. pp. 2-171; hereafter cited as *Rhetoric.*

[75] *Rhetoric,* II, i, 4-6, pp. 170-1; see also I, ii, 3-6, pp. 16-17.

[76] Ibid.,I, ii, 8- I, iii, 9; pp. 26-38.

[77] See the interpretation of Kenneth Burke in *The Rhetoric of Religion* (Berkeley: University of California Press, 1970) and *A Rhetoric of Motives* (Berkeley: University of California Press, 1969).

them genetically would require a book. My point here is simply to indicate that in classical examinations of rhetoric, there is already an attempt to indicate how rhetoric implies the authenticity of the speaker and the implication of the audience.

If rhetoric is the at least organizing name for what is called prayer among religious people, then sacrament labels the authentic rhetoric of Christian conversion. They are prayers in which finite and infinite speaker meet in a dialogue of persuasion and conviction. Sacrament has the internal logic of rhetoric, making use of affective invitation and ornament, partial argument, and the enabling example. To negotiate one's Christian conversion requires not only the "inner" turning toward the Transcendent Other, but the constitutive expression of sacrament. Indeed, it is precisely through sacrament that one is assured in a public, communal language that mediation through Christ is warranted. They are the continuing appeal of his historically incarnate meaning; their mediation through affect, image, rituals of social passage, and political integration, negotiates one's own Christian conversion and presence, the self-mediation of Christ's cross. As authentic rhetoric, they effect what they signify! Thus ritual is not simply a matter of the "external relations" of theology,[78] but rather part of the internal objectification of dialectics in foundations. Not only must Christian theologians be involved in their own speech but participate in the authentic mediations of the community at large.[79]

Sacrament is one of those factors which Christian theologians thematize when understanding their own tradition; and because of the very nature of sacramental rhetoric, it requires self-implication. Nor is sacrament a private event. Christian theologians must involve themselves in (i.e., appropriate) their own reflective speech, but also must participate in the gestural mediations of the community at large. Sacrament invites the theologian to the fundamental inter-subjectivity (horizontal and vertical) which is the very essence of Christian conversion. The "content" of those inter-acting subjects is articulated and can be analyzed in the verbal interchange which takes place in prayer, its included narratives, and figures of speech.

It has been said upon occasion that sacrament should be compared to art-symbol, that its evocation of feeling and invitation into

---

[78] See Nicholas Lash's criticism of Lonergan, *Lonergan's Method*, pp. 139-40; Vergote makes a distinction between prayer and rite with which this author would not altogether agree, see *Interprétation*, p. 211.

[79] See the comparisons of Joseph Kroger, "Polanyi and Lonergan on Scientific Method," *Philosophy Today* 21(Spr., 1977):2-20 and John Apczynski, *Doers of the Word: Toward a Foundational Theology Based on the Thought of Michael Polanyi* (Missoula, Mont.: Scholars Press, 1977).

the world of the narrative or a painting which transforms ("metaphorizes") the individuals so involved best parallels the language of art. There is some problem here, however, as I have indicated briefly in another context.[80] Human gesture and speech are for communication, and are born in an intersubjective matrix. All language includes that intersubjective reference, even where severely limited (as in natural science, for example). Art, as described in a post-Kantian context, is frequently called disinterested.[81] The art object is isolated from its original environment, its original communicative intent, and studied for its formal interrelationships. It is those structural relations which please. If sacrament is compared to artifact in this interpretive context, it operates irrespective of its intersubjective intent. Indeed, should a religious text seem to function in a similar fashion, it too is reduced in its ultimate efficacy. We simply do not say that the Bible or the Koran is the Word about God; it is the Word of the Speaking God. Sacraments do not simply evoke a utopian societal possibility; they are an effective language of intersubjective actuation according to the tradition. It is likely that without a meta-language which thematizes subject and inter-subjectivity neither art, religious text, nor Christian sacrament will be understood as they are experienced. The inclusion of prayer and sacrament as the religious rhetoric of love in foundations remedies this cultural problem as well as makes coherent a theological method which hopes to recover Christian life as a whole.

But inclusion of the intersubjectivity and self-involvement of prayer and sacrament within theology need not destroy the "critical" character of the discipline. Participation in Christian symbol means sharing in other intersubjective symbols as well—both religious and civil. Reflection upon sacrament in foundations requires an evaluative comparative investigation of symbolics, which specifies the adequacy or inadequacy of each to the matter at hand. Just as Paul Ricoeur has compared various symbols of evil, so Christian theologians must compare, both existentially and theoretically, the past and present of competing symbols as well as concepts.[82] Rituals abound in religion; comparison of structures, themes, intersubjective communication, referents has barely begun at any normative level, i.e., a level in which deliberation toward critical praxis is at issue. Sacrament is at once a private and political act, the speaking of a transformed and transforming intersubjective encounter.

---

[80] See this author's response to William Van Roo in *Proceedings of the Catholic Theological Society of America* 32(1977): 116-7, fn. 3 and 5 for appropriate bibliography.

[81] Cf. I. Kant, *Critique of Judgment,* trans. J. H. Bernard (New York: Hafner, 1968), pp. 38-39.

[82] P. Ricoeur, *Symbolism of Evil,* trans. E. Buchanan (Boston: Beacon Press, 1967).

Conclusion. I trust that this perhaps audacious attempt to outline an intersubjective and sacramental spirituality flowing from Bernard Lonergan's reflections upon theological method does no major injustice to his positions. I believe that it may ultimately be faithful to some of the earliest thrusts of his own work, though it argues for the inclusion of symbol and sacrament at the level of dialectics and foundations. Lonergan is sometimes accused of an intellectualist bias; but the biases of his mind tend toward clarity of definition, logical argument, and the self-appropriation of one's ultimate loving. In such a way, perhaps he understands best what Bernard of Clairvaux said well: "He who understands truth without loving it, or loves without understanding, possesses neither one nor the other."

Consciousness in Christian Community

by Tad Dunne

I. Catholicity in Religious Experience

One of the most important contributions of historical criticism has been the insight that no significant event exists prior to people's interpretation of what the event means. Human events are occurrences in a world mediated by acts of meaning, and so we can properly say that the first historians are the participants themselves. We can discover this wrinkle in the nature of human events also in the resurrection of Christ. From a fully historical point of view, that event included the interpretations of it suggested by Jesus and proclaimed by his disciples — interpretations which sprung from conscious acts of faith. It is an illusion to think of the resurrection as the "real" event and then ask whether anybody had any faith in it. We can plausibly imagine that when the earliest disciples proclaimed that God had fulfilled his promises from of old, they included their own acts of faith within this act of God in their time. In fact, what seems highly implausible is that the disciples would have regarded their acts of faith as not part of that act of God. God, then, not only raised Jesus up and made him Lord, but, as part of the same salvific act, also raised up the faith of Christians over the centuries.[1]

---

[1] I do not mean to propose any new doctrine here. And while, like Pannenberg, I want to recognize a historical universality in the Christ-event, I do not conceive of history primarily in terms of revelation, nor do I think that the historian qua historian can legitimately state dogma. My purpose is to understand the elements in consciousness which make Christian faith something that can be held in common.

That raising up of faith is a significant experience. As experience, it begs interpretation. But as significant, it must include not only sense data (the voice of witnesses, the texts of evangelists) but something in the data of consciousness too—otherwise no one would find that faith significant in their lives. What is it in consciousness that makes Christian faith something that can be held in common? If we can answer this, we will understand (in, I hope, a transcultural way) what the common experience is that makes Christian community possible.

Let me approach the question again, this time from the angle of hermeneutics. Do we all agree on what the various formulas for resurrection mean? We have to understand their meaning in our lives if we are to judge in faith that they are true. For example, what does it mean to say "Jesus is Lord" or Jesus "is risen" or Jesus "was raised" or that we are "saved" or that our "sins are forgiven"? I once tried to reëxpress the truth behind these formulas in a more basic and quite broad formula that I thought might be more intelligible to our times. My formula went like this: *Through Christ, God is now giving himself on our behalf.* Still, this formula too has its limitations. It suggests a view that God did not always act on our behalf; it neglects to mention sin; and there are certainly other valid difficulties with it.

But how do you and I recognize such difficulties? Do we not test it against our living faith? And in what does that testing consist? We appeal, I believe, not to another formula, but to a truth which we know, in spite of the fact that all formulations of that truth are revisable. In stating that through Christ, God is now giving himself on our behalf, I can only hope that persons with faith know what I'm talking about. This presumes that all genuine Christians enjoy a knowing which correctly understands the meaning of a certain relevant set of data. Without the possibility of such common and correct judgments, of course, Christian community would be impossible. But there also has to be a common set of data too; otherwise the judgments would not be about the same reality. So there seems to be some base in experience which is properly universal or "catholic." The catholicity of faith, we might say, is the appearance in knowledge of a prior catholicity in experience. In terms of my own limping formulation, God "now giving himself on our behalf" refers to an understood set of experiences—both of sense data and of my own operations as a subject—which I presume to be commonly recognizable. With the word "is" I judge my understanding of those experiences to be the same understanding of the same experiences which all genuine Christians have, beginning with Jesus and his disciples.

Furthermore, Jesus himself must have had this same universal element in experience as well as its verified understanding in judgment, not only because he too is human but also because otherwise his disciples would have nothing meaningful in common with him. When I say "verified understanding in judgment" I do not mean the further objectifications which follow upon judgment, be they artistic, dogmatic, evangelical, confessing, dreamt, theological, scholarly, or dramatic. I mean rather the act of knowing the real meaning of a set of experiences — the act against which one measures the validity of all its objectifications.

There seems to be, then, a reality in conscious experience which Christians have in common with Christ and with one another and whose meaning can be correctly grasped through faith. I am speaking not of all the experiences which faith affects, but of those experiences "through which faith reaches its proper object. One might think of such experiences" as reading Scripture, or being encouraged by the witness of a Christian, or feeling some awe at the thought that God is on the move in one's life. In these examples, the objects as experienced are different complexes of data and they differ somewhat in meaning. However, in the subject who experiences, there is one experience that is common to them all. It is the experience of a self-in-relation, with the relation being to God, to Christ, to other Christians. All experience is intrinsically ambiguous; otherwise it would not stand in need of correct understanding. The same is true of one's self-experience. Is the self I am conscious of in all my activities a self in relation to God or not? Is this self really part of a "we" with Jesus and the community of his disciples or not? Did not even Jesus experience a self in union with God, prescinding from the various understandings of that union by Paul, John, and perhaps Jesus himself? Whatever other experiences may be relevant to a Christian faith, certainly the experience of a self-in-relation to God will be worth some investigation.

II. We-consciousness

With these experiences in mind, I would like to pursue some answer to the following question: What, in terms of human consciousness, is the ontological structure of Christian community? Bernard Lonergan offers the only basic clarity I know of on this subject.[2] For my part in this tribute to him on his seventy-fifth birthday, I in-

---

[2] For clear statements on what "consciousness" means for Lonergan, follow the leads given in the index of *Insight* and see "Christ as Subject: A Reply," in *Collection,* ed. F.E. Crowe, S.J. (New York: Herder and Herder, 1967), p. 175 and *passim.* For evidence that Lonergan had not arrived at this clarity much before *Insight,* see David Burrell's index to his edition of the *Verbum* articles: the entry "consciousness" refers to passages in which the idea is present but the term is absent.

tend to begin with his notion of consciousness and develop its social dimensions within the larger framework of his thought. More specifically, I want to investigate the idea of a "we-consciousness," to understand how it develops and what sort of knowledge it is. Along the way, I will touch briefly on how the category can be used for expressing such doctrines as the sufficiency of Christ for salvation, the necessity of prevenient and cooperative graces, and the possibility of finding God's will.

First, then, I will review Lonergan's understanding of consciousness to clear up a chronic ambiguity that afflicts the majority of discussions one comes across on the topics of Christ's consciousness and of human experience. Lonergan distinguishes between consciousness-as-perception and consciousness-as-experience. Consciousness-as-perception is the non-technical and ordinary meaning of the term found in such expressions as "I was quite conscious of the fact that you felt uneasy" or "I became conscious of a deep feeling of peace." It simply means known or perceived. The "con-" in this use of "conscious" has become an etymologically useless appendage. Consciousness-as-experience, on the other hand, means the awareness of oneself and one's act which accompanies one's knowing or perceiving any object whatsoever. In this technical usage, the prefix "con-" is justified because it specifies an awareness of self simultaneous with thoughts, feelings, and actions directed towards objects, including the times when that object happens to be oneself. I want to use "consciousness" in this technical sense.

The notion of a common consciousness—that is, of an unreflective awareness of a "we" to which the self belongs—first occurred to me while reading Lonergan's early work "Finality, Love, Marriage" (1943).[3] There he had written, "the compenetrating consciousness of lives shared by marriage is dynamic and reaches forth to will and to realize in common the advance in Christian perfection that leads from the consummation of two-in-one-flesh to the consummation of the beatific vision."[4] And earlier in the same article, following Aristotle: "a man is to himself in consciousness of his being, and he is conscious of his being through activity; hence to be to his friend as he is to himself, the common consciousness of mutual other selves has to find a common activity."[5]

---

[3] *Collection*, pp. 16-53. I believe I am also indebted to Alfred Schutz for directing my attention to the importance of understanding how the structure of social relations are founded on the structures of relations in consciousnesses. His "The Dimensions of the Social World," (*Collected Papers II*, ed. Arvid Brodersen [The Hague: Martinus Nijhoff 1964], pp. 20-63) is a phenomenology of the experiences in which another person's consciousness becomes accessible.

[4] p. 37

[5] p. 35

Readers familiar with Lonergan's thought will justifiably wince at the meaning of the term "consciousness" in this early work. It is questionable whether he means precisely the self-awareness which accompanies acts that intend objects, as he will define it in later works. He identifies "common consciousness" here with the *"totius vitae communio, consuetudo, societas"* of a marriage.[6] On the other hand, Lonergan does say that a person "is conscious of his being through activity." This indicates that at least he does not merely mean consciousness-as-perception, since the activities through which the person or the group are "conscious" of themselves are obviously not strictly activities of mutual perception or self-reflection but may be any common activities whatsoever. It seems, then, that by "common consciousness" Lonergan here means not only a wide range of shared views and purposes but also the sheer awareness which accompanies common operations.

Whatever Lonergan meant by "common consciousness" in these passages, we can ask about its reality. Is there such a thing as a consciousness, defined as a subject's self-awareness which accompanies the subject's intending of objects, which can properly be called common? I believe it is easy to demonstrate that there is. Take a card game. Because the acts of dealing and deploying the cards are conscious acts, I am certainly aware of myself, even though I am thinking only about trouncing my opponents. But as an act which is common, I am also aware of the "we" who make up the compound subject who plays. Should someone ask me what *I* was doing, I spontaneously answer that *we* were playing cards.

To say that several persons have a common consciousness does not imply that each lacks the self-awareness that accompanies his or her participation. Nor does it imply a Hegelian supra-subject whose self-transcendence makes the authenticity of individuals merely a means to a larger end. Nor am I thinking here of what liberation theology calls "conscientization" or "consciousness-raising," since these seem to deal mainly with consciousness-as-perception. I am simply adverting to the verifiable phenomenon that when people engage in a common activity, each one is aware of a "we" even though no one may be thinking about it.

Besides this common consciousness given in common activities, there may also be given a common intention to form a "we." Of course, this is not always the case. Martin Buber has discerned three distinct types of dialogue, two of which seem to bear no intention at all of forming a "we":

---

[6] Ibid.

> There is genuine dialogue—no matter whether spoken or silent—where each of the participants really has in mind the other or others in their present and particular being and turns to them with the intention of establishing a living mutual relation between himself and them.
>
> There is technical dialogue, which is prompted solely by the need of objective understanding.
>
> And there is monologue disguised as dialogue, in which two or more men, meeting in space, speak each with himself in strangely tortuous and circuitous ways and yet imagine that they have escaped the torment of being thrown back on their own resources.[7]

In what Buber calls "genuine dialogue," the purpose of establishing a community accompanies other purposes held in common. This seems essential to any self-constituting community. In "technical dialogue," persons may reach a common understanding and a common judgment about the state of things, so common meanings may be reached cognitively, and a "we-consciousness" would certainly be present. Still, as long as the will-to-community is lacking, no full community can be realized. In "monologue-disguised-as-dialogue," a mere formal common understanding is not even desired, and so the possibilities for community are extremely low.

Prior to any thought about it, the difference between genuine dialogue and the other two types is experienced in one's feelings. In a genuine dialogue, besides the feelings which respond to the qualitative values in the purposes pursued together, there are feelings which respond to the ontic values of the persons pursuing them.[8]

Experience tells us that this response to the ontic values of other persons occurs in two modes. In the first, each responds to the ontic value of the other. In the second, each responds to the ontic value of the "we." Marian the Librarian, in the musical "Music Man," sang about both of these in her pining for her "White Knight":

---

[7] Martin Buber, *Between Man and Man,* trans. Ronald Gregor Smith (London: Fontana Library, Pb., 1961), p. 37.

[8] See Lonergan, *Method in Theology,* (New York: Herder and Herder, 1972), p. 31. Lonergan refers the reader to Dietrich von Hildebrand's *Christian Ethics;* what Lonergan calls "ontic" value von Hildebrand calls "ontological" value. The faculty psychology that von Hildebrand uses there, while much more systematic than Buber's phenomenology, still fails to get at a dynamic account of the process of responding to the person of another. And although Lonergan sets von Hildebrand's general account of value within a dynamic account of feelings, he does not develop the ontic/ontological aspect. See *Christian Ethics* (New York: David McKay, 1953), pp. 129-139 and *Method in Theology,* pp. 31, 38-50.

And I would like him to be
More interested in me
Than he is in himself
And more interested in us
Than in me.

A genuine dialogue, then, seems to have two distinguishable modes. The first I would like to call "personal address." In this mode, two persons welcome one another for the unique value that the other is, prescinding from the other's talents or beauty or possibilities. It is the mode of I and Thou. The second mode I would like to call "togetherness." This is the mode in which each welcomes the unique union being formed, again prescinding from the qualities of that union. (I have been speaking of a relationship between two persons. The two modes, however, are present in larger groups: One person can "dialogue" with either one other member or the entire group; and any number of persons can be consciously together in a common activity.) In the early stages of a developing relationship, each participant may welcome both the others and the union without, however, knowing whether the other participants do too. A genuine dialogue does not blossom until the point is reached where everyone not only welcomes the others and the union, but everyone knows that everyone does.

I do not mean to ignore the fact that a developing relationship intends and welcomes objects outside of it. To respond to the ontic values of others has to include an appreciation of the others' self-transcending openness to the real world and to enduring values. It would be difficult to imagine a growing "we" between persons who have closed themselves against reality and against the inner questions that may prove to be "we-transcending." I would like, however, to focus on the kinds of common consciousness that accompany the shared activities of persons in a genuine dialogue — the persons, that is, who intend community. In particular, I want to reach some sort of explanation, in terms of consciousness, of how communities develop. Anybody who attempts to understand the constituents of community without examining development runs the risk of overlooking the permanently self-transcending nature of its members and implying by default that an ideal community is an unchanging one.

III. Development

Lonergan has shown that to understand developments genetically, we should specify operators and integrators — operators being the routines that instigate change and integrators being the routines that consolidate change.⁹ To determine what the operators and integrators are in consciousness which generate that developing personal relationship, let us look at what kinds of interpersonal activities are intrinsically common: activities that have no meaning unless two or more persons are involved — activities, therefore, that give a common consciousness.

We have already seen that there appears to be two main modes of genuine dialogue, a personal address mode and a togetherness mode. Included in the personal address mode are any activities whose structure involves two or more persons acting at different poles of a single activity and responding to the others' ontic values. For example, in activities such as encounter, communicating, waiting for someone, caring or being cared for, giving or receiving, one is conscious of "we" but one's consciousness of the polarity of I and Thou dominates the structure of the experience because one is conscious of oneself as responding to the ontic value of someone else, and of being a subject who is similarly being responded to. On the other side, there is togetherness — activities whose structure involves two or more persons at the same pole of the activity, yet carry with them a response to the ontic value of the "we." For example: singing together, being part of an audience, acclamation, commiserating, believing together. In all of these, the felt response to the ontic value of the "we" dominates each one's response to the ontic value of the others. (Besides these examples, there are many activities which, although they might be done alone, are in fact done together.)

A genetic outline of the ascent of "we" through the levels of a blossoming friendship follows straightaway. Personal address acts as an operator and togetherness acts as an integrator. In other words, when a person who intends community with others either addresses them or is addressed, some portion of the common meaning which constitutes that community is being questioned for the sake of development, and simultaneously that person is aware of being a "we" in the mode of personal address. And when such a person finds agreement or cooperation with those others, some common meaning has been achieved, and all such genuine participants are aware of being a "we" in the mode of togetherness.

Now the forms of togetherness are simply: common experience, common understanding, common judgment, common decision. But we recognize this as Lonergan's heuristic of community,¹⁰ and so we have already come full circle. If community is "an achievement of common meaning," we have merely called that common meaning

---

⁹ See Lonergan, *Insight,* pp. 465-467, and especially p. 546.
¹⁰ Lonergan, *Method in Theology,* p. 79.

"togetherness," regarded it as a genetic integrator in consciousness, and clarified what "achievement" means in terms of the genetic operator "personal address."

Further, while it is true that a community which is continually self-transcending provides its members with an ambiance of tested values, it is also true that the origin of each of those values is not the common meanings that constitute the community but the originating value which some member or another happens to be. Let me express this in genetic terms: While togetherness is an integrator and personal address is an operator in community, within that operator are the two poles of I and Thou. Of these two poles, the role of operator generally falls to one self-transcending subject who, while engaging in genuine dialogue, shares experiences, ideas, judgments, or decisions and leaves them open to question by the other. Otherwise it is monologue disguised as dialogue. The point is that a self-transcending community is not automatic. It is a direct function of self-transcending individuals.[11]

IV. The Ambiguity of Consciousness

But there's a gremlin in the operator. Persons in community can raise questions that divide as well as unite. In free countries, both the biased and the unbiased enjoy equal freedom to speak their minds. So we try to fashion a dialogic forum for resolving differences in opinions and proposals, in stages of development, and in basic horizons. Still, the gremlin does his mischief in consciousness too, because the data of consciousness alone are insufficient grounds for knowing oneself to be a "we" with others. Experience, as we have said, is intrinsically ambiguous: it begs correct understanding. Consciousness, as inner experience, also begs a correct understanding. Among the common activities which mediate a common consciousness, some may be as immediate as sawing together with a two-handled buck-saw, but others are mediated almost entirely by

---

[11] I have been talking about what Lonergan calls the "top" level of consciousness — being in love as the dynamic principle of being responsible, reasonable, intelligent, and attentive. We shouldn't overlook, however, the phenomenon that a pet dog and a man or woman can "befriend" one another, with the dog showing responses of glee, remorse, longing (and evidence of having learned to delay satisfactions) which it ordinarily does not show to any other dog. So although the "topmost" scheme of recurrence in humans is a being in love, such love has more evident roots in the subhuman than do the "lower" schemes of human responsibility, reason, and intelligence. This suggests that the spontaneous intersubjectivity which we seem to share with animals and which is sublated by our capacity to be in love ought to be the principle object of any study of what human learning and animal learning have in common. The genetic structure of personal address/togetherness, when considered as operator/integrator, will be useful for organizing the data on this "pet phenomenon."

mental and emotional acts—such as being a Democrat or sitting on a committee. The "we-consciousness" which accompanies common activities of understanding, judging, and deciding is itself a product of understanding, judging, and deciding. One can ask "Do you know what I mean?" or "Isn't that right?" or "Are we together on this project?" and never lose the intention of community. But one can also ask "Do you really want anything to do with me?" And no matter whether the other persons answer Yes or No, one still must make a judgment about what the others' intentions really are and whether it is worthwhile believing them. In the data of consciousness, then, the experience of thinking and deliberating together is not enough to justify the judgment that all parties have chosen to form and consolidate a "we."

I don't intend to untangle the slew of projections and recriminations found in relationships that break down. Rather I want to examine the dynamism of consciousness found when the new relationship blossoms with God through Christian faith. The most fundamental experience of ourselves in all our self-transcending operations is the experience of an oriented self. We are oriented to intelligibilities, realities, and values—particularly to the ontic values of a loving community—in an open-ended manner. But an oriented self will forever be an ambiguous self without the judgment in faith that the term of that orientation is being given in one's here and now. After all, it is one thing to be consciously oriented and quite another to be knowingly a "we" with the term of that orientation. If orthodox doctrine states that through Christ and the Holy Spirit we are "divinized" or "elevated" as well as forgiven and healed, then to judge this proposition to be true would seem to have this effect in consciousness: It resolves the radical ambiguity of whether the self I experience in all my self-transcending operations is part of a "we" with God or not. More specifically, I know that I am not the autonomous origin and manager of my own self-transcendence. For even my very experiences of having questions, as well as reaching answers, can be known in faith to be experiences, respectively, of God's personal address upon me and of his togetherness with me. Such experiences may well have been what Augustine understood when he formulated his doctrines of prevenient and cooperative grace.

V. Assurance

This judgment—that one is a "we" with the absolutely transcendent—is a special form of knowledge. It is not like the judgments of fact which reach a reality that has no dependence on the judgment in order to be real. Nor is it like the judgment of value that sees the worth of believing the good news. I would like to name this form of knowledge "assurance." Its general anthropological effect is to assure a person that intelligent inquiry, reasoned judgment, and responsible action are worthwhile, despite piecemeal insights, limited certainties, and halting convictions. Its special religious effect is to assure a person that all experience is experience of God, that the world as one finds it is an instance of divine personal address, that the ultimate significance of world process derives from the historical significance of divine action in Christ Jesus, and that one's very spirit of wonder is an act of togetherness with God.

Before elaborating upon its special religious effect, I want to point out how at least some form of assurance is absolutely necessary for the achievement of any community. In our times, there is already an assurance which underpins contemporary philosophy of empirical science. From physics on up to the human sciences, investigators work with the assurance that there are reasons behind the way things work, even though no one investigator is assured of discovering them. Still, this assurance of intelligibility is not enough to generate the criteria needed to create community. For besides understanding how things work, scientists such as sociologists help shape policy, family psychologists must suggest therapies, and philosophers of history speak not only of history's pattern but of history's purpose too. What assurance have they that these goals are worthwhile? No doubt, people achieve common purposes; it's the one achievement that makes a community fully alive. And no doubt, people act with at least implicit criteria for agreeing on purposes, criteria beyond sheer consensus. But there must also be some assurance that the very effort to define one's purpose is itself worthwhile. Few people speak with absolute conviction about their decisions. Rather than saying "I did *the* best," one says "I did *my* best." Yet those who have achieved the common meanings of a stable community speak with an assurance that *the* best is reached by people doing *their* best. Such an assurance is given in moral consciousness, in the self-awareness of persons whose minds and hearts are set on doing good. Without it, there could be no human community at all, because there would be no properly moral base for developing criteria on how to choose the good. We would be left—indeed, Western liberal thought has been left[12]—with only the cognitive criteria suited for understanding how things work. In the end, the only criteria for choosing between equally workable proposals would be the will of the more powerful.

I have been speaking hypothetically. At least some assurance of

---

[12] See Roberto Mangabeira Unger, *Knowledge and Politics* (New York: The Free Press, 1975), pp. 38-41, 51-55, 76-81, 88-100.

objective values lurks in the consciousness of even the most self-indulgent among us. So genuine communities do rise up. Unfortunately, we have not yet developed the sciences of final causality anywhere near as extensively as we have the sciences of formal causality. That explains somewhat why the full dimensions of world and human purpose — especially the questions of morally self-transcending subjects bound in common consciousness — have not been adequately dealt with.

The religious form of the question of common purpose is whether we share a common purpose with God. The knowledge that we do is an assurance in consciousness of being "we" with God in all that we do, save sin. It is this element in consciousness that I believe all Christians have in common with one another and with Christ Jesus. This assurance — that one's oriented self is also a self-in-relation which will not be ultimately frustrated in its most self-transcending desires — forms the *basso continuo* in the consciousness of Christ. It seems to underpin the changes in strategy Jesus made as he went from teaching and healing, to gathering a small group of disciples, and finally, to facing a death which all the world would deem a failure. Even from an ordinary historian's point of view, Jesus seems to have acted with an assurance, unprecedented in the history of Israel, that his acts were the acts of God.

As for us Christians, we believe that communion with Christ in his Church is enough for our salvation and that there is no need to look for some second divine mediator in order to be in communion with him. Translated into terms of consciousness, we believe that the gospel of Christ is his personal address on us — a standing invitation to continual conversion. And we believe that when we preach the gospel to the world, it is in togetherness with Christ that we preach — with an eloquence and wisdom which he promised he would give us (Lk 21:15). It is no coincidence, I believe, that Christian liturgies comprise a "word" liturgy and a "eucharist" liturgy. With these two rites we express the two ways in which we act in genuine dialogue with God. In the Liturgy of the Word we are addressed by God, and in the Liturgy of the Eucharist we act in togetherness with Christ offering our lives in communion with him.

One of the most consoling scenes in all the New Testament is the first scene Luke portrays after Jesus' ascension into heaven (Acts 1: 12-26). About one hundred and twenty believers were gathered together, and Peter asked them to choose a successor to Judas. So they prayed, asking God to "show us which of these two you have chosen," and then they quite simply "gave lots." Whether "giving lots" meant a vote or else the equivalent of flipping a coin to decide between equally worthy alternatives, they seemed to have used a rather ordinary decision-making process and trusted that the outcome was indeed God's own choice. If that isn't acting with assurance, I don't know what is. Such assurance is the effect in the consciousness of Christians of what we call the guarantee of the Holy Spirit to the Church. And this reassuring scene of the very first "Acts of the Apostles" represents the archetypical finding of God's will— conceived not as a plan to be discovered through a judgment of fact, but as a judgment of value of persons in togetherness with God.

Ethics

Moral Development: Is Conversion Necessary?

by Walter E. Conn

During the last twenty years Lawrence Kohlberg's theory of moral development has become increasingly influential not only in developmental psychology, but also in philosophical and theological ethics and, especially, moral and religious education. The popular appeal of Kohlberg's six-stage theory of moral reasoning development is dependent in no small way on the fact that it approaches perennial issues of conscience and values in an empirical fashion, and offers a vision of apparent clarity, precision, and simplicity which affirms the common sense perception that the moral reasoning of children, adolescents, and adults differ significantly. Kohlberg outlines these differences in three levels of moral development, specifying two stages within each level:

Level I   Preconventional

   Stage 1   Obedience and Punishment Orientation
   Stage 2   Instrumental-Relativist Orientation

Level II   Conventional

   Stage 3   Interpersonal Concordance or "good boy-nice girl" Orientation
   Stage 4   Authority and Social-Order Maintaining Orientation

Level III   Postconventional

   Stage 5   Social Contract, Legalist Orientation
   Stage 6   Self-chosen Universal Ethical Principle Orientation[1]

---

[1] See Lawrence Kohlberg, "The Claim to Moral Adequacy of a Highest Stage of Moral Judgment," *The Journal of Philosophy* 70/18 (October 25, 1973), pp. 631-32.

Like every theory that achieves a significant degree of popularity and influence, Kohlberg's has also received its share of criticism.[2] One of the most important and interesting critical discussions of Kohlberg's work is John Gibbs' attempt to clarify its central concept of stage development.[3] Gibbs' critical strategy is based on a fundamental distinction he finds between two groups of Kohlberg's "stages": *natural* stages at the first two levels, and *existential* orientations at the third, postconventional level.

In this essay I will briefly review Gibbs' constructive critique of Kohlberg, and then offer a different interpretation of Gibbs' natural/existential distinction based on Bernard Lonergan's analysis of moral conversion. I will argue that in order to appreciate the existential theme of postconventional morality one must view it from the perspective of self-creation, and especially from the existential moment of that process I call critical moral conversion. Gibbs correctly points to the existential theme as dominant in Kohlberg's principled morality. But I will argue that by emphasizing the formal, reflective, philosophical dimension of principled reasoning, and not its self-chosen character, Gibbs does not do full justice to the existentialist theme nor thus to the radical difference between what he calls the first four "natural" orientations in Kohlberg's theory and the last two "existential" orientations.

I. Postconventional Morality as Existential

The specific context of Gibbs' discussion is the relationship of Kohlberg's work to the developmental stage theory of Jean Piaget, the preeminent psychological theory of development, and clearly the single greatest influence on Kohlberg's entire project. Gibbs' critique begins with Kohlberg's claim that the moral judgment stages in his theory satisfy the criteria for stages in the strong Piagetian sense of the term.[4] Stated briefly, Piaget's criteria for stages, as Gibbs understands them, are: (1) evidence of an underlying structure; (2) an upward tendency and stability in development; (3) facilitated develop-

---

[2] See, for example, the essays by R. S. Peters, J. Nicolayev and D. C. Phillips, and B. Crittenden in D. B. Cochrane, C. M. Hamm, and A. C. Kazepides (eds.), *The Domain of Moral Education* (New York: Paulist Prss, 1979); W. Kurtines and E. C. Greif, "The Development of Moral Thought: Review and Evaluation of Kohlberg's Approach," *Psychological Bulletin* 81/8 (August, 1974), pp. 453-70; and E. L. Simpson, "Moral Development Research: A Case Study of Scientific Culture Bias," *Human Development* 17 (1974), pp. 81-106.

[3] John C. Gibbs, "Kohlberg's Stages of Moral Judgment: A Constructive Critique," *Harvard Educational Review* 47/1 (February, 1977), pp. 43-61.

[4] See Jean Piaget, *Biology and Knowledge* (Chicago: The University of Chicago Press, 1971), pp. 16-25.

ment in an experientially "rich" environment; (4) gradual and consecutive sequential movement; (5) commonly found among species members; and (6) achieved through spontaneous and essentially unconscious processes.

The central point of Gibbs' criticism is that while there is evidence that Kohlberg's first four preconventional and conventional stages satisfy all these criteria, his last two postconventional or principled stages do not. Gibbs claims that the admitted rarity and explicitly reflective character of the postconventional stages argues against their fulfillment of the last two criteria. Gibbs' point is not to deny the existence of what Kohlberg calls postconventional moral reasoning, nor even to deny that there are postconventional stages. His proposal, rather, is that an accurate understanding of moral development requires that Kohlberg's fifth and sixth postconventional stages be recognized as a significantly different *kind* of stage from the first four.

The six criteria for stages listed above relate, according to Gibbs, to four basic features of Piaget's developmental-structural stage theory: holism (underlying structure), constructivism (upward tendency), interactionism (facilitated development), and naturalism (necessarily gradual, common, and achieved through spontaneous and essentially unconscious processes). In Gibbs' view naturalism is the most fundamental of these features: "At the heart of Piaget's theory is a naturalistic theme that human mental development reflects a deep biological significance. Building upon this theme are the assumptions of holism, constructivism, and interactionism." [5] As an important example of how these features of Piaget's thought interrelate, it should be noted that a correct understanding of Piaget's naturalistic emphasis on "a continuity between the human species and other forms of life" and the "deep biological significance" of "normative human behavior" includes the constructionist view on evolution "that human intelligence extends, but does not reduce to, organic regulatory processes and structures." [6]

To repeat Gibbs' basic point now in terms of Piaget's fundamental theme of naturalism, research evidence indicates that Kohlberg's first four stages meet *all* the Piagetian stage criteria and therefore qualify as Piagetian *natural* stages in the fullest sense. Kohlberg's postconventional fifth and sixth stages, however, because they fail to meet the specific criteria of being universal and unconscious which are related to Piaget's naturalistic theme, cannot be considered as *natural* stages in the full Piagetian sense, though they may be seen as stages in terms of other criteria.

---

[5] Gibbs, p. 53.
[6] Ibid., p. 52.

In recognizing Kohlberg's first four stages as valid natural stages in the full Piagetian sense, Gibbs is pointing to naturalism as one of the two key themes he finds in Kohlberg's work, themes which are among the most fundamental in modern psychology. While naturalism argues that "the development and expression of human behavior reflect spontaneous constructive processes reflective of life in general," the second theme Gibbs identifies in Kohlberg's work, the existentialist theme, argues that "awareness of self and efforts to come to terms with this awareness are keys to understanding the human phenomenon."[7] Gibbs' claim, therefore, is that moral development in Kohlberg's theory will be understood more accurately if stages one through four are seen as *natural,* and stages five and six as *existential.* Gibbs is able to point to suggestions of this distinction in Kohlberg's more recent work, where Kohlberg admits that the construction of the postconventional stages "seems to require experiences of personal moral choice and responsibility usually supervening upon a questioning period of 'moratorium'."[8] As Gibbs understands it, "post-conventionality is the existential experience of disembedding oneself from an implicit world view and adopting a detached and questioning posture."[9]

Whereas Kohlberg views his postconventional, principled stages as "natural structures" out of which ethical theories may be systematically constructed, Gibbs sees them not as natural stages but as reflective, philosophical formalizations based on implicit achievements of earlier, natural stages.[10] In particular, Gibbs understands the social contract ethic of Kohlberg's fifth orientation (he uses "orientation" as a general, descriptive term, reserving "stage" for those orientations which satisfy all the Piagetian criteria) as a highly formal theory informed by the pragmatic intuition that "*a priori* rational people must simply temper their desires with the recognition that others want their lives and freedom as they themselves want theirs." In Gibbs' view, the social perspective taking involved in the meta-ethics of Kohlberg's fifth orientation "does not seem to go beyond that necessary for the natural moral stage 2." In the social perspective taking required for the meta-ethics of orientation 6's ideal role taking, says Gibbs, "*a priori* rational people must be capable of moderating their immediate interests and reconstructing

---

[7] Ibid., p. 43.

[8] Lawrence Kohlberg, "Continuities in Childhood and Adult Moral Development Revisited" in P. B. Baltes and K. Warner Schaie (eds.), *Life-Span Developmental Psychology* (New York: Academic Press, 1973), p. 180.

[9] Gibbs, p. 56.

[10] Ibid.; also see Kohlberg, "The Claim to Moral Adequacy of a Highest Stage of Moral Judgment," p. 634.

them into ideal or mutual sentiments." Such third-person perspective taking and the meta-ethics of orientation 6, then, according to Gibbs, are those of the stage 3 rational person. In summary, then, Gibbs sees persons reasoning from orientations 5 and 6 as philosophers, and understands "the principled orientations themselves as 'constructive systematizations' starting from natural intuitions about morality and human nature."[11] While natural stages subsume and dominate preceding ones, Gibbs claims that "formal ethical philosophies [i.e., moral reasoning or orientations 5 and 6] may override but do not eliminate the relevance of the natural stages of moral judgment." Stage 3 and 4 possess a maturity of permanent significance for everyday life. Gibbs' fundamental objection to Kohlberg's view of all six orientations as natural stages is that it "fails to take into account the crucial distinction between implicit theories-in-action [natural stages 1-4] and detached reflections upon one's theories-in-action [orientations 5-6]."[12] On the other hand, and this is Gibbs' central positive contention, "explicitly distinguishing the existential and naturalistic themes in Kohlberg's theory permits each theme to assume an important role in his work on the development of moral judgment."

II. Existential Orientation as Self-Chosen

The preceding review of Gibbs' "constructive critique" of Kohlberg's theory clearly shows, I think, that Gibbs' distinction between two types of stages or orientations has identified an important issue in Kohlberg's interpretation of moral development. As we noted, Kohlberg has dealt with the question of the existential dimension of principled morality himself. In so doing, however, he takes a significantly different tack from Gibbs: Kohlberg's approach is to account for principled moral reasoning as a distinctively adult reality by reinterpreting the concept of structural stage in a way wide enough to include the existential experiences of personal moral questioning, choice, and responsible action — realities excluded from his earlier view which denied the existence of a *structurally* distinctive adult morality.[13] Gibbs, as we have seen, moves in the opposite direction by defining the concept of stage in such narrowly Piagetian terms that Kohlberg's fifth and sixth stages are considered no longer as true natural stages but as existential orientations of a reflective, meta-ethical character.

---

[11] Gibbs, p. 57.

[12] Ibid., p. 58.

[13] See L. Kohlberg and R. Kramer, "Continuities and Discontinuities in Childhood and Adult Moral Development," *Human Development* 12 (1969), pp. 118-19. Also see my "Postconventional Morality: An Exposition and Critique of Lawrence Kohlberg's Analysis of Moral Development in the Adolescent and Adult," *Lumen Vitae* 30/2 (June, 1975), pp. 227-28.

Clearly, the important issue here is the most adequate understanding of moral development, not whether Kohlberg or Gibbs is right or wrong. Surely, if a stage in the full sense must be universally found, then Kohlberg's fifth and sixth stages do not qualify. It is not clear, however, even in Piaget's own theory of cognitive development, that the full realization of the formal operational stage is found universally.[14]

Gibbs' second key point about the spontaneous and unconscious nature of stages is more complicated. Gibbs claims that stages in the full sense are *implicit* theories-in-action rather than detached, *explicit* reflections upon one's theories-in-action. By interpreting Kohlberg's principled stages as "constructive systematizations" of reflective, philosophical meta-ethics, Gibbs easily places the principled stages or orientations in the category of detached explicit reflections upon theories-in-action rather than that of implicit theories-in-action. Gibbs' interpretation on this point deliberately contradicts Kohlberg's explicit understanding, and Gibbs does not argue for his interpretation but simply asserts it in one sentence. The question which remains for us, then, is whether or not principled moral reasoning should be understood as necessarily explicitly reflective, philosophical meta-ethics.

Answering in the negative, my response to this question will be developed within the context of a positive alternative interpretation of Kohlberg's principled moral reasoning based on an understanding of moral conversion derived from the critical methodological thought of Bernard Lonergan.

Perhaps the most significant point about Gibbs' critique is what he does after drawing the natural/existential distinction and emphasizing the importance of the existential theme, which he says is in Kohlberg's theory but not clearly distinguished there. Although he makes very brief references to such sub-themes as meaning, authenticity, and self-actualization as well as to such authors as Victor Frankl, Rollo May, and Abraham Maslow, Gibbs explicates the existential theme he finds in Kohlberg almost entirely in terms of formal meta-ethical philosophies.[15] This perspective echoes Gibbs' interpretation of Kohlberg's stage 6 as an orientation "justifying moral prescriptions or evaluations by appeal to the results of ideal role taking."[16] Here, and with Kohlberg's other stages, Gibbs is on target, in my judgment, in emphasizing the "orientation" character

---

[14] See Lawrence Kohlberg and Carol Gilligan, "The Adolescent as a Philosopher: The Discovery of the Self in a Postconventional World," *Daedalus* 100 (Fall, 1971), p. 1065.

[15] Gibbs, pp. 56-57.

[16] Ibid., p. 54.

of stages and in stressing "justification" as their central element. Gibbs misses the bull's-eye in his interpretation of stage 6, however, by sighting exclusively on the "appeal to the results of ideal role taking" as the stage's defining element.

While the moral point of view of any rational person (ideal role taking) is clearly part of Kohlberg's characterization of stage 6, an accurate interpretation of this stage must focus sharply on the defining element of "following self-chosen ethical principles," universal principles of justice.[17] In order to emphasize the existential theme of Kohlberg's postconventional, principled moral reasoning, especially that of stage 6, I will focus here on its "self-chosen" character. If there is anything "existential" about postconventional moral reasoning it is precisely the fact that the stage 6 person reasons in terms of—justifies moral evaluations or prescriptions by appeal to—*self-chosen* principles, whereas the person of conventional moral reasoning appeals to the rules of the given social system as justification. This is a crucial difference, indeed, a *critical* difference (I use this word deliberately in anticipation of the following discussion of conversion), one that Gibbs unfortunately neglects in his interpretation of the existential theme in Kohlberg's theory.

III. Self-Chosen Principles, Self-Creation, and Critical Moral Conversion

Self-chosen ethical principles are an essential part of the existential process of authentic self-creation in which Bernard Lonergan has identified the ground of a contemporary empirical theology—the personal reality of conversion. For authentic self-creation, in Lonergan's view, demands conversion, conversion which in its fullest realization is affective, intellectual, moral, and religious.[18] Here, for the purpose of illuminating the existential theme in Kohlberg's interpretation of moral development, I will concentrate on the personal reality of moral conversion.

Conversion, in Lonergan's view, is the "about-face" by which a person moves into a radically new horizon. More than a direct continuation or expansion of previous development, conversion "begins a

---

[17] Lawrence Kohlberg, "Moral Stages and Moralization: The Cognitive-Developmental Approach," in Thomas Lickona (ed.), *Moral Development and Behavior* (New York: Holt, Rinehart and Winston, 1976), p. 35.

[18] See Bernard Lonergan, *Method in Theology* (New York: Herder and Herder, 1972), p. 238; On affective conversion, see Lonergan, "Natural Right and Historical Mindedness," *Proceedings of the American Catholic Philosophical Association* 51 (1977), pp. 240-41. Also see my Columbia University doctoral dissertation on *Conscience and Self-Transcendence* (Ann Arbor, MI: University Microfilms International, 1973), pp. 524-525.

new sequence that can keep revealing ever greater depth and breadth and wealth." [19] "As lived," says Lonergan, conversion "affects all of a man's conscious and intentional operations. It directs his gaze, pervades his imagination, releases the symbols that penetrate to the depths of his psyche. It enriches his understanding, guides his judgments, reinforces his decisions." [20]

Moral conversion in the most basic sense, Lonergan tells us, "changes the criterion of one's decisions and choices from satisfactions to values"; it "consists in opting for the truly good, even for value against satisfaction when value and satisfaction conflict." [21] Such moral conversion should be seen as independent of the other conversions, inasmuch as this shift of criterion does not necessarily presuppose an intellectual, affective, or religious conversion. It would, however, definitely presuppose some significant level of affective and cognitive development. In fact, to be understood properly in its full existential reality, moral conversion in the basic sense of a shift of criterion for decision must be interpreted in this concrete context of personal development. For Lonergan, personal development is to an important degree a process of self-creation, which when authentic is a personal realization of the radical dynamism of the human spirit for self-transcendence.

In connection with this process of self-creation, Lonergan says: "by deliberation, evaluation, decision, action, we can know and do, not just what pleases us, but what is truly good, worthwhile." [22] In other words, on the topmost level of consciousness (which includes the cognitive levels of critical understanding) the subject is "at once practical and existential: practical inasmuch as he is concerned with concrete courses of action; existential inasmuch as control includes self-control, and the possibility of self-control involves responsibility for what he makes of himself." [23] As Lonergan points out, however, self-control can be grounded in quite different personal realities. If that ground be mere selfishness, says Lonergan, "then the process of deliberation, evaluation, decision is limited to determining what is most to one's advantage, what best serves one's interests, what on the whole yields a maximum of pleasure and a minimum of pain."

---

[19] Lonergan, *Method,* pp. 238-39.

[20] Ibid., p. 131.

[21] Ibid., p. 240.

[22] Ibid., p. 35. The discussion of self-creation in the following paragraphs is developed more fully in my *Conscience and Self-Transcendence,* pp. 503-18.

[23] Bernard Lonergan, "Faith and Beliefs" (mimeographed version of paper presented at the Annual Meeting of the American Academy of Religion, Newton, Ma., October, 1969), p. 6.

But self-control can, at the opposite pole, proceed rather from a concern with value, and in the measure that one's living is a response to value, in that measure one effects a real self-transcendence. In every decision, every action, every achievement that is a response to value and not the mere gratification of personal desire, in other words, one moves beyond, transcends one's self in a real way. And to the degree that one achieves such real self-transcendence, one becomes a source, a principle, as Lonergan puts it, of "benevolence and beneficence, capable of genuine collaboration and of true love." [24] But, as Lonergan is quick to add, it is one thing to transcend oneself in response to value "occasionally, by fits and starts. It is another to do it regularly, easily, spontaneously." For only from a long process of development involving every facet of the conscious human subject does there emerge the *sustained* self-transcendence of the virtuous person. The crucial factor in this long process of self-creation or personal, moral development, of course, is the transformation of horizon, the shift in criterion of choice that Lonergan names moral conversion.

Of course, one does not need to be morally converted to realize self-transcendence in particular choices any more than one needs to be intellectually converted to attain cognitive self-transcendence in given instances of true judgment. Still, as intellectual conversion is a special instance of cognitive self-transcendence, so too, moral conversion is a special instance of moral or real self-transcendence—special in the sense that it grounds, provides the programmatic base for the conscious, deliberate development of the sustained moral self-transcendence of human authenticity.

If moral conversion, then, is the beginning of a deliberate movement toward an ever more complete authenticity, it is also the end of a process of many years of fundamental cognitive and affective developments that form the very condition for the possibility of a radical moral conversion. The fact is that a normative personal conscience is in no way given as an accomplished fact. From the very beginning in the early years of childhood even the most rudimentary moral sense must be developed. Thus, even the emergence (let alone conversion) of what Lonergan calls the fourth level of responsible consciousness, the level of deliberation, evaluation and choice, is a slow process that only begins to occur at around the age of three as "the child gradually enters the world mediated by meaning and regulated by values and, by the age of seven years, is thought to have attained the use of reason." [25]

---

[24] Lonergan, *Method,* p. 35.
[25] Ibid., p. 121.

Such use of reason is, of course, only a bare minimum, as Piaget and Kohlberg have amply indicated, and is, as Lonergan says, only the beginning of human authenticity. It is a seed that must develop over many years with careful nurture. In childhood, as Lonergan says, we must be "persuaded, cajoled, ordered, compelled to do what is right."[26] But as the very being of the subject is becoming, one slowly and painfully becomes oneself. And as each year, month, day passes, the subject has more and more to do with his or her own becoming. The subject also, of course, *wants* more and more to do with his or her becoming. And because, as Lonergan points out, "development is a matter of increasing the number of things that one does for oneself, that one decides for oneself, that one finds out for oneself," the young subject, resenting adult interference, wants to do, decide and discover more and more for her or himself, despite the fact that desire for doing and deciding quickly outruns ability for reasonable judgment and thus responsible deciding.[27] This fact seems responsible for a good measure of the tragic quality of human existence, for, as Lonergan puts it in *Insight,* "man develops biologically to develop psychically, and he develops psychically to develop intellectually and rationally. The higher integrations suffer the disadvantage of emerging later. Then are the demands of finality upon us before they are realities in us. They are manifested more commonly in aspiration and in dissatisfaction with oneself than in the rounded achievement of complete genuineness, perfect openness, universal willingness."[28] And during the process of self-development "one has to live and make decisions in the light of one's undeveloped intelligence and under the guidance of one's incomplete willingness."[29] Indeed, it is for this reason that "one has to have passed well beyond the turmoil of puberty before becoming fully responsible in the eyes of the law."[30]

But, at the same time, "as our knowledge of human reality increases, as our responses to human values are strengthened and refined," parents and teachers and superiors of one kind or another more and more let us do, decide, and discover things on our own, leaving "us to ourselves so that our freedom may exercise its ever advancing thrust toward authenticity."[31]

---

[26] Ibid., p. 240.

[27] Bernard Lonergan, *Collection,* ed. F. E. Crowe (New York: Herder and Herder, 1967), p. 241.

[28] Bernard Lonergan, *Insight: A Study of Human Understanding* (New York: Philosophical Library, 1957), p. 625.

[29] Ibid., p. 627.

[30] Lonergan, *Method,* p. 121.

[31] Ibid., p. 240.

And in such a thrust toward authenticity there is the possibility of moral conversion, of the concrete human subject reaching that critical point, that existential moment within a long and gradual process of development and increasing autonomy when she discovers that her judging and choosing affect herself, the subject, no less than the objects of her judgments and choices, and that it is up to herself to decide for herself what she is to make of herself.[32] Such discovery, such realization of oneself as an originator of value who creates herself in every deed, decision, and discovery of life that all accumulate as dispositions, habits, and character determining what one's very subjectivity is and is to be, demands that the subject through a radical exercise of her fundamental, vertical freedom take hold of and responsibly choose herself precisely as the originating value she has realized herself to be (in which case originating and terminal values coincide). Such a radical appropriation of oneself as a free and responsible creator of value establishes an entirely new horizon defined by the choice of value as criterion of decision and choice, a criterion, indeed, of one's living. Even before this conversion, this discovery and choice of oneself as responsibly free, and the consequent reorientation and reorganization of one's priorities and values, the self is its own creator; the essential point to note about moral conversion is that after conversion the self's creation of itself is open-eyed and deliberate. As Lonergan puts it, "autonomy decides what autonomy is to be."[33]

And even if, before the discovery of ourselves as moral persons, we have made ourselves what we are without any significant awareness of what we were doing, still, after that discovery, it is to a large extent possible to recreate ourselves in the light of better knowledge and fuller responsibility. To refuse the opportunity of such re-creation of self offers no escape, for it means, ultimately, the assumption of responsibility, whether we want it or not, for whatever we have inadvertently made of ourselves in the past.[34] The opposite to the open-eyed, deliberate control of the self-appropriated autonomy emerging from moral conversion, is, quite simply, drifting. As Lonergan puts it,

> the drifter has not yet found himself; he has not yet discovered his own deed and so is content to do what everyone else is doing; he has not yet discovered his own will and so he is content to choose what everyone else is choosing; he has not yet discovered a mind of his own and so he is content to think and say

---

[32] Ibid.; also see *Collection,* p. 242.

[33] Lonergan, *Collection,* p. 242.

[34] Bernard Lonergan, "Notes on Existentialism" (mimeographed notes for lectures at Boston College, July, 1957), sec. IV, p. 11.

what everyone else is thinking and saying; and others too are apt to be drifters, each of them doing and choosing and thinking and saying what others happen to be doing, choosing, thinking, saying.[35]

The moral conversion we have discussed here must not be confused, of course, with moral perfection, of which it falls far short. To opt for a new horizon, to choose a new criterion of decision is one thing; to live within that horizon fully, to choose consistently according to that new criterion is another. As Lonergan says, "deciding is one thing, doing another."[36] It is, indeed, difficult enough for one to overcome the resistance that one spontaneously throws up against the possibility of conversion, of moving into a radically new horizon. For horizons define not abstractions but the shape of concrete living. And for anyone to experience, anticipate, or even seriously contemplate a change in the style of concrete living that has up until now more or less successfully synthesized and integrated the key elements of one's personality—unconscious as well as conscious, practical as well as interpersonal—is to invite an experience of anxiety or dread. And the spontaneous and resourceful resistance that this dread releases not only attempts to defend the given horizon that is being challenged, but necessarily does so from within it, employing a logic of common sense based on its own meanings and values that is unimpeachable on its own grounds.[37] From the viewpoint of logic, then, conversion to a radically new horizon is a leap, and such a leap is necessarily effected not by logical argument, but by more concrete and symbolic means that do not attack logical defenses but reach immediately to the very core of horizon, tunneling directly to its imaginative and affective ground, the "heart" of the subject.

As difficult as such a leap of conversion may be, however, it is, as I have already suggested, more a beginning than an end. As Lonergan has put it, "in this life the critical point is never transcended." For, again, "it is one thing to decide what one is to make of oneself; ...it is another to execute the decision. Today's resolutions do not predetermine the free choice of tomorrow, of next week, or next year, or ten years from now. What has been achieved," says Lonergan, "is always precarious: it can slip, fall, shatter. What is to be achieved can be ever expanding, deepening. To meet one challenge is to effect a development that reveals a further and graver challenge."[38]

---

[35] Lonergan, *Collection*, p. 242.
[36] Lonergan, *Method*, p. 240.
[37] Lonergan, "Notes on Existentialism," sec. IV, pp. 10-11.
[38] Lonergan, *Collection*, pp. 242-43.

Moral conversion is not moral perfection. Still, meeting the challenge of moral conversion not only brings the meaning of personal responsibility into sharp focus, but also highlights in an intensely personal fashion the ideal of authentic human living, as well as the distance between it and one's present achievement. Thus moral conversion is not so much an achievement as a call to commitment. For insofar as through conversion a person realizes how drastically one's effective freedom is limited,[39] one must commit oneself to the seemingly endless task of conquering the jungle of one's personal prejudices and biases, of developing one's knowledge of concrete human realities and possibilities, of scrutinizing one's intentional responses to values and their implicit scale of preferences, of listening to criticism and protest, and of learning from others. For, as Lonergan says, "moral knowledge is the proper possession only of morally good men and, until one has merited that title, one has still to advance and to learn."[40] And even after "meriting the title," a person must continue to advance and learn, of course.

Having sketched the profile of moral conversion, we must now draw a basic distinction, for the shift in criterion of decision from satisfaction to value which constitutes moral conversion can be made critically or uncritically.[41] In other words, in moral conversion one can *critically* recognize and accept the responsibility of critically discovering and establishing one's own values (in dialogue with one's community), or one may merely turn *uncritically* toward and accept a *given* set of values, be they given by parents, church, peers, "society," or whomever. Moral conversion in this second uncritical sense is a real enough conversion (from satisfaction to values), but it presupposes no intellectual conversion, and could follow very easily, or so it seems, from religious motivation. Moral consciousness that is converted in this uncritical way sublates the empirical, intelligent, and rational levels of consciousness, but these levels as intellectually unconverted.

If the shift in criterion, however, is rooted in the existential moment when we discover for ouselves "that it is up to each of us to decide for himself what he is to make of himself"[42] a truly critical moral conversion is involved, for the existential discovery that it is up to each of us to decide for ourselves what we are to make of our-

---

[39] See Lonergan, *Insight,* pp. 619-33.

[40] Lonergan, *Method,* p. 240.

[41] For a fuller development of this distinction as discussed in the following paragraphs, see my *Conscience and Self-Transcendence,* pp. 530-37, and "The Ontogenetic Ground of Value", *Theological Studies* 39/2 (June, 1978), pp. 328-35.

[42] Lonergan, *Method,* p. 240.

selves presupposes at least what I would call an *implicit* intellectual conversion, that is, a subject's tacit but nonetheless real recognition and choice of her or himself as the criterion of the real and the truly good in her or his own self-transcending judgments and choices of value.

In the fully explicit, philosophical sense, Lonergan understands by intellectual conversion a "radical clarification and, consequently, the elimination of an exceedingly stubborn and misleading myth" that "knowing is like looking, that objectivity is seeing what there is to be seen and not seeing what is not there, and that the real is what is out there now to be looked at."[43] But if intellectual conversion eliminates this myth of naive realism, it does so because it consists essentially in what Lonergan calls the "discovery of the self-transcendence proper to the human process of coming to know," the recognition and appropriation, in other words, of the radical dynamism and structure of one's own cognitive capacities and operations.

I have specified "at least" an implicit intellectual conversion as being involved in a critical moral conversion because while such a critical moral conversion could follow upon a fully articulated philosophical version of intellectual conversion, it seems that the implicit or tacit intellectual realization spelled out above is, while necessary, also sufficient for a critical moral conversion. And given the rarity of philosophically articulated intellectual conversions, this implicit intellectual conversion (which, though hardly a common phenomenon, is less rare, I think, than Lonergan's strictly philosophical conversion) would seem to be the usual basis for a critically grounded moral conversion. In the same way, while postconventional moral reasoning can be given explicitly reflective, philosophical expression in a meta-ethics, it is the practical reasoning in terms of self-chosen universal ethical principles of justice, and not their philosophical articulation, which constitutes postconventional morality.

This differentiation between a critical and an uncritical moral conversion is based on Lonergan's own analysis of the fundamental structure of conscious operations. For, basically, moral conversion is a decision or choice on the fourth level of consciousness, a choice of value over satisfaction as criterion for decisions, and a choice of oneself as responsible. And this choice, like any other, is just as good — no more, no less — as the understanding and judgment from which it proceeds and on which it depends. The fourth level of consciousness itself involves two moments, two different kinds of responses: judgments of value, and decisions or choices. While it may not

---

[43] Ibid., p. 238.

always be easy to distinguish judgments of value from judgments of fact, one can distinguish decisions or choices from judgments, and one's decisions will be critical insofar as they proceed from realistic judgment, authentic insofar as they conform to objective judgment. Thus a moral conversion proceeding from an intelligent grasp and reasonable affirmation of one's own interiority is a truly critical self-appropriation. Moral conversion as a mere shift in criterion for decision from satisfaction to value, on the other hand, lacks fundamental self-knowledge, and, while adequate perhaps for getting along in untroubled times, is vulnerable to exploitation from every side, and, because its values are held uncritically, is like a ship without captain or rudder during stormy times. The fact of the matter is that in our complex world critical self-appropriation is no moral luxury; it is an essential part of authentic human living.

While intellectual conversion is of great importance for making fundamental clarifications in various philosophical fields, for most people its really crucial significance is to be found in the kind of personal, existential self-appropriation that we have been discussing, the appropriation of oneself as a free, responsible, and self-constituting originator of value who in one's own self-transcending judgments and choices is the criterion of the real and the truly good. And in this area, the basic realization, more than its technical philosophical expression, is of paramount importance.

Indeed, moral conversion would seem to be not only a possible, but also a very natural and highly likely context for such an implicit intellectual conversion. For, clearly, nothing is closer, more personal to the subject than his or her own decisions and choices, and thus the reflection, deliberation, and evaluation leading up to them. And if the choice is more important than the restaurant for tonight's dinner or of more personal concern than the color of one's new automobile, the centrality of one's subjectivity can be exposed in a sometimes all too harsh fashion, for one finds it difficult to surround oneself with the defenses of "objective" criteria when one faces personal decisions about the military draft, aborting a fetus, or withholding the means of life from an incurably sick, elderly parent suffering unendurable pain; or when one decides on a spouse, or a career, or must choose between marriage and career. Because one does not want to decide or choose blindly, without reflection, one usually discovers before too long in his or her attempts at intelligent and reasonable reflection that there are neither easy, simple answers to concrete questions of life and death nor a predetermined, easy-to-follow program for one's life somewhere "out there" to be hit upon if only one looks long and hard enough. This discovery, what Lonergan calls an "inverse insight," that no pre-packaged life scripts or solutions to human problems exist, and that the pursuit of them leads one into the maze of endless blind alleys of unauthentic decisions, has the singular power of leading one to the positive discovery of oneself, in the authentic, self-transcending insights, judgments, decisions, and choices of one's own subjectivity, as the only truly objective source and criterion of human meaning and value. I must emphasize that this intellectual conversion is implicit *not* in the sense that one accidentally and almost without noticing falls upon it during the course of life, but in the sense that it occurs along with, within, and as part of a moral conversion upon which attention is focused. Insofar as this happens, the focal conversion is not simply a moral shift, but also a critical self-appropriation.

Such an implicit intellectual conversion forms an adequately critical ground for a full moral conversion whose shift in criteria for decision will be to the appropriation of personally discovered and developed values rather than to an uncritical conformity with a moral code or set of values given by some external authority. Thus, in summary, while moral conversion in the simplest sense of a shift to values as criterion of decision may be independent of and presuppose no intellectual conversion, the deeper critical moral conversion does involve intellectual conversion, either implicitly or explicitly.

IV. Conclusion: Conversion to Postconventional Morality

Having distinguished moral conversion in its critical and uncritical forms, we can now direct this distinction back to Kohlberg's theory of moral development, in an effort to illuminate the existential theme which Gibbs has identified as dominating its postconventional, principled stages.

Focusing first on uncritical moral conversion, it is clear enough from the very meaning of conventional moral reasoning that an uncritical shift from satisfaction to value as criterion for choice can occur at Kohlberg's third or fourth stages of moral reasoning. In fact, it is very "natural" for the younger or older adolescent to turn from excessive concern with obedience/punishment and pragmatic self-interest to a genuine desire to be and do good, interpersonally and socially. Because of the developmental limitations of the adolescent's affective and cognitive resources, however, the desired good, while understood as value rather than satisfaction, is identified uncritically in terms of interpersonal and social givens, as we have seen.

Turning now to critical moral conversion, we should note how Kohlberg has pointed out that moral judgments of a stage 6 principled conscience require such complex affective and cognitive development along with a depth of personal experience that, even in the small minority of people who reach it, the psychological maturity for such a principled conscience emerges at the earliest only in young adulthood.[44] Taking a clue from this point, I want to argue — and this is my basic thesis — that the realization of Kohlberg's stage 6 principled conscience is substantially identical to a critical moral conversion. The key to understanding this identity lies in seeing the *self-chosen* character of the ethical principles of Kohlberg's stage 6 as constituting the *critical* dimension of moral conversion. Unlike the rules and principles of conventional moral reasoning, which are rooted — at stage 4 — in societal authority, ethical principles are chosen at stage 6 on the *self's* authority because one has become personally convinced of their moral truth, as well as of one's own radical obligation as a responsible person to make such ultimate judgments and choices for oneself. And unlike conventional moral rules or principles which one is socialized to accept, principles at stage 6 are freely and deliberately *chosen,* with open eyes, as Lonergan would say.

Of course, the fact that principles are chosen at stage 6 on one's own authority as a responsible person does not necessarily mean that the values earlier accepted on society's authority are rejected. The same values may be substantially reestablished on a new basis. From a structural perspective, the postconventional stages, in subsuming lower stages, preserve their positive advances and eliminate only their limitations. An example of this is the member-of-society perspective of stage 4. Persons at stages 5 and 6 have moved beyond the member-of-society perspective, but only in the sense of relativizing it, not in the sense of eliminating it. A relativized member-of-society perspective, in fact, is essential for principled moral reasoning, a point which makes Gibbs' claim that stages 5 and 6 are, respectively, only philosophical versions of the perspective-taking of stages 2 and 3, difficult to accept.[45]

---

[44] Kohlberg and Gilligan, "The Adolescent as a Philosopher," p. 1071.

[45] Gibbs does not attempt to explain why a philosophical version of stage 2, for example, would not be simply a type of meta-ethical egoism.

Gibbs refers to the "existential crisis" which sometimes results from "confronting alternative moral viewpoints, and discovering hypocrisy and societal corruption" (p. 54), but he does not explicitly discuss Kohlberg's stage 4½ of moral relativism. To move beyond conventional morality requires an insight into the relativity of any society's values. While that insight is necessary and true, it does not of itself advance a person beyond the relativism of stage 4½. To move to postconventional morality in a positive sense, a further insight is necessary to overcome extreme relativism and provide an intellectual grounding for fundamental human values; in short, an intellectual conversion.

From one important angle Kohlberg's interpretation of stage 6 can be seen as explicating the structure of reasoning of the critically converted conscience, at least in its most highly developed cognitive form. At the same time, however, I am arguing that in order to appreciate the existential theme of postconventional morality one must view it from the perspective of self-creation, and especially the existential moment of that process I have called critical moral conversion. Gibbs correctly points to the existential theme as dominant in Kohlberg's principled morality, but by emphasizing the formal, reflective, philosophical dimension of principled reasoning, and not its self-chosen character, he is not able to do full justice to the existentialist theme and thus to the radical difference between what he calls the first four "natural" orientations in Kohlberg's theory and the last two "existential" orientations. In order to really do justice to this difference and to the existential theme of Kohlberg's postconventional morality, in my view, one must interpret moral development in the context of the self-creation of the concrete personal subject, highlighting the possibility that within this process of spontaneous, natural self-creation there may occur that existential moment when we discover that it is up to each of us to decide for ourselves what we are to make of ourselves.

Is conversion necessary for principled morality? Yes, in the sense of the critical moral conversion we have discussed. This conversion may not be natural in the sense of occurring spontaneously and unconsciously, but, if and when a person experiences an existential crisis in the human environment of value, this conversion is necessary for normative development to continue, and in that sense may be thought of as natural. In this sense of the authentically human, the natural and the existential become one.

Bioethics as Anamnesis: What Lonergan has Understood and Others Have Overlooked

by David J. Roy

I. My Purpose

I could well write this paper as an expression of gratitude. Wentzel's introduction to the *Bardo Thödol*, the Tibetan Book of the Dead, relates the story of Milarepa, the Tibetan monk, who finished his life with a song of gratitude. He lived out his finest and supreme moments integrating all of his days and experiences in an activity of thinking recollection. *Anamnesis* becomes *eucharistia;* "*Wiedererinnering*" comes to express itself in an active "*Wiederholung*", a new, integrating communication of one's self which takes up all of one's experiences and gives a new form to one's choices, decision, acts. Careful attention to the character of one's origins delivers the understanding that, at all levels of existence, one is both gift and achievement. *Eucharistein*, a living out of oneself as gift, as a communication of gratitude in word, decision, and deed, then corresponds to a fundamental dimension of human existence. As such, *eucharistein* and its accompanying activity of *anamnesis* are foundations of ethics.

I am deeply grateful to Bernard Lonergan for so much of what I have come to understand. However, I write to direct attention not to Lonergan, but to his axial insights that so many of us have forgotten or overlooked. We are at the threshold of a new era of eucaryotic biology. Discoveries are coming rapidly, each spawning a new generation of theoretical and biotechnological advances. The feel of new power is heady—and distracting. The cumulative results of powerful new methods in biomedicine are so strikingly obvious. We are not so ready at this time to grasp that profound mistakes can set up an equally cumulative process of decline.

I work in circles where Lonergan's work is rarely, more accurately to my knowledge, never cited. That, of itself, would be hardly an occasion for this paper if a number of Lonergan's fundamental insights were actually operative, illuminating and guiding biomedical research and the application of new biotechnologies. In so many critical instances, this really is not the case. I write this paper to identify a number of these instances.

II. My Context

I work within a clinical research institute, in close association with twenty-five biomedical laboratories; within hospitals, attempting with doctors and health care personnel to design guidelines for medical decision-making; within medical schools, socratically trying to coax students to pit their fundamental beliefs and options against those of others in an arena of critical discussion.

Biomedicine and bioethics are new words in our language. They indicate that we now enjoy and also have to deal with very new kinds of knowledge and technology. Innovative specializations in the life sciences promise the power to introduce changes in the networks of life on our planet, changes that may well affect human beings very profoundly, for long periods of time, perhaps, even irreversibly.

Some of the developments in medicine today are *technically phenomenal, though ethically prosaic:* they simply buttress traditional values. Other developments are *ethically paradoxical:* they set up difficult value conflicts. A number of advances in the broader domain of biomedicine are *socially and ethically dramatic:* they promise to radically alter traditional patterns of behavior and relationships, to profoundly modify institutions that have been marked by stability. A further class of biomedical innovations could prove to be *philosophically and humanly meta-dramatic:* they would appear capable of taking us beyond, outside of the human drama as we have known it to be for centuries.

In a range of cases, the power of biomedicine today—its ability to effect changes—reaches far beyond earlier, more restricted notions of therapy. The reconstruction of human beings and of social institutions—not simply the restoration of health and the containment of the ravages of disease—increasingly appears to be a less utopian, less science-fictional expectation of what contemporary biomedicine is and will be able to deliver.

It is really no longer possible to ignore a new science and complex biotechnology directed, in part at least, towards transforming "human nature as principle" into "human nature as project." It is quite likely true that we have not yet seen what man can make of man.

Within this context we face the question: where, on radically new frontiers, do we find our guidance to determine what we should do, what we may do, what we should not do amongst all the innumerable and untested things we can do to, with, or for human beings?

In the face of these developments and this question I turn to Lonergan's position that "The root of ethics...lies neither in sentences nor in propositions nor in judgments but in the dynamic structure of rational self-consciousness."[1] Of course, in any given person this structure works itself out within a community of other instances of more or less rational and conscious expressions of selves. So I turn also to Karl Otto Apel's concept of dialogue as method. Lonergan's "dialectical criticism of subjects" is really what is at the root of Apel's *Kommunikationsgemeinschaft,* at least in so far as this community works towards ethical norms for activities which affect the entire community. Biomedical innovations are this sort of activity.

III. A Turn to Lonergan's Insights

My turn to Lonergan's insights is selective, hence restricted. I refer to a set of value conflicts and ethical controversies in contemporary biomedicine that illustrate an ignorance of or failure to attend to insights which, if properly grasped and utilized, could or would be decisive for the given controversy, for medical practice, and for biomedical research.

1. Defective Newborn Children and Finality

Contemporary neonatalogy is the scene of an increasingly intense debate.[2] The issue, in its crudest and most unqualified form, is: to treat or not to treat seriously defective newborn babies. At an earlier period, many or even most of these babies would simply have died, indeed, quite quickly. Because little could then be done for these babies, little had to be decided.

Things have changed. Medicine has advanced. Many of these babies now need not die as a direct and quick result of their defects

---

[1] Bernard Lonergan, *Insight: A Study of Human Understanding* (New York: Longman, 1958), p. 664.

[2] Cf. David J. Roy, ed. *Medical Wisdom and Ethics in the Treatment of Severely Defective Newborn and Young Children* (Montreal: Eden Press, 1978).

at birth. Their lives can now be "saved" or at least prolonged for a very significant period.

In some cases, the prolongation resulting from medical treatment amounts to little more than an extension of the dying process. The anencephalic, the hydranencephalic, the child with major neurological and multi-system defects are examples.

In other cases, vigorous and prolonged medical treatment will save the baby's life. The child, later, the teenager and young adult will, however, be more or less handicapped. Depending on the circumstances, the handicap will be both physical and mental in character. Babies born with spina bifida and myelomeningocele are examples.

In a third set of cases, babies are born with a physical defect which can be treated successfully and is lethal if left untreated. These babies, however, are also marked by other sorts of defect that are not lethal but also at the moment, untreatable. Such, frequently, are the Down's syndrome or mongol babies.

It is with respect to babies such as these that the question of selective nontreatment, with death as a consequence, arises in contemporary neonatalogy. Some hold tenaciously to a "sacredness of life" principle and argue that no selection whatsoever should be made. Every effort to prolong every infant life should be made. Others hold with equal tenacity to a "quality of life" principle and use measures of natural endowment at birth to prognosticate or guess future likely levels of I.Q., productivity, etc., of the given infant.

The best possible medical decisions for these infants surely call for attention to a host of concrete physiological and neurological factors. The ultimate basis for a decision in these matters, nevertheless, is more in character. The medical community is divided in opinion and conflicting treatment policies are proposed and followed precisely because of a deep divergence of view on the worth or value of these babies.

Both sides of this divergence have frequently overlooked the ethically normative force of Lonergan's theorem or principle of finality.

Those who hold absolutely to a given "sacredness of life" principle tend to forget that this sacredness covers a curve or spiral of development. "Man develops biologically to develop psychically, and he develops psychically to develop intellectually and rationally."[3] Ignorance of this principle can generate a misplaced passion for the sacred. One then goes forward to overlook the purposes and limits of medicine.

---

[3] Lonergan, *Insight*, p. 625.

A basic canon of ethics centers on these purposes and limits. "When biological damage is so extensive that curative, restorative, and corrective medical interventions cannot aid the patient's development, but only succeed in perpetuating or prolonging a patient's fixation at a level of development that is not meant to be final and is far short of the variety of purposes and levels of life to which biological human life is ordained—when this obtains, then, so the canon, medical intervention has reached its limits, works contrary to its calling in perpetuating such fixations, and should not be employed."[4]

Honoring this canon presupposes a recognition of Lonergan's principle of finality.

Others ignore this principle in quite different ways. Non-treatment decisions are frequently taken today and mean death for babies who have real chances to reach levels of genuine human development. Of course, the infants will develop only with our continued help, only with the support of medical and educational expertise. Those who allow or help these babies to die forget the correlation part of Lonergan's principle of finality. "The higher integrations suffer the disadvantage of emerging later. They are demands of finality upon us before they are realities in us."[5]

To argue for the death of a defective newborn baby or, as is frequently done today, for the death of a fetus after positive prenatal diagnostic results, on the basis that neither *now* manifests a capacity for the higher integrations and behavior characteristic of human beings is to fatally ignore that these higher integrations are moral demands of finality upon us so that they may become realities in others.

2. PRENATAL DIAGNOSIS FOR THE DETERMINATION OF SEX: SPONTANEOUS DESIRES VS. VALUES

Fetal euthanasia after positive prenatal diagnostic tests calls for a much more extensive discussion than could ever be attempted here. However, the request for prenatal diagnostic procedures for the purposes of selecting fetuses for birth/death on the basis of sexual differentiation illustrates the frequently fragile moral base of decision-making in medicine.

Prenatal diagnosis reveals the sex of the fetus. Some parents have requested these procedures for this precise purpose. They wanted only one more pregnancy and desired a child of a given sex. They were ready to demand an abortion if the diagnosis revealed the fetus to be of the undesired sex.

---
[4] David J. Roy, "The Severely Defective Newborn," *Health and Christian Life* (Ottawa: Catholic Health Association of Canada), p. 22.
[5] Lonergan, *Insight*, p. 625.

A recent article by John Fletcher in the *New England Journal of Medicine* discusses the question of whether parents should be dissuaded from using prenatal diagnosis for this purpose.[6] The Hastings Center Genetics Research Group published "Guidelines for the Ethical, Social and Leagal Issues in Prenatal Diagnosis." When discussing the issue of prenatal diagnosis for sex selection, the report recalled that the guidelines had been written "in a moral framework favoring the protection of individual choice and autonomy of parents."[7] Sex choice, i.e., aborting a fetus because it is not of the sex desired by the parents, can, as the report mentions, appear to parents to be justifiable.[8]

Decisions to abort fetuses because they are of an undesired sex and guidelines which offer a moral framework to protect such decisions identify objects of desire with values. They ignore the fact that not all things important in human living are equally important. They overlook or reject the position that "values are hierarchic."[9] If "objects of desire are values only in as much as they fall under some intelligible order,"[10] then that order delivers the norm for the choice of values in a case of value-conflict. I know of no *intelligible* order which can place parental desire for this or that sex of an infant on the same level of a value hierarchy with the life of that infant or unborn child. *Intelligibility,* however, appears hardly necessary to be justifications offered by "spontaneous-desire" ethics.

3. Normative Ethics and the Root of Ethics

The greatest confusion reigns in medical and biomedical science circles on the difference between right and wrong as well as on the basis for determining that difference.

Daniel Callahan has noted a widespread tendency "to justify actions with an ethical slogan or a one-sentence general principle."[11] Callahan has observed a range of bases upon which popular ethical thinking distinguishes between right and wrong, either with respect to personal or public behavior:[12]

---

[6] John C. Fletcher, "Ethics and Amniocentesis for Fetal Sex Determination," *The New England Journal of Medicine,* 301 (1979):550-53.

[7] Tabitha M. Powledge, and John Fletcher, "Guidelines for the Ethical, Social and Legal Issues in Prenatal Diagnosis," *The New England Journal of Medicine* 300 (1979):171.

[8] Ibid., p. 172.

[9] Lonergan, *Insight,* p. 611.

[10] Ibid.

[11] Daniel Callahan, "Normative Ethics and Public Morality in the Life Sciences," *The Humanist,* Sept./Oct., 1972, p. 5.

[12] Callahan's discussion is paraphrased and abbreviated at this point.

- *The religious school:* something is right or wrong because a religious or church tradition says so.

- *The emotive school:* feelings or "gut reactions" determine what is right or wrong.

- *The conventionalist school:* what is or has been generally accepted as right *is* right.

- *The simple utilitarian school:* what produces the greatest good for the greatest number is right.

- *The "barefoot civil liberties" school:* one position is as good as another. At any rate, one should be free to make up one's own mind. One should not impose one's ethical views on others.

- *The majoritarian school:* courses of action enjoying majority support are right. Legality is identified with moral justifiability.

Callahan cautioned that these descriptions should not be taken as caricatures or exaggerated simplifications. "These decriptions are not parodies. Every one is an expression I have either heard repeatedly in discussions with scientists and physicians, or found in scientific and medical literature. Moreover, the kinds of expressions I have quoted often represent total ethical positions." [13]

A tendency is fairly rampant in biomedical circles to turn to law, to conventional expressions of public opinion, to authoritative statements of a religious, ecclesiastical, or professional nature, and finally, to simple spontaneous reactions as the basis for distinguishing right from wrong—at least where this moral distinction has not been completely subsumed within a simple risk-benefit or preference calculus.

Hans Jonas is a rarity in the circle of those writing on the ethics of biomedical developments. He has faced the question of the foundations of ethics.

Jonas has mentioned being called from "theoretical detachment to public responsibility" and finding a new task for his philosophizing. The source of the call was a question latent in the "growing realization of the inherent dangers of technology as such—not of its sudden but of its slow perils, not of its short-term but of its long-term threats, not of its malevolent abuses which, with some watchfulness, one can hope to control, but of its most benevolent and legitimate uses which are the very stuff of its active possession." [14]

---

[13] Ibid.

[14] Hans Jonas, "Introduction," *Philosophical Essays* (New Jersey: Prentice-Hall, 1974), p. XVI.

The latent question is really a quest for an effective ethics for a technological culture shaped by fundamental changes in the characteristics of human action. "Modern technology has introduced actions of such novel scale, objects, and consequences that the framework of former ethics can no longer contain them." [15]

How can one best pursue this quest? An effective ethics would have to be based upon and emerge from a philosophy of organism, a philosophy of mind, and—more generally—a philosophy of nature. "Only an ethics which is grounded in the breadth of being, not merely in the singularity or oddness of man, can have significance; and whether he has it we must learn from the interpretation of reality as a whole. But even without any such claim of trans-human significance for human conduct, an ethics no longer founded on divine authority must be founded on a principle discoverable in the nature of things, lest it fall victim to subjectivism or other forms of relativity. However far, therefore, the ontological quest may have carried us outside man, into the general theory of being and life, it did not really move away from ethics, but searched for its possible foundation." [16]

Jonas is seeking the possible foundation of ethics. He comes close with his recognition that ethics must be founded in a principle discoverable in the nature of things. He begins to lose his way when he overlooks the fact that the principle of man's singularity in the universe is also the principle of his universality.

Even wide ranging philosophies of mind, organism, and nature will not, as a complex set of propositions, serve as the foundation of ethics. If ethics deals with the consistency between knowing and doing, then the foundation of ethics will have to be a principle which is discoverable as a dynamic function that delivers this consistency.[17]

This is what Lonergan has understood with his position that "the root of ethics, as the root of metaphysics, lies neither in sentences nor in propositions nor in judgments but in the dynamic structure of rational self-consciousness. Because that structure is latent and operative in everyone's choosing, it is universal on the side of the subject; because that structure can be dodged, it grounds a dialectical criticism of subjects. Again, because that structure is recurrent in every act of choice, it is universal on the side of the object; and

---

[15] Jonas, "Technology and Responsibility: Reflections on the New Tasks of Ethics," *Philosophical Essays,* p. 8.

[16] Jonas, "Epilogue. Nature and Ethics," in *The Phenomenon of Life: Towards a Philosophical Biology* (New York: Harper and Row, 1966. Paperback; New York: Dell Publishing Co., A Delta Book, 1968), p. 284.

[17] Lonergan, *Insight,* p. 600-02.

because its universality consists not in abstraction but in inevitable recurrence, it also is concrete."

On this view of things, the real principles of ethical precepts and codes "are not propositions or judgments but existing persons."[18] Existing persons live in community. "Community is not just an aggregate of individuals within a frontier, for that overlooks its formal constituent, which is common meaning....The genesis of common meaning is an on-going process of communication, of people coming to share the same cognitive, constitutive, and effective meanings."[19]

This on-going process of communication defines Karl Otto Apel's *Kommunikationsgemeinshaft* and motivates his turn to *Dialog als Methode*.[20]

It is enough at this point to emphasize that the community of argumentation presupposed by logic and scientific discourse is not simply a community of scientists and logicians. "Science" stands not simply for a set of methods, specializations, and propositions. The scientific interest itself is only one amongst many characteristics of the human community. Over and above particular scientific propositions, the scientific interest itself and its claims have to be argued and justified.

The community of argumentation, presupposed by logical argument and scientific discourse, demands not only an attempt to achieve unbounded verification of propositions but, equally so, an attempt to achieve unbounded justification of interest claims.

The process of rational argumentation as the counterpoint to a dogmatic or obscurantist imposition of propositions, views, beliefs, and claims reaches very far. Its demands are high. The imperative is for an at least implicit recognition of all possible claims of all members of the *Kommunkationsgemeinschaft*. That can be justified by rational argument. The second imperative is for a willingness to justify all one's own claims by rational argument, indeed, before the entire community of communication.

Of course, the real community within which all discourse is embedded is all too often marked by the forms of ego, group, and general bias that block the quest for unbounded verification and justification of propositions and claims.[21] So, dialogue as method

---

[18] Lonergan, *Insight*, p. 604.

[19] Lonergan, *Method In Theology* (New York: Herder and Herder, 1972), pp. 356-357.

[20] Karl-Otto Apel, "Das Apriori der Kommunikationsgemeinschaft und die Grundlagen der Ethik," in *Transformation der Philosophie*. Band II (Frankfurt am Main: Suhrkamp Verlag, 1973), pp. 359 ff.

[21] Lonergan, *Insight*, pp. 217-44.

calls not only for rational justification of propositions and claims. This dialogue must also take the form of a "dialectical criticism of subjects" and a "dialectical analysis to reveal how situations are to be corrected." [22]

4. Recombinant DNA, Effective Freedom, Liberation

Amongst the many kinds of contemporary biomedical developments, one class could well prove to be philosophically meta-dramatic. These innovations would be, at least at this moment, capable of taking us beyond the drama, capable of radically altering the nature or condition we have called "human" for thousands of years.

The power to design new genetic combinations represents a category of technological innovation that may have the longest-term consequences and bring us to the frontier of pressing questions we have never before had to consider.

DNA recombination technology is young and immature. This has not blocked a recent sharp and prolonged debate as to whether these techniques should be employed, let alone further developed. The debate has centered predominantly on the issue of biohazards, their magnitude and likelihood of occurrence. To reduce both, guidelines have been proposed, notably by the United States, Great Britain, and Canada.

Biohazards define a central issue. Frequently forgotten, however, is the equally momentous issue that emerges with the question about where recombinant DNA technology is likely to take us. May we reasonably expect that further refinements and cumulative progress in the development of this technology will one day deliver the power to redesign the genetic correlates of human nature? Are we prepared to assume control over the evolutionary process?

Some would doubt that so much is at stake. However, it would be naive to assume that recombinant DNA techniques represent little more than some localized pattern of molecular technology, of prime interest only to geneticists and molecular biologists. If this technology continues to develop as other technologies have — and the will to press in this direction is very strong — then it is reasonable to claim that "man will have a dramatically powerful means of changing the order of life. I know of no more elemental capability, even including the manipulation of nuclear forces....It should not demean man to say that we may now be unable to manage successfully a capability for altering life itself." [23]

---

[22] Ibid., p. 614.

[23] Prof. Shaw Livermore quoted in: William Bennett and Joel Guerin, "Science that Frightens Scientists: The Great Debate over DNA," *The Atlantic Monthly,* Feb. 1977, p. 59.

The development of recombinant DNA techniques raises a range of questions which transcend the domain of activity properly amenable to scientific method.

One set of questions deals with the possibility and consequence of our acquisition of power over the evolutionary process. Robert Sinsheimer has formulated these questions as follows:

> How far will we want to develop genetic engineering? Do we want to assume the basic responsibility for life on this planet — to develop new living forms for our own purpose? Shall we take into our own future evolution?[24]

Great power calls for proportionate knowledge. However, what kind of knowledge is really proportionate to a power over the origins and forms of life? We arrive at a second question.

> We begin to see that the truth is not enough, that the truth is necessary but not sufficient, that scientific inquiry, the revealer of truth, needs to be coupled with wisdom if our object is to advance the human condition....In the nucleic acids of the cell we have penetrated to the core of life.
> When we are armed with such powers I think there are limits to the extent to which we can continue to rely upon the resistence of nature or of social institutions to protect us from our follies and our finite wisdom. Our thrusts of inquiry should not too far exceed our perception of their consequence. There are time constants and moments in human affairs. We need to recognize that the great forces we now wield might — just might — drive us too swiftly toward some unseen chasm.[25]

Our follies and our finite wisdom do not necessarily begin only where our perception of consequences stops. Nevertheless, Sinsheimer comes close to formulating what Lonergan has called the problem of liberation.

Recombinant DNA technology stands, even in its inchoate forms, as a symbol of a desire for unrestricted power over life. Such a desire, all the more such a power, tends towards a dictatorship of the arbitrary unless balanced by an unrestricted desire to know and an unrestricted capacity of matching one's doing, the exercise of power, to that knowledge. That capacity is willingness. It is here that the profile of the problem of liberation begins to emerge, for "to reach the universal willingness that matches the unrestricted desire to

---

[24] Robert Sinsheimer, "Troubled Dawn for Genetic Engineering," *New Scientist*, Oct. 16, 1975, p. 150.

[25] Sinsheimer, from a talk given at University of California, June, 1976 and quoted in: Nicholas Wade, "Recombinanat DNA: A Critic Questions the Right to Free Inquiry," *Science* 194 (1976):304.

know is indeed a high achievement, for it consists not in the mere recognition of an ideal norm but in the adoption of an attitude towards the universe of being, not in the adoption of an affective attitude that would desire but not perform but in the adoption of an effective attitude in which performance matches aspiration." [26]

If persons are the root of ethics, then an orientation and emancipation of persons is required that permits performance to match the reach of aspiration. The problem of liberation "lies in an incapacity for sustained development." [27] Sustaining development is a process of transcendence. Transcendence occurs with the recurrence of the dynamic structure expressed in the transcendental imperatives: be attentive, be intelligent, be reflective, be responsible.

The problem of liberation occurs when this structure fails to recur. On one level the problem appears as a "succession of ever less comprehensive viewpoints." [28] On this level the solution "has to be the attainment of a higher viewpoint." [29] On another level the problem appears as a break-down of the process of on-going communication. How could it be otherwise? On the level of the mind, transcendence occurs when an unconditioned is grasped. On the level of human living transcendence occurs when an unconditioned is realized, made real. Human communication reaches its full scope in such an achievement, the achievement of unconditioned acceptance and unconditioned gift. However, when one can or will no longer grasp the unconditional in the level of the mind, how can one achieve the unconditional in human living? So on this level the solution to the problem of liberation "has to be a still higher integration of human living." [30]

The decisive insight, however, defines the order governing higher viewpoint and higher integration within the solution to the problem of liberation: "The needed higher viewpoint is a concrete possibility only as a consequence of an actual higher integration." [31]

If the attainment of an effective ethics awaits a solution to the problem of liberation, then bioethics does little unless it functions as *anamnesis*.

IV. Bioethics as Anamnesis

Bioethics does not only stand for moral theory and moral decision-making which takes account of biological and biomedical know

---

[26] Lonergan, *Insight*, p. 624.
[27] Ibid., p. 630.
[28] Ibid., p. 231.
[29] Ibid., p. 234.
[30] Ibid., p. 632.
[31] Ibid., p. 633.

ledge. Nor is bioethics just a more complicated term for traditional medical ethics. Bioethics stands for interdisciplinary concern with the total range of conditions necessary for a responsible stewardship of life, particularly human life, in a context of rapid and complex biomedical development.

The challenge is to face both the promises and the perils of new knowledge releasing new power over human beings, power of a depth and duration not really encountered before in human history. Meeting this challenge means advancing effectively towards wisdom. That advance starts as we begin to devise new frameworks of value to balance choices and decisions, and new networks of communication to heighten the participation of the entire human community in the design and the realization of the common good.

How can this challenge be met? Surely not only with the construction of ever more precise codes of medical and biomedical ethics. For the problem that constitutes the challenge is the problem of emancipation. The solution to that problem "is not to discover a correct philosophy, ethics, or human science. For such discoveries are quite compatible with the continued existence of the problem. The correct philosophy can be but one of many philosophies, the correct ethics one of many ethical systems, the correct human science an old or new view among many views. But precisely because they are correct, they will not appear correct to minds disorientated by the conflict between positions and counter-positions. Precisely because they are correct, they will not appear workable to wills with restricted ranges of effective freedom." [32]

A higher viewpoint surely is needed to devise codes of biomedical ethics that can resolve value conflicts capable of tearing apart the human community. But higher values have to be grasped, chosen, made the effective basis for decision and action. If higher viewpoints condition the grasp of higher values it nevertheless remains true that such viewpoints are "a concrete possibility only as a consequence of an actual higher integration." [33]

If such an integration has occurred as an historical event, then appeal to that event and the elaboration of codes, guidelines, and policies in the light of that event is surely as much a function of bioethics as is the interpretation and application of ancient and recent ethics documents. The appeal will achieve little if it is only a recall. The appeal has to take place as an appropriation, as a realization.

Dialogue is method in bioethics. An on-going process of communication that tumbles determinisms and frees from the bondage of bias

---

[32] Ibid., p. 631.
[33] Ibid., p. 633.

has to be real. That is why bioethics fails if, at its limits, it is not the communication of the historical verification that all human beings have been accepted unconditionally by the Unconditioned. Communication, precisely as the realization of the unconditioned, is at the root of bioethics. The appropriation of the historical communication of unconditioned acceptance and unconditioned gift is *anamnesis*. To the extent that bioethics functions as *anamnesis* it will find the higher viewpoint required to illuminate what man can make of man.

The Theory-Praxis of Social Ethics: The Complementarity Between Hermeneutical and Dialectical Foundations

by John A. Raymaker

In order to appreciate the possible relevance of Lonergan's metamethod to social ethics one must first advert to the reality of and interrelationships among the three levels of ethics, and how these interrelate with other disciplines and the concrete praxis of everyday life.

The first level of ethics, or practical morality, is the level of moral rules or imperatives as such. It deals with the application of particular moral codes. The second level of ethics deals with the basic question of the ground or essence of what makes an action "good." This level also tries to integrate moral imperatives or rules into coherent systems. Finally, the third or meta-ethical level investigates the very presuppositions that inform the various ethical theories (second level) behind particular patterns of behavior (first level).[1] These three levels are integral to sound social, religious, and theological development.

Space does not permit us to delve into all these complex relationships. Although metamethod is relevant to all three levels of ethics, I will restrict myself primarily to some potential interdisciplinary contributions of Lonergan's dialectical-foundational method on the third meta-ethical level as it might interface with Gibson Winter's social ethics. I begin with various contextual backgrounds which impinge on the foundational praxis of ethics.

---

[1] Franz Wiedman, s.v. "Ethics" in *Marxism, Communism, and Western Society,* C. D. Kernig, ed. (New York: Herder and Herder, 1972) III, p. 219. See also W. H. Werkmeister, *Theories of Ethics* (Lincoln, Neb.: Johnsen, 1961) pp. 7-8, 409.

I. Contextual Background

1) Ethical theory-praxis became dichotomized in Kant's deontology. Facing the question of whether there is a causality outside the laws of nature which allows for human freedom, Kant "resolved" the problem by bifurcating reality into the worlds of theoretical and practical reason. He placed the basis of obligation not in the nature of man, but *a priori* simply in the conceptions of pure reason. On the basis of the transcendental subjectivity of man Kant fell back upon an unmediatable categorical imperative or maxim to act in such a way that one could will that the action should become universal law. His formally grounded deontology tried to establish a general practical philosophy "solely from a priori principles without any empirical motives."[2]

I believe that Kant's insistence on a *foundational* difference between form-contents and those contents' "objectivity" resulted in a conceptualist or extrincisist mediation of praxis. For in stressing the "contents" he overlooked a) the prior question of the praxis of subjective acts giving rise to the contents and their objectivity and b) the mutual interaction and the complementarity of the theory-praxis between contents and the subjective acts of the intentional operations. A conceptualist mediation is an insufficiently critical mediation of ethical praxis. In contrast to Lonergan's basic horizon I call it an inverted horizon because it gives an inverted priority to concepts rather than to the subjective acts generating the concepts. The conceptualist dichotomization of theory-praxis in Western thought has resulted in the tragic dissociation of disciplines from one another. Science is dissociated from ethics, and both of these are dissociated from philosophy and theology.

2) The Kantian and positivist dichotomizing legacies have at long last given way to a few meaningful convergences among meta-ethicians and meta-scientists on the issue of the complementarity of theory-praxis.[3] Such scattered efforts to overcome the fatal dissociations among their various disciplines have led to a convergence for instance between phenomenology and axiology in Scheler. His value ethics rethought Kant's presuppositions. Granted that Kant had rescued ethics from the relativism of a merely empirical approach of

---

[2] Immanuel Kant, *Fundamental Principles of the Metaphysic of Morals* (Chicago: Regnery, 1949), p. 3. See also pp. 69-70, and 83.

[3] E.g., the representative works of the Frankfurt School of *Ideologiekritik,* such as Theodor Adorno, *Negative Dialektik* (Frankfurt: Suhrkamp, 1966;) Max Horkheimer, *Critical Theory,* tr. M. H. O'Connel, (New York: Herder, 1972) and Jürgen Habermas, *Knowledge and Human Interests,* tr. by J. Shapiro (Boston: Beacon Press, 1972). Also Gerard Radnitzky, *Contemporary Schools of Metascience,* vols. 1 and 2 (New York: Humanities Press, 1970).

a Hume, Scheler showed that Kant's ethics cannot provide guidance for actual conduct. For Scheler apriorism need not be merely formal, but can also be based on the non-formal values which had heretofore been the exclusive domain of empirical ethics.[4] In their ethical thought both Lonergan and Winter have been influenced by Scheler.

3) I want to at least allude to two divergent appraisals of the possibilities of Lonergan's method for social ethics: a) Charles Curran has, I believe, failed to understand the radicality of conversion in metamethod, its applicability to social ethics, and its central theory-praxis focus. He has further confused the issue by trying to reduce its conversions to two, the intellectual one, and an "existential" one.[5] b) Curran's misunderstanding of the various levels on which method is operative is partially, though indirectly, answered by Donald Johnson. Johnson explains that Lonergan transposes the universality and necessity of moral problems to the invariance of the subject as subject's normative operations, i.e., a self-corrective praxis. Method has two poles, a subject pole or the conscious human subject's evaluation of the data relevant to any particular moral question, which is Lonergan's principal concern; and an object pole which deals with the total complex of data evaluated before any decision.[6] Method is of its essence amenable to input from the object pole as furnished by any discipline. This basic openness can lead to what I call a horizonal complementarity between method and social ethics for example. I will sketch how one might develop such an horizonal complementarity between the works of Lonergan and Winter as subject and object poles respectively.

---

[4] Max Scheler, *Vom Umsturz der Werte,* vol. 3 of *Gesammelte Werke* (Bern: Francke Verlag.) Also Herbert Spiegelberg, *The Phenomenological Movement,* 2nd ed. (The Hague: Nijhoff, 1965, Vol. I, pp. 228-68.

[5] Charles Curran, "Christian Conversion" in Philip McShane, ed., *Foundations of Theology* (South Bend: Notre Dame, 1972), pp. 41-59. Elso Curran, "Is there a Catholic and/or Christian Ethic?" *Proceedings of the Catholic Theological Society of America* 29 (1974): 125-54. I am not faulting Curran for his emphasis on the reality of sin, but his methodological attempt to reduce Lonergan's conversions to two. As I will suggest, metamethod offers open, ongoing, critical norms to dialectically counter evil. I believe that Curran's pessimistic notions as to the finality of sin and negation of a specifically Christian ethic reflect Kant's position in Book One "On the Radical Evil in Human Nature" in his *Religion Innerhalb den Grenzen der Blossen Vernunft,* tr. (New York: Harper: 1960).

[6] Donald Johnson, "Lonergan and the Redoing of Ethics" in *Continuum* 5, (1967-1968), pp. 211-20. There are two problems with Johnson's interpretation, as I see it. First, I do not believe that the competence of ethics lies merely in the subject pole. Otherwise, the particular methods within the object pole will continue to err on the side of objectivism and unhealthy dissociations of disciplines. Second, while Johnson lets ethical precepts depend on the "common meanings constitutive of community" as they are concretely developed in history, I would say that this is the case *only if* a given community is self-transcending.

II. Initial Context

There is an initial context to develop a horizonal complementarity in Lonergan's high praise of Winter's *Elements for a Social Ethic*[7] as an outstanding model of interdisciplinary work. Winter not only interrelates the four various styles of sociology, but he also relates them to social ethics in a critically constructive sense. In questioning, for instance, whether the behaviorists', functionalists', and voluntarists' sociological judgments are scientific or ideological in nature, Winter transposes the discussion to a recognition of the need for philosophically grounded ethics *and* social science. Winter proposes the intentionalist style of such seminal sociologists as G. H. Mead and Alfred Schutz as pointing the way to philosophically grounding the other three social scientific styles.

Winter's ability to meet head on issues in the social sciences that are not resolvable by empirical methods occurs, I believe, primarily on the second hermeneutical-dialectical level of social ethics. I see Lonergan's method achieving the same success on the third dialectical-foundational level of ethics. Both methods, each on its respective level, have taken the transcendental turn, asking the conditions of the possibility for any such studies.

Lonergan offers a suggestion as to one way theology and the social and religious sciences can fruitfully cooperate. If the philosophy of religion contains a genuine account of religious experience, then it will be open to a theology, to moral theology, and from these one can go on to a religious policy. The result would be a *praktische Theologie*, so that such praxis as preaching or sociological group action could be studied as to their results by empirical scientists. In turn, the evaluated results of the results could lead to an ongoing feedback process, i.e., fruitful cooperation setting forth "not timeless truths but the adaptations of attitudes and actions needed at each particular time and place."[8]

Winter and Lonergan offer, I believe, complementary hermeneutic and dialectical foundations through which an ongoing cooperation between disciplines can work in a feedback model. Let us prepare for a sketch of such a feedback model by recalling method's foundational praxis of conversion.

---

[7] Gibson Winter, *Elements for a Social Ethic* (New York: Macmillan, 1968). On Lonergan's comments see Bernard Lonergan, *Method in Theology* (New York: Herder, 1972) pp. 86, 248-49, and *Second Collection,* ed. B. Tyrrell. (London: Darton, Longman and Todd, 1975), pp. 215-27.

[8] *Second Collection,* p. 192.

III. Foundational Praxis of Conversion

Lonergan has not worked out a code of ethics, but he has indicated both what the foundations and the general development of an ethics might be. The foundations would lie in the praxis of subjects authentically appropriating the inner dynamism of their intentional operations in the three conversions.[9] Let us illustrate the "radical" nature of the foundational praxis of the conversions through a contextual analogy.

The analogy may be glimpsed from Lonergan's going back behind the procedures of ancient, medieval, and modern sciences, philosophy, theology, and ethics, and the actual performances of the people involved in those various disciplines, whether today or previously. For example, between scientific thought today and Thomist thought he discovers an isomorphism or a protracted analogy of proportion that "concentrates on a structural similarity to prescind entirely from the materials that enter into the structures."[10] The key point is to grasp the mental structures operative in both modern science and previous patterns of thinking. The contextual analogy can be more precisely understood by joining Lonergan's appreciation of H. Butterfield's *The Origins of Modern Science, 1300-1800*[11] and its depiction of the development of the needed historical contexts to shift from one paradigmatic understanding and doing of science to another. The scientific materials and methods change, but the mental structure understanding the changes is invariant.

Butterfield distinguishes between new ideas and the context or horizon for expressing and developing the new ideas. New scientific ideas actually date from the fourteenth century, but it was not until the seventeenth century that the break-boundary emerged to shape these ideas into the modern scientific context we have experienced since. I believe that philosophical ethicists reacted to the modern context by either withdrawing into rationalism (Descartes, Leibniz, Spinoza,) proposing empiricism (Locke, Hume,) or proposing the inverted horizon of transcendentalism (Kant).

The metacontextual analogy helps us understand the radical shift in ethical foundations. The dialectical-foundational approach avoids the dichotomization of theory-praxis while integrating both empi-

---

[9] See Lonergan, *Second Collection*, pp. 39-40. The development of ethics, like Lonergan's metaphysics, would be "explicitly aware of itself as a system on the move."

[10] Lonergan, *Collection* I, F.E. Crowe, ed. (N.Y. : Herder and Herder, 1967), pp. 142-143.

[11] Herbert Butterfield, *The Origins of Modern Science, 1300-1800*, 2nd ed. (London: Bell and Sons, 1965).

rical and rationalist, as well as transcendental ethics. The new foundational praxis consists not in a set of verbal propositions named first principles, or in enouncing either rules to be followed or theories subject to revision. Rather it consists in the appropriation of the inner dynamism leading to a radical transformation or a transvaluation of values. Conversion occurs in the concrete dynamic reality, is capable of generating knowledge of, and change in, particular, concrete, dynamic, as well as communal, social, and historical praxis. Any positive change in socio-ethical communal praxis can yield redefining processive structures for redemptive praxis.

The foundational praxis of conversion, however, must somehow interrelate the three levels of ethics in order to effect individual and social change. The horizonal complementarity I have proposed can help us in the very complex task of interrelating the three levels in social ethics. Let us indicate how the horizonal complementarity *might* be developed through a two-fold dialectic.[12] Each dialectic should interrelate the three levels of ethics, the first dialectic as to their hermeneutical-dialectical and dialectical-foundational complementarity, and the second as to the collaboration of the various ethical levels with foundational, political, and liberation theologies.

IV. Dialectic of Complementarity

In a fully worked out dialectic of complementarity between Lonergan's dialectical-foundational and Winter's hermeneutical-dialectical structures[13] I would make a one for one correlation between the four scientific styles as treated by Winter and the four levels of intentional consciousness thematized by Lonergan. I would then endeavor to show how the scientific styles once correlated with the operational levels impact on the three ethical levels. The whole enterprise would be set within and applied to the intersubjective praxis of actual social and ecclesiastical life. Such a procedure would treat at length how hermeneutic and dialectical foundations complement one another in interrelating the three levels of ethics. It would strive to redefine socio-ethical structures for an emancipatory redemptive praxis.

---

[12] A fully developed horizonal complementarity would be based on the two basic mediating and mediated phases of Lonergan's *Method,* pp. 133-36. The two phases correspond to my abbreviated complementarity and collaboration dialectics. Again in this paper I speak of the three levels of ethics for the sake of simplicity of treatment. But from a fully developed dialectical-foundational standpoint there are actually four levels corresponding to the four cognitional levels or the four functional specialties in each basic phase. The integration of moral imperatives into coherent systems should be differentiated into two distinct levels.

[13] I attempted a fuller treatment in my PhD thesis, *Theory-praxis of Social Ethics: The Complementarity between Lonergan's and Winter's Theological Foundations* (Milwaukee: Marquette U., 1977), available from University Microfilms, Ann Arbor. See also note 12.

I stress the complementarity and mutual interdependence of the four socio-scientific styles, the four cognitional levels, and the three ethical levels. Lonergan's and Winter's works can both be interpreted in theory-praxis terms to bring out a horizonal complementarity between hermeneutical-dialectical and dialectical-foundational redefining ethical structures. It is a matter of merging their hermeneutical-dialectical and dialectical-foundational horizons[14] to reinforce one another's potentialities. I will indicate mainly on the foundational level some mutual theory-praxis reinforcements or "correctives" that our two authors can offer one another. I believe that Lonergan's theory-praxis mediation is particularly relevant in grounding the value judgments of an intentionalist ethic and in objectifying the intersubjective feedback character of such judgments. Winter's mediation of social and intersubjective praxis, on the other hand, can help offset the limitations of Lonergan's mostly methodological mediation of praxis with an informed mediation of a) the categorial procedures of social science and b) the meaning and function of symbols in the intersubjective matrix which is Christianity. Let us treat these four points briefly.

Firstly, Lonergan has succeeded in grounding the praxis of value judgments. This is surely one of his major achievements. Having shown at length the fallacy of Kant's original synthetic unity of apperception which left no room for a consciousness of the generative principle of the categories, Lonergan was able to thematize the dynamic state that leads to grounded judgments of fact.[15] He thematized the law or structure immanent and operative in cognitional process and allied it to the experiential component in knowing to show that one's power of questioning leads to an unconditional affirmation of one's heuristic nature in an unconditioned judgment of self-affirmation. In ethics he showed how the practical insights leading from the third to the fourth level of consciousness result in judgments of value which differ in content but not in structure from judgments of fact.[16] A major point which needs to be stressed is the *complementarity* that exists a) among the four different levels of our consciousness, and hence b) between their self-corrective praxis and

---

[14] In a parallel case, as I see it, Gadamer's hermeneutical-dialectical fusion of the content of being into image or form *(Verwandlung ins Gebilde)* in a "total mediation" of a new being must be carried further on the dialectical-foundational level of transformatively changing Church structures to be instruments of the truth of the Spirit.

[15] See *Insight,* pp. 340-341. One of Lonergan's key distinctions is on the one hand between analytic propositions whose terms are abstract, as for example those involved in Kant's question of universal and necessary judgments, and on the other, analytic principles, whose terms are existential.

[16] Lonergan, *Method,* p. 37.

the revisable theories they generate. The complementary dynamism of the mutually interdependent and immanent operations yields the basic link between theory and praxis which on any level of discourse results in a self-corrective process of reflection for action.[17] In application to Winter's *Elements for a Social Ethic,* for instance, this complementarity and the pivotal precedence of grounded value judgments in the transition to potential action can help ground the intentionalist style in its relation with the other three sociological styles.

Secondly, while Winter is the master of the theme of intersubjectivity, Lonergan can furnish a crucial step of objectifying the praxis of intersubjectivity, which in turn leads to a breakthrough in providing a feedback, self-corrective process among the three levels of ethics. The reduplicative direct and reflective modes of consciousness permit a mutual subject as object relationship. Lonergan has clarified Scheler's axiology on this point.[18] True, a person cannot be apprehended cognitively as an "object" taken in a naive realist, Kantian, or positivist sense. But a person as ontic value, known and loved in a self-transcending way, can be a subject as object, not merely a subject as subject. It is a matter of applying the operations as intentional to the operations as conscious. It leads to a self-corrective process both within any intersubjective matrix and in the course of reflecting on such a matrix.

Thirdly, we have already touched on Lonergan's enthusiastic acceptance of Winter's innovative construction of basic sociological terms and relations to ground a critique of the four sociological styles. In answer to Charles Curran,[19] I believe that Lonergan would readily admit that his own efforts in the ethical sphere have been restricted to thematizing the praxis of the dialectical-foundational level of ethics. But that does not betray any inherent limitations in his method or its socio-ethical application. On the contrary, having understood the distinction and interrelatedness among the three ethical levels, Lonergan's metamethod needs to be complemented by methods like Winter's which specify the praxis and procedures of first order socio-scientific methods, and how ethical content is operative within society. Only such hermeneutical procedures can help determine whether the various scientific styles conflict with a society's ethical intentions.

---

[17] I am indebted for this formulation and other insights in theory-praxis to Matthew Lamb, e.g., his "The Theory-Praxis Relationship in Contemporary Theologies," paper delivered at C.T.S.A., 1976.

[18] Lonergan, "Natural Knowledge of God," *Collection* II, p. 120.

[19] See note 5. In his own answer in *Foundations of Theology,* Philip McShane ed. (Dublin: Gill and MacMillan, 1971), pp. 226 ff., Lonergan intimates that Curran has overlooked the implications of the dialectical-foundational grounding of authentic subjectivity as the specific theological principle.

Fourthly, in order to do justice to Winter's contribution in our horizonal complementarity, I must stress that his accomplishments go much beyond the just noted hermeneutical breakthroughs in macro-sociology. His first interests were in the field of Christian micro-sociology. There he showed adroitness in everyday ethical problem-solving. He studied family, parochial, and metropolitan group dynamics. His original interest was in how the family might be able to extend the sphere of personal community beyond the home, and so reshape the large community in the metropolis. He was able to show the ambivalent character of symbolic processes at work in these intersubjective matrices. Since 1960 Winter's hopes for community seem to have been gradually dashed with the realization that the ideal of *privacy* and community within the home often degenerated, among Christian parochial "elites", into a *privatizing* abuse and destruction of the interdependent metropolitan community.[20] He offers Lonergan a needed emphasis on the intersubjective praxis of actual social and ecclesiastical life and on how the meanings of symbols function within such intersubjective matrices.

In a fully worked out dialectic of complementarity, I would interrelate the above mutual correctives in a much more systematic way. The point to be made is that an integrative social ethic is possible by reconciling the different socio-ethical levels functioning within a differentiated unity on the basis of the very complementarity existing between theory-praxis as manifested in our cognitional and volitional processes. This fundamental complementarity needs to be tapped to restore harmony among and within dissociated disciplines and within society. The primary task of our first dialectic of complementarity consists in fully sublating any residual conceptualist theories operative within the various levels of ethics by recalling the theorists' own immanent dynamic praxis potentially leading them to a collaborative self-transcendence. Collaborative self-transcendence, i.e., one way of describing our second dialectic of collaboration,[21] is the other half of what I see as a fully integrative psycho-social feedback process of self-corrective socio-ethical praxis.

V. Dialectic of Collaboration

I have been arguing that the pre-systemic self-transcending praxis thematized by Lonergan can be extended cooperatively to social praxis thematized by critical hermeneutical-dialectical methods such

---

[20] See Gibson Winter's *Love and Conflict* (New York: Doubleday, 1957); *The Suburban Captivity of the Churches* (New York: Macmillan, 1963); *Being Free: Reflections on America's Cultural Revolution* (New York: Macmillan, 1970).

[21] Both dialectics are dialectics of complementarity, the second one specifying the collaborative aspect.

as Winter's. Both men agree that the three levels of ethics in the socio-ethical domain include foundations, policy, and practice. Our dialectic of collaboration will indicate how these three levels of social ethics actually correspond to foundational theology, political theology, and liberation theology respectively, and how the correspondence helps us develop an integrative social ethic within the actual intersubjective matrices of Church and societal structures. The two dialectics together are an attempt to apply Lonergan's generalized self-correcting process of reflection for action.

A foundational theological social ethics. I have already touched on the foundational praxis of conversion. This radical shift in foundations, concretized in value judgments, guides decisions which must be made to effect societal structural changes for the implementation of religious liberating praxis. Let us sketch how the foundational praxis of the dialectical-foundational structure offers a key theory-praxis link for the emancipatory redefinition and restructuring of basic theologico-ethical terms and issues. We shall then be in a position to outline how this theory-praxis link, operative in our horizonal complementarity, helps effect a socio-ethical policy mediation demanded by political theologians and an effective strategy for emancipation from structures of domination as advocated by liberation theology.

An integrative theological socio-ethical method holds up as crucial the proper structuring of social issues in relation to political theology's hermeneutic. The crucial nature of the foundational reality stems from its ability to dialectically handle the contradictions of the many unmediated pluralisms that stem from inverted and absolutizing philosophical horizons. Lonergan conceives foundations as what is first in an ordered set of ongoing, developing reality. What is first in such a set is the immanent and operative set of norms that guides each forward step in the process. One is freed from deductivism and what becomes of paramount importance is a control of meaning through a process whereby the foundational reality, having rejected counterpositions in dialectic, can adopt a radical horizon of conversion which is *not* a set of propositions but a move to a new set of roots. It is a move from one set of roots in theory to a set derived from the differentiation of consciousness in the realm of interiority as praxis.

Foundations reveal the basis of the general and special categories to be our intentional operations and God's gift of His love.[22] The question of the derivation of the categories must be kept distinct from that of the existence of the bases from which they are derived. The praxis of self-appropriation reveals the existence of the bases. The manner of derivation of the categories from these bases, how-

---

[22] Lonergan, *Method*, pp. 281-93.

ever, is decisive as to whether a theological social ethics will be truly redemptive social praxis or not. The first crucial point is an advertence to, and appropriation of the bases themselves, which as foundational reality exist whether they are adverted to or not. The distinguishing factor between hermeneutical-dialectical and dialectical-foundational structures is, I believe, in the latter's explicit thematization and the former's mere implicit use of the transcultural, foundational bases. I believe that political theologians' and Winter's hermeneutical-dialectical socio-ethical mediations of redemptive praxis are authentically derived special theological categories. They need to advert more closely, however, both to the existence of the foundational reality in their own performance and to the manner in which they themselves derive such praxiological categories.[23] An integrative approach to the three levels of ethics through a horizontal complementarity furnishes one possible theory-praxis link between dialectical-foundational and hermeneutical-dialectical levels in structuring socio-ethical issues, and points to their contributing interaction with political and liberation theologies' interests in the same issues.

VI. Political Theologians' Demand for a Christian Social Ethic of Change.

Winter's thematization of such carriers of meaning as symbolism and intersubjectivity and his insistence on a social ethic are not only similar to, but also antedate political theologians' demand that a redefining hermeneutic be conducted regarding our present understanding of the symbols of Christian faith. In this section I will indicate the point of insertion between dialectical-foundational and hermeneutical-dialectical methods to achieve socio-ethical praxis, some minimum parameters of that praxis, and how the praxis acts back on the system.

The complexity and pluralism of the modern situation demands the development of psycho-social feedback models, in which the problems of bias and distortion afflicting the individual might be dealt with through moral social praxis.[24] The Christian churches' redemptive process must be a fully conscious process of self-constitution. It requires illumination from other human sciences. A social ethics founded in the self-transcending praxis of the three conversions makes possible a theory-praxis link or horizontal complemen-

---

[23] In foundations one merely accepts the categories as models, or interlocking set of terms and relations. Only in the later specialties does a theologian commit himself to such categories as hypothesis about reality. Ibid., p. 292.

[24] See Lamb, "Implications Méthodologiques" in *La Pratique de la Théologie Politique* (Bruxelles: Casterman, 1974), pp. 66-67.

tarity wherein Winter's works function as integrative social ethic within a larger theological method. Lonergan indicates such a possible point of insertion:

> Corresponding to doctrines, systematics, and communications in theological method, integrated studies would distinguish policy making, planning, and the execution of the plans. Policy is concerned with attitudes and ends. Planning works out the optimal use of existing resources for attaining the ends under given conditions. Execution generates feedback.[25]

Our horizonal complementarity is such a feedback attempt. Winter is able to deliver on Lonergan's demand and stress that a principle of subsidiarity be observed. This principle is to the effect that theology can only be integrated with other studies, and so be effective in undoing evil, when the necessary intermediary studies regarding policies have been conducted as to how particular methods function in concrete situations.

Some of the minimum parameters of a redemptive social praxis include political theology's critique of the privatization of theology, and the call for a new hermeneutic which is necessarily orientated to societal action. Such a praxis critically accepts the implications of a secularized world. It recognizes that there is no immediate transition from faith to action. It relies on the mediation of an ethics as "determinate negations" of society.[26]

A horizonal complementarity's theory-praxis articulation of an integrative theological and socio-ethical method deepens both the new foundational thrust toward emancipatory theological categories, and the more effective socio-ethical mediational ability between foundations and practice which political theology is researching. We are led to the level of practice in which a self-corrective process of reflection acts back upon the system.

VII. Effective Strategies for a Theology of Liberation

The level of reflective practice is the most concrete. As Winter had anticipated the political theologians' hermeneutical task, so he had anticipated liberation theology's emphasis on developing transformative strategies for economic and cultural emancipation from ghetto bonds.

---

[25] Lonergan, *Method,* pp. 365-366.

[26] See, e.g., Johann B. Metz, *Theology of the World* (New York: Seabury, 1973); *Sacramentum Mundi,* III, Col. 1237 ff.; Francis P. Fiorenza, "Political Theology and Liberation Theology" in Thomas McFadden, ed., *Liberation, Revolution and Freedom* (New York: Seabury, 1975), pp. 3-29.

From a dialectical-foundational perspective there are two forms of alienation and ideology. The first is the basic form of refusing conversion. The second stems from the basic type, and it is the one liberation theology confronts when it addresses the ontological meanings and societal structures which tend to perpetuate the derivative forms of alienation and ideology. One cannot, in practice, overcome basic alienation without concurrently changing the structures which promote and maintain derivative alienation, and vice versa.

Accordingly, our theory-praxis link would take cognizance of the fact, bemoaned by black writers and Winter, that not only have blacks been deprived of their cultural heritage, but that whites have failed to learn many possible lessons from that heritage, such as the care and protection of children, the advocacy roles of extended families and of the churches, and the resiliency and interaction within the community and social systems. Our theory-praxis link within the horizonal complementarity is aimed at the development of viable institutions both within ethnic groupings and among any would-be cooperators. It would help in "reversing the ancient and contemporary practices of exclusion and negative valuation."[27] It would draw upon and complement concrete and effective developmental strategies aimed at transformative truth in persons and in communities.[28]

For instance, one recalls the phrase "Black Power" coined in the heat of the civil rights movement. Although the exponents of the phrase are not agreed on its precise meaning or methods for attaining it,[29] it and comparable consciousness-raising slogans have helped transform black-white cooperative patterns in the U.S.A. The black is now on his way to being respected. What interests us here is how insight interactionism in concrete situations can and does redefine old theories in the light of new emergent praxis. The civil rights movement against negative valuation and exclusionism is a classical example of determinate negation, and of what should lead to positive cooperative value judgments among men and women of good will. It takes the three levels of ethics, working in tandem, to fashion and implement cooperative value judgments that can over-

---

[27] Andrew Billingsley, *Black Families in White America* (Englewood Cliffs, N. J.: Prentice Hall, 1968), p. 151.

[28] This is not to negate liberation theologians' arguments against a developmentalism which would leave existing structures of domination and exploitation intact. See Gustavo Gutiérrez, *A Theology of Liberation* (New York: Orbis, 1973), pp. 22-23, 25-27, 82-84; Philip Berryman, "Latin American Liberation Theology," in *Theological Studies* 34, (Sept., 1973):358-64.

[29] James Cone, *Black Theology and Black Power* (New York: Seabury, 1969), pp. 5-30.

come both the basic and the derivative forms of ideology and alienation.

From concrete examples of cooperative value judgments there is effected a feedback process back to the foundational and policy levels. These three-levelled value judgments are reconciled and integrated through complementarity and collaboration dialectics. The two dialectics show the possibility of grounding the voluntarist element at work in the theologies of liberation, revolution, and hope. Because they are shown to flow downwards from critically grounded foundations, and because they can, in turn, have ongoing critical feedback input into the cognitive, effective, and constitutive meanings of church and societal policies, political and liberation theologies are successfully integrated within larger socio-ethical and theological methods. Underlying the integration is a recognition and appropriation of the theory-praxis of social ethics' hermeneutical and dialectical foundations, which are complementary and mutually indispensable.

Aristotle's Notion of Epieikeia *

by Garrett Barden

I.

Aristotle, when he comes to treat of *epieikeia,* or equity, is faced with two largely opposed traditions: the popular and the philosophic. In the popular tradition *epieikeia* is a virtue of the heroic conqueror who demands from the defeated less than he could, of the man who does not always insist on every detail of observance, of the man who is not small minded. However, the popular tradition reached an aporia in the matter of the administration of the law. If law was to rule, then equitable judgments, which did not insist upon perfect observance, seemed to bend the law, to go outside it, to go beyond it or be less than it, to be, in short, illegal. And yet, as the popular tradition realized, to apply the law rigidly was small-minded, mean, often absurd and unjust.[1]

Plato in *The Laws* and particularly in *The Statesman* takes up the issue and clarifies the problem: the law is a universal statement, the situation is particular, so the law cannot always adequately cover the situation.[2] Such is the problem of equity as it was adumbrated in the

---

* Prof. Barden has chosen a more exact translation of ἐπιείχεια as *Epieikeia,* rather than the more familiar rendition of the Greek term as *Epikeia* –Editor's note.

[1] Consult Liddell and Scott, *A Greek-English Lexicon* under *epieikeia* and *epieik-euomai* to discover that popular usage — especially early usage — gives *epieikeia* a positive value. However the idea that it may be opposed to the law appears for example in Herodotus *polloi tón dikaión ta epieikestera protitheisi.* (III, 53, Sect. 4)

[2] *The Statesman* (294a-b): "Law can never issue an injunction binding on all which really embodies what is best for each: it cannot prescribe with perfect accuracy what is good and right for each member of the community at any one time. The differences of human personality, the variety of men's activities and the inevitable unsettlement attending all human experience made it impossible for any art whatsoever to issue unqualified rules holding good on all questions at all times."

popular tradition and as it was accepted by Aristotle. Plato, acknowledging the inadequacy of the law, preferred the government of the Royal Ruler precisely because the Royal Ruler had the knowledge which would allow him to judge correctly on each occasion. However, since the Ruler could not always be present, it was necessary that there be laws to govern activity and that these laws be not deviated from. These laws came from the Royal Ruler and were, therefore, correct. Their application, on the other hand, would inevitably give rise to injustice or error because the concrete situations would deviate from the universal situations envisaged in the law. This inevitable injustice or error was, for Plato, part of the human condition. To deviate from the laws would be, however, considerably worse for it would be to descend into a chaos from which the image of the Form of Justice, dimly perceived in the laws, would be totally hidden. For Plato equitable judgment was bad judgment in that it was a deviation from and a diminution of law. The judge who would judge in equity would be like the painter in *The Republic* who would paint a chair without seeing the Form. His painted chair is a deception. So the judge who does not follow the law deceives. His judgment is no more than a misleading appearance of justice. Only the Royal Ruler saw the Form of Justice and so only he could discern justice in the concrete.[3] Plato's solution takes up the popular tradition and develops it in one direction; where the popular tradition saw the absurdity of the rigid application of laws Plato saw the unavoidable tragedy of the human condition. For Plato, then, justice can be achieved only through the application of the just laws of the Royal Ruler. The problem in Plato's position is that if it is sometimes impossible for the universal law to cover adequately the particular case, as he thought it was, then sometimes justice could not be achieved. Plato was aware of this problem but thought it without solution.

In the popular tradition, however, *epieikeia* had generally a positively valued sense. To judge in equity is to judge well. *Epieikes* has the senses of "fitting," "noble," "appropriate," "good." Equity is somehow better than the law because somehow the application of the law does not always seem appropriate. Aristotle's discussion of *epieikeia* in

---

[3] However one may settle the question of the development of Plato's political thought from the *Republic* to the *Statesman* it is clear that in the latter the Ruler discerned what was just in a particular case—and so, in the limit, had no need of laws—as the ship's captain discerned how to guide the vessel in a particular case: "The ship's captain fixes his attention on the real welfare at any given time of his ship and crew. He lays down no written enactments but supplies a law in action by practical application of his knowledge of seamanship to the needs of the voyage." (296e) This would serve very well as a metaphor for Aristotle's equitable judge.

the *Nicomachean Ethics* is an effort to sustain this popular sense of what is fitting against Plato's formalism.

In Bk. VI of the *Nichomachean Ethics* (1143a20) Aristotle, having already discussed *epieikeia* at length in Bk. V., associates it with *sungnome,* or sympathetic judgment: *ton gar epieiké malista phamen einai sungnomonikon, kai epieikes to ekhein peri enia sungnómén. Hé de sungnómé gnómé esti kritiké tou epieikous orthé. Orthé d'hé tou aléthous.* Ross's translation is: "(We) identify equity with sympathetic judgment about certain facts. And sympathetic judgment is judgment which discriminates what is equitable and does so correctly; and correct judgment is that which judges what is true." In this passage we have the kernel of Aristotle's conclusion concerning equity. It is a conclusion notably at variance with that of Plato. For Plato sympathy (often translated "indulgence") was indeed associated with equitable judgment, but such judgment was erroneous. Aristotle preserves the association but claims without equivocation that the sympathetic judgment is correct and true.[4]

Thus the non-sympathetic, non-equitable judgment is neither correct nor true. For Plato too the non-equitable judgment in the concrete might well be neither correct nor true. The difference between them lies in this, that where Plato saw an impasse Aristotle sees a way through.

II.

Aristotle distinguishes between "law" and "justice" *(nomos* and *to dikaion)* in a number of ways. First denotatively: "law" covers all aspects of action, "for the law bids us to practise every virtue and forbids us to practise any vice" (1130b 25) and the term "just" is sometimes used in this sense; "justice"—or "particular justice" which is a part of virtue and not virtue entire—is concerned with exchange between men, either with the distribution of honors, etc. or with the rectifying of transactions between men. The modern English "fair-

---

[4] *Sungnome,* or sympathetic judgment, has the sense of fellow-feeling, forbearance, lenient judgment, compassion. It thus overlaps considerably with *epieikeia.* As *epieikeia* became a technical word it had the tendency to mean "mistaken", "erroneous", "warped" judgment led astray by indulgence and clemency. This meaning becomes paramount in Plato who writes in the *Laws* at 757e: *to gar epieikes kai sugnomon tou teleou kai akribous para diken ten parthen esti paratethranmenon.* Aristotle, when he retains the association between *sungnome* and *epieikeia* and further associates both with correct judgment, quite deliberately restores and develops the earlier usage and morality against a later formalism. For a longer discussion of this point see Marie P.T. Baker, *Epieikeia in Aristotle's Philosophy of Law* (unpubld. M.A. thesis U.C. Cork, 1979) esp. part I, although the entire thesis repays study. For the relation between feeling and judgment in Aristotle see Pierre Aubenque, *La Prudence chez Aristote* (Paris: P.U.F., 1976).

ness" is in some ways a better rendering of Aristotle's term. This distinction between *nomos* and *to dikaion* is crucial to Aristotle's legal philosophy, as we shall see.[5]

A second distinction between "law" and "justice" and one which has a bearing on the present topic is the more familiar distinction between the formulated universal law, whether written or unwritten, and the particular situation to which the law is to be applied. Here there is supposedly a justice to be found in the situation which may not be found by the automatic application of the law.

A third distinction, again familiar, is the distinction between a just and unjust law. This distinction is important for Aristotle but it is not the distinction which gives rise to the question of equity. Throughout the central discussion of equity in the *Nichomachean Ethics* (1137a31-38a3), Aristotle always assumes that he is talking about just laws.[6] The discussion of the application of unjust laws is in the *Rhetoric* Bk. I, ch. 13 & 14.

With these clarifications Aristotle can deal with the problem of the equitable although he is still left with the terminological difficulty of the tendency to identify the just with the law. He talks, therefore, of two kinds of justice in Bk. V (1137b 1): the legal and the equitable. For the history and development of legal philosophy this way of dealing with the problem is unfortunate because for Aristotle there is in the end only one justice, namely the equitable. The legal justice, of which the equitable is said to be a correction, is not concretely justice at all and is wrongly so called.

An example will illustrate the two kinds of justice. A ferry-boat company informs intending passengers that they will not be permitted to embark later than thirty minutes before departure. A bus company runs a service between the city center and the ferry-port. The bus is scheduled to arrive forty-five minutes before departure of

---

[5] Michel Villey is one of the few modern philosophers of law to make anything of this distinction between *nomos* and *to dikaion*., cf. his *Critique de la Pensée Juridique Moderne* (Paris: Dalloz, 1976). From the beginning the philosophy of law has tended to become the philosophy of commands and since Hobbes' *Leviathan* and *A Dialogue Between a Philosopher and a Student of the Common Laws of England* it has been almost exclusively that even in languages where the distinction between *to dikaion* and *nomos* is retained in common use.

[6] It is worth pointing out that if equity is an interpretative procedure, a way of reading statutes, then there is also an equitable approach to unjust laws (that is, laws that according to some other criterion are unjust) for the measure of interpretation is what Aristotle calls the "thought of the legislator." Without hoping to resolve the dispute between Betti and Gadamer on this point, the text suggests that one discovers the thought of the legislator by understanding the statute in its context. An unjust law has a context just as much as a just one. When Aristotle writes that the "law is not at fault" he must be taken seriously, for to understand *epieikeia* as the correction on an unjust law by a just but higher law is to miss the point entirely.

the boat. The bus breaks down and by the time another is provided the passengers are later than the stated time and arrive only ten minutes before the ferry is due to sail. They are not permitted to embark, the boat sails and they are left behind. The irate passengers sue the company. For whom should the judge find? The company claims that they contracted to carry the passengers under certain conditions. One of these conditions was not fulfilled. So it was within its rights to refuse admission. The passengers, on the other hand, claim that they could reasonably expect the company to wait for the passengers from the normal bus and certainly to delay embarkation.

What Aristotle calls legal justice would be fulfilled by finding for the company. If the judge was concerned only with this "legal justice" he would inquire no further but merely ask whether or not the passengers had fulfilled their part of the bargain. However, he might think it good to inquire further and weigh up all the pros and cons. This further inquiry would be, in Aristotle's terms, equitable.

Legal justice is the application of the relevant law. Hans Kelsen remarks that it is always possible to apply the law and that the result of doing so seems absurd only to someone who does not share the presuppositions or political attitudes behind the law. Aristotle agrees that it is always possible to apply the law: the result of doing so inappropriately is what he calls here "legal justice." An absurd result comes about when the intention of the law is frustrated. Kelsen seems to think that the presuppositions of a law are wholly articulated in the written statute; Aristotle thinks that they are not.

Legal justice is the application of the relevant law. This is not an adequate description, for in the case above one judge might find for the company without having asked any further questions while another judge might find for the company having investigated the situation in detail. In other words, to judge equitably is not necessarily to come to a conclusion different from that arrived at by the mere mechanical application of the law; it is to consider the case in a particular manner. Thus the correction of legal justice involved in equity is fundamentally the correction of a procedure rather than of a conclusion.

Although it is initially adequate to distinguish legal and equitable justice it is clear that Aristotle thinks that in the concrete circumstances of the case there is a just solution, however difficult it may be to find. The just solution is not to be found by the mechanical application of the universal law, for such a mechanical application is just only by chance. The term "legal justice" is therefore a misnomer. The basic distinction is between mechanical and equitable judgment, and justice is discovered through the latter.[7]

Why will a mechanical application of the law not do? The general answer is that the law is universal and the case particular: "the error is not in the law nor in the legislator but in the nature of the thing, since the matter of practical affairs is of this kind from the start" (1137b 18). The law takes the usual case whereas the case under consideration is particular and may or may not be an instance of the usual.

Aristotle does not analyze the difference between his two distinctions: the universal and the particular, or the usual and the exception. The law is universal because it is an understanding and all understanding is universal. But that understanding which is expressed in a law is legally relevant because it is an understanding of a usual case. The application of the law to a case always requires the insight that this case is an instance covered by the law, that is, that this particular case is a member of the class of usual cases and that, therefore, there is no need to inquire further. What Aristotle here distinguishes as equitable judgment depends on the insight that the case is unusual and so must be understood differently. But the understanding which yields the judicial sentence is universal and would apply to any similar future cases; hence the importance of precedent. What Aristotle does not clearly see here is that every judicial determination of what is just is equitable. His identification of equity as a special case of prudence in Bk. VI, ch. 11 would, however, point in this direction.[8]

The law is a statement of what is thought to be just in a case. Contract law tells how just contracts are to be made. When there is dispute concerning a contract the effort is to determine the just in this particular case and a first step is to discover how similar this case is to the case envisaged in the law and to other cases where judgments have been given. A great deal of forensic dispute is in fact concerned with establishing or denying relevant similarity. If relevant similarity is established, then by the principle that similars are similarly understood, precedent or the law can be applied without further ado. Mere individual difference is not taken as relevant; if it were

---

[7] The term "mechanical application" is shorthand and strictly there is no such thing, for in all cases the judge has to discover whether or not the case, X, is covered by the law, Y. What is here called mechanical application of the law occurs when the judge insists that a situation *partially* described by a statute is *wholly* described by that statute.

[8] There are, then, two aspects to equity. One deals with the particular case in the light of universal laws and here every judgment concerning a particular situation should be equitable, for there is no science of particulars. See on this F. E. Crowe, "Universal Norms and Concrete 'Operabile' in St. Thomas Aquinas", *Sciences Ecclésiastiques*, Vol. 7, 1955, pp.115-149 and 257-291. The second aspect, which deals with exceptional cases, is a special case of the first.

there would be no law, for law assumes that there are usual cases.⁹

The law is a statement of what is thought to be just in a kind of case. This means that the society's sense of justice is specified in a given situation. To talk of a sense of justice may seem unduly vague; the phrase needs some clarification. Initially a sense of justice is this: that within a community there is some idea that people can behave well or badly towards one another. What precisely constitutes well and badly has yet to be determined; what is important is that some sense of this difference exists. In a contract this sense of good or bad behavior is often specified as fulfillment of the contract. To behave well is to fulfill the contract; to renege is to behave badly. To say this is to specify, however minimally, a sense of good or bad behavior.

The sense of justice, although it is not and cannot be fully articulated, is specified and expressed in, but is not contained by law. Each situation provides a new opportunity for a further specification of the sense of justice. Thus it happens that, even when situations are relevantly similar, precedents are overturned because the sense of justice has changed. Thus it happens too that laws, the more formal expression of that sense, are likewise repealed or reformed.¹⁰

The fact that the world diverges from the norm yields situations which are by definition abnormal and not covered by the understanding of the usual case. These unusual cases must now be understood. Plato's theory was that only the Royal Ruler could understand and legislate for them and that in his absence the only thing to do was to follow the law even though it fitted the case badly. Aristotle thought that the judge could himself understand this new case but not *ab ovo*, not as if he were an alien figure without a background. He could understand the new case because he knew the laws and so knew how the communal sense of justice had been articulated.

In the unusual case the judge must judge not mechanically according to the law but still in the light of the law. He must "say what the

---

⁹ Where Aristotle writes of "usual cases" one may also write "envisaged cases" for there is a case envisaged in the law and it is a further judgment that this case is also usual. Law is abstract in much the same way as discoveries in the natural sciences are abstract. To apply the law always requires the addition of insight into the concrete. So there is no mechanical application but, in the end, good and bad judgment.

¹⁰ Within the presuppositions of an extreme command theory there is literally no problem about changing laws, for all laws depend on the will of the lawgiver and change as he wills. Kelsen assumes that laws are changed for reasons that seem good to the lawgiver but the further discussion of these reasons is beyond the scope of a pure theory of law. Within the presuppositions of a natural law theory that considers the laws as statutes there is hardly room for any change. Within the presuppositions of a theory of justice which considers the just as something to be discovered there is room for change, but precisely how it comes about requires further analysis.

legislator himself would have said had he been present" (1137b 20). And how is he to know what the legislator would have said? In fact here the legislator is a metaphor for the sense of justice for it is impossible to know what the legislator would have said except by knowing the sense *(dianoia)* of what has already been said. In other words to know what the legislator would have said is to know the sense of justice contained in the law but not totally specified by it. It is not to know this completely; it is to know it sufficiently to be able to make a judgment in the light of the law. This judgment will not be infallible. It may be overturned later by other judgments that will themselves not be infallible. Finally the legislature may overturn all previous judgments by developing the law which itself may be repealed or reformed as the society develops. Infallibility cannot be had and it is the curse of legal philosophy to think that it can.

In doing something other than applying the law the judge is attempting to determine the justice of the case. His solution is "not better than absolute justice but better than the justice which arises from the absoluteness of the statement" (1137b 25). As has been said earlier, the wording here is unfortunate and misleading for Aristotle does not think that justice is achieved by mechanically applying the law; a better rendering of his meaning (not, however, a better translation of his words) would be: equitable judgment is not better than justice but better than the legalism which arises from the absoluteness of the statement.

Throughout the entire operation, including the making of the law, the comparison of the case with the law, and the final judgment, the effort is to determine what is just. The judge is the final link in that cooperative chain. Because the question is asked in the concrete the answer must be given in the concrete, but in the light of tradition and precedent.

The tradition in the light of which the judge works includes past legislation, past jurisprudence, and the general discussion and writing concerning justice in his society. All these make up the presuppositions of judicial inquiry. So Aristotle thinks that a good judge needs a good education in the jurisprudence of his community. For the Royal Ruler with his vision of the Form of Justice Aristotle substitutes the judge. It is the judge, not just anybody at all, who can act equitably in legal matters.[11]

---

[11] Aristotle does not think that it is easy to judge well: "To know what is just and unjust requires, men think, no great wisdom, because it is not hard to understand the matters dealt with by the laws...; but how actions must be done and distributions effected in order to be just, to know *this* is a greater achievement than knowing what is good for health." *Nic. Eth.* 1137a 10-15. Again, "The law affords judges a special formation to enable them to administer and determine those things left indeterminate by the law" (*Politics,* III, 16, 1287a 27) and "magistrates judge well when

The analysis of Aristotle's theory of *epieikeia* has so far avoided an examination of the naturally just or natural law. There is, however, a tradition which interprets *epieikeia* as an appeal to natural law against the positive law of the statute.

In his discussion of *epieikeia* in the *Rhetoric*, which is more diffuse than the discussion in the *Nicomachean Ethics*, Aristotle on one occasion speaks of the general law and equity in the same sentence (1375a 30): "if the written law is counter to our case, we must have recourse to the general law and equity." The "general law" is "*tói koinói nomói.*" Earlier (1373b 5) he writes: *koinon de ton kata phusin*, "by general I mean those based on nature," and in that earlier passage he goes on to discuss Antigone's refusal to obey Creon when she claims that "it is just, though forbidden, to bury Polynices, as being naturally just" (1373b 12). By the general law based on nature as opposed to those laws "established by each people in reference to themselves" Aristotle has in mind those laws that are found either everywhere or almost everywhere, those found for the most part or usually (MM.1195a3).

According to the *Rhetoric* "equity is justice that goes beyond the written law" (1374a 250) and "equity is constant and never changes" (1375a 31).

When Aristotle recommends that we go beyond the written law[12] if it runs against us (he is here giving advice to advocates) and suggests that recourse be had to the general law and equity is he advocating recourse to one or two things? Are equity and the general law identical? If they are, then to judge in equity is to judge in accord with a higher law contrary to the posited statute. If they are not identical then the interpretation of equity given above can stand although the relation between natural justice and equity has still to be worked out.

One thing must be quite clear: Aristotle did think that it was possible to criticize a written statute by comparing it with the unwritten general law as the example of Creon and Antigone shows. But that is not an example of equity, for equity comes in when the law does not fit the situation, whereas Creon's refusal to allow Antigone to bury

---

they have received an adequate education in the laws". (idem 1287b 27). Finally, in the *Rhetoric* (1375b 28-29) we are told that the judge is not to seek to be wiser than the laws. The laws stand to equitable judgments as the universals stand to the particulars in wise judgments in general (cf. *Nic. Eth.* 1142a 15): "(practical) wisdom is concerned not only with universals but with particulars", which implies that it is concerned not only with particulars but also with universals.

[12] The distinction "written/unwritten" law is fluid in Aristotle. He takes it over from the tradition but does not make much of it. It does not always correspond to the distinction "natural/conventional" or "general/particular" for "the particular laws established by each people in reference to themselves,...are divided into written and unwritten...." (*Rhetoric* 1373b 5).

her brother Polynices fitted the situation exactly. This example is clearly and unequivocally a case of the criticism of a particular statute by the unwritten general law.[13] Although this is certainly a way of seeking justice beyond the written law, it is not the way of equity.

The appeal to equity is not an appeal to another statute nor to a specific precedent (which, in the common law at least, is recognized to have many of the characteristics of a statute and in the civil law is more influential than is sometimes recognized according to the principle, common to both systems, that similar cases are decided similarly). Equity is appealed to precisely when there is no statute and no precedent that adequately covers the case in hand. Equity, then, is not an appeal to a natural law conceived as a set of statutes standing behind the written law of the community.

And yet, according to the *Rhetoric* and in one passage in the *Nicomachean Ethics,* although not in the section where equity is treated at length, "equity is constant and never changes." In its constancy equity is compared by Aristotle to the general law that is based on nature (R.1375a ad fin): *kai'oti to men epieikes aei ménei kai oudepote metaballei, oud ho koinos (kata phusin gar estin)....* We must ask about the source of this eternal and unchanging character of equity.

First, it is important to remark on the peculiarity of speaking of equity as eternal and unchanging for equity deals precisely with the temporal and the changing about which, as Aristotle reminds us, there can be, *epistémé.* (*Eth. Nic.* VI. 3, 11396b 18ff).

The paradox is resolved by the principle that there is in every situation a just solution to be discovered, while denying that the posited law can always or necessarily provide that solution. Equity is constant, unchanging, and common to all because there is this just solution to be found. But because situations differ and cannot always be foreseen there is not an *epistémé* of situtations so that the equitable judgment is not the application to the situation of a natural, and supposedly higher law conceived as a statute, albeit unwritten.

In so far as equity is common to all it is because something is shared, and since the equitable judgment is an intellectual act what is shared must be an intellectual virtue or habit. It is to this habit that the vague term "the sense of justice" refers. There are then three elements in the move towards the equitable judgment. The judgment itself discerns the just; this is based on a traditional specifica-

---

[13] The example of Creon and Antigone is a case of conflict of laws within a system although the system in question has two sources — the conventional source to regulate what was originally indifferent and the natural to express what is in itself just or unjust.

tion of the kind of thing that is just; and this in turn is based on the fundamental presupposition that in human affairs there is a just and an unjust to be distinguished.

At this point the sharp and crucial difference between the Aristotelian and the positivist approach appears. For the positivist the posited law arbitrarily discriminates between the just and the unjust; for Aristotle the posited law is the statement of what is thought to be the just and the unjust. The law, for Aristotle, records a discovery. In this sense it is like a law in the natural sciences.

In this sense, too, equity is natural. The equitable judgment is an attempt to discover what is the case, to answer the question: what is the just solution in this particular case?

The equitable judgment — indeed the court judgment in general — is an indicative not an imperative. The judge says what is just. In the legal system some imperatives follow from this indicative; the just is accepted or imposed on the community. The legal system may have bailiffs, police, and various officers of the court to see that the just is done, but prior to all this is the indicative statement of what is just.

Equity, then, is not an appeal to natural law as a statute, and yet it is conceived as natural. In the light of this let us analyze the traditional example of equity which, found as early as the commentary of Andronicus of Rhodes, persists through the Middle Ages through Albert, Thomas, St. German as far, in the English tradition at least, as Plowden: the example of the stranger on the city walls.

A city is being attacked. A stranger, against the law of the city which forbids it under pain of death, climbs the ramparts to assist in its defense. When the attack is repulsed what is to be done with the stranger? Only a character from *Alice in Wonderland* would suggest that the stranger be punished. But why? Aquinas suggests that we have recourse to the natural justice: *Esset enim contra jus naturale ut benefactoribus poena rependeretur. Et ideo secundum justum naturale oportet hic dirigere justum legale.* (Lect. XVI, 1086)

Does Aquinas mean here that we should lay aside one statute in favor of another well known higher statute? Certainly there has been a tendency to interpret Aquinas and the tradition generally in this way, but whatever the correctness of this approach it seems to me that it is demonstrably not Aristotle's.

In both the *Rhetoric* and the *Nicomachean Ethics*, Aristotle refers to what the legislator would have said had he been there, or to the intention of the legislator:

> *kai to mé pros ton nomon alla pros ton nomothetén skopein kai me pros ton logon alla pros ten dianoian tou nomothetou* (R1374b 17).

In the traditional example one would grasp that the force of the law was to protect the city. But when a stranger climbs the walls to help defend the city then the law is discovered no longer to apply, i.e., the situation appears as unlike the situation envisaged in the law, and the stranger appears only as a benefactor and is to be treated as such. Is it naturally just to treat benefactors well? Certainly, at least in one Aristotelian sense: it is something that holds for the most part. This is what men are discovered spontaneously to do; there is a natural justice discovered in the way men interact together.

That spontaneous natural justice is of course cultural — it goes beyond a single culture in so far as different cultures share a common attitude — so the appeal to natural justice is an appeal to a spontaneous cultural attitude. The appeal is successful only in so far as the common cultural attitude is shared, but when the attitude is shared the appeal is to the unformulated sense of justice which is the background of the formulated rules.[14] This unformulated background is not another set of rules but is rather that attitude which makes us think of the laws as just for the usual cases.

The sense of justice which gives rise to the specific equitable judgment is the sense of justice which gave rise to the law, and it is only because of this that it is possible to think that the law does not adequately fit this case.[15]

One of the dangers in speaking of equity is that one may begin to assume that the judge who attempts to judge equitably will always be right, that is, will always succeed in judging equitably. Plato was so aware of the possibility of error that he considered it better to refuse equity altogether as a diminution of justice. Aristotle does not forget the danger and is at pains to stress that to know "how actions must be done and distributions effected in order to be just...is a greater achievement than knowing what is good for the health..." (1137a 10). He is aware of the bias of self interest (cf. 1134b1ff), of the bias caused by love and hate, etc. (R.1354b5ff). Aristotle does not

---

[14] K. Kuypers in his well known article in *Mnemosyne,* Vol. 5, 1937 at p. 294, "Recht und Billigkeit bei Aristoteles" speaks of a "natural sense of justice" but wants to distinguish this from natural right in a way that is not attempted here. This unformulated sense of justice is referred to in the draft of the Civil Code of the Netherlands (Burgerlÿkwetboek 1955, sect. 7): "In order to determine the equitable the following must be considered: the universally recognized principles of law, the common opinions held about law by the Dutch people, and the social and personal interests in each case." Quoted by J. L. M. Elders in "Equity in Dutch Law" in Ralph Newman (ed.), *Equity in the World's Legal Systems* (Brussels: Bruylant,1973), p.363.

[15] A law fits a case in as much as the justice intended by the law is realized when the law is applied to the case. If the judge has another idea of justice which he decides to realize in his judgment, he is bypassing the law not, in Aristotle's sense, judging equitably.

mean, therefore, that to attempt to discover what is just is to be infallible. He means simply this: to answer the question as to what is just in a particular situation requires more than the mechanical application of the universal law.

Every forensic judgment regards the specific case so that in a sense every judgment attempts to be equitable, for on each occasion the judge must discover whether or not this case is relevantly similar to the one envisaged in the law. If he discovers that it is then he applies the law, but not mechanically; he applies the law because the law adequately states what is just in this situation. The statute is, so to speak, an algorithm for arriving at the desired solution. To accept the law as just means to accept it as yielding the just solution to the case which it envisages. When laws are repealed, reformed, or allowed to lapse this is because they are no longer considered to be statements of what is just in the situations they envisage. Equity, as Aristotle sees it, is not law reform, for in equity "the law is not in error."

The operator in the whole process is the question: what is just either in this or this kind of situation? But that question does not arise in a void. It arises within a living community with its actual problems associated with its cultural, scientific, personal, industrial, and commercial development. It arises within what we call human experience. But it arises because human experience is moral experience. The formulated question specifies a basic human experiential fact: that men feel that in their life together there is a distinction between good and evil. That fundamental feeling develops into cultural habits, attitudes, injunctions, customs, songs, and stories of praise and blame that begin to tell what is courage, what is honor, what is disgrace. Such songs, stories, dramas tell and clarify communal attitudes. They would be fundamentally unintelligible if people did not share the basic experiential fact, if their experience was not moral. They would be difficult to understand if the audience did not share the less fundamental attitudes concerning courage, honor, shame, etc. which characterize and differentiate a culture. They are actually understood because these attitudes are in fact shared. The law is another way of formalizing such cultural moral attitudes and the court specifies them by the question, what is just in this situation? The moral attitude of the community must sometimes be stated and acted upon. The legal system is the community's way of doing this.[16]

---

[16] If a community's sense of justice can develop so too may it decline. This is an aspect of the crucial dialectical insight that eventually leads Lonergan to the development of the functional specialties. But no scheme can guarantee truth, and so there are identified the fundamental precepts of attentiveness, intelligence, reasonableness, and responsibility. These, too, do not guarantee truth, but they allow argument, which is the ground of the possibility of its emergence. Intrinsic to the entire process is a critical dynamism guaranteed by questioning.

To conclude, then, Aristotle's equitable judgment is the answer to the question: what is just in this situation? That answer is arrived at through the habit of justice and the investigation of the situation. The habit of justice is the communal sense of justice which the judge learns by his living in the community and by his study of the laws and precedents of the community which are the expression of that habit. And that habit, finally, is based on the conviction, arising from the fundamental morality of human communal experience, that the question of justice properly arises.

Language and Literary Criticism

Lonergan, Wittgenstein, and Where Language Hooks Onto the World

by Hugo Meynell

On the fundamental philosophical problem of how language is related to the world, the opinions of Wittgenstein and Lonergan are in some ways similar, in others antithetical. But I think that a great deal is to be learned from the comparison and contrast of the views of these two philosophers on the topic. Such comparison has up to now been largely lacking. This is because in general those who have concerned themselves with Lonergan's work have been philosophers of the Neo-Scholastic or phenomenological style; while it is on members of the analytic school that Wittgenstein has exerted an overwhelming influence. That the absence of detailed comparison up to the present has not been due to any lack of intrinsic interest in the topic itself, I hope to show in what follows.

Very roughly, according to the doctrine set out by Wittgenstein in the *Tractatus,* some propositions are true or false by virtue of the truth and falsity of other propositions, while others are true or false by virtue of whether they "picture" the facts of which the real world consists.[1] In the *Investigations,* this view seems largely abandoned;[2] language is to be seen against the background of human activity and

---

[1] L. Wittgenstein, *Tractatus Logico-Philosophicus* (London, 1961), 2.1-3.01.

[2] How far it is actually abandoned is disputed; Anthony Kenny, in *Wittgenstein* (Cambridge, Mass.: Harvard Univ. Press, 1973), p. 226, argues that the later doctrine of meaning as use was meant rather to supplement than to rival the picture theory. For the contrary view, cf. G.N.A. Vesey's introduction to *Understanding Wittgenstein,* ed. Vesey (New York, 1974), p. xv.

intercommunication, and the manner in which it may reflect the extra-linguistic world cannot be reduced to any such comparatively simple formula.[3] According to Lonergan at all the stages represented by his published work, the real world is what is to be known through judgments, which are to be arrived at by putting successively two types of questions, those of understanding and those of reflection, to the data of our experience. The question for understanding is that demanding a possible explanation for such a set of data; the question for reflection is that asking whether such an explanation is probably or certainly true or false.[4]

Few would dispute that some propositions are true or false by virtue of the truth or falsity of other propositions. Thus for the Jones family to be in London is for Tom Jones to be in London, Hortensia Jones to be in London, and so on and so on. But it may easily be seen that one will be involved in a vicious circle or an infinite regress if one claims that this is the case with all propositions; thus some at least, it may reasonably be maintained, must be true or false by representing or misrepresenting, picturing or failing to picture, what lies beyond language, in the world or in human experience or both. Wittgenstein in the *Tractatus* distinguished the latter class of propositions as "elementary";[5] he put it that every proposition is a "truth-function" of elementary propositions.[6] (For proposition a to be a truth-function of propositions p, q, r, is for the truth or falsity of a to be dependent on the truth or falsity of p, q, r.) According to the radical empiricist or logical positivist interpretation of the *Tractatus*, the facts pictured by elementary propositions are data of sensation.[7] Wittgenstein did not hold this view when he wrote the *Tractatus*, but he is said to have come round to it for a while later.[8]

One can see why the logical positivist interpretation of the *Tractatus* is a tempting one. Our ordinary judgments about what is the case are largely confirmed as true, or shown up as false, by experience. What could be a more natural conclusion than that these judgments are nothing but compendious ways of making a huge array of judgments, each one of which is verified or falsified by an instant of

---

[3] There is a good short summary of Wittgenstein's earlier and later philosophies by A. M. Quinton in G. Pitcher, ed., *Wittgenstein: The Philosophical Investigations* (London, 1968), pp. 1-21.

[4] A convenient short account is to be had in the first chapter of Lonergan's *Method in Theology* (London: Darton, Longman and Todd, 1972).

[5] The earliest translation had "atomic" for "elementary" propositions.

[6] *Tractatus*, 4.21, 5.

[7] The most well-known exposition of logical positivism, A. J. Ayer's *Language, Truth and Logic* (London: V. Gollancz Ltd., 1936), regards the work in this light.

[8] Cf. Quinton, p. 4; Kenny, pp. 9, 130.

experience? However, the plausibility of the *Tractatus* account of the relation of language to the world does not stand or fall with the empiricist interpretation. That I am sitting in this room now depends on various material objects being in juxtaposition with one another, which depends on various chemical elements being compounded and mixed in particular proportions, which in turn depends on protons, neutrons, electrons and so on being related to one another within a series of recurrent patterns.[9] The *Tractatus* view might be applied phenomenalistically or materialistically;[10] and it is by no means clear that this exhausts the possibilities.

Lonergan would by no means deny that we can have experiences or talk about them, or that these experiences are in a crucial way relevant to the truth or falsity of the judgments that we make. But for him the main clue to the relationship between language and extra-linguistic reality is not a hierarchy of truth-functionally related propositions, with those at the basis of the hierarchy "picturing", through experience or in some other way, the basic states of affairs of which the world consists. It is that the world, the sum-total of things and facts, is what is to be known by putting questions to the data of experience, propounding possible explanations, and accepting as probably or certainly true those explanations which best account for the data.[11] Lonergan's cognitional theory and the metaphysics erected upon it, one might say, amount to the thorough application of what Collingwood called a "logic of question and answer." [12]

Such an account would not entail a denial of the doctrine that propositions may often be truth-functionally related to one another; but it would put the emphasis very much elsewhere in approaching the problem of the relation of language or thought to the world. Lonergan would agree with the corollary of a materialist rendering of the *Tractatus* doctrine, that for a man to be sitting writing at a table, an immense number of chemical events have to be occurring, which in turn depend on an even larger number of micro-physical events.[13] And he would have no reason to contest a consequence of a phenomenalist interpretation of that doctrine, to the extent that for there to

---

[9] This thought seems to be followed through in J. J. C. Smart's *Philosophy and Scientific Realism* (London: Humanities Press, 1963).

[10] Cf. W. D. Hudson, *Ludwig Wittgenstein* (London, 1968), pp. 22, 73. J. Hartnack is cited for the view that Wittgenstein implied that the elements of reality must be empirically observable; G. E. M. Anscombe for the contrary view.

[11] Cf. B. J. F. Lonergan, *Insight: A Study of Human Understanding* (London: Darton, Longman and Todd, 1957), p. 348.

[12] Cf. R. G. Collingwood, *Autobiography* (London: Oxford Univ. Press, 1939), pp. 33, 39.

[13] On the manner in which types of states of affairs depend upon other types, cf. *Insight,* pp. 437-440.

be sensory evidence for such an occurrence, appropriate visual, aural, or tactual data have to be available in appropriate circumstances. But he would oppose very strenuously the atomism which is characteristic of the doctrine on any interpretation. On his view, for example, electrons and protons both are, and are what they are, by virtue of conformity to certain intelligible laws, which have been excogitated by physicists and verified by observation and experiment. But at the chemical, biological, and specifically human level, things and events no less exist and are what they are by virtue of conformity with intelligible laws, such as have been or may be excogitated and verified by chemists, biologists, and psychologists. The existence and occurrence of things and events, and the intelligible laws constitutive of them, at the micro-physical level, is admittedly a *necessary condition* of the existence and occurrence of things and events at the higher levels. But this does *not* imply that they are *nothing but* mere aggregates of things and events of the lowest level. If the criterion of the real existence, occurrence, or obtaining of things, events, and laws of any kind is verification of judgments arrived at by putting questions to experience, then men and animals exist no less than electrons and protons.

Few philosophers have held such a physicalist reductionism as the one just outlined; but it is important to see that similar arguments may be adduced however the "elementary facts" at the basis of the system of the *Tractatus* are concretely conceived. And the postulation of such "elementary facts" is inevitable when the relation of language to extra-linguistic reality is conceived as a matter of truth-functional connections supplemented by a more or less determinate "picturing". But if language hooks onto the world to the extent that its user intelligently conceives and reasonably judges on the basis of attention to his experience, as is the case on Lonergan's view, such postulation is quite unnecessary.

According to the *Tractatus,* all significant discourse consists of truth-functions of elementary propositions; and talk about how elementary propositions "picture" elementary facts, or indeed about how propositions may be truth-functionally related to one another, cannot itself be reduced to such truth-functions of elementary propositions. There follows the notorious consequence drawn by Wittgenstein himself, that on the criterion proposed in the *Tractatus* itself, the propositions of which the *Tractatus* consists are strictly speaking senseless; but he defends himself with the plea that his particular set of senseless propositions has the advantage over other such sets that one may employ it as a device for coming to see the world rightly.[14]

---

[14] *Tractatus,* 6.54.

A similar paradox can be derived from all forms of empiricism which are thorough and consistently worked out, and for similar reasons; one cannot in the nature of the case test by experience the meaningful non-analytic proposition that all meaningful non-analytic propositions are testable by experience.[15]

It may be protested that every account of the relation of thought or language to what is supposed to exist independently of them is bound to run into such paradoxes; but it is by no means obvious that Lonergan's account is liable to such strictures. The real world, according to him, is nothing other than what conscious subjects tend to get to know by intelligent inquiry and reasonable reflection on the basis of their experience; that is, by proposing hypotheses which might account for this experience, and selecting some of these as actually or probably the case. (For example, we have no direct experience of such aspects of the real world as the fate of Edward II, the properties of positrons, or the thoughts and feelings of our neighbors; but we can come to know about them as a result of thinking out, on the basis of the relevant experiences, possibilities as to how these things *might* be; and judging that one set of these possibilities is in each case more likely to be the case than its rivals as accounting better for these experiences.) But nothing is more intelligent and reasonable to suppose — no hypothesis accounts better for the relevant evidence — than that conscious subjects can come to make true judgments about the world by intelligent and reasonable assessment of their experience. Thus Lonergan's general account of the relation of language or thought to the real world can perfectly well be applied to itself without self-destruction.[16] And all rival accounts, if they present themselves as the most intelligent and reasonable assessment of the relevant evidence, may be said covertly to presuppose that account; whereas if they do not, there is no reason to take them seriously. It is of some historical interest that, from a point of view like Lonergan's, Wittgenstein's repudiation of Russell's earlier attention to the human subject and his judgments in favor of the propositional sign as such is to be regarded as a retrograde step.[17]

According to Anthony Kenny, it is a fundamental feature of Wittgenstein's philosophy from the period of the *Tractatus* onwards that

---

[15] For such self-destructive positions and what is to be learned form them, cf. especially G. Grisez, *Beyond the New Theism* (Notre Dame, Ind.: Univ. of Notre Dame Press, 1975).

[16] There is an amusing demonstration of the self-defeatingness of the opposed positions in *Method in Theology*, pp. 16-17.

[17] Cf. Guy Stock, "Wittgenstein on Russell's Theory of Judgment," in Vesey.

there is no *a priori* component in our knowledge of the world.[18] (There are traces of the opposite view in the early *Notebooks* [19]). What tends to do duty in Wittgenstein's later philosophy for the *a priori* is what he calls "grammar" — "deep" as opposed to "surface grammar" — which seems to consist of very general and more or less inalienable features of *our* discourse about the world. (Who "we" are is a question of some consequence; whether a particular "grammar" is intrinsic to human language as such, or whether "grammar" differs according to period, culture, or community, has been something of a crux among Wittgenstein's interpreters). We cannot justify "grammar", since it is presupposed in all justification; thus it seems that we have no grounds for saying or assuming that its structures are mirrored in the world as it might exist prior to and independently of human language.[20] So far as any "picturing" relationship remains between language and the world in this later philosophy, its poles are reversed; "grammar" determines the structure of "our" world, rather than *vice versa*.[21] Lonergan's philosophy, on the contrary, consists basically of a working-out of a certain conception of the *a priori* — briefly, that knowledge cannot but be the term of intelligent and reasonable inquiry into experience, and that the real world cannot but be what such knowledge is of. For him, the *a priori* principles must characterize the world prior to and independently of human thought as well as human thought and the language in which it is expressed. All men understand and judge on the basis of their experience; but few, even in societies which have taken that procedure far enough to yield mature sciences, have followed through its implications far enough to replace "mythic consciousness" with an articulate theory of knowledge and of reality. It is largely to this fact that the amazing variety of world views which have prevailed in different human communities is to be attributed.[22]

It is interesting to note that the corollary of Wittgenstein's early logical atomism for the understanding of causation is much the same as that of the psychological atomism of David Hume. For Hume, belief in causal connections has no better foundation than our habits of mind;[23] for Wittgenstein, superstition is belief in the causal nexus.[24] For Hume events are connected to one another by psychological

---

[18] A. Kenny, "The Ghost of the *Tractatus,*" in Vesey, p. 12.

[19] L. Wittgenstein, *Notebooks 1914-16* (Oxford: B. Blackwell, 1961).

[20] On these points, cf. Bernard Williams, "Wittgenstein and Idealism," in Vesey.

[21] Cf. Kenny, "The Ghost of the *Tractatus*"; in Vesey, p. 12.

[22] Cf. *Insight,* pp. 536-42.

[23] David Hume, *An Inquiry Concerning Human Understanding,* Section VII, Part II.

[24] *Tractatus,* 5.1361.

glue, whereas for Wittgenstein the glue is truth-functional.[25] It seems hardly necessary to point out that there are no such disturbing consequences to be inferred from Lonergan's account. The fact that I can have no more direct *experience of* a causal connection than of Edward II or of positrons does not affect the issue, if knowledge is to be had by intelligent inquiry and reasonable reflection *on the basis of* experience. I can have excellent reason to judge, on the basis of a consideration of my experience, that the occurrence of event A is due to the occurrence of event B or the agency of person C. And this implies, on Lonergan's account of what knowledge is, that one can come to know of real causal relations between the things and events which constitute the world.

It is in parts of *On Certainty,* the work on which Wittgenstein was engaged at the very end of his life, that one is most forcibly reminded of central aspects of Lonergan's theory of knowledge.[26] As Wittgenstein maintains in a number of passages in that work, one cannot properly doubt in a manner so radical that the meanings of the very words used to express the doubt are called into question.[27] Even if it were possible to doubt separately each single one of the facts presupposed by what we say and do, we could not possibly really doubt them all.[28] One can only doubt where some test of what is doubted is possible;[29] and tests presuppose what is not doubted or tested,[30] propositions which in relation to our doubts "are as it were like the hinges on which those turn."[31]

All these points are of course strongly reminiscent of those relating to scepticism made in the eleventh chapter of *Insight,* where it is pointed out that, even to defend his scepticism, the sceptic has to make a case for its being the most intelligent and reasonable option on the evidence available to experience; but to presuppose, as this does, that such in general is how one comes to know what is so, is itself destructive of scepticism.[32] In *Insight* generally, and in this chapter in particular, Lonergan is in effect showing clearly just what are the hinges of *a priori* certainty upon which doubt turns, or rather *ought to* turn. Of course, the circumstances in which doubts in fact *do*

---

[25] I cannot remember who it was that first hit on this striking analogy.

[26] L. Wittgenstein, *On Certainty* (Oxford: Blackwell, 1969), referred to as OC in subsequent notes. Chapter XI of *Insight,* in particular, may be cited by way of comparison.

[27] Cf. OC, pp. 114, 306, 369, 456, 486, 507.

[28] OC, p. 232; cf. Kenny, *Wittgenstein,* p. 206.

[29] OC, p. 125.

[30] OC, pp. 163, 337.

[31] OC, p. 341; cf. Kenny, p. 207.

[32] *Insight,* pp. 331-2.

arise notoriously differ from person to person, and from society to society; and are affected at least as much by wishes, fears, and ingrained mental habits as by the principles which Lonergan describes. A crucial question which arises with regard to Wittgenstein's views on this matter is whether one can say, in accordance with them, that there is just one set of principles in relation to which one ought to doubt, if doubt is to be employed as a useful instrument for getting at the real truth about things, as on Lonergan's view; or whether one is to infer from them that these principles vary from place to place and from time to time. That Wittgenstein seems at best to leave the way open for, at worst to assert, the latter view, is perhaps the most disturbing feature of *On Certainty;* many, whether in agreement or in disagreement, have seen what he says as implying idealism, or a thoroughgoing social relativism such that truth in statements and validity in arguments are determined in the last resort simply by the conventions of one's society.[33] Wittgenstein does say that our world-view is the inherited background against which we distinguish between true and false; pointing out that we do not come by it as a result of satisfying ourselves of its correctness.[34] And in getting someone of a more primitive outlook to adopt our worldview, he says, we do not provide him with grounds which prove its truth; rather we have to convert him to the new way of looking at the world, with appeal perhaps to its greater "simplicity" or "richness" as compared with the old one.[35] To assess these remarks from a point of view like Lonergan's, one would have to distinguish world-views which are actually maintained on the one hand, from the human conscious capacities for attentiveness, intelligence, and reasonableness whose greater or lesser application underlies all such worldviews on the other. World views as they are are determined not only by the exercise of these capacities, but also by those individual desires and fears and those group and class ideologies which tend to inhibit their exercise.[36] While it is true that we do not as individuals take on our world view mainly by the exercise of these capacities, it remains that we can use them to correct this or that aspect of what we have inherited, as in fact has been done to a notable extent by all considerable scientists, philosophers, and religious reformers. And by such corrections we tend to come closer to knowledge of what is actually the case about the world. When a person is brought from

---

[33] Cf. Williams; also David Bloor, "Wittgenstein and Mannheim on the Sociology of Mathematics," *Studies in the History and Philosophy of Science,* Vol. 4, 1973.

[34] OC, p. 94.

[35] OC, pp. 92, 286; cf. Kenny, p. 217.

[36] Cf. chapters VI, VII, XII, and XIV of *Insight;* and chapter 2 of *Method in Theology.*

one world view to another, given that he is conscientious about the matter, it will be due to conviction that the second world view is the result of a more thorough application of intelligence and reason to a wider range of experience than the first. The mention of "simplicity" and "richness" suggests that such an account of the matter would not be completely alien to one tendency at least of Wittgenstein's thought at the time he wrote *On Certainty.*

In one passage, Wittgenstein raises the question of why it is that he is tempted to call the rules of "grammar" arbitrary, in a way that those of, say, cookery are not. The answer he gives is that whereas the rules of cookery are determined by the ends to be realized by cookery, this does not apply to language and its "grammar". The case of "grammar", he says, is more like that of chess; if you follow other rules than those prescribed, you are playing another game; and the same is to be concluded if someone follows "grammatical" rules different from those of any particular set.[37] This seems true for language in general, which, as Wittgenstein notoriously insisted during the later period of his philosophy, has a large and heterogeneous collection of uses.[38] But what about that aspect of it which is concerned with stating what is the case about the world? At least the rules for the "grammar" of *this* aspect of language would seem to be determined by how far they realize an end beyond themselves, and in this sense analogous rather to those of cookery after all.

If Wittgenstein's remarks on the limits of doubt in his very last writings are reminiscent of some aspects of Lonergan's philosophy, the accounts of mental events and activities given by the two philosophers appear at first sight to be as opposed as they could possibly be. What is perhaps the central thesis of the whole of Lonergan's thought, that there is a generic resemblance between all cases of coming to understand, is directly contradicted by Wittgenstein.[39] And the whole tenor of Wittgenstein's later philosophy is to discourage the use of introspection as a device for solving problems in the philosophy of mind; whereas Lonergan, though he opposes one kind of introspection, is strongly committed to another.[40] It is central to his position that, if we are to get the hang of human thought and its relation to the world, we must attend to our own conscious activities of questioning, coming to understand, weighing evidence, judging, and so on.

---

[37] L. Wittgenstein, *Philosophische Grammatik* (Oxford: B. Blackwell 1969), p. 189; and *Zettel* (Oxford: B. Blackwell, 1967), p. 320; cf. Kenny, p. 177.

[38] Cf. especially L. Wittgenstein, *Philosophical Investigations* (Oxford: B. Blackwell, 1958), I, p. 12, where language is compared with the various handles in the cabin of a locomotive.

[39] *Grammatik,* p. 65; cf. *Investigations,* I, 151-5; Kenny, p.142.

[40] On the two types of introspection, cf. especially *Insight,* pp. 320-324.

It may appear that the collection of arguments which Wittgenstein directed against the notion of a "private language" is crucial to this issue.[41] However, I think that this appearance is deceptive; and that even assuming the validity of the arguments, the procedure followed by Lonergan is not really impugned. It is important to be clear about what Wittgenstein means by a "private language". On his own account, it is a language of which the words "refer to what can only be known to the person speaking: to his immediate private sensations."[42] Of course, if the manner in which the meanings of words are learned is envisaged in this way, doubt inevitably arises as to whether the private sensations from which one person has learned the meaning of, say, "blue", are at all similar to those from which another has learned it — since in the nature of the case the sensations in question could never be compared. While Wittgenstein, as Kenny has expressed it, disagreed with behaviorists in his conviction "that particular mental events could occur without accompanying bodily behavior," he agreed with them that "the possibility of describing mental events at all depends on their having, in general, an expression in behavior."[43]

Now Lonergan nowhere states or implies that we could speak about having experiences, wondering about them, hitting on a possible explanation of them, and so on, *unless* such conscious acts of ours had a characteristic expression in external behavior; but he does insist that, given that we can thus come to talk about them, each of us can deepen his own apprehension of their nature and significance by attending to his own performance of them. The whole of *Insight* is an invitation to do just this; and it seems to me very regrettable that some have been deterred from accepting this invitation through a mistaken belief about what was demonstrated by Wittgenstein's arguments. And it is at first sight odd to deny, at least without very strong reasons indeed, that the kind of attention recommended by Lonergan is ever possible or in the least fruitful; that, for example, I may advert to the fact that I judged on a particular occasion out of habit or through fear or desire rather than as the evidence required, and may attend with particular care to what I am about when a similar case next arises. And it should be emphasized that Lonergan would agree with Wittgenstein, against radical empiricists and followers of Descartes, that what judgment is primarily about, and hence what the statements of language in the first instance refer to, is the public world of things and events. Equivalent to Wittgenstein's

---

[41] *Investigations,* I, 243; Kenny, p. 179.
[42] Cf. Kenny, pp. 179, 16-17.
[43] Kenny, p. 17.

insistence on the essential publicity of language is Lonergan's assertion that it is at the level of judgment that we apprehend a shared and public world.[44] And Lonergan's view that knowledge is a matter of judgment with good reason, and not merely of experience, is parallel to Wittgenstein's that knowledge is possible only on matters about which doubt is conceivable. That I am enduring a pain here and now, or having an impression of red, is not something which I could conceivably be mistaken about; and therefore, according to Wittgenstein, I cannot be said to know it.[45] On Lonergan's view, one might put it that the paradigm cases of knowledge are to the effect that something *is so* in the public world, of which the *evidence* is apt to be provided in sensation; the knowledge *that* one was having this or that sensation would be allowed, but as a special as opposed to a typical case.[46]

It seems worthwhile very briefly, in conclusion, to compare the views of Lonergan and Wittgenstein on the practice of philosophy itself, on ethics, and on religion. From the point of view set out by the *Tractatus*, philosophical, ethical, and religious propositions are all strictly speaking senseless. However, as Anthony Quinton has pointed out, the senselessness of such propositions is on this account deplorable in varying degrees.[47] Least excusable is the senselessness of traditional metaphysics. In contrast to this stands the senselessness attributed to the propositions of the *Tractatus* itself, which enable one to come to see the world rightly and finally to eschew senselessness. In yet a third category there is the senselessness of those utterances by which one tries to indicate what is inexpressible, yet apparently to be taken seriously; as in ethical and religious utterances. According to the view advanced in the *Investigations*, the business of philosophy is to examine language as tt is actually used, and to leave everything as it is—with the significant exception of the language of traditional philosophy, which is symptomatic of a misunderstanding of these uses. On Lonergan's view, traditional philosophies all illustrate a fact which most of them fail to assert about the relation of thought and the language in which it is expressed to the world.[48] If the world is what is to be known by intelligent inquiry and reasonable reflection on the basis of experience, empiricism exaggerates the role of experience in knowing; while idealism,

---

[44] *Insight*, p. 378.

[45] *Investigations*, II, p. 221; Kenny, p. 185.

[46] For similar points, cf. R. Bambrough, "How to Read Wittgenstein," in Vesey, pp. 130-2; and A. J. Ayer, "Wittgenstein on Certainty," ibid., pp. 229 ff.

[47] Quinton, pp. 7-8.

[48] *Investigations*, I, p. 124; *Insight*, pp. 385-9.

in seeing what is wrong with this, exaggerates the creative role of understanding, and overlooks the manner in which its speculations are to be controlled by reasonable reflection. One might put it that while empiricism represents a crude view of how our knowledge corresponds with the real world, idealism, in rightly rejecting this crude view, is driven to abandon the truth that such correspondence is possible — that there is a world of things and facts prior to and independent of human thought and language to which these aspire to conform.[49] As to ethics, Lonergan believes that truth about moral matters tends to be arrived at by intelligent and reasonable questioning of the relevant evidence in much the same way as the truth about other matters; one tends to get to know and do what is good so far as one attends to the evidence on the long-term desires and needs of all who may be affected by one's actions, and does not allow one's attentiveness, intelligence, and reasonableness to be blocked by the biases deriving from one's personal circumstances or those of one's group or class.[50] When it comes to religion, Lonergan argues that reflection on the world, as having the nature which it must have if we are to get to know it, provides a basis by which one may establish whether or not it is intelligent and reasonable to believe in a God; while, given that there is a God, other religious questions may be tackled by asking what a God *might* have done, and possibly actually *has* done, if one examines the relevant historical evidence, to remedy the plight of mankind.[51]

It is a cardinal doctrine of the later Wittgenstein that ordinary language is all right, and certainly cannot be improved upon by philosophers. From Lonergan's point of view, the presuppositions of ordinary language and the common sense which underlies it certainly cannot be all wrong; but it needs science and a fully critical philosophy to set out accurately what are their scope and limits.[52] Ordinary language as it actually exists at any given time and place not only encapsulates the accumulated experience, understanding, and judgment of the community within which it prevails;[53] it also conceals the neglect of experience, the flight from intelligence and reason, which have characterized that society or the dominant

---

[49] On the misunderstanding of the correspondence theory of truth, cf. Lonergan, *A Second Collection* (Philadelphia: Westminster), pp. 14-16.

[50] Cf. *Insight,* chapter XVIII; *Method in Theology,* chapter 2.

[51] Cf. *Insight,* chapters XIX and XX.

[52] On the scope and limits of common sense, cf. *Insight,* pp. 175-81, 293-99, 416-21.

[53] Cf. J. L. Austin, *Sense and Sensibilia* (Oxford: Clarendon, 1962), p. 63. "It is advisable always to bear in mind that the distinctions embodied in our vast and, for the most part, relatively ancient stock of ordinary words are neither few nor always very obvious, and almost never just arbitrary."

groups within it. Thus philosophy has no business leaving everything as it is. In this respect Lonergan's thinking is more reminiscent of that of Marx than of that of Wittgenstein. In a striking and memorable analogy, Wittgenstein likens language to a city, the old center of which, with its haphazardly arranged streets and squares, is comparable to ordinary language, and the regularly planned suburban landscape to the technical and specialist languages of the sciences.[54] Applying the analogy from a point of view like Lonergan's, one might put it that the modern planner must not merely add the boulevards and supermarkets of suburbia, leaving the ancient city just as it was; he also has to remove health hazards, and make modern comfort possible, in the older part of the city.

Lonergan provides an account of how, by means of our thought and language, we may come to think and speak the truth about a world which exists independently of and prior to our thought and language about it. His account does not self-destruct, in the manner of the *Tractatus;* and seems open to acknowledgment of the various roles played by language, apart from speaking the truth about things, insisted on by the later Wittgenstein, without the tendency to relativism plausibly ascribed to him.[55] A student of Lonergan who admired Wittgenstein might put it that the former had provided a Hegelian synthesis of the thesis and antithesis represented by the latter's earlier and later philosophies.

---

[54] *Investigations,* I, p. 18; cf. Kenny, p. 155.
[55] On various functions of meanings, cf. *Method in Theology,* chapter 3.

The Question of Belief in Literary Criticism: Prospectus for a Systematic Approach[1]

by Mary Gerhart

The question of belief is generally understood to be an affair of the religious consciousness. Yet whether one states one's position as a belief or as an unbelief, the same issues determine its intelligibility and its relation to faith. I shall try to show in this essay that by examining what has happened to the question as it has been raised in the field of literary criticism, one has a new way of retrieving and reformulating the issues in whatever field disciplined reflection occurs, as well as in the field of religion.

This essay has two parts. The first part is a brief historical-critical sketch of the question of belief in Anglo-American criticism from 1920 to the present. Here, the knowledgeable reader will recognize my utilization of Bernard Lonergan's epistemology, specifically his explication of consciousness, to identify the issues in the early debates over the question of belief—issues which I argue, persist implicitly in literary criticism even when the question of belief is not itself explicit. The second part of the essay is an attempt to reformulate the question of belief by readdressing each of the issues raised in part one and to redefine belief in the light of those issues.

---

[1] The author's book-length development of this approach is published as *The Question of Belief in Literary Criticism: An Introduction to the Hermeneutical Theory of Paul Ricoeur* (Stuttgart: Akademischer Verlag Hans-Dieter Heinz, 1979).

The question of belief is considerably more complicated today than fifty years ago when T. S. Eliot remarked that the question is probably quite insoluble.[2] Meyer Abrams, for example, in his English Institute essay of 1958, reminds us that the problem of belief, in one or another formulation, has been present since the beginning of criticism. Perhaps more importantly, Abrams cautions that we inherit not only the problem but the largely unvoiced aims and assumptions which control the way it is posed and answered.[3]

It seems clear that each generation must reflect on the question of belief anew in relation to the science, culture, and history of its own time. This is especially evident today in view of the extensive specialization of language. Although it has been conventional to understand the problem of belief almost exclusively in a religious or ethical sense, there is good reason to suspect that to understand it in contemporary literary criticism will involve other disciplines as well.

My interest in the problem proceeds from the now generally acknowledged recognition that, while religious discussions of belief have paid too little attention to the factor of imagination, literary critical discussions have in general all too exclusively taken imagination as their focus. Moreover, if literary critics have not excluded the specific problem of belief from their discussions altogether, they have often naively slighted its importance. By pointing out the inadequacies of the positions of certain major literary critics, I shall argue against the nineteenth century as well as contemporary notion that, traditional religion being now in irreparable ruins, it is to literature that we must turn for the interpretation of our highest destinies. For it seems to me that whether modern theory reckons with the question of belief under the aegis of religious or literary criticism, just how literature enables us to arrive at propositions about "our highest destiny" is the crucial phenomenon to be understood.[4] At the same time, I am wagering that only by means of an adequate formulation

---

[2] T. S. Eliot, "Shakespeare and the Stoicism of Seneca," *Selected Essays, 1917-32* (New Edition; New York: Harcourt, Brace and Company, 1932), p. 118. For an excellent summary of the question of belief in literary criticism, see the entry, "Belief, Problem of," in Alex Preminger, *Encyclopedia of Poetry and Poetics* (Princeton, N.J.: Princeton Univ. Press, 1965), pp. 74-76, where Murray Krieger points out that the formulation of the question of belief depends on the view taken toward poetic truth. In turn, the relation of poetic truth to the "truth of actual reality as maintained by the reader...has been seen to be crucial to our valuing of the poem."

[3] Meyer Abrams, ed., "Belief and the Suspension of Disbelief," *Literature and Belief: English Institute Essays* (New York: Columbia Univ. Press, 1958), pp. 1-2.

[4] See Matthew Arnold, "The Study of Poetry," *Essays in Criticism,* Second Series (London and New York: Macmillan and Company, 1891), for a statement of the classical position advocating the substitution of poetry for religion. Curiously enough, it has been Arnold's polarization of poetry and religion, rather than his argument for commitment to criticism, that is best remembered.

of the question of belief in literary criticism will there be the possibility of a satisfactory theological treatment of that question in relation to written texts, both "sacred" and "secular."

My historical-critical analysis of the question of belief spans three generations. If one begins with the question of belief at a point in Anglo-American criticism where it was discussed in a highly self-conscious way, one invariably returns to the T. S. Eliot-I. A. Richards debate of the 1920's, where the context of the discussion was a *practical* one. In essence they asked, How does agreement or disagreement with the author's beliefs affect the reader's enjoyment and understanding of a poem? Northrop Frye represents the critics of the '40's and '50's who transposed the question to a *theoretical* level: How is criticism a science, Frye asked, and how does it relate to other sciences? More recently, there are the hermeneutical critics, such as E. D. Hirsch, who seek *normative* principles for the interpretation of meaning.

I will be setting forth the problem of belief in three issues: one, an issue of meaning pertaining to the understanding of beliefs as they are embodied in literature; two, an issue of verification involving the truth or falsity of such beliefs; and three, an issue of commitment concerning investment in such beliefs. These three issues become closely identified with more conventional philosophical problems in criticism. The problem of meaning is rooted in the philosophical problem of the dichotomy between feeling and thought. The problem of verification is attached to the dispute over polysemy. And the classical problem of commitment is related to the need to argue for and arbitrate among various principles of interpretation. The issues, I maintain, remain constant among the conceptions of the question of belief posed by the three representative groups of Anglo-American critics I will discuss, even though one or another issue takes precedence as the question passes from open debate, through a transposition of status, to the beginnings of a retrieval. Let us examine each of these positions in turn.

I. An Historical-Critical Sketch of the Question of Belief, 1920 to the Present

I. A. Richards and T. S. Eliot afford us some of the best common sense reflections on the question. The progress of Eliot's considerations on the issue of meaning, which for him pertained to how beliefs are embodied in literature, can best be followed in his three essays on Dante in 1920, 1929, and 1950. In the 1920 essay, he is responding to Paul Valéry, who, according to Eliot, reduces the function of poetry to that of producing "states" in the reader.[5] Against Valéry's conception of poetics, Eliot asserts that most great poetry is composed upon some belief or philosophy, even if the latter happens to be — by itself — only "odds and ends of still life and stage properties." He is ambivalent about the separation of poetry from thought, holding on the one hand that the poem is enriched by the thought informing it, and on the other that the best poets do no "real" thinking. In the 1929 essay, noting that most readers are not at all disturbed at the discrepancy between their own and the author's beliefs, Eliot modifies his previous position. Here, he points out that the *intensity* of the poem is its most important element and sees *meaning* as contributing to that intensity. Indeed, he says, the test of genuine poetry is that it can communicate before it is understood. In this later view, "clear visual images are given much more intensity by having meaning."[6] This leads him to state what I consider to be the key insight of his position: "Every precise emotion tends toward intellectual formulation."[7]

As several studies of Eliot have asserted, the issue of commitment becomes more important in his later work.[8] In his 1950 essay on Dante, for example, he speaks of his indebtedness, or commitment, to that poet as a matter of fact — a debt which had accumulated over many years of re-reading and appreciation.[9] His commitment to Dante's poetry, however, contrasts with his understanding of *religious* commitment, which is closely allied to the principle of orthodoxy. For Eliot, the issue of commitment involves the "holding" of some beliefs rather than others.

For Richards, *verification* is the paramount issue. He opens his discussion of the question of belief in *Principles of Literary Criticism* (1924) with the first of several distinctions he makes between different kinds of belief.[10] Although his continual attention to the issue of

---

[5] See especially Eliot's response to Richards' formulation of the question of belief: Notes to Section Two of the essay on Dante in *Selected Essays,* pp. 229-31.

[6] Eliot, *Selected Essays,* pp. 199-237, esp. p. 218.

[7] Ibid., pp. 115-16.

[8] Cf., for example, Joseph D. Margolis, *T. S. Eliot's Intellectual Development, 1922-1939* (Chicago and London: The Univ. of Chicago Press, 1972).

[9] Eliot, *To Criticize the Critic* (New York: Farrar, Straus and Giroux, 1965), esp. pp. 125-26.

[10] I. A. Richards, *Principles of Literary Criticism* (London: K. Paul, Trench, Trubner and Co., Ltd; New York: Harcourt, Brace and Co., Inc., 1925 (1924)), esp. pp. 272-87. Richards' initial reflections on the issue of verification are in many respects similar to those discussed in the British linguistic analysts' debate about ten years later. See, for example, the introduction to the second edition of Alfred Jules Ayer, *Language, Truth and Logic* (New York: Dover Publications, Inc., 1952), pp. 5-26.

verification eventually leads him to do philosophical reflection in his later work, his earliest and most often quoted position on the issue is also his most radical: "It is evident that the bulk of poetry consists of statements which only the foolish would think of attempting to verify. They are not the kind of things which can be verified." In this first essay on belief, Richards attempts to differentiate between emotive and scientific belief. Scientific beliefs, he thinks, refer to some object whereas emotive beliefs are objectless and are simply directly toward feelings and attitudes themselves. The early Richards' reason for making this distinction is pedagogical rather than theoretical: he thinks it necessary to develop "a habit of mind which allows both reference and the development of attitudes their proper independence."[11] Later, in *Coleridge and Imagination* (1934) he overcomes all previous distinctions in his definition of belief as "Accordant Action," which for him includes intellectual assent as well as feelings and attitudes.

The second stage of reflection, which emphasizes the theoretical status of the question of belief, is best represented by Northrop Frye. One way of plotting the scene for his position is that which R. S. Crane attempted in his 1952 Lecture at the University of Toronto. One group of critics, he says, try to find in the poem "the primary intuition which had enabled its poet to synthesize his materials into an ordered whole," whereas other critics approach the poem with certain *a priori* concepts, in search of rhetorical or mythological meaning. The latter method Crane calls "dialectical criticism," since it supposedly employs two critical principles, one formal and the other didactic; it is, as he says with some distaste, a criticism that has "special interests" of an "extraliterary" kind.[12] Among the dialecticians named by Crane, Northrop Frye is preeminent. His position is particularly important: influenced as he was by Crane's formulation of theoretical criticism, Frye declares that the question of belief ought to be excluded from literary criticism:

> In belief you're continually concerned with questions of truth or reality: you can't believe anything unless you can say "this is so." But literature never makes any statement of that kind: what the poet and novelist say is more like "let's assume this situation." So there can never be any religion of poetry or any set of beliefs founded on literature.[13]

---

[11] Richards, *Principles of Literary Criticism,* pp. 273, 278, 281.

[12] R. S. Crane, *The Languages of Criticism and the Structure of Poetry* (Toronto: The Univ. of Toronto Press, 1953), esp. p. 146.

[13] Frye, *The Educated Imagination* (Bloomington: Indiana University Press, 1964), pp. 76-77.

Nevertheless, in spite of his exclusion of the question of belief from literary criticism, Frye deals with the same issues that Richards and Eliot raised, that is, the issues of meaning, verification, and commitment, even though he formulates them differently. Whereas Richards, for example, is preoccupied with the kinds of claims that may be made regarding the truth status of literature, Frye takes the "truth" of literary experience for granted, and for him, the great question is not how literary meaning is to be verified but rather how it is to be distinguished from historical, philosophical, or scientific meaning. "Belief" in his view obscures the problems of polysemy (multiple meaning) and eclecticism (multiple critical methods), which he considers to be fundamental to all literary interpretation. Nevertheless, Frye himself can be interpreted as having provided a new possibility for reconsidering the problem of belief in *Anatomy of Criticism* (1949) where he proposes that literary criticism be reconceived systematically as a science.[14] That is, his own categorical exclusion of the question of belief on the assumption that it is a threat to imagination is to be questioned on the basis of his own more extensive view of criticism.

The third stage of reflection, which brings linguistic and hermeneutical theory to bear on the question, brings us to the present. While Richards, Eliot, and Frye are writing about the question of belief in terms of "pure" critical theory, other critics since 1940 attempt to broaden the very foundations of literary criticism by means of philosophical inquiry. Instead of focusing directly on the issues disclosed in the earlier discussions, these latter critics deal with more general problems, such as the relation of feeling to thought and the analysis of mythic form. The earliest philosophical critics were the Neo-Kantians, such as Ernst Cassirer and Susanne Langer, distinguished for their work on symbolic and mythic forms of thought. Of all that should be said about the Neo-Kantian contribution to criticism, there is time here only to reiterate what is best known about them—they effect a radical shift from the notion of truth to that of meaning. They insist on the credibility of mythic form and deemphasize the need for propositional form in belief. For this same reason, however, the Neo-Kantians have not been very helpful in providing theoretical principles for criticism.

The more recent hermeneutical critics, distinguished by their attempts to formulate principles of meaning and criticism, hold that the problem of interpretation has priority over the problem of

---

[14] Frye, *The Anatomy of Criticism*, p. 14. Cf. Premise Four below for another scientific conception of literary criticism.

myth.¹⁵ Theologians influenced by Heidegger, for example, have in their religious criticism taken the spoken word as the model for principles of interpretation.¹⁶ E. D. Hirsch, an American literary critic influenced by Husserl, takes the written word as the starting point of his hermeneutical theory and claims that the only stable norm in criticism is the intention of the author.¹⁷ Hirsch's main contribution has been to show how the goal of interpretation is best stated as a matter of probability rather than of certainty.

In summary, three issues have dominated the discussion of the question of belief in American criticism since 1920: an issue of meaning pertaining to how beliefs are embodied in literary texts; an issue of verification, pertaining either to the truth and falsity of such beliefs or to the difference between literary and other kinds of meaning; an issue of commitment, pertaining to the "holding" of some beliefs rather than others. These issues, however, have not been presented in a systematic relation to one another. I wish to suggest, therefore, how a general theory of interpretation, or hermeneutics, enables us profitably to reformulate and interrelate these issues.

II. An Outline of the Question of Belief Reformulated

The following five premises comprise the substance of my reconstruction of the question of belief in literary criticism. One, a phenomenological distinction between first and second naiveté is helpful for understanding the act of belief. Two, following upon this distinction, the traditional object of belief in literary texts may be understood as a "possible-mode-of-being-in-the-world." Three, within hermeneutics, or a general theory of interpretation, the issues disclosed in the earlier discussions of belief can be redefined. Four, the implication of the question of belief for religious and literary critics is that they have similar methodological responsibilities toward the literary text. Five, having been saturated by means of hermeneutical reflection on texts, philosophical reflection has the task of arbitrating the cognitive (or truth) status of belief. The first two premises define

---

¹⁵ Cf. Stanley Romaine Hopper and David L. Miller, eds., *Interpretation: The Poetry of Meaning* (New York: Harcourt, Brace and World, Inc., 1967), pp. xivff.

¹⁶ See, for example, Gerhard Ebeling's essay, "Word of God and Hermeneutic" in James Robinson and John Cobb, Jr., eds., *The New Hermeneutic* (New York, Evanston and London: Harper and Row, Publishers, 1964), esp. pp. 93-94. For an excellent evaluation of theological uses of Heidegger's theory, see George Steiner's *Martin Heidegger* (New York: Viking Press, 1978); for a critical analysis of literary theorists' employment of Heidegger, see Robert Magliola's *Phenomenology and Literature* (West Lafayette: Purdue Univ. Press, 1977), esp. pp. 57-80.

¹⁷ E. D. Hirsch, *Validity in Interpretation*. See also the eight critical articles of his theory of interpretation in *Genre*, I (July, 1968), and his response to them in *Genre*, II (March, 1969).

the terms of the problem, and the last two state the implications of and conditions for successfully implementing them.

I have found contemporary hermeneutical theory to provide the best framework for reformulating the question of belief intelligibly for our time. Paul Ricoeur, in particular, has brought together some of the most important aspects of continental and Anglo-American traditions of thought. Along with Heidegger and Gadamer, he stands in the Greek and biblical hermeneutical traditions, which can be interpreted as having taken two decisive moves since the beginning of the nineteenth century. These shifts are from regional to general hermeneutics, best seen in Schleiermacher and Dilthey, and from general to fundamental hermeneutics, most evident in Gadamer's and Heidegger's subordination of epistemological considerations to ontological ones. In this brief summary, I shall indicate the usefulness of some aspects of Ricoeur's theory for addressing the issues raised in part one, specifically, for the task of interrelating the issues of meaning, verification, and commitment.

First Premise: Ricoeur's distinction between first and second naiveté is helpful for understanding the phenomenon of belief. Ricoeur initially presents belief in relation to the essential structure of the human, that is, in the dynamic relationship of the voluntary and the involuntary.[18] He sees belief as being most like other expressions of judgment—like surmise, wager, or discernment. Accordingly, we may say that the language of belief, as potentially the most complex form of judgment, attempts to expose the transition between primordial feeling and its development in consciousness. In this sense, language is intrinsic to meaning, that is, to the tentative meanings of "the network of signs covering our field of perception, action and living."[19] Since the primordial can be *known* only on the side of consciousness, the other side remains obscure, blind, and possibly illusory.[20] All that can be known is that which appears, that is, the significant gestures and words of meaning.[21] Any gesture, word, or belief can be said to be meaningful as soon as we dwell on the fact that we have noticed it.

If everyday life, events, action remain on the level of the nonreflective and the pre-critical, the expressions of faith are said to be beliefs of first naiveté, because they spring from "primitive consciousness" or the natural attitude:

---

[18] See Ricoeur, *Freedom and Nature: The Voluntary and the Involuntary* (Chicago: The Univ. of Chicago Press, 1966), pp. 173-74, 180.

[19] Ricoeur, "New Developments in Phenomenology in France: the Phenomenology of Language," *Social Research*, XXXIV (Spring, 1967), pp. 8, 11.

[20] Ricoeur, *The Symbolism of Evil*, pp. 7-10.

[21] In the context of inquiry and reflection (as distinct from the context of undifferentiated experience), conscious, specified meanings can be distinguished from their initial meaning*fulness* (i.e., plenitude of meaning or polysemy).

> For if I lose myself in the world, I am then ready to treat myself as a thing of the world. The thesis of the world is a sort of blindness in the very heart of seeing. What I call living is hiding myself as naive consciousness within the existence of all things.

The difference between first and second naiveté is best understood in terms of contrasting intentionalities: first naiveté is the forgetting of consciousness; second naiveté is consciousness discovering itself as given.[22]

According to Ricoeur first naiveté, or a literal understanding of traditional beliefs and myths, has been irremediably lost for contemporary adults. But lest we think that a critical understanding — that is, second naiveté — is by itself sufficient, he points out that just as there was in first naiveté the endless reengagement of the natural attitude upon objects, so too, there can be in second naiveté a self-defeating concentration on critical consciousness: "this naiveté may be more difficult to overcome than that of the natural attitude. An even more tenacious illusion imprisons it in the very matrix of its subjectivity."[23] In other words, the vanity of the Ego as existing, thinking, and positing itself is by itself a sterile consciousness. Fascinated with itself, it cannot "receive the nourishing and inspiring spontaneity, which breaks the circle of the constant return to itself."[24]

With this brief analysis as a foundation, we can redefine faith as a new mobility between first and second naiveté. In this relationship, all experience can be described as movement from ground to recognition of ground. As such, all experience is initially meaningful, that is, a ground of potential meanings. With regard to the problem of interpretation, a literary text might be approached with first or second naiveté, depending on the purpose or mood of the reader. But the formal critical task of interpreting the text demands that the interpreter have an attitude of second naiveté toward certain expressions of belief in the text, or toward the whole text taken as proposing a kind of belief.

Second Premise: The object of belief is best formulated as a "possible-way-of-being-in-the-world."

It is essential to consider the object of belief in relation to a believing subject or person, but the converse is also true: unless we are able to consider the object of belief abstractly, in relation to other meanings, we run the risk of becoming a prey to irrational beliefs, superstitions,

---

[22] Ricoeur, *Husserl: An Analysis of His Phenomenology* (Evanston: Northwestern Univ. Press, 1967), p. 20.
[23] Ibid.
[24] Ricoeur, *Freedom and Nature,* p. 14.

or fears. The first premise was an important preliminary to our reformulation of the question of belief, for in earlier discussions the verifiability of belief was denied because the object of belief was detached from the performance of the believer. In order to overcome this detachment of object from the believer, it is necessary in the second premise to presume a fundamental confidence in common human experience taken as the theoretical context for all objects of belief.

The distinction that Ricoeur makes between discourse and written texts is helpful for understanding the object of belief in literary texts:

> In spoken discourse...the intention of the speaking subject and the meaning of the discourse overlap each other in such a way that it is the same thing to understand what the speaker means and what his discourse means. With written discourse the author's intention and the meaning of the text cease to coincide....The tie between the speaker and the discourse is not abolished but distanced and complicated....What the text says now matters more than what the author meant to say.[25]

By virtue of this distance, beliefs, in the literary text, are best conceived of as having broken their moorings from the author's beliefs, either as man or as poet (to use Eliot's distinction).[26] The proper goal of interpretation is not the author's experience nor even his/her understanding of it, even if shared by a majority of interpreters (which is Hirsch's norm).[27] Nor is the goal of interpretation merely to analyze the text. The fact of its being a written text allows for the possibility of continual reenactment of meaning. We can say, then, that the written text surpasses the immediate situation common to the author and his/her hypothetical readers, and presents a sense, an ideal meaning to beliefs which call for verification—"an ensemble of references which can constitute a world of its own." In turn, we shall

---

[25] Ricoeur, "Interpretation Theory" (unpublished paper). See also Ricoeur, *Interpretation Theory: Discourse and the Surplus of Meaning* (Fort Worth: The Texas Christian Univ. Press, 1976), pp. 29-30.

[26] Eliot, *Selected Essays,* p. 118. Eliot's distinction allows for a distanciation between the private and artistic life of the poet. Ricoeur's theory not only allows for a more significant distanciation, but also explains its function in the art of interpretation. See Ricoeur, "The Hermeneutical Function of Distanciation," *Philosophy Today,* XVIII (Summer, 1973), pp. 129-41. One might say that in this sense the poem "creates" the poet.

[27] Ricoeur agrees basically with Hirsch's notion of "validation." He differs from Hirsch on the *normativeness* of authorial intention and is able to demonstrate, as Hirsch cannot, the role of the sciences in interpretation. I have retained the term "verification" in the following discussion, in order to be faithful to Richards' classical statement of the issue and to suggest how Ricoeur's use of the sciences as diagnostics and notion of appropriation overcomes Richards' dichotomy between emotive and scientific beliefs.

see that these non-situational references are "offered as possible modes-of-being, as symbolic dimensions of our being-in-the-world."²⁸ *Third Premise: In the context of hermeneutics, or general interpretation theory, we are able to reformulate the issues of meaning, verification, and commitment, now interrelated as the first, second, and third stages of interpretation, respectively.*

As a second level discourse about interpretation, hermeneutics provides a framework for reformulating the question of belief in literary criticism. Moreover, by giving boundaries to the foregoing discussions of the phenomenon and object of belief, hermeneutics allows for the possibility of interrelating the issues raised earlier in my historical-critical analysis of the question of belief. Although these issues are best comprehended in terms of their interrelationship, they are here presented as a heuristic progression from one stage of interpretation to the next.

Whereas the earlier critics were concerned with identifying beliefs embodied in the literary work, the first issue of meaning is better understood as the task of determining the meaningfulness of the literary text. The new critics' description of the text in terms of rhetorical or linguistic analysis can be seen as available models for this first stage of criticism, in which the reader gives an account of the aesthetic effect of the work. Such an account leads to a reflective discovery of what Eliot calls the *sensibilité* of work, or in Frye's terms — its subtlety, delicacy, refinement — or perhaps even its "terrible clairvoyance."²⁹ This epoché — the initial suspension of the desire to make sense in terms of known systems of meaning, or to refer to objects, events, or ideas outside the literary work — is precisely the condition of the possibility for reflecting upon the work as self-contained and autonomous. Theoretically, it becomes possible for the reader to find any belief meaningful because of the aesthetic mode of presentation.

Whereas the earlier critics were concerned with the truth or falsity of beliefs embodied in poetry, the second issue is better understood as the task of verifying the meaningfulness and sense of the text. In the first stage of interpretation, sense and meaning begin to emerge

---

²⁸ Ricoeur, "Metaphor and the Main Problem of Hermeneutics," *New Literary History*, 6 (Autumn, 1975), pp. 95-110.

²⁹ Frye, *T. S. Eliot* (Edinburgh and London: Oliver and Boyd, 1963), p. 28. Throughout Premise Three it should be noticed that Frye's concern for the essentially *literary* qualities of meaning, for the preservation of polysemy, and for the utilization of multiple critical methods — which considerations he finds missing in previous discussions of the question of belief in literary studies — is taken into account and satisfied in Ricoeur's theory.

from the descriptive account of the work and to set a certain direction to the reader's thought. It is the business of the second stage to explain the sense, that is, to specify what meanings may be present and to account for them in the text taken as a whole. The specification of meanings initiates the formal process of verification and relates literary criticism to the other sciences which also claim to explain the literary text. At this stage, polysemy, or multiple meanings, manifests itelf as a problem. The direction of my argument is that the multiple meanings of texts makes possible the multiple meanings of smaller elements, such as words: every text is born out of and into multiple worlds of meaning. To cope with the problem of multiple meaning, the interpreter is obliged to pass through the various worlds of meaning in order to set forth, explicitly or implicitly, the possible meanings of the text.

Ricoeur's notion of the sciences as diagnostics provides us with a useful way of understanding the verification process, which, in fact, does occur in all good practical criticism, but which, for lack of adequate formulation, is misunderstood or understood only vaguely as common sense in theoretical criticism. To conceive of the sciences as diagnostics is to avail ourselves of a patterned background and a range of possible meanings. To employ the sciences as diagnostics is to afford opportunities for "thickening" the significance of what has emerged as being meaningful at the first stage of description. It is also to provide contexts and conflicts for the emergence of new meaning.[30]

The interpreter's construction of the meanings of the text might well be understood as a model for understanding the text, which previously lacked any mapping. If the text, to use Frye's terms, is a hypothetical situation—a "suppose this is"—then the constructed meaning can be understood as a hypothetical model—a "suppose this is the meaning of the text." The model, in turn, enables the interpreter to talk about the complexities of the text as a single object and even provides a context for communicating what cannot be otherwise understood about it.

Whereas the earlier critics were concerned with the investment in some beliefs rather than others, the third issue is better understood

---

[30] That is, texts "speak" not so much of embodied, known meanings and beliefs, but of "possible worlds and of possible ways of orienting oneself in those worlds." (See Ricoeur, "Metaphor and the Main Problem of Hermeneutics": "speak" is used figuratively here, for Ricoeur finds the dialogue model of text-interpretation inadequate for the general consideration of the problem.) For an explication of Ricoeur's use of the sciences as "diagnostics," see the author's "Paul Ricoeur's Notion of Diagnostics: Toward a Philosophy of the Human," *Journal of the American Academy of Religion* (September, 1977), pp. 137-56.

as having to do with *appropriating* the text as it refers to (1) a model for self-understanding, (2) a model for a way-of-being-in-the-world. These two models, self-referent and world-referent, are to be taken as the respective subject- and object-poles of both emergent and ideal meaning. The sense or meaning of the text, having been constructed in the second stage of interpretation, is no longer hidden but now is a model held out in front of the reader, pointing to a possible world. In this way, the third stage of interpretation becomes the grasping of world-propositions which have been opened up by the non-situational references of the text.

What does this reformulation mean for "belief" as it has been viewed traditionally? In this schema, belief is not properly referred to as proposition—in the sense of its being proposed for appropriation—until the third stage of interpretation. For the interpreter's own expression of the multiple meanings of the text, his/her judgment of what is probable for self-reference and world-reference is a late moment in the completed performance of belief. And these propositions are not so much about "things" or "the external world" (as they were in the earlier discussions) as they are propositions which point through meaning toward "limit situations, death, suffering, sexuality." The factor of giving assent to propositions, so much emphasized in earlier religious discussions at least, is still operative, but in a much more complex way than the simple alternative "yes" or "no". The judgments made during the process of conflicting interpretations help us to see the possibility of varying degrees of assent to particular expressions of life-meaning, as well as of denial to others. Assent to particular meanings—dependent, of course, upon the way the reader understands the text, the act of intepretation, and the meaning of assent itself—then, would seem always to result in an "irreversible gain of truthfulness, intellectual honesty, objectivity." [31]

In what way can this gain be said to be in faith? Precisely what has been appropriated and how? Primarily, it is the self who appropriates his/her own desire and will to exist. By engaging in the task of acquiring a true consciousness, the innermost self comes to understand what it means to transcend the self because by relinquishing an *immediate* self-consciousness, s/he experiences, through the act of interpretation, an act of the *totally centered* self. Through the process of interpretation, second naiveté tears a person "away from the conveniences of neutralized belief." Because the person of second naiveté is able to move from text to abstract thought informed by experience and back again, s/he is free to hear more clearly the invitation "to situate himself better in being." In this sense, the text not

---

[31] Ricoeur, *The Symbolism of Evil*, p. 356.

only gives rise to thought, but holds out to a person "an index of his situation at the heart of the being in which he moves, exists and wills." [32]

Fourth Premise: The implication of the question of belief for theology and literary criticism, considered as sciences, is that religious and literary critics have the same kind of methodological responsibility toward the text at the second stage of interpretation: namely, to verify whatever meaning appears in terms of their respective disciplines. At this stage, theologians must also function as literary critics—or responsibly employ the results of literary critical analysis (both positive and negative) in their comparison and construction of the possible religious meanings of the text. Similarly, literary critics must also function as theologians—or responsibly employ the results of theological research (both positive and negative) in their comparison and construction of the possible literary meanings of the text.[33] By religious meanings I have in mind such concepts as ultimacy, transcendence, limit-situation, sin, holiness. I assume that the concept "God" understood as the most comprehensive object of religious experience, will be central to most discussions of religious meaning. By literary meanings, I have in mind such regulative concepts a genre, style, mode, persona, catharsis, myth, symbol, informing principle. This implication is functional, of course, in the case of any science which investigates literary text. For what is to be understood has multiple meanings, and conflicting meanings, have ultimately to be judged on the evidence presented in the text, according to the two general criteria of internal coherence and fullness of meaning.[34]

Fifth Premise: Having been saturated with intelligibility by means of hermeneutic reflection on texts, philosophical reflection has the task of arbitrating the cognitive (or truth) status of beliefs.

During the third stage of interpretation, the interpreter must transcend the eclecticism that was essential to the first and second stages of criticism. Just by participating in the dynamics of criticism, of course, the interpreter has already abandoned the "exile of the disinterested spectator." As Ricoeur says, "By the adoption of one [fiction], the appropriation of all of them becomes possible, at least

---

[32] Ibid., pp. 354-56.

[33] By initially emphasizing the distinction between religious and literary meanings, I mean to affirm that significant experience usually gives rise to both kinds of meanings.

[34] The criterion of "internal coherence" requires that an interpretation disclose organizing principles or patterns that are highly persuasive with power to illuminate the literary work. The criterion of "plenitude" requires that an interpretation account for a greater number of diverse elements in the literary work than does another interpretation.

up to a certain point."[35] But to break out of the circle of thought and belief, to go beyond being an intelligent spectator, it is finally necessary to reappropriate the mode of imagination itself, as distinct from the works of literary imagination. For by finding meaning in imaginative texts — that is, existential meanings which become his or her *beliefs* — the interpreter can be said to "believe," at least performatively, that imagination is itself a mode of being in the world. As such, imagination needs to be reconciled with other "ways of being," such as religious and ethical ways. For the task of understanding these fundamental ways of being as world-referents, the interpreter needs not only several disciplined languages, but *a* conceptual language — namely, philosophy — which is capable of showing their interrelationship. It has always been the case that the greater literary works evoke a plurality of kinds of questions, for example, theological, psychological, aesthetic, philosophical. What has not been available is a sufficient account of this plurality as it occurs in the performance of man or woman as questioner.

The very least that can be said is that philosophy, theology, and aesthetics together share the common problem of bringing to language those basic experiences of life — the desire for truth, love, and beauty — which have to do with not only our fundamental understanding of ourselves, but with the very energy by which we will to live.

To put it another way, if any interpreter claims that literature is a means of "deciphering human reality," it becomes incumbent upon him or her to verify the power of literature "to raise up, to illuminate and to give order" to those regions of human experience which, without his or her own commitment to this final stage of philosophical reflection are "all too easily reduced to error, habit, emotion, passivity" — or, we might add, to chance or "pure" imagination.

In another sense, both the literary critic and the theologian can be seen as engaged in quests for texts which most adequately and powerfully re-present aesthetic and religious dimensions of belief for themselves and their time. The literary critic who pursues the philosophical level of interpretation does, in fact, choose to work with certain literary texts which give repeated evidence that the experience and aesthetic meaning of literature is part of a *meaningful* way-of-being-in-the-world. The theologian, freed by philosophical reflection from the obligation to defend the intelligibility of *every* traditional religious meaning, will in fact begin to commit himself or herself to the appropriation of certain literary texts which are inexhaustible sources of experience and of possibly universal religious meaning. If

---

[35] Ricoeur, *The Symbolism of Evil*, p. 306.

their literary and religious criticism is truly a counterpart of the imaginative text, his or her interpretations will in turn invite other interpreters to investigate the beliefs which they can reconstruct from the text.

The question of belief in literary criticism, reflected on philosophically, has led us to a tentative comprehensive definition of belief that transcends, yet includes the various kinds of beliefs. Belief is a judgment, linguistically expressed as having a self-referent and an object-referent, made about a way of being-in-the-world. If the belief involves a claim for existential ultimacy and universality, it is to be regarded as manifestly religious. Regardless, belief must be understood concomitantly as an aesthetic disposition toward a field of meaning. In articulations of belief that are both religious and aesthetic, commitment is an ethical decision made later according to philosophical reflection on the degree of truth determined to be present in a certain way of being-in-the-world. As disposition, belief is seen to be a recurring factor of human inquiry, manifested most clearly in everyday judgment-making. As decision, belief is seen to be a fully reflective and ideal articulation of this disposition, most often in a communal context.[36]

* * * * *

From the foregoing reformulation, we can conclude, I think, that the question of belief in literary criticism has an important function within and beyond that particular discipline: (1) it provides a concept which focuses on the proper interrelationship of all elements in the literary enterprise: namely, poem, poet, reader, worlds of meaning; (2) it requires a definition of literary criticism by which the latter can be understood both as autonomous and as related to other human sciences which investigate literary texts; (3) it demonstrates that hermeneutics—or a general theory of interpretation—provides that larger context wherein literary criticism can be understood in relation to philosophical reflection, and wherein an interpreter can be seen to function as aesthete, scientist, and philosopher. Finally, by its nuanced explication of the language factor, it provides a new entry point for understanding religious belief in itself.

---

[36] See Bernard Lonergan for an explication of the communal aspect of belief: "...however personal and intimate is religious experience, still it is not solitary. The gift can be given to many, and the many can recognize in one another a common orientation in their living and feeling, in their criteria and goals....Community invites expression, and the expressions may vary." *Method in Theology* (New York: Herder and Herder, 1972), p. 118.

Phenomenology

The Transcendental Reduction According to Edmund Husserl and Intellectual Conversion According to Bernard Lonergan

by W. F. J. Ryan

The aim of this paper is to show that the Transcendental Reduction (or, Epoche) in Edmund Husserl and Intellectual Conversion in Bernard Lonergan are kindred methodological starting points. They are kindred, not because Lonergan is influenced by Husserl like a disciple, but rather because both Husserl and Lonergan share the conviction 1) that a philosopher must begin with a type of intentionality analysis and 2) that, armed with intentionality analysis, a philosopher will go on to throw out empiricism with its impedimenta of claptrap dogmatism. We will be examining the thought of the later Husserl in *The Crisis of European Sciences and Transcendental Phenomenology* and some other works, and then the thought of Lonergan principally in *Insight* and *Method in Theology*. In *The Crisis,* Husserl speaks of the Transcendental Reduction as almost like a religious conversion.[1] For his part, Lonergan openly names in *Method in Theology* an Intellectual Conversion,[2] whereas in *Insight* he speaks of

---

[1] See Edmund Husserl, *The Crisis of European Sciences and Transcendental Phenomenology,* trans. David Carr (Evanston: Northwestern University Press, 1970), p. 137; cf. pp 100 and 89.

[2] See Bernard J. F. Lonergan, S.J., *Method in Theology,* 2nd ed. (New York: Herder and Herder, 1973), pp. 238-240. See further Lonergan, *A Second Collection,* ed. William F. J. Ryan, S.J., and Bernard J. Tyrrell, S.J. (Philadelphia: The Westminster Press, 1974) with its works, "The Subject" (pp. 5-79), "An Interview with Fr. Bernard Lonergan, S.J. (p. 228), and "Revolution in Catholic Theology" (p. 237).

the necessity of abandoning the myth that knowing is a type of intuition, a type of taking a good look out there. This paper comprises three parts: 1) The Transcendental Reduction, or Epoche, in Husserl: 2) Intellectual Conversion in Lonergan; 3) a brief comparison of basic elements in the two notions.[3]

I. The Transcendental Reduction According to Edmund Husserl

After the self-admitted Cartesian attempt to perform the Transcendental Reduction in *Ideas I* (1913) and the *Cartesian Meditations* (an elaboration of two lectures which Husserl delivered at the Sorbonne in 1929; Husserl never published a final German text of the *Cartesian Meditations*), Husserl in some unpublished lectures comes to the conviction that one can only initiate the Transcendental Reduction (Epoche) by starting with the Life-world.[4] Putting the Epoche into operation, one can uncover the correlation of the intending subject and the intended object. Since Husserl at the end of his life asserts that one must take the way *(Weg)* from the intentional products founded upon the Life-world—intentionality as it embedded in the Life-world—one would find it imperative, then, to determine at the outset of Husserl's phenomenology just what the Life-world is insofar as one is able to do so. The conception of the Life-world is capital in *The Crisis*. Without exaggeration it could be said that to reach an understanding of the Life-world and its relation to the Transcendental Reduction is to find and cross the *pons asinorum* of Husserl's phenomenology.

Although Husserl writes much on the Life-world in *The Crisis,* the notion nonetheless would seem to allow for several interpretations. One may take as agreed that Husserl explains clearly what an intending subject and an intending community within its tradition

---

[3] The conviction that Husserl and Lonergan are involved in very similar methodological work is the basis for the two articles by the present author, "Intentionality in Edmund Husserl and Bernard Lonergan," *International Philosophical Quarterly,* 13 (1973), 173-190, and "Passive and Active Elements in Husserl's Notion of Intentionality," *The Modern Schoolman,* 45 (1977), 37-55. A book review of the present author's "Trinification and Phenomenology," in *Trinification of the World,* ed. Thomas A. Dunne and Jean-Marc Laporte (Toronto: Regis College Press, 1978), 97-109, by Walter E. Conn is the immediate incentive and occasion for the specific topic of this paper. (Conn's book review is found in *Theological Studies,* 40 (1979), 369.) Conn seems to have reservations about the closeness of Husserl and Lonergan in the Reduction and Intellectual Conversion.

[4] See *Erste Philosophie,* ed. Rudolph Boehm (The Hague: Martinus Nijhoff, 1959), II, pp.44-46. See also Rudolf Boehm, "Basic Reflections on Husserl's Phenomenological Reduction," trans J. Quentin Lauer, S.J., *International Philosophical Quarterly,* 5 (1965), 183-202.

are with their correlative, intended objects. One may further take it as agreed that according to Husserl such a state of intentionality is ceaselessly going on in the Life-world. One may not take it for granted, however, that Husserl defines precisely what the Life-world is. Without being unfair to Husserl, one can list two quite distinct meanings of Life-world that occur in his writings. The first meaning: the Life-world is the intentionality found in Passive Constitution and the objective correlative of this Passive Constitution. The second meaning of Life-world: the Life-world is this objective correlative of *Passive Constitution* in conjunction with the cultural objects constituted by the intending of *Active Constitution*. The cultural object of Active Constitution is founded upon the intending of Passive Constitution. There are other points to remark. In Husserl's thinking, the intentionality in the Life-world occurs "anonymously" for the Epoche has not uncovered the structure of the Life-world and identified it. For phenomenology the Life-world is precisely the *Weg* which one must follow to perform the Epoche, therewith laying bare intending subject and intended object with their correlation. Having subjected the Life-world to the working of the Transcendental Reduction, one can then grasp that either conception of the Life-world excludes any empiricist tainted account of the Life-world. Or, to put the matter in Lonergan's fashion of speaking, a person can understand how both conceptions of the Life-world are total rejections of the blunder that reality is "the already out there now real."

Of these two meanings for Life-world, we will use the first, namely, the meaning that the Life-world is the objective correlative of Passive Constitution. It would seem evident that one should have clearly in mind what he means when he is talking about Husserl's notion of the Life-world, not just for understanding the Life-world for itself, but also for grasping its indispensable relationship to the Transcendental Reduction. This paper, then, inasmuch as its main concern is the Transcendental Reduction cannot neglect the Life-world which is the "way" to performing the Transcendental Reduction.

Husserl explicitly distinguishes Passive Constitution and Active Constitution from each other.[5] A fundamental difficulty, however, remains: there is really just one, primal intending of which Passive and Active Constitution are two cycles. Husserl would say that all intending heads from Passive Constitution towards Active Constitution. In *Experience and Judgment* Husserl flatly asserts that only with the emergence of the judgment through Active Constitution may

---

[5] See Ryan, "Passive and Active Elements in Husserl's Notion of Intentionality," pp. 37-55.

one correctly speak of the existence of an object in the proper sense of the term.[6] We must accept Husserl's explicit assertion about the judgment and objectivity at its face value. Husserl means the following: *only* the judgment constitutes cultural objects, such as F = ma and the totality of physics; the writ of *habeas corpus* and the totality of the American legal system; the cathedral of Amiens and the totality of French Gothic architecture; a single word and the totality of language. The level of intending where cultural objects are constituted is totally different from the level of intending where cultural objects are not intended, i.e., Active Constitution presupposes but still is different from Passive Constitution. Thus put simply: no judgment and Active Constitution, no cultural object.

We have very briefly assembled the basic elements of the cultural object, Active Constitution, and judgment. We will proceed to align them with the Life-world and the Epoche. For our purposes — according to the two meanings of Life-world — we will examine intending in the Life-world as occurring on a level prior to the level of the intending of cultural objects. In other words, we have distinguished the Passive Constitution and the Active Constitution in Husserl without claiming that they are essentially unrelated. As Hegel might say, Active Constitution sublates Passive Constitution. In summary, then, there are two kinds of constitution but only the one intending.[7]

The Transcendental Reduction has as its field for application any intending with any intended object. As has been stated, the only genuine — that is, complete — object of Husserl is that which Active Constitution effectuates. The Transcendental Reduction, then, in order to reveal intentionality in the intending subject and the intended object, must begin with cultural objects where intending has reached its culmination. Perhaps to grasp most concisely and most quickly what Husserl has in mind to do with the Transcendental Reduction one ought to examine the Appendix in *The Crisis* entitled "The Origin of Geometry." This Appendix is an excellent primer for finding in clearest form the fundamental concepts of Husserl's phenomenology: Passive constitution, Active constitution with its ideal objects (the cultural objects of Galilean geometry), and then the Transcendental Reduction.

Although to understand adequately the Transcendental Reduction in Husserl, a person must understand its source, and its results, still it is possible to detach the three moments, and consider them

---

[6] *Experience and Judgment*, trans. James S. Churchill and Karl Ameriks. (Evanston: Northwestern University Press, 1973), p. 77, n. 1.

[7] See Ryan, "Intentionality in Edmund Husserl and Bernard Lonergan," pp. 173-90, and "Passive and Active Elements in Husserl's Notion of Intentionality," pp. 37-55.

alone, and thereby reach several wide-ranging conclusions about Husserl's phenomenology. The first moment of the Transcendental Reduction is the suspension of acceptance of the positing and the valuing in all one's intending, in all one's Active Constitution (which subsumes Passive Constitution) of cultural objects. This first moment is the "bracketing," the "putting out of play" of all common postulates that rest upon the unexamined grounds of one's positing and valuing. When Husserl asserts, then, that one must "suspend" all the "existential claims" of one's uninterrupted positing and valuing in all areas, he means that one must lay open the structure that grounds all positing and valuing, and thus endows them with their validity. Any positing and any valuing are instances of Active Constitution. Such Active Constitution, as in positing something as true or in valuing something as noble, has what may be called "existential claims," that is to say, the positing and the valuing put forth claims about *how something really exists,* for example, Organic Chemistry or family loyalty. Thus Husserl means that one must correlate the Active Constitution and the cultural object in the intending subject. Husserl does not mean that one's positing and valuing are to be declared null and void, that they are not correlated with objective reality ("existence"), that one's positing and valuing are at best a Kantian performance in a phenomenal world and at worst a flow of solipsistic acts. Were Husserl to make such claims about positing and valuing would be for him to ignore his own Transcendental Reduction and make the ungrounded "existential" claims that he is combatting.

The second moment of the Epoche is the return to the "living present." The living present is the cumulatively advancing consciousness-point in which the subject can be said himself to be constituted as a constant source of intending acts while the object is constituted by this subject in Active Constitution and Passive Constitution.[8] This consciousness-point is all-embracing, both with respect to every individual act that emerges and to the object that is thus constituted.

The third moment of the Epoche is the Eidetic Reduction. The term "eidetic" is most unhappy, for it conjures up the notion of intui-

---

[8] There is absolutely never any indication in Husserl that the subject *creates* the object. See Edmund Husserl, *Ideas,* trans W. R. Boyce Gibson, 3rd impression (London: George Allen & Unwin, Ltd., 1958), "Author's Preface to the English Edition," p. 21. See further Rudolf Boehm, "Les Ambiguîtés des concepts husserliens d' 'immanence' et 'transcendence,'" *Revue Philosophique de la France et de L'Etranger,* 84 (1959), pp. 504-517; Robert Sokolowski, *The Formation of Husserl's Concept of Constitution* (The Hague: Martinus Nijhoff, 1964), pp. 126-131.

tion and seeing as the norm for human knowing.⁹ The Eidetic Reduction has as its function to reveal the Eidos, or invariant structure, of intentionality in the subject with the subject's relationship to any intended object.

Even such a sketchy outline of the Transcendental Reduction can permit one to grasp a wide-ranging conclusion: Husserl rejects any empiricist account of knowing. The empiricist imagines that there is doubtlessly a confrontation between the subject and a ready-made empirical thing of some sort. One might simply ask oneself why Husserl would reject the assumptions of philosophers like Thomas Hobbes, A. J. Ayer, and B. F. Skinner.

Whatever a cultural object may be in the thinking of Husserl, it is not a ready-made object out there to know, like something found in a sack.¹⁰ In pursuing his goal of uncovering the structure of intentionality, Husserl holds that Active Constitution, which is the culmination of knowing, is nonempirical (though, of course, it subsumes the empirical elements provided by Passive Constitution). The cultural object of Active Constitution, then, is nonempirical. Further, one can make use of it as a clue *(Leitfaden)* to reach the invariant structure of intentionality in the subject. This invariant pattern is in no way whatsoever essentially empirical in the sense that empirical psychology alone can know it. Husserl's Transcendental Reduction thus is the ground for rejecting empiricism. When Husserl, therefore, employs such terms as "Passive Constitution," "Life-world," "perception," "the living presence of the object," or "intuition," one must be chary. One must always toss overboard any meaning of these terms that in any way is tinctured with the empiricist confrontational theory of knowing.

What is left to do with Husserl's Transcendental Reduction, Active Constitution, and objectivity? One must first acknowledge Husserl's rout of empiricism, begun in the *Logical Investigations* and continued to *The Crisis,* as the context in which to always interpret Husserl. Granted that Husserl's vocabulary may be misleading; the goal of his phenomenology is not. Although the goal of the Transcendental Reduction is not exclusively the repudiation of empiricism, nonetheless anyone performing the Transcendental Reduction must realize what its major effects are. The repudiation of empiricism is one of the major effects of the Transcendental Reduction.

---

⁹ It can be shown that in spite of the pervasive use of the term "intuition" in Husserl, it is inferior to his other term, "constitution." See Ryan, "Intentionality in Edmund Husserl and Bernard Lonergan," pp. 173-190, and "Passive and Active Elements in Husserl's Notion of Intentionality," pp. 37-55.

¹⁰ See Edmund Husserl, *The Idea of Phenomenology,* trans. William P. Alston and George Nakhnikian (The Hague: Martinus Nijhoff, 1964), p. 59.

Husserl insists that the Transcendental Reduction is an attitude of mind permanently adopted. As far as Husserl is concerned, the Transcendental Reduction demands something as radical as a type of conversion. Husserl does not hesitate to compare it with a religious conversion:

> Perhaps it will even become manifest that the total phenomenological attitude and the epoche belonging to it are destined in essence to effect, at first, a complete personal transformation, comparable in the beginning to a religious conversion, which then, however, over and above this, bears within itself the significance of the greatest existential transformation which is assigned as a task to mankind as such.[11]

II. Intellectual Conversion in Lonergan

Bernard Lonergan in his post-*Insight*, later writings describes the condition of possibility for doing philosophy as an "intellectual conversion."[12] Through such a conversion, according to Lonergan, one grasps the range of intentionality as intentionality manifests itself in a cumulative pattern of operations. The intentionality unfolds itself through experiencing, understanding, and judging. Intellectual Conversion enables one to grasp that intentionality and knowing are a set of functionally interrelated elements. Converse to Lonergan's insistence that knowing comprises a pattern of operations is his rejection of the belief that knowing is a simple, homogeneous act whose finest paradigm is intuition, or looking, or perceiving. Furthermore, in accord with Lonergan's affirmation of what knowing is and what knowing is not is his rejection of any sort of empiricism.

Insight's purpose, among others, is to show the pernicious effect of the assumption that a theoretical account of knowing is best modeled upon some kind of intellectual intuition. Lonergan finds that the attachment to such intuitionism hamstrings an adequate theory of knowledge. Such intuitionism Lonergan does not hesitate to call a "blunder." For intuitionism proposes a dualism in which the subject and the object confront each other; the subject is really in here and the object is really out there; the subject intuits the object as essentially ready-made. The classical example of intuitionism for Lonergan is Kant with his self-contradicting noumenon and phenomenon.

Intuitionism, however, does not come to an end with Kant, whose Transcendental Analytic and Transcendental Dialectic are inventive but desperate attempts to escape from the "self-incurred tutelage" of his dualism. At root empiricism depends upon intuitionism. Empiri-

---

[11] Husserl, *The Crisis*, p. 139.
[12] See note 2 above for references.

cism is content with the notion that knowing is basically an intuiting of a subject that confronts an object. In a discussion of empiricism, the names of Thomas Hobbes and David Hume come readily to mind. B. F. Skinner, however, represents well the contemporary empiricist. His blithe dogmatism never advances beyond the reductionism that an empiricist forces himself to accept.[13] That reductionism consists essentially in considering knowing as a mechanistic affair. Empiricists and behaviorists cannot overcome their unquestioned belief that knowledge is a meeting of an in here and an out there, that knowledge is of the "already out there now real." Empiricism as found in Hobbes, Hume, and Skinner shows the effect of an absence of Intellectual Conversion. Intellectual Conversion can start with the empiricist-behavioristic assumptions about objectivity and work back to the basic components of the type of subject that would have to be related to such objectivity. The basic components would be: an intuiting subject; an object out there. One might add that Kant's *Critique* is to a certain extent a rehabilitation of this subject and its object, engineered through an intricate empiricism.

Intellectual Conversion, according to Lonergan, occurs in the individual subject as a fundamental orientation grounding all his knowing.[14] Intellectual Conversion could be more concisely described as a consciously grasped set of judgments about the structure of knowing that one possesses. One should always have clearly in mind that Intellectual Conversion exists in a subject who is a conscious, intending, knowing, and valuing person. Since Intellectual Conversion is a personal, conscious performance, it is not a mélange of assumptions. Though perhaps best described as a fundamental orientation in one's thinking about the subject and the object, the description should never be allowed to become so abstract that one loses sight of the fact that there are usually very specific incidents that stir the wonder that leads to Intellectual Conversion. At times one incident alone will be enough to fillip one out of the mythical belief that knowing is passive looking at what is already out there. To grasp some of the main points of R. G. Collingwood's *An Autobiography,* Jean Piaget's *Genetic Epistemology,*[15] Erwin Schrödinger's *Science, Theory, and Man,* or Albert Einstein's famous paper of 1905, "On the Electrodynamics of Moving Bodies," is to witness Intellectual Conversion in others and perhaps to appropriate some Intellectual Conversion from them for oneself. Each of these men is talking about intending, knowing, objectivity, and reality so differently from our own common-sense beliefs or the solemnized accounts of

---

[13] See, for example, *Beyond Freedom and Dignity,* ch. 9: "What is Man?"
[14] See Lonergan, *Method in Theology,* pp. 238-240
[15] See especially ch. 2.

the empiricists. The four men, at a crucial point in their works, reject the simplistic, reductionist belief that knowing is taking a look. R. G. Collingwood first of all repudiates intuitionism as a viable account of knowing and then repudiates the historians who practise intuitionism in their work as "scissors and paste" historians. Collingwood demonstrates that the intuitionism of the scissors and paste historians is their prolegomenon to any future work they may undertake.

One who has Intellectual Conversion has a reflective grasp of the relations and terms that exist in his knowing structure. Lining up the relations and the terms, he can uncover the invariant pattern of knowing in himself. He can name the main component of the pattern. He can correlate the intending pattern with the intended object. He can further correlate the levels of his conscious knowing with the different components of objectivity. As an example, one might take R. G. Collingwood and Hadrian's Wall. The Wall has stood there in northern England for centuries. People have looked at it and walked upon it, including historians. Some people thought that the Wall was a defensive fortification similar to the Great Wall of China. Collingwood, however, asks: "Why is the Wall so low and narrow if it is in fact a defensive fortification?" Collingwood concludes that Hadrian's Wall was Hadrian's Sentry Walk—an ancient DEW Line. A scissors and paste historian, believing in intuitionism, might reach the same conclusion as Collingwood. The scissors and paste historian, however, would never have Collingwood's theory of knowledge to proceed to inquire about what evidence is, what a hypothesis is, what a correct judgment is, or even why he is asking questions.

A person lacking Intellectual Conversion cannot understand the significance of establishing what data are, what insights and hypotheses are, what a correct judgment is. Lonergan constantly names three levels of knowing. Taken together they are very kindred to the types of knowing activity as held by Collingwood. Lonergan claims that these levels belong to the basic terms and relations in the structure of knowing. He insists the levels are functionally interrelated, like the parts of a living organism. No single level, insists Lonergan, is knowing, much less the paradigm for understanding what human knowing might be.

And so Lonergan's principal fashion of showing what Intellectual Conversion consists in is to show it as the abandonment of the myth that knowing may be neatly imagined as a kind of intuiting. In a sense, Lonergan starts with the consequences of Intellectual Conversion and then goes back to an examination of the invariant pattern of knowing. In doing so he finds what the implications of that examination are. One of them is most certainly the unequivocal exclusion of all empiricism.

III. Comparisons

The Transcendental Reduction of Husserl and the Intellectual Conversion of Lonergan each have, we could say, two main results. First of all, each enables one to inspect the structure of intending, knowing, and objectivity. Secondly, each drives home a rejection of empirihism. One might ask: Why do Husserl and Lonergan both reject empiricism? Does their rejection have anything to do with their notions of intentionality? The rejection of empiricism follows directly from Husserl's and Lonergan's notions of what the structure of intending is. They have in a way trapped themselves so that they must exclude empiricism. Their disclaimer of empiricism points back to their notions of the structure of intentionality.

Both Husserl and Lonergan hold that there are levels of knowing brought about by the one, primal intending of the subject. The levels are functionally interlinked such that no one level alone and by itself could arrogate the title of knowing in the manner that intuitionism does. If, then, there are levels of knowing, there are levels of objectivity. Further, the culminating act of knowing for Husserl is the judgment that he calls a "complete satisfaction" [16] of intentionality in its drive to come to a limited act of knowing upon a determined set of evidence. The culminating act of knowing for Lonergan is the judgment. It too is a limited act of knowing, for it is the grasp of a fact, of something that happens to have a limited number of conditions fulfilled.

Finally, Husserl's notions of the Life-world and of cultural objectivity, which might seem to put Husserl and Lonergn at odds, really reinforce their kindred theories of knowledge. The Life-world is not out there. The cultural object is not out there. What remains to do, Husserl and Lonergan would assert, is to perform the Transcendental Reduction or undergo Intellectual Conversion. Then, they would say, the structure of knowing appears and the myth of empiricism disappears.

---

[16] Husserl, *Experience and Judgment*, p. 214.

Maréchal, Lonergan, and the Phenomenology of Knowing

by Michael Vertin

Introduction

Bernard Lonergan has often remarked that in developing his theory of human knowing he was influenced in part by the views of Joseph Maréchal, even though his knowledge of the Belgian Jesuit's writings was largely second-hand, coming "by osmosis" from a Louvain-trained fellow student rather than acquired through first-hand study.[1] The consequences of that influence were such that in recent years it has become a commonplace for writers to associate Lonergan's cognitional theory very closely with that of Maréchal. Indeed, the two positions, along with those of other thinkers—notably Karl Rahner and Emerich Coreth—who also show a Maréchalian influence, frequently are grouped together under a common label, "transcendental Thomism," in order globally to contrast them with other groups of positions in the broad tradition stemming from Aquinas.[2]

---

[1] Lonergan frequently has told the story of his indirect familiarity with Maréchal, in responding orally to questioners at conferences. For a written account, see Lonergan, "*Insight* Revisited," in William Ryan & Bernard Tyrrell, eds., *A Second Collection* (Philadelphia: Westminster, 1974), pp. 265, 276. The "five great *Cahiers*" to which Lonergan refers in this account are the five volumes of Maréchal's *magnum opus,* entitled, *Le Point de départ de la métaphysique: Leçons sur le developpement historique et théorique du probléme de la connaissance* (henceforth *PD,* with the appropriate volume and page numbers). The first edition of the first volume—or, to use Maréchal's somewhat whimsical term, *"cahier"*—appeared as early as 1922; while a revised edition of the fifth appeared, posthumously, as late as 1949. (For the details of each volume's publication-history, and, more generally, a complete list of Maréchal's writings, see "Bibliographie du Pére J. Maréchal," *Mélanges Joseph Maréchal* [Bruxelles: L'Edition Universelle, 1950], I:47-65.) The editions (Bruxelles: L'Edition Universelle) cited here are dated thus: I−1944; II−1944; III−1944; IV−1947; and V−1949.

The publicity given to the similarities between the cognitional theories of Lonergan and Maréchal, however, has tended to obscure the differences between the two, differences which—if perhaps less obvious—are of no less philosophical import. Relatively few studies advert in more than cursory fashion to the differences, and even fewer attempt to order and appraise them.[3]

My concern in this article, then, is more with those points of divergence than with the points of convergence. Specifically, my aim is fourfold: (i) to recount, albeit in highly condensed fashion, Maréchal's phenomenology of knowing; (ii) to review, with comparable brevity, Lonergan's phenomenology of knowing; (iii) to indicate three important differences beside the evident similarities between the two theories; and (iv) to offer a brief comparative assessment.[4]

---

[2] The term, "transcendental Thomism," was coined by Joseph Donceel. See his "Philosophy in the Catholic University," *America*, 115 (1966): 330-31; "Thomism: How Much to Keep?" *America*, 116 (1967):580-82; "Introduction," in Emerich Coreth, *Metaphysics* (New York: Herder & Herder, 1968), pp. 7-14; "On Transcendental Thomism," *Continuum*, 7 (1969):164-68; and "Transcendental Thomism," *Monist*, 58 (1974):67-85. Donceel considers Maréchal to be the original transcendental Thomist, but he also applies the term to Rahner, Coreth, and, on occasion, Lonergan, as well as others. Nonetheless, he remains aware that Lonergan stands much further removed from Maréchal than do many of the others. (See esp. 164-65 of the fourth item just noted.) Save in Donceel's writings, however, the term has generally come to be applied to Maréchal, Rahner, Coreth, Lonergan, etc., without distinction. See, e.g., Richard Hinners, *et al.*, "The Transcendental Method," *Continuum*, 6 (1968):221-45; Leslie Dewart, "On Transcendental Thomism," *Continuum*, 6 (1968):389-401; Eric Mascall, "Transcendental Thomism," in *The Openness of Being* (London: Darton, Longman & Todd, 1971), pp. 59-90; Gerald McCool, "The Philosophical Theology of Rahner and Lonergan," in Robert Roth, ed., *God Knowable and Unknowable* (New York: Fordham University, 1973), pp. 123-57; and Frederick Wilhelmsen, "The Priority of Judgment over Question: Reflections on Transcendental Thomism," *International Philosophical Quarterly*, 14 (1974):475-93. For other examples of studies noting the similarities between Lonergan's position and those of Maréchal, Rahner, Coreth, etc., though not under the "transcendental Thomist" label, see Coreth, "The Problem and Method of Metaphysics," *International Philosophical Quarterly*, 3 (1963):403-18; Harald Holz, *Transzendentalphilosophie und Metaphysik* (Mainz: Matthias-Grünewald, 1966); Otto Muck, *The Transcendental Method* (New York: Herder & Herder, 1968); and Muck, "The Logical Structure of Transcendental Method," *International Philosophical Quarterly*, 9 (1969):342-62.

[3] One of the more lengthy efforts to elucidate fundamental differences as well as similarities among Maréchal, Rahner, Coreth, Lonergan, etc., is Otto Muck's book, cited in the previous note. Unfortunately, it is marred by the author's inadequate understanding of Lonergan and consequent tendency to assimilate him unduly to the Maréchalian group. For one of Muck's misunderstandings, though by no means the only or even the most serious one, see Lonergan, *Method in Theology* (New York: Herder & Herder, 1972), p. 13, n. 4. A suggestive, but hardly extensive, indication of differences between Lonergan and a thinker more obviously in the Maréchalian line is provided by the following three items: Lonergan, "Metaphysics as Horizon," in Frederick Crowe, ed., *Collection: Papers by Bernard*

I. Maréchal on the Stages in Knowing

1. *(Implicit) Transcendental Affirming.*[5] For Maréchal, the very first stage in one's knowing process is the "transcendental act of affirming," the "transcendental act of judging." Logically prior[6] to any particular knowledge whatsoever, it is a dynamic structural element of human intelligence as such. More precisely, it is one's anticipatory positing of any proximate objective term of intellectual finality as a cognitional means to the ultimate objective term of intellectual finality. It is the *a priori* attribution of conditioned absolute unity, necessity, intelligibility, or "limited real existence"—and thus of ultimate dependence upon unconditioned absolute unity, necessity, intelligibility, or "unlimited real existence"—to any possible object of knowledge. It is the utterly general cognitional compounding of real existence and anticipated content, the dynamic pure synthesizing that is presupposed in all particular knowledge and whose static expression is the principle of identity (or, negatively, the principle of contradiction). And hence by implication it is the anticipatory positing of the ultimate objective term of intellectual finality, the *a priori* asserting of unlimited real existence.

2. *(Implicit) Sensing.*[7] On Maréchal's analysis, the second stage in one's knowing process, and the first stage in "this" by contrast with "that" particular knowing, is the cognitional grasping of sensible data

---

Lonergan (New York: Herder & Herder, 1967), pp. 202-20, esp. 219-20; Coreth, "Immediacy and the Mediation of Being: An Attempt to Answer Bernard Lonergan," in Philip McShane, ed., *Language, Truth and Meaning* (Notre Dame: University of Notre Dame, 1972), pp. 33-48; and Lonergan, "Bernard Lonergan Responds," ibid., p. 311. Cf. Giovanni Sala, "Seinserfahrung und Seinshorizont," *Zeitschrift für Katholische Theologie,* 89 (1967):294-338.

[4] By "phenomonology of knowing" I mean an account of the recurrent features of human knowing, framed expressly from the standpoint of the knowing subject as such, or, again, a philosophical description of human knowing. The contrast is with "metaphysics of knowing," an account of the recurrent features which is framed expressly from the universal standpoint, a philosophical explanation of human knowing. Though the term is mine rather than Maréchal's or Lonergan's, it corresponds to (the results of) Maréchal's "transcendental analysis," and to Lonergan's "cognitional theory." Secondly, the human knowing with which I am especially concerned in this article is not necessarily more than merely factual: I prescind from all consideration of evaluative knowing as such. More precisely still, the focus is the process of factual knowing in its most basic instances, rather than inferential knowing or, further, believing.

[5] *PD*, I, 24-25, 41-56, 254-55; V, 81-99, 532-68. (Since detailed references to the works of Maréchal and Lonergan are hardly feasible in a brief article, my citations for each stage in the knowing process are rather general and/or merely representative.)

[6] The logic of the priority is *transcendental* logic. See *PD*, V, 47-71, 492-514, 518-31. Cf. III, 110-20.

[7] *PD*, V, 131-84, 520-21.

and the organizing of them into a concrete spatio-temporal image or "phantasm".

3. *(Implicit) Conceiving.*[8] Next, the Maréchalian knower forms an abstract intelligible similitude, or concept, of what is given concretely and sensibly in the phantasm. As a similitude, the concept is identical in content with that which the phantasm embodies; but as abstract, the concept is universal and thus differs in mode from that which, embodied in the phantasm, is concrete and therefore particular.

4. *(Implicit) Converting to Phantasm.*[9] The fourth stage in the knowing process, according to Maréchal, is "converting to phantasm," effecting a particular "concretive synthesis." It is the first of the two stages of (implicitly) objectifying the conceptual content, or, again, the first of the two stages of (implicit) judging. It consists in attributing the abstract intelligible form to the concrete sensible data, referring the universal concept back to the particular "this" whence it was abstracted.

5. *(Implicit) Affirming.*[10] The next stage in knowing, on Maréchal's theory, is "affirming," effecting a particular "objective synthesis." It is the second of the two stages of (implicitly) objectifying the conceptual content, or, again, the second of the two stages of (implicit) judging. It is nothing other than bringing the particular concretive synthesis under the transcendental act of affirming, positing the particular concretive synthesis as a cognitional means to the ultimate objective term of intellectual finality, attributing limited real existence to the concretive synthesis and thus referring the latter to unlimited real existence. Hence it is mediately, through intellectual attributing to a particular concretive synthesis the real existence that in utterly general fashion one knows *a priori,* rather than immediately, through intellectually intuiting real existence in the concretive synthesis, that one achieves that knowledge of particular existence which is proper to human intelligence. That is to say, human knowledge of particular real existence is "discursive," not intuitive.

6. *Explicit Judging.*[11] In Maréchal's view, what I have characterized as the fifth stage marks a certain completeness in one's knowing process but nonetheless is not the final stage. For human awareness as such is correlative with reflection. One is aware of an object precisely insofar as one distinguishes self from that object; and

---

[8] *PD,* V, 185-279, 521-22.

[9] *PD,* V, 281-96, 522-23.

[10] *PD,* V, 296-315, 346-61, 524-26.

[11] *PD,* V, 110-31, 210-14, 242-43, 301-302, 396-405, 408-409, 452-61, 481, 525. Cf. III, 123-24, n.; IV, 118.

such a distinction arises precisely insofar as one's activity is directed toward the object and then returns upon itself, regards the object and then takes itself in turn as object, is not merely "centrifugal" but "centripetal" as well. In transcendental affirming, and in sensing, conceiving, converting to phantasm, and affirming, however, the return of one's activity upon itself is merely partial, "reflection only in the wide sense." Consequently, one's awareness of other and of self in these activities is merely "lived," "exercised," "implicit," "unconscious" or "subconscious" or "preconscious," "conscious merely in the wide sense"; and the activities themselves are performed not "consciously" and "freely" but merely "naturally" and "necessarily." And although at the fifth stage the conceptual content is completely objectified "in consciousness," it is not yet objectified "for consciousness"; or, again, the object is known but not yet known *as* object —i.e., as clearly distinct from the knowing subject.

"Explicit judging," then, is the remaining development. It is "reflection in the strict sense," one's complete return upon self and, more specifically, upon the preceding cognitional activities and their terms. It is one's reflexive bringing of the implicit to explicitness, one's articulating a judgment whose predicate-subject union expresses the particular concretive synthesis and whose very being-articulated expresses the particular objective synthesis. It gives rise to awareness of other and of self that is "recognized," "signified," "explicit," "conscious," "conscious in the strict sense"; and it opens the possibility of one's operating not just "naturally" and "necessarily" but "consciously" and "freely." In it the conceptual content is completely objectified "for consciousness," the object is known *as* object.

II. Lonergan on the Stages in Knowing

1. *Experiencing.*[12] For Lonergan, the first stage in one's knowing process is "experiencing," and it has two dimensions. In its "external" dimension experiencing is identically the "intentional" dimension of sensing, i.e., that dimension in which one is aware of sensible contents and organizes them into a perceptual image. In its "internal" or "conscious" dimension experiencing is identically the "non-intentional" dimension of sensing and of all subsequent acts of awareness as well, i.e., that dimension in which one is primitively aware of one's acts themselves and, more radically, of oneself as actor. This internal experiencing, consciousness, primitive awareness of self and

---

[12] *Insight: A Study of Human Understanding* (New York: Philosophical Libary, 1957), pp. 181-91, 272-75, 320-38, 381-83; *De constitutione Christi ontologica et psychologica* (Romae: Pontificia Universitas Gregoriana, 1956), pp. 83-88, 130-34; "Christ as Subject: A Reply," in *Collection*, pp. 222-27; and *Method*, pp. 6-20.

acts, is not reflexive in the least. It is not in any way a return of activities upon themselves, but rather the non-reflexive presence of the actor to himself in and through his acts. In its external dimension experiencing is the first stage in one's knowing of objects (including other subjects); and in its internal dimension it is the first stage in one's knowing of oneself.

2. *Transcendental Intending.*[13] Following on experiencing, according to Lonergan, is "transcendental intending," the pure question seeking its integral objective, the *a priori* notion of "being," the dynamic anticipation of intelligibility and affirmability, the unrestricted intellectual yearning for "essence" and "existence" (or "occurrence").[14] Transcendental intending is not knowing. Rather, it is the pure desire to know, the eros of the human mind as such, the *a priori* drive which motivates one's entire cognitional process and renders it not just materially but formally dynamic. Awakened by experiencing, it is manifested initially in questions about the intelligibility and, in turn, the affirmability of "these" or "those" experiential data (whether of sense or of consciousness); but it finds its adequate expression only in questions about the intelligibility and affirmability of all that can be asked about. Moreover, although it is a natural, given element of one's cognitional structure, transcendental intending is in no way automatic or unwitting. On the contrary, it is that whereby one is non-reflexively self-present and self-constituting as intelligent and critical questioner, possesses in advance the fundamental criteria for measuring the intelligence and reasonableness of one's answers, and is constitutionally opposed to all stupidity and foolishness.

3. *Direct Insight.*[15] The next stage in one's knowing process, on Lonergan's analysis, is concrete direct understanding or "direct insight." It is apprehending a universal in the particular, cognitionally grasping an intelligible whole in, or similarity among, the concrete experiential data of sense or of consciousness, attaining the

---

[13] *Insight,* pp. 4, 9, 220-22, 348-74, 380-81, 636-39; *"Insight:* Preface to a Discussion," in *Collection,* pp. 152-63; "Metaphysics as Horizon," pp.202-20; "Cognitional Structure," in *Collection,* pp. 227-39; and *Method,* pp. 6-20, 213-14, 238-40, 263-64. (Consonant with the restriction made explicit above in note 4, I am concerned in this article with Lonergan's transcendental intending insofar as it is an intending of intelligibility and reality, and I prescind from it insofar as it is also an intending of value.)

[14] Lonergan anticipates the distinction between the existence of things, on the one hand, and the occurrence of properties, on the other. See *Insight,* pp., 248, 437. Cf. *"Insight:* Preface to a Discussion," p. 162.

[15] *Verbum: Word and Idea in Aquinas* (Notre Dame: University of Notre Dame, 1967), pp. 1-46, 141-81; *Insight,* pp. 3-32, 271-75, *et passim;* "Cognitional Structure," pp. 222-27; and *Method,* pp. 6-20.

intelligible form of a concrete "thing" or "property." The act of direct insight, by no means blind or mechanical, is one's achievement precisely as an intelligently conscious and self-constituting subject; and the content of direct insight partially satisfies one's pure desire to know intelligibility.

4. *Conceiving.*[16] In Lonergan's view, conceiving is a stage in a particular knowing process only insofar as the objective of that process is more than merely immediate, restricted, non-systematic, practical. One apprehends the universal apart from the particular, expresses abstractly the intelligible whole or similarity, formulates the intelligibility of the thing or property. That act of conceiving—often difficult and always requiring at least minimal shrewdness—is a further operation, beyond that of direct insight, which one performs precisely as an intelligently conscious and self-constituting subject. The content of conceiving is a further partial satisfaction, beyond that provided by direct insight, of one's pure desire to know intelligibility.

5. *Reflective Insight.*[17] On Lonergan's phenomenology of cognition, the operation following on concrete direct understanding—and, perhaps, conceiving—is reflective understanding, "reflective insight." The pure desire to know, manifested now in questions about the real existence or occurrence of the thing or property that one has grasped as intelligible, presses one onward; and in due course one lays hold of evidence as sufficient (or insufficient) for grounding an affirmation of existence or occurrence. To grasp evidence as sufficient is to grasp (i) the prospective affirmation as being conditioned, (ii) an intelligible connection between that conditioned and its conditions, and (iii) the fulfillment of the conditions. This is equivalent to grasping the affirmation as "virtually unconditioned"—i.e., as having conditions which nonetheless are fulfilled.

The prospective affirmation is the prospective positing of a concrete intelligible unity or similarity. The intelligible connection between conditioned and conditions is some normative procedure immanent and operative within cognitional process as such, some internal governing pattern that — prior to and even apart from being reflexively objectified—guides cognitional process. It links the prospective affirmation to criteria of affirmability, criteria of existence or occurrence, that are given *a priori* in the very structure of the pure desire to know. The precise nature of the intelligible connection and

---

[16] Ibid.

[17] *Verbum,* pp. 47-95; *Insight,* pp. 271-316, 377-83; "*Insight:* Preface to a Discussion," pp. 152-63, esp. 160-63; "Metapysics as Horizon," pp. 202-20; "Cognitional Structure," pp. 222-39; and *Method,* pp. 6-20, 213-214, 238-40, 263-64.

thus of the conditions to be fulfilled varies with the nature of the prospective affirmation. In the most basic cases, the conditions are fulfilled by grasping the experiential data which are intelligibly unified or related in the thing or property whose concrete existence or occurrence is in question.

To achieve reflective insight is not yet to know existence or occurrence. Rather, it is merely to grasp the cognitional reason which justifies actually making the affirmation, with the affirmation itself left as the act in and through which one knows existence or occurrence. Again, the act of reflective insight, often laborious and always requiring at least minimal sagacity, is an operation which one performs precisely as a rationally conscious and self-constituting subject.

6. *Affirming.*[18] The final stage in one's process of knowing other or self, according to Lonergan, is "affirming." Rationally compelled by reflective insight, one posits the conditioned as virtually unconditioned, actually carries out the envisaged assertion, makes a positive judgment of real existence or occurrence; and in and through this affirmation, assertion, judgment, one knows that the thing in question really exists or that the property in question really occurs. For just as grasping a prospective affirmation as virtually unconditioned is the cognitional reason for making the affirmation, so the latter is the cognitional reason for claiming to know. And thus it is mediately, through affirming in a given instance the real existence or occurrence that one anticipates *a priori*, rather than immediately through intellectual intuition in the given instance, that one achieves that knowledge of real existence or occurrence which is proper to human cognitional capability.

The act of affirming is a further operation, beyond that of reflective insight, which one performs precisely as a rationally conscious and self-constituting subject. Again, the content achieved through affirming brings to completion one particular partial satisfaction of one's pure desire to know factual intelligibility; on the other hand, at least two additional such partial satisfactions are required for manifesting the distinction of the subject (or one of its properties) from the object (or one of its properties).

III. Lonergan and Maréchal: Similarities and Differences

1. *The Similarities of Lonergan to Maréchal.* It is obvious that Lonergan's phenomenology of cognition is similar in more than one respect to that of Maréchal. Both claim a basic role for sensing. Both

---
[18] Ibid.

declare that knowing includes cognitionally grasping some concrete intelligible unity or similarity. Both argue that it is in judging that one knows the real existence (or occurrence) of that concrete intelligibility. Surely their most important point of agreement, however, and identically their most distinctive point of common disagreement with the theories of many other thinkers, is the contention that this judging is discursive and not intuitive.[19] To judge is not intellectually to intuit, perceive, see, in the concrete intelligibility a content that one may conceptualize subsequently — *a posteriori* — as "real existence" (or "real occurrence"). On the contrary, to judge is to affirm of, attribute to, assert of, the concrete intelligibility a content that one anticipates — *a priori* — as "crowning component of the objective of intellectual dynamism," and in that sense "real existence" (or "real occurrence").

2. *The Differences of Lonergan from Maréchal.* There are no less than three important differences between Lonergan's phenomenology of knowing and that of Maréchal. I should like to suggest that one of these, a difference between the respective accounts of self-awareness, is more basic than the other two and stands in large part as their antecedent.

For Maréchal, self-awareness arises insofar as one's activity, initially directed toward an object, returns upon itself. A partial self-return gives rise to primitive self-awareness, "self-consciousness in the wide sense," and a complete self-return gives rise to fuller self-awareness, "self-consciousness in the strict sense." Primitive and fuller self-awareness differ merely in degree, therefore, in correspondence with their respective degrees of reflection, and not in kind.

For Lonergan, on the other hand, self-awareness is of two distinct kinds. Primitive self-awareness, "internal experiencing" or "consciousness," is the non-intentional, non-reflexive presence of oneself to oneself in and through acts which in their other dimension are intentional. Fuller self-awareness, "self-knowledge," is the reflexive, introspectively intentional self-presence that arises by virtue of grasping an intelligibility in the data of internal experiencing, and affirming it.

Now, on Maréchal's account of self-awareness, it is by virtue of reflection that one is aware of one's transcendental anticipating, sensing, cognitionally grasping some concrete intelligibility, and affirming. But reflection does not constitute that which it reflects upon: it merely manifests it as already constituted. The constitution of those cognitional activities, therefore, occurring prior to reflec-

---

[19] For an excellent example of the other view, see Joseph Owens, *An Interpretation of Existence* (Milwaukee: Bruce, 1968), pp. 14-43.

tion, must be merely "natural," lacking in self-awareness, opaque.[20] Moreover, certain aspects of the naturally-constituted sequence which are not manifested by reflection may be reached—indeed, can be reached only—by transcendental-logical inference. And thus on Maréchal's phenomenology one infers (i) that cognitionally grasping some concrete intelligibility is a matter of conceiving and then converting to phantasm, and (ii) that (particular) affirming is a matter of "applying" to the concrete intelligibility the "real existence" that, prior to all particular acts in a knowing process, one transcendentally affirms.

On Lonergan's account of self-awareness, by contrast, it is non-reflexively, by virtue of internal experiencing, that one is radically aware of one's sensing, transcendental anticipating, cognitionally grasping some concrete intelligibility, and affirming. But internal experiencing is not merely self-manifestive. It is self-constitutive as well, the self-presence of the acts exactly as acts and of oneself exactly as actor. The constitution of those cognitional activities, therefore, is not merely "natural," lacking in self-presence, opaque. Rather, it is an empirically, intelligently, and rationally conscious self-constituting. As self-constitutor, moreover, one has immediate, and not just inferential, awareness of every key aspect of the cognitional sequence. Thus, on Lonergan's phenomenology, one internally experiences, and can also reflexively know, (i) that cognitionally grasping some concrete intelligibility is a matter of direct insight, perhaps but not necessarily followed by conceiving, and (ii) that affirming is a matter of attributing to the concrete intelligibility, precisely on the basis of reflective insight, the "real existence" (or "real occurrence") that prior to affirming, though subsequent to experiencing, one transcendentally intends but does not as yet know.

IV. The Superiority of Lonergan to Maréchal

A phenomenology of knowing purports to set forth recurrent features of human cognitional subjectivity as such. To assess one or more given phenomenologies, however, ultimately is nothing other than to measure them against the only concrete subjectivity of which one is directly aware, namely, one's own.[21]

On the basis of my own self-awareness as a knowing subject, therefore, I conclude, in the first place, that on those points of cognitional phenomenology wherein Lonergan's position accords with

---

[20] More exactly, Maréchal maintains that the constitution of any activity prior to *complete* reflection cannot be more than just "natural." Still less, therefore, can the constitution of an activity prior even to *partial* reflection be more than just "natural."

[21] More broadly, of course, for those who argue that judging is discursive, the basis of *any* assessment finally is a personal one.

that of Maréchal, that common position is correct. In particular, I find their common claim that judging is discursive rather than intuitive to be concretely indisputable.

In the second place, I conclude that on the three important points wherein Lonergan's position differs from that of Maréchal, it is the Lonerganian view that is correct.

First, my primitive and fuller self-awareness differ in kind, as non-reflexive and reflexive, and not just in degree, as partially and completely reflexive. That is to say, my own concrete evidence confirms Lonergan's account of self-awareness and disconfirms Maréchal's account. I attribute Maréchal's mistake on this matter to an incompleteness in his knowledge of his own concrete self-awareness, plus the latent influence of the philosophically popular but essentially uncritical principle that all human knowing—or, more generally, awareness—is exclusively intentional.[22]

Secondly, my failures as well as my successes in attempting to grasp and, perhaps, abstractly formulate some concrete intelligibility, and, again, the frequent narrowness as well as the occasional breadth of those successes, are among the most incontrovertible features of my cognitional life. Moreover, I am keenly aware of a direct correspondence between the failure or success, or, again, the narrowness or breadth, on the one hand, and the dullness or intelligence, stupidity or shrewdness, with which I constitute myself in making the attempt to understand, on the other. Lonergan's theory, propounding direct insight and conceiving as acts of an intelligently self-present and self-constituting subject, does full justice to these features. Maréchal's theory, however, does not; and I ascribe its deficiency to an incompleteness in the Belgian Jesuit's knowledge of his own concrete acts of understanding, plus the influence of his mistaken account of self-awareness. Because Maréchal views self-awareness as exclusively reflexive, he cannot claim that the activity of cognitionally grasping some concrete intelligibility is originally self-constituting; for there cannot be self-constitution where there is not even self-presence. Consequently, he must view the original constitution of that cognitional grasping, subsequently manifested by reflection, to be merely "natural," automatic, and more or less exhaustive; and thence he is led further to infer merely "natural,"

---

[22] On this point, see the pages of Lonergan cited above in note 12. It is perhaps ironic that Maréchal should be caught up in a variant of the global but uncritical tendency to characterize all human awareness on the perceptual model, given his unswerving opposition, throughout *Le Point de départ de la métaphysique*, to what is but another variant of the same perceptualist tendency, namely, the principle that all human knowing—and, in particular, all human knowing of real existence—is fundamentally direct, unmediated, intuitive.

automatic, and more or less exhaustive conceiving and converting to phantasm in order to explain it.

Thirdly, it is painfully obvious to me that at some times I am less able to make judgments than at others, and that I am prone to make erroneous judgments as well as true ones. Furthermore, I cannot but notice a direct relation between the difficulty or ease with which I judge, or, again, the error or truth of the judgments, on the one hand, and the unreasonableness or reasonableness, foolishness or sagacity, with which I constitute myself in making the attempt to judge, on the other. Lonergan's phenomenology, proposing reflective insight and true affirming as acts of a rationally self-present and self-constituting subject, is fully adequate to these elements of my cognitional subjectivity; while Maréchal's phenomenology again falls short. Consonant with my previous diagnosis, I suggest that the Maréchalian theory's flaw in the present respect stems from its author's incomplete advertence to his own concrete acts of judging, plus the influence of his mistaken contention that self-awareness is exclusively reflexive. The activity of (particular) affirming cannot originally be self-constituting, since until it returns upon itself it is not even so much as self-present. Consequently, Maréchal must consider that activity at least originally to be merely "natural," automatic, and more or less infallible. And in order to explain how such an activity is effected, he is driven to infer that transcendental anticipating is in fact nothing other than transcendental affirming.

It remains only to reiterate that this assessment of the cognitional phenomenologies of Lonergan and Maréchal is based ultimately upon the evidence of my own concrete self-awareness. Whether or not the reader's concrete self-awareness, in turn, impels the same assessment is, of course, for him or her to determine.

Socio-Political Orientations

Method and the Social Appropriation of Reality

by William Mathews

I.

Human knowing, the twentieth century has indelibly impressed upon us, is inherently a socially distributed activity and attribute. Extending an insight of T. S. Kuhn, the terms physics, chemistry, biology, or more generally science, common sense, history, philosophy, and theology, as well as being the names of types of inquiry and knowledge can also be understood as the names of communities who, collectively, pursue and possess the knowledge and the power it gives.[1] Science or history are not the names of some one solipsistic questioner. Rather they are the names of socially distributed groups of questioners. Human knowing is also inherently incomplete and in process, spurred on by the creative restlessness of the human spirit of inquiry and its discontent with ignorance. But it is also being impressed upon us that the explosion of human knowin and knowledge in society is also a process of considerable discord. Quietly at first there has emerged a multiplicity of sciences, the natural, life, behavioral, human, and social. To these have been added the historical and hermeneutic disciplines. Everyday common sense living has declared its independence as a realm of human inquiry and knowing.[2] From quiet beginnings this emergence has built up into

---

[1] T. S. Kuhn, *The Structure of Scientific Revolutions* (Chicago: University of Chicago Press, 1962, 1970), p. 179 where "optics," "electricity", and "heat" are interpreted as the names of scientific communities.

[2] The exploration of the everyday common sense world and its autonomy seems to have been the central concern of Alfred Schutz. See his *Collected Papers I* (The Hague: Martinus Nijhoff, 1973), pp. xxv f.

something like a crescendo of discordance at the present time. There now no longer exists any commonly accepted notion of what science is. The common sense community can view scholars and scientists, now with adulation, now with suspicion. The multiplication and fragmentation of the realms of knowing has brought with it considerable discord and division within the fabric of society and even within the consciousness of an individual. Modern society is characterized by a considerable ignorance of how the different sub-communities relate to one another in the progressive appropriation of reality. Progress seems very much a matter of chance, of separate, discordant, or out of phase development, of booms and slumps as fashions emerge and prestige and fame are sought. In recent theology we have witnessed something akin to booms and slumps in exegesis, doctrines, and catechetics. Classical science boomed from Newton to Einstein and effectively held back the complementary development of statistical and other scientific methods.

The question which the present essay addresses itself to is simply, what might be the norms governing the manner in which a social group appropriates reality as a group. Its aim is not to discover social and other factors which condition the beliefs of a group. Rather it will suggest that human wonder, interpreted as a socially distributed attribute, is the possible dynamic first principle from which the whole discordant crescendo has built up. It will view society from the viewpoint of knowing as a community of questioners, of notions of being. The current discord, it will be suggested, is the result of a fairly total neglect of questioning and its implications as a social attribute. It will ask, does anarchy rule, or might an understanding of human wonder help establish a "framework for collaborative creativity"[3] which would promote in some harmonious manner the many otherwise discordant questioners? In raising this question it will invite the translation of some of the central notions in Lonergan's *Insight* and *Method in Theology* into a more explicitly social context.

II.

In Chapter XII of *Insight* Lonergan invites us to discover that our wonder or pure desire to know is a notion of being, of what there is, of reality. The resulting treatment, although it has to be read in the context of the earlier chapters dealing with scientific and common sense wonder, and on which it is built, is highly impersonal. It prescinds from biographical, social, and historical contexts. It in-

---

[3] See B. J. F. Lonergan's *Method in Theology*, (London: Darton, Longman and Todd, 1972), p. xi.

vites us to discover something about our wonder, that it is unrestricted in anticipation, spontaneous, all pervasive, the core of meaning, puzzling, and an anticipation of what there is. Through inviting us to discover something about our own wonder it is tacitly inviting us to discover something about every other human being. But because *Insight* is an exercise in *self*-appropriation, the former seems to be the focus. But being is also the objective of the wonder of the whole historico-social community of individuals. In order to interpret it as such there is a need to build up an image of an historical and social community of questioners.

Much recent biographical material illustrates the foundational role in science of human wonder. A sense of curiosity about the world is one of the key characteristics of the life of Einstein.[4] In his later life he recalled:

> A wonder of such nature I experienced as a child of 4 or 5 years, when my father showed me a compass. That this needle behaved in such a determined way did not at all fit into the nature of events.... I can still remember—or at least believe I can remember—that this experience made a deep and lasting impression upon me. Something deeply hidden had to be behind things.[5]

Around the age of twelve his wonder was again aroused by the problems of Euclidean geometry and with much effort he succeeded in puzzling out Pythagoras' theorem. Einstein contrasts ordinary everyday attitudes to falling bodies, wind, and rain, the fact that the moon does not fall down, and to the differences between living and non-living matter, with that attitude that is brought about by the emergence of wonder.[6] He was to remark that "he was brought to the formulation of relativity theory in good part because he kept asking himself questions concerning space and time that only children wonder about."[7] A similar sense of wonder is to be found in Kepler, Newton, and Darwin. Kepler in the context of the emerging Copernican world view:

---

[4] The theme of Einstein's wonder runs through Jeremy Bernstein's book *Einstein*, (London: Fontana, 1973), particularly pp. 21-3, 68-9, 137f., especially pp. 138 n. 9, 140.

[5] 'Autobiographical Notes' p. 9. These are published in *Albert Einstein, Philosopher Scientist,* edited by P. A. Schilpp (N.Y.: Tudor, 1949).

[6] Ibid., p. 9.

[7] Quoted by Erik H. Erickson in his *Toys and Reasons* (N.Y.: Norton, 1976), p. 140.

began to wonder why there existed just six planets 'instead of twenty or a hundred' and why the distances and velocities of the planets were what they were. Thus started his quest for the laws of planetary motion.[8]

Later he was to remark:

> I would have concluded my researches on the harmonies of the spheres if Tycho's astronomy had not fascinated me so much that I almost went out of my mind.[9]

His initial interest grew into an obsession. Likewise Newton, according to Keynes, had the ability to stay with a problem for days and weeks and months until it yielded its secret to him.[10] Darwin was brought up to believe in the permanence of biological species. His observation of the fact that each of the Galapagos Islands had its own form of finch, tortoise, and mocking bird, called his inherited beliefs into question and presented him with a problem which he remarked "haunted him." [11] For years he pondered over the explanation of the variability of species.

If we turn from biography to philosophy of science we find further acknowledgement of science as a questioning activity. For Kuhn scientific problems and wonder are of two kinds, normal and revolutionary.[12] The problems of normal science are well defined and their resolution is analogous to puzzle solving. They are pursued by a community who are in agreement about the kind of solution that is acceptable. Revolutionary scientific questioning deals with anomalies generated by the development of normal science. Such questioning is not well defined, unpredictable, and in turn either modifies or replaces the problem solving framework. It is then acknowledged that the community of scientists is a community of questioners. Human wonder is the life principle of that community. Were it to dry up the community would die.

Questioning is not confined to the realm of science. It is also a central characteristic of everyday common sense living. Dramatic narratives, although fictional, do in very many instances mirror the 'real life' drama of such common sense living. An examination of the narrative structure of very many dramas reveals the significance in them of the interrogative mood. Consider in this light the opening

---

[8] Arthur Koestler, *The Sleepwalkers*, (London: Penguin, 1964), p. 250.

[9] A. C. Crombie, *From Augustine to Galileo* (London: Mercury, 1964), vol. 2, p. 187.

[10] Bernstein, *Einstein*, pp. 137-8.

[11] *The Autobiography of Charles Darwin and Selected Letters*, edited by Francis Darwin (N.Y.: Dover, 1958), pp. 42, 175f.

[12] *The Structure of Scientific Revolutions*, Chapters IV and IX.

scene of Arthur Miller's *Death of a Salesman* which, it could be claimed, is representative of many similar human situations:

> LINDA: (hearing WILLY outside the bedroom, calls with some trepidation): Willy!
> WILLY: It's all right. I came back.
> LINDA: Why? What happened? (Slight pause.) Did something happen, Willy?
> WILLY: No, nothing happened.
> LINDA: You didn't smash the car, did you?
> WILLY: (with casual irritation): I said nothing happened. Didn't you hear me?
> LINDA: Don't you feel well?
> WILLY: I'm tired to the death....[13]

A central feature of the drama is Willy's flight from the fearful question "what happened at Boston?".[14] The interrogative mood of the opening is reminiscent of that of Hamlet where Barnardo asks: "Who's there?" That remark according to Maynard Mack sets the tone, not simply of the opening, but rather of the whole of the drama.[15]

Alfred Schultz has reflected on the process by means of which a stranger, an immigrant for instance, comes to understand the bewildering common sense world into which he has been transplanted. He concludes:

> The adaptation of the newcomer to the ingroup which at first seemed to be strange and unfamiliar to him is a continuous process of inquiry into the cultural pattern of the approached group.[16]

It is interesting to consider, imaginatively, what might be our own response on finding ourselves so transported. Would we be afraid or would we be curious? In everyday living on a deeper level and in contrast with the formalized questioning of the questionnaire there is the playful and artistic wonder by means of which people can wonder about and in a creative manner come to know each other. Equally, there can be many unwanted and feared questions close to the surface of such living. An individual or a group can invest a great deal of emotional energy in ensuring that a question will never surface or if it does in discrediting it with rhetorical eloquence.

As well as in the realms of science and common sense, wonder is also a characteristic of the realm of scholarship, of history and bio-

---

[13] Arthur Miller, *Death of a Salesman* (New York: Penguin, 1961), p. 8.
[14] Ibid., p. 74.
[15] William Shakespeare, *Hamlet* (N.Y.: The Signet Classic Shakespeare, 1963), p. 237.
[16] A. Schutz, 'The Stranger', *Collected Papers II* (The Hague: M. Nijhoff, 1976), p. 105.

graphy, for instance. Biographers, interpreters, and historians are not merely passive observers of life. Scissors and paste history and chronicle biography are now recognized as inadequate ideals. The sources have to be actively and imaginatively questioned. J. L. Clifford remarks that in the course of his biographical research on Johnson he became interested in Mrs. Thrale, Johnson's friend. As his knowledge of her grew so also did his questions:

> What had the lady really been like? Was she essentially selfish and heartless?...Or did she truly deserve Johnson's long devotion?...The more I thought about the problem, the more curious I became, and in a desultory way I began collecting books about her.[17]

Collingwood's experiences of archaeological excavations taught him that one learned nothing at all if one dug without having a definite question in one's mind.[18] It is only through raising and answering an extended sequence of questions that the life or the historical movement becomes understood. In a fine study of what he terms "The Art of Historical Questioning" James Collins provides a great range of illustrations of the different types of questions posed by historians, from textual criticism, through problems of interpreting the meaning of a text, to those concerned with understanding what was happening in an historical movement from Kant to Heidegger, for instance, and also those concerned with the study of continuative problems.[19] He concludes that:

> Searching speaks more powerfully than does finding—an observation that holds good in history of philosophy as elsewhere. Just as the great modern philosophers are those who raise powerful questions about human experience and who keep up the search in the face of efforts to render everything in our existence obvious and settled, so also the great historians of philosophy are those who remain forever queryful in the presence of the source works.[20]

Again it becomes clear that questioning is the common method of the community of biographers, historians, and interpreters.

Finally, wonder is also acknowledged as a central and vivifying characteristic of the community of philosophers. Socrates wondered —what is the definition of piety, justice, temperance, courage, wis-

---

[17] J. L. Clifford, *From Puzzles to Portraits: Problems of a Literary Biographer* (London: Oxford U.P., 1970), p. 13.

[18] R. G. Collingwood, *Autobiography* (London: Oxford U.P., 1970), pp. 24f. See also his *The Idea of History,* (London: Oxford Univ. Press, 1970), pp. 269ff. for his comments on the role of questioning in history.

[19] 'The Art of Historical Questioning' is the title of Chapter III of James Collins' *Interpreting Modern Philosophy* (Princeton N.J.: Princeton Universtiy Press 1975) where again the role of questioning in interpretation and history is emphasized.

[20] Ibid., p. 99.

dom, and virtue—and with great questioning intensity searched for answers.[21] In the *Theaetetus* he remarks:

> This sense of wonder is the mark of the philosopher. Philosophy indeed has no other origin, and he was a good geneaologist who made Iris the daughter of Thamus.[22]

In the first chapter of the *Metaphysics* Aristotle asserts that all men by nature desire to know, and he goes on to reaffirm the role of wonder in philosophy. In our own time it is fairly widely accepted that questioning is a basic method in philosophy. There are some seven hundred and eighty four non-rhetorical questions in Wittgenstein's *Philosophical Investigations*: "How do words refer to sensations?" "In what sense are my sensations private?" "What happens when a man suddenly understands?" Hacker points out that the philosophical method of the later Wittgenstein is a dialogue form structured by an interrogative method:

> If one discovers through questioning that someone is using different conflicting rules for one and the same word, then one brings him to see a source of confusion, and the necessity for decision. But the decision should be his, not the therapists'.[23]

Again we find that an intellectual realm such as philosophy can be interpreted as a community of questioners. Wonder is its life principle.

These brief profiles can be used as a base from which to build up an image of questioning as a socially distributed activity. Realms of mental activity such as science, common sense, scholarship, philosophy, and theology are the names of communities of questioners. Obviously one and the same individual can belong to more than one of those realms but the names do refer to types of questioning that enjoy some overall common characteristics. Different individuals or groups within the scientific or scholarly communities, for instance, can apply their wonder to different fields of study, to the study of different chemical elements, biological organisms, or historical periods.[24] The collective wonder of the group will be its life principle. Within each of those communities individuals can engage in routine, normal, idle, obsessive, pathological, imaginative, innovative, playful, ecstatic, and revolutionary types of wondering. Their motives for so doing might be the pursuit of fame or of prestige or of truth. They may have open or

---

[21] The questions, what is piety, justice, temperance, and courage are posed in the *Euthyphro, Crito, Charmides,* and *Laches.* J. A. Stewart in his *Plato's Doctrine of Ideas* (Oxford: Clarendon Press, 1909), p. 16 remarks that these dialogues have been referred to by Grote as dialogues of search.

[22] *Theaetetus*, 155D.

[23] P. M. S. Hacker, *Insight and Illusion* (London: Oxford University Press, 1972), p. 117.

[24] What Lonergan refers to as field specialization *(Method in Theology,* p. 125) Kuhn refers to as subject matter specialization *(The Structure of Scientific Revolutions,* p. 179). Obviously a community can be defined in terms of its field or subject matter as well as in terms of its methods.

closed minds. Their actual achievement of openness to the incredible complexity of the real, both individually and socially, may vary considerably. This in no way invalidates the fact, whether they recognize it or not, that their wonder, their desire to know is a notion of being, of reality, of what there is. Being is the objective of the collaborative wonder of the human community.

III.

An image has been built up of a community of questioners or notions of being. Human wonder, the well spring of mental creativity, is the basic method of coming to know the world. In each instance it promotes the human mental performance of coming to know something, it effects the transition from ignorance to knowledge. Wonder, however, is not some "inner, indescribable, and private" mental activity "already in here now real."[25] Unlike Descartes, Hume, and Kant, Lonergan does not work with a closed box notion of mind and mental acts. For him such activities are intentional where intentional names a relation between the mental activity of the agent and the object. Such objects are not "in our minds" but are actual attributes of the world. The object of wonder is the world. It follows that self-appropriation, the appropriation of how it is that one's questioning promotes the performance of coming to know something in the world, far from amounting to some kind of private knowledge about oneself, really amounts to a social objectification, an objectification of what it is for anyone to be a questioner and come to know something. That objectification can only take place through participating, questioningly, in the social enterprises of science, common sense, and scholarship. It cannot be achieved by a Cartesian withdrawal from those realms. In fact the contrary might be the case. In order to appropriate one's questioning and knowing one might have to engage in more science and scholarship. The more highly developed those realms are and one's participation in them, the greater will be the clarity of the self-appropriation.

If, then, one truly appropriates what it is to raise, for instance, a statistical type of question and understands how the questioning unfolds and what is made present to oneself through its resolution, a probability distribution, in so doing one has not simply understood something about oneself but rather about the whole community of statisticians. Similar considerations apply, for instance, to an his-

---

[25] Normal Malcolm's attack on the notion of mental acts as inner, indescribable, and private in his "Wittgenstein on the Nature of Mind," *American Philosophical Quarterly Monograph No 4,* 1970, p. 18, is something like a critique of mental acts as 'already in here now real'.

torical type of question. In understanding how one's historical questiontng unfolds and what it makes present to us one understands something about the whole community of historians. Through understanding the most general attributes of one's questioning and its objects in science, common sense, and scholarship one understands something about the total community of questioners. When one understands the rules of chess one has understood the common framework of every chess game and of the chess playing community. When one understands the creative and unchanging norms of one's own mind and the attributes of the world that correspond to one's questioning and knowing one has understood something about the common mental and ontological framework of the whole human community. Without that understanding the practitioners of the human and social sciences are like prospective chess players who don't yet know the rules.

Taking one's wonder about the world seriously is a step, the difficulty of which must not be underestimated.[26] For some it will be transparently obvious that we question, that knowledge is a matter of answering questions, and that so far the text has simply stated the obvious.[27] Is it not the case that there really is no problem here at all? Part of the difficulty in recognizing one's great ignorance about oneself as a questioner is that through language we become quite familiar with the names of mental activities such as perceiving, inquiring, understanding, thinking, critically questioning, and judging. The trouble is that when named linguistically many conclude that that is the end of it. Hamlet's complaint could in this instance be addressed to the language, that it "would pluck out the heart of my mystery."[28] It took a Socrates to persuade us that knowing the name of virtue is not at all the same as knowing what virtue is. The name simply names an unknown. It is like the x in an algebraic equation. But many confuse it with the actual solution. There is a parallel here with learning the name of another person. When named, many assume the other is known. But all the name does initially is to name a total unknown. Recall how difficult it is really to understand some other person. When you cease wondering about them they are totally taken for granted and the relationship is dead. When one ceases to wonder about one's own wonder one is taking oneself totally for

---

[26] I have no wish to reproduce *Insight* here but am commenting on the kind of project it sets forth.

[27] When Collingwood attempted to draw attention to the significance of questioning he was accused of stating the obvious, *Autobiography*, p. 26.

[28] *Hamlet*, Act III, Scene ii, pp. 370f.

granted and is dead to the deepest realities of being human. The acknowledgment of ignorance is the beginning of wisdom.

What sort of human attribute is wonder, the pure desire to know? Through questioning we become interested in and come to know objects in our common sense, scientific, and scholarly worlds. But our own wonder is not an activity that can be found like an historical personality, a human state of affairs, or a probability distribution, in those worlds. Rather it is the unquestioned condition of possibility of coming to know such objects. Accordingly, in a sense the analysis of that activity is beyond the scope of science, common sense, and scholarship. Where then is wonder "inside" you, inside your skin? How is it inside you? What does it feel like to wonder or be curious? Is it something like having a mental pain? What might be right and wrong with these questions? Does one's wonder change throughout one's lifetime? Is it the same for the child, adult, senior citizen? We talk about changing our minds, but that usually refers to what we wonder about and think about, not to our questioning and thinking faculties which do not seem to change over a lifetime. How does questioning unite the successive moments in our living when we are engaging in an inquiry? Is it an operation that unites stages in our lives or even all of our lives? Is it the same activity that is involved in science, common sense, scholarship, philosophy, and theology? If so is it a human absolute, an absolute presupposition, a basic activity?[29] Is it the unchanging and unrevisable principle of all revision?

It is then, one thing to use one's mind in science, common sense, and scholarship; it is quite another matter to have any clear grasp what mental activities are involved and how our questioning organizes them. Most of us have only a very dim appreciation of how our wonder reorganizes our perception of texts in exegesis, of our hearing in listening to a conversation, or of our perceptions of scientific data or human states of affairs. Questioning in every instance is an anticipation. What is it an anticipation of and how are the anticipations made present? Are they made present through questioning reorganizing our looking so that we see what we are looking for? Or is questioning nothing at all like looking and might its anticipations be made present through some mental activity that is totally different from seeing, understanding for instance. If so what kind of anticipated objects could it possibly have? We see colours and shapes. What we see, allowing for the velocity of light, coincides with our seeing. We can wonder about the past, present, and future, the law

---

[29] See R. G. Collingwood, *Essay on Metaphysics* (Chicago: Gateway, 1972), Chapter V; P. Geach, *God and the Soul* (London: Routledge, 1969), pp. 32f.

of gravity, and another person's intentions. The possible anticipations of our wonder are made present through acts of understanding, moments of insight. We exclaim, "suddenly it all fell into place, I'm not stuck any more, I can go on, I can continue." What exactly falls into place in a moment of insight? How is it different from a gestalt shift? If understanding is nothing at all like looking, what possible sorts of objects could it make present to us and where could they possibly be — in Plato's noetic heaven? Insights in turn generate hypotheses. Our wonder now becomes critical; it becomes concerned with the evidence for or against a hypothesis. In our waking living there is hardly a moment that goes by when we are not performing some one of these mental activities. We experience our mental activity as a conscious and given experience. But for the vast majority T. S. Eliot's remark holds, "We had the experience but missed the meaning."[30]

Consider then some distinct types of wonder. Statisticians wonder — what is the probability distribution $P(E_i)$ of some random aggregate; historians wonder — what was going forward from A to B, from Kant to Heidegger for instance; scientists wonder — what are electrons, atoms, plants, animals? A statistician will claim with great certainty that he knows what a probability distribution is. Likewise an historian will claim that he knows what history is, a scientist that he knows what an electron or a biological organism is. On one level this is obviously true and not to be denied. Through their work they understand probability distributions, historical movements, and various things or individuals. But they don't understand their own understanding, how it differs from looking, and how it makes a probability distribution, an historical movement, or various things known to them. Because they might be vague about the distinction between looking and understanding they tend to equate understanding with looking and when asked, what is an electron, a probability distribution, or history, they try to draw some kind of visible picture of it.

Now in fact it is the present position that understanding and judging, the activities by means of which the anticipations of our wonder are made present to us, are utterly unlike looking. Again understanding is not some kind of totally inner, private, and indescribable activity. Its object is not an attribute of an agent but rather of the world. Its object is in fact the probability distribution of the aggregate, the actual historical movement, or the thing. It follows that because statisticians and historians neglect their own understanding and the manner in which it makes the anticipations of their question-

---

[30] T. S. Eliot, *Four Quartets* (London: Faber, 1958), p. 39.

ing present there is a sense in which they are radically in the dark both about themselves and about what a probability distribution, an historical movement, and a thing are. But it will take something of a Socrates to so persuade them.

The exercise of self-appropriation will then invite us to cease being naive realists' it will invite an unavoidable ontological stance. Questioning is an anticipation of the attributes of the world. Those attributes are made present to us, not simply by looking, but only through perceiving, questioning, understanding, thinking, and judging. Until one has undergone a prolonged process of self-clarification in which the distinction between looking, understanding, and judging, and the objects of those activities becomes clear one is *in a sense* in the dark, not only about oneself and everybody else, but also about the kind of world it is that is proportionate to our collaborative wonder.

In his late fifties Sartre remarked: "Atheism is a cruel and long-range project. I think I have carried it through."[31] The ascent of self-appropriation is long and steep and demanding, but it is not cruel. It is an ascent out of atheism, out of materialist philosophies of man and reductionist philosophies of the world. Somewhere along the ascent one discovers one's immortality. But it is also paradoxical. The ascent cannot be divorced from participation in science, common sense living, and scholarship. Participation in those realms at a high level of development aids it. But in every instance the result is an objectification, not of something personal and private, but rather of the common reality characteristic of every human being. The greater the success of any individual in appropriating his own wonder about the world, the more deep will be his understanding, not simply of himself and his world but also of everybody else and their world.

IV.

An image has been built up of an historical and social community of questioners. A contrast has been drawn between a member of that community who takes the fact that he is a questioner and its implications seriously and a member who although he does question totally ignores that fact. The former is moving towards a deepening understanding of how his and everyone else's wonder organizes the performance of coming to know something and the attributes of the world that correspond to and become known through that performance. The latter is in the dark about it. The question now arises, can the standpoint of the former be made the basis for an understanding of

---

[31] J. P. Sartre, *The Words* (N.Y.: Braziller, 1955), p. 158.

how a community comes to appropriate reality? What is distinctive about the standpoint is that the personal and social role of wonder is allowed its full scope. For the latter it will not be acknowledged as of any particular significance. Self-appropriation is concerned with determining the most general properties of the questioning performance, of how it organizes coming to know across the various mental realms, and of what becomes known. But the question now arises, can one use that standpoint as a basis for discovering the particular anticipations of the questioning of the scientific, common sense, and scholarly communities?

The central suggestion is that although questioning occurs in all the realms of mental life and corresponding communities, it does not occur in a totally random, but rather in a recurrently structured fashion. Science, scholarship, common sense, philosophy, and theology originate from very obscure origins. But in their historical evolution there emerges and recurs throughout their subsequent history permanently recurring *types* of questioning. Those types are not discarded in revolution such as occurred in the transition from Newton to Einstein, or in the shift from pre-critical to critical history. Rather there is apprehended with increasing clarity through the revolutionary process the type of questioning that is involved in explaining movement or history.[32] An indefinite number of particular instances of the type of questioning emerge but they all belong to the same type. To wonder what the Councils of Nicea, Chalcedon, Trent, and Vatican I, meant respectively by consubstantial, *prosopon,* transsubstantiation, and Papal Infallibility, is to raise four distinctive instances of the interpretative type of questioning. The particular instances can be multiplied indefinitely yet they all belong to one and the same type. To wonder what was going forward from Nicea to Chalcedon or from Trent to Vatican I is to raise two distinctive instances of the historical type of questioning. Such types of questioning and their anticipations are obviously distinct from but related to the interpretative types. Accordingly there emerges the suggestion that scholarship and the scholarly community are characterized by *a set* of interdependent types of questioning, or a set of systems of searching or paradigms.[33]

Similarly the scientific community seems to be characterized, not by homogeneous questioning, but rather by a set of distinct but

---

[32] Both Einstein and Newton anticipated the same kind of laws, those involving functional relations. Space does not allow me to comment on how in fact revolutions can throw light on a type of questioning.

[33] On paradigms see Kuhn, *The Structure of Scientific Revolutions;* on systems of searching see L. Wittgenstein, *Philosophical Remarks* (Oxford: Blackwell's, 1975), pp. 170f.

related types of recurring questions and anticipations. One type of scientific questioning is concerned with discovering functional or structural relations. It is an anticipation of some unknown function $f(x,y,z,t)$ or of the set of terms and their structural or functional relations constitutive of the chemical elements, biological organisms, human knowing, an economy, and so forth. A whole host of questions of the type "why is this strip of space time an X?" will find their answer in terms of "because of its structure or functional relations." Likewise there are many different kinds of random aggregates or events or populations. To them all we can address the statistical question: what is the probability distribution $P(E_i)$ of the aggregate or population? Further distinctive types of scientific questioning seem concerned with development, evolution, and things. As those different types of questioning seem interdependent, science like theology might be characterized by functional specialties.[34] Science, like scholarship, can be interpreted as the name of a community characterized by a set of interdependent types of questions and anticipations, a set of systems of searching or paradigms.

Now although the number of distinctive individual questions we might ask in any mental realm seems totally unlimited, the number of types of human questioning involved might not be so unlimited. In fact, numerically it might be quite small. There follows the possibility of defining a realm of mental life and the social group who participate in it in terms of the emergence and recurrence of a finite set of interrelated and permanently recurring types of human questioning. Nor would there seem any alternative unless we want to earn for ourselves the title, obscurantist, and remain in our mental and social chaos. The suggestion will of course horrify the philosophical philistines but it cannot be easily rejected. But it will be difficult to take seriously if one neglects one's wonder.

So much for the suggestion. What then is involved in the process of objectification? In elementary algebra students are recurrently presented with problems of the type, find the unknown x.[35] Part of their strategy in finding the unknown is to articulate everything that is known about it prior to actually discovering it. They can proceed by stating, let x be the unknown, and then attempt to work out an algebraic equation in which it figures. Similarly in statistics they can say, let $P(E_i)$ be the unknown probability distribution, in history let X be the unknown historical movement. An important point to

---

[34] In Chapter IV of *Insight* Lonergan establishes the complementarity or functional interdependence of classical and statistical questioning. It could be concluded that those methods are functional specialties in science.

[35] For a multitude of illustrations consult W. W. Sawyer, *Vision in Elementary Mathematics* (New York: Pelican Original, 1964).

appreciate is that although the many problems of elementary algebra are all different, their solutions all enjoy a similar structure. The same kinds of insights are involved in making them present. So instead of asking, what are the characteristics of the anticipated x in this specific problem?, we can ask, what are the common structural attributes of the totality of solutions of this type? Similar questions can be posed for statistical and historical questioning. Algebra or statistics or history are also the names of communities who participate in the corresponding types of problem solving. Accordingly to ask what are the common anticipations of all the questions of algebra is really to ask a disguised question about the anticipations of the questioning of the whole community. It is to raise a question about the common framework, paradigm, system of searching, the heuristic anticipations or structures of the group. Lonergan's articulation of the classical and statistical heuristic structures can then be interpreted as an attempt to articulate the anticipations of the shared questioning of the corresponding groups.[36] As Wittgenstein puts it, "Tell me how you are searching, and I will tell you what you are searching for."[37] But what exactly is a paradigm or a shared system of searching? Most attempts to articulate such systems are on the conceptual level, on the level of the analysis of the shared language and concepts of the group. Lonergan is not necessarily in conflict with that approach but he goes beyond it in a most important manner. For his emphasis is on the shared questioning and understanding of the group, the activities that generate the shared concepts and language. Understanding makes present what one is searching for. Accordingly, to articulate the attributes of statistical or historical types of understanding and their proportionate objects is to make clear the anticipations of the searching of the group. The object of questioning and understanding is in every instance some attribute of the world that is wondered about. So there is an unavoidable ontological stance involved. Again, as mentioned, if understanding is neglected there is a sense in which a group can talk about probabilities and history and not be clear about what they are talking about.

But science, common sense, and scholarship are the names, not simply of homogeneous types of questioning, but rather of sets of distinctive types of questioning. It follows that in order adequately to articulate the anticipations of the wonder of such communities one has to move from simple systems of searching or heuristic structures

---

[36] Lonergan distinguishes between a heuristic notion, heuristic structure, and integral heuristic structure, *(Insight,* Chapter II and pp. 391f). The present invitation is to interpret the last two of those terms as social categories.

[37] Wittgenstein, *Philosophical Remarks,* p. 67.

to sets of systems or what might be termed integral heuristic structures. The attempt to work out an interdependent set of systems or an integral heuristic structure is really a disguised way of working out the questioning orientation of a community. *Method in Theology* must rank as a paradigm illustration of the execution of such a program, the articulation of an interdependent set of anticipations tacit in the set of types of questioning of the theological community.

How might that task be achieved? In working out *Method in Theology* Lonergan had to participate himself in the historical and social enterprise that is theology. The goal of the involvement is to objectify the complete set of types of questioning that one cannot avoid raising when doing theology and the kinds of objects they anticipate and make known. One has to discover that research raises questions of the type, who wrote such and such a text and when? Interpretation is concerned with questions of a type, what did A mean by B? History is concerned with questions of the type, what was going forward from the New Testament to Nicea, and so forth for all the distinctive types of questioning in the set. The anticipated text, interpretation, and history are named unknowns. In every instance a particular type of understanding will be involved in making the unknown known. It is one thing to understand the meaning of a specific text or to understand what was going forward in an historical movement; it is quite another to identify one's acts of interpretative and historical understanding, how they differ from plain looking, and the kinds of objects in the world they make present. But it is only by taking that further move that one can in an unconfused manner become clear about the anticipations of the community and the real world that is proportionate to them. The term of the analysis, if successful, is the discovery not simply of how one cannot avoid doing theology oneself, but rather of how the community is or ought to be doing theology. The programme can obviously be extended from theology or scholarship to science, common sense, and philosophy itself. Again in every instance self-objectification, if correct, will also be a social objectification.

In the initial stages of their history the different types of questioning which characterize the different groups will obviously be very undifferentiated and the group will be in need, then as always, of permanent openness to the emergence of new types. The task of objectification is a continuing and interacting one. Its goal is a reorientation of the questioning of the community. Through understanding the functional relations between the different types of questioning the possibility of replacing discordant or out of phase development, of booms and slumps, by more harmonious development emerges. Nor will the group find itself trapped in a logical straight jacket by this process. Rather the contrary, it is a most demanding definition. The group is being defined, not statically but dynamically in terms of an unrestrictedly dynamic principle, its collaborative wonder. If the group is true to it, it will progress in its appropriation of the real; if not, its appropriation of reality will be distorted. Without that objectification progress is in the hands of chance.

To conclude, it has been suggested that philosophy of mind and ontology are really social sciences. Self-appropriation is a social objectification. The notion of being, self-affirmation, differentiations of consciousness, heuristic structures, and functional specialties should be interpreted as explicitly social categories.

Politics and Self-Acceptance

by Geoffrey L. Price

I.

In his work on *Method in Theology,* Lonergan has been concerned to show that the diverse concerns of the theological community—from textual scholarship to dogmatics and pastoralia—can be understood not as disjointed specialisms, but as interlocking activities that stem from the theologians' capacity for unrestricted inquiry[1] into the present situation of the church and the possibilities for responsible action in the future. Such an inquiry[2] will bring an awareness of the grounding of religious tradition in the primary accounts of its founding events and subsequent controversies, and this will engage the theologian in the problems of interpreting those events. As he becomes aware of divergences in interpretation, and their relation to divergences among religious communities, the theologian may learn that in the resulting conflicts and dialogues of the past, fundamental disagreements concerning truth, value and religious experience are at stake. Centrally therefore, the theologian stands in need of discernment: from his growing awareness that his whole evaluation of the past is affected by the scope of his existing value-judgments, he needs to be drawn to foundational judgments upon which he can rest his conclusions concerning the truth and value of the alternatives mediated to him by the past. Thus for Lonergan the religious experience of the theologian is intertwined with his systematic reflection: for insofar as he encounters God whose love sought him out, so he is set free to discern that which is truly valuable in life, and thus to grasp the worth of adhering to an account of truth which does full

---

[1] Bernard Lonergan, *Method in Theology* (London: Darton, Longman and Todd, 1972), pp. xii, 133. (Hereafter cited as *Method*).

[2] *Method*, chs. 5-11.

justice to his own capacity for reflective intelligent inquiry. So it is that Lonergan sympathizes with Voegelin's insistence[3] that the gospel comes to us not as information, but as the existential discovery that God himself seeks and draws us as we encounter the alternatives of living in integrity and love or in the death-like refusal to attain them. So too it is that Lonergan affirms that as the theologian engages in dialectical analysis and takes his stand on foundational judgments, he is experiencing and sorting out the pulls and counter-pulls of just such alternative modes of existence.[4] It follows that only the theologian's personal appropriation of love, goodness and truth can allow him to select, within the alternatives uncovered, those doctrinal principles on which he will approach the different spheres of the church's activity—pastoral, moral, liturgical or any other.[5] Within that integrity of reflection that makes possible his selection of doctrines, he may go on to work out a detailed understanding of their interrelation, thus developing an intelligent grasp that will allow the significance of the church's teaching in changing human circumstances to be effectively communicated.[6]

It is paradoxical that, while Lonergan has clearly indicated the bearing of his analysis of theological enquiry upon the corresponding problems of the human sciences with which theology must collaborate, his work has so far received little attention from those political theorists who are concerned with recovering and communicating a basis for order and integrity in human communities. For Lonergan suggests that within the human sciences arise problems of discernment whose scope parallels those experienced by the theologian.[7] The conflicting accounts of the past and its bearing on analysis of the present that face the political theorist, demand of him a capacity to distinguish those elements in situations which are the seeds of true human community, and those which lead to enmity and the conflict which springs from self-alienation. In effect, therefore, he sketches the possibility of a 'method in politics' in which the diverse human sciences could find a basis for cooperation that would enable them to discern and counter the sources of social alienation. The discernment of the political theorist would be grounded in his experience of conversions that unlock his capacity to orient his value judgments by his understanding of goodness, and free him to form judgments

---

[3] Eric Voegelin, 'The Gospel and Culture', in *Jesus and Man's Hope,* ed. D. G. Miller and D.Y. Hadidian, (Pittsburgh: Pittsburgh Theological Seminary, 1971), pp. 80, 88-91 (Hereafter cited as 'Gospel and Culture').

[4] Bernard Lonergan, 'Theology and Praxis', *CTSA Proceedings* 32 (1977), pp. 6-10.

[5] *Method,* pp. 267-9.

[6] *Method,* chs 5, 12-14.

[7] *Method,* pp. 364-5.

of truth upon the full implications of his capacity for inquiry. Thus a principle of selection in political analysis is established: of the conflicting policy alternatives, the theorist may distinguish those which embody and support the possibilities for good latent within a situation. A principle of coordination now follows: the theorist may now plan efficiently in order to bring out the implications of his general policy stance within that particular situation. A principle of action is established: *praxis* finds its orientation and meaning as the outcome and completion of systematic reflection on the significance of a changing situation.[8]

At the heart of such an analysis of the political theorist's need for discernment, therefore, stands an insistence on the three-fold reorientation in his stance on truth, his estimate of value and his affective orientation within life. Now for all that Lonergan finds Aquinas' development from Aristotle's account of intellectual and moral judgment to be more coherent than the Platonic positions,[9] nevertheless Lonergan's account of the breakthroughs that are intellectual and moral conversion remains closely reminiscent[10] of Plato's symbolism of the prisoners in the Cave.

> The transition from the neglected and truncated subject to self-appropriation is not a simple matter. It is not just a matter of finding out and assenting to a number of true propositions. More basically, it is a matter of conversion, of personal philosophical experience, of moving out of a world of sense and of arriving, dazed and disoriented for a while, into a universe of being.[11]

Now Plato's symbolism reflects an account of the human dilemma which Lonergan's analysis both confronts and extends. For the imagery of the Cave grounds an insistence that the problem of freeing human knowledge from delusion involves changes in habitual false beliefs which are bound up with disoriented moral judgments.[12] It follows that a knowledge of the reality for which the shadows of the

---

[8] *Method*, pp. 365-6; compare Sir Geoffrey Vickers *Value Systems and Social Process* (Harmondsworth: Pelican Books, 1970), *passim*.

[9] Bernard Lonergan *Verbum: Word and Idea in Aquinas*, ed. David B. Burrell (Notre Dame: University of Notre Dame Press, 1967), pp. 16-33; compare R. J. Henle, *St. Thomas and Platonism* (The Hague: Martinus Nijhoff, 1956) *passim.*, and David B. Burrell, *Aquinas: God and Action* (London: Routledge and Kegan Paul, 1979), pp. 120-2.

[10] Bernard Tyrrell, *Bernard Lonergan's Philosophy of God* (Dublin: Gill and Macmillan, 1974), p. 34.

[11] Bernard Lonergan, 'The Subject', in *A Second Collection*, ed. William Ryan and Bernard Tyrrell (London: Darton, Longman and Todd, 1974), p. 79.

[12] Plato, *Republic* 586 a, b; Robert Cushman *Therapeia: Plato's Conception of Philosophy* (Westport, Connecticut: Greenwood Press, 1976 reprint of original 1958 edition), 144-6. (Hereafter cited as *Therapeia*).

Cave were formerly mistaken, involves a new moral disposition.[13] On the other hand, escape from the illusions of the Cave is for Plato a necessity in the establishment of a true morality founded on understanding.[14] Hence there is disclosed what Cushman considers the 'weak link in Plato's *therapeia*', the dilemma that the Socratic attempt to bring about intellectual and moral reorientation by provoking an awareness of the cave-like ignorance that men are trapped in

> at one and the same time is designed to induce, and yet itself presupposes, a suitable condition of character.[15]

Lonergan considers that this problem is insoluble in its own terms, because man's will does not match 'the detachment and unrestricted devotion' of his capacity for intellectual inquiry. The problem of emerging from the confusion of mistaken beliefs lies in the mistaken individual:

> A critique of mistaken beliefs is a human contrivance, and a human contrivance cannot exorcise the problem of human evil...As long as will fails to match the desire of intellect, intellect may devise its efficacious methods, but the will fails to give them the cooperation they need.[16]

However, this conclusion leads Lonergan not to pessimism, but to the task of understanding the solution to the dilemma of man's weakness, a solution that comes from God, that can be affirmed because of his wisdom, goodness and omnipotence, and that is effective as man believes in and cooperates with it.[17] Thus in his more recent work on theological enquiry, Lonergan affirms that:

> From a causal viewpoint, one would say that first there is God's gift of his love. Next, the eye of this love reveals values in their splendor, while the strength of this love brings about their realization, and that is moral conversion. Finally, among the values discerned by the eye of love is the value of believing the truths taught by the religious tradition, and in such tradition and belief are the seeds of intellectual conversion.[18]

By arguing that the human sciences raise problems of method parallel to those of theology, Lonergan affirms that the religious transfor-

---

[13] *Therapeia* pp. 147-50.

[14] Plato, *Republic* 509a.

[15] *Therapeia*, p. 150.

[16] Bernard Lonergan, *Insight: A Study of Human Understanding* (London: Darton, Longman and Todd, 2nd edition, 1958), p. 717. (Hereafter cited as *Insight*.) Compare David Tracy, *The Achievement of Bernard Lonergan* (New York: Herder and Herder, 1970), p. 182.

[17] *Insight*, p. 720.

[18] *Method*, p. 243.

mation of the social theorist is just as central to the possibility of his reaching true discernment and wise action, as it is for the theologian.

> Now as in theology, so in historical and empirical human studies scholars and scientists do not always agree. Here too, then, there is a place for dialectic that assembles differences, classifies them, goes to their roots, and pushes them to extremes by developing alleged positions while reversing alleged counter-positions. Theological foundations, which objectify the horizon implicit in religious, moral and intellectual conversion, may now be invoked to decide which really are the positions and which really are the counter-positions. In this fashion any ideological intrusion into scholarly or scientific human studies is filtered out.[19]

Now the notion of an articulated understanding of the interrelation of the diverse human sciences is surely to be welcomed, even though it is clear that much needs to be done to elaborate the detailed bearing of Lonergan's analysis on the ambiguities of political judgment in concrete human situations. However, objections may be raised even before that task of explication begins, and it is likely that these will include questions concerning the role Lonergan assigns to religious conversion in the political theorist's emergence from the distortion of ideologies into true discernment. Douglass, commenting recently on the political role envisaged for Christianity in the work of Voegelin, concludes that:

> while in principle Christianity is viewed as an ally of philosophy in the quest for a rightly ordered existence, it is also considered a somewhat unreliable ally.[20]

This estimate is largely based on Voeglin's paper 'The Gospel and Culture,' in which he readily concedes the strength of the gospel movement to be its 'concentration on the one point that is all-important,' that in man's struggle between the forces of life and death (discerned in the notion of *metaxy* in the earlier movement of classic philosophy) God himself is present. We have already noted Lonergan's concurrence with this exposition of the gospel as encounter and decision. But Vogelin goes on to express the fear that

> This very strength (sc. of the gospel) . . . can cause a breakdown, if the emphasis on the centre of truth becomes so intense that its relations to the reality of which it is the centre are neglected or interrupted.[21]

---

[19] *Method,* p. 365.

[20] Bruce Douglass, 'The Gospel and Political Order: Eric Voegelin on the Political Role of Christianity', *Journal of Politics 38* (1976), p. 27.

[21] 'Gospel and Culture', p. 97.

Under those conditions, man's experience in society and nature is lost sight of; thus Christianity tends to undermine the civil theologies that symbolized social order in traditional societies by desacralizing them, and yet tends to be uninterested in providing a durable substitute for them. Douglas concludes that

> It is clear that it is primarily to philosophy to which [Voeglin] looks for the therapy modern culture requires. At issue is mainly the reformation of reason, and this is mainly a philosophical task. Christianity can help in this process to the extent that it absorbs philosophical criticism. But to the extent that it does not, it only contributes to the problem.[22]

Two questions may therefore be asked concerning the notion of 'method in politics': is it the case that, in reaching full discernment, the political theorist encounters problems in his own experience that can only be resolved at the religious level of intentionality? Secondly, does Lonergan's account of religious conversion as a falling in love which brings to full actuality our capacity for moral and intellectual inquiry, imply a role for the gospel in political order that averts Voegelin's fears?

II.

We may approach the first question by considering the problem of the emergence of unrestricted intellectual and moral inquiry as an individual develops from childhood. He may slowly gain confidence in the inferences of his own questioning in limited fields, perhaps those of technical or scientific reflection, which interact least with accepted patterns of behaviour. But in social existence, he will find that appropriate models of behaviour are tacitly assumed within his culture, and he will experience pressure to conform to those models as the price of his own survival. Insofar as his own emerging judgment of moral issues conflicts with such social norms, he will experience fear as the needs of adjustment conflict with the demands of integrity: a fear which affects him if he seeks to embark on political analysis no less than for other members of his society.[23]

Eric Neumann was extensively concerned with the political correlates of these tensions and fears. He develops the notion of the 'old ethic', whose central principle is the representation of an ideal type of personality as an absolute value, tacitly implying that individuals can and should adapt to that ideal by eliminating incompatible qualities. Only if they succeed in adapting will they be said to have a

---

[22] Douglas, *op. cit.* note 20, p. 45.

[23] John Haught, *Religion and Self-Acceptance* (New York: Paulist Press, 1976), p. 157.

'good conscience'. But complete adaptation is impossible, because the general social ideal is not adjusted to the reality of any particular person: and so the individual is faced with the outstandingly difficult task of conforming.[24]

Following Jung, Neumann distinguishes two principal mechanisms of such adjustment. In *suppression,* the conscious self deliberately works to perfect its behaviour, but contrary tendencies remain known to it; the price of denying them satisfaction is accepted, and hence the suppressive reaction involves suffering. This is the usual adaptive mechanism of moral élites. By contrast, the most frequent mechanism used to secure conformity is *repression.* Here, the unacceptable side of the personality is forced out of sight: it becomes unconscious or forgotten, although still with an active and independent function capable of interference with the person's actual behaviour. Both processes allow the formation of a semi-conscious or unconscious 'shadow' personality, as compensation for the presentation of a facade social role or *persona.*[25] Neumann is clear that the formation of this facade is in conflict with the emergence of the desire for understanding:

> A large part of education will always be devoted to the formation of a *persona* which will make the individual "clean about the house", and socially presentable, and will teach him, not what is, but what may be regarded as, real; all human societies are at all times more interested in instructing their members in the techniques of not looking, of overlooking, and of looking the other way, than in sharpening their observation, increasing their alertness, and fostering their love of truth.[26]

The political consequences are far-reaching. Within the community, the 'orthodox' members are forced into an inner doubt by suppression or repression of the unacceptable self. This doubt is exacerbated if dissident minorities seek to appeal to alternative moral, political or religious authorities. The 'orthodox' members may sense a superiority in the dissidents and fight to eliminate or denigrate them, as in Scheler's analysis of *ressentiment.*[27] Alternatively they may feel the dissidents to have chosen an inferior life, in which case the

---

[24] Eric Neumann, *Depth Psychology and a New Ethic* (London: Hodder and Stoughton, 1967).

[25] Neumann, *Depth Psychology and a New Ethic,* pp. 34-5; Carl Jung, 'The Relations between the Ego and the Unconscious', in *The Collected Works of C. G. Jung,* ed. G. Adler, M. Fordham, H. Read, (London: Routledge and Kegan Paul, 1953), vol. VII.

[26] Neumann, *Depth Psychology and a New Ethic,* p. 38.

[27] Max Scheler, *Ressentiment,* trans. William W. Holdheim, (New York: Free Press, 1961), pp. 43-78.

'orthodox' may preserve their self-image by heaping on them the blame for their disturbance of social life.[28] If the dominant orthodoxy depends on asceticism and repression, then its doubt-laden fight will be a sadism in conscious and rationalized form, stemming from a sense of inner disturbance that is relatively near the conscious level.[29] If the dominant group holds itself in check by repression, then it will have no conscious capacity to acknowledge or evaluate the feelings of insecurity aroused by the hated group, and its sadism will be of the wildest emotionality.[30]

Now the political analyst may in his own development have adapted his behavior through elements of repression or suppression. The problem of moving beyond self-rejection is therefore central if such an individual is to make social judgments stemming from his own capacity for reflective inquiry, rather than conform to collective norms or fight to eliminate those who disturb those norms. Yet the whole thrust of Neumann's argument is that the 'old ethic', within which there is no scope for unrestricted questioning, is sustained by the fear of one's own unacceptability. John Haught's recent analysis, while not addressed directly to Neumann's work, clearly suggests that such experiences of fear in facing the possibility of adulthood, raise problems with a religious dimension. The sensed possibility of responsible freedom

> ...generally brings with it both a sense of self-esteem and an increasing anxiety in the face of the developing experience of autonomy. If one is not capable of appropriating the loneliness of his emergent freedom, he will experience the temptation to regress to a heteronomous state of existence once more . . . In order to prevent the imperatives from appearing as though they spring from the inmost depths of oneself, the individual may, among other defenses, cling desperately to the heteronomous image of God that is the religious correlate of the child's extrinsicist experience of the norms of his mind. This God then becomes the screen on which he projects his desire to be governed from outside.[31]

Thus at the limit of questioning within political existence, the question of God arises: not as a term in a logical sequence, nor as an irruption from a sphere beyond that of the social order, but as an

---

[28] Neumann, *Depth Psychology and a New Ethic*, pp. 52-5.

[29] Neumann, *Depth Psychology and a New Ethic*, p. 55; compare Albert Camus, *The Rebel* (Harmondsworth: Pelican, 1962), pp. 156-210.

[30] Camus, *The Rebel*, 146-55.

[31] Haught, *Religion and Self-Acceptance*, p. 157.

issue that is sensed within the conflict between emerging into personal integrity, and the security of extraneous projected norms.[32] For the question may dimly be perceived: does God indeed reject us as we reject ourselves? If it were the case that God is caring, accepting and affectionate in a manner dimly mirrored in the capacity of another person who loves and accepts even our darkest side, then our deepest fear could be dissolved. If God's acceptance is commensurate with our own capacity for self-deception, then our capacity for inquiry need no longer be blocked, our energy need no longer be consumed in maintaining our 'distance' from ourselves. As Haught says,

> What makes a religious story, such as that of God's unconditional love, a story which promotes the quest for truthfulness towards oneself, is the narrative "world" that it constitutes in such a way as to eliminate any fear of uncovering one's darker side. One is accepted in any case. Nothing that he can do or leave undone will change this basic situation.[33]

Thus the experience of forgiveness, on this analysis, is precisely the point at which our capacity for unrestricted integrity in our political reflection and behaviour, is unlocked. The political theorist stands in need of self-acceptance no less than any other member of his society. It follows, then, that in placing the experience of God's grace and goodness at the heart of any individual's conversion to truth and value, Lonergan is going to the heart of the problem, not only of the discernment of the theologian, but also of the political theorist. Only if we know ourselves to be accepted without reservation can we abandon the self-deception that we generate out of fear of revealing ourselves to others, and commit our intelligence, our feelings and our love to discerning the common good of the community as it faces the future.

III.

By juxtaposing Haught's analysis of self-acceptance with Neumann's study of the political consequences of repression and suppression, we have focussed on 'narrative revision' as the key to allowing inner integrity to become the central desire in life. Is there not a danger, however, that this focus may be misunderstood, particularly where the gospel has been collapsed to propositional form

---

[32]. *Method*, pp. 38-9, 102-3.
[33] Haught, *Religion and Self-Acceptance*, p. 173.

divorced from experience? Voegelin is aware of the phenomenon of church communities which constitute

> ... an environment where it is not customary to ask questions, where the character of the Gospel as an answer has been so badly obscured by its hardening into self-contained doctrine that the raising of the question to which it is meant as an answer can be suspect as a "non-Christian attitude." [34]

Thus Voegelin repeatedly warns that the primary experiences of personal encounter may be lost sight of; the truth of revelation is not to be abased to a piece of information. In our earlier analysis we concluded that the political analyst is confronted with the dilemma of self-rejection. Let us now inquire in more detail into the personal process of appropriating the gospel of forgiveness and acceptance, and its consequences for the possibility of a politics of integrity.

At this point we may find help in recent studies by Sebastian Moore, which focus on the paradox that the *initial* encounter with the message of acceptance is deeply disturbing. For the 'source and matrix of the Christian conviction of God's forgiving love is the guiltless consciousness of Jesus.' Yet the actual encounter with one who is completely free from self-rejection is complex:

> For one who is free of guilt altogether, free even of the generic guilt, will be a terrible accusation to me. He will make me conscious of the guilt in my whole build-up as a person . . . I am bewildered by the terrible presence of an alternative to what has seemed to me and to everyone else to be the only way to live, the only way to become. [35]

To say that, we may reflect, is to say that the gospel narrative of a forgiving God who is not the coercive deity whom we project as guardian of the 'old ethic', is not easy to accept. As Moore argues, we have a paradox:

> The *presence* of the guiltless one accuses my guilt, awakens guilt long ago forgotten, and indeed hardly perceived as guilt; while the *message* of the guiltless one is precisely that I am not guilty, that the charge against my freedom was falsely pressed and mistakenly accepted. [36]

The gospel narratives repeatedly assert that Jesus himself had a growing realization that there was only one way out of the paradox

---

[34] 'Gospel and Culture', pp. 61-2.

[35] Sebastian Moore *The Crucified Jesus is No Stranger* (New York: Seabury Press, 1977), p. 108.

[36] Moore, *The Crucified Jesus is No Stranger*, p. 108.

that his encounter with self-alienated man provoked,[37] a way whose meaning Moore recovers thus:

> Totally without guilt, totally deprived of my private self-affirming, I would fall apart, I would die. The only resolution is for him to undergo the death that I would die if I could accept his message of acceptance by God. *He* must die the death of the old world. *He* must fall apart. The love with which he offers man the sinner God's acceptance must turn back on him as death.[38]

The possibility of self-acceptance therefore hinges on the concrete possibility that we may find peace through the transfer of our own inner conflict onto the very person whose acceptance arouses our fear. Thus it is only

> ... in the death of Jesus that our perception of him as accusation dissolves into the true perception of him as the sign of our acceptance. For, as we have seen, it is his death that resolves the paradox which held his message of acceptance trapped in the form of accusation.[39]

Thus our inner anger, generated by the threat to our repressive or suppressive adjustments to the 'old ethic', is vented on one who does not turn aside from its force, but accepts in full the price of our death-dealing blows. At first we stand amazed: we had always feared to defy the coercive God of our childhood projections, lest he should really prove to be the cement of the universe. Yet now that our anger *has* been drawn out by the even more threatening possibility of an *accepting* God, we find that instead of destroying the world, our anger has been the means of showing us that we were loved and accepted from the beginning.

Yet later our fears may return. Moore argues elsewhere that the fear of the first disciples is then our fear: has the kind of God that lived in the life of Jesus actually *died?* In that case the guilt-shadow would return, once more to be played out in our loneliness. The implication is that

> With the quarrel with God dissolved in the soul's inner emptiness, with the virulence of guilt shrunk back into the originating self-dislike—which surely *is* the inner emptiness—the absence of God becomes associated uniquely with self-dislike, and self-dislike with the absence of God.[40]

---

[37] Matthew 16:21; Mark 10:32-4.
[38] Moore, *The Crucified Jesus is No Stranger*, p. 108.
[39] Moore, *The Crucified Jesus is No Stranger*, , p. 109.
[40] Sebastian Moore, 'The Humanity of God: The School of the Heart', Typescript, Boston College Lonergan Workshop, 1979, p. 13

Yet the gospel narratives recount that for despondent followers the totally unexpected happened: the embodiment of God's love returned from that chaos which enemies finally heaped on the threat he presented, and from that isolation in which even those who once trusted him had left him to die. It follows that in the resurrection, the possibility of our living beyond self-rejection, of giving full rein to our inner imperatives to consistency in knowing, doing and loving, is established. If Jesus took on himself the full outcome of the projected hostility of those whom he threatened, then he himself allowed men to act out the possibility that God (in the person of one in whose guiltlessness men sensed his divinity) was to be destroyed because he made their former lives seem unbearable. Yet in returning from death, Jesus showed himself to be stronger than that chaos of self-alienation which men broke over his head, and more faithful than the treachery which led them in self-disquiet to try to efface his memory. It follows that for an individual to emerge from the cocoon of rationalizations by which he adapted to the 'old ethic', is not to emerge to death, but to a life in which he is set free to be himself. The resurrection of Jesus has cleared from before him the final threat: he may follow his desire for understanding, responsibility and love in the knowledge that that desire is simultaneously his own, and one that is established by one who transcends him.[41]

Now if we understand the appropriation of the gospel of forgiveness in the concrete encounters which lead through fear and hostility to new life, we may go further in our analysis of the bearing of religious conversion on the political theorist's need to escape the dilemmas of self-rejection. If his knowledge of the gospel is derived from meeting a community which has lost sight of the question to which its founding narratives intended to answer, the theorist will at best find the propositions presented to him to be unsettling, and at worst irrelevant. But the theorist may encounter a community whose members have themselves found that in their own search for integrity of knowing and doing, the culminating and anchoring experience is their own acceptance by God. By extension of Moore's analysis, we may conclude that the initial effect of such an encounter can only engender fear and hostility in the theorist. The very fact that the community he meets has found a basis for being at peace with itself, unsettles the last defence of his rationalizations. Thus the encounter with Jesus will be mirrored in the encounter with those for whom he has already made possible the transition from absurdity through death to resurrection. Once again the possibility of acceptance will be misunderstood as a threat. The more the community of

---

[41] Compare Haught *Religion and Self-Acceptance*, pp. 160, 162.

new humanity is at peace with itself, the greater will be its tension with an uncomprehending world. Can there be any resolution of *that* paradox unless that community stands alongside the one from whom the Good News stems, and follows him in enduring the brunt of the hostility that cements an individual in the 'old ethic'? Without a willingness from that community to share in taking the force of the death-dealing suspicions projected by the inner conflicts of others,[42] it will be a living denial of the truth of the narrative by which it claims to live. But if the community has discovered in its unity with Christ that there is a resurrection life beyond the acceptance of suffering,[43] so it will be able to show that the worst that the 'gods' who sanctioned the 'old ethic' can do to man has been encountered and overcome. Thus in the midst of suffering it can be the beginnings of a truly human community, a hope-filled foretaste of a return to self-liking in human politics. The effect on the political theorist who encounters it may then be like that of the early Christian converts, whose lives led Saul, the Pharisee of the Pharisees, to kick against the pricks:

> Perhaps in a moment of reflection on the God proclaimed by the followers of Jesus, Paul suddenly felt the congruity between their dramatic accounts and the repressed elements of his own sentient consciousness. His conversion, then, took the form of a sudden flooding into harmony of the various levels of his world-involvement.[44]

IV.

We have argued that the political theorist cannot escape his own self-rejection; that the fulfillment of his capacity for self-transcending inquiring and valuing depends on his appropriation of God's acceptance of him as capable of living by those inner imperatives; and that the concrete possibility of his making that personal appropriation involves an encounter with individuals whose own religious conversion enables them to accept in love the hostility initially generated towards the gospel they proclaim. But what of Voegelin's fears that the very strength of the gospel's focus on man's relations with God tends to a characteristic neglect of the legitimation of civil society, and thus opens a way for a resurgence of gnosticism? Now Lonergan's own inquiry into dialectic confronts the fact that religious conversion is not necessarily the anchoring and fulfillment of moral and intellectual conversion; he recognizes that any individual's horizons

---

[42] I Peter 2:21, 4:12-26.
[43] Romans 6:5-11.
[44] Haught, *Religion and Self-Acceptance*, p. 172.

may be shaped by the affirmations of any one of the conversions, any two, all three, or none at all.[45] It follows that the religious experience of falling in love with God may not be grasped as a context in which moral action makes sense, in which the suffering involved in undoing the effects of social decline can be accepted. Even if religious conversion reveals the grounds of all true value, the subject may not grasp the moral value of establishing a basis for truth on his capacity for unrestricted understanding. Alternatively, intellectual conversion alone may lead to a firm cognitional basis for the natural and human sciences without proceeding to a firm basis for the consequent issues of value; moral conversion alone may result in an ethical critique of the social situation that, lacking a comprehensive understanding, results merely in idealistic but impractical suggestions;[46] intellectual and moral conversion conjointly may reveal the true issues in social progress and decline, but not the significance of love and suffering in the subject's struggles with his own and others' alienation. Nevertheless, the notion of 'method in politics' depends on individuals whose discernment stems from their fundamental judgments in all three spheres of experience: intellectual, moral and religious.[47] And this is no abolition of their human capacities, no other-worldly derailment of the gospel of the possibility of a new humanity. Rather, it is their complete surrender to their latent exigences for careful attention to the natural and social world they inhabit, intelligent inquiry into its meaning, reasonable judgments concerning the implications and possibilities of the situations it presents to them within it, and responsible decisions to foster true values as they are revealed, all in the loving realization that

> ... there is nothing in death or life, in the realms of spirits or superhuman powers, in the world as it is or the world as it shall be ... nothing in all creation that can separate us from the love of God in Christ Jesus our Lord.[48]

Although the watersheds of living that are denoted by the term 'conversions' are intensely personal, they are not purely private. For as for the theologian in Lonergan's analysis,[49] so for the political theorist in whom they occur it can mean the decision to align himself with a different social group, or to align himself with the group of his origins in a different way. Thus it will be in his social existence that he bears witness to the narrative of forgiveness that transformed his

---

[45] *Method,* p. 247.
[46] *Method,* p. 38.
[47] Compare, *Method,* p. 268.
[48] Romans, 8:38-9.
[49] *Method,* p. 269.

affective existence, his moral horizon, his intellectual norms. It will be in his social existence, too, that he and his neighbours demonstrate their allegiance not to their own interests but to the good of others.

It follows that the integrity of political thought and action which is implicit in the notion of 'method in politics' will be embodied in a strategy of communal living which seeks to discern and undo the root causes of social decline.[50] The discernment of such a community will be rooted in a conversion of intellect and feeling which is grounded and inspired by the discovery that God has accepted the cost of its attaining its true humanity, through the suffering of His incarnate Son. That discovery will allow the community to accept the hostility and suffering it endures in its turn.[51] Hence by conjoining religious conversion with moral and intellectual in his suggestions for the foundations of reflective method in the human sciences, Lonergan's stance is not in conflict with Voegelin's hope of restoring the life of reason as the foundations of human order. Rather, the notion of 'method in politics' implies a community whose discernment and action is moved by the love of understanding, of integrity and of responsibility, and whose love is grounded and inspired by the very self-disclosure of God within concrete human existence which has met and overcome the ultimate threat to ordered human existence.

---

[50] *Insight*, pp. 225-242.
[51] *Method*, p. 242.

Horizonal Diplomacy

by Mark D. Morelli

Bernard Lonergan's methodological studies have generated a nucleus of foundational insights whose intellectual expansion and deliberate and methodical implementation, if undertaken as a collaborative cultural project, would transform significantly a wide range of human endeavors. Lonergan has carried out the major portion of the work of intellectual expansion himself in one especially noteworthy case. From the basis provided by his foundational objectification of the intelligent and reasonable subject in *Insight*, he has developed the eight functional specialties outlined in his more recent *Method in Theology,* thereby accomplishing single-handedly the primarily intellectual portion of the transposition of theological endeavor from a classical to a modern context.[1] By carrying out this fundamental reorganization in the theological domain, Lonergan has greatly facilitated the task confronting those of us who would reorganize other human endeavors which fall under the broad heading of human studies. For, the eight specialties with which Lonergan has reorganized theological endeavor may be used to structure any discipline that investigates a cultural past in order to constitute and

---

[1] For Lonergan's affirmation of *Method*'s dependency upon *Insight*, see *Method in Theology* (New York: Herder and Herder, 1972), pp. 7n.2, 17, 260. F. E. Crowe has explored the relationship between *Insight* and *Method* at length in "An Exploration of Lonergan's New Notion of Value," *Science et Esprit,* XXIX, 2 (1977), 123-143,. On the fivefold shift of emphasis characterizing the transition from the classicist to the modern world-view, see Lonegan's essay in *A Second Collection,* eds. William Ryan and Bernard Tyrrell (London: Darton, Longman & Todd, 1974), pp. 43-54, esp. pp. 49-52.

guide a culture's future.² In the present essay I will attempt to expand Lonergan's nucleus of fundamental insights in the direction of reorganization in the domain of philosophy. However, I shall not attempt to transport the eight specialties from the theological to the philosophic context; this task is far too intricate to be handled in a short essay. Instead of presuming to think adequately here in terms of eight tasks, I propose to speak more cautiously, in terms of two distinguishable phases of philosophic activity. Moreover, because what I take to be the emphases of philosophy's first phase are illustrated sufficiently not only by the work completed by Lonergan in the first eighteen chapters of *Insight* but also by all more or less successful, predominantly intellectual philosophic work, I propose to concentrate my attention on the second phase of philosophy. Accordingly, I will present an account of a philosophic *praxis* which, to my mind, flows naturally from a personal grasp of the foundational enucleation of subjectivity engaged in the full range of endeavors. The self-appropriated methodologist is peculiarly suited for a type of cultural participation which actively promotes ongoing cultural collaboration by acknowledging and then reducing a range of cultural tensions which severely inhibit cultural development.

I. Horizonal Relations

The range of human endeavors may be conceived as a range of horizons.³ Each endeavor has its own standpoint, mode of conscious and intentional operation, and world.⁴ Six contemporary horizons have been distinguished by Lonergan: common sense, art, science,

---

² See Lonergan's remarks in "Bernard Lonergan Responds," in *Foundations of Theology*. Papers from the International Lonergan Congress 1970, ed. Philip McShane (Dublin: Gill and Macmillan Ltd., 1971), p. 233. Lonergan has made the same assertion with particular regard to philosophy in response to a question posed by me. See the Question Session following his Address to the Canadian Philosophical Association at the University of Toronto in 1974 (Tape-recording, The Lonergan Centre, Toronto).

³ The ideas presented in this section have been presented in greater detail in my unpublished doctoral dissertation, *Philosophy's Place in Culture: A Model,* University of Toronto, 1979.

⁴ Outstanding employments of the notion of horizon are those of Kant and Husserl. For Kant "the horizon thus concerns judgment on, and determination of, what man *can* know, what he *needs* to know, and what he *should* know." He employs the notion to discuss the extensive and intensive magnitude of cognition. This is the notion in its familiar analogous sense. See Kant's *Logic,* trans. Robert Hartman and Wolfgang Schwarz (Indianapolis and New York: Bobbs-Merrill, 1974), pp. 44-45. Husserl also employs the notion in its typical analogous sense. The horizon is the *"co-present* margin" of perception, "a *dimly apprehended depth or fringe of indeterminate reality."* See Husserl's *Ideas: General Introduction to Pure Phenomenology,* trans. W. R. Boyce Gibson (London: Collier-Macmillan, 1962), Section 24. While Lonergan begins in

scholarship, philosophy, and religion.⁵ A group, set, or cluster of distinct horizons of subjects who are at least present to one another and who may be understood and known as horizons by one another may be named a horizonal constellation. A constellation may be merely potential, in which case it has not yet been made problematic by the emergence in at least one of the member subjects of a recognition of horizonal dissonance. By a recognition of horizonal dissonance I mean a determinate and articulate or indeterminate or indirectly expressed apprehension of differences between standpoints, modes, and worlds. For example, if a man of common sense and a scientist pass their time together playing cards, the constellation is merely potential. Their mutual presence could be made problematic by a recognition of dissonance, but this recognition has not emerged. However, if their conversation turns to a topic which bears scientific treatment, an actual constellation is in the making. A constellation is potential inasmuch as one of the member subjects may diverge from ordinary concerns and operations in virtue of previous extraordinary development, but in fact does not. A potential constellation becomes virtually actual as one or more of its member subjects diverge from the ordinary mode of operation in virtue of the introduction of a topic which bears extraordinary treatment. A constellation is fully actual if the mutual presence of the members has become

---

Method with the analogous notion, according to which a horizon corresponds to one's concern, he also employs the notion to mean "the group of operations one has mastered" and "the range of things the subject is conscious of." Accordingly, the world of a horizon includes the mode of operation and standpoint as at least self-present. See the unpublished transcription of his *Lectures on the Philosophy of Education,* 1959 (The Lonergan Centre, Toronto), Lecture 4, p. 10 and Lecture 8, p. 25; see also his unpublished *Lecture on the Philosophy of History,* 1960 (The Lonergan Centre, Toronto), p. 22. Other usages of the notion of horizon by Lonergan may be found in the following: *Collection,* ed. F. E. Crowe (New York: Herder and Herder, 1967), pp. 200, 213-214; *A Second Collection,* pp. 69, 142, 162; his unpublished Introduction to his doctoral dissertation *Gratia Operans: A Study of the Speculative Development in the Writings of St. Thomas Aquinas,* ca. 1943 (The Lonergan Centre, Toronto), pp. 17-18; *Insight: A Study of Human Understanding* (New York: Philosophical Library, 1958), p. 639; his unpublished *Notes on Existentialism,* 1957, Thomas More Inst. Typescript (The Lonergan Centre, Toronto), p. 17; his unpublished *Dublin Lectures on Insight,* 1961 (The Lonergan Centre, Toronto), pp. 41-50; his unpublished lecture *The Mediation of Christ in Prayer,* 1964 (The Lonergan Centre, Toronto), p. 7; "Merging Horizons: System, Common Sense, Scholarship," *Cultural Hermeneutics*, (1973), 89, 93; his unpublished paper "Method: Trend and Variations," 1974 (The Lonergan Centre, Toronto, pp. 5-9; "Aquinas Today: Tradition and Innovation," *The Journal of Religion* 55, no. 2 (1975), 166-174; "Theology and Praxis," *CTSA Proceedings* 32 (1977), p. 11 N. 42.

⁵ See *Method,* the Index under "differentiations of consciousness". Similar lists have been presented by others. See, for example, R. G. Collingwood, *Speculum Mentis, or the Map of Knowledge* (Oxford: Clarendon Press, 1924, 1970), p. 42; Peter Winch *The Idea of a Social Science and its Relation to Philosophy* (London: Routledge & Kegan Paul, 1963), pp. 41, 100-101.

problematic in virtue of the emergence in at least one of the members of a recognition of horizonal dissonance.

Horizonal relations may be conceived as functions of efforts made by subjects with different horizons to accommodate the perplexity generated by recognitions of dissonance. Horizonal dissonance, and the horizonal multiplicity which underlies it, are perplexing. Every horizon is a more or less integrated unity of standpoint, mode, and world; and this unity, if not known clearly and distinctly, is at least self-present. As potential constellations become actual, the self-present unity of horizons is threatened. There are many horizons, and each one is a unity. If the emergent perplexity were given explicit expression, it might take the form of a question of the following type: How can the existence of a multiplicity of horizons be reconciled with the self-present unity of my own horizon? This perplexity is related, it seems, to the twofold orientation of horizons. On the one hand, the subject of a particular horizon is determinately directed by horizon-specific ideals. On the other hand, every subject is indeterminately directed by the ideals of human subjectivity in general. While each of us has a horizon, each of us is also human. Now, a determinate mode of operation from a determinate standpoint with regard to a determinate range of objects and objectives may or may not be a partial realization of the ideals of subjectivity in general. But, normally, the development of a horizon is attended by an identification, more or less complete and more or less deliberate, of the ideals proper to the emergent horizon with the ideals of subjectivity in general. For example, the developing scientist tends naturally to identify his emergent standpoint, mode, and world with *the* adequate standpoint, *the* adequately objective mode, and the universe of being.[6] This identification seems to have its root in the apparently self-validating unity of the developing horizon. As potential constellations become actual, this natural identification is temporarily dissolved; other apparently self-validating unities are recognized to exist. The adequacy of the identification is called into question: Are my world, mode, and standpoint coincident with the universe of being, the adequately objective mode of operation, and the basic ideals of subjectivity in general? In the philosophic horizon, this perplexity attains explicit expression as the threefold problem of the identity of worlds, modes, and standpoints. The notions of a

---

[6] Collingwood has noted the same phenomenon: "Every person who is actually absorbed in any given form of experience is by this very absorption committed to the opinion that no other form is valid, that his form is the only one adequate to the comprehension of reality....When artists and scientists, who after all do inhabit a common world of fact, meet and discuss their aims, each is apt to accuse the other of wasting his life on a world of illusions." See *Speculum Mentis,* p. 307.

universe of being, a transcendental mode of operation, and ideals of subjectivity in general, taken together, constitute the heuristic notion of the basic horizon of human existence. If an account of this horizon were acquired, and if the account were also generally known, a culture would be in possession of the ultimate frame of reference for the fully adequate intellectual integration of the variety of human endeavors. However, inasmuch as an ultimate frame of reference does not orientate human endeavors relative to one another at the present time, at least explicitly, subjects have no ultimate court of appeal to which they may turn to alleviate the perplexity generated by recognitions of horizonal dissonance. Consequently, attempts to accommodate perplexity take a variety of forms, rather than a single set of complementary forms, and they give rise to a limited variety of types of intersubjective relationships.

As constellations are actualized, member subjects acquire a new or renewed awareness of the distinction between horizon-specific ideals and the ideals of subjectivity in general. As horizonal integrity is called into question, so also is the presumed coincidence of horizon-specific ideals and the ideals of subjectivity in general. Once perplexity has emerged and the normal identification has been dissolved, efforts to accommodate perplexity are governed by one or the other of two possible ideals of cultural unity. By an ideal of cultural unity or cultural ideal I mean a more or less articulate conception of the unity of the variety of co-existing endeavors. There seem to be two fundamental, concrete cultural ideals, corresponding approximately to two different notions of unity. On the one hand, there is the ideal of differentiated unity, that is, the ideal of a harmonious blending of elements which retain their individual autonomy and integrity. On the other hand, there is the reductionist ideal of cultural unity, that is, the ideal of a monolithic unity which emerges subsequent to the annihilation or relegation to inferior positions of all but one of the elements. Horizonal perplexity is accommodated by appealing to these ideals and by entering into relationships under their governance. The pursuit of the reductionist ideal involves either a reversion to the original identification of horizon-specific ideals with the ideals of subjectivity in general or a transformation of the original identification through substitution. That is, pursuit of the reductionist ideal results either in claims of hegemony for one's own horizon in a given constellation or in the attribution of authoritative status to another horizon in the same constellation. Guided by the reductionist ideal, the perplexed subject mitigates his perplexity by arrogating to his own horizon the ruling position in the constellation of which he is a member, or he supports total domination by a co-existing horizon. On the other hand, the pursuit of the ideal of differentiated unity involves a concerted effort to preserve the autonomy and integrity of each of the co-existing horizons by resisting the natural tendency to identify the ideals of subjectivity with the determinate ideals of one horizon in a given constellation. Guided by the collaborative ideal, the perplexed subject mitigates his perplexity by granting equal status to every horizon in the given constellation. However, neither pursuit of the reductionist ideal nor pursuit of the collaborative ideal fully eliminates the tension which is brought to consciousness by the dissolution of natural identification. Reductionism does not eliminate the tension, because the perdurance of those horizons whose elimination or subjugation is sought remains to be explained. Pursuit of differentiated unity does not eliminate the tension, for the maintenance of the dissolution of natural identification in a culture lacking an ultimate court of appeal is extremely difficult.

The two guiding cultural ideals provide the ground out of which six basic types of intersubjective activity, relating co-existing horizons to one another, emerge. Under the governance of the reductionist ideal, subjects (1) totalize their horizons with an intention to annihilate co-existing horizons, (2) totalize with an intention to relegate co-existing horizons to inferior positions in the constellation, (3) capitulate in a self-abandoning fashion to a co-existing totalizing horizon, or (4) capitulate in a subservient fashion to a co-existing totalizing horizon. Under the governance of the collaborative ideal, subjects (1) collaborate with co-existing horizons or (2) resist the totalizing and capitulating activities of co-existing horizons. Constellations whose member horizons are governed by the ideal of differentiated unity may be named collaborative constellations. Those whose member horizons are governed by the reductionist ideal of a monolithic cultural unity may be named reductionist constellations. When a constellation is constituted partially by horizons governed by the collaborative ideal and partially by horizons governed by the reductionist ideal, it may be named a heterogeneous constellation. Heterogeneous constellations may be complicated further by internal horizonal differences. Subjects sharing the same horizon may differ from one another as collaborating, resisting, totalizing, or capitulating.

II. Two Phases of Philosophy

In both of its phases, philosophy stands in a deliberate and methodical relation to co-existing horizons. The world of philosophy in its first phase is the full range of existing horizons. The ideal of first-phase philosophy is an intellectual integration of existing horizons.

The mode of operation in the first phase is identification, differentiation and correlation of existing horizons. Among existing horizons the philosophic horizon is unique, for it alone takes for its world the standpoints, modes, and worlds of the other horizons.[7] As standpoints and modes are not sensible but conscious, and as worlds are always mediated by meaning and are in some cases constituted by meaning, the philosophic mode in the first phase involves a methodical exploitation of a given access to data of consciousness.[8] Because it acknowledges explicitly the mediating and constituting functions of standpoints and modes, first-phase philosophy culminates in a *methodological* unification.[9] The results of the first phase are recorded in a cognitional theory, an epistemology, and a metaphysics. But the metaphysics which results from the successful pursuit of a methodological integration is of a peculiar sort.

The successful first-phase philosopher is equipped with a knowledge of the integral heuristic structure of proportionate being.[10] He has a grasp of the heuristic notion of the basic horizon of human existence.[11] By an alternation of his efforts, from the self-attentive task of self-appropriation to the perhaps more exacting task of self-development and back again, the first-phase philosopher achieves selfknowledge as he raises himself to the level of his culture.[12] The dynamic structure of conscious and intentional operations, which was operative implicitly in the philosophic novice, becomes explicit in the maturely philosophic subject. So it is that metaphysics is to be conceived, not as something recorded in a book, not as something to be learned by rote, but as the integrating subject himself, deliberately and methodically implementing his knowledge of transcenden-

---

[7] On the data of philosophy, see *Method*, pp. 94-95, 259 and "Aquinas Today: Tradition and Innovation," 169, 174-175.

[8] On meaning, see *Insight*, pp. 177, 568-573; *The Mediation of Christ in Prayer*, p. 7; "Time and Meaning," in *Bernard Lonergan: 3 Lectures*, ed. R. Eric O'Connor (Montreal: Thomas More Institute for Adult Education, 1975), pp. 29-54; *Collection*, pp. 243-244, 252-268; *A Second Collection*, pp. 20, 218-219, 220, 227; *Method*, Ch. 3, pp. 107, 114-115, 120, 257-262, 265-266, 272-273, 304, 306, 328, 330, 348-349. On self-presence, see *Understanding and Being: Bernard Lonergan's Halifax Lectures on Insight*, eds. Elizabeth A. Morelli and Mark D. Morelli (Toronto: Mellen Press, 1980), Ch.1; *Dublin Lectures on Insight*, pp. 28-29; *Collection*, pp. 248, 226-227; *Method*, p. 8. On data of consciousness, see Lonegan's unpublished *Notes on Intelligence and Reality*, 1950 (The Lonergan Centre), p. 9; *Insight*, pp. 72, 235-236; *Method*, pp. 8-9. On the all-important distinction between consciousness and knowledge, see *Insight*, p. 672 and *Collection*, pp. 164-197, 226-227.

[9] *Insight*, pp. 390-396, 421-423.

[10] *Insight*, pp. 390-396.

[11] *Insight*, pp. 387, 389, 530; Lonergan's unpublished *Notes on Hermeneutics*, 1962 (The Lonergan Centre, Toronto), p. 13; *A Second collection*, p. 14.

[12] *Insight*, p. 387; see also *Understanding and Being*, Chs. 1 and 4.

tal method.[13] Explicit metaphysics requires, not only a cognitional appropriation of the truth of cultural self-knowledge, but also further sensitive and volitional appropriations.

> Cognitional theory, epistemology, and metaphysics...have to be subsumed under the higher operations that integrate knowing with feeling and consist in deliberating, evaluating, deciding, acting.[14]

Accordingly, the world of philosophy in its second phase is the full range of endeavoring subjects. Its ideal is a concrete synthesis of endeavoring subjects. Its mode of operation is the implementation of an intellectual integration in harmonizing social conduct at the level of the times. Explicit metaphysics stands to ongoing human endeavors, not as a dam to a river, but as the bed to the flowing waters.[15] As Lonergan remarks,

> when the natural and the human sciences are on the move, when the social order is developing, when the everyday dimensions of culture are changing, what is needed is not a dam to block the stream but control of the river-bed through which the stream must flow.[16]

In the successful first-phase philosopher a portion of the river-bed has become deliberately unobstructive. In the second phase, this deliberate passivity becomes methodical activity as it is transformed into philosophic *praxis*.

III. Horizonal Diplomacy

For second-phase philosophic activity I propose the name "horizonal diplomacy". This name is not only less awkward than "second-phase philosophic activity", and less misleading than "explicit metaphysics", but it also calls to mind international diplomacy and evokes in that way an analogous understanding.

Diplomacy, in an ordinary sense, is the management of international relations by negotiation. Similarly, horizonal diplomacy is the management of horizonal relations by tactful intervention in constellations. Again, in a more technical sense, international diplomacy is the intelligent and tactful implementation of a foreign policy in the conduct of official relations between the governments of independent

---

[13] *Insight*, pp. 396, 397, 398; "Theology and Praxis," p. 15; *A Second Collection*, pp. 203-204; *Lecture on the Philosophy of History*, p. 9.

[14] *A Second Collection*, p. 204; also, *Insight*, pp. 391-392, 558-559, *xii-xiii* on sensitive and volitional appropriation.

[15] "Theology and Praxis," p. 15.

[16] *A Second Collection*, pp. 51-52.

states.[17] Similarly, horizonal diplomacy is the methodical implementation of an intellectual integration for the promotion of collaborative relations between subjects of autonomous horizons. Just as the international diplomatist practices on the basis afforded by a study of the history of international negotiations, an analysis of treaties, and an investigation of the ambitions, resources, and weaknesses of individual nations; so the horizonal diplomatist practices on the basis afforded by a study of the history of horizonal relations, an analysis of coalitions and disputes, and an investigation of the ideals, modes, and worlds of existing horizons. Again, international diplomacy, if it is collaborative, is practiced with an appreciation of common interests. The Greeks of the fifth century B.C. recognized an implicit 'law' which was thought to be above immediate national interests and momentary expediency; the Romans employed a vague notion of *ius naturale* or natural right. Similarly, horizonal diplomacy, because it is collaborative, is practiced with an appreciation of common interests; it is guided by a heuristic notion of the basic horizon of human existence which includes in its scope all perduring horizons.

Besides the similarities there are notable differences. For the most part, international diplomacy is practiced with specific national interests in mind. So it is that even the earliest diplomatists, the heralds of the Homeric period, were placed under the tutelage of Hermes, symbol of charm, trickery and cunning. In contrast, the horizonal diplomatist is not an agent of a particular horizon. This is the paradox, as it were, of philosophic activity. While the horizonal diplomatist is a philosopher, it is also true that philosophy happens to be that horizon which promotes a general, collaborative accommodation of horizonal perplexity. The horizonal diplomatist stands to co-existing horizons as a diplomatic agent of the entire human world stands to co-existing nations. He differs greatly, then, from Plato's philosopher who holds that our troubles will not cease unless philosophers becomes kings in our states.[18]

This analogy with international diplomacy conveys a general idea of the role I have in mind for the practical philosopher who has been relatively successful in his pursuit of an intellectual integration of human endeavors. I will turn now to a consideration of the thing-itself which I envisage.

---

[17] The definition is that of Sir Ernest Satow. It is quoted by Sir Harold Nicolson, *Diplomacy* (London: Oxford University Press, 1969), pp. 24, 122. In the present section I shall rely upon Nicolson's account of the development of organized international diplomacy. See pp. 1-14 of his essay.

[18] *Republic* 473c-e.

The occasion for the initiation of diplomatic activity is constituted by the emergence of perplexity in members of a constellation. For the horizonal diplomatist to promote collaborative relations successfully, he must block immediate accommodations and promote deliberate accommodations. It may appear, then, that there is no need for the horizonal diplomatist in a collaborative constellation, on the one hand, and that there is no point of insertion for the horizonal diplomatist in a reductionist constellation, on the other. It seems that occasions for the initiation of diplomatic activity arise only in heterogeneous constellations, those constellations which include at least one totalizing horizon and at least one resisting horizon. However, this apparent limitation on the role of the horizonal diplomatist has its root in a static conception of constellations. Horizons are gradual developments of subjects; every culture, if it is to survive, must take appropriate measures to reproduce itself. Consequently, horizonal perplexity regularly emerges during the acculturation process in all types of constellations as developing subjects are introduced to existing extraordinary endeavors. In every constellation, there is a point of entry for the horizonal diplomatist in the educational process. Through this opening, there passes the *horizonal diplomatist-as-teacher*. In situations calling for diplomacy-as-teaching, the dispute to be mediated normally involves the ordinary horizon as one of its parties. Besides the diplomatist-as-teacher, there is the *diplomatist-as-instigator*. The philosopher in a predominantly reductionist constellation, who somehow discovers a basis for promoting collaborative relations, becomes himself a resisting subject. But, because he is a diplomatist, his resistance is a self-conscious instigation of perplexity in contemporaneous subjects; he exploits the paradox of philosophic activity to promote perplexity, block immediate accommodation, and promote deliberate accommodation. Finally, reflection on the nature of heterogeneous constellations gives rise to the notion of the *horizonal diplomatist-as-mediator*. In heterogeneous constellations the stage is set regularly for diplomatic intervention; the co-existence of totalizers, capitulators, and resisters virtually guarantees the frequent emergence of perplexity not only in the educational process but also in the recurrent interactions of the educated.

The horizonal diplomatist may function as a teacher, as an instigator, and as a mediator in all three types of constellations. But clearly, the present constellation is heterogeneous. Accordingly, the notion of horizonal diplomacy may be qualified here by an emphasis upon mediation. What are the steps to be taken by the diplomatist-as-mediator? I envisage two stages of diplomacy-as-mediation. The first stage is impersonal, empathic, and definitive of the particular situation. The second is interpersonal, communicative, and transformative of the situation.

In the first stage the diplomatist *identifies* the horizons of the perplexed subjects, *distinguishes* them from one another, and *relates* them to one another. This procedure is impersonal, for as yet the diplomatist has not entered into dialogue or discussion, verbally or in writing. But the procedure is nevertheless empathic. The identification, distinction, and relation of the horizons constitutive of the actual constellation is at once a re-enactment of the dialogue or discussion which is heard or read and a correlation of the meanings expressed by the participating subjects with the standpoints, modes, and worlds distinguished and related previously in a relatively adequate intellectual integration. Finally, this procedure is definitive of the particular situation; for its conclusion is a judgment of the following type: The present situation is constituted by horizons of this type which differ from one another in these ways and are related to one another in these other ways.

In the second stage the diplomatist *intervenes* in the constellation; he *enucleates* the dispute by bringing to light the transcendental mode informing the horizon-specific modes, the ideals of subjectivity reflected in the horizon-specific ideals, and the universe of being partially objectified in the horizon-specific worlds; he *transposes* horizon-relative expressions from one horizon to another by adverting to the horizon-relative employments of key variable terms such as 'being', 'object', 'objectivity', 'knowing', and 'knowledge'. This procedure is interpersonal and communicative, for it is an engagement in the dialogue or discussion through the expression of meanings, verbally or in writing. It is transformative of the particular situation, first, because it is a complexification of the constellation by the addition of an explicitly collaborative member and, second, because enucleation and transposition, if successful, have mediated a common rudimentary realization that collaboration could displace conflict in the future.

Clearly, the task of the horizonal diplomatist, whether it be teaching, instigating, or mediating, is not an easy one. It is more complicated than the complex task of conceptual analysis and linguistic clarification which has won the hearts and engrossed the minds of so many philosophers in our century. The conflicts with which the diplomatist is concerned have deeper roots than conceptual confusion and imprecise use of language. Again, the diplomatist's task is more difficult than the labor of communicating a body of 'truths'. While there is a sense in which an intellectual integration may be called a body of truths, the diplomatist's task is not its communication but its *implementation* in an indefinite range of concrete situations. Perhaps the greatest difficulty associated with the practice of horizontal diplomacy derives from its dramatic nature. Diplomacy is a performance which makes far-reaching demands upon the actor. The dynamic stance of the diplomatist is a precarious posture, one requiring simultaneous detachment and involvement. When the diplomatist intervenes, he complexifies the constellation, he becomes part of it, and the paradox of philosophic activity is easily transformed into an oscillation between deliberately collaborative implementation of an integration and virtually totalizing activity designed to impress the participants of philosophy's relevance to cultural life. Consequently, just as the international diplomatist, ideally, should be calm, accurate, patient, good-tempered, and modest, so too should the horizontal diplomatist be psychologically well-adjusted.[19] For the diplomatist is, above all, an exemplar of possible success in the transformation of contentious heterogeneity into collaborative unity in human endeavor. The relationship of psychological constitution to practical philosophic efficacy, it seems to me, cannot be ignored by aspiring practitioners of horizontal diplomacy. As Otto Bird has observed in his study *Cultures in Conflict*, the imperialism typical of adherents of intellectual ideals has had its root invariably in *hubris*.[20]

IV. The Need for Horizontal Diplomacy

Horizontal diplomacy may not be an easy task, but it is nevertheless demanded by the contemporary cultural situation. Returning to our analogy, modern international diplomacy, as the art of negotiation, first acquired a significant place in the political sphere during the thirteenth and fourteenth centuries in Italy. It was inevitable, Sir Harold Nicolson has argued, that Italy should have become the mother of professional diplomacy; the time was ripe. The Italian city states "were interconnected by countless common interests as well as

---

[19] Sir Harold Nicolson, *Diplomacy*, pp. 62-63. As the psychological therapist should be psychologically healthy, so the horizontal diplomatist should be well-adjusted. However, horizontal diplomacy is not to be conceived strictly as a type of therapy, except insofar as it is governed by the following guideline: "The therapist's skill and art lie in keeping things simple enough so that something can happen: in other words, he clears the field for favorable change, and then tries to avoid getting in the way of its development." See H. S. Sullivan, *The Psychiatric Interview*, eds. Helen Swick Perry and Mary Ladd Gawel (New York: W. W. Norton, 1970), p. 227. Psychological constitution has its effects in cognitive work as well; consequently, the philosopher's psychological constitution may have a detrimental influence upon his pursuit of an intellectual integration. See Abraham Maslow's list of cognitive pathologies in *The Psychology of Science: A Reconnaissance* (Chicago: Henry Regnery Company, 1969), pp. 26-29.

[20] Otto Bird, *Cultures in Conflict: An Essay in the Philosophy of the Humanities* (Notre Dame; London: University of Notre Dame Press, 1976), pp. 178-184.

sundered by ferocious rivalries; they were constantly engaged in a competition for power and preoccupied by those combinations and alliances which might render that power predominant."[21] Similarly, while the horizonal constellation has been complex for centuries, only recently has the complexity become explicitly sixfold. Moreover, our constellation is heterogeneous; proponents of interdisciplinary studies are barely heard above the clamor of totalizers and resisters. As this heterogeneity becomes more acute, the need for horizonal diplomacy or some basically similar philosophic praxis becomes more urgent. Whole bodies of expression, whole meaningful worlds, whole modes of inquiry, discovery and creativity, and whole sets of ideals stand in danger of being subjugated or even discarded. Only the subject of that horizon whose world is the full range of horizons is specifically suited to restore methodically and equitably the balance.

Philosophy as intellectual integration of the arts and sciences has long been recognized as a separate pursuit. Philosophy as the pursuit of the unity of science has also acquired a distinct place. But philosophy as concrete synthesis has yet to receive full recognition as philosophic activity deserving serious reflection and clear delineation. Just as international diplomacy was associated for many centuries with the preservation of archives, the analysis of treaties, and the study of the history of negotiations, so properly philosophic activity has been identified, virtually to this day, with the *study* of horizons and their relations. It was not until the beginning of the last century at the Congress of Vienna, long after the heralds and orators had been displaced by diplomatists, that the rules, conventions and presumptions of international diplomacy as the actual conduct of international relations were given a definite if fragile form. Second-phase philosophy has yet to reach a similar level of self-consciousness. In light of the disheartening collapses of admirable intellectual monuments, this deficiency is somewhat understandable. One can hardly proceed confidently to enunciate in detail the canons of horizonal diplomacy if guiding intellectual integrations remain controversial. However, inattention to second-phase philosophy is rooted partially in an expectation of the ideal case of sequentially-ordered philosophic phases. In fact, the phases are reciprocally constitutive, just as negotiation and foreign policy are mutually transformative. Horizonal diplomacy is the implementation of an intellectual integration; but, concretely, it is the manner in which evidence is obtained and tentative integrations are tested. Moreover, Lonergan has provided a thoroughly modern, methodological integration

---

[21] Sir Harold Nicolson, *Diplomacy*, pp. 12-13.

which, he claims, is not subject to *radical* revision. Because it stands upon an advertence to modes of operation, Lonergan's first-phase integration has a plasticity that precludes the kinds of collapses characteristic of conceptual systems. Such an integration, if it has indeed been accomplished, invites us to initiate serious reflection upon its implementation.

As a testament to the need for an elaboration and legitimation of second-phase philosophy we have the perduring *symbol* of Socrates. Even though Socrates' death illustrates the need for serious reflection upon the canons of practical philosophy, other elements of the Socratic symbol tend to obscure that need. Nowadays the symbol is recalled to console us. A most distressing question recurs within philosophy and outside it: *What is philosophy?* In our internal dialogues, the symbol is recalled to support us in a poorly-defined pursuit, to inspire us, and to renew us. In fact, the death of Socrates, rather than stimulating reflection on the canons of practical philosophy as it should, seems to function as an indirect confirmation of a conviction of our profundity and the inability of the ordinary mortal to understand us.[22] In our conversations with non-philosophers, on the other hand, the symbol is employed as a device to help others situate us. To the Socratic symbol as a consoling, inspiring, and renewing force in our philosophic lives I have no serious objections; but the use of the symbol as a situating device has its drawbacks. First, the symbol as such is ambiguous. Socrates is synoptic inquiry; but he is also perduring *aporia*. He exemplifies the ideal of philosophy's first phase; but he also exhibits the pursuit of that ideal as virtually interminable. Second, Socrates symbolizes emergent philosophy; but modern philosophy is a variety of activities rooted in centuries of wondering. Third, Socrates practiced in a constellation with a relatively low level of complexity; but the present constellation has a six-fold complexity. Fourth, Plato's Socrates of the *Republic* reflected at length on the problems attendant upon the implementation of a reductionist integration; but the perdurance and resilience of a multiplicity of horizons constitutes a serious chal-

---

[22] As Hannah Arendt has noted, "The reason Plato wanted the philosopher to become the ruler of the city lay in the conflict between the philosopher and the polis, or in the hostility of the polis toward philosophy, which probably had lain dormant for some time before it showed its immediate threat to the life of the philosopher in the trial and death of Socrates. Politically, Plato's philosophy shows the rebellion of the philosopher against the polis. The philosopher announces his claim to rule, but not so much for the sake of the polis and politics (although patriotic motivation cannot be denied in Plato and distinguishes his philosophy from those of his followers in antiquity) as for the sake of philosophy and the safety of the philosopher." See *Between Past and Future: Eight Exercises in Political Thought* (New York: The Viking Press, 1961), p. 107.

lenge to the adequacy of the reductionist ideal of cultural unity. As a device for situating ourselves in relation to co-existing horizons, the Socratic symbol may have outlived its usefulness. While the memory of Socrates may orient, inspire, and renew the philosophic enterprise, it may inhibit it as well by providing a symbolic justification, as it were, of our inattentiveness to second-phase philosophic activity. The philosophic horizon awaits its own version of the diplomatists' Congress of Vienna. Lonergan's foundational insights provide boundaries for common reflection which might give such a congress direction and cohesion.[23]

V. The Limits of Horizonal Diplomacy

The task of the horizonal diplomatist is difficult and demanded by our times, but horizonal diplomacy is not a panacea. The activities of identification, distinction, relation, intervention, enucleation, and transposition are undertaken in the atmosphere of a selective attention to the horizonal variable. The horizonal variable is just one among many which must be taken into account in the pursuit of a complete understanding and adequate resolution of the conflicts that fragment the cultural community. As the horizonal diplomatist must abide in the paradox of philosophic activity, so he must retain and nourish an awareness of just what he can and cannot accomplish. I will conclude with a brief discussion of the ideal which guides the horizonal diplomatist.

The ideal governing horizonal diplomacy is cosmopolitan rather than utopian. H. G. Wells interpreted the drama of world history as the tension between man's animal affection for the narrow comforts of tribe and village and his self-surpassing search for the widest possible community of thought, wealth, and work. W. Warren Wagar has translated this distinction into the antithesis between Utopia and Cosmopolis.[24] If the ideal governing horizonal diplomacy were utopian in this sense, then horizonal diplomacy would be more appropriately named philosophic totalization. The process of creating a utopia, like the process of totalizing a horizon, is a terminal process; the aim of the process is a relatively static, monolithic unity. As monolithic cultural unity is characterized by the totalization of the

---

[23] I do not mean to imply that the Socratic method should be excluded from consideration when we pursue an adequate notion of second-phase philosophic activity. However, it remains that we must be attentive to the possible disadvantages of motivating and governing our actual performance by adverting to the symbol of Socrates. As Lonergan has noted, feelings are evoked by symbols, and they provide the mass, momentum, and drive of our conscious living. See *Method,* p. 65; also, *Insight,* pp. 188-198, 237.

[24] W. Warren Wagar, *The City of Man. Prophecies of a World Civilization in Twentieth-Century Thought* (Baltimore: Penguin Books, 1967), p. 14.

ideals, mode, and world of a single horizon, so utopian unity is characterized by parochialism and ethnocentrism.[25] On the other hand, the process of creating a cosmopolis, like the process of promoting differentiated cultural unity, is open-ended. Wagar writes that cosmopolis

> is the quintessence of a civilization, the gathering of all its vital human resources into a living organic unity. A cosmopolis is not a utopia; it is not the best of all possible worlds, but the boundless community of the best in the world-that-is. . . . Cosmopolis is simply the world in a state of optimal integration.[26]

It follows that, as horizontal diplomacy differs from horizontal totalization, it differs also from that terminal process by which the personal and interpersonal tensions generated by self-surpassing encounters are supposed to be eliminated.

Moreover, my description of philosophy as a two-stage process is ideal-typical, and so it differs from what is meant by the popular notion of a utopian scheme. Numerous problems attend the personal appropriation of any intellectual integration, and these problems are intellectual, psychological, and social. Again, horizontal diplomacy has been conceived in abstraction from personality and class differences, differences of the level of mastery of an intellectual integration, and differences of the level of facility with which an integration is tested and verified as it is transposed to actual practice. The conception of horizontal diplomacy is only an ideal-type useful for exposing the virtual tendencies of the philosophic horizon. Actual discrepancies can be identified and investigated in the light of this ideal-type. Utopian schemes, on the other hand, tend to force signs of failure into the shadows.[27]

Finally, Karl Mannheim introduced, early in the present century, a notion of utopia which differs from Wagar's technical notion and from the popular notion of a utopian scheme. "A state of mind is utopian when it is incongruous with the state of reality within which it occurs."[28] By analogy, a conception is utopian when its implementation implies a reconstitution of the existing order. The notion of horizontal diplomacy is a conception of a manner in which both philosophy and the horizontal constellation generally might be renovated. In Mannheim's sense, then, the notion of horizontal diplomacy is a utopian conception.

---

[25] Ibid., pp. 13-17.

[26] Ibid., p. 15.

[27] For a general discussion of typologies and their uses, see Edward A. Tiryakian, "Typologies," in *International Encyclopaedia of the Social Sciences,* pp. 177-185.

[28] Karl Mannheim, *Ideology and Utopia,* trans Louis Wirth and Edward Shils (New York: Harcourt, Brace & World, 1936), pp. 192-193.

Natural Science and Mathematics

Lonergan on the Foundations of the Theories of Relativity

by Patrick H. Byrne

In a paper[1] recently presented before the Boston Colloquium for the History and Philosophy of Science, Prof. Max Jammer of Bar-Ilan University surveyed the history of the attempts to provide axiomatic (or conceptual) foundations for the Special Theory of Relativity (hereafter abbreviated as "STR"). Among other things, Prof. Jammer's paper revealed that, in contrast to quantum mechanics, no generally accepted axiomatic foundations for STR has yet emerged. Furthermore, Jammer's paper showed that several attempts at axiomatic foundations were beleaguered with problems not to be found in the use of the theory by Einstein or the successive generations of practicing physicists.

The shortcomings of these efforts to develop axiomatic foundations for STR—and indeed of any parallel efforts directed toward the search for axiomatic foundations for the General Theory of Relativity as well—are, in my judgement, inherent in the theories themselves. That is, the proper foundations of the theories of relativity reside, not in conceptual axioms, but in the foundational reality of the subject as subject. It is not my purpose in this paper to enter into a detailed critique of the various attempts at axiomatization discussed in Prof. Jammer's paper. Rather, on this occasion celebrating the achievements of Fr. Bernard Lonergan, I simply intend to

---

[1] Max Jammer, "The Conceptual History of Special Relativity," delivered to the Boston Colloquium for the History and Philosophy of Science on November 28, 1978.

show how his phenomenological appropriation of the structure of consciousness has opened up the possibility of approaching the question of the foundations of the theories of relativity from the viewpoint of the subject as subject.

I. Inverse Insight and the Subject as Subject

Lonergan's principal discussions of the theories of relativity are to be found in his philosophical *opus, Insight: A Study of Human Understanding.*[2] In particular, he first took up the topic of STR in the section of Chapter 1 devoted to the analysis of the conscious act he called "inverse insight." It will be helpful, therefore, to review the nature of inverse insight and to situate this act within the dynamism of the subject as subject.

Lonergan both compared and contrasted inverse insight with direct insight—the act of understanding which his book is intended to help the reader appropriate. Like direct insight, inverse insight presupposes some positive content presented in sensation or imagination (that is, in consciousness at the level of experiencing). Again, as with direct insight, inverse insight responds to the spontaneous desire for understanding manifested in an inquiry. Yet, unlike direct insight, inverse insight is not a grasp of a positive intelligible content (intelligibility). Rather, inverse insight "apprehends that in some fashion the point is that there is no point, or that the solution is to deny a solution, or that the reason is that the rationality of the real admits of distinctions and qualifications."[3] Furthermore, Lonergan claims that, relative to the frequency of direct insights, occurrences of inverse insight are rare. Finally, Lonergan states that "inverse insights occur only within the context of far larger developments of human thought...that positively exploit their negative contribution."[4]

Lonergan regards these remarks concerning inverse insight as "descriptions." In most of the first half of *Insight,* Lonergan's objective was to merely "describe" conscious activities such as direct insight, formulation, and inverse insight. By "description" Lonergan meant a form of expression which helps a person understand something in relation to his or her self.[5] It is for this reason that Lonergan

---

[2] Bernard Lonergan, *Insight: A Study of Human Understanding,* (N.Y.: Philosophical Library, 1958). Hereafter cited as *"Insight."*

[3] Ibid., p. 19.

[4] Ibid., p. 20.

[5] Ibid., pp. 37, 291-292, 295-296. Lonergan first introduced the term 'classification' in the early sections of *Insight,* but the term 'description' (which has the same definition as 'classification') is used more frequently in subsequent sections.

followed his descriptive remarks concerning inverse insight with several examples or exercises in inverse insight, in order to evoke the relevant experiences of having inverse insights.

Yet Lonergan did not regard descriptions of conscious activities as ends in themselves. Indeed, if the accounts of conscious activities remain in the mode of description, any philosophy rising from these accounts is vulnerable to the charges of "psychologism" and "naturalism" (that is, the reduction of questions regarding the objectivity of thought to the empirical conditions under which thought arises).[6] Thus Lonergan regarded description of conscious acts simply as an essential propaedeutic to their explanation in terms of cognitional theory,[7] and it is only in such an explanatory context that the foundational character of the subject as subject can be grasped fully. It is in explanation that one moves from an understanding that grasps relations to the peculiarities of oneself toward an understanding of relations that prescind from such peculiarities. In particular, the explanatory account of conscious acts in cognitional theory grasps the relations these acts have to one another in the self-transcending, dynamic pattern of the subject as subject. In such an explanatory account, the charge of "psychologism" and "naturalism" are overcome, for acts such as direct insight are understood as constitutive of the subject's self-transcendence into objective knowledge of being.

While it is true that Lonergan provided an explanatory account explicitly relating such conscious acts such as experiencing, direct insight, formulating, reflecting, and judging in his writings on cognitional theory, it remains that the relations among those acts and the act of inverse insight have not been made explicit in any explanatory context. In other words, acts of inverse insight have not been explicitly situated within the foundational reality of the self-transcending subject as subject. Yet, an explicit account is required if one is to establish the way in which the subject as subject can provide answers to questions regarding the foundations of STR. Fortunately such an account can easily be reconstructed from the descriptions of

---

[6] "Psychologism" has been coined to refer to the antagonist of Gottlob Frege's critiques. See, for example, his *The Basic Laws of Arithmetic,* (Berkeley: University of California Press, 1964), pp. ix, 12-25, "Naturalism" was coined by Edmund Husserl to refer to a similar problem. See Edmund Husserl, *Phenomonology and the Crisis of Philosophy* ed. Q. Lauer, (N.Y.: Harper and Row, 1965), pp. 79ff.

[7] Bernard Lonergan, *Method in Theology* (N.Y.: Herder & Herder, 1972), pp. 261-262, and *Insight,* pp. 332-335. The explanatory account of the acts of consciousness (cognitional theory) is stated most succinctly in *Insight,* pp.272-275, 319-328 and in Bernard Lonergan, "Cognitional Structure" in Bernard Lonergan, *Collection,* ed. Frederick Crowe, (N.Y.: Herder and Herder, 1967), pp. 221-239.

inverse insight and the elaborations of cognitional theory. Therefore, this essay will first make explicit what is implicit in Lonergan's writing, and then consider his treatment of foundations of the theories of relativity.

It is perhaps unnecessary to recapitulate all the details of Lonergan's explanatory account of the structure of human consciousness. Yet a few points should be stressed. First Lonergan drew upon David Hilbert's innovation of "implicit definition" in the field of geometry—where terms and relations mutually define one another — as the paradigm for fully explanatory accounts.[8] Yet there is a significant difference between Hilbert's use of implicit definition and Lonergan's use. While the terms and relations of Hilbert's geometry are conceptual, the terms and relations of Lonergan's cognitional theory are the consciously occurring acts and dynamisms of a concretely existtng subject.[9] It is for this reason that cognitional theory cannot be properly separated from the personal achievements of self-appropriation. The statements employed to formulate cognitional theory will appear merely formal or abstract if this intrinsic connection with actually occurring conscious activities is overlooked or forgotten

Second, the approach via implicit definition makes clear that conscious acts and dynamisms never occur in isolation. The terms are conscious acts. These acts can be distinguished, according to their inherent degree or level or quality of consciousness, into acts of experience, intelligence, reasonableness, and responsibility. The relations are the dynamisms of a level of consciousness bringing itself to act in awakening, inquiry, reflection, or deliberation. Thus, an act of experience is defined as that which is presupposed by an act of insight through intelligent inquiry. An insight is defined as what presupposes acts of experience which have been inquired into, and what is presupposed by acts of formulation and judgement. The rest of the definitions follow this pattern.

Third, the relations between acts are not abstract universals, any more than experiencing, understanding, judging, or deciding are abstract universals. In Lonergan's cognitional theory, the appeal to the subject as subject means an appeal to a concretely existing unity, identity, whole of experiences, thoughts, judgments, feelings, values, and acts. Yet, the subject as subject is not merely the unity of distinct acts, but the unity of acts as concretely related to one another. Furthermore, such relations go beyond the particular inquiries which relate particular experiences to particular insights and feelings to particular judgments of value and decisive actions. Beyond these

---

[8] *Insight*, pp.12-13.
[9] Ibid., pp. 334-335.

particular relations of acts there is the overarching dynamism of the unrestricted desire to know and love which, in a concretely existing human subject, relates whole series of insights to one another, contexts of judgements to one another, and ranges of decisions to one another in a unique, developing (and even declining) pattern. Thus, Lonergan arrived at the foundational character of the subject as subject, not by means of some impoverishing abstraction about the subject, but by being more concrete than any other philosopher in this regard. Through his more concrete approach, Lonergan discerned the self-transcending dimension of consciousness which is immanent in the concrete activities of the subject as subject.

It follows that in an explanatory account, the act of inverse insight must also be understood in terms of its concrete relations to other conscious acts. It is now possible to make such an explanatory account explicit. First, inverse insight is an act of consciousness which, through an intelligent inquiry, presupposes acts of experiencing. Second, such an act is, like direct insight, an act of consciousness as intelligent. However unlike direct insight, inverse insight has no direct intelligible content *(noema)* for it grasps only that the intelligibility anticipated in the inquiry is not to be found. Third, inverse insight is related to subsequent direct insights as the unrestricted desire to know and love gives rise to questions about its implications and seeks to positively exploit its negative contribution. Fourth, the inverse insight is further related to acts of judgment when the unrestricted desire desires to determine whether the positive implications constitute instances of the virtually unconditioned. Any instance of inverse insight will occur within such a pattern of terms and relations, for the explanatory account prescinds from particularities to grasp things in their relations to one another. Finally, such a pattern, like the instances of inverse insight themselves, only occur concretely, and thereby presuppose the existence of a concrete, conscious, unity, identity, whole—that is, the subject as subject.

II. Inverse Insight and the Special Theory of Relativity

From this explanatory account of inverse insight and the subject as subject, it is now possible to show how Lonergan approached the question of the foundations of STR. It is generally held that STR is based upon two postulates: the relativity postulate and the postulate that the speed of light is a constant magnitude for all inertial observers. Discussions of the foundations of STR revolve around the conceptual status and grounds for justification of these two postulates. Lonergan focuses his attention on the first of these—the relativity postulate. Thus, I will limit myself for the present to an explication of his discussion of the relativity postulate.

Lonergan's statement of the relativity postulate reads as follows:

> The mathematical expressions of physical principles and laws is invariant under inertial transformations.[10]

Of course the meaning of this statement must be made clear before questions concerning its foundations can be taken up. First, then, a mathematical expression is a formulation of a relationship among numbers and/or magnitudes. According to Lonergan, relationships are apprehended by insights.[11] Thus, mathematical expressions are the formulations of insights into the relationships among numbers or magnitudes. The expression of such relationships often takes the form of a mathematical equation, for example, $z = x^2 + y^2$, which states that the number or magnitude designated by 'z' is related to the numbers or magnitudes designated by 'x' and 'y' as the sum of their squares.[12]

Second, a physical law or principle is a relationship among measurable quantities. The mathematical expression of a physical law or principle, is therefore, a mathematical equation of the relationships which, it is claimed, hold among the measurable magnitudes. Lonergan credited Galileo with this discovery, and coined the terms

---

[10] Ibid., p. 23. Albert Einstein did not, of course, use exactly these words. Compare, however, his own formulations, for example: "the same laws of electrodynamics and optics will be valid for all frames of reference for which the equations of mechanics hold good." H.A. Lorentz, A. Einstein, et. al., *The Principle of Relativity* (N.Y.: Dover Publications, Inc., 1923), pp. 37-38. "The laws by which the states of physical systems undergo change are not affected, whether these changes of state be referred to one or another of two systems of coordinates in uniform translatory motion." Ibid., p. 91. The preceeding two quotations are taken from the 1923 translation by W. Perrett and G. B. Jeffery of Einstein's 1905 article, "Zur Elektrodynamik bewegter Körper," *Annalen der Physik*, 17 (1905), pp. 891-921. Slightly later Einstein wrote: "Natural laws are independent of the state of motion of the reference system, at least in the case where the latter is an acceleration-free reference system." A. Einstein, "Über das Relativitätsprinzip und die aus demselben gezogenen Folgerungen," *Jahrbuch der Radioaktivität*, 4 (1907), p. 416. Again, in a 1916 statement, we may read: "If, relative to co-ordinate system K, K' is a uniformly moving co-ordinate system devoid of rotation, then natural phenomena run their course with respect to K' according to exactly the same general laws as with respect to K." *Relativity: The Special and General Theory* (N.Y.: Crown Pubishers, Inc., 1961), p. 12. Translated by R. Lawson from the 1917 original *Über die spezielle und die allgemeine Relativitätstheorie, Gemeinverständlich* (Barunschweig: Wieweg, 1917). Finally, Einstein used essentially the same 1916 formulation in his 1921 lectures at Princeton University, A. Einstein, *The Meaning of Relativity* (Princeton, N.J.: Princeton University Press, 1956), p. 25. In all cases, Einstein's statements focus on the *laws* rather than their *mathematical forms of expression*. However, the contexts of these five statements make clear that Einstein intended that mathematical expressions should likewise be the same. Subsequent developments in the tensor formulations of STR further substantiate the correctness of Lonergan's formulation.

[11] *Insight*, p. x.

"classical correlation" and "classical law" to mean "mathematical expression of physical laws and principles." [13]

Third, as with physical principles and laws, co-ordinate transformations are expressed as mathematical equations or functions, and represent correlations among physical measurements. What is the difference? Physical principles and laws are intended to express intelligible relationships among measurements made by one and the same observer—for example, measurements of positions and times made by the same subject. Transformations of co-ordinates, on the other hand, represent relationships among different observers—for example, the relationships between my measurements of the position of something and your measurements of the position of the same thing. While human subjects differ primarily because of the distinctness of their acts of existence (central acts), insofar as the subjects are observers they also differ by their positions in space and time. Such spacio-temporal differences give observers different perceptual perspectives—that is, differently experienced data. These differences in data lead to different measurements. Thus, different observers would tend to disagree about the values of their measurements of the

---

[12] Mathematical equations may also be regarded as expressions involving functions—i.e., correlations (relations) among ranges of numbers or magnitudes. In the example, values of the variable, z, would be functionally correlated with values of x and y by means of the summation of squares. In other words, z is a function of x and y. One can easily transform any mathematical equation into an equation involving a function of *all* the variables by subtracting the set of terms appearing on one side of the equation from both sides. Thus, in the example, one derives the new equation, $z - x^2 - y^2 = 0$ or, in more general notion, $f(x,y,z) = 0$. Thus, '$z - x^2 - y^2$' (or 'f(x,y,z)') expresses a functional relationship among the ranges of numbers and magnitudes designated by 'x', 'y', and 'z'. The equation states that, for some determinate set of those numbers or magnitudes, the value of that function is zero. This explains how, despite the fact that physicists usually express their discoveries in terms of *equations,* Lonergan can claim that they seek to determine some indeterminate function, $f(x,y,z,...) = 0$. *Insight,* p. 38.

[13] Ibid., pp. 37-38. Lonergan does not intend to restrict his use of the terms "classical correlation" and "classical law" to the correlations proper to physics, although his paradigm of a classical correlation is a mathematical functional relationship among measurements. He wrote, for example, that "when one mounts to the higher integrations of the organism, the psyche, and intelligence, one finds that measuring loses both in significance and efficacy." Ibid., p. 463. Nevertheless, it is clear that Lonergan expects biology, sensitive psychology, and cognitional theory, as well as physics and chemistry to arrive at classical correlations. See, for example, ibid., pp. 255-257, 459-460. It would be an important service to the development of Lonergan's thought if "classical correlation" could be defined in such a completely general way as to free it from the limitations imposed by the paradigm from physics. Such an attempt would have seriously to consider whether such a definition could also be free of negative conceptual elements—for example, that an understanding is of things, *not* as related to us, but as related to one another, or that "immanently intelligible" relations are those *not* concerned with efficient, final, or material relations.

same things. Fortunately, understanding can grasp how differences in perceptual perspective can be correlated with differences in data. Such acts of understanding can give rise to correlations among the differences in measurements. When such correlations are expressed mathematically, they are called "coordinate transformations." Co-ordinate transformations correlate or "transform" one set of measurements into another. Such transformations enable different observers to resolve their disagreements about measurements.

The idea of a co-ordinate transformation can be illustrated by means of an example. Suppose an observer (A) is walking away from a building. His measurements of the position of the building will vary from moment to moment. Observer A can measure the moments by means of a watch, and can grasp a correlation among these positions and times. Such a correlation could be expressed as a mathematical equation. Suppose another observer (B) is walking toward the same building as A leaves it. Observer B could also measure positions and times, and could also formulate a mathematical expression of the correlations among B's measurements. These expressions of correlations by A and B would be like mathematical expressions of physical laws.

B's perspective — and therefore B's data and measurements of the positions of the building — will differ from A's. Yet, if A can grasp how B's perspective changes in relation to A's perspective, A can determine a correlation between his own measurements of position and time, and the measurements made by B. When formulated in mathematical terms, this correlation constitutes a co-ordinate transformation

Finally, in Lonergan's statement of the relativity postulate there is an element of denial, and this element also requires some clarification. The element of denial is that the form of mathematical expression is invariant — i.e., does *not* vary with the transformation of coordinates. It is natural to expect that, since A can determine how B's measurements relate to his own, A can also grasp how B's expressions of physical laws will relate to his own. It is also natural to expect that, since B's perspective, data, and measurements all differ from A's, B's correlations of his measurements will also differ from A's. The remaining element in the statement of the relativity postulate asserts that despite all the other differences, there will be no difference in the expression of the correlations (and hence no differences in the correlations themselves), as long as the differences in A and B's perspectives are merely inertial (i.e., do not involve accelerations).

Lonergan's way of stating that there will be no difference in mathematical expression of the correlation is to say that the expression is "invariant" under inertial transformation. In the contemporary physics community the term "co-variant" is used where Lonergan has employed "invariant." In order to avoid confusion, I will adopt the more generally accepted term, "co-variant." [14]

Given this clarification of the relativity postulate, it is now possible to return to Lonergan's treatment of the foundations of the postulate. The question concerning the foundations of the postulate can be stated as: "On what *grounds* do scientists assert that the expression of physical principles and laws is co-variant under inertial transformations?"

Lonergan's way of answering this question begins by noting some parallels between the statement of the relativity postulate and the account of inverse insight. Clearly the relativity postulate, like inverse insight, implicitly presupposes a positive, sensible content, since there are empirically different magnitudes for different observers to measure. Again, the relativity postulate, as with inverse insight, involves a denial—in this case the denial of the anticipation that some difference in intelligible explanation must correspond to these

---

[14] In the practice of contemporary physicists, the term, 'invariant', is reserved for *numbers or magnitudes* which are constant for all observers (i.e., do not change their *values* under co-ordinate transformations). Thus, for example, the numerical value of the speed of light is said to be invariant under inertial transformations, within the context of STR. (The speed of light is *not* invariant for all observers, once non-inertial transformations are permitted, as in the General Theory of Relativity.) The word, 'co-variant', was coined to mean that the set of measurements performed by one observer kept the *same set of relationships* among themselves as for another observer. Thus, for the sake of illustration, suppose that the equation E/F = ½ were regarded as co-variant. Suppose further that, because of his perspective, one observer measured E to have a value of 8 and F to be 16, while another observer, because of the difference in his perspective, would measure E as 6 and F as 12. Thus, despite the differences in their perspectives, both observers would claim that the correlation between E and F was the same. As a factual example, the special relativistic formulation of one of the laws of electromagnetism is written as

$$\frac{\partial F^{\mu\nu}}{\partial x^\nu} = j^\mu$$

The equation states relationships between measurable electromagnetic field quantities ($F^{\mu\nu}$), the current density (j^μ), and the measurements of position (x^ν). This equation is generally held to be co-variant within the context of STR. Thus, if $\frac{\partial F^{\mu\nu}}{\partial x^\nu} = j^\mu$ expresses the correlations among measurements from observer A's perspective, and observer B's perspective differs only inertially from A's, the co-variance of the equation means that B will express the correlation among his measurements as $\frac{\partial F^{\mu\nu\prime}}{\partial x^{\nu\prime}} = j^{\mu\prime}$ where the apostrophes ("primes") mean that the measurements are made, not from A's perspective but from B's. Clearly $\frac{\partial F^{\mu\nu}}{\partial x^\nu} = j^\mu$ differs from $\frac{\partial F^{\mu\nu\prime}}{\partial x^{\nu\prime}} = j^{\mu\prime}$ by the appearance of three apostrophes, so that the two expressions are not exactly the same (not "invariant"). Yet, the apostrophes are merely intended to show the reader that the measurements differ, while the relations among them are the same. Thus, Lonergan's terminology that the expression is "invariant", while at variance with common usage, is essentially correct.

empirical differences. (The denial is limited, however, to empirical differences which are completely reducible to inertial differences among observers.) Lonergan concludes, therefore, that the relativity postulate is in part grounded in the occurrences of an inverse insight. The inverse insight is that differences among observers (and differences in what they observe and measure) which are due solely to differences in their inertial state, do not have a corresponding intelligibility. In particular, rest and unaccelerated motion, though observably and measureably different, do not differ intelligibly.

The inverse insight Lonergan refers to is *not* a philosophical conclusion (i.e., a conclusion from cognitional theory). It does *not* arise from the data of consciousness. It is an act that arises from sensible empirical data. If it is correct, its consequences will be instances of the virtually unconditioned whose conditions are given in sensation. Nor is the inverse insight some transcendental deduction of what must necessarily be so. It is certainly *conceivable* that differences due merely to inertial state have some intelligible explanation. After all, ordinary common sense, Aristotle's physics, and even Maxwell's electromagnetics all propose, at least implicitly, intelligible correlations among inertial differences. Yet, the inverse insight indicates that conceivability is irrelevant, for as a matter of empirical fact, no such explanation is to be found. Hence, while this inverse insight is indeed an occurrence in the conscious development of some concrete subjects, it remains that one does not need a cognitional theory of the subject as subject in order to have this insight or to grasp its proximate significance for an understanding of sensible data.

Yet, the concern here is not about this particular inverse insight into inertial motion, but about the use made of it in the relativity postulate. The relativity postulate does not assert that there is intelligible difference among empirical data which differ inertially. It asserts that there is no difference in the form of expression of physical laws under inertial transformations. In order to justify or ground this second assertion, something more than the veracity of the inverse insight is required. That "something more" is the explanatory account of the subject as subject. Lonergan's great contribution has been to demonstrate that the justification for this part of the postulate lay in the *de facto* cognitional structure of the subject as subject.

Lonergan demonstrated that cognitional theory, in combination with the inverse insight into inertial motion, led to the relativity postulate in the following way. From cognitional theory, it is clear that any expression or formulation corresponds to an insight. Hence, there is a general cognitional theorem that the differences in expressions must be due to differences in insights. Again from cognitional theory it follows that insights are grasps of intelligible relations among sensible or imagined data, so that in general, difference in insights correspond to differences in data. One major exception to the last statement, however, is that when an inverse insight occurs regarding differences in sensible or imaginable data, there is no corresponding intelligible difference. Where there is no intelligible difference, there can be no difference in the acts of understanding, for such difference in the acts would imply a difference in contents — i.e., a difference in intelligibility. Thus, there follows a second general cognitional theorem, that when an inverse insight is correct, there will be a difference in sensible content without a corresponding difference in the expression of intelligible relations. Combining these general cognitional theorems and the specific inverse insight into the non-intelligibility of inertial differences, Lonergan constructed the following syllogism to account for the foundation of the relativity postulate:

> When there is no difference in a physicist's insights, there should be no difference in the form of the mathematical expression of physical principles and laws.
> But when an inertial transformation occurs, there is no difference in a physicist's insights.
> Therefore, when an inertial transformation occurs, there should be no difference in the form of the mathematical expression of the physical principles and laws [i.e., they are covariant].[15]

The major premise in Lonergan's syllogism is a conclusion from: (a) the cognitional theoretic grasp that expressions are formulations of insights and; (b) the self-appropriated application of cognitional theory to equations used in physics. The application mentioned in (b) grasps that physicists' equations are formulations of the insights appropriate to physicists as physicists. The minor premise is a conclusion from: (c) the general cognitional theorem relating formulations, direct insights, and inverse insights; (d) the analytic understanding that what is meant by 'an inertial transformation' is a correlation between measurements performed on two sets of data which differ only inertially; (e) the recognition that by 'physicists' insights' is meant insights with respect to measurements of one or the other of these sets of data, in accordance with cognitional fact; and (f) the inverse insight, which originates with sensible data and is probably verified with respect to the givenness of sensible data, that there is no intelligible difference between sets of data which differ only inertially. The conclusion, therefore, is virtually unconditioned insofar as the analytic meaning of (d) is grasped, insofar as the affirmations of cognitional theory (particularly (a), (b), (c), and (e)) are instances virtually unconditioned for the self-appropriated subject, and to the

---

[15] *Insight*, p. 24.

extent that (f) is empirically verified in the data of sense. It is clear, then, that the relativity postulate is largely based, not on sensibly empirical fact, but upon cognitional fact—upon the *de facto* structure of the concretely acting subject as subject.

What is problematic in the question of the foundations of the relativity postulate is not the truth or falsity of the particular inverse insight into inertial motion. Roughly speaking, the inverse insight is subject to the same general empirical procedures of verification as any other insight into physical nature. Moreover, the inverse insight did not originate with Einstein. Einstein himself spoke of Galileo and Newton as the originators of the relativity principle,[16] while Lonergan traces the same inverse insight back to Zeno's paradoxes.[17] Yet, there is a vast difference between Einstein's formulation of the relativity postulate, and the formulation which preceeded his. That prior formulation is found in Newton's principles. In those principles, Newton positively exploited the negative contribution of the inverse insight into inertial motion in the context of the theory of external physical forces. Now while the precise meaning of Newton's concept of "force" was the subject of prolonged and serious debate, it is clear enough that Newton intended that the formulation of his principles—like the inverse insight itself—should be wholly based upon matters of empirical fact.

What is problematic in the foundations of the relativity postulate is the way Einstein exploited the inverse insight. As Lonergan puts it, Einstein "raised the issue to the methodological level."[18] That is, Einstein's principle of relativity is not an empirically verifiable law or principle, but a principle for generation and selection of empirically verifiable principles and laws. Thus, Einstein's positive exploitation of the negative contribution of the inverse insight cannot be substantiated by means of empirical methods of investigation, for his exploitation is on the same level as those methods. It is only by addressing the foundations, not of the laws of physics, but of the methods of physics that the problem of the foundations of STR can be resolved. Lonergan's life work has been largely devoted to showing how the subject as subject provides the proper foundations for method *in general*. The foregoing discussion has shown how Lonergan was able to identify the foundations of the particular methodical innovation wrought by Einstein in STR.

---

[16] See, for example, A. Einstein, *Ideas and Opinions* (N.Y.: Dell Publishing Co., Inc., 1973), p. 225.

[17] *Insight*, p. 25.

[18] Ibid.

III. The Subject as Subject and the General Theory of Relativity

Lonergan's discussion of the foundations of Einstein's work was not limited to the Special Theory of Relativity. Lonergan took up the problem of the foundations of General Theory Relativity (GTR) as well. His contributions here are probably more significant for, while many scientists have a notion that STR has some empirical foundation (in the probably verified inverse insight into inertial motion), the problem of an empirical justification for GTR has, at one time or another, puzzled almost all scientists and philosophers of science familiar with the theory. Lonergan's approach is remarkable, for it shows that, in the ordinary sense of "empirical" (i.e., what is based upon the data of sense), there is no empirical foundation for GTR. Rather, it is only when one moves to the perspective of a "generalized empirical method" [19] — a method which deals with the data of consciousness as well as the data of sense — that the foundations of GTR can be shown. In Lonergan's view, while STR is partially dependent upon the sensibly empirical validity of the inverse insight into merely inertial difference, GTR is wholly dependent upon cognitional fact. Let us, then, consider Lonergan's explication of this position.

The core of GTR is the Principle of Equivalence — that is, the assertion that physical laws and principles are equivalent, not simply for inertial observers, but for all observers. Stated more precisely, this fundamental postulate of GTR is that the mathematical expression of physical principles and laws is co-variant under the group of all continuous transformations. Clearly, this is a generalization of the relativity postulate of STR, for it removes the restriction that transformations be inertial (hence, the *General* Theory of Relativity). Most significantly, the postulate implies that the mathematical expression of physical principles and laws will be the same for observers undergoing complex forms of relative accelerated motion as for observers moving with relative constant velocity or even at relative rest.

The Principle of Equivalence is implemented in GTR by the insistence that all physical principles and laws be expressed in terms of tensor equations. There is a general theorem of tensor calculus that tensors and functional correlations among tensors are co-variant under the group of continuous transformations. Thus, the insistence that physical principles and laws be formulated in terms of tensors is one way of guaranteeing that the Principle of Equivalence is maintained.

---

[19] Ibid., p. 41.

Lonergan states that this Principle of Equivalence is "a conclusion...based on cognitional theory."[20] The basis for Lonergan's contention is his cognitional theoretic clarification of the type of insight which is the objective of modern scientific investigation. According to Lonergan's analysis of modern scientific practices, modern science specializes in a certain type of understanding. Lonergan refers to this type as the understanding of "correlation"—that is, the understanding of the relations among things themselves. He clarifies what he means by the understanding of correlation by contrasting it with another type of understanding which he terms "classification". Classification involves the understanding of things in relationship to a subject's senses. In order to show how Lonergan can claim that the Principle of Equivalence is a conclusion from cognitional theory it is first necessary to explicate his cognitional theoretic discrimination between these two types of understanding.

The clarification of what Lonergan meant by "classification" is perhaps best achieved by means of examples. How do people ordinarily understand what ammonia is? Common understanding of ammonia is usually expressed as "Ammonia is whatever smells like this smell I am presently smelling." Such an act of understanding is entirely dependent upon the concrete occurrence of a sensation or a memory. Without that concrete occurrence, the understanding is lost. Consider again, what is ordinarily meant by 'far away.' Although no one would put it in these words, the average person's understanding of "far away" would be expressed something like this: "Something is far away if it would require what I regard as considerable exertion for me to move to where I could touch or grasp this thing with my hands." Here, two types of sensations—one kinesthetic, the other prehensile—provide the essential referents of the understanding of the relationship. By extension, one might say that classification is the type of understanding which relates things to a human subject's sensations or practical purposes. Thus a "pest" is understood as whatever interferes with the attainment of one's practical purposes in life. Further sub-classifications of pests (into rats, bugs, etc.) would be based on further relations to one's sensations or purposes.

By way of contrast, the maturation of the modern sciences has been accompanied by rather deliberate attempts to minimize or eliminate relations to human sensations or purposes. The seventeenth century revolution in astronomy had to overcome the fact that humans have no *sensation* of their motion when they are standing "still" on the earth.[21] Galileo's contributions to the parallel revolution

---

[20] Ibid., p. 41.

[21] Herbert Butterfield, *The Origins of Modern Science* (N.Y.: Free Press, 1957), pp. 13-17.

in mechanics were cut short by his inability to break with the limitations of circular images—limitations rooted in the experience of the human body as a center. The developments of analytic geometry and the calculus were essential in order that Newton could overcome these limitations.[22] Again, Linneaus initiated the trend toward a new, "natural" terminology for ordering plants and animals by partially prescinding from the peculiarities of human interests.[23] Likewise, Lavoisier began the reordering of modern chemistry by developing a new nomenclature for chemical substances based upon their relations to one another, rather than upon their relationships to human sensations or purposes.[24]

Along similar lines, the importance attached to measurement in modern scientific practice testifies to a difference between classification and the type of understanding sought by modern science. One may have a very refined understanding of alcohol in relation to one's senses and, as well, a sophisticated understanding of sugar in relation to one's senses. Yet these two understandings fail to provide an adequate basis for the understanding of the relationships between alcohol and sugar. Again, baseball all-stars have very astute understandings of the motions of baseballs in relation to their sensations, and accomplished sailors have keen understandings of the movements of stars in relationship to their senses. However, a baseball all-star who was also an accomplished sailor would have a pitiful basis for understanding the relationships between the movements of baseballs and stars. Measurement provides the adequate basis required for the understanding of things in relationship to one another.

Measurement consists in the understanding of relationships among data on things being measured and data on a reproducible standard of measurement (e.g., a ruler, a watch, or scales). Because the standard of measurement is reproducible, either the same standard or its equivalent can be applied to data on other things, and their relationships grasped. Thus, measurement enables one not only to relate different things to the standard of measurement, but also, by means of that standard, to grasp relations of those things to one another. Furthermore, it is not the data either on the things measured or the data on the measuring standard, but rather the understanding of the relationship between the standard and the measured which is crucial to measurement. Thus, when scientists seek correlations, not among

---

[22] Ibid., pp. 81-84, 160.

[23] L. Eisley, *Darwin's Century* (N.Y.: Doubleday and Co., 1961), pp. 14-26.

[24] S. Toulmin and J. Goodfield, *The Architecture of Matter* (Chicago: University of Chicago Press, 1977), pp. 216-221.

perceived data but among measurements, they are methodically prescinding from relationships to their sensations. Modern scientists therefore seek, not relations between the relationships to their senses, but "relations between the measured relations of things to one another." [25]

To recapitulate, a variety of modern scientific practices (including the reliance on measurement) have all been developed in order to help scientists attain understandings of things in their relationships to one another. Cognitional theoretical analysis reveals that this type of understanding is radically distinct from classification, and that special efforts must be made to overcome the common tendency to understand things in relationship to one's sensations or purposes. Such a discrimination between these two types of understanding presupposes a grasp of what understanding is and is not. It further presupposes a grasp of how the understanding of classifications and the understanding of correlations are differently related to acts of experiencing. Since it is the task of cognitional theory to discover the distinctions and relations among acts of consciousness, the clarification of the understanding of correlations is a conclusion from cognitional theory.

From this clarification of the objective of modern science it is now possible to show how the Principle of Equivalence follows as a conclusion from cognitional theory. First, the ways things relate to human sensations (especially visual sensations) depend in large measure upon the human subject's spacio-temporal perspectives and changes in those perspectives (that is, states of motion of the human observer). In general there seem to be few limits to the states of motion possible for human observers, except that these motions be continuous in space and time. Since the variations in perspectives affect how things are perceived by observers, they will naturally affect how things are understood in relation to the observers' sensations. Yet such variations cannot be allowed to influence the understanding of how things are related to one another. But unless some special effort is made, the common tendency to understand classifications will undermine the attempt to understand correlations. A solution to this problem is provided by insisting that the insights which grasp correlations (physical principles and laws) must be the same for all observers, regardless of their state of motion. In other words, of all the insights into data which can be possibly had, the only ones which will be admitted as potential candidates for physical principles and laws will be those insights which are *not* influenced by the ways various states of observers' motions affect observers' perceptual perspectives.

---

[25] *Insight,* p. 41.

This solution follows from the cognitional theoretic clarification of the type of understanding proper to correlation, and from knowledge of how states of motion affect the relationships of things to human sensation. The derivation of the Principle of Equivalence requires one further cognitional theoretic premise, along with an understanding of what is meant by a coordinate transformation. From cognitional theory, it is clear that formulations are directly related to the insights they formulate. If there is no difference in the insights into physical principles and laws, there should be no difference in their formulations. Thus, the formulations of physical principles and laws should be the same for all observers, regardless of their states of motion. From what has been said in the earlier section regarding coordinate transformations, it follows that the mathematical formulations of physical principles and laws must be co-variant, not merely for inertial transformations, but for all continuous coordinate transformations. This is the Principle of Equivalence.

Lonergan speaks of this conclusion from cognitional theory—the Principle of Equivalence—as "no more than a general anticipation." [26] That is, from an understanding of the type of understanding which is the specialty of modern science, it follows that any potential candidate for the title, "physical principle or law," must satisfy the Principle of Equivalence. This general anticipation does not, however, render up any specific insight into physical correlations, nor does it determine which ones are correct. It merely provides heuristic guidance by, so to speak, narrowing down the field of insights worthy of consideration.

Incidentally, this heuristic character of the Principle of Equivalence and the closely affiliated insistence that physical laws and principles be formulated in terms of tensors provides the answer to a frequent objection to Einstein's GTR. It has been commonly objected that any physical principle or law (for example, Newton's laws of motion) can be easily reformulated in terms of tensors. The upshot of this objection is that the tensor requirement is trivial and inconsequential. However, the Principle of Equivalence and the tensor requirement only constitute minimal requirements of eligibility. They do not determine the correctness of principles or laws so formulated. Thus, while it is true enough that any physical principle or law can be reformulated in terms of tensors, it is not the case that principles or laws, once they are so formulated, will be verified. Einstein did not assert that every tensor law was correct; he merely held tensor-formulation was a minimum criterion for admissibility.

---

[26] Ibid.

One further point remains. Lonergan notes that the upshot of Einstein's Principle of Equivalence was to situate physical principles and laws "completely outside the range of observational activity." [27] One can read this statement without recognizing the radical implications of the word, "completely." Yet, if one is caught by that radicalness, one is struck by the sense of "startling strangeness," where the seemingly solid foundations of natural science have been lost. Are the physical principles and laws of modern science, then, merely arbitrary? Where is the solidity upon which science can be founded if not, as John Locke put it, upon the "testimony of the senses"? It is as if at the apex of the development of modern science, Einstein's General Theory of Relativity has caused the very foundations of modern science to dissolve right from under the monumental edifice.

Fortunately, this problem is only a pseudo-problem. It arises only because the search for foundations has been mislead by the metaphor of "solidity." The metaphor of "solidity" derives its force and sense of reality from the "already out there now" of biological extroversion — an extroversion continuous with observational activity. GTR demonstrates conclusively that the foundations of physical principles and laws (their reality) *cannot* be found in the solidity of observation.

The foundations of physical principles and laws must be sought instead in the non-solid activity of the human subject. Lonergan did not claim that GTR eliminated foundations altogether. He did not claim that physical principles and laws lie outside *all* activity of the human subject — only outside *observational* activity. Clearly, Lonergan situates the foundations of physical principles and laws within the self-transcending normativity of the intelligent and reasonable activity of the subject. Activity that is intelligent and reasonable is hardly arbitrary. Thus from Lonergan's perspective, Einstein's achievement in the General Theory of Relativity goes beyond the discovery of an empirical principle or law. It removed the illusion of a "solid" foundation for modern science, and threw us all back upon the foundational reality of the self-transcending subject as subject.

---

[27] Ibid.

Body to Thing

by Joseph Flanagan

In considering the problem of intellectual conversion in Lonergan's *Insight,* a great deal of effort has been given to explaining the shift from counter-position to position in terms of Lonergan's cognitional theory. I would like to examine this same conversion in terms of the shift from the notion of body to that of thing, focusing primarily on chapters four and eight in *Insight.* The themes that I am going to analyse were treated by Lonergan in several articles published before *Insight,* and it may clarify my focus if I briefly describe this earlier context of the problem.

The two articles I have selected are "Finality, Love, Marriage" and "The Natural Desire to See God." The theme common to both articles is referred to, in the contemporary context, as a world-view; but in the more traditional context was discussed as the classification of things according to their transcendental generic and specific relations. The popular version of this world-view is the scheme that divides the world up into minerals, plants, animals, humans and gods without specifying the relations between the classes. In the traditional scholastic context, the world of things was analysed and dissected according to the four basic causes of their being, then reassembled as a hierarchy of higher and more perfect essences reaching up to the divine essence or perfect being. In "Finality, Love, Marriage" Lonergan proposed that such a scheme had emphasized the horizontal finality of things but tended to overlook vertical finality. In horizontal finality it was stressed that things seek ends proportioned to their essences, hence, it emphasized the different ways that things operated according to the grade of being they had received. Such a world-ordering of things according to their essences was abstract and overlooked the concrete, dynamic interaction of things with one another not only on their own appropriate levels but also the interactions that occured between levels. It is this interaction between levels that Lonergan labels vertical finality. Thus the nitrogen cycle involves plants, animals, minerals and humans in a vast web of interactions interconnecting four different grades of being in a complex scheme of cooperation that benefits all of the things involved. The reason for the neglect of vertical finality by medieval and renaissance scholastics was that the workings of vertical finality were not known in any concrete or detailed way until recent developments in the natural sciences made it more explicit.

The second article, "The Natural Desire to See God," also involves the problem of world-order and contrasts two different ways of approaching and constructing a world-view. The first tends to result in a closed, static order since it assumes that the natures of things are already fixed and that God orders the design and interaction of things according to these pre-determined natures. The contrasting framework is open and dynamic, assuming that world-order is prior to the natures of things and that things come to their natures through the concrete interactions of things with one another. The obvious connection between the two articles is that vertical finality, stressing the interconnections of the hierarchically arranged levels of things, becomes a working assumption of the dynamic, open, world-order, while exclusive emphasis on horizontal finality leads to the closed, static world-order. This contrast is somewhat oversimplified, but it does point up the problem of conversion as a shift from one view of world-order to its opposite.

In *Insight* Lonergan has reconceived the entire context of the problem so that none of the terms in the above contrast were used; what emerged in *Insight* was an explanation of why the scholastic emphasis on horizontal finality had tended to bring about the formation of a closed, abstract, static world-order. Rather than a shift from abstract, fixed essences to concrete, dynamic interacting natures *Insight* proposed a shift from a world of bodies that are already-out-there-now to a world of things existing in and through their recurrent schemes. The problem in *Insight,* then, is to convert a person from thinking of things as out-there-now-real bodies to understanding them as existing in their recurrences concretely conditioned by other recurring things. The key step to this conversion is to understand the notion of a recurrent scheme which is the central term in Lonergan's own account of world-order.

The first interesting point to note about Lonergan's account of world-order in chapter four is that there is no mention of things, genera and species. The discussion of these terms takes place in chapter eight after the mistaken notion of things as bodies has hopefully been eliminated and a world-order of recurrent schemes has been established. A second interesting feature of recurrent schemes is that schemes cannot be explained by a law but only by a combination of many laws interconnected. Thirdly, schemes are not only combinations of laws but of events, and while events are of various kinds, still the emphasis is on the event—the actual occurrence or non-occurrence. With this brief description of world-order in terms of recurrent schemes we can turn to an actual example of a recurrent scheme and proceed to a more detailed analysis of the steps leading to a shift from the closed static world-order to an open dynamic one.

Our first example of a recurrent scheme will be the circulation of water over the planet. The water rises out of the warm, tropical seas steaming upward, forming clouds that are carried on wind currents to the northern and southern hemispheres where the rains fall on the land, run down the mountains into rivers and lakes, flowing out to the ocean where the water circulates back to the tropical seas to repeat the scheme. This account provides us with a concrete, descriptive account of how the scheme recurs. However, one of the most important distinctions made in the first half of *Insight* is between a point of view based on descriptive relations and one based on an explanatory framework. To explain a series of events one has to move from a world-order that relates things to ourselves through descriptions to one that relates things to one another through explanatory correlations. Such a move involves abstractive procedures that prescind from the sensible relation of things to us to discover the intelligible, explanatory relations of things to one another. From the history of science we know it took over a thousand years of scientific analyses before scientists were able to develop an explanatory perspective freed from descriptive, sensible relations of things to observers. However, from the same history of science we learn that an even more difficult problem is to reverse from an abstract, explanatory perspective back to the concrete order in which verification must take place. Put somewhat succinctly, the problem is to reverse from an explanatory framework back to a descriptive view in such a way that the explanatory correlations ground and control the descriptive relations. If we examine three of the world-orders given in chapter four, we can illustrate this point.

In chapter two Lonergan analyses the two major explanatory procedures that scientists have developed—classical and statistical. Scientists working with classical procedures seek to discover and verify systematic or regularly recurring relations between things, while statistical investigators seek to understand and verify non-systematic or irregularly recurring relations among these things. The procedures are opposite but complementary and Lonergan connects them in his scheme of recurrence. Since both procedures are necessary to understand how the world is concretely ordered, a failure to understand and employ the procedures can lead to a confused account of the way things work together to form the world. Thus, Lonergan, contrasting his own world-order with those of Aristotle, Galileo and Darwin, focuses on their failure to clarify these two basic procedures. Aristotle's abstractive procedures led to the development of a classical, explanatory framework for systematic relations; however, he failed to clarify the difference in the way we verify descriptive and explanatory properties of things. Galileo's world-order compounded the problem by simply denying the reality of descriptive relations. Darwin's world-order, however, is especially interesting since he was one of the first scientists to develop an explanatory framework using statistical procedures, and since statistical procedures employ descriptive relations he was able to restore the objectivity of these relations. However, Lonergan makes the rather surprising assertion that both classical and statistical procedures are abstract and both fail to give a completely concrete account of world-order. This claim needs some explanation.

If we examine the relation between the recurrent scheme of water circulation and Galileo's and Darwin's theories, we can clarify the problem of determining a concrete explanation of world-order. To give a causal account of how water falls from the clouds onto the earth, a scientist needs to know Galileo's law of falling bodies, but this law will be of little help in explaining why water rises up and forms clouds. Scientists, therefore, could not verify Galileo's law under ordinary, concrete circumstances; such classical correlations can be verified only under ideally or artificially constructed conditions, usually involving the building of special instruments. This does not mean that Galileo's law has no explanatory power with regard to the way that world-order concretely operates. What it does mean is that in verifying Galileo's law, scientists have verified not the actual nor probable ways that things accelerate and decelerate but rather the concretely possible ways that things will change if certain concrete conditions are fulfilled. Galileo was certainly aware that his spatio-temporal patterns were ideal but what he was not aware of, nor did he even suspect, was that the concrete pattern of interactions could vary from these idealized possibilities in irregular ways. For example according to the classically conceived spatio-temporal patterns of Newton, the earth should travel in a perfect elliptical orbit. In the actual, concrete order, the earth does not fulfill the expected ideal pattern. The next question we should consider, then, is whether the actual variations fall into a regular or irregular pattern. Are there slight decreases in planetary accelerations or slight increases in their decelerations that might lead to the gradual loss of any elliptical pattern? Next, are the gains or losses of speeds classically predictable or are they only probably predictable and, if so, how probable; do the probabilities admit exceptions that are very small, even unique, etc. This line of questioning points out that there are three concrete orderings that have to be taken into account in dealing with world order. These are the concretely, possible ordering between things, the concretely probable, and finally, the actual order. Classical scientists like Galileo, Newton, Lavoisier and Pasteur were trying to discover how things interact with one another, but not how frequently they interacted. When they attempted to verify their correlations between things, they set up laboratory procedures that were not naturally or actually given, but were man-made, artificial conditions deliberately aimed at eliminating concrete conditions that would interfere with their proposed verifications. And so, what these scientists verified was not the way that world order concretely operates, nor the way it probably would operate, but the possible ways that it might actually or concretely operate. Verified classical laws, therefore, reveal not just possible orders but concretely possible orders. We can make a similar point if we shift to statistical scientists such as meteorologists.

Meteorologists assume all the classical laws that connect together and explain the concrete possibilities for water circulating up, around, down and across the earth's continents. Their preoccupation is with distribution of water in various places and at various times and they know that this distribution varies in non-systematic or irregular ways, yet they assume that despite the non-regular relations the probable distribution and amount of rainfall can be predicted. It would seem, then, that this combination of classical and statistical procedures would provide the scientist with a completely concrete account of the events of world-order. But such a procedure does not give an account of each and every event but of only the average run of events. This can be seen even more clearly if we look at Darwin's approach to world-order.

Darwin's method of study seemed to be thoroughly concrete since he took into account not only the generic likenesses among birds, not only the specific differences between birds that were generically similar, but he also paid attention to the individual differences of particular birds, as when he drew a series of heads of finches that drew attention to the individual shapes of their beaks. Yet despite the apparent concern with every concrete detail of particular things, Darwin's interest was primarily with species, not individuals, with specific things, not individual things. Darwin was like the mathematical gambler trying to figure out the odds of rolling sevens or elevens. Such a gambler notes every individual roll but he does so only to figure out averages. Just as the meteorologist gives the specific probabilities of the generic possibilities of rain falling, so Darwin gives us the successive sets of alternative potential developments for present and future schemes within certain specific boundaries. But, beside these concretely possible and concretely probable schemes of recurrence, Lonergan would add the concretely actual schemes that are presently operating or have in fact operated in the past. By this Lonergan means not only how rain falls, not only how much rain might fall today, but how much in fact did fall today and yesterday and the day before. When Lonergan distinguishes his world-order from Darwin's he states he is concerned, at least in chapter four, not with species, nor with things, but with possible, probable and actual recurring schemes.

Anticipating briefly the context of chapter eight where Lonergan does deal with genera, species and things, we can say—things exist and schemes recur, but we must add, these things exist only in and through their recurring schemes. One and the same thing can be affirmed from two united but distinguishable frameworks—things and schemes of recurrences. Trees exist but they do so only in a conditioned series of recurring schemes; the continuous existing of trees and animals is through their actual recurring schemes and the probable, alternative ones that may emerge in view of concrete possibilities. I shall return to a further discussion of this aspect of world-order, but for the present I would like to draw attention to another aspect of recurrent schemes.

The key to the design of Lonergan's world-order is, as we have explained, schemes of recurrence, but not as single schemes, rather as a series emerging in such a way that earlier schemes provide conditions that make later schemes not only possible and probable but more and more probable as more and more of the conditions for the further, higher scheme actually emerge. As illustrative of this conditioned series of schemes we can take the examples given by Lonergan, beginning with the planetary system, which conditions the emergence and actual operation of the water circulation over the earth's surface which in turn conditions the nitrogen cycle, which in turn conditions the routines of animal life, which in turn conditions the human, economic rhythms, etc. The emergence of any scheme in the series depends on the operation of the prior recurrent scheme. The schemes form a conditioned series and only as long as the prior schemes continue to operate can we expect the later schemes to continue to recur. Further each scheme depends on a large number of conditions that must continue to be given if the scheme is to recur. The scheme by itself is quite regular, even circular, but, for the circuit to keep repeating itself, prior conditions that led to the emergence of this kind of a circle of events must continue to provide the ground for each of the emerging events that together form the circle of occurrences of any given scheme. In other words, to give a full explanation of any single cycle involves the scientist in the task of explaining all the conditions actually operating and providing the basis for the particular scheme he is explaining. Furthermore, these conditions diverge not only backward in time, in that prior schemes must already be operating, but they also diverge spatially in that, for example, the nitrogen cycle depends on the prior water circulation scheme, which in turn depends on a system of interacting planets, and so on outward to the entire universe of galactic systems. Such a focus suggests the complexity of meaning that Lonergan attaches to the word "concrete" when he proposes that the concrete is not only everything about this thing but everything about everything. In contrast to this meaning of the concrete there is the way a person thinks of the concrete when operating, not in a scientific pattern of experience with its two basic explanatory perspectives, but in the common-sense pattern which is always descriptive. This difference needs to be stressed.

Besides living in the scientific context of relations, scientists also live in a common-sense patterning of experience as happens when driving cars, eating meals, writing checks, talking with neighbors and the myriad other aspects of ordinary living. Such a pattern of experience is very concrete and, while people recur and operate in economic, political, social and religious recurrent schemes, they do not ordinarily deal with these schemes in an explanatory fashion, but as particular, immediate, and practical everyday matters of concern. Science, on the other hand, tries to understand reality in terms of its concretely possible and probable schemes of recurrences; common-sense deals with the same reality as immediate, particular and practical. The problem is how to put these two apparently opposed yet actually complementary methods of knowing together so that they yield a meaning of reality that does not limit the concrete to particular immediate realities but also includes those possibilities and probabilities that have been verified as concretely possible and probable.

This is the task Lonergan sets for the metaphysician in chapter fourteen where he speaks of a "reoriented science and common-sense" that will provide the philosopher with the set of secondary minor premises, while the primary set will come from the series of repeated affirmations of self as a self-recurring knower. In this paper

I have not dealt with the primary set that focuses on knowing as a recurring scheme, but have suggested that this reversal of science and common-sense involves shifting from a closed, conceptualistic world-order to an open, dynamic framework. More specifically, this means shifting from thinking about material objects as bodies to thinking about them as things operating in recurrent schemes. I have suggested that such a reversal can be effected through a series of stages. First, one must shift from a descriptive to an explanatory framework. Second, the problem is to reverse back to the descriptive framework in such a way that the explanatory framework is not governed by the descriptive perspective but rather mediates and controls it. Thirdly, the key step to this reversal and control of frameworks is the scheme of recurrence understood as a conditioned series of schemes that can order the concretely possible, probable, and actual schemes into a world-order whose grounding conditions form a non-systematic aggregate of events from which emerge the conditioned series of schemes. The fourth and final step is to grasp the unity and identity between things and the schemes within which they operate. This final step has yet to be completed since one further problem remains.

In contrastng body and thing in chapter eight Lonergan connects the meaning that is usually given to body to a spatio-temporal framework organized and controlled by a biologically extroverted awareness. It is a framework shared by both animals and men, and since this framework is operative in human beings from the first moment when infants seek nourishment, it is a rather difficult experience to appropriate; it is only because of recent developments in the study of spatio-temporal frameworks that this problem has come to explicit awareness. The problem can be stated quite simply: we must first distinguish descriptive and explanatory spatio-temporal frameworks, then, combine them into a concrete ordering that allows for verified possible, probable, and actual spatio-temporal frameworks. The difficulty of this problem can be seen in a scientist like Galileo who, at least in a limited way, distinguished explanatory and descriptive frameworks when he separated the primary and secondary qualities of things. However, he failed to apply this distinction to the spatial and temporal qualties of things. Newton continued the problem and intensified it, combining descriptive and explanatory spatio-temporal perspectives into an absolute framework that enclosed all of reality. Such an absolute framework would certainly find a discussion of space or time as something possible or probable quite puzzling. To speak about space as something probable suggests that space has certain limits, and for Newton, space was unlimited and absolute, and time had the same characteristics.

Renaissance and Enlightenment scientists did not distinguish descriptive from explanatory spatio-temporal recurrences because their Euclidean framework fitted in so nicely with their biological, extroverted, spatial awareness. In the biological sphere objects are bodies out-there that can be seen, touched, picked up, thrown, pushed up against, struck with a stick, etc. This chair, for example, is out-there right now and it was already there before the child bumped into it. It is a solid, stable, and very real object, as are all bodies, except those that are soft, spongy, or watery. Even fire is such a body. Such bodies are real, then, because they are right-out-there-now in the empty spaces they occupy. In this context space is what is between bodies, the unity of all the empty places completely homogeneous and undivided. Time has similar characteristics. Just as bodies move about in space without changing space itself so bodies change in time without time itself changing; it just flows by smoothly and continuously without ever stopping or ending. In such a context time seems to be timeless, an everlasting now present before all particular nows, while space appears spaceless, empty but capable of containing any and all particular places. All of reality is within this spaceless space and flows along in timeless time; particular realities are subdivider parts of this spatio-temporal whole which in itself has no parts or subdivisions but is given all at once independent of anything it may happen to contain. Such was the explanation of space by Newton, and it blended in with his ordinary experiences of space, which in turn were grounded in a biological, extroverted awareness.

Someone might object that the ordinary, geocentric, experience of the world is quite different than the explanatory, heliocentric view of the same experience. Such a claim is quite correct, but the point I am proposing is that this distinction between descriptive and explanatory ordering of spatial experiences does not alter or even question the prior and more fundamental, spatial experiences associated with our biological awareness of a palpable, outward thereness with its corresponding, inwardly centered hereness. Somewhere around eight or nine a child learns how to form two different viewpoints of one and the same spatial arrangements. Anyone, then, knows what it is to change spatial frameworks for ordering the motions of the sun — one geocentric and the other heliocentric. Both frameworks can be centered with certain basic directions and sizes, all of which can be related to a centering axis. Whether the axis is centered in the earth or in the sun is not important since our biological awareness of an inner, feelable here correlated with an outer experienced there is not radically challenged when you shift from earth-centered here to a solar-centered there; in both perspectives there is a privileged or absolute center from which and to which all measurements can be referred. Newton's explanatory centered universe can still be harmonized with his biologically centered spheres. If Newton had proposed a spatial ordering that had no extroverted, objective center, no special out-there, then, the possibility for distinguishing descriptively sensed spaces and times from explanatory spatio-temporal frameworks could have emerged. Such a distinction became possible once Einstein eliminated Newton's absolute, explanatory framework.

In the nineteenth century Newton's absolute space was modified into what the scientists labelled aether, but it still retained all the essential properties of Newton's absolute space. Nobody had ever been able to detect aether, to prove that it did in fact exist, and so, scientists decided to try and verify its reality by testing its effects on light waves. They hypothesized that as the earth circled around the sun it would tend to drag the aether around with it, creating an aether wind. To test this hypothesis they measured the velocity of light moving with the aether wind and against it. The result expected was based on the ordinary experience that you run faster with the wind at your back than when running into the wind; the difference in speeds supposedly could be explained by adding or subtracting the wind velocity. However, if after running with the wind and against it, you discovered that your speeds were the same both ways, this would certainly puzzle you since one expects that the force of wind will increase or decrease velocity. Several interpretations could be given. First, you might say that you were mistaken, no wind was blowing. Second, you might say that you were running as fast as possible and so any further added force would not accelerate you beyond that maximum limit. Both interpretations could be given if you supposed that your maximum running velocity was faster than wind-velocity, and so, at your top speed you could not even detect a tail-wind since you were outrunning it. Einstein's interpretation of the famous Michelson-Morley experiments was similar to my example. Scientists had expected that the velocity of light would be increased or decreased by the aether wind, but when the measurements did not yield the expected increase or decrease scientists hypothesized that the increases and decreases did in fact occur but that their measuring instruments were also affected so that the spatial and temporal measurements of the instruments themselves were changed. Einstein agreed with this hypothesis; namely, that accelerations would actually change the sizes of rulers and the speeds of clocks, but he suggested that the reason for the change was not the aether but that the spaces and times of matter will vary with their velocities, and that there are no spaces and times apart from or independent of the material substances themselves. Space was not the empty, immovable reality through which things traveled, but rather space was itself material and matter was spatial. Moreover, time did not flow independent of material bodies, but was itself material and all matter was temporal. When you stand watching a bird or plane travel across the skyline you can see the beginning and end of the spatial path all at once, while the time of the flight is apparently inside your watching, independent of the spaces traversed. Time seems to be something spiritual, impalpable, independent, and outside of material changes, but Einstein proposed time was intrinsic to matter, which also was intrinsically spatial, or rather, matter was essentially a spatio-temporal field that was not separable from matter.

If we now briefly sketch the shift from the descriptive, ordinary spatiotemporal frameworks to Newtonian explanatory frameworks and a similar shift to Einsteinian explanatory frameworks we can again illustrate the problem of a concrete ordering of all the possible, probable and actual spatiotemporal frameworks. We have suggested that the root of the problem is the biological basis of human awareness. There are generic differences in the ways that animals and humans sense spaces inside and outside their bodies, but besides these generic differences, both humans and animals are conscious and their consciousness is biologically grounded in an inner sphere that feels a need for food, sex, and security, and an outer sphere where these appetites can be satisfied. The cultural spaces and times that human societies develop and hand on through successive generations can vary, but they remain biologically conditioned toward and by bodies already-out-there and by inner based centers that are already-in-here. Bodies can change their places and times, but people tend to "sense" that these places and times can all be related to a space and time that does not change, an ultimate unchanging out-there to which all inner subjective variables can be correlated. The real is out-there, it is objective, and it ultimately grounds all interior, sensed experiences. Newton's explanatory spatiotemporal framework did not ultimately challenge this biologically based notion of reality and objectivity. In certain ways it actually reinforced it since Newton utilized a coordinate, axial system based on Euclidian presuppositions which blended in with the biological grounding of human awareness.

In the Euclidean world bodies were thought of in terms of points, lines, planes and angles. Such geometric bodies, it was assumed, did not change their shapes and sizes when accelerated. Sizes of trees vary with their ages and their ages vary with their stage of development, but rocks, mountains and planets are not expected to change their sizes and shapes as they move about, nor would a well-made clock be expected to give different times at different speeds, and certainly the enveloping space that contained all these geometrized bodies never changed since it never moved, but was already in its place before there were any bodies to occupy it. In Einstein's spatiotemporal world all the physical objects including atoms were like trees; their sizes varied with their ages and their ages varied with their successive speeds. Most importantly there was no space and time apart from the material objects themselves, and so, there was no need for an empty space between things, since these spaces are not empty but are either gravitational or electromagnetic fields resulting from the interactions of various physical entities. Supposed empty spaces, then, can change their sizes and shapes, since they are identical with the interacting entities that change as they interact. Spaces and times are physical realities interacting, and so, there is no ultimate shape or size to such a finite, spatiotemporal universe, but rather a series of possible, probable, and actual shapes and sizes that can vary through a series of sizes and shapes, with the velocity of light fixing the limit of the variations.

The Einsteinian explanatory framework of spaces and times not only fixes the generic possibilities for the situations and durations within which the recurrent schemes of world-order can emerge and function but it also undermines the mistaken notion of things as bodies already-out-there-now existing. What exists and operates in such schemes as the nitrogen cycle are plant, animal, and human things, not bodies. Bodies are biologically based realities that are out-there-now clearly separable, frequently far apart from one another with empty spaces between them. Things, on the other hand, are not separable from their schemes. Things and schemes are simply two ways of understanding one and the same reality. As human things, they are individual unities that perdure in their identity through spatiotemporal changes, chemical and biological changes, psychological and intellectual changes. These same things, considered in terms of their schemes, are not individual identities, but interconnected unities involved in a vast web of schemes conditioning one another so that no one of them can continue to recur without the others continuing to provide the conditions for their recurring functions. World-order is not something already out-there, but rather world-order is what in fact is actually recurring in the light of verified possibilities and probalities; nor is world-order one reality and things another. Rather world-order recurs in and through things while things exist in their world recurring schemes. Just as things are not bodies already-there before the world is ordered, so the world is not already there before the things existing in their recurring scheme realize the possible, probable, and actual workings of world order. Once bodies have been eliminated from the universe by eliminating their ground in pre-existing spaces and times there is left a universe of existing things none of which can continue to exist unless the conditions for their existence continue to be provided. The very existence of such a universe, therefore, is completely contingent and cannot explain itself. Such a universe is full with the mystery of unanswered questions.

A Dialogue on Learning Mathematics

by R. Eric O'Connor

The Thomas More Institute of Montreal (founded 1945) offers annually to its 600 students some 40 university-level courses which are designed specifically for older adults. One full-year course in mathematics is among the requirements for those who are working for a B.A. degree, though such a requirement is not often maintained elsewhere. B. Lonergan has been associated with the Institute — in lectures, interviews or discussions — since its beginning. The success of his 1945-46 course "Thought and Reality" assured the founding directors that a certain quality of adult education would be viable in Montreal.

Early in the Spring of 1980, Eric O'Connor (EOC), Cathleen Going (CG), and Charlotte Tansey (CT), the participants in this dialogue, attended an exhibition of the recent work of the painter Louis Belzile, a director of Thomas More Institute, one of its B.A. degree graduates in 1965, and a co-founder of the Plasticien movement in Montreal years before. The pictures were filled with light and with structure. "He referred to his new work as a breathing between the structured and the unstructured", was the report of Cathleen Going. And someone kept marvelling at the strong shapes as suggesting granite-like commitments, though Belzile's reactions were spontaneous and he seemed easy-going. The event became the background for the discussion which revolved around the following questions:

> Why have we insisted that adult students have a course in mathematical ideas as part of the B.A. degree? What does mathematics add to the intellectual, the imaginative, development of a person? What is real about mathematics?

EOC: I remember seeing in a painting a sphere that looked more like a sphere than any I'd ever been able to imagine; it looked perfect. But a sphere that one sees or makes isn't the perfect sphere the mathematician thinks of. The one he thinks of just never was. The perfect circle never was. The line is of no thickness, and so it can't be seen. The point occupies no space; it can't be seen. In the world of such ideas there is a clarity and a precision that are not in the world, but both are strangely prophetic of what is found in the world.

I compare the reality of the world of mathematical ideas with the reality of stories. These also never were as they are told, but they are highly intelligible when you listen to them. They refer to life, and they are like life. They evoke in the reader an *idea* of life. But "Did it really happen like that?" is not a question you ask when a good story is told. In mathematics "Is any existing like that?" is not a question asked. "It *could* be" is all that matters.

CT: Verifying that it happens that way is for empirical science.

CG: So mathematics is an internal world?

EOC: Strictly. Once you have the image of a circle, you don't need to keep looking at the wheel.

CT: Because you've seen the relationships involved?

EOC: Yes, you've seen them and people say you've abstracted. But you've abstracted creatively; that is, you've said "The circle is a line of no thickness, every point equidistant from a mid-point, and that point has no area." From those facts (and on a plane) you can with very simple common sense deduce amazing results.

CG: Is it exactly there that you would start the mathematics course in an adult student's pattern of degree studies?

EOC: I'd start it like the geometry lesson in the *Meno*. It might be a little while before students would come themselves to the definition of a circle as a line equidistant from a given point, and I think I'd give some experience of lines and triangles before coming back to discuss the differences from any circle they know about in the world.

CG: In order to transport them into their new world?

EOC: Exactly. Similarly when you start with number theory, you don't start with "The wonder of numbers;" you let them work with numbers, or play with numbers, finding the relationships among them. Out of their finding those relationships you could help them to get aware of their cognitional activity.

CT: Are you saying it is part of mathematics to be made aware of one's cognitional activity?

EOC: All I'm saying at the moment is that I wouldn't move to that immediately. I've been troubled about getting people to manipulate the mathematical images easily.

CT: In your mathematics classes I generally got the point, but I didn't appropriate it sufficiently because I didn't do the exercises. The easy thing for me is to look at the cognitional aspect but bypass the discipline of the mathematics. This is a flirtation with a subject which is interesting but which doesn't imply a thawing into being able to operate within a whole new world of thought.

EOC: If students don't do the problems, they won't ordinarily acquire the operational ease that is "learning mathematics." There is need for working on their own.

In classes years ago, when I used *What is Mathematics?*, by Courant and Robbins, almost exclusively, there would always be four or five people in the class who were very curious about the book. I felt they would get very well the mathematical insights — and then in some other course, philosophy perhaps, they could renew these insights and become aware of their thought process.

I think flirtation with a subject may be more important for some people than for others. If a person isn't going to use the mathematics, flirtation may be more valuable than the careful doing of a certain number of problems every day until he or she is tired.

CG: In teaching mathematics to the older adult, do you find that there are any gains or are there only hazards, only drawbacks, for trying to step into that world when one is older?

EOC: There are drawbacks of unfamiliarity and fear, but it is a world that has been a fascinating one for so many minds, for so many millennia, and no other world is just like it.

CT: I'm thinking of all the people in senior-citizens' residences, and sixty percent of our discussion leaders there, who say they can't "do" poetry. They always seem to stand outside it. There must be a certain level of being familiar, of crossing the threshold into mathematics. What does that require?

EOC: I think it requires, just as in poetry, fundamentally and absolutely a catching of what the poet or mathematician is trying to do, to be able to be in sympathy with him and think in somewhat the same way.

CG: The "flirtation" you were speaking of, sounds to me very different from merely "standing outside" a subject.

Is mathematics like many other courses at the Institute in being more than a flirtation but still just a beginning? And wouldn't you despair if you were hoping for more than a beginning?

EOC: I guess the difference is that in mathematics it's well known that — provided persons have already had some basic start — they can begin to be utterly certain of their judgment very early in a course. "I know it's a fact that there is an infinity of primes. I know it's a fact that if a structure can be thought of as a group, it will have certain properties, and then necessarily certain other properties." They can be completely sure of those judgments within a few weeks. Now in history, or in literature, persons can be sure they love the direction they are taking, but it is very hard to say what they can be sure they know.

CG: Is that because interpretation in philosophy, literature and history depends so much on personal development, and in mathematics doesn't?

EOC: I would think so as regards the relative need of development. But there's hardly any problem of interpretation in mathematics. Once one has had the idea of the circle, and has been led to see what one can deduce from it by ordinary commonsense postulates, one can be sure that these do follow — even though not explicitly in a first understanding.

CG: Lonergan says there is no literature of interpretation of Euclid.

EOC: Because you know what's being said. Euclid wasn't just getting a person aware of simple shapes and simple relationships and the more complicated relationships you could get from those. What he was interested in and what he taught the human race how to do was theory. He made simple statements about mathematics and proved everything as logically as he could from those postulates. That is Euclid as he is understood by a mathematician, by anyone who's been with it for quite a while.

CG: Isn't that a good example of the kind of point a person flirting can get, and be excited about? But first: what didn't Euclid prove that he seemed to prove?

EOC: Well, he was very careful in his postulates, but he didn't have the most modern ways of saying them. He took for granted that you knew what a straight line was. He said "It lies evenly between two points."

CG: So Euclid was *counting* on our picture-thinking.

EOC: He was counting on it as our basis for moving along, but then he would use the notion in his argument. He said "A line. Straight. You know what straight is." And then he said (in effect): "One of my postulates is that two lines can be parallel to one another and can *stay* parallel."

Now it was only in the first two decades of the 1800's that Gauss got the point that it is possible that no two lines stay straight and at the same distance from one another. This led to an alternative postulate that there are no parallels, and that was Lobachevsky's geometry. Only then it began to be realized that the world of geometry is not the world we have imagined as real, that we take for granted in physics. So there has been the recognition that mathematics and physics are completely separate sciences — a point not grasped when geometry seemed to be the way the world was.

Another interesting point: someone two centuries before non-Euclidean geometry, had worked out the value of *pi* (the ratio of the circumference of a circle to its diameter) to 35 decimal places. No measurement that you could make could do anything like that. The Chinese had gotten to 7 places before 500 A.D. (At first it was thought that they had learned from Greeks and from Ptolemy though these did not have it to that accuracy. It is thought now that they must have worked it out themselves.) When you say a circle has a certain ratio, and give *pi* to 35 decimal places, you don't mean that it is so in the world; you mean it in Euclid's geometry. You were asking me as the discussion began: "What is real in mathematics?" The relationships are real. They're intelligently affirmed. They don't have to be checked.

CG: What does "not having to check" mean?

EOC: Without having to check means you don't have to go to external experience to see whether you are right. The delight reported by the very best adult students I've taught has to do, I think, with an experience of knowing something for the first time without belief.

CT: I'm trying to see whether the experience of someone like that, vibrating with all sorts of insights that have an abstract quality, is close to having an ecstatic experience — you know, the moment in the second act of a ballet where the pattern falls into place and for a short period everything is perfect, and you are surprised it could happen.

EOC: It's very like that experience, I think.

CT: So while we started by talking about structure, "ecstatic experience" seems to be almost the opposite of structure, doesn't it?

EOC: The point is, though, as people are delighted by some of these things, and want to be sure they've seen them correctly, they recognize that they need a logical structure to build up what they have seen. That's the structure of theory. By defining things precisely and going logically, you can make sure you're right.

CG: In terms of people's development: you're not afraid to get them trapped in a logical world they haven't known before?

EOC: No. I don't like the notion that mathematics *is* logic. It is the easiest example of logic. But the high intelligibility of mathematical ideas is what draws one on. I understood Euclid's gift only after studying Lonergan; the logic makes explicit what the insight is.

CT: So your statement about the great liberation which insight gives — a statement Fred Lawrence refers to repeatedly — relates to this?

EOC: Yes. The insight is of what things will follow from which, if articulated sharply.

CT: I wonder if you should explain to students your advising them against getting a tutor in mathematics, by insisting more dramatically that mathematics is something one does oneself.

EOC: It certainly doesn't always get across. One student this year learned it only at the end.

CT: Would you let any students write a lyric in which they touched all the points raised (to show that they had, in fact, caught the insights) if they didn't want to do the problems attached to the lessons? We do sometimes allow lyrics in other subjects.

EOC: A person would have to be good because he or she wouldn't have the symbolism to think or write in, and things get complicated terribly soon. The person needs to have stayed with the matter long enough to be able to meet, with some ease, the complications of the precisions.

CT: I could perhaps relate what you have been saying to "thawing" into a subject, the slow orientation after which there can be questioning. Lonergan speaks of a deep curiosity that is submerged yet motivating, "the pure desire to know." It is hard to question until one is sufficiently into a subject to have the vocabulary, and not to question certainly cuts one off from any development. We have recognized that many mature persons are trapped within their "pure desire to know" and we have wished to give them means to question and to enter the world of theory. Whatever intellectual conversion means, we have wanted to put them on the track for it. Can we make other claims about our intentions over thirty-five years? You refer to some of them as if their taking mathematics was a test of goodwill more than a test of intelligence. You now trust their commitment in other areas because they caught the point of the mathematics course and carried that through?

EOC: Yes, it has seemed to me that persons who mastered the mathematics course, caught the point of catching the point—and knew when they hadn't in mathematics and in other subjects.

CG: I'm wondering about the element in mathematics that gives some people a needed practice in logic—the more "literary" persons, and the ones who write essays such as we've all had to deal with; lots of interesting things recorded but no hanging-together. Is it because you didn't want to teach them logic that you taught mathematics?

CT: You were trying to demonstrate, weren't you, what the world of explanation is as opposed to the world of description? Surely anybody who doesn't know the difference doesn't know fully what rationality is.

EOC: In mathematics you can work for a while and be quite expert in doing all the problems yet not know why they work. I went through a mathematics course for my B. A. degree, and I was interested in calculus and did good work. Later on, as a young Jesuit in philosophy, I wondered about the relation of the derivative and the integral but there was no one around, and the books were too complicated or too old, and I knew it was just one of those things I should have understood beforehand. Here I was, using the relation — and I *could* use it — but I didn't know why it worked. I remember having that question when I got into a course at the University of Toronto; the professor could point out the answer in just a few moments, and I got what it was.

The ideal people for the mathematics course for adults at the Institute I have thought to be those who have had a course in analytic geometry and calculus, and are able to do the ordinary problems; perhaps without having understood some of them.

CT: In fact you've been getting people who have less and less fundamental mathematics.

EOC: Yes. When they put 2^3, they're not sure really what it means.

CG: In earlier years at the Institute, was it important to stop judgments from coming too fast because people were brought up on judgments — ones they had learned? In recent years what is missing may be different. There are insights all around but no rock because no one knows what a grounded judgment is. Was insisting on mathematics partly to cut people loose from the "real world" and prepare them for insights not needing verification in a commonsense world?

EOC: But having verification in their minds.

CG: Or, more important at that time, did mathematics highlight the catching-on that is prior to verification?

EOC: But catching on to something precise, too.

I guess the trap I'm most aware of in people is the trap of arguing logically from a purely conceptual grasp.

CG: Worse than the infamous picture-thinking? A memorized logic?

EOC: Arguing logically from some concept and not having an idea of the whole thing, and not knowing that there's any point of having an idea of the whole thing. I volunteered once to say that I didn't know whether I had had any intellectual conversion. But I remember trying, in topology, to conceptualize first before I understood. I didn't have clearly the notion of understanding as separate from conceptualizing. That's something I've learned since. I've ordinarily done it correctly in things that I knew well, but in subjects that I didn't know well, I'd go in for the concepts and be satisfied with them and not come to grips with the underlying question.

CT: The topology is what I can still chuckle over when I recall doing the mathematics here. I was right on the edge of picture/non-picture, and it was a delight.

CG: When I took the math course (I hadn't had any in my own undergraduate program) I could see new kinds of thinking—perhaps not possible to *me,* but possible. For example, I'm not sure I did grasp correctly the infinity of primes but I saw that if one were to understand it, it would forever be a correction to picture-thinking. Or I could see what a pluralism of number-systems or of geometries would do to certain myths. It was like an opening into the function of language.

CT: One leader said something poignant about her little group in a senior-citizens' residence. She said that these were people who had lived in the judgments of others, that their pattern had been not to question, that in their middle-aged world of thirty-five years ago the reality of that world was given by authority, that they were humble people with much knowledge of friendship, but not of questions. I think Cathleen was right that this was the worldview we wanted mathematics to break into.

CG: And mathematics could do it because it was "neutral"?

EOC: Yes, that was certainly the reason no one in the Society raised trouble when I went to the University of Toronto in 1931. Mathematics was a safe subject.

CT: About intellectual conversion and psychic conversion; those who have the gravest difficulty at the Institute are mature people who are totally commonsense people. The problem has something to do with attention-span, and so with motivation, but most of all with the threshold into any subject.

CG: You used to say you would prefer not to have to give a degree to persons in whom an intellectual conversion had not occurred during their six, eight or ten years of study.

EOC: The stages, or insights, by which the larger conversions happen, seem to me most pressing to make possible.

CG: Could there be in all subject areas a common move away from image-as-trap?

EOC: To read a whole book and understand what its author means, certainly takes longer than a week if it is a solid book. That experience may demand a conversion, at least out of speaking easily about what an author is saying.

CT: Part of being on the way to intellectual conversion is relaxing, being able to wait, to trust, to suspend judgment. A participant no longer bristles.

EOC: And also really wondering what the author means by the whole. It isn't just relaxing; it's also working with some vigor.

CT: "Attending," as Doran suggests, is important too. It brings one into subject areas in which one has not been motivated enough to get to work.

I can think of students at the Institute who have been with us for decades, but sometimes seem half dead. They always take the course they consciously know they are interested in. Sometimes they become leaders, and will only lead in the kind of course we know they are already curious about and well-read enough in. They don't consider entering into something like genetics or theatre or mathematics, and this is partly because they are under a myth about scholarship's being more and more precise knowledge in a more and more limited area. They no longer enter the bloody field where knowledge comes by the vigorous exploration you are suggesting.

EOC: So we will keep trying.

CT: I wonder whether in mathematics, Chinese civilization or contemporary music, where the challenge is so daunting, we might do better to offer short courses over a sustained period of years, so that a person can dip in, work hard, recover, and then dip in again. With Chinese culture that is the pattern I have promised myself over ten years.

CG: In the study we did a while ago of the differing processes by which two students learned within the degree pattern, Charlotte suggested that there were personal themes by which they chose the courses they did, and that this is the essential motivation that can be discerned. Perhaps also the gaining of the degree?

CT: At their best, many have a trust that the learning process is part of a human development, and that development is wished for. There is a theme in that too.

EOC: As an argument against the short touches of challenging areas; one does need a time long enough to gain some kind of competence and serious interest.

CG: Yet you have tried more than once, and recently, short sections in the mathematics course.

CT: And working from aspects which are all around people; raffles, lotos, games of chance, public opinion polls.

EOC: I know that in mathematics an easy way of catching a pattern can be lost as one was lost in late Greek times and the first few Christian centuries. A very careful historian of mathematics has recorded that something that was quite simple to people like Archimedes got lost for a millenium and a half (to about the year 1400) because there was no one to pass over how to think of it. Studying probability, which I'm interested in, I come across areas that are especially obscure. When I am working alone, I have to decide whether any one of them is important enough to stay with until I have it easily. If the easy pattern were completely lost, it is possible that no one would find it again for several hundred years.

CG: Would learning a pattern for doing long division be an example?

EOC: It was a harder thing than that. It was dealing with the theory of proportion as that came through Euclid. It was there for everybody, but because of the irrational numbers they had to dodge, they had to use geometry, and there was no one to say, "Look, I'll show you how to do it." They couldn't catch it from a book, just as I could not catch that fundamental theorem of calculus until I met the professor at Toronto who understood it, and then there was no problem.

CT: What you mean is certainly what Plato was worried about in the Seventh Letter.

EOC: Yes, loss of operational insight where there had been an unusual way of thinking.

CG: People seem to have different imaginations. Some have an easy time with algebra, some with geometry. Why won't everyone's unconscious toss up a suitable image for getting a needed mathematical insight?

EOC: Generally without serious searching and perhaps asking, there aren't enough operational images.

CG: You mean there is only the incapacity of will-power; there is no incapacity of psyche?

EOC: There is sometimes incapacity of psyche. Sometimes there is a too strong expectation of a definite kind of answer.

CG: But imagine things at a better level than that; suppose a person consciously situated in a more willing way. Why won't the appropriate image come?

CT: It seems to me that in discussion courses, one of the roles of the parallel student participant is to toss up another example or a half-suggestion which is stimulating for another person in the group, who can take it and carry it further. That doesn't happen in the mathematics course because you lecture in it, and sometimes your example is *too* clear and too fast. One year we tried to include a few questioners in the class, in the hope that something like that could happen, but the students went to them for advice instead, and the images, the half-formed questions, didn't come as suggestions from equals in search.

EOC: It certainly did not come off as we had hoped.

CT: We might say that in discussion-courses, the leaders, because they are learners but also on-the-spot interested initiators of questions, ask with a kind of passion. Others catch some of that passion, then more are involved. The rest think there must be something there, and an edge comes to everyone's effort.

CG: One used to hear talk, about mathematics especially, of a discipline where the emotions aren't involved. We were talking earlier about a people brought up in judgments with powerful feelings attached, and very threatened by change. In mathematics they didn't need to feel this threat; mathematical insights don't depend on how you feel on any particular occasion. It doesn't matter how you're feeling when you come to discuss *Transatlantic Blues* either, but would that fact be clearer in mathematics? Would it be a neater, tidier, antiseptic area?

CT: One of the good students this year reported that she was unprepared for how totally absorbed she could get in the mathematics. She could and did lose her sense of time, and spent hours and hours without noticing it.

EOC: The concepts you are dealing with (I use the word "concepts" consciously, as opposed to insights) become so all-engrossing, once they are familiar, and your question is so clear, that you just want to get concepts and questions together, and you almost *have* to. It's a pure puzzle, a beautiful puzzle.

CT: Why do you often start to do mathematics at night?

EOC: I'm going to something I'm able to think of easily. I can get a problem within *probability* very quickly — one I can't see how to handle. By focusing on it, a whole lot of other things become familiar — and I want that familiarity. It's completely engrossing.

CT: And deeply reassuring, too?

EOC: Oh, yes.

CT: One of our directors has told us that he and his wife go away every year to a forest so they can rescue each other and then come back to their ordinary existence for another year. I'm suggesting that there is positive reinforcement, as Skinner would say, in solving a problem in an area you love and are familiar with.

EOC: If it's an area I'm completely familiar with, I don't think I'd bother trying.

CT: I mean that it is reassuring to solve something, and then your ordinary life takes a different perspective.

EOC: That's right. And it's completely restful from the disturbance of things that one can't do anything about at the moment.

CT: One of the ways I think Voegelin has been important to us has to do with his witness to, his preoccupation with, the "in-between." The whole of human existence is lived in that "in-between," and the human search is for the ground of that existence; the person holds himself open for revelation, for being attentive to burning bushes, and for understanding.

CG: You are saying that we live in the tension of the in-between, and that a recognized social way to help is to devise courses which put us into the unfamiliar and therefore lure us to recognize, in a limited way, the tension that is basic to existence.

CT: And bring to light some concerns that are just under consciousness. Then one begins to sharpen, explore, organize, understand, where one is in the "in-between."

CG: I wonder if there is a whole view of human existence in Lonergan's saying that the distinctive matter of mathematics is the empirical residue? What does he mean by that?

EOC: It seems to me he gets there somewhat like this; the "empirical residue" means those aspects of our experience which are not themselves data for any of the empirical sciences. Space, time, chance events, a continuous line, do not appear significant in themselves. A place, a moment, have significance only for what occurs in them. But we can pattern space by thinking of various shapes in it. Or we can indicate "up," "to west," "to north," and say space is three-dimensional. We pattern time by assigning hours to it. We mark off a continuous line by numbers $1, 2, 3, \ldots, \frac{1}{2}, \frac{1}{3}, \frac{2}{3}, \ldots$. This patterning of the unpatterned is, of course, not limited to real space, or patterns of nature. Each pattern is pushed to its utmost of intelligibility.

CT: But are all patterns mathematical?

EOC: They seem to become mathematical when they are found to be intelligible. For example: topology's development is fairly recent. Mazes are found to be mathematical. Earlier, movement was. When an intelligible pattern is found to apply to experience, then that experience becomes much more significant than it was. The tremendous advance of physics in the eighteenth century came from recognizing the mathematical form of the laws of mechanical motion. Statistical science came from the development of the mathematics of probability. If I could point out yet unpatterned aspects of the empirical residue I would probably be indicating where mathematics will be developing, and what sciences will benefit. But I can't.

CG: Would economics be an area of experience to which a mathematical pattern could be applied?

EOC: I should have thought of that. Lonergan has worked out how in an industrial economy, the productive pattern clarifies when you distinguish the production and distribution of capital goods (the surplus stage) from the production and distribution of consumer goods (the basic stage). The significant aspects are the acceleration of these stages and acceleration is the idea that Newton caught as basing Newtonian mechanics. Acceleration is a mathematical concept. My guess as to why economists have not picked it up is because they are not easy enough with the mathematics of acceleration.

CT: Early in our discussion, we were talking about your interest in story.

EOC: Northrop Frye has suggested that, just as mathematics was the basis of the early physical sciences (physics, chemistry) and of later ones, so stories hold together sociology, psychology —

CG: — and theology? Theologians have a great interest in narrative nowadays.

EOC: Yes. What strikes me is that the story is a unique way of catching significant human change. It isn't mere description. It isn't as "neat" as calculus is in catching movement. But perhaps there is no "neat" way of catching all the myriad possibilities. When you think of a story as description, you miss its power of expression.

CT: It seems to me the reason you have a real sympathy with Frye is that he finds the pattern under the stories. You don't find that upsetting the way most people do. You don't object that the patterns are always the same and never new.

EOC: Oh no, I find it marvelous.

CG: Why is it that pointing out pattern in two famous stories we know moves us to the reader as subject?

EOC: Yes, why is it that it does? That stories carry us is obvious. Frye points out that we may come to admire the author, but certainly the story is us. We recognize ourselves in it.

CT: Certainly one identifies with Gilgamesh as subject.

EOC: If a story captures you it is certainly, as Frye says, the hopes and fears and loves and hates of human beings that get expressed. As in mathematics, the expression is in a way that never was in time or space with such perfection. You meet bravery in life but not in the simple way you meet it in stories — the simple, abstract way. And in life you don't really meet horribleness in quite the abstract way of the story. The perfection of the art comes when, with a worrisome character, you see the keys to his worrisomeness, and you can even identify with it. That is abstract as a line is abstract, and you catch the point of movement in it.

What I'm fascinated with is how that movement can be created. It's so terribly hard. I haven't done any great creative mathematics. So much that is creative in me is understanding something that someone else has done. But it's a joy like a story. When reading and failing to understand, I've got to stop and work it out for myself.

CG: So mathematics, like the story, brings one back to the subject-as-subject.

CT: Erikson has a recent study on Jefferson and American identity, a study in which I sense a disturbance because he is struggling with a question not yet fully formulated. He says the American is a self-made man, and that this mythic way of seeing himself helps him to excuse the fact that the immigrant became American by cutting the memory of the past, shedding his roots in Europe, Asia, Africa.

It gave psychic energy to the whole endeavour of creating America and the American. Do you think that part of our original intuition about the mathematics requirement was that there has to be a subject you get into where you lose yourself? That you will never tranform yourself if at every stage you carry all the memory of yourself — you will never have a pure experience of self as knower that is separate from your continuous life?

EOC: I think that's utterly true. One of the joys of music, and one of the joys of mathematics, is that pure experience of self as knower.

CG: Then the experience of having mathematics is more and more necessary, not less and less, in the midst of all the talk of self-development and self-awareness — which are all really rather external. The self-made man is the subject-as-object, surely? The more there is preoccupation with the self, the more necessary is the mathematics?

CT: You're transported out of yourself.

CG: You're not concerned that it is yourself.

EOC: No. You see a problem. You grasp it.

CG: Is this another way of recognizing what is meant by intellectual conversion?

EOC: It certainly is an insight into it; I don't think it is the whole of it. I think a person can find in mathematics a completely satisfactory life for himself, and at the same time say of all the other things that are going on around him in people, "I just can't make anything of them at all." I know competent mathematicians who, I think, haven't had any great psychic conversion either. It's possible to get interested in mathematics so early in one's thinking career that one doesn't consider what goes on in oneself. Coming to know that one has to sleep on a problem, might be the extent of psychic conversion in some.

CG: Could R. Doran, and you, be saying of some philosophers also that they have not had a psychic conversion?

EOC: Yes.

CT: What do you understand by "psychic conversion"? I see it as something on the way elsewhere. I don't think that is quite how Doran sees it; he thinks it comes fairly late. But when he's appealing for the aesthetic (because through that, all other movement happens) that isn't something ultimate; it is a helping kind of thing that affects us.

EOC: We all realize that a question is something that one has to feel somehow; it's not just in the head.

CG: In mathematics you are concentrating on the "question in the head"?

EOC: In mathematics the first questions you meet are questions in the head. They are clear questions, and you try to handle them. You can go through a full course, you can become an expert user of mathematics and not go further than that. In my own learning about topology, I didn't realize that one needs to feel the shapes. And to come to judgment depends on being familiar with the matter.

CG: For a long time we've recognized that if you can say, "I am a knower", then you aren't *at the mercy of* feelings. Perhaps what we've learned more recently is that the two can't be separated.

EOC: I think some people get a basic recognition of intelligence, of their intelligence, through a mathematics course; I think some won't. But this is true of almost every area we do. Our vision of liberal education was at least to give the different possibilities because you couldn't be sure of what would be *the* way.

CT: Yes, but we said; it's good if you take music appreciation, but you *must* take mathematics; you *must* take three philosophies.

EOC: Yes, we did.

CT: Now the way we have worked on the affective realm in getting people to philosophy over the years has been very different from the approach to mathematics. We've brought them in through stories about concrete social and psychic realities, we've demonstrated concern for what the good, or justice, or beauty is. We've allowed them to stay at that level in their first philopshy. This process has not been possible in bringing them to mathematics — except for using as examples public-opinion polls, or Las Vegas.

With people who don't wish to take theology, when we ask them the formal question "Will you choose the ground of your own deepest concern and take two courses there?" we're asking them to identify what is close to consciousness, what they can identify as serious further questions for themselves. But mathematics, for many, is an almost unknown world, one towards which there is no psychic stirring. In Lonergan's terms, the first is the known unknown, the second is the unknown unknown. The invitation is important in both cases.

CG: In mathematics did you find yourself trying functional specialties from Lonergan's "generalized empirical method" when you first met them in *Method in Theology?* Or subsequently?

EOC: No. I did not think them relevant.

CG: History of mathematics is clearly one functional specialty, I suppose?

EOC: One of the ways you can study mathematics is by its history, but the trouble is that unless you have a certain competence in the ideas, you can't read it properly.

CG: Having an eight-fold collaboration or division of functions, rather than field or subject specialization, doesn't appeal to you for mathematics?

EOC: You don't need the history to grasp the validity of your understanding, in mathematics.

I think mathematics is in need of a new focusing because, as Lonergan suggests, the problem of how to build a mathematics that would be relevant for biology or social sciences is real, but there is little sense of direction. I was conscious of this ten years ago. Nobody knows where to move. There are many constructions in mathematics that nobody gets interested in because they seem arbitrary. Serially analytic principles, which Lonergan points to as constituting the reality of mathematics, are not easy to come by. They are the discoveries of genius. A lot of the recent development of mathematics has been in the pure analytic propositions which are interesting to look at, and which are patterns. Some day enough of them will be looked at so that someone who can grasp them all can put them together. That *could* provide a new basis for a human science, as calculus did for physics. But I don't think that day has come yet. In the meantime there is a sort of dead end for new things. That doesn't mean that tomorrow may not be different. Something may be already in the works, but I don't know about it.

CG: Could there be some apportioning of collaborative tasks for what *is* available in mathematics? Again, history of mathematics is the easiest of the functions to imagine.

EOC: Well, if someone who is a historian in mathematics turns up some new fact about it, most of us can understand that fact. We don't have to be into the commonsense of another time to understand it. Also if we put a little time on it, we can see whether the person writing saw the point or didn't see the point.

CG: You're emphasizing again how minimal the field of interpretation is in mathematics. Is there a dialectic in mathematics? A dialectic of fundamental positions?

EOC: Now that's very interesting. There are positions on the "foundations of mathematics," as with Bertrand Russell: mathematics is logic. Or with the so-called intuitionists. But most mathematics is not affected by those positions. Most accounts deal with the validity or invalidity of theorems concerning infinite sets — whether they can be thought of as actually existing or only potentially existing. But these different "positions" don't affect the applications of mathematics in clarifying empirical knowledge.

CG: The dialectic of positions is important to philosophy and not to mathematics as such?

EOC: It would be important for that part of mathematics known as "foundations," but it is not at all clear that dialectic would liberate the genius who might discover a mathematics applicable to the human sciences. To illustrate: A man who was at one of the Canadian Mathematical congresses (Brouwer was his name) wouldn't allow certain irrational numbers to be used. They weren't intuitively constructible. His seemed to me a primitive philosophical position, but that is all you can say about it.

CG: There are positions and counter-positions only in something beyond the sciences (including, in this context, mathematics as science)?

EOC: I don't know. It isn't a question I have found interesting to explore or have expected to be productive for mathematics. No important mathematical insights seem to depend on the answer. There is a theorem of set theory that every set can be well ordered. It means that you can put its elements in a proper order, first, second, third, and exhaust them all. It's interesting to know that using that as a logical basis you can formulate certain theorems that you can't otherwise. But many don't want the theorems, so it's like talking about analytic propositions. Many mathematicians have no great sympathy with that. The one thing of mathematical logic that interests everybody is the theorem of Goedel. Bertrand Russell disturbed me years ago with the ideal of postulational thinking. Goedel's theorem shows beautifully, out of the same tradition, that anything more complicated than the infinity of the system of integers cannot be expressed postulationally in a way that renders all propositions either provable or disprovable. There would have to remain undecidable propositions. What the theorem proves, I find quite convincingly established by what I know from Lonergan's clarification of the role of postulates in expressing the details of an insight. The theorem adds precisions, of course.

CT: In your view, has Lonergan's quest come full circle? The first chapters of *Insight* take mathematics very seriously and he is now concerned with mathematics to underpin his work in economics.

EOC: A *story* begins the preface to *Insight* — recalling the clues of a detective story — and the first chapter exploits the simple intelligibility of mathematics to help the reader become aware of basic cognitional operations. To me, his early profound grasp of mathematics stands out in his economics where he recognizes the need of a rigorous analysis of dependencies in the productive process prior to the application of mathematics. I think the unfruitful directions that economics has taken come from the lack of the premathematical preparation of the materials. I know he is looking for enlightened patterning of the empirical residue (i.e., really new mathematics) and he may provide us with keys for this presently locked door.

Macroeconomics

Insight and Emergence:
an Introduction to Lonergan's
Circulation Analysis

by Michael Gibbons

I. The Context

To discover that Bernard Lonergan has written a treatise on economics will no doubt come as a surprise to many. From the many published sources that recount "in cameo" the prehistory of *Insight* and *Method in Theology,* one finds little reference to any interest in economic problems, much less to a highly theoretical analysis available in manuscript since 1945. It is tempting to conclude that this treatise constitutes merely a passing interest of the young Lonergan; that its relationship to the Lonergan *corpus* is peripheral. This would be an error for at least two reasons. One cannot read the chapters on commonsense in *Insight* without suspecting that the delicate balance of images and insights presented there summarizes volumes of reading and years of thought. The verbal expression is too economical to allow any other interpretation. Secondly, Lonergan's more recent writing on the themes of progress and decline continue to exhibit a similar perspicacity in relation to contemporary social developments.

Recently, Lonergan has described the origins of his interests in economics in the following way:

> My interest in economics goes back to the course on ethics when I was a student of philosophy at the Jesuit House of Studies at Heythrop in Oxfordshire.... I returned to Canada in 1930 to find the country in the pit of a depression. Theories and fads about what was wrong were current. In particular, there was a theory called Social Credit that argued that purchasing power

was systematically deficient and that banks should issue and distribute money to make up for the deficiency.... The argument for Social Credit was clear and simple; the fallacy in the argument could be uncovered only through dynamic analysis. *I tinkered with the problem of working out a dynamic analysis off and on; and finally about 1943 or 44 I had a 128 page manuscript* (emphasis mine).[1]

Of what transpired between 1945 and the present in relation to Lonergan's interest in economics much has yet to be uncovered. In what is clearly a reference to the Circulation Analysis, Lonergan has recently stated:

"I worked on the question for fourteen years.... I wrote one hundred and twenty eight pages but didn't find anyone who could see any sense in it. Six or seven years later a colleague read it, found it extremely interesting and helpful, and agreed to collaborate — but he went off to Zambia to teach. The question is still genuine and authentic. Next term I shall be attacking it publicly." [2]

On the basis of what evidence there is, it seems reasonable to conclude, therefore, that economics was certainly of more than peripheral concern to Lonergan. Nonetheless, his personal situation and his developing interest in method meant that further exclusive work in economics would have to await the completion of the major project represented in the works on Aquinas, in *Insight* and in *Method in Theology*.

As a matter of fact, the Circulation Analysis responded to problems of the depression that afflicted North American and Western Europe in the early 1930's. If the economic situation of the 1970's does not yet constitute a depression as socially damaging as that of the inter-war years, still it is serious enough to have engaged some of the best economic talent in the world — albeit with apparently little effect so far. Yet, one can never totally suppress the suspicion that the failure of contemporary economics to deal with inflation and unemployment lies in the network of images, insights and propositions that make up contemporary economic science; it is to this complex that the Circulation Analysis is primarily addressed. The phenomena of "booms and slumps" are apparently recurrent and, as Lonergan seeks to show, derive from an inadquate theoretical

---

[1] B. Lonergan, "Macroeconomics and the Dialectic of Decline", unpublished notes prepared for a seminar on the above mentioned subject at Boston College, 1978-79, p. 1.

[2] *The Question as Commitment - A Symposium* Thomas More Institute Papers/77 edited by E. Cahn and C. Going, Montreal, (1979) p. 32. The colleague was Fr. Kevin Quinn, S.J.

understanding of the nature of the productive process in an industrial economy and, therefore, of the sorts of human behaviour necessary to keep the economic system functioning smoothly.

There can be no doubt that a great deal has changed socially, economically, and politically since Lonergan completed the Circulation Analysis in 1945. But a strong case could be made for the relevance of Lonergan's 1945 analysis to the underlying problems of today. In economics particularly, the Keynesian revolution pointed a way to "solving" the problems which faced the major Western economies in the 1930's. When Lonergan was drafting the circulation analysis the capitalist world was crippled by the stagnation brought upon by underinvestment and high unemployment. The contemporary reappearance of inflation and high unemployment leads one to suspect that the Keynesian "solution" was really part of the problem. The problem was diagnosed as being due to the lack of aggregate demand. Keynes showed that by increasing public spending governments could—via the multiplier—stimulate investment thereby expanding the demand for labour, actualizing latent aggregate demand, and so bring the Depression to an end. In the 1970's when Lonergan returned to his economic manuscripts, the economies of the West after twenty five years of unprecedented (and virtually uninterrupted) growth, were once again experiencing the characteristics of a depression (now called a deep recession). This time, however, the recession was characterized not by lack of demand and unemployment but rather by excess demand and inflation. But the Keynesian methods which were aimed at expanding the economy at full employment do not appear to be working in the contemporary context. Indeed, a heated debate has emerged between the Keynesians and the Monetarists about the possibility of achieving simultaneously economic growth, low unemployment, and low rates of inflation.[3] It would appear that we have reached a stage in the development of capitalism where reasonable growth can be achieved only with unacceptably high rates of unemployment; otherwise, inflation results. This seems to indicate, as Galbraith has mentioned, how capitalist economics is in a sorry state indeed. My purpose here is not to provide a history of the ups and downs of capitalist economies but merely to advert to the fact that the ups and downs are recurrent. Further, the existence of economic fluctuations provided the concrete context within which Lonergan began his investigation of circulation analysis, and therefore it is necessary to make this explicit. Within this context the central question posed by Lonergan in

---

[3] M. Friedman, *The Counter-Revolution in Monetary Theory*, The Institute of Economic Affairs, Occasional Paper No. 33, (London:1970).

this analysis is "Is the uniform expansion of an advanced economy which avoids the pitfalls of booms and slumps, possible and/or probable?" In other words, assuming an economic order based on the principle of monetary exchange between participants in which the function of capital goods has been discovered, is it possible to raise the standard of living in the long run while at the same time avoiding such effects as chronic inflation and unemployment? Even the briefest glance at the historical record of capitalism would seem to provide sufficient evidence for a negative answer. Altough there can be little doubt that the so-called advanced industrial societies have been characterized by a general growth trend, still the pattern has been irregular; so much so, in fact, that a separate specialization within economic science concerned with fluctuations has emerged.

Nonetheless, at the time Lonergan was working on the circulation analysis, economic fluctuations and other wave-like phenomena were considered a peripheral theoretical problem; fluctuations were then, and to some extent still are, regarded as pathological symptoms of an otherwise healthy economic system.[4] According to neoclassical theory, which is still the dominant paradigm in Western economics, the economy should tend to an equilibrium position — though it may from time to time exhibit small scale fluctuations about this position. After the Second World War, as interests in economics shifted from problems of equilibrium to those of growth, theory returned once again to the problem of sustained economic expansion and within this context developed the notion of dynamic equilibrium.[5] Economic fluctuations still remained a residual phenomenon caused more often than not by the untimely interference of government — the new economic actor introduced by Keynes — with the natural working of the market system.

Lonergan does not belong to the long and distinguished line of equilibrium theorists, though he is certainly aware of their work.[6] By contrast, though perhaps without deliberately trying to establish a position outside the then mainstream, the circulation analysis is an inherently dynamic theory; it is concerned with the *rates and volume of change in the different parts of the production process.* Lonergan's theory is concerned with processes in motion; with the flows of goods and services through the production process and with the parallel flows of

---

[4] See, for example, R. Gordon, *Business Fluctuations* (London: Harper and Row, 1961).

[5] N. Kaldor, "The Irrelevance of Equilibrium Economics", *The Economic Journal,* December, 1972, pp. 1237-1252.

[6] B. Lonergan, "An Essay in Circulation Analysis", an unpublished manuscript Copyright 1978, p. 1. Hereafter this work will be referred to as the *Circulation Analysis.*

payments as they move from investment to consumption. To borrow a phrase frequently used by Lonergan; economics is concerned with "systems on the move".

The Circulation Analysis because it is a theory within a concrete heuristic is abstract only in the sense that it omits the inessential.[7] Following what he was later to call classical and statistical heuristic structures, the analysis moves from things related to our senses to the relationships of things to one another. What Lonergan is trying to do is to get us to understand the functionally normative and heuristic relationships which connect flows of goods to the circulations of payments made and received. It is in respect to the theoretical development of these *functional interdependencies* that, it seems to me, Lonergan has moved beyond contemporary thinking. Thus:

> On such a methodological model circulation analysis raises a large superstructure of terms and theories upon a summary classification and a few brief analyses of typical phenomena.[8]

To those unacquainted with economic analysis this "large superstructure of terms and theories" is bound to appear somewhat forbidding. To those who have struggled with other parts of Lonergan's work the style of thought and the mode of expression will be familiar enough; sharp definitions, overwhelming logic, terse conclusions. But as in the case with *Insight* and so many of his other works the struggle is well worth the price. For few, even amongst economists, would deny that economic theory at least in its present state of articulation is inadequate to meet our present travail; the presence of such diametrically opposed views on the sources and cures for inflation, to name just one example, indicates the need for insight at the most fundamental levels. Lonergan provides a fresh starting point for considering the essential dynamics of an exchange economy and in doing so provides a new perspective on many of the economic mechanisms that have been regarded as unproblematic.

So, to all those who would meet the intellectual challenges of circulation analysis, it may be useful to have a description of what Lonergan is doing. He himself makes clear that he intends us to do most of the work of reconstruction ourselves:

> Out of the endless classificatory possibilities one selects not the one sanctioned by ordinary speech nor again the one sanctioned by facility of measurement but the one that most rapidly yields terms which can be defined by the functional interrelations in which they stand. To discover such terms is a lengthy and painful process of trial and error.

---

[7] B. Lonergan, *Insight: A Study of Human Understanding* (New York: Philosophical Library, 1956), pp. 35-45.

[8] *Circulation Analysis,* p. 3.

> *Experto crede.* To justify them, one cannot reproduce the tedious blind efforts that led to them; one can appeal only to the success, be it great or small, with which they serve to account systematically for the phenomena under investigation. Hence it is only fair to issue at once a warning that the reader will have to work through pages, in which parts are gradually assembled, before he will be able to see a whole and pass an equitable judgment upon it.[9]

Lonergan is right, but perhaps the occurrence of insight can be facilitated if a little attention is given at the outset to setting up appropriate images.

II. Exposition of the Central Question

In order to answer the question about the possibility of uniform expansion of an exchange economy — that is, one in which goods and services are exchanged through some sort of price mechanism — one needs an image or a model which captures the essential elements of the production process. The production process is the characteristic way in which things are made in a given economic order. What distinguishes an industrial economy from other economic orders is the presence of a dynamic capital goods sector. There are very strict limits to the possibilities if economic expansion without the prior existence of a group of individuals, firms, and industries concerned with making machinery whose purpose is not to be directly consumed but to be used by another sector of the economy whose function it is to make things for consumption. As long as the bulk of the population is producing things for immediate consumption — such as food, clothing, and shelter — the prospects for expansion are determined by the prospects for increasing the population. But as the countries of the developing world are painfully aware, the potential for expansion latent in increasing population is all too soon eroded by the abililty of the natural resources available to the community to provide the basic necessities to sustain life. Malthus grasped this limitation in the 18th century when he pointed out the fact that populations tend to increase at a geometric rate while food production continues at an arithmetic rate; the result is starvation and the consequent reduction of the population to a level more in line with the capability to produce food.

But the insight upon which capitalism is founded is that it is possible to break out of this routine by diverting part of the population away from producing for immediate consumption to producing the means of production. The way in which this insight was elaborated

---

[9] Ibid., p. 9.

and worked out in the concrete is available in the multitude of papers, monographs, and books which document the history of industrialization.[10]

The process of industrialization is by no means a simple affair but its real potential lies, not in the division of labour as Adam Smith thought but in the increases in productivity made available by the application of machinery to the production process itself.

Lonergan began his description of the production process from the point at which a mature capital goods sector already exists and the image of machinery produced in one sector of the economy being consumed by another sector which in turn produces goods for mass consumption is precisely articulated. The basic idea is of a dynamic system whereby the potentialities of nature are transformed into a standard of living:

> Thus the productive process, which proceeds from the potentialities of nature, terminates in a standard of living in as much as the goods and services it renders become elements in the standard of living. But it may also terminate indirectly in a standard of living in as much as the goods and services it renders complement the potentialities of nature to make the process capable of effecting a higher standard of living. Consumer goods and services enter directly into the standard of living. Producer goods enter indirectly into the standard of living; directly they are improvements upon nature that facilitate the production process and increase its power and efficacy; and only indirectly through this increased power and efficacy do they affect the standard of living by improving and increasing the supply of consumer goods and services. [11]

From this point, Lonergan develops a multi-stage model of the productive process and formulates the notions of point-to-point, point-to-line, point-to-surface and point-to-volume correspondences within the productive process. These correspondences fill the gap between the potentialities of nature and the emergent standard of living. Because the process is dynamic, the various levels are defined in terms of the flow of goods and services from one level (or correspondence) to another. It is important to remember that throughout the Circulation Analysis the basic unit is "so much every so often", that is, a quantity in a given time interval - *a flow*. Expansion of the productive process will then be a positive change in the flow of goods and services.

A further point concerning this structure should be made. The various stages of the productive process

---

[10] D. Landes, *The Unbound Prometheus* (Cambridge: University Press, 1969), especially Chapter 1.
[11] *Circulation Analysis,* p. 8.

> (are) not based on propriety differences, for the same firm may be engaged at once in different correspondences with the standard of living. Again it is not a division based upon the properties of things: the same raw materials may be made into consumer goods and capital goods; and the capital goods may be in point-to-line, or point-to-surface or higher correspondences; they may have one correspondence at one time and another at another....
>
> The division is neither propriety nor technical. *It is a functional division of the structure of the productive process; it reveals the possibilities of the process as a dynamic system,* though to bring out the full implications of such a system will require not only the next section but also a later section on cycles (emphasis mine).[12]

Although the elaboration of a multi-level (or multi-stage) economy is important, heuristically, in guiding the imagination to grasp the functional relations of the structure, it does not figure prominently in the subsequent analysis. The analysis explores the dynamics of an economy in which the higher order correspondences are described simply as the surplus stage and the lowest order correspondences as the basic stage. Thus the basic stage is defined as "the aggregate of rates of production of goods and services in process and in a point-to-point correspondence with the elements in the emergent standard of living." Besides the basic stage there is, as we have seen, a series of surplus stages. "Each of these surplus stages is an aggregate of rates of production of goods and services in process and in point-to-line, point-to-surface, or higher correspondences with elements in the standard of living." The fundamental point to be grasped is that while the ultimate products of the basic stage enter into the standard of living the ultimate products of the surplus stage do not. Thus machinery for producing shoes or textiles are not consumed by people with cold feet — they are interested in the shoes themselves. Rather, the machinery which is produced in the surplus stage (or stages) is used by and depreciated in the basic stage which in turn produces a flow of shoes and so contributes to the emergent standard of living.

We are now in a position to make a first attempt to answer the central question of the circulation analysis — "Is a uniform expansion of the economy possible?" It seems clear that the flow of shoes into the emergent standard of living will be a function of the number of machines available for the production of shoes. From this we can see that any positive increase in the flow of shoes (what is usually implied by the concept of economic growth) into the standard of living can be met only by providing a steady flow of machines from the

---

[12] Ibid., p. 15. As functional, Lonergan's analysis applies to both capitalist and communist economies.

surplus stage; each new machine makes it possible to add a certain increment to the flow per unit time. In other words, if it is possible to produce a continuing series of machines it is possible, in principle, to imagine the continuous acceleration of the basic stage. So at first blush it looks as if the uniform expansion of the economy is a theoretical possibility.

At this point Lonergan makes an important distinction between short and long term accelerations of the productive process. If we follow up the example of shoe production, it is of course possible to make improvements (i.e. to increase the efficiency) with which existing machinery is used and so it is possible to conceive ways in which the flow of shoes into the standard of living might be enhanced without making any further demands on the surplus stages of production. But, and this is the point, the possibilities of expansion following this route are limited. Thus, short term accelerations — changes in the flows — are possible but they are limited by the degree of technical development itself. So after a period the flow of shoes assumes once again a constant albeit higher rate and acceleration moves to zero. It is clear, then, that long term acceleration of the basic stage will be possible only if there is a flow of new machines into the service of the basic stage:

> A long term acceleration is an increase in rates of production due to the introduction of more capital equipment. The latter is termed a long termed acceleration because it changes the basis on which short term acceleration works: the short term acceleration improves and increases the equipment which a corresponding short term acceleration will use in the fullest and most efficient manner. [13]

Two important points follow from this: in a long term acceleration the basic and surplus stages are coupled together; and, further, long term accelerations take place in virtue of the dependence of each lower stage on the next higher:

> Thus the structure of the productive process is a series of stages, where each stage is an aggregate of rates of production, and each lower stage receives from the next higher stage the means of long term acceleration of its rates.[14]

With this in mind let us return to the central question about the uniform expansion of the economy in the long term, and ask what happens when the demand for shoes is such as to call forth a change in the flow of machines from the first surplus stage. It is clear that the rate of expansion of the basic stage is determined in the long run by

---

[13] Ibid., p. 21.
[14] Ibid., p. 21.

the ability of the first surplus stage to accelerate. How is this possible? In the first place it must be possible to build more machines per unit time interval. At the very least this will require an increase in the flow of gears, wheels, levers, etc. from the second surplus stage — that is, from the machine tool sector. But, how is this increase in the production rates of the second surplus sector to be attained? Are we not in a position of saying that this will in turn require an expansion into a third surplus stage and so be faced with the problem of an infinite regress? On the other hand if the infinite regress is curtailed at some level other than the first, it would seem that the prospect of uniform expansion of the economy is curtailed as well.

If the problem expressed in this way provides a negative answer to the question posed initially, it also points to the reason for the failure of a long term uniform acceleration to occur. Reverting to the example of shoes, any increase in the demand for shoes will be felt more or less instantaneously in the basic stage and information as to the need for more machines and more component parts will be fed back through the various stages of the production process. But the response of the surplus stages cannot be infinitely rapid. As Michael Kalecki has observed, there is a finite time lag between the decision to invest and the realization of a flow of machines; between the production of one stage and its consumption by another.[15] Further, a long term acceleration is likely to be a massive affair:

> In the first place, it is a matter of long term planning; the utility of capital formation emerges only over long periods; hence long term planning is involved in capital formation and, since one is settling one's fate for years to come, it is generally worthwhile to do so in the best possible manner. In the second place, the introduction of more efficient units of production is not to be expected to take place in a random fashion: the supply of a single product depends on the activities of many units, so that it is worthwhile for many units to develop when it is worthwhile for any one of a series to develop; on the other hand, increased demand does not concentrate upon some one product but it divides over several so that if there is an increase in the demand for one there will be an increase in the demand for many; and as the increased demand for one justifies the development of a series of productive units, so the increased demand for many justifies the development on a series of series of units[16]

The acceleration that Lonergan envisages is one that emerges over a decade or so, and because this overall acceleration depends on

---

[15] G. R. Feiwel, *The Intellectual Capital of Michal Kalecki: A Study in Economic Theory and Policy* (Knoxville: University of Tennessee Press, 1975), pp. 138 ff.

[16] *Circulation Analysis*, p. 24.

accelerations *at different times in different parts of the productive process, the possibility of a long term cycle is inherently present in that process.*

There is one further aspect of long term accelerations to be considered that is independent of the cyclic effect introduced into the productive process by the time lags that are intrinsic to the various stages of the productive process; long term accelerations are limited for any given field of natural resources and population operating at a given level of cultural, political, and technical development. It arises from the fact that with these limitations there is a ceiling beyond which it is impossible to acquire the necessary natural resources or manpower to devote to the making of further equipment in the surplus stage. Thus:

> The ground of the limitation is that both the greater complexity of more efficient equipment and the greater quantity of more equipment postulate proportionate rates of replacement and maintenance. The process accelerates against an increasing resistance, so that every element of acceleration reduces the room for further accelerations. In the limit the whole effort of the surplus stage is devoted to replacement and maintenance of capital equipment, and then the only possibility of further acceleration is to depart from the assumption of a given level of cultural, political and technical development.[17]

The elements are now in place for a descriptive account of the pure cycle that is inherent in the productive process. Lonergan further points out that this pure cycle is different from the familiar trade cycles which he holds result from insufficient understanding of the nature of the inherent cycle:

> This dynamic structure has now to be connected with the idea of cycles. Let us distinguish two totally different types. There is the familiar trade cycle which is characterized by a succession of positive and negative accelerations of the productive process; there are booms and there are slumps. Quite different from this trade cycle one may conceive a pure cycle that has no necessary implications of negative acceleration. A pure cycle of the productive process is a matter, simply, of the surplus stage accelerating more rapidly than the basic stage, then of the basic stage accelerating more rapidly than the surplus.[18]

Thus, we have an intimation of Lonergan's answer to the question of the possibility of the long term expansion of an exchange economy: such expansion is possible but it cannot be uniform. The pure cycle itself cannot be smoothed out and, further, if it is not managed properly it collapses into the more familiar trade cycles. The correct

---

[17] Ibid., p. 22.
[18] Ibid., p. 27.

management of the pure cycle requires certain specific conditions of human adaptation which involve massive redistributions of wealth, functionally defined, during the phases of surplus and basic expansions. We have, according to Lonergan, learned a good deal about the management of capital accumulation that concerns the acceleration of the surplus stage. But, what about the acceleration of the basic stage?

> ...it is of the nature of a surplus expansion to prepare the way for a far greater basic expansion, for surplus activities stand to basic as a flow to a flow of flows. But a surplus expansion calls for saving, and a massive surplus expansion calls for massive saving. In contrast, the basic expansion calls for ever increasing consumption. So the practical wisdom cherished in the surplus expansion has to give way to a quite different type of practical wisdom in the basic expansion.
>
> The difference is not merely an internal difference, a change of mentality and attitude. For the simplest way to obtain great savings and so promote surplus expansion is to increase the income of the rich who can hardly spend more on their standard of living. Again, the simplest way to promote consumption is to increase the income of the poor and thereby make it possible for them to improve their standard of living.
>
> Now to change one's standard of living in any notable fashion is to live in a different fashion. It presupposes a grasp of new ideas. If the ideas are to be above the level of currently successful advertising, serious education must be undertaken. Finally, coming to grasp what serious education really is, and, nonetheless, coming to accept that challenge constitute the greatest challenge to the modern economy.[19]

III. Conclusions: Image and Emergence

What has been attempted here is not the presentation of a piece of economic theory nor even a piece of Lonergan's economic theory. Rather, I have been trying to "dispose the phantasm" — to set up a set of images which can function as a pivot between insight and theory. The model of the production process functions to provoke further understanding of the possible correlations between flows and flows of flows of goods and services. The image contains already within it the possibility of a differential acceleration of the various stages of the productive process — what Lonergan refers to as the pure cycle. But the image as it is developed appeals in a general way to our understanding of the dynamics of technological change in an industrial context. The notion that the sequence of development is one in which surplus expansion acceleration proceeds at first more rapidly

---

[19] Ibid., p. 65.

than the basic stage emerges within, and appears not inconsistent with, a general broad view of the process of industrialization.

If brief, our sympathetic understanding is engaged, but the theoretical problem has yet to be worked out. The insight which must be added to the dynamics of the productive process concerns the role of money in the exchange economy. What are needed are concepts to tie up the various flows of goods and services through the multistage production process and the key to this is the notion of monetary payments and their classification.[20] In other words the complex of flows of various goods and services can be represented or mapped in terms of the flows of payments through the different stages of the production process. But it should be remembered that the model of the process which Lonergan develops is a functional one: the basic and surplus stages are distinguished not on the basis of property or technical differences but on the basis of functional performance; the basic stage functions as consumer to the surplus stage while the standard of living is consumer to the basic stage. The parallel which Lonergan develops throughout the remainder of the analysis is based upon the notion of monetary functions and attempts to work out a set of terms and relations between monetary functions. This is a complex undertaking which, unfortunately, cannot be discussed here, but by following Lonergan into the intricacies of this analysis one finds oneself with new insights into such phenomena as profit and entrepreneurship, deficit financing and fiscal policy. Although it is a difficult undertaking, one which I have by no means completed, I do not think that anyone else, economist or otherwise, has even begun to explore the potentialities of this functional approach to monetary circulation. To be sure, there have been many who have used the notion of circulation analysis to describe what they are doing, but no one so far as I am aware has hit upon, much less developed, the image in terms of dynamic functional relationships. Perhaps this brief paper will help to encourage the unpacking of the many valuable insights contained in this manuscript.

---

[20] Ibid., pp. 65-66.

Features of Generalized Empirical Method and the Actual Context of Economics

by Philip McShane

"How does one diagnose the health of a body that has long been acknowledged to be immortal? Joyce had indicated that he intended for his work to keep the scholars busy for 300 years, so that anyone who has been at work on *Finnegans Wake* for the past 20 years, still has 280 to go. Not every *Wake* commentator has accepted the full measure of dedication apparently, for some have paused for long respites along the way." [1] And what of Lonergan? [2] In this contribution to the celebration of his seventy-fifth birthday, I should like to pause briefly to reflect on (1) the features of generalized empirical method, and (2) Lonergan and the actual context of economics.

I. A Bridge Too Far?

The fifth bridge, according to the war reports on which Cornelius Ryan's epic are based, was suggested to be a bridge too far. [3] The question mark in the title invites my reader to join me strategically

---

[1] Bernard Benstock, "The State of the Wake", *James Joyce Quarterly* 14 (1976-7): 237.

[2] For my previous paralleling of Lonergan and Joyce, see McShane, *The Shaping of the Foundations: Being at Home in Transcendental Method* (Washington, D.C.: University Press of America, 1976), especially pp. 2-5.

[3] "But, sir, I think we might be going a bridge too far." Lieutenant General Browning's remark at the final conference on Operation Market-Garden, cited by Cornelius Ryan, *A Bridge Too Far* (New York: Popular Library, 1974), p. 9.

on page 250 of *Method in Theology*. Many of my readers, I know, will be much younger than I in following Lonergan's clues to generalized empirical method: then my invitation will be to a risk of larger learning and there may even be some who would accept such an invitation echoing Stephen McKenna, "This is worth a life."[4] There will be other readers, and I think here especially of those steeped in present theological and philosophical trends, familiar indeed, even to a measure of enthusiasm, with Lonergan's work, for whom nonetheless my invitation smacks of a mission impossible, of too many bridges too far. Of these I would ask a distinction: are these bridges in principle too far, or are they rather beyond the reach of the armoury of past education and present responsibilities? If the latter is the answer regarding any bridge then I would ask that the distinction be made operative in teaching and writing. As I remarked elsewhere, "our generation's challenge would seem to be to reach indeed, but more to point, to encourage, so that a later generation might live a more improbable dream."[5]

I write here primarily of changes in "the turn to the idea"[6] adequate to modernity. What I say may well be recognized as "making conversion a topic,"[7] particularly intellectual conversion, but the seven bridges I present are, in fact, integral challenges to levels of maturity for subjects incarnately seeking a foundational reflective mediation of the transformation of "the monster that has stood forth in our day."[8]

Some of the bridges are indicated more fully than others, either because I have previously signposted them, or because I face still the discomfort of their challenge. In general, I must note that I am in agreement with Fr. Lonergan who regularly refers to the difficulty of reaching adequately differentiated consciousness, and that I am

---

[4] Confided to his private journal on his 36th birthday, regarding the task of translating Plotinus.

[5] McShane, *Lonergan's Challenge to the University and the Economy* (Washington, D.C.: University Press of America, 1979), p. vi.

[6] *Die Wendung zur Idee* is axially transformed by Lonergan's focus on "the profounder meaning of the name, intelligible", B. Lonergan, *Insight* (London: Longmans, Green and Co., 1958), p. 647 with a Praxis of functional specialization.

[7] B. Lonergan, *Method in Theology* (London: Darton, Longman and Todd, 1972), p. 253.

[8] Ibid., p. 40. The monster, of course, is not some naively decadent world. It is the mesh of our polymorphic selves, and to the discussion of inner bridges to follow one might apply Jung's comment "If a man is a hero, he is a hero precisely because, in the final reckoning, he did not let the monster devour him, but subdued it not once but many times." Jung, "The Relations between the Ego and the Unconscious," *Two Essays in Analytic Psychology,* trans. R.F.C. Hull, *Collected Works* (Princeton: Princeton University Press, 1966), VII, p. 173.

uneasy about an opposite impression given by some of his disciples. Let me say then that what I signpost here is a challenge for much more than a decade of devotion, "not a great sacrifice," as I wrote ten years ago for the Florida Conference, "for the enormous benefit of coming intellectually into the twentieth century." [9]

I have given the bridges helpful names and put them in relevant sequence. But the names and the sequence will, I hope, not distract the reader from the basic dialectic challenge: are these bridges personal spannings to a modern metaxy?[10] Is this bridge a bridge too far?

1. THE BRIDGE OF GEMS

The bridge requires the identification and cultivation of Generalized Empirical Methodological Strategies, GEMS. It also is the bridge of non-discipleship. In order to throw light both on the elusiveness of the identification and on the irrelevance of discipleship, I would recall 16th century Italian science and the achievement of Galileo Galilei.

Modern science is called, not Galilean, but experimental. Stillman Drake notes that before Galileo there was no dearth of mathematical reasoning but "the systematic appeal to experience in support of mathematical laws seems to have been lacking....The design of experiments to discover new mathematical laws comes after Galileo's time."[11] Drake notes the difficulty of believing this, and so goes on to describe the inadequate strategies of such men as Tartaglia (1546), Cardano (1570), and Ubaldo (1577) in seeking out laws of force for bodies on inclined planes.

Lonergan's lasting achievement is the identification of generalized empirical method and its basic strategy: "It does not treat of objects without taking into account the corresponding operations of the subject: it does not treat of the subject's operations without taking into account the corresponding objects."[12] The strategy is present throughout *Insight;* so, one treats of roundness in tandem with

---

[9] *The Shaping of the Foundations,* p. 41. The paper in question, "Image and Emergence: Towards an Adequate *Weltanschauung,*" serves well as a larger prologue to the present essay.

[10] I am sublating here Voegelin's notion of the In-between, central to his *The Ecumenic Age* (Baton Rouge, La.: Louisiana State University Press, 1974).

[11] Stillman Drake, *Galileo Studies* (Ann Arbor, Mich.: The University of Michigan Press, 1970), p. 44.

[12] Lonergan's developed view of generalized empirical method appears in The Donald Mathers Memorial Lectures, three lectures delivered at Queen's University in March 1976. I quote from the first lecture, "Religious Experience" which appears in *Trinification of the World,* ed. T. Dunne and J.-M. Laporte. (Toronto: Regis College Press, 1978).

treating of one's procedures in treating of roundness.[13] But I note that the strategy is regularly missed. Analogous to 16th century Italy, the 20th century shows no dearth of philosophical debate. Furthermore, so-called Lonergan scholars can be as eloquent as Tartaglia or Cardano, and as lacking in experiment.

The central issue is the emergence of a precise experimental method. The basic specimens are particular insights. The fundamental irony is the misreading of the first paragraph of the first chapter of *Insight*.

The need for generalized empirical method is an epiphany of the twentieth century, whether one considers the planning and practice of business, the frontiers of human searching, or the structuring of education on any level. So, for example, modern government, economics, literary criticism, musicology, physics, all stumble along in procedural obscurity.[14] What such obscurity shows is not just a need for a new "core programme" in universities; not, one might say, a need for a new deal, but for a new deck. Yet a committee of Harvard University can pathetically restructure undergraduate education in a manner that perpetrates the continued avoidance of the central sickness.[15] And present departments of education blindly ensure the survival of the sickness in later generations.

Galileo's followers, like Castelli and Toricelli, pushed on to understand and change the world. Einstein, a later follower, going beyond Galileo in content rather than method, could describe Galileo as "a man who possessed the passionate will, the intelligence, and the courage to stand up as a representative of rational thinking against the host of those who, relying on the ignorance of the people and the indolence of teachers in priestly and scholarly garb, maintained and defended their positions of authority."[16] Lonergan, a passionate representative of a *praxis* of concomitant self-and-world empirical understanding, will not be remembered in later centuries because of present studies of Lonergan in relation to dated thinkers. He will be remembered through the manifest all-pervading fruits of his tandem method, fruits that are only seeds in our time.

---

[13] *Insight,* pp. 7-13.

[14] The two books cited in notes 2 and 5 above spell out this procedural obscurity.

[15] *The Chronicle of Higher Education,* March 6, 1978 (Vol. XVI, no. 2) gives the report, pp. 15ff. The principles laid out by the committee cry out for generalized empirical method: "an educated person should have a critical appreciation of the ways in which we gain knowledge and understanding of the universe, of society and of ourselves," but the cry goes unheard.

[16] A. Einstein, in his foreword to Galileo Galilei, *Dialogue Concerning the Two Chief World Systems,* trans. S. Drake (Berkeley: University of California Press, 1967), p.vii.

2. The Bridge of Size

"By size will be meant magnitude apart from any geometrical conceptions. It is an elementary experiential conjugate, and it is to be characterized in terms of simple experiences."[17]

One hopes for an ABC of generalized empirical method, and, indeed, I have tried elsewhere to provide what is commonly meant by such an ABC.[18] but here I cast around on a large canvas of history — or should I say foundations?

The foundational ABC of generalized empirical method, I would suggest, can be located in Lonergan's noting of "the natural bridge over which we may advance from our examination of science to our examination of common sense."[19] To put the issue in its largest context, I would note that in the metaxy of historical intelligence there is a lower ground of loneliness and an upper ground of loneliness. Questing the lower ground of loneliness throws one back to such questions as "why are the distances AB, BC, CA, different?"[20] It turns one discomfortingly to "begin by distinguishing (1) size, (2) length, and (3) measurement."[21]

Like Thomas beginning his discussion of the nature of God with, for some, a silly question, "Whether God is a Body,"[22] the present issue may seem trivial. Yet for Lonergan it offers "considerable light."[23] The question of chapter five of *Insight* invites one to move beyond Newton's oversight regarding Space, Kant's mistake regarding an *a priori* form of sensibility, and Hoenen's view that only Euclidean three-dimensional extension is known as possible.[24] Without some-years-long preoccupation with that question one can disagree only nominally with Newton or Kant or Hoenen, and one is easily trapped in myth whether one's interest is in physics or chemistry, in dream-analysis or art, or in a heuristic conception of the finality of being.[25]

---

[17] *Insight*, p. 167.

[18] *Wealth of Self and Wealth of Nations: Self-Axis of The Great Ascent* (New York: Exposition Press, 1975).

[19] *Insight*, p. 140.

[20] Ibid., p. 27.

[21] Ibid., p. 167.

[22] *Summa Theologica* I, q.3, a.1.

[23] *Insight*, p. 140.

[24] Lonergan, "A Note on Geometric Possibility," *Collection* (New York. Herder and Herder, 1967), p. 97.

[25] Since, in physics, the clash is direct, paradoxes are more manifest. Most recently, in "The Quantum Theory and Reality," *Scientific American,* November 1979 (Vol. 241, no. 5), 158-81, Bernard d'Espagnat struggles in naive Euclidean realism. Relevant here, too, is the point made by the lengthy citation on dreams at n. 54, below.

3. The Bridge of Strangeness

"One escapes only through the discovery (and one has not made it yet if one has no clear memory of its startling strangeness) that there are two quite different realisms, that there is an incoherent realism, half-animal and half-human, that poses as a half-way house between materialism and idealism and, on the other hand, that there is an intelligent and reasonable realism between which and materialism the half-way house is idealism." [26]

I recall vividly the strangeness of the beginnings of my own escape, and the concomitant shift in sensibility, when I was 26, with four years of mathematical science and two years of philosophy behind me. The pivotal text, oddly enough, was not *Insight* but the fifth element in the general notion of inner word in the first of the *Verbum* articles.[27] Since then I have found it easy to keep track of the few students I have helped towards and into that strangeness, and I have no doubt that Maslow's statistic, "less than 1% of adults grow," [28] holds sway for the population of philosophers with regard to this bridge. The statistic can change only if we seriously and incarnately make this bridge a topic, and the difficulty of its crossing a topic.

The difficulty I write of is, of course, the difficulty of insightfully taking a stand on the position presented on page 388 of *Insight*. I would note in passing that "the position" is not something proven in *Insight;* one is rather invited to share thematically an existentially invulnerable assumption. The difficulty of taking this stand is clearly related to the difficulties noted regarding the previous two bridges. The full crossing of the second bridge is not essential to the stand. But the ghost of it that haunts chapter eight of *Insight* is central to the development of strangeness, and again I recall, as paradoxical encouragement to those willing to learn, the winter months of 1964 that I spent getting some distance towards some understanding of the notion of a thing; and I am only normally slow-witted.

I recall Lonergan's own comment on the difficulty of the present bridge:

> Unfortunately, some people have the impression that while Tertullian and others of his time may have made such a mistake, no one repeats it today. Nothing could be further from the truth. For until a person has made the personal discovery that he is making Tertullian's mistake all along the line, until he has

---

[26] *Insight*, p. xxviii.

[27] Lonergan, *Verbum: Word and Idea in Aquinas*, ed. D. Burrell, (Notre Dame: University of Notre Dame Press, 1967), p. 7.

[28] A. Maslow, *Towards a Psychology of Being*, (Princeton, N.J.: Van Nostrand, 1968), p. 204.

gone through the crisis involved in overcoming one's spontaneous estimate of the real, and the fear of idealism involved in it, he is still thinking just as Tertullian did. It is not a sign that one is dumb or backward. St. Augustine was one of the most intelligent men in the whole Western tradition and one of the best proofs of his intelligence is in the fact that he himself discovered that for years he was unable to distinguish between what is a body and what is real.²⁹

This, I must admit, is hard to take as a project³⁰ in the modern academic world. But so is the project of differentiating animals by their psychic differences, a project closely meshed with the present one.³¹ In this tandem of issues there must be a slow learning of proper business;³² "its business is not to follow some line of least resistance but to triumph in surmounting apparently insoluble difficulties...The animal pertains to an explanatory genus beyond that of the plant...."³³ The business requires the taking of a bridge uncomfortably far; the locating of oneself and plant and animal—and friends—in a modernly adequate answer to the question of, the questing for, the meaning of "is it?" and "Yes!"³⁴

4. THE BRIDGE OF BONES

"There is the law of integration. The initiation of development may be organic, psychic, intellectual or external, but the development remains fragmentary until the principle of correspondence between different levels is satisfied."³⁵

Here my interest is in a follow-through in intellectual development, particularly that development constituted by the third bridge. Elsewhere I have touched on the topic "memory of its startling strangeness,"³⁶ drawing especially on Proust. Here I am returning to the apparently less complex hints of Lonergan; the mind's discovery of realism is in the mesh of brainwaves and neural demand functions, rapid-eye-movement-dreams and rituals of worship,

---

²⁹ Lonergan in an unpublished talk on "Consciousness and the Trinity," delivered in Rome in 1964.

³⁰ I use 'project' in Gibson Winter's sense: "the project is the total intentionality with which subjectivity as a totality is stretched towards the world as possibility," *Elements for a Social Ethic* (New York: MacMillan, 1968), p. 135.

³¹ The meshing is discussed at the conclusion of my article, "The Core Psychological Present of the Contemporary Theologian, *Trinification of the World,* ed. T. Dunne and J.-M. Laporte, (Toronto: Regis College Press, 1968), pp. 84-96.

³² See *Lonergan's Challenge to the University and the Economy,* pp. v ff.

³³ *Insight,* p. 265.

³⁴ For the discomfort of the issue within literary studies see *Lonergan's Challenge to the University and the Economy,* pp. 69 ff.

³⁵ *Insight,* p. 471.

³⁶ *The Shaping of the Foundations,* pp. 105 ff.

coffee conversations and evenings in the rhythms of the moon or the symphony or the sea.

The crucial issue is the challenge, and the discomfort, of boning up on realism, of membering and remembering, so that dying thus alive would slowly seed a new spontaneity, a lift beyond fantasy[37] to basic intersubjectivity and intersubjective meaning. Chesterton and Joyce together could enlarge on this; at issue is the Gethsemane of the transition from primitive compact consciousness to a mediated integration of later millenia

Fr. Lonergan points up the unity-in-tension, the polymorphic, in human consciousness, and goes on to note that "the intellectual pattern of experience is supposed and expressed by our account of self-affirmation, of being, of objectivity. But no man is born in that pattern; no one reaches it easily; no one remains in it permanently; and when some other pattern is dominant, then the self of our self-affirmation seems quite different from one's actual self, the universe of being seems as unreal as Plato's noetic heaven, and objectivity spontaneously becomes a matter of meeting persons and dealing with things that are 'really out there.' "[38]

But might it not be that even in some less distant years the law of integration, passionate in human history, would engender both a solitude and a dialogue of positional transformation in which "this transformation of sensitivity and intersubjectivity penetrates to the physiological level,"[39] in which eye-seeing and I-saying, eyeball to eyeball, Jack and Jill,[40] reach to an embodiment of critical realism?

5. THE BRIDGE OF IMPS

To take seriously the challenge of *Insight, Method in Theology, Praxis, Sargawit*,[41] the challenge of *IMPS*, is the fifth bridge.

'Sargawit' is a Joycean word denoting here the adequate foundational person, who faces incarnately the challenge to reach what I have elsewhere described as an IMProbable vision,[42] a vision of

---

[37] One may note here an interweaving of bridges: fantasy is the proper object of the sixth bridge, the Bridge of Oxen.

[38] *Insight*, p. 385.

[39] Ibid., pp. 741-42.

[40] See Lonergan, "Cognitional Structure," *Collection* (New York: Herder and Herder, 1967), pp. 236 ff.

[41] A marginal note in the "Triv and Quod" section of *Finnegans Wake*, p. 294, indicates "Sarga, or the path of outgoing." *Sarga* is the sanskrit for "process of world creation or emanation."

[42] *Lonergan's Challenge to the University and the Economy*, pp. 92 ff.

IMPerceptibles,[43] a total tandem heuristic vision. Furthermore, my bridge title draws attention to the role of imp—in both an archaic and a modern sense—a role played in the vortex of functional specialization.

The issue is the content and the use of the general categories noted in *Method in Theology*, pp. 286-87. These categories clearly cover and reach beyond the contents of *Insight* and *Method in Theology;* they present a precise challenge to an adequate modern *Praxisweltanschauung*. And this is a discomforting message for the vast majority of modern academics.

Lonergan remarked in *Insight* that his view on hermeneutics would be just as unacceptable to scholars as tensor fields and eigenfunctions were to physicists earlier in this century.[44] And in this context I am not, of course, expecting miracles; present theologians, especially, cannot be expected to bridge a centuries-old gap to modernity. But it will greatly help the implementation of *Method in Theology* if those working towards new biblical studies and historical studies would strive, with prayer, to remain incarnately alert to Lonergan's view that "the use of the general categories occurs in any of the eight functional specialties."[45] Otherwise the "gap" will emerge only in that as yet undeveloped and discomforting specialty, dialectics, and the massive "transposition"[46] to the genetico-dialectic patterned systematics[47] needed to give modern people a culturally-incarnate story of stories and story-tellers to live by, will remain for centuries cribbed.

The book *Insight* invites one to begin the task of developing an adequate modern view.[48] The insights it investigates are not a random selection; their sequential understanding is required if one is to have categories adequate to generate deep progress. I am here, of course, merely circling round the unwelcome message. Foundations persons are mischievous, trouble-makers. They "make conversion a topic",[49] or bridges. But they also may appeal to the archaic mean-

---

[43] A strategy I find useful is to take the text at *Insight*, p. 464, beginning, "Study of the organism begins from the thing-for-us, from the organism as exhibited to our senses," and follow it through replacing the word "organism" by the word "daisy," "Christ," "the Mystical Body," "history," etc.

[44] *Insight*, p. 581.

[45] *Method in Theology*, p. 292.

[46] See F. E. Crowe, "Doctrines and Historicity in the Context of Lonergan's Method," *Theological Studies* 38 (1977), also McShane, *Lonergan's Challenge to the University and the Economy*, pp. 104 ff.

[47] Relevant here are Lonergan's comments regarding a treatise on the Mystical Body, *Insight*, p. 742.

[48] *Method in Theology*, p. 260.

[49] Ibid., p. 253.

ings of the word "imp": to implant, graft; to repair; to furnish with wings. This bridge cannot surely be too far if its grafting into the vortex of method could furnish with wings the task of transforming the global network of neurotic aggressions and greeds with larger novel patterns of kindness, and success, and hope.

6. THE BRIDGE OF OXEN

There is an episode in Joyce's *Ulysses* which goes by the title "Oxen of the Sun." It is an awaiting of a birth, and Joyce moves brilliantly through centuries of English prose style, ending in a babel and a birth. I take the episode and the title as a symbol of this bridge, a bridge of concrete fantasy and hope. Generalized empirical method and the emergence of the third stage of meaning, the second time of temporal subject,[50] is the possibility and probability of profound changes in meaning.[51] To begin scheme-wise, to seriously envisage such longterm concrete changes is to cross this Bridge of Oxen. "Without fantasy, all philosophic knowledge remains in the grip of the present or the past and severed from the future, which is the only link between philosophy and the real history of mankind,"[52] and the task here requires what I have called elsewhere concrete fantasy.[53] It is a task which calls for an impossible serenity to the upper passion and lower potency of loneliness. The goal is an impossible dream, but the labour may be a patient effort to release more humdrum dreams from conventionalization:

> The distortion of a dream thought which resistance wants to keep from awareness has to be distinguished from the process of conventionalization, which more or less *all* dream elements undergo because the medium of dream language is incompatible with the medium of the conventional world of waking life. In the degree of this incompatibility there are, of course, considerable variations between different people and, even more so, between different cultures. But modern Western civilization with its streamlined efficiency, uniform mass culture, and emphasis on usefulness in terms of profitable and material production is particularly and strikingly at the opposite pole from the world of dreams.... It is the trans-schematic quality of early childhood experience as well as of dreams which makes it difficult or impossible for the memory schemata to preserve and recall voluntarily such experience. Yet it is also this quality in

---

[50] Lonergan, *De Deo Trino: Pars Systematica* (Rome: Gregorian Press, 1964), p. 199.
[51] Lonergan, "Dimension of Meaning," *Collection,* pp. 255-56.
[52] Herbert Marcuse, *Negations: Essays in Critical Theory,* translated by J. J. Shapiro (Boston: Beacon Press, 1968), p. 155.
[53] *The Shaping of the Foundations,* pp. 111 ff.

which potentialities of progress, of going beyond the conventional pattern, and of widening the scope of human life are forever present and waiting to be released.[54]

The impossible dream is the communal mediated human integration of the third stage of meaning, and to live with its present remoteness and its systematic exclusion by East, West, and South is to reach for the patience of God with and within history; the second million years is on our side.

The enormity of the topic is overwhelming and I will only hint at three aspects that I have touched on more fully elsewhere: the transposition of language, of the arts, of economics.

Aggreformic[55] structuring of consciousness coupled with the strategy of subject-referent linguistic feedback[56] will slowly lift scientific language out of its decayed present patterns[57] and mediate a redemption of common language currently derhythmatized by the truncated tenchnologists of the two elementary sciences.[58] A basic condition is an emergent probabilistic shift in community towards the suspicion that we are not at the end of time, that spoken and written language has, at present, only embrionic maturity. And so an integral mediation of that redemption will be a transposition — itself mediated by a humble openness to primitive compact consciousness — of contemporary aesthetic consciousness.

Susanne Langer wrote of a bridge of asses in art relating to a liberation from represenatation.[59] Boulez reached, within the presence of Mallarmé's lyrics and Joyce's prose, for a grasp of music "as an object of its own reflection."[60] The third stage of meaning should spiral forth art to a profound novelty of genuine realism.[61] So, for exam-

---

[54] E. G. Schachtel, "On memory and Childhood Amnesia," *Psychiatry*, 10 (1947): 17-18.

[55] See *The Shaping of the Foundations*, pp. 120 ff.

[56] See *Method in Theology*, p. 88, note 34.

[57] For illustrations of present deficient expression in botany, zoology, and musicology see *The Shaping of the Foundations*, pp. 27-8, 62, 90-1.

[58] One must entertain a perspective in which the scientific revolution is not something that has passed, but is something beginning.

[59] Susanne Langer, *Mind: An Essay on Human Feeling*, I (Baltimore: Johns Hopkins Press, 1967), p. 97, note.

[60] Pierre Boulex, "Sonate, Que me veux-tu?", *Perspectives of New Music* 1 (1963):32.

[61] I recall here *La Spirale,* the title of a novel sketched by "the father of realism," Flaubert, of which Maurice Nadeau remarked "if La Spirale had been written it might have prevented the stupid label of 'realist' from ever being attached to Flaubert." *The Greatness of Flaubert,* trans. B. Bray (New York: The Library Press, 1972), p. 286. Flaubert's sketch is in *Oeuvres complétes,* XII (Paris: Club de l'honnête homme, 1974), pp. 229-32. Recall also note 25 above on physics and dreams, and a related entrapment of the plastic arts.

ple, if sculpture "effects the objectification of self and environment for the sense of sight,"[62] then one must expect an axial difference in objectification and in its reception tandem to transformed subjects.

Finally, it seems to me that it is this bridge which gives one the courage to take seriously the concrete implementation of Lonergan's economic analysis. Schumpeter wrote of crossing the Rubicon in economics:

> By the phrase "crossing the Rubicon", I mean this: however important those occasional excursions into sequence analysis may have been, they left the main body of economic theory on the 'static' bank of the river; the thing to do is not to supplement static theory by the booty brought back from these excursions but to replace it by a system of general economic dynamics into which statics would enter as a special case...An increasing number of workers see the new goal; but for the time being this is practically all....[63]

To envisage adequately the dynamic bank is to walk in one's own time and place, but now with leadership, the bridge of normative economic modernity which Lonergan paced out alone between 1930 and 1944. To reach adequately that dynamic bank is to walk the bridge of cosmopolis,[64] of oxen, of hope. It is to envisage quite new patterns of education, quite new criteria of human success, the emergence of microautonomy as key to the control of meaning,[65] the end of economics as a branch of politics.[66]

Clearly, to envisage this million-year transposition of "man's intersubjective awareness of the sufferings and the needs of mankind"[67] is quite literally beyond present hopes and dreams.

7. The Bridge of Straw

With these seven bridges I am sketching a project which is a programme, not for undergraduates or graduates, but for slow foundational adult growth. The title of this last bridge should indeed recall to the reader's mind the latter days of Aquinas, but in the present context I am thinking not of mystical transports but of "a slow, if not a bloody, entrance. To learn thoroughly is a vast undertaking that

---

[62] S. Langer, *Feeling and Form* (New York: Scribner, 1953), p. 91.

[63] J. Schumpeter, *History of Economic Analysis* (New York: Oxford University Press, 1974), pp. 1160-61.

[64] *Insight*, pp. 238 ff.

[65] McShane, *Wealth of Self and Wealth of Nations,* pp. 92 ff.

[66] Lonergan's analysis of the drift of political modernity lies hidden in manuscripts and typescripts from the period 1930-44.

[67] *Insight*, p. 241.

calls for relentless perseverence. To strike out on a new line and become more than a week-end celebrity calls for years in which one's living is more or less constantly absorbed in the effort to understand, in which one's understanding gradually works round and up a spiral of viewpoints with each complementing its predecessor and only the last embracing the whole field to be mastered."[68] And the mastery here is the paradoxical mastery by Mystery, authentic nescience. It is mastery, however, carried on by history in its calling forth of dedicated human inquiry. One can find its patterns both in the humbling growing-pains of modern science or in the lengthier and loftier perspective of Voegelin's later work. The growing-pains of modern science recall previous bridges and the present bridge becomes a thinker's task only through an ontogenetic mirroring of those painful differentiations. One comes slowly to appreciate the micro-thinness of our understanding of the complexity of history; a message implicit in modernity's growing sensitivity to method as against content in science.

I find it necessary at this stage to reemphasize this humbling aspect of detailed science because of a pervading tendency among philosophers, theologians, and methodologists to head for generalities, and I impishly recall once more the first sentence of *Insight:* "In the midst of that vast and profound stirring of human minds, which we name the Renaissance, Descartes was convinced that too many people felt it beneath them to direct their efforts to apparently trifling problems."[69] To theologians who debate various views regarding history as revelation I would put such questions as "Is the mind of Galileo part of history as revelation, or the self-energy of the electron, or animal thirst?"

It may be clearer now that I am writing here about a particular type of *Final Integration in the Adult Personality.*[70] Far from lapsing "into the error of those that forget men to be potency in the realm of intelligence,"[71] the foundations person seeks, through the previous bridges, to remain open to an ontogenetic anamnesis and prolepsis[72] of the phylogenetic message of history. "Through the differentiations

---

[68] Ibid., p. 186.

[69] Ibid., p. 3.

[70] The title of a book by A. R. Aresteh, Leiden, 1965. His remark on page 18 regarding the psychologist may be transposed to the present issue of foundations persons: "Unless the psychologist has himself experienced the state of quest of final integration in the succession of identities he will hardly acquire an understanding or incentive for doing research on it."

[71] *Insight,* p. 748.

[72] The topic of the epilogue to *The Shaping of the Foundations:* "Authentic Subjectivity and International Growth: Foundations," pp. 119-140.

of consciousness, history becomes visible as the process in which the differentiations occur...History is discovered as the process in which reality becomes visible for the movement beyond its own structure; the stucture of history is eschatological." [73]

The movement is of self and history towards an incarnate appreciation of the essential incompleteness[74] of the passion of being in time. It is a vortex movement of the seven bridges, remaining still a challenge to strange old bones. And from that growing vortex, balanced in a greying metaxy between life an death, art and nature would speak, and be spoken of, in new ways: for "art draws attention to the fact that the splendour of the world is a cipher, a revelation, an invitation, the presence of one who is not seen, touched, grasped, distinguished by a difference, yet present" and "man is nature's priest and nature is God's silent communing with man." [75] And dying bones may clutch at gemstraws for the sake of time.

II. Lonergan and the Actual Context of Economics

Having asserted, with aphorisms and acronyms, the significance of generalized empirical method under the metaphor of "a bridge too far," I should like now to spell out in prose fashion the relevance of generalized empirical method for the actual context of economics.

> Lacking any coherent theory of how the market should operate, the Yugoslav government and the academic economists alike have been content to meet pricing and market crises as they arise, and to advocate changes in business behavior and institutions on an ad hoc basis.[76]

The Yugoslav experience in its recent years of working away from centralized economic planning to some form of self-management may seem very different from the Western experience, but in that one respect of "lacking any coherent theory of how the market should operate" we have a common characteristic of economic practice of any colour. *Business Week* recently spoke of "Yugoslavia's game plan for 1980" which included a curtailment of credit while "government policymakers are shooting for a 6% rise in exports coupled with a drop in imports" [77] and one is surely tempted to take the words

---

[73] E. Voegelin, *The Ecumenic Age,* p. 304.

[74] In continuity with the heuristic perspective of *Insight,* p. 686, and the perspective on mystery of *De Deo Trino: Pars Dogmatica* (Rome: Gregorian Press, 1964), p. 274.

[75] The quotations are from an unpublished talk on art by Lonergan, given during a summer institute on education at Xavier University, Cincinnati, 1959.

[76] Joel B. Dirlam and James L. Plummer, *An Introduction to the Yugoslav Economy* (Columbus, Ohio: Merrill, 1973,) p. 63.

[77] *Business Week* (May 5, 1980):p. 79.

"game" and "shooting for" in the meanings they would have in a foggy morning shoot. Washington and Ottawa too have their game plans, with wobbling credit control and other shots in the mist.

The fundamental issue is whether "lacking any coherent theory of how the market should operate" is an inevitability of the human condition and its economic practice. Further, one should note that a denial of that inevitability coupled with an exclusion of inalienable characteristics of the human condition, such as is implicitly available either in a Marxist perspective or in capitalist centralist growth theoretics, does not respond to the fundamental issue. And the failure to meet or even seriously raise that fundamental issue in twentieth century economic thinking has, decade by decade, led us into the makeshifts that Lonergan wrote of nearly forty years ago:

> ...as makeshift follows makeshift, it becomes increasingly difficult to distinguish between a democratic and a totalitarian economy.
> But economists can be champions of democracy as well as advisers to dictators or planning boards. The proof of the possibility is an historical fact: the old political economists were champions of democracy; and if the content of their thought has been found inadequate, its democratic form is as valid today as ever. That form consisted in the discovery of an economic mechanism and in the deduction of rules to guide men in the use of the economic machine, a rule of laissez faire for governments and a rule of thrift and enterprise for individuals. It is now fully apparent that these rules serve their purpose only in particular cases, but it is still insufficiently grasped that new and more satisfactory rules have to be devised. Without them human liberty will perish. For either men learn rules to guide them individually in the use of the economic machine, or else they surrender their liberty to be ruled along with the machine by a central planning board.
> The reality of that dilemma measures the significance of an effort, however tenuous and incomplete, to formulate the laws of an economic mechanism more remote and, in a sense, more fundamental than the pricing system. Now there is little dispute that the dilemma is real, for the liberal dream of an automatic economy has, like all dreams, at long last broken. The necessity of rational control has ceased to be a question, and the one issue is the locus of that control. Is it to be absolutist from above downwards? Is it to be democratic from below upwards? Plainly it can be democratic only in the measure in which economic science succeeds in uttering not counsel to rulers but precepts to mankind, not specific remedies and plans to increase the power of bureaucracies, but universal laws which men themselves administer in the personal conduct of their lives. Thus the breaking of the liberal dream of automatic progress provokes a

revision of judgment on the old political economists. Their greatness lay not in fostering an amoral devotion to automatism but in developing an economic science and from it issuing universal precepts of proper economic conduct. The automatism is a husk that has withered and fallen, and to cling to it is to fall into the totalitarian abyss. The old science and the old precepts have gone the way of Ptolemy and Newton. But to deny the possibility of a new science and new precepts is, I am convinced, to deny the possibility of the survival of democracy.[78]

That Lonergan has had a serious and prolonged interest in economics will come as a surprise to many. That he faced the fundamental issue, the possibility of a new science, over a period of about fourteen years, to bring forth the actual context of the new science by 1944, will be found incredible by most. Indeed, as we shall indicate briefly here, it has been found incredible or incomprehensible. As Lonergan wrote recently, "I beg to note that such an analysis has not been tried and found wanting. Rather, to speak with Chesterton, it has been thought hard and not tried".[79] It seems that Lonergan's work on economics is at present in the first stage of the fate of creative theory: "First...it is attacked as absurd; then it is admitted to be true but obvious and insignificant; finally it is seen to be so important that its adversaries claim that they themselves discovered it."[80]

We have here what will surely become a classic instance in the tradition of Kuhn's *Structure of a Scientific Resolution*. Hywel Jones wrote recently, "there can be little doubt of the difficulty of changing any ingrained habit of thought or thinking. Keynes spoke of his 'long struggle to escape' from the conventional approach to the analysis of unemployment. Given that the neo-classical approach dominates the teaching of economics in the Western world, it would be surprising if a non-neoclassical growth theory attained any large measure of acceptance independently of a transformation in economic theory in general".[81] As we shall try to intimate, Lonergan's shift in economic thinking goes much deeper than the usually cited instances of scien-

---

[78] The quotation comes from an early typescript associated with Lonergan's work towards *Circulation Analysis*.

[79] The quotation is from some recent (1980) notes communicated to me by Lonergan. Lonergan's work on economics still remains entirely unpublished. I would like here to note my indebtedness to him throughout this essay. Since he first indicated to me the existence of *Circulation Analysis* in 1968 he has been most generous in keeping me informed of his work.

[80] William James, *Pragmatism* (London: Longmans, 1912) p. 198.

[81] Hywel Jones, *An Introduction to Modern Theories of Growth* (London: Nelson, 1978), p. 71.

tific revolution. It has been described elsewhere as a transposition;[82] it relates to "changes in the control of meaning that mark off the great epochs in human history";[83] it calls for what Lonergan names the second time of the temporal subject;[84] it can blossom only in the emergent light of the third stage of meaning.[85]

Within that massive transposition there are included, of course, corrections of more evident disorientations. So, for example, in the citation given already, Lonergan speaks of something "more fundamental than the pricing system" and Nicholas Kaldor gives substance to the suspicion of a massive disorientation of systematic economics: "The difficulty with a new start is to pinpoint the critical area where economics went astray....I would put it in the middle of the fourth chapter of Vol.I of *The Wealth of Nations*.... In (that) chapter, after discussing the need for money in a social economy, Smith suddenly gets fascinated by the distinction between money price, real price, and exchange value and from then on, hey presto, his interest gets bogged down in the question of how values and prices for products and factors are determined. One can trace a more or less continuous development of price theory from the subsequent chapters of Smith through Ricardo, Walras, Marshall, right up to Debreu and the most sophisticated present-day Americans."[86] Lonergan's early, incomplete, manuscripts show his struggle to determine the significance of price, and his manuscript of 1944 locates price properly as ranking low in an adequate analysis.[87]

Secondly, there is the disorientation expressed in the remark made by Hansen in his presidential address to the American Economic Association at their annual meeting, December 1938: "The business cycle was *par excellence* the problem of the nineteenth century. But the main problem of our times, and particularly in the United States, is the problem of full employment."[88] Since then theoreticians have produced a vast literature on steady growth, and governments have tried to realize it with a nice balance of unemployment

---

[82] McShane, *Lonergan's Challenge to the University and the Academy* (Washington: University Press of America, 1980) pp. 107 ff. The final chapters of this book deal with Lonergan's economics and complement the present essay.

[83] B. Lonergan, *Collection* (New York: Herder and Herder, 1967), pp. 255-56.

[84] B. Lonergan, *De Deo Trino* II (Rome: Gregorian Press, 1964), p. 199.

[85] B. Lonergan, *Method in Theology* (London: Darton, Longman and Todd, 1972) pp. 93-99.

[86] N. Kaldor, "The Irrelevance of Equilibrium Economics," *Economic Journal* 82 (1972):1240-41.

[87] I have dealt with this, and some of the points to follow, more fully in chapters 6 and 7 of op. cit. note 82.

[88] Alvin Hansen, "Economic Progress and Declining Population Growth", *American Economic Review*, Vol. XXIX, No. 1 (March 1939): 4.

and inflation. The orientation is towards smoothing out cycles. It has not been very successful: as the economist Martin Feldstein remarked recently: "We know enough to move the economy out of a trough but not enough to control the business cycle."[89] Lonergan, on the other hand, grasps economic process as intrinsically cyclic, with the possibility not only of the trade cycle but also of what he calls the pure cycle, of which he writes: "One may say that it is solidly grounded in a dynamic structure of the productive process; and one has only to think of the practical impossibility of calculating the acceleration ratios...to smile at the suggestion that one should try to 'smooth out the *pure* cycle'."[90] One is led to smile, but sadly, at the suggestions of Hansen and Feldstein.

Thirdly, there is what Robinson and Eatwell call "the central problem of economic philosophy — the nature of profits,"[91] and they discuss Sraffa's work in order to throw light on that problem. But what Sraffa's work shows is that profit is not the central problem of economics. The central problem of economic philosophy is an adequate analysis of the productive process, and within that analysis the issue of the nature of profit is precisely relocated and resolved.

Fourthly, there is the issue of sufficient disaggregation: "the need for a model which takes account of the sectional differentiation of the process of production can hardly be denied. As we have seen, the task is not one of merely adding more variables to the Keynesian set. Nor is it one of disaggregation in general. In the latter case Leontief's input-output table would present the ideal solution....The task consists in choosing a level of aggregation between those chosen by Keynes and Leontief — high enough to permit analytic manipulation of complex dynamic processes, low enough to reflect those physical properties of an industrial market which affect its general stability."[92] Lowe, in the article cited, gives a brief history of such sufficient disaggregation and settles for two circular flows related to capital and labour (the capital flow subdivided to allow for machine tools) which include a cross-over not unlike that introduced by Lonergan.[93] One must note however that Lonergan's distinction is precisely functional,[94] cutting across industries, and would, no doubt, call forth comments similar to that made by Domar with regard to the Feldman model: "it is impossible

---

[89] Martin Feldstein, quoted in *Time*, August 27, 1979, p. 27.

[90] Lonergan, *Circulation Analysis*, p. 73.

[91] Joan Robinson and John Eatwell, *An Introduction to Modern Economics* (Maidenhead, England: McGraw Hill, 1973), p. 183.

[92] Adolf Lowe, "A Structural Model of Production", *Social Research* (1952): 140-41.

[93] See McShane, op. cit., note 82, p. 121.

[94] Ibid., pp. 117 ff.

to give it any but the roughest empirical meaning simply because an economy is not organized in this manner." [95] The points to follow will suggest that Lonergan, but not Domar, reaches empirical meaning.

Fifthly, an analysis of the productive process does not essentially involve proprietory social relations. In contrast to Lonergan's clarity in this, there is the effort of Robinson and Eatwell "to go back to the beginning and start again." [96] They open chapter two with the remark: "The foregoing analysis was designed to illustrate the importance of social relations in the process of production." Such designing could put the analysis out of focus.

Sixthly, there are the blind alleys of perfect competition and monopoly. "Between 1926 and 1933, economic theory, particularly in Anglo-Saxon countries, subjected to penetrating criticism the claims that these two extremes were representative of capitalist markets in the real world. This criticism developed along lines which were rather different from those advanced by Schumpeter." [97] An analysis which focuses on flows and cycles in a dynamic economy does not react to Sraffa by seeking a middle ground, riddled with indeterminacies, of imperfect competition, monopolistic competition, or degrees of monopoly. Rather it would note, with Lonergan and Schumpeter, that perfect competition and monopoly belong to a statics where there is no real business, that competitive business is a matter "of doing things better or at any rate more successfully than the fellow next door". [98]

Seventhly, there is the broader issue of indeterminacies and unmeasurables. It is an issue associated with "The Capital Controversy" which divides the two Cambridges.[99] The issue takes on far more realism when one moves in the world of development planning. As Paul Streeten notes regarding the application of "capital-

---

[95] E. D. Domar, *Essays in the Theory of Economic Growth* (New York: Oxford University Press, 1957), p. 227. Chapter nine deals with Feldman, a Marxist engineer-economist whose work dates from the late twenties.

[96] op. cit., note 16. On the relation of Robinson's efforts to neo-Marxist analysis, see Ludo Cuyvers, "Joan Robinson's Theory of Economic Growth," *Science and Society,* XLII (1979):326-48.

[97] Claudio Napoleoni, *Economic Thought of the Twentieth Century,* edited and translated by Alessandro Ciono (who adds an introduction and chapter 9), (London: Robertson, 1972), p. 52. Chapter 3 deals with Schumpmter; chapter 4 deals with reactions to Sraffa. Chapter 8 deals with later attempts to patch up equilibrium theory.

[98] J. Schumpeter, *History of Economic Analysis* (New York: University Press, 1974), p. 975.

[99] For a survey and bibliography see chapter 6 of Hywel Jones, *An Introduction to Modern Theories of Economic Growth* (London: Nelson, 1978).

output ratio": "If a series of investment projects are interrelated, either sectorally or temporally, each depending on the others for its success, the very notion of a capital-output ratio for any one of them in isolation becomes as meaningless as the question, What is the contribution of the first violin to the Ninth Symphony?" [100] Later, in discussing the Little-Mirrlees method of project analysis,[101] he notes among a variety of dangers that "complete rationality about a sub-system can be worse than sub-rationality about the whole system." [101] He sides with Aristotle, "the man of education will seek exactness so far in each subject as the nature of the thing admits," [103] and notes the usual reply to such criticism as he makes: "what else can you put in its place?" [104]

A short essay introductory to a work yet to be published cannot be expected to supply that work's answer to this question. It can hint, as in the previous seven points, at flaws, blind-alleys, needs, clues. It can suggest the notion and difficulty of an actual context which would give an integral perspective on these points, But the *Festschrift* requires also some account of the emergence of Lonergan's interest in economics and of his present work in that area. To this we turn immediately.

An early stimulus was from Fr. Lewis Watt, the ethics professor in Heythrop College, Oxfordshire, where Lonergan studied philosophy in the late twenties. Fr. Watt was working on a book, *Capitalism and Democracy* and Lonergan recalls him posing the problem bluntly: you starve the workers to keep capitalism going, or you feed the workers and ruin capitalism. A further stimulus to his interest, on his return to Canada in 1930, was the actuality of the depression and the theoretical background to William Aberhart's Social Credit movement emerging in Alberta. The movement was based on the view of a Scottish engineer, Major Clifford Douglas (1878-1952). As assistant director of the Royal Aircraft Works in England during the first world war, Douglas made comprehensive studies of cost accounting which led him to the view that, in over 100 industrial establishments, the weekly sum-total of wages and salaries was con-

---

[100] Paul Streeten, *The Frontiers of Development Studies* (New York: Macmillan, 1972), p. 75. The book contains solid critical chapters on this and larger issues such as the applicability of growth theories to which we turn briefly in the text. Chapter 12 discusses the multinational corporation, a topic of present interest to Lonergan but beyond the scope of this short article.

[101] M. D. Little and J. A. Mirrlees, *Manual of Industrial Project Analysis in Developing Countries* (Paris: Development Centre of OECD, 1969).

[102] Streeten, p. 365.

[103] Ibid., p. 347. The Aristotle text is *Nicomachean Ethics,* 1094b.

[104] Ibid., p. 365.

tinually less than the weekly collective price of the goods produced. This led him to his famous A + B theorem: according to Douglas, there is a permanent discrepancy between A (the purchasing power of consumers) and A + B (the total cost of production). The view leads to a requirement of consumer credit, a requirement manifest in the Social Credit Movement launched by Aberhart in the autumn of 1932. Lonergan has remarked about his continued interest in economics in the thirties: "I wanted to find out what was wrong with social credit." So, into what appears to be a full schedule of teaching classics until 1933, studying theology, writing a doctorate thesis, and teaching his first years in theology, Lonergan moved towards his 1944 typescript entitled *Circulation Analysis.* Years later, in the autumn of 1977, in a symposium entitled *The Question as Commitment,* he noted "I worked on one question for fourteen years, getting nowhere. I wrote one hundred and twenty pages but didn't find anyone who could see any sense in it....The question is still genuine and authentic. Next term I shall be attacking it publicly".[105] He has, in fact, now given three spring seminars on the topic in Boston College, while concomitantly broadening the scope of his previous work to provide a perspective on other directions of modern economic theory and practice.

But let us return to the early thirties. The final product *Circulation Analysis,* is a massive achievement. Obviously, then, Lonergan was getting somewhere in the previous years. Still, his statement "getting nowhere" is legitimate. What he noted later regarding his study of Aquinas may be applied here: "Only by the slow, repetitious, circular labor of going over and over the data, by catching here a little insight and there another, by following through false leads and profiting from many mistakes, by continuous adjustments and cumulative changes of one's initial suppositions and perspectives and concepts, can one hope to attain such a development of one's own understanding as to hope to understand what Aquinas understood and meant." [106] But Lonergan's added difficulty in economics was that there was no Aquinas. Even Schumpeter's work, which might be considered a halfway house, seems to have been discovered by Lonergan when Lonergan's own views had already developed along a parallel direction.

Lonergan's unpublished notes and typescripts of this period may not be easy to date. There are several substantial but incomplete

---

[105] *The Question as Commitment,* Thomas More Institute Papers, 1977, (Montreal: Perry Printing Ltd., 1979), p. 32.

[106] B. Lonergan, *Verbum: Word and Idea in Aquinas,* ed. D. Burrell (Notre Dame, Ind.: University of Notre Dame Press, 1967), p. 216.

typescripts that would seem to antedate the final *Circulation Analysis,* and these show his struggle towards what we name an adequate actual context for economics. There is a great deal more in these typescripts, for instance, on the nature and dialectic of prices. Perhaps a single page from one early typescript on the latter topic would give some indication of the vigour and direction of his thought (possibly in the early forties):

> Within the last hundred years economic thought has moved steadily away from the view that fluid prices and competition are the panacea for all economic ills and the guarantee of ever greater benefits. Underlying this change of thought there is the very simple fact that, while the price system is an exquisite mechanism, still it is not a mechanism into which one can put little knowledge and less wisdom and then reasonably expect to receive notable amounts of both. The price system will strike a balance of any present set of preferences; but it will not make the preferences wise, nor will it make the expectations, on which they are based, turn out to be true. On the contrary, it will find the economic mean, so to speak, of wise and stupid, intelligent and foolish preferences; it will weigh true and false expectations with the money that backs them; and with relentless accuracy it will work out the anomaly one may expect a machine so controlled to yield. In the long run one is presented with a dilemma: either eliminate from every strategic post in the economy the unenlightened freedom of choice that works ruin through exchanges and through prices, or else, if you would preserve that freedom, take effective steps to enlighten it. The alternatives are socialism or an enlightenment of insufficiently enlightened self-interest.

Besides the typescripts there is a bulky collection of handwritten quotations and graphs, with his own comments on such writers as Heinrich Pesch, F. H. Knight, L. Robbins, F. Hayek, E. R. Lindahl, J. Schumpeter. There is, as far as we know, no mention of Keynes, and it may be suspected that Lonergan's view of Keynes might coincide with that of Schumpeter.[107] These handwritten notes bear witness both to Lonergan's attention to economic detail and to his struggle to specify adequate enlightenment.

It is time that we focused, in some brief introductory fashion, on that adequate enlightenment, on the actual context for economic theory and practice.

---

[107] I refer in particular to the essay on Keynes in J. Schumpeter, *Ten Great Economists from Marx to Keynes* (New York: Oxford University Press, 1951). Schumpeter remarks, at one point, that "Professor Myrdal's gentle sneer at 'that Anglo-Saxon kind of unnecessary originality' is amply justified," p. 277.

First we must say something in general about the meaning of actual context. The general notion derives from Lonergan: "Actually, context is the interweaving of questions and answers in limited groups.... It is limited inasmuch as all the questions and answers have a bearing, direct or indirect, on a single topic....The single topic is something to be discovered in the course of the investigation. By persistence or good luck or both one hits upon some element in the interwoven set of questions and answers. One follows up one's discovery by further questions. Sooner or later one hits upon another element, then several more....One reaches a point where the overall view emerges....The single topic, then, is something that can be indicated generally in a phrase or two yet unfolded in an often enormously complex set of subordinate and interconnected questions and answers...." [108]

Now interested economists may wonder at this long preamble on actual context when their focus in on some possible novelty in economic theory. We crave their patience and prolonged interest. Adolf Lowe, who worked over fifty years on growth theory, recently remarked on the economic masters: "if so many astute minds have failed to come up with answers satisfactory at least to themselves, we cannot suppress a suspicion that they may not have asked the right question." [109] Coming to ask the right question is like coming to a determining heuristic of "the single topic." Lonergan's experience, and my own, of the incomprehension of economists, has led me to try to specify the grounds of that incomprehension. There is, then, the difficulty of focusing adequately on "the single topic," a difficulty due to the abstractive determinist mindset of much of contemporary economic thinking; there is the larger difficulty was faced by Lonergan in the thirties and early forties: its first published expression was in 1943. [110] In so far as one does not personally face that same difficulty, I suspect that Lonergan's analysis will appear vague and impractical. It will appear all the more so if one is caught in the prior difficulty which prevents an adequate focus on "the single topic": the actual productive process in its rhythms of growth in modern economies.

A parallel may help here. There is a type of modern chemist who studies plant growth in a doubly-deficient manner. The actual context for such a study is an evolutionary and aggreformic perspective; the single topic is the growing plant, grasped adequately only

---

[108] *Method in Theology*, pp. 163-64.
[109] A. Lowe, *The Path of Economic Growth*, Cambridge University Press, 1976, 7.
[110] I refer to Lonergan's essay, "Finality, Love, Marriage," republished from *Theological Studies*, 1943, in *Collection*.

through a notion of development thematized as genetic method. Lonergan's *Circulation Analysis* is like the upper blade of genetic method in botany, and falls like it within a larger actual context. Returning to the economic context one may say that Lonergan represents a double methodological shift across the Rubicon of which Schumpeter wrote: "By the phrase 'Crossing the Rubicon', I mean this: however important those occasional excursions into sequence analysis may have been, they left the main body of economic theory on the 'static' bank of the river; the thing to do is not to supplement static theory by the booty brought back from these excursions but to replace it by a system of general economic dynamics into which statics would enter as a special case....An increasing number of workers see the new goal; but for the time being this is practically all...."[111] A first shift moves away from current dynamic analysis which, despite appearances, is solidly rooted in comparative statics, regularly omits what is essential to "the single topic," and frequently ends up in the static "golden age."[112] Lonergan moves in a context, not of abstract modelling, but of concrete heuristics; his focus is not on well-behaved functions in a world of automatons but on the possibility of well-behaved people enlightened about a world governed by emergent probability. The second, positive, shift, then, is this move to meet the economic issue as it arises in such a world. Lonergan's perspective generates a concrete normative heuristic of possible, probable, and actual seriations of relatively stationary and evolutionary interacting economies. Its centerpiece is the analysis of a normative possibility; the evolution of a closed economy from one dynamic stationary state to another through the intussusception of new technological and institutional horizons. That perspective and its fruits will eventually be more at home with Rostow than with Solow, more acceptable to genuine goodwill in the Third World than to growth theoreticians and global managers. Perhaps at this stage a simple illustration of economic evolution would be helpful. It only gives hints of the relevant concrete functional analysis and policy, but later we will see how modern growth theory might handle the same island in the absence of Lonergan's dual methodological shift.

Envisage, then, an isolated island community, with a non-horsepower technology. Envisage some sub-group grasping the innovative idea of the plough, with horse, oxen, whatever. Insofar as the sub-group carries the community towards the realization of a plough

---

[111] J. Schumpeter, *History of Economic Analysis* (New York: Oxford University Press, 1974), pp. 1160-61.

[112] A convenient survey is *Growth economics,* ed. A. Sen, Penguin Books, 1970: see the index under 'Golden age'.

culture, there occur definite fluctuations in the exchange economy (inclusive of banking etc.) of the island. The fluctuations are associated with the fact that for a period energy and money are being devoted to the carpentry, tannery, horse-training, etc., which is to make concretely possible the plough culture. What is evident is that the community is building towards a period of higher consumption, greater leisure. Less evident are the fluctuations in the flow of finance on the island required to make the innovation possible and eventually to make increased consumption a reality. But clearly one may note an initial period of reorientation of present resources preparatory to the emergence of a new aggregate of capital ventures associated with horse-ploughing; there is a following period when production of horse-ploughs is underway, accelerating, gradually levelling to the demands of maintenance and replacement; there is the later period when the benefits emerge in consumption goods and better times.

Of course, this rhythm of evolution internal to the productive process calls for human adaptation, ideally human adaptation grounded in microautonomy[113] educated to an unusual perspective on what constitutes success. The human adaptation can be lacking: the subgroup may want the Linus blanket of extra money mistakenly called profit. They may add woodworms to the plough; they may advertize the myth of the necessity of a new plough every year; they may turn to persuading neighbouring islands of fruit-gatherers that they too need ploughs; they may find ways to benefit from taxes imposed on origin or destination principles; they may eventually have the fruit-gatherers making cheaper ploughs; and so on. More profoundly evil, they may generate an economic theory which gives their mistaken notions of profit and success an axiomatic status.

The island illustration calls for detailed functional analysis of the circulation of goods and monies. Similarly, the following illustration from neo-classical growth theory calls for detailed criticism, in particular in relation to the seven disorientations mentioned above, and the absence of actual context; but as Robinson's half-way house shows,[114] such criticism is a tricky and lengthy matter. Suffice it that the first illustration gives a hint of the concrete problem of global progress faced by Lonergan, and that the second manifests what emerges in some minds in the absence of actual context.

In the kingdom of Solovia "a policy-maker was heard to say 'Forget grand optimality. Solovians are simple people. We need a simple

---

[113] See McShane, *Wealth of Self and Wealth of Nations* (New York: Exposition Press, 19,4), p. 93.

[114] Joan Robinson, *Economic Heresies: Some Old-Fashioned Questions in Economic Theory*, (New York: Basic Books, 1973).

policy. Let us require that the fraction of output accumulated be fixed for all time....' "[115] A brilliant peasant, Oiko Nomos, comes up with his idea of a Golden Age: "By a Golden Age I shall mean a dynamic equilibrium in which output and capital grow exponentially at the same ratio...." His short lecture pleased the crow, especially his introduction of a lemma. " 'A lemma, a lemma', the crowd shouted. It was plain that the Solovians were excited by the prospect..."[116] Oiko Nomos' solution was all the more acceptable when "the King's econometricians were eventually satisfied that production in Solovia took place according to a Cobb-Douglas function...."[117]

I. F. Pearce takes Phelps to task, noting that Alice (nineteen year old granddaughter of Oiko), though "at first she accepted, like every properly indoctrinated Solovian of the Post-Oiko era, that capital must be accumulated at the constant growth rate,"[118] began to think out a new strategy of saving which eventually gave rise to a new party, and indeed a civil war.

Phelps has a comeback: "Alice preferred to save differently, and this fact appears as a prima facie argument against the desirability of the growth policy. But the growth policy could be carried out through a government budgetary surplus (deficit) coupled with the purchase (sale) of public or private securities. This would make individuals free to save and bequeath whatever they desired to the fiscal-credit environment created by Government."[119] Phelps ends with a plea: "Let us take for granted that we do not wish necessarily to grow exponentially. Should we forget Oiko, like a bad dream? Is Oikonomics an impractical subject? Does it say nothing about desirable growth, or undesirable growth?"[120] Apart from the aspect of fable, such economic model-building and mathematizing is not untypical, especially of North American economic journals. Should we forget Oiko? Fully developed mathematics will always be relevant where countabilities and measureabilities are present, but it is high time that predictive mechanics ceased parading as preceptive economics and history. The elaborate mathematical constructs of most of

---

[115] E. S. Phelps, "The Golden Rule of Accumulation: A Fable for Growthmen", *American Economic Review (1961):638-43*. Reprinted in A. Sen, op. cit., note 112, pp. 193-200, from which my quotations are taken, p. 194.

[116] Ibid., p. 196.

[117] Ibid., p. 199.

[118] J. F. Pearce, "The End of the Golden Age in Solovia: A Further Fable for Growthmen Hoping to be 'One-Up' on Oiko", *American Economic Review* (1962):1088.

[119] E. S. Phelps, in his reply to Pearce, ibid., p. 1098.

[120] Ibid.

modern growth theory do not, of course, flow into policy.[121] Ronald Britto, in "Some Recent Developments in the Theory of Economic Growth: An interpretation", remarks "We must admit that the recent developments outlined here will not be of much help in explaining growth patterns in the real world".[122] Even Hicks, a master in the field, comments as follows on his own and other contributions, "It is the dynamic problem of positive economics—of the actual behavior of an economy, with imperfect foresight—that, when even considered in this much detail, becomes so baffling...."[123] What flows into the policy of developed nations is, indeed, much more Hicks' famous simplification of Keynes, the backbone of most North American textbooks in economics.[124] What flows into the policy of underdeveloped nations is regularly an uncomfortable and destructive mix of Hicks, Friedman, Harrod-Domar, and the Multinationals.[125] What should flow into both types of policy, on the other hand, is the fruit of Lonergan's functional distinctions. Recall the earlier clues regarding adequate disaggregation. One is not dealing with a GNP = Y. One is dealing with two circuits, a basic circuit with which one associates Y' and a surplus circuit with which one associates Y''. Furthermore, the distinction of the circuits makes manifest the existence of a crossover, and the operation of the circuits in an evolutionary dynamic reveals normative oscillations of profits and prices making manifest the inefficiency or destructiveness of a great deal of present monetary, fiscal, centralist, and growth policies.

The fundamental issue, of course, is not government policy: the issue, as we noted in the beginning, is the future of democracy. Recent writings of both R. Heilbroner and A. Lowe see it otherwise;

---

[121] Elements of them have, of course, been tried: "If there is one concept that has dominated recent discussion on growth theory and development planning, it is that of the capital-output ratio, or the capital-coefficient as it is sometimes called. It has been extensively used in various growth models, e.g., those of Harrod, Domar, Kaldor, and Mahalanobis, and it has also helped the formulation of our First and Second Five Year Plans." Pankaj Kumar Sen, "Use of the Capital-Output Ratio in Economic Planning", *The Indian Economic Review* I (1960):23.

[122] *Journal of Economic Literature* (1973):1360.

[123] John Hicks, *Capital and Growth,* (New York: Oxford University Press, 1965), p. 201.

[124] J. Hicks, "Mr. Keynes and the 'Classics': A Suggested Interpretation", *Econometrica,* p. 5 (1937):147-59. For a treatment which includes later views on the demand for money see F. R. Glahe, "A Permanent Restatement of the IS/LM Model", *The American Economist,* XVII (1973): 158-67.

[125] The Third World economic journals increasingly give evidence of flawed policies.

Heilbroner looks to the emergence of a socialism akin to religion;[126] Lowe focuses on the need for Control.[127] Their views are asymptotic with the dynamics of the non-communist world particularly since the second world war. In that sense they represent good Machiavellian science. But against such massively organized alienation stands human subjectivity in its total religious reality. The economic rhythms of the second million years, and the third stage of meaning, are on the side of intelligence and of the glory of history. But it is to be expected that in these next decades we may well paint ourselves into the corner that Yugoslavia sought to escape:

> Their experience with centralized planning disillusioned the Yugoslavs. A very complicated hierarchical mechanism of federal, republican, and local state agencies was created. Factories piled up inventories of unwanted products in the midst of terrible shortages of other goods; management and workers alike were unconcerned about efficiency; investments were badly planned; and there was no concern for innovation and research. The period is remembered as a kind of nightmare. Some desperately needed reconstruction was achieved but conditions were ideal for wholesale evasion of resonsibility, corruption and exercise of power by incompetents.[128]

Getting out of that corner depends on the emergence of Global elders who can take a comprehending stand against the Global managers, neurotically and other-directedly reaching for the Linus blanket of corporate stability or growth, and against politicians, bureaucrats, and militants whose profound self-neglect breeds a thirst for the establishment or prolongation of petty power, in a universe upsurging with human loneliness and hunger. It depends on the emergence of adequate economists.

Lonergan's work offers an invitation. Of it I might say, borrowing from Solow's remark on the difficulty of Uzawa's two-sector model of economic growth:

> It requires only a little arithmetic and the bare elements of the calculus of functions of one variable. Any economist who cannot read it ought at least to insist that his students do so.[129]

---

[126] Most recently in R. L. Heilbroner, *Marxism: For and Against* (New York: Norton, 1980), p. 168.

[127] A. Lowe, *On Economic Knowledge. Towards a Science of Political Economics* (New York: Harper and Row, 1965), p. 130. Lowe does require "the formation of enlightened public opinion capable of understanding the primary Control," (ibid., p. 283), but his emphasis is on public control: see the index of his later book, *The Path of Economic Growth,* under Control.

[128] op. cit., note 76, pp. 21-22.

[129] R. W. Solow, "Note on Uzawa's Two Sector Model of Economic Growth", *Review of Economic Studies* (1961):50.

III. Epilogue

I have sketched briefly a project that has preoccupied me in the twenty years since I first encountered Lonergan's writings. The sketch is the expression of my own dim reach towards an achieved larger project in methodology which, as Lonergan told me in rich conversations when he was in Ireland in 1971, drew his interest when he first went to London University in the late twenties.

In discussing the first bridge, I noted it as a bridge of non-discipleship. Yet I am clearly a disciple, like a second-rate musician in the presence of Beethoven. I am increasingly puzzled by the difference between the community of mind and the community of music. The community of intellect seems to be, as Leo Strauss points out, a community "of impressarios or lion-tamers."[130] The community of great musicians is reverent. Chopin endlessly returned to Bach. Mahler's last word was "Mozart." Recently Herbert Von Karajan conducted Beethoven's fourth and fifth symphonies, three weeks after having listened to them more than 200 times in editing his *Deutsche Grammaphon* recording of the nine. "From the moment I began," he remarked of the concert, "they were new works to me."[131]

Like Karajan with Beethoven, I cannot read Lonergan's works, even after more than twenty years, as familiar; they are quite beyond me. He has bridgeheaded generalized empirical method, the tandem incarnate academic challenge of the twenty-first century and beyond; he has done so in towering solitude. We could best honor him in his seventy-fifth year by, primarily in solitude, coming to grips afresh with his invitation to slowly discover our modern selves in the tandemness of his method.

He wrote, in concluding *Verbum* more than thirty years ago: "a completely genuine development of the thought of St. Thomas will command in all the universities of the modern world the same admiration and respect that St. Thomas himself commanded in the medieval University of Paris."[132]

But respect can die in the mesh of death, disregard, and condemnation. What followed Aquinas all too quickly were correctors of correctors of Brother Thomas.

It seems to me that the cost of a genuine development of Aquinas, of "the transposition of his position to meet the issues of our own day,"[133] of implementing generalized empirical method, is, in these coming decades, precisely the cost of discipleship.

---

[130] Leo Strauss, *Liberalism: Ancient and Modern* (New York: Basic Books, 1968), p. 3.
[131] The remark is quoted on page 23 of the text published with the *Deutsche Grammaphon* edition (1977) of Beethoven's Nine Symphonies.
[132] *Verbum: Word and Idea in Aquinas,* p. 220.
[133] Ibid.

List of Contributors

Dr. Garrett Barden, Professor of Philosophy and Dean of the Faculty of Arts, University College, Cork, Ireland.

Dr. Patrick H. Byrne, Associate Professor of Philosophy, Boston College, Massachusetts, U.S.A.

Dr. Walter E. Conn, Associate Professor of Religious Ethics, Villanova University, Pennsylvania, U.S.A.

Rev. Robert M. Doran, S.J., Associate Professor of Philosophical Theology and Interdisciplinary Studies, Regis College, Toronto, Canada.

Rev. John S. Dunne, C.S.C., Professor of Theology, University of Notre Dame, Indiana, U.S.A.

Rev. Tad Dunne, S.J., Assistant Professor of Systematic Theology and Founder of the Spiritual Integration Program, Regis College, Toronto, Canada.

Rev. Joseph Flanagan, S.J., Professor of Philosophy and Chairman of the Philosophy Department, Boston College, Massachusetts, U.S.A.

Dr. Mary Gerhart, Associate Professor of Religious Studies, Hobart and William Smith Colleges, New York, U.S.A.

Dr. Michael Gibbons, Professor of Interdisciplinary Studies and Departmental Director, Department of Liberal Studies in Science, The University, Manchester, England.

Rev. Vernon Gregson, S.J., Associate Professor of Theology, Loyola University, Louisiana, U.S.A.

Rev. Stephen Happel, Associate Professor of Systematic Theology, St. Meinrad School of Theology, Indiana, U.S.A.

Rev. Joseph A. Komonchak, Associate Professor of Theology, Department of Religion and Religious Education, Catholic University of America, Washington, D.C., U.S.A.

Rev. Matthew L. Lamb, Associate Professor of Theology, Marquette University, Wisconsin, U.S.A.

Dr. Frederick Lawrence, Associate Professor of Theology, Boston College, Massachusetts, U.S.A.

Dr. William P. Loewe, Associate Professor of Theology, Department of Religion and Religious Education, Catholic University of America, Washington, D.C., U.S.A.

Rev. William Mathews, S.J., Associate Professor of Philosophy, Milltown Institute of Philosophy and Theology, Dublin, Ireland.

574   List of Contributors

Dr. Sean E. McEvenue, Professor of Biblical Studies and Director of Lonergan University College, Concordia University, Montreal, Canada.

Dr. Philip McShane, Professor of Philosophy and Interdisciplinary Studies, Mount St. Vincent University, Nova Scotia, Canada.

Dr. Ben F. Meyer, Professor of New Testament Studies, McMaster University, Ontario, Canada.

Dr. Hugo Meynell, Professor of Philosophy, The University, Leeds, England.

Rev. Sebastian Moore, O.S.B., Assistant Director of Campus Ministry and Lecturer in Spirituality and Theology, Marquette University, Wisconsin, U.S.A.

Dr. Mark D. Morelli, Assistant Professor of Philosophy, Loyola Marymount University, California, U.S.A.

Rev. Michael O'Callaghan, Associate Professor of Systematic Theology, Newman College, Alberta, Canada.

Rev. Eric O'Connor, S.J., (1907-1980) Former Co-Founder and Director of the Thomas More Institute for Adult Education, Montreal, Canada.

Dr. Geoffrey L. Price, Lecturer in the Department of Liberal Studies in Science, The University, Manchester, England.

Dr. Quentin Quesnell, Professor of Religious Studies, Smith College, Massachusetts, U.S.A.

Rev. John A. Raymaker, Independent Research in Social Ethics and Transcultural Philosophy, Military Chaplaincy, Japan.

Dr. Nancy Ring, Assistant Professor of Systematic Theology, Le Moyne College, New York, U.S.A.

Rev. David Roy, Director of the Bioethical Research Center, Clinical Research Institute of Montreal, Quebec, Canada.

Rev. William F. J. Ryan, S.J., Associate Professor of Philosophy, Gonzaga University, Washington, U.S.A.

Dr. William M. Shea, Associate Professor of Religious Studies, University of South Florida, Tampa, Florida, U.S.A.

Rev. David Tracy, Professor of Philosophical Theology, Divinity School, University of Chicago, Illinois, U.S.A.

Rev. Bernard J. Tyrrell, S.J., Associate Professor of Religious Studies, Gonzaga University, Washington, U.S.A.

Dr. Michael Vertin, Associate Professor of Philosophy and Religious Studies, St. Michael's College, University of Toronto, Ontario, Canada.

Name Index

Abbott, W., 178
Abelard, 177
Aberhart, W., 562f.
Abrams, M., 384
Ackroyd, P., 187, 192
Adelmann, F., 80
Adey, G., 74
Adler, G., 449
Adorno, T., 43, 65, 216, 340
Aesop, 239
Ahlstrom, S., 154, 156f.
Albert, 363
Alexandra, 193
Allison, D., 283
Alston, W., 406
Ameriks, K., 404
Anderson, J., 4
Anderson, P., 65
Andronicus, 363
Angyal, A., 15, 26f.
Anscombe, G., 371
Anselm, 218
Apczynski, J., 106, 288
Apel, K., 74, 327, 333
Aquinas, Thomas 17f, 38, 58-60, 80, 93, 101-104, 110, 176f., 198, 216, 222, 358, 363, 445, 465, 547, 554, 563, 571
Archimedes, 517
Arendt, H., 472
Aresteh, A., 555
Aristotle, 39, 268, 287, 294, 353-366, 431, 445, 486, 498, 562.
Arnold, M., 83, 384
Athanasius, 71
Aubenque, P., 355

Augustine, 16f., 87f., 177, 193 245, 286, 300, 428, 547.
Austin, J., 380
Avineri, S., 40, 56f.
Ayer, A., 370, 379, 386, 406.

Bach, J., 571
Baker, M., 355
Baltes, P., 310
Balthasar, H.U. von, 80, 285
Bambrough, R., 379
Barden G., 353
Barnet, R., 67
Barth, K., 84, 90, 249
Bauer, G., 74
Baum, G., 36, 40, 55, 64, 66, 73
Baum, W., 20
Baumgartner, H., 74
Becker, E., 230, 232, 236, 239
Becker, W., 56
Beeck, F. van, 215
Beethoven, L., 571
Bellarmine, R., 193
Belloc, H., 47, 230
Belzile, L., 509
Benjamin, W., 43, 45, 65, 81
Bennett, W., 334
Berger, P., 84
Bernard, 290
Bernard, J., 289
Bernstein, J., 427f.
Bernstein, R., 35f., 271
Berryman, P., 351
Betti, E., 356
Betz, O., 204
Bien, J., 43

Name Index

Billings, M., 154
Billingsley, A., 351
Bindley, T., 174
Bird, O., 470
Bitter, G., 136
Bloor, D., 376
Bodin, J., 269
Boehm, R., 402, 405
Boehme, J., 94
Bonhoeffer, D., 75
Boniface VIII, 193
Bonino, J., 194
Bottomore, T., 58
Boulez, P., 553
Braaten, C., 275
Brahe, Tycho, 428
Brand, G., 283
Braxton, E., 68, 72, 276
Bray, B., 553
Britto, R., 569
Brodersen, A., 294
Brouwer, 525
Brown, R., 73
Buber, M., 295f.
Buchanan, E., 289
Buck-Morss, S., 40
Bultmann, R., 84, 87, 203, 221, 249
Burke, K., 287
Burns, J., 110
Burrell, D., 38, 59, 93, 280, 293, 445, 548, 563.
Bushnell, H., 153-169
Butler, B., 276
Butler, H., 287
Butterfield, H., 343, 490

Cafferty, P., 45
Cafone, J., 156
Cahn, E., 530
Callahan, D., 330f.
Campbell, K., 207
Camus, A., 450
Cano, M., 83, 102
Caplan, H., 286
Cardano, G., 545f.
Carr, A., 58
Carr, D., 401

Cassidy, R., 47, 70
Cassirer, E., 388
Castelli, F., 546
Channing, W., 156
Charlemagne, 193
Chauncy, C., 155
Cheney, M., 155
Chenu, M., 80, 83
Chesterton, G., 550, 558
Childs, B., 186
Chopin, F., 571
Churchill, J., 283, 404
Clebsch, W., 167
Clement, 268
Clifford, J., 430
Cobb, J., 84, 389
Cochrane, D., 308
Coleman, J., 36
Coleridge, S., 154, 156f., 159, 161f., 387
Colletti, L., 65
Collingwood, R., 207, 371, 408f., 430, 433f., 461f.
Collins, James 430
Collins, Joseph 67
Comte, A., 79
Cone, J., 47, 351
Conn, W., 19, 23, 307, 402
Corcoran, P., 132, 276
Coreth, E., 411-413
Cormie, L., 71
Correy, G., 11
Couchoud, P., 203
Courant, 511
Crabb, L., 20
Crane, R., 387
Crittenden, B., 308
Crombie, A., 428
Crosby, D., 154, 156f., 168
Cross, B., 155
Cross, F., 192
Crossan, J., 284
Crowe, F., 61, 79 f., 83, 88, 252, 277, 293, 316, 358, 412, 459, 461, 479, 551
Curran, C., 19, 341, 346
Cushman, R., 445f.
Cuyvers, L., 561

Cyprian, 268

Dabrowski, K., 11, 26, 28-30
Dahl, N., 200, 266
Dalman, G., 203, 204, 206
Danielou, J., 47
Dante, 385f.
Darwin, C., 427f., 498f., 500
Darwin, F., 428
Davies, J., 194
Davis, C., 41, 58
Dawson, C., 47
Debreu, G., 559
Derrida, J., 283
Descartes, R., 87, 124, 343, 378, 432, 555.
Dewart, L., 412
Dewey, J., 36f., 164
Dierkens, J., 284
Dilthey, W., 284, 390
Dirlam, J., 556
Dix, G., 197
Dixon, J., 278
Dodd, C., 205f.
Domar, E., 560f., 569
Donceel, J., 412
Donovan, L., 127
Doran, R., 25, 53f., 62f., 94, 105, 109, 111f., 218, 256, 276, 282-284, 516, 522
Dostoevsky, F., 92, 239
Douglas, B., 447f.
Douglas, C., 562f.
Drake, S., 545
Dreyfus, H., 287
Duffy, R., 12
Dulles, A., 84, 214f.
Dunne, J., 3, 284
Dunne, T., 40, 58, 109, 291, 402, 545, 549
Dych, W., 58

Easton, D., 56
Eatwell, J., 560f.
Ebeling, G., 389
Eccles, J., 231
Edward II, 373, 375
Edwards, J., 155f., 162, 167

Eicher, P., 58f., 125, 136
Eichner, A., 67
Einstein, A., 408, 427f., 437, 477, 482, 488f., 493f., 504-506, 546.
Eisley, L., 491
Eissfeldt, O., 190
Elders, J., 364
Eliade, M., 117, 141
Eliot, T., 9, 47, 233, 235, 384-386, 388, 392f., 434.
Ellul, J., 46
Emerson, R., 154, 156-158
Engels, F., 41, 55
Engnell, I., 203
Erickson, E., 427, 521
Espagnat, B.d', 547
Euclid, 503, 505, 512f., 518, 547.

Fairchild, J., 156
Farrer, A., 198
Feiwel, G., 538
Feldman, G., 560f.
Feldstein, M., 560
Fessard, G., 15
Feuerbach, L., 56
Fichte, J., 55, 154, 253
Fierro, A., 120
Finance, J. de, 22
Finney, C., 156
Fiorenza, E., 75
Fiorenza, F., 36f., 58, 75, 350
Fischer, K., 125, 129f.
Flaubert, G., 553
Flanagan, J., 283
Fleet, M., 73
Fletcher, J., 330
Foard, L., 168
Fohrer, G., 186, 189
Ford, D., 276
Fordham, M., 449
Foster, F., 154
Franck, F., 83
Frankl, V., 11, 312
Frazer, J., 3
Frege, G., 479
Freese, J., 287

Name Index

Freud, S., 53, 188, 191
Freund, E., 4
Frick, F., 191
Friedman, M., 531, 569
Frisby, D., 74
Frye, N., 283, 385, 387f., 393, 521
Funk, R., 284

Gadamer, H., 39f., 42-45, 81, 88, 99f., 282, 345, 356, 390.
Gager, J., 71
Galbraith, J., 531
Galileo, 404, 428, 482, 488, 490 498f., 502, 545-547, 555
Gauss, C., 512
Gawel, M., 470
Geach, P., 434
Geertz, C., 41
Geffré, C., 79, 81
Gelpi, D., 25
George, S., 67
Gerhart, M., 383
German, 363
Gervais, M., 99
Gibbs, J., 308-313, 322-324
Gibellini, R., 66
Gibson, W., 405, 460
Giddens, A., 271
Gilkey, L., 47, 84, 276
Gill, J., 12
Gill, R., 284
Gilligan, C., 312, 323
Gilmour, S., 70
Givord, R., 285
Glahe, F., 569
Glasser, W., 11
Glen-Doepel, W., 284
Goedel, K., 525
Goethe, J., 276
Goguel, M., 203
Going, C., 509, 516, 530
Gollwitzer, H., 84, 86, 89f., 94f.
Goodfield, J., 491
Goodwin, H., 154
Gordon, R., 532
Gottwald, N., 47, 70, 191

Gould, J., U1
Gouldner, A., 40f., 54, 57, 64
Gramsci, A., 57
Grant, R., 71
Greeley, A., 45, 238
Green, D., 56
Greene, T., 70
Gregory VII, 268
Gregson, V., 53f., 141
Greif, E., 308
Grisez, G., 373
Gross, M., 58
Guddat, K., 56
Guerin, J., 334
Gunn, D., 186
Gunn, G., 284
Gustafson, J., 271
Gutiérrez, G., 41, 194, 351
Güttgemann, E., 285

Haar, M., 253
Habermas, J., 37, 40, 42f., 45, 81, 340
Hacker, P., 431
Hadidian, D., 38, 444
Haight, R., 48
Hamm, C., 308
Hansen, A., 559
Happel, S., 154, 275
Harnack, A., 70
Harrington, D., 71
Harris, M., 58
Harrod, R., 569
Hart, R., 94, 284
Hartman, R., 460
Hartnack, J., 371
Hartshorne, C., 90
Harvey, V., 58, 84
Hauerwas, S., 38
Haught, J., 448, 450f., 454f.
Haughton, R., 72
Hayek, F., 564
Hazard, R., 154
Hebblethwaite, P., 41
Hegel, G., 54-58, 60, 252, 275, 404
Heidegger, M., 4, 58, 81, 87f., 97-101, 230, 283, 389f., 430

Name Index   579

Heijden, B. van der, 125
Heilbroner, R., 369f.
Henle, R., 445
Hennelly, A., 73
Herder, J., 155
Herodotus, 353
Hicks, J., 569
Hilbert, D., 480
Hildebrand, D. von, 296
Hinners, R., 412
Hinson, E., 280
Hirsch, E., 84, 385, 389, 392
Hobbes, T., 269, 356, 406, 408
Hobsbawm, E., 65
Hodgson, P., 37
Hoenen, P., 547
Hoffmann, J., 203
Holdheim, W., 449
Holz, H., 412
Hooker, M., 202
Hopkins, G., 174, 231, 234
Hopper, S., 284, 389
Hora, T., 11, 13-15
Horkheimer, M., 43, 61, 216, 340
Howard, R., 65
Hudson, H., 70
Hudson, W., 371
Hull, R., 544
Hume, D., 163f., 341, 343, 374, 408, 432
Husserl, E., 100, 164, 283, 389, 401-407, 410, 460, 479
Hutchison, W., 48

Iersel, B. van, 55, 283
Ignatius of Antioch, 21
Ignatius of Loyola, 15, 19f., 126

James VI, 193
James, W., 36, 164, 167, 208, 280, 286, 558
Jammer, M., 477
Jaspers, K., 77, 87, 97
Jay, M., 40
Jefferson, T., 521
Jeffery, G., 482
Jeremias, J., 205f.

John of the Cross, 21
John Paul II, 238
Johns, R., 59
Johnson, A., 154
Johnson, D., 341
Johnson, R., 87
Johnson, S., 430
Johnson, W., 162
Johnston, W., 102, 280
Jonas, H., 87f., 331f.
Jones, H., 558, 561
Jossua, J., 276
Joyce, J., 543, 550, 552f.
Julian of Norwich, 233
Jung, C., 25, 62, 94, 105, 117, 121, 188, 191, 218, 237, 246, 276, 449, 554
Jüngel, E., 84, 86, 89f., 94

Kaldor, N., 532, 559, 569
Kalecki, M., 538
Kant, I., 54f., 58, 70, 86f., 93, 99, 124, 154, 289, 340f., 343, 345, 407f., 430, 432, 460, 547
Karajan, H. von, 571
Kasper, W., 86, 123, 136
Kay, D., 204
Kazepides, A., 308
Kee, H., 70
Keefe, D., 73
Kelly, W., 59
Kelsen, H., 357, 359
Kelsey, D., 58
Kenny, A., 369f., 373-378
Kepler, J., 427
Kernig, C., 339
Keynes, J., 428, 531f., 558, 560, 564, 569
Kierkegaard, S., 6, 87, 97, 176, 280
King, A., 286
King, M., 37
Kitagawa, J., 141-143
Klare, K., 65
Knight, F., 564
Koestler, A., 428
Kohl, M., 204

Name Index

Kohlberg, L., 307-313, 316, 322-324
Kolakowski, L., 40, 54
Komonchak, J., 265
Korsch, K., 65
Kramer, R., 311
Krieger, M., 384
Kroger, J., 288
Krzywon, E., 284
Kuhn, H., 206
Kuhn, T., 425, 428, 431, 437, 558
Kümmel, W., 70
Küng, H., 19, 45, 73
Kurtines, W., 308
Kuypers, K., 364

Laflamme, R., 99
Lamb, M., 35f., 40, 43f., 53, 55, 58-60, 63-65, 67-69, 72, 74, 116, 284, 346, 349
Langer, S., 388, 553f.
Landes, D., 535
Laporte, J., 40, 58, 93, 109, 402, 545, 549
Lappé, F., 67
Lash, N., 288
Lauer, Q., 402, 479
Lavoisier, A., 491, 499
Lawrence, F., 40, 67, 79, 275, 513
Lawson, R., 482
Leibniz, G., 92, 343
Lenin, V., 57
Leo I, 268
Leontief, W., 560
Lernoux, P., 67
Lessing, G., 55, 83
Levasseur, J., 83
Lewis, C., 236
Lickona, T., 313
Liddell, H., 353
Lidzbarski, M., 204
Lincoln, A., 37
Lindahl, E., 564
Linneaus, C., 491
Little, M., 562
Livermore, S., 334

Lobachevsky, N., 512
Lobkowicz, N., 35
Locke, J., 163, 343, 494
Loewe, W., 61, 71, 213, 217
Lohfink, N., 192
Lonergan, B., 3, 11, 15, 22f., 25, 37-40, 53-55, 58-72, 74-77, 79-83, 86, 88f., 92f., 98-123, 131-144, 147-150, 164, 169, 173, 176, 183, 185, 187, 190, 198f., 214, 216-227, 229, 233, 249f., 252-262, 265f., 269-272, 275-285, 287f., 290, 293-299, 308, 312-321, 323, 325-329, 332f., 335f., 339-348, 350, 365, 369-381, 383, 398, 401-403, 407-413, 415-421, 426, 432f., 438-440, 443-448, 451, 455-457, 459f., 465f., 471-473, 477-490, 493-498, 500-502, 512-514, 520, 523-525, 529-541, 544-552, 554, 556-567, 569-571
Lorentz, H., 482
Lowe, A., 560, 565, 569f.,
Löwith, K., 56
Luther, M., 87
Lutz, H., 206

Machiavelli, N., 194, 570
Mack, M., 429
Macquarrie, J., 84, 283
Magliola, R., 389
Maquire, D., 230
Mahalanobis, 569
Mahler, G., 571
Malcolm, N., 432
Malherbe, A., 71
Mallarmé, S., 553
Malthus, T., 534
Mannheim, K., 376, 474
Manno, B., 45
Marcuse, H., 552
Maréchal, J., 280, 411-414, 418-421
Margolis, J., 386
Marković, M., 65
Marsh, J., 203

Marshall, A., 559
Martin, D., 64
Marty, M., 36
Marx, K., 35, 53-57, 64-66, 381, 564
Mascall, E., 412
Maslow, A., 312, 470, 548
Mason, D., 47
Massie, R., 193
Maxwell, J., 486
May, R., 284, 312
McBrien, R., 84
McCann, D., 43
McCarthy, T., 40, 43
McCool, G., 412
McCready, W., 45
McEvenue, S., 185
McFadden, T., 37, 350
McGovern, A., 73
McKenna, S., 544
McLellan, D., 53f.
McShane, P., 93, 106f., 113, 132-134, 136, 139, 185, 275f., 341, 346, 413, 460, 544, 551, 554, 559f., 567
Mead, G., 342
Melanchthon, P., 83
Merleau-Ponty, M., 65, 287
Metz, J., 35-38, 41, 43-45, 47f., 59, 73, 75, 82, 94-96, 194, 249, 284, 350
Meyer, B., 70, 74, 197, 202
Meyers, M., 157
Meynell, H., 369
Michelson, A., 504
Miller, A., 429
Miller, D.G., 38, 444
Miller, D.L., 284, 389
Miller, G., 136
Miller P., 156
Mills, C., 95
Mirrlees, J., 562
Misgeld, D., 43
Moltmann, J., 47f., 84, 86, 89f., 94f., 215
Moore, S., 53f., 229, 452-454
Morelli, E., 465
Morelli, M., 465

Morland, D., 281
Morley, E., 504
Mosheim, J., 83
Mozart, W., 571
Muck, O., 412
Mueller, D., 70
Müller, R., 67
Mumford, L., 114f.
Murray, J., 36
Mussner, F., 201
Myrdal, G., 564

Nadeau, M., 553
Nakhnikian, G., 406
Napoleoni, C., 561
Navone, J., 284
Needleman, J., 21
Nesbitt, M., 13f.
Neumann, E., 448-451
Newman, R., 364
Newton, I., 427f., 437, 488, 491, 493, 498f., 502-505, 520, 547, 558
Nicholas, 193
Nicolayev, J., 308
Nicolson, H., 467, 470
Niebuhr, R., 36f., 84
Nietzsche, F., 56, 81f., 87, 90, 97
Nilson, J., 60
Nisbet, R., 58
North, H., 286
Noth, M., 186, 189, 192
Novak, M., 208
Nygren, A., 84

O'Callaghan, M., 123
Occam, W., 193
O'Connel, M., 340
O'Connor, E., 465, 509
O'Donovan, C., 71
Oelmüller, W., 55
Ogden, S., 47, 73, 84, 86, 89-91, 169
O'Malley, J., 55-57
O'Neil, J., 43
Origen, 71
Orsy, L., 23f.

582 Name Index

Ott, H., 84, 89, 91, 94
Ott, L., 214
Owens, J., 419

Pannenberg, W., 84, 132, 291
Park, E., 154
Parsons, T., 64
Pasteur, L., 499
Pauck, W., 48
Paul, St., 16f., 21, 87, 234-236, 267f., 445
Pearce, J., 568
Percy, W., 232
Perrett, W., 482
Perry, H., 470
Pesch, H., 564
Peters, R., 308
Peterson, E., 73, 75
Peukert, H., 35, 43, 58, 74
Phelps, E., 568
Phillips, D., 308
Piaget, J., 137, 308f., 316, 408
Pierman, A., 21
Pitcher, G., 370
Plato, 194, 353-355, 359, 364, 435, 445f., 467, 472, 518, 550
Plotinus, 544
Plowden, 363
Plummer, J., 556
Polanyi, M., 106, 288
Porte, J., 154
Powledge, T., 330
Preminger, A., 384
Proust, M., 549
Pseudo-Dionysius, 268
Ptolemy, C., 513, 558
Puhl, L., 20
Pythagoras, 94, 427

Quesnell, Q., 70, 76, 83, 173
Quinn, K., 530
Quintilian, 286f.
Quinton, A., 370, 379

Rad, G. von, 187, 192
Radnitzky, G., 340
Rahner, K., 23, 58f., 84, 92, 94, 123-132, 135-140, 161, 195, 249, 281, 284, 411f.

Rasmussen, D., 276
Raymaker, J., 65, 339
Read, H., 449
Reitzenstein, R., 203
Renthe-Fink, L., 74
Ricardo, D., 559
Richards, I., 385-388, 392
Ricoeur, P., 25, 43, 62, 82, 87, 94, 105, 161, 216, 218, 276, 284f., 289, 383, 390-397
Riedel, M., 44, 56
Ring, N., 249
Ritschl, A., 70
Robbins, L., 511, 564
Robinson, E., 283
Robinson, James, 87
Robinson, Joan, 560f., 567
Rogers, C., 25
Roo, W. van, 289
Ross, W., 355
Rostow, W., 566
Roth, G., 64
Roth, R., 412
Rousseau, J., 83, 253
Roy, D., 325, 327, 329
Ruether, R., 42
Rupp, G., 48
Russell, B., 373, 524f.
Ryan, C., 543
Ryan, J. A., 36
Ryan, J.J., 193
Ryan, W., 70, 107, 138f., 277, 401, 403-406, 411, 445, 459
Rynin, D., 154

Sala, G., 60, 413
Saner, H., 97
Satow, E., 467
Sartre, J., 436
Sauter, G., 58
Savage, D., 284
Sawyer, W., 438
Schachtel, E., 553
Schaie, K., 310
Scheler, M., 239-341, 346, 449
Schelling, F., 86f., 94, 154, 252f.
Schillebeeckx, E., 38, 55, 92, 243, 249, 283

Schiller, F., 276
Schilpp, P., 427
Schilson, A., 136
Schindler, A., 73
Schlegel, F., 253
Schleiermacher, F., 83, 154, 156, 161, 390
Schmidt, A., 56
Schrödinger, E., 408
Schumpeter, J., 66, 554, 561, 563f., 566
Schutz, A., 294, 342, 425, 429
Schwarz, W, 460
Schwemmer, O., 55
Scott, N., 284
Scott, R., 353
Segundo, J., 41, 66, 73
Seliger, M., 41
Sellin, E., 186
Semler, J., 83
Sen, A., 566, 568
Sen, P., 569
Shakespeare, W., 429
Shapiro, J., 340, 552
Shea, W., 36, 153
Shils, E., 474
Siebert, R., 35
Simon, R., 83
Simpson, E., 308
Sinsheimer, R., 335
Skinner, B., 406, 408, 519
Smart, J., 371
Smith, A., 65, 535, 559
Smith, D., 59
Smith, J., 93
Smith, R., 296
Smith, W., 141f., 151
Smyth, K., 281
Snell, R., 276
Socrates, 430f., 433, 436, 446, 472f.
Sokolowski, R., 405
Sölle, D., 84, 221, 284
Solow R., 566, 570
Spener, P., 83
Spiegelberg, H., 341
Spinoza, B.,83, 343
Spülbeck, V., 59

Sraffa, P., 560f.
Staël, Mme. de, 253
Stalin, J., 57
Steere, D., 6, 280
Stegemann, H., 206
Steiner, G., 389
Stewart, D., 43
Stewart, J., 431
Stock, G., 373
Strain, C., 41
Strauss, L., 40, 81, 571
Streeten, P., 561f.
Suarez, F., 193
Sullivan, H., 470
Sullivan, T., 45
Swartz, B., 143

Tansey, C., 509, 517
Tartaglia, N., 545f.
Taylor, C., 56
Taylor, N., 156
Tertullian, 71,174, 268, 548f.
Theresa of Avila, 21
Theissen, G., 70f.
Theunissen, M., 56
Thompson, F., 15
Thorold, A., 280
Tiebout, H., 30
Tillich, P., 84, 249-256, 258f., 261f., 275
Todes, S., 287
Toricelli, E., 546
Torrance, T., 282
Toulmin, S., 491
Tracy, D., 35, 45, 59, 72, 84, 86, 89, 91, 94, 101, 132, 169, 249, 276, 446
Trible, P., 70
Trotsky, L., 57
Tyrrell, B., 11f., 53f., 70, 93, 107, 138f., 277, 342, 401, 411, 445, 459

Ubaldo, 545
Unger, R., 301
Uzawa, S., 570

Valéry, P., 385f.

Vaux, R. de, 191
Vergote, A., 280, 285, 288
Vesey, G., 369, 373f.
Vickers, G., 445
Villey, M., 356
Vincent of Lerins, 181
Voegelin, E., 37f., 40, 81f., 107f., 114, 116f., 119, 190, 233, 444, 447f., 452, 457, 519, 545, 555f.
Voltaire, F., 83

Wach, J., 141f.
Wade, N., 335
Wagar, W., 473
Walras, M., 559
Wang, T., 21
Watt, L., 562
Weber, M., 64, 195, 268
Weil, S., 81
Wellhausen, J., 190
Wells, H., 473
Wentzel, 325
Werkmeister, W., 339
White, L., 76
Whitehead, A., 90
Wiedman, F., 339
Wilder, A., 284
Wilhelmsen, F., 412
Williams, B., 374, 376
Wilson, E., 58
Wilson, W., 14
Winch, P., 461
Winter, G., 339, 341f., 344-351, 549
Wirth, L., 474
Wittgenstein, L., 369f., 372-381, 431f., 437, 439
Wittich, C., 64
Wolf, W., 37
Wolffe, H., 192
Wood, A., 70
Woodruff, C., 30
Wordsworth, W., 230
Wright, G., 47

Xhaufflaire, M., 56, 59

Yahalom, I., 284
Young, J., 156

Zaidan, C., 161
Zeller, M., 121
Zeno, 488